Second Edition
Curriculum Leadership

Dedication

This book is dedicated to Dr. Allan A. Glatthorn (1924–2007), who had a romantic concept of education. He directed his view not to the past but to the day after tomorrow. As coauthors of the second edition of Curriculum Leadership: Strategies for Development and Implementation, *we hope this book will continue to provide completeness in curriculum thought and theory.*

—Floyd Boschee
—Bruce M. Whitehead

Second Edition

Curriculum Leadership

Strategies for Development and Implementation

Allan A. Glatthorn

Floyd Boschee
The University of South Dakota

Bruce M. Whitehead
Principal, Missoula School District #4
University of Montana

Los Angeles • London • New Delhi • Singapore • Washington DC

For information:

SAGE Publications, Inc.
2455 Teller Road
Thousand Oaks, California 91320
E-mail: order@sagepub.com

SAGE Publications India Pvt. Ltd.
B 1/I 1 Mohan Cooperative Industrial Area
Mathura Road, New Delhi 110 044
India

SAGE Publications Ltd.
1 Oliver's Yard
55 City Road
London, EC1Y 1SP
United Kingdom

SAGE Publications Asia-Pacific Pte. Ltd.
33 Pekin Street #02-01
Far East Square
Singapore 048763

Printed in the United States of America.

Library of Congress Cataloging-in-Publication Data

Glatthorn, Allan A., 1924-2007
Curriculum leadership: strategies for development and implementation/Allan A. Glatthorn, Floyd Boschee, Bruce M. Whitehead. —2nd ed.
    p. cm.
Includes bibliographical references and index.
ISBN 978-1-4129-6781-5 (cloth)
  1. Curriculum planning—United States. 2. Educational leadership—United States. I. Boschee, Floyd. II. Whitehead, Bruce M. III. Title.

LB2806.15.G57 2009
375'.001—dc22   2008028753

This book is printed on acid-free paper.

08 09 10 11 12 10 9 8 7 6 5 4 3 2 1

Acquisitions Editor:	Diane McDaniel
Editorial Assistant:	Leah Mori
Production Editor:	Tracy Buyan
Copy Editor:	Tony Moore
Typesetter:	C&M Digitals (P) Ltd.
Proofreader:	Jennifer Gritt
Indexer:	Will Ragsdale
Cover Designer:	Gail Buschman
Marketing Manager:	Christy Guilbault

Brief Contents

Detailed Contents

PART III. CURRICULUM MANAGEMENT 235

PART IV. CURRENT TRENDS IN THE CURRICULUM   333

13. Current Developments in the Subject Fields   334

Preface

The second edition of *Curriculum Leadership: Strategies for Development and Implementation* is intended for teachers and administrators presently functioning as curriculum leaders and those preparing for such roles. Its goal is to provide readers with the knowledge and the skills needed to exercise leadership in curriculum at several levels and in many roles and to help prepare curriculum leaders to meet the challenges of our globally connected classrooms.

DEVELOPING CURRICULUM LEADERSHIP

Becoming an effective curriculum leader requires being totally committed to an important idea, having unwavering faith in the process, and understanding and promoting the value of positive change. It is crucial that leaders have the knowledge to apply curricula solutions that are working in one school with the changes that are needed in another. Leaders must understand problems and link similar innovations together to amplify their impact in education. It is through hard work, commitment, an inquiring mind, and the ability to learn from experiences that curriculum leaders are able to go from a local to a global understanding. The challenges for curriculum leaders are many, but the satisfaction of developing and implementing solutions is worth the effort. This book is designed as an invitation for those in leadership positions to assume an active role in curriculum development.

The overriding aim of curriculum leadership is to improve the opportunity for all children of whatever background in our public and private schools. Curriculum leaders need to constantly look for ways to achieve excellence in our schools. Like many other professionals, they must understand that changes in society require them not only to improve their performance but to substantially redefine education's mission as well. Curriculum leaders cannot continue to use their equivalent of the Model-T Ford for curriculum development and implementation. Education for all children requires the delivery capacity of a supersonic jet, a postindustrial information-age model, if we are to educate youth for the workplace and for social cohesion in the 21st century. As curriculum leaders we are on the frontline of this change.

The second edition of *Curriculum Leadership: Strategies for Development and Implementation* is designed to help administrators and teachers understand how to address the educational challenges before them in curriculum development and implementation.

NEW TO THE SECOND EDITION

The second edition has been significantly refined to incorporate important new research and strategies needed by curriculum leaders today. We've included a comprehensive list below of many of the new features to be noted in this second edition:

Expanded coverage of multicultural education. This new edition provides an expanded historical overview of multicultural education and literature as well as tips for improving multicultural education and integrating it into the curriculum.

Some examples of how multicultural education has been further integrated in this new edition are listed below:

- Chapter 1 includes additional discussion of curriculum diversity and multicultural education as well as expanded discussion of cultural variables in regards to curriculum development.

- Chapter 2 incorporates discussion of how American educators have learned from differing cultural and socioeconomic groups. It also includes a new section on the development of multicultural education and incorporates a section under "The Exemplary Leaders" about James Banks, one of the pioneers of multicultural education.

- Chapter 13 includes tips for improving multicultural education and integrating it into the curriculum. New exercises that incorporate discussion of multicultural education have been included in the "Applications" section at the end of Chapter 13.

Expanded coverage of global education. Because American students for the 21st century must be globally literate, information on global education has been expanded throughout the book.

Some examples of how global education has been further integrated in this new edition are listed below:

- Chapter 2 includes an expanded discussion of global education, which includes a checklist of central and structural goals.

- Chapter 13 includes a discussion of global education and the need to incorporate global and international components into the subject fields. New end-of-chapter exercises that incorporate discussion of global education are included in the "Applications" section in Chapter 13.

Significantly revised Chapter 10: Curriculum Development and Implementation. This revised chapter includes a step-by-step approach on how to plan an effective curriculum program. This includes the following steps:

- The development of a program philosophy and rationale (for which samples are provided)
- A typical 5-year curriculum development cycle

- Methods for choosing teacher representation

- A scope and sequence, program goals, objectives, learning outcomes, and authentic tasks (for which samples are provided)

- Taxonomy of thinking

- Textbook selection guide

- The process to initiate and develop curriculum

- An expanded case study about choosing teacher representation

Expanded technology strategies for the teaching and learning process. This new edition incorporates significant discussion of technology and implementation in the curriculum. It also includes an added emphasis on E-learning.

Some examples of how technology has been further integrated in this new edition are listed below:

- Chapter 1 includes a discussion of online testing programs that help ease the alignment of local testing and state and national standards as well as of new technologies in neuroimaging research.

- Chapter 3 provides an expanded discussion of technology and futurists, technology as a catalyst of curriculum change, and some discussion of the theoretical classroom of the future and its reliance on technology.

- Chapter 3 also discusses the National Association of Elementary School Principals commissioning of the Institute for Alternative Futures (IAF) to explore areas of uncertainty and opportunity for schools as part of its Vision 2021 project and their nine forecasts about a preferred future.

- Chapter 5 includes technology planning goals and an expanded discussion of technology and the curriculum database.

- Chapter 7 includes a discussion of Microsoft's Live Meeting and its significance for education, and it also incorporates examples of Web-based learning and assessment.

- Chapter 8 includes expanded discussion of integrating technology into instruction and provides expanded discussion of distance learning courses.

- Chapter 12 includes discussion of technology use for corrective activities.

- Chapter 13 includes discussion of the Read/Write Web in regards to technology and reading improvement and also includes an expanded discussion of technology, inquiry-based instructional strategies, and science.

- Chapter 14 provides an extensive look at technology and curriculum and includes an expanded discussion of the Internet and technology in the curriculum; coverage of project-based multimedia learning and school technology realities; discussion of technology as a tool in the classroom and how elementary teachers are currently using it; a discussion of how technology is helping to improve the collection, management, and analysis of data in the classroom; a new, extensive discussion of Web-based applications used by principals/teacher leaders/teachers and their impact on teaching and learning; and an expanded discussion on E-learning as an alternative choice and opportunity for both students and educators

Additional teaching strategies and resources. To help curriculum leaders implement key ideas discussed in the book, we have provided a variety of teaching strategies and resources throughout the book.

Some examples of how teaching strategies and resources have been further integrated in this new edition are listed below:

- Chapter 5 includes a classroom needs assessment and provides strategies for integrating it into the classroom.

- Chapter 7 includes a discussion of curriculum mapping as a tool to help teachers and students and includes an expanded discussion of differentiated instruction within the diagnostic–prescriptive approach.

- Chapter 8 provides some expanded discussion and suggestions for how teachers can assess the needs of learners.

Additional focus on the role of teacher as curriculum leader. This new edition provides expanded coverage on teachers as leaders in curriculum development and implementation. Examples have been incorporated throughout the book to illustrate teachers' involvement as leaders. In addition, some of the case studies have been revised with a teacher–leader focus.

Some examples of how the role of teacher as curriculum leader has been further integrated in this new edition are listed below:

- Chapter 1 includes expanded discussion about teachers as leaders.

- Chapter 9 includes expanded discussion about the importance of motivating teachers to be leaders and collaborative professionals and to achieve the goals of the school district.

- Chapter 14 includes a case study that has been revised to discuss a teacher–leader and colleague solving a problem.

Additional discussion of high-stakes testing, accountability, standards, and legislation. The new edition includes an expanded look at the influence of standards and No Child Left Behind (NCLB) in curriculum development and implementation.

Some examples of where this discussion has been expanded are included below:

- Chapter 2 includes new discussion of NCLB under predominant trends in modern conservatism, which includes a checklist to explore your perceptions of NCLB.

- Chapter 4 includes expanded discussion of NCLB in regards to the curriculum-influence process and high-stakes testing, standards, and accountability. There is also discussion of the future of NCLB. This chapter also includes a discussion of the National Council for Accreditation of Teacher Education (NCATE) standards for teacher preparation that is presented with pros and cons about institution accreditation.

- Chapter 7 includes a discussion of high-stakes testing and keeping assessment and testing in perspective, and the case study in Chapter 7 has been revised to discuss incorporating NCLB guidelines and differentiated instruction.

New and updated graphics throughout each chapter. This new edition includes an increased number of exhibits, tables, charts, and worksheets to visually enhance curriculum leaders' understanding of chapter concepts.

Some examples of these new graphics are listed below:

- Chapter 1 includes new charts to illustrate the discussion of prescriptive and descriptive definitions of curriculum.

- Chapter 2 includes a chart of the historical eras of curriculum theory and practice and a revised exhibit on the elements of curriculum theory.

- Chapter 4 includes a new exhibit that shows the NCATE standards for teacher preparation and an exhibit about the NCATE institutional accreditation pros and cons.

- Chapter 9 includes a new chart about Maslow's Higher Hierarchy of Needs.

- Chapter 10 includes a new table that depicts methods for choosing teacher representation for curriculum development and also includes a Taxonomy of Thinking chart and a textbook selection guide.

- Chapter 12 includes a Curricular Program Components chart.

- Chapter 13 includes a new exhibit about mathematics curriculum focal points.

- Chapter 14 includes several new graphics, including a chart that provides descriptors for each step to be used in writing and teaching the writing process, a chart that offers several NCTE principles that should guide effective teaching practice in writing, a chart that looks at National Educational Technology Standards (NETS) Project Partners, and a chart that looks at are several sample online virtual high school programs that are offering courses.

- Chapter 15 includes a new exhibit that depicts principles for fostering equity and excellence across academically diverse learners and a new figure that shows the

What Works Clearinghouse report findings indicating that reading recovery leads to positive effects on students' alphabetic skills and general reading achievement.

Expanded discussion of important research and key issues. In addition to the topics addressed above, we have extensively revised and updated all chapters to reflect key issues and discussions in curriculum leadership.

Some of the areas where they have expanded this coverage are listed below:

- Chapter 2 includes expanded discussion of homeschooling and P–16 education. Also in this chapter, new major publications have been added under the "Modern Conservatism" section, including *Fair Isn't Always Equal: Assessing & Grading in the Differentiated Classroom* by Rick Wormeli, *Response to Intervention: A Practical Guide for Every Teacher* by William Bender, and *The World Is Flat: A Brief History of the Twenty-First Century* by Thomas L. Friedman.

- Chapter 3 includes additional discussion of brain-based research.

- Chapter 4 includes an expanded discussion of the role of the federal and state governments in education, discussion of the role of professional organizations in education, including international professional organizations, and expanded discussion of the role of the principal and teacher–leaders in curriculum development.

- Chapter 5 includes an expanded discussion of the community-based learning model.

- Chapter 6 includes an expanded discussion of restructured programs of study.

- Chapter 7 includes an expanded discussion of best practices of staff development.

- Chapter 8 includes an expanded discussion of the need for curriculum leaders to find and develop planned corrective activities to meet state and national requirements.

- Chapter 9 includes an expanded discussion of differentiated professional development.

- Chapter 11 includes an expanded discussion on adapting teaching and educative models of professional development.

- Chapter 13 includes an expanded discussion of the importance of literacy skills, differentiated instruction, and integrating the arts into the broader curriculum.

- Chapter 14 includes an expanded discussion on the effects of a semester-long listening skills program on listening comprehension and reading.

- Chapter 15 includes an expanded discussion on providing for academically challenged learners, which includes an expanded discussion of the Response to Intervention (RTI) guidelines and a case study that looks at RTI guidelines and their implementation in the classroom.

In addition to the many features listed above, the text now includes **part openers** that provide an overview of the material in each part prior to moving into the chapter discussions. Also, the references have been significantly updated throughout the book where applicable. Lastly, the new edition includes revised **"Keys to Leadership"** and **"Curriculum Tips"** sections throughout each chapter to provide guidance for administrators, teachers, and teacher leaders.

We hope that these new elements will make this text even more useful to you as you exercise leadership in curriculum or prepare to meet the challenges of the globally connected classroom.

ORGANIZATION OF THE TEXT

Part I: Foundations of Curriculum begins by exploring the foundations of the field so that decisions are made from a broad perspective and with a deep knowledge. The chapters in this part examine the general concepts of curriculum, curriculum history, curriculum theory, and the politics of curriculum—the way that power and influence affect curriculum decision making at the federal, state, and local levels.

Part II: Curriculum Processes focuses on processes. Beginning with an overview of the curriculum-planning process, the general goal of this part is to help the reader acquire the skills needed to bring about major curricular change.

Part III: Curriculum Management addresses management and development and implementation of curriculum. If the process of developing and implementing curricula is to be truly effective, it must be managed well.

Part IV: Current Trends in the Curriculum examines trends in the subject fields, presents trends across the curriculum, including the use of computers, and concludes with a focus on trends linking individualizing the curriculum with the needs of special students.

FEATURES OF THE TEXT

Several special features make the second edition of *Curriculum Leadership: Strategies for Development and Implementation* more accessible to you.

Key to Leadership

Each chapter begins with a Key to Leadership, which provides a practical and insightful view into the world of what works in the area of curriculum leadership.

Curriculum Tips

Innovative Curriculum Tips are scattered throughout each chapter. These tips present ideas and strategies that will help curriculum leaders address present and future professional curricula needs.

Summary

Each chapter concludes with a summary of the main points covered in the chapter.

Applications

This end-of-chapter feature encourages readers to think carefully and reflect on the issues presented. The applications are designed to reinforce the chapter content and to help readers explore their own ideas and beliefs.

Case Study

This end-of-chapter feature gives the reader an opportunity to spend additional time investigating controversial issues and topics that affect education today. Each issue or topic highlighted has been chosen because of its direct impact on schooling and its potential for affecting curriculum leadership. Each case study concludes with a Challenge and Key Issues/Questions. The Challenge is a thought-provoking exercise that stimulates discussion and promotes self-understanding. The Key Issues/Questions are designed to stimulate discussion and help readers analyze and develop deeper insights into the issues and concepts being discussed.

Webliography

This end-of-chapter feature encourages readers to explore Web sites where they can learn more about the curriculum process by researching issues, learning more about current curriculum applications, and looking at practical applications of the material being presented in the text. Readers should note that Web resources are time and date sensitive; therefore, the Web sites listed may become inactive at any time.

Key Terms

Important terms are bolded and defined throughout the book. These terms and their definitions are included in the glossary for easy reference.

Ancillary Materials for Instructors

Instructors' Resource CD

An Instructors' Resource CD is available to further support and enhance the learning goals of *Curriculum Leadership: Strategies for Development and Implementation,* Second Edition. The CD includes sample syllabi, PowerPoint slides, and a comprehensive test bank with multiple-choice, true/false, short-answer, and essay questions.

ACKNOWLEDGMENTS

Special thanks must go to acquisitions editor Diane McDaniel and editorial assistant Leah Mori from SAGE for their assistance in collecting reviewer data and their constant willingness to help with the production of the book.

We have been fortunate in obtaining the assistance of graduate students and a number of colleagues in making suggestions and reviewing the initial and second edition drafts of the book.

The following colleagues participated in the development of the first edition:

Cynthia Chapel, Lincoln University

Mary C. Clement, Berry College

Robert Ferrera, Notre Dame de Namur University

Barbara Gonzalez-Pino, University of Texas at San Antonio

David L. Grey, University of South Alabama

Andrew L. Hunt, University of Arkansas at Little Rock

Charles Lamb, Texas A&M University

Phil McKnight, University of Kansas

Kristine Reed, University of South Dakota

Allen H. Seed, University of Memphis

Chris Zirkle, Ohio State University

The following colleagues participated in the development of the second edition:

Debra J. Anderson, Minnesota State University, Mankato

Patricia D. Clark, Lincoln Memorial University

Shanan Fitts, California State University, Fullerton

Sharon L. Gilbert, Southern Illinois University, Carbondale

Alan P. Grimsley, State University of New York at Albany

Marilyn Koeller, National University

Amany Saleh, Arkansas State University

Clyde Winters, Governors State University

Marsha Zenanko, Jacksonville State University

Chris Zirkle, Ohio State University

We are especially appreciative of the comments and suggestions offered by the following graduate students in the School of Education, Division of Educational Administration, at the University of South Dakota (USD), and colleagues at other colleges and universities:

Jason Alons

Brian Corlett

Donavan G. DeBoer

Beth Dykstra

Tim Frederick

Robert Hirsch

Jerry Joachim

Preston Kooima

Sheryl Knutson

Dean Kueter

Joe Meyer

Ronda Zinter

We also acknowledge the continuing and supportive help received from our wives, Marlys Ann Boschee and Charlotte Whitehead. They helped us give meaning and coherence in an age in which change and flux in education reign supreme. Also, a special thank you is extended to Barbara Glatthorn for her assistance and continued support in completing this book.

Foundations of Curriculum

Curriculum planners have tried to characterize curriculum with very little guidance. The purpose of Part I is to present an overview of curriculum, so that curriculum planners can begin to comprehend the essential elements for curriculum development and implementation and gain a fundamental foundation upon which to firmly build a sound curriculum.

CHAPTER 1

The Nature of Curriculum

The intent of this introductory chapter is to provide curriculum leaders with a general overview of the curriculum field and a set of concepts for analyzing the field. To accomplish these related goals, the discussion that follows focuses on these outcomes: defining the concept of curriculum, examining the several types of curricula, describing the contrasting nature of curriculum components, and analyzing the hidden curriculum. Some fundamental concepts essential for understanding the comprehensive field of curriculum can be established at the outset.

Questions addressed in this chapter include the following:

- What is curriculum, and why is it important?
- What are the types and components of curricula, and how have they changed over the years?
- What are mastery, organic, and enrichment curricula, and what roles do they play in the development of curriculum?
- Why is knowledge of the "hidden curriculum" important to curriculum leaders?

Key to Leadership

Curriculum leaders should review and monitor curriculum policies to make sure that the policies align with curricular goals and that they support student learning.

THE CONCEPT OF CURRICULUM

In a sense, the task of defining the concept of curriculum is perhaps the most difficult of all, for the term *curriculum* has been used with quite different meanings ever since the field took form.

Curriculum, however, can be defined as prescriptive, descriptive, or both. "Prescriptive [curriculum] definitions provide us with what 'ought' to happen, and they more often than not take the form of a plan, an intended program, or some kind of expert opinion about what needs to take place in the course of study" (Ellis, 2004, p. 4). Analogous to prescriptive curricula are medical prescriptions that patients have filled by pharmacists; we do not know how many are actually followed. "The best guess is that most are not" (p. 4). This is parallel to the prescribed curriculum for schools where the teacher, like the patient, ultimately decides whether the prescription will be followed. In essence, "the developer proposes, but the teacher disposes" (p. 4).

To understand the nature and extent of curriculum diversity, it is important at this juncture to examine the prescriptive and descriptive definitions offered by some of the past and present leaders in the field. The prescriptive definitions in Exhibit 1.1, arranged chronologically, have been chosen for their representativeness.

The descriptive definitions of *curriculum* displayed in Exhibit 1.2 go beyond the prescriptive terms as they force thought about the curriculum "not merely in terms of how things ought to be . . . but how things are in real classrooms" (Ellis, 2004, p. 5). Another term that could be used to define the **descriptive curriculum** is *experience.* The experienced curriculum provides "glimpses" of the curriculum in action. Several examples, in chronological order, of descriptive definitions of curriculum are listed in Exhibit 1.2.

The definitions provided for prescriptive and descriptive curricula vary primarily in their breadth and emphasis. It would seem that a useful definition of *curriculum* should meet two criteria: It should reflect the general understanding of the term as used by educators, and it should be useful to educators in making operational distinctions.

Curriculum Tip 1.1	The following definition of *curriculum* is offered and will be used in this work: The curriculum is the plans made for guiding learning in the schools, usually represented in retrievable documents of several levels of generality, and the actualization of those plans in the classroom, as experienced by the learners and as recorded by an observer; those experiences take place in a learning environment that also influences what is learned.

Several points in this definition need to be emphasized. First, it suggests that the term *curriculum* includes both the plans made for learning and the actual learning experiences provided. Limiting the term to the plans made for learning is not enough, because, as will be discussed below, those plans are often ignored or modified. Second, the phrase "retrievable documents" is sufficiently broad in its denotation to include curricula stored in a digital form—i.e., software and/or shared on the Internet. Also, those documents, as will be more fully explained below, are of several levels of specificity: Some, such as curricular policy statements, are very general in their formulation; others, such as daily lesson plans, are quite specific. Third, the definition notes two key dimensions of actualized curriculum: the curriculum as experienced by the learner and that which might be observed by a disinterested observer. Finally, the experienced curriculum takes place in an environment that influences and impinges upon learning, constituting what is usually termed the *hidden curriculum.*

Although the definition, for the sake of brevity, does not deal explicitly with the relationship between curriculum and instruction, an implicit relationship does exist. Instruction is viewed

EXHIBIT 1.1	Prescriptive Definitions of Curriculum	
Date	*Author*	*Definition*
1902	John Dewey	Curriculum is a continuous reconstruction, moving from the child's present experience out into that represented by the organized bodies of truth that we call studies . . . the various studies . . . are themselves experience— they are that of the race. (pp. 11–12)
1918	Franklin Bobbitt	Curriculum is the entire range of experiences, both directed and undirected, concerned in unfolding the abilities of the individual; or it is the series of consciously directed training experiences that the schools use for completing and perfecting the unfoldment. (p. 43)
1927	Harold O. Rugg	[The curriculum is] a succession of experiences and enterprises having a maximum lifelikeness for the learner . . . giving the learner that development most helpful in meeting and controlling life situations. (p. 8)
1935	Hollis Caswell in Caswell & Campbell	The curriculum is composed of all the experiences children have under the guidance of teachers. . . . Thus, curriculum considered as a field of study represents no strictly limited body of content, but rather a process or procedure. (pp. 66, 70)
1957	Ralph Tyler	[The curriculum is] all the learning experiences planned and directed by the school to attain its educational goals. (p. 79)
1967	Robert Gagne	Curriculum is a sequence of content units arranged in such a way that the learning of each unit may be accomplished as a single act, provided the capabilities described by specified prior units (in the sequence) have already been mastered by the learner. (p. 23)
1970	James Popham & Eva Baker	[Curriculum is] all planned learning outcomes for which the school is responsible. . . . Curriculum refers to the desired consequences of instruction. (p. 48)
1997	J. L. McBrien & R. Brandt	[Curriculum] refers to a written plan outlining what students will be taught (a course of study). Curriculum may refer to all the courses offered at a given school, or all the courses offered at a school in a particular area of study.
2007	Pennsylvania Department of Education	Curriculum is a series of planned instruction that is coordinated and articulated in a manner designed to result in the achievement by students of specific knowledge and skills and the application of this knowledge. (n.p.)

In your opinion, which definition is appropriate today? Why?

here as an aspect of curriculum, and its function and importance change throughout the several types of curricula. First, in the written curriculum, when the curriculum is a set of documents that guide planning, instruction is only one relatively minor aspect of the curriculum. Those retrievable documents used in planning for learning typically specify five components: a rationale for the curriculum; the aims, objectives, and content for achieving those objectives; instructional methods; learning materials and resources; and tests or assessment methods.

EXHIBIT 1.2	Descriptive Definitions of Curriculum	
Date	*Author*	*Definition*
1935	Hollis Caswell & Doak Campbell	All the experiences children have under the guidance of teachers.
1941	Thomas Hopkins	Those learnings each child selects, accepts, and incorporates into himself to act with, on, and upon, in subsequent experiences.
1960	W. B. Ragan	All experiences of the child for which the school accepts responsibility.
1987	Glen Hass	The set of actual experiences and perceptions of the experiences that each individual learner has of his or her program of education.
1995	Daniel Tanner & Laurel Tanner	The reconstruction of knowledge and experience that enables the learner to grow in exercising intelligent control of subsequent knowledge and experience.
2006	D. F. Brown	All student school experiences relating to the improvement of skills and strategies in thinking critically and creatively, solving problems, working collaboratively with others, communicating well, writing more effectively, reading more analytically, and conducting research to solve problems.

In your opinion, which definition is appropriate today? Why?

Instruction is a component of the planned curriculum and is usually seen as less important than the aims, objectives, and content at the actualized level; when the planned or written curriculum is actually delivered, instruction takes on a new importance. The administrator or supervisor observing the curriculum as the total learning experiences of a classroom seems to focus on instruction—how the teacher is teaching.

THE TYPES OF CURRICULA

The definition stipulated above suggests that there is a major difference between the planned curriculum and actualized curriculum. Yet even these distinctions are not sufficiently precise to encompass the several different types of curricula. It is important to note that the word *curriculum* (as defined from its early Latin origins) means literally "to run a course." If students think of a marathon with mile and direction markers, signposts, water stations, and officials and coaches along the route, they can better understand the concept of types of curriculum (Wilson, 2005).

As early as the late seventies, Goodlad & Associates (1979) were perhaps the first to suggest several key distinctions. As Goodlad analyzed curricula, he determined that there were five different forms of curriculum planning. The *ideological curriculum* is the ideal curriculum as construed by scholars and teachers—a curriculum of ideas intended to reflect funded knowledge. The *formal curriculum* is that officially approved by state and local school boards—the sanctioned curriculum that represents society's interests. The *perceived curriculum* is the curriculum of the mind—what teachers, parents, and others think the curriculum to be. The *operational curriculum* is the observed curriculum of what actually goes on hour after hour in the classroom. Finally, the *experiential curriculum* is what the learners actually experience.

While those distinctions in general seem important, the terms are perhaps a bit cumbersome and the classifications are not entirely useful to curriculum workers. It seems to be more useful in the present context to use the following concepts with some slightly different denotations: the **recommended curriculum**, the **written curriculum**, the **supported curriculum**, the **taught curriculum**, the **tested curriculum**, and the **learned curriculum**. Four of these curricula—the *written,* the *supported,* the *taught,* and the *tested*—are considered components of the **intentional curriculum**. The intentional curriculum is the set of learnings that the school system consciously intends, in contradistinction to the **hidden curriculum**, which by and large is not a product of conscious intention.

The Recommended Curriculum

The recommended curriculum is the curriculum that is recommended by individual scholars, professional associations, and reform commissions; it also encompasses the curriculum requirements of policy-making groups, such as federal and state governments. Similar to Goodlad's "ideological curriculum," it is a curriculum that stresses "oughtness," identifying the skills and concepts that ought to be emphasized, according to the perceptions and value systems of the sources.

Curriculum Tip 1.2	Recommended curricula are typically formulated at a rather high level of generality; they are most often presented as policy recommendations, lists of goals, suggested graduation requirements, and general recommendations about the content and sequence of a field of study, such as mathematics.

Several influences seem to play key roles in the shaping of recommended curricula. First, societal trends seem to have a strong influence on policymakers. The prevailing conservative mood of the 1980s in the United States and the concern about competing with Japan were undoubtedly factors that influenced many of the reform reports of that period. Second, advancements in technology also play a role. The widespread use of technology in the nation's schools has influenced several of the professional associations to include aspects of technology across the curriculum in their recommendations. Advancing excellence in technological literacy in our schools is vital because

citizens of today must have a basic understanding of how technology affects their world and how they coexist with technology. Attaining technological literacy is as fundamentally important to students as developing knowledge and abilities in the traditional core subject areas. Students need and deserve the opportunity to attain technological literacy through the educational process. (Dugger, Meade, Delany, & Nichols, 2003, pp. 316–317)

Professional associations and individuals also seem to have an impact. First, the professional associations representing the several disciplines, such as the National Council of Teachers of Mathematics, and those that represent school administrators, such as the National Association for Secondary School Principals, have been active in producing recommended curricula. Also, there seems to be a network of opinion shapers in the profession, who through their writing and consulting have a strong impact on recommended curricula as they attempt to translate the latest research into recommendations for content and methodology. Also, as will be discussed in Chapter 4, federal and state legislation and court decrees play a significant role. Public Law 94-142, requiring the "least restrictive environment" for handicapped pupils, and Public Law 107-110, the No Child Left Behind Act, as well as charter schools, homeschooling, school choice, and vouchers, have had a profound influence on all those developing recommended curricula for these groups of learners.

All of this new legislation is being judiciously reviewed. For example, Amy Azzam (2007), a senior associate editor for educational leadership, notes, "Everyone interested in NCLB needs to be very careful about raising conclusions based on flawed or simplistic interpretations of data" (p. 92). As a result, national educational organizations have launched a series of ambitious projects to define voluntary standards for science, mathematics, art, music, foreign languages, social studies, English language arts, and other subjects. These efforts have served as catalysts in a wide-ranging national conversation about the needs of students and the instructional approaches of their teachers. This also adds to the national dialogue by presenting the consensus that exists among thousands of educators about what all students in K–12 schools should know and be able to do in the various subject fields. The authors endorse the act of defining standards by the national organizations because it invites further reflection and conversation about the goals of public schooling. Those recommended curricula serve some useful functions. First, as recommendations about policies and requirements, they identify important boundaries, emphases, and endpoints for curriculum planning: All high school students should study one semester of computer science and related technological skills. Second, they promote equity and excellence for all students: learning how to learn, equal access to resources, adequate staffing, and safe, well-equipped schools. Finally, as we reviewed the standards set forth by the various learned societies in the 1990s, it was concluded that curriculum specialists and teachers should consider the following points for the 21st century:

- Standards are not a national curriculum.

- Standards are an attempt to define what students should be able to know and do.

- The standards are informed by the latest theory and research regarding the various curricula.

- Standards are field based; they build on past successes of teachers and students.

- Standards can be met through a variety of teaching styles and strategies.

- The standards project emphasizes that *all* students can learn and achieve at high levels if their background, needs, and interest are considered.

- Standards should be a source of professional conversation and critique about what to do and how to do it.

- Teachers are members of a professional community, and a variety of professional organizations are available to support teacher growth.

- The literacy demands of the 21st century will require students to construct meaning with a variety of tools and texts. (Wilhelm, 1996, pp. 2–13)

It is interesting to note that the recommended curriculum, as posited by the learned societies, remains remarkably accurate today.

Raising standards in the core curriculum subjects continues to gain momentum in states and school districts across the country. In essence, "the process of setting standards for state assessments should follow the suggestions of many experts—good judgment and pragmatism must guide the final standard setting" (Pellegino, 2007, p. 541). In this regard, states have begun to use academic standards to make clear what students should learn and what teachers should teach. The recommended curricula by the learned societies will help curriculum coordinators and teachers make decisions about developing their instructional programs.

In addition to recommendations for the core curriculum by the learned societies, there must be a focus on curriculum diversity in our public schools. The authors perceive **multicultural education** as a response to the changing demographics of the United States. This perception is supported by Hanley (1999), who cites J. A Banks and C. A. M. Banks (1996), who predict that "by the year 2020, 46% of the students in public schools will be children of color and 20.1% of all children will live in poverty" (n.p.). Subsequently, "the need to address the various learning needs of such a diverse student population and the subsequent pluralistic society for which those children will be responsible is an urgent task faced by American public schools" (n.p.).

The Written Curriculum

Generally similar to Goodlad's (1984) "formal curriculum," the written curriculum is intended primarily to ensure that the educational goals of the system are being accomplished; it is a curriculum of control. Typically, the written curriculum is much more specific and comprehensive than the recommended curriculum, indicating a rationale that supports the curriculum, the general goals to be accomplished, the specific objectives to be mastered, the sequence in which those objectives should be studied, and the kinds of learning activities that should be used. Note, however, that Glatthorn (1980) questioned such comprehensiveness and recommended that the written curriculum be delivered to teachers as a loose-leaf notebook, containing only a scope-and-sequence chart, a review of the research, a list of course objectives, and a brief list of materials to be used. This simpler format, he believed, would make the written curriculum more likely to be used.

Curriculum Tip 1.3	The written curriculum is an important component of authentic literacy—the ability to read, write, and think effectively.

As school administrators and curriculum leaders, the authors believe that the written curriculum must be authentic. Schmoker (2007) supports the authors by saying, "there is every reason to believe that these capacities [the ability to read, write and think effectively], if acquired across the disciplines, will change lives by the millions and will redefine the possibilities of public education" (p. 488). As an aspect of authentic literacy, Walker (1979) was one of the first to note that written curricula can be both generic and site specific. Let's review both the concepts of generic and site specific curricula.

Generic curricula are those written for use in various educational settings. During the 1960s, numerous generic curricula were produced by federally funded research-and-development laboratories; now, more typically, they are produced by a state curriculum office and intended for use throughout the state, with some local leeway provided. Site-specific written curricula are those developed for a specific site, usually for a local school district or even for a particular school.

Site-specific written curricula are influenced by several different sources. First, as will be explained more fully in Chapter 4, federal and state legislation and court directives play a role. The passage of PL 94–142 prescribing that schools provide the "least restrictive environment" for handicapped learners undoubtedly precipitated much local curriculum work to help teachers work toward "inclusion." The textbooks and standardized tests in use in the district seem to influence decisions about the inclusion and placement of content. The expectations of vocal parent and community groups seem to have at least a constraining influence on what can be done.

In general, however, the guides seem to reflect the preferences and practices of a local group of elites: a director of curriculum, a supervisor of that subject area, a principal with a strong interest in curriculum, and experienced teachers. They, in turn, seem most influenced by the practice of "lighthouse" districts. It is important to note that we are entering a new kind of shard leadership in the 21st century. Teacher leadership is evolving because it can connect teachers and principals in their mutual mission: improving learning for students (Scherer, 2007). The authors know that people will support what they help to create, so all stakeholders, especially teachers, share the commitment of curriculum leadership.

The chief functions of written curricula seem to be three: *mediating, standardizing*, and *controlling*. They first mediate between the ideals of the recommended curriculum and the realities of the classroom; in this sense they often represent a useful compromise between what the experts think *should* be taught and what teachers believe *can* be taught. They also mediate between the expectations of administrators and the preferences of teachers. The best of them represent a negotiated consensus of administrative and classroom leaders. An example on the "how to" in developing and implementing curriculum is illustrated in Chapter 10.

They also play an important role in standardizing the curriculum, especially in larger districts. Often they are produced as a result of directives from a superintendent who is concerned that students in School A are studying a social studies curriculum or using a reading series quite different from those in Schools B and C.

Standardizing and centralizing curricula are often used by district and school administrators as management tools to control what is taught. This control function seems to be perceived differently by administrators and teachers. Administrators believe that controlling the curriculum is an important management responsibility; they point to the research on school effectiveness that seems to indicate that in schools with higher pupil achievement there is a principal actively monitoring the curriculum to ensure that the written curriculum is being delivered. Waters, Marzano, and McNulty (2003) compiled more than three decades of research on the effects of instruction and schooling on student achievement and found a substantial relationship between leadership and student achievement (see Exhibit 1.3). The results of this study have provided practitioners with specific guidance on the curricular, instructional, and school practices that, when applied appropriately, can result in increased achievement.

EXHIBIT 1.3 Principal Leadership Responsibilities	
Responsibilities	*The extent to which the principal . . .*
Culture	establishes a set of standard operating procedures and routines.
Discipline	protects teachers from issues and influences that would detract from their teaching time on focus.
Resources	provides teachers with material and professional development necessary for the successful execution of their roles.
Curriculum, instruction, assessment	is directly involved in the design and implementation of curriculum, instruction, and assessment practices.
Focus	establishes clear goals and keeps those goals at the forefront of the school's attention.
Knowledge of curriculum, instruction, assessment	is knowledgeable about current curriculum, instruction, and assessment practices.
Contingent rewards	recognizes and rewards individual accomplishments.
Communication	establishes strong lines of communication with teachers and among students.
Outreach	is an advocate and spokesperson for the school to all stakeholders.
Input	demonstrates an awareness of the personal aspects of teachers and staff.
Affirmation	recognizes and celebrates school accomplishments and acknowledges failure.
Relationship	demonstrates an awareness of the personal aspects of teachers and staff.
Change agent	is willing to and actively challenges the status quo.
Optimizer	inspires and leads new and challenging innovations.
Ideals/beliefs	communicates and operates from strong ideals and beliefs about schooling.
Monitors/evaluates	monitors the effectiveness of school practices and their impact on student learning.
Flexibility	adapts leadership behavior to the needs of the current situation and is comfortable with dissent.
Situational awareness	is aware of the details and undercurrents in the running of the school and uses this information to address current and potential problems.
Intellectual stimulation	ensures that faculty and staff are aware of the most current theories and practices and makes the discussion of these a regular aspect of the school's culture.

Walcott (1977), however, discovered in his ethnographic study of a district monitoring plan, that most teachers have historically viewed such attempts to control the curriculum as intrusive and counterproductive and will work hard to subvert such plans. Guilfoyle (2006) echoes Walcott's predictions by stating that "any system that hinges the evaluation of an entire school on one test score average from one group of students at one grade level cannot hope to accurately assess that school" (p. 13).

Predictably, written curricula, especially site-specific ones, are of uneven quality. The best of them seem to represent a useful synthesis of recommended curricula and local practice; they seem well conceptualized, carefully developed, and easy to use. Too many, however, lack those qualities. Careful reviews of a large number of such curriculum guides reveal that they suffer from some common faults: The objectives are often not related to the stated goals, instructional activities are not directly related to the objectives, the activities do not reflect the best current knowledge about teaching and learning, and the guides are generally cumbersome and difficult to use.

The Supported Curriculum

The supported curriculum is the curriculum as reflected in and shaped by the resources allocated to support and deliver the curriculum. Four kinds of resources seem to be most critical here: the time allocated to a given subject at a particular level of schooling (How much time should we allocate to social studies in Grade 5?); the time allocated by the classroom teacher within that overall subject allocation to particular aspects of the curriculum (How much time shall I allocate to the first unit on the explorers?); personnel allocations as reflected in and resulting from class-size decisions (How many teachers of physical education do we need in the middle school if we let PE classes increase to an average of 35?); and the textbooks and other learning materials provided for use in the classroom (Can we get by with those old basals for one more year?).

The patterns of influence bearing upon the supported curriculum seem rather complex. First, the state seems to exercise a strong influence on the supported curriculum: State curriculum guidelines often specify minimum time allocation, and some state-approved lists of basic texts restrict the choice of textbooks to a relatively small number.

The local school board, under the leadership of its superintendent, seems to play a key role. In many districts, boards will adopt curriculum policies specifying minimum time allocations to the several subjects, will approve district-purchased texts, and will make major budget decisions that strongly affect the personnel and material support provided. At the school level, principals also seem to have a major influence. They usually have some discretion in the allocation of funds for textbooks and other learning materials. They often are given some latitude in their requests for additional staff. The school master schedule is the major means for translating school priorities into decisions about curricular support.

Of course, the classroom teacher plays a crucial role. All teachers exercise a great deal of influence in determining how much time is allocated to particular subjects, despite the attempts of principals to limit such autonomy. All teachers have much autonomy about how time is allocated to given units or aspects of the curriculum.

Obviously the supported curriculum needs to be examined. The data are clear that several aspects of the supported curriculum have a major bearing upon what and how much is learned. First, early studies indicate that time is an important factor. In her review of the research,

Stallings (1980) concluded that "the body of knowledge emanating from the research on teaching in the 1970s suggests that teachers should allocate more time to academic subjects, keeping in mind ability levels, and students should be kept engaged in the tasks" (p. 12).

Berliner (1984) also cited examples of the dramatic differences in the way time is allocated in elementary school classrooms. One fifth-grade teacher devoted only 68 minutes a day to reading and language arts; another teacher, 137 minutes. Karweit (1983), however, questioned one aspect of this concern for time. In a review of the research on time-on-task, Karweit noted that "by a variety of criteria for the importance of an effect, the most outstanding finding relating the effects of time-on-task to learning is that the effects are as small as they are" (p. 46).

Second, does class size make a difference?

In a study of 20,000 fourth- and eighth-graders in 182 school districts across the country, the Educational Testing Services Policy Information Center found that fourth graders from classes of 20 students or less scored higher on the National Assessment of Educational Progress (NAEP) than did their peers in larger classes. (Chambers, 1999, pp. 1–2)

Several studies have been conducted regarding class size. The results reveal the following conclusions: The Tennessee class size experiment demonstrated that students learn better when class sizes are reduced (Finn & Achilles, 1990; Mosteller, 1995). Achilles (1997) has shown that having 15 students per class, especially in the first grade, has the greatest effect on student achievement. Farber and Finn (2000) found that fourth graders who had experienced small classes through the third grade were more engaged in learning than those who had experienced larger classes with teacher aides.

Achilles, Finn, Prout, and Bobbett (2001) found different behavior patterns between teachers who had small classes (15–17) and regular classes (20–28). Their findings revealed that as the day wore on, teachers in regular classes became irritable, edgy, and tired. "They wiped their eyes, sat down, and slowed or regimented instruction, often neglecting students' indiscipline, lassitude, and off-task misbehavior. All [teachers] seemed hassled" (p. 2). In contrast, teachers with small classes "remained full of energy all day. Time-on-task stayed high and constant with students remaining well behaved, engaged, and energetic. Student and teacher behavior were reciprocal, but positive" (p. 2). Another factor that the study revealed was carbon dioxide (CO_2) levels. "CO_2 is related to the number of persons in a space, is cumulative, and causes drowsiness and lethargy that may influence teaching and learning. Class size and time of day seemed to be key variables" (p. 2).

More recently, the National Education Association (NEA) (2007) indicated that a class size of 15 students in regular programs and even smaller in programs for students with exceptional needs is the key. NEA officials noted that while many education reform proposals remain controversial, reducing class size to allow for more individualized attention for students is strongly supported by parents, teachers, and education researcher. It is believed that teachers with small classes can spend time and energy helping each child succeed. Smaller classes also enhance safety, discipline, and order in the classroom. When qualified teachers teach smaller classes in modern schools, kids learn more.

Finally, the quality of the textbook and other learning resources as an aspect of the supported curriculum seems to play a central role. In reviewing the literature, Doyle (1983) noted several deficiencies of textbooks that researchers have discovered. For example, many textbooks present information in a confusing manner; the instructional procedures in the teacher's manual are often unnecessarily complicated for students; textbooks provide little explanation and direct instruction, but a great deal of practice and assessment material; and the overlap of textbooks and standardized tests is very low.

Allington (2002) noted that "many students in Grades 5–12 struggle to learn from content area textbooks that don't match their reading levels" (p. 16). As Chall (as cited in Allington, 2002) noted, the demands of reading increase dramatically for students in fourth grade as their learning begins to rely more on textbooks. For example, "the vocabulary for fourth graders is less conversational and less familiar, with more specialized, technical terms (delta, plateau, and basin) and abstract ideas (democracy, freedom, civilization)" (Allington, 2002, pp. 16–17). In essence, "the syntax of texts becomes more complex and demanding" (pp. 16–17). Also, "the reasoning about information in textbooks shifts, with a greater emphasis on inferential thinking and prior knowledge. (For example, what stance is the author taking on industrial polluters? Is there another stance that others might take?)" (p. 17). As Baumann and Duffy (as cited in Allington, 2002) indicated,

> Schools have typically exacerbated the problem by relying on a single-source curriculum design—purchasing multiple copies of the same science and social studies textbooks for every student. This one-size-fits-all approach works well if we want to sort students into academic tracks. It fails miserably if our goal is high academic achievement for all students. (p. 17)

Problems with textbooks continue to be a recurring problem. It should be noted that current elementary school reading series appear to contain several flaws: Stories written for use in the primary grades do not give enough insight into characters' goals, motives, and feelings; many of the so-called stories do not actually tell a story; textbooks lack a logical structure, often emphasizing a trivial detail rather than a fundamental principle. Harder textbooks, as well as media-related texts, unfortunately, have captured the attention of educators and policymakers who want to raise academic achievement.

This, however, does not have to be the case. According to Kirschenbaum (2006), author of *Goodbye Gutenberg*, "The debate about the future of the book is not between print and screen. It is between rectangular blocks of black-and-white text and colorfully designed pages. . . . What our students are screaming for is visually stunning, multi-sensory ways of reading and writing" (pp. 49–50). Allington (2002) parallels the harder textbooks to one's own experience—for example, building a Web site. "Do you reject many of the books because they are too easy? Do you say to yourself, 'Gosh, only 11 words on this page I can't pronounce—not hard enough for me!'" (p. 18). With that thought, there needs to be a rethinking of what curriculum and instruction should look like.

It should be noted there are aspects of supportive curriculum other than textbooks. For example, noted curriculum author Carol Ann Tomlinson and her colleagues (2002) indicated that the supported curriculum can also involve the use of flexible options and the formation of a parallel curriculum model. Tomlinson noted in *The Parallel Curriculum* that parallels can be used to develop or support curriculum for individuals, small groups, and entire classes. The term *parallel* indicates several formats through which educators can approach curriculum design in the same subject or discipline. Tomlinson refers to the four parallels as Core Curriculum, Curriculum and Connections, Curriculum of Practice, and Curriculum of Identity.

These parallel processes can be deductive or inductive and can be used as a catalyst to discover student abilities and interests or in response to student abilities and interests. Tomlinson believes that these parallels act as support for thematic study and help connect content that might otherwise seem disjointed to learners. Using her model, a teacher might establish a definition of change, identify key principles related to change, and introduce students to key skills as well as specify standards that need to be covered. Tomlinson's parallel model for curriculum development is only one of the many approaches that can be used to help support curriculum.

The supported curriculum plays a central role at several stages of the curriculum cycle. First, in developing curricula, educators should give specific attention to the supported curriculum, paying special attention to time allocations and the materials of instruction. Second, in implementing the curriculum, administrators should be sure that adequate support is provided. Next, as Chapter 11 indicates, those involved in aligning the curriculum should assess to what extent there is a good fit between the written, the supported, and the taught curricula. Finally, any comprehensive evaluation of the curriculum should assess the supported curriculum, because deficiencies in support will probably be a major factor in student achievement.

The Taught Curriculum

The extent to which there is consonance between the written curriculum and the taught curriculum seems to vary considerably. At one extreme are those school systems that claim to have achieved a high degree of consonance between the two by implementing curriculum-alignment projects. At the other extreme are schools where a state of curricular anarchy exists: Each teacher develops his or her own curriculum, with all sorts of disparate activities going on across the school.

Curriculum Tip 1.4	The taught curriculum is the delivered curriculum, a curriculum that an observer sees in action as the teacher teaches.

How does the taught curriculum, regardless of its fit with the written curriculum, become established? The question is a complex and an important one that can best be answered by synthesizing several studies of teachers' thinking, planning, and decision making.

Thus, teachers' decisions about the curriculum are products of many interacting variables. Rather than being mindless choices or acts of willful rebellion, those decisions instead seem to represent the teacher's considered judgment about what compromises will be best for that teacher and a particular class.

The Tested Curriculum

The tested curriculum is that set of learnings that are assessed in teacher-made classroom tests, in district developed curriculum-referenced tests, and in standardized tests. To what extent are these several types of tests related to the taught curriculum? The answers seem to vary. First, there were early problems in test preparation. Tests previously concentrated on assessing students' comprehension and memory of objective information, and their attempts to measure understanding of concepts resulted in multiple-choice items that really assessed students' guessing ability.

The evidence on the congruence between curriculum-referenced tests and instruction suggests a somewhat different picture. In districts using curriculum-referenced tests as a means of monitoring teacher compliance, the test seems to drive instruction. The result is a closer fit. Yet here the congruence is not reassuring to those who value higher-order learning. An examination of a curriculum-referenced test used in a large district's alignment project indicated that the test items were concerned almost exclusively with such low-level objectives as punctuating sentences correctly, spelling words correctly, and identifying the parts of speech.

Finally, the research suggests that a gap is widening between standardized tests and what some instructors are teaching. The consequences of inadequate alignment and poor testing are serious.

From a historical perspective, Berliner took the lead in 1984 to point out that achievement was lower in schools where there was not a close fit between what was taught and what was tested. Students were put at a disadvantage when the teaching and testing did not match, and their grades and scores were probably not a valid measure of what they had learned. Finally, there were serious legal consequences when poorly fitting tests were used to make decisions about promotion and graduation. The courts ruled that when tests were used for purposes that denied constitutional guarantees of equal protection or due process (as in retention or denial of graduation), schools needed to provide evidence that those tests assessed skills and concepts actually taught in the classroom.

Today, educators are facing similar if not greater problems with testing. James Popham (2007), a noted author, states, "If we plan to use tests for purposes of accountability, we need to know that they measure traits that can be influenced by instruction. . . . Instructionally insensitive tests render untenable the assumptions underlying a test-based strategy for educational accountability" (p. 147).

The good news is that many more teachers are using online-based programs to ease the alignment of local testing to state and national standards. Teachers are also using data analysis of student strengths and weaknesses. Web site programs such as Exam View now allow classroom teachers to create pre- and posttests online easily and quickly. Valid and reliable test questions aligned with state and national standards are selected from large banks of test items. Online testing programs also provide possible teaching strategies to address specific areas of need.

Curriculum Tip 1.5	Components of the curriculum determine the fit between what is taught and what is learned.

It might be useful at this juncture to note again that the four curricula discussed above—*written, supported, taught,* and *tested*—might be seen as constituting the intentional curriculum, which comprises that set of learning experiences that the school system consciously intends for its students.

The Learned Curriculum

The term *learned curriculum* is used here to denote all the changes in values, perceptions, and behavior that occur as a result of school experiences. As such, it includes what the student understands, learns, and retains from both the intentional curriculum and the hidden curriculum. The discussion here focuses on what is learned from the intentional curriculum; the last part of the chapter analyzes what is learned from the hidden curriculum.

What, then, do students learn and retain from the intentional curriculum? Obviously, the answer varies with the student, the teacher, and the curriculum. Creating a solid infrastructure with history, pedagogy, and philosophy is critical, but practical experiences are equally as valuable (Fleck, 2007). There are some subtle transformations, especially between the taught curriculum and the learned curriculum, that occur in most classrooms, regardless of the specific conditions. (The discussion that follows draws primarily from the review of the research on academic work.)

To begin with, the students seem especially sensitive to the accountability system at work in the classroom and take seriously only that for which they are held accountable. Regardless of what objectives the teacher announces or what the teacher emphasizes, the students seem to assess the importance of classroom transactions in relation to their value in that accountability system: "Will this be on the test?"

To achieve success in that accountability-oriented classroom, the students invent strategies for managing ambiguity and reducing risk. They will restrict the output they provide teachers, giving vague and limited answers to minimize the risk of making public mistakes. They also attempt to increase the explicitness of a teacher's instructions, asking the teacher for more examples, hints, or rephrasing of the question. Furthermore, they pressure teachers to simplify curriculum complexity, strongly resisting any curriculum that forces them to think, inquire, and discover.

According to Booher-Jennings (2006), the theory of accountability is simple. She believes in giving students regular benchmark assessments—use the data to identify individual students' weaknesses, and provide targeted instruction and support the curriculum that addresses those areas. It is therefore assumed that accountability systems will provide reliable data on which to base educational policy. However, McGill-Franzen and Allington (2006) are not as positive. They maintain that four overlooked factors—summer reading loss, retention in grade, test preparation, and testing accommodations—are consistently producing skewed pictures of student achievement. Their contention is that unless accountability policies are substantially revised and current practices modified, estimates of school effectiveness will remain unreliable, and the public and policymakers will continue to be misled.

In sum, students learn what is assessed and remember those learnings as discrete answers to questions, and if this holds true, their learning is somewhat disorganized and unconnected.

COMPONENTS OF THE CURRICULUM

Although several texts in the field seem to treat curriculum development as if it were one undifferentiated process, the realities are quite different. The concept subsumes several distinct entities that might best be described as components of the curriculum. They are as follows. Each of these will be analyzed briefly below and then discussed more fully in the chapters that follow.

Curricular Policies

No education reform is ever going to be long lasting unless it becomes institutionalized, and none is going to become institutionalized until we first change the culture of schools and schooling (Boles & Troen, 2007). The best way to institutionalize curriculum is to formulate sound curricular policies.

The term *curricular policies*, as used here, designates the set of rules, criteria, and guidelines intended to control curriculum development and implementation. Kirst (1983) led the way, noting that there are macropolicies, such as a board policy on courses required in high school, and micropolicies, such as a set of recommendations for a curriculum unit in mathematics. Policymaking, as he noted, is essentially the "authoritative allocation of competing values" (p. 282). Thus, as a board makes a policy requiring 3 years of science in the high school curriculum, but does not require any study of art, it is perhaps unwittingly according a higher value to science as a way of knowing than it does to aesthetics. Saylor, Alexander, and Lewis (1981) made a useful distinction between de jure policy making (as implemented in court decisions, state legislative acts, and local agency regulations) and de facto policy making (as carried out by community networks, testing bureaus, accrediting associations, and advisory boards).

Curriculum Tip 1.6	Educators, administrators, and teachers are well advised to reexamine policies affecting curriculum and the accepted practices at their schools.

The decisions that a school makes regarding established policies and practices can affect students enormously. For example, teachers' instructional decisions influence students' feelings about (and success with) the curriculum, but the policies and practices in both classrooms and in the entire school provide the context for teacher–student interactions around instruction (Danielson, 2002).

Schools have multiple policies and practices that can and do affect curriculum development. Some policies are deliberately set in place, while others evolve with time.

Curricular Goals

Curricular goals are the general, long-term educational outcomes that the school system expects to achieve through its curriculum. Three critical elements are included in this definition. First, goals are stated much more generally than objectives. Thus, one goal for English language arts might be "Learn to communicate ideas through writing and speaking." One objective for fifth-grade language arts would be much more specific: "Write a letter, with appropriate business letter form, suggesting a community improvement." Second, goals are long-term, not short-term, outcomes. The school system hopes that after 12 years of formal schooling, its students will have achieved the goals that the system has set.

Finally, curricular goals are those outcomes that the school system hopes to achieve through its curriculum. Here it is important to make a distinction between educational goals and curricular goals. Educational goals are the long-term outcomes that the school system expects to accomplish through the entire educational process over which it has control, as Brown (2006) found from a survey that was conducted with educators, parents, and employers as to what type of skills they believed students should be developing. The following is a prioritized list of survey responses:

1. Critical-thinking skills5

2. Problem-solving strategies and effective decision-making skills

3. Creative-thinking processes

4. Effective oral and written communication skills

5. Basic reading, mathematics, and writing abilities

6. Knowledge of when and how to use research to solve problems

7. Effective interpersonal skills

8. Technology skills

9. Knowledge of good health and hygiene habits

10. Acceptance and understanding of diverse cultures and ethnicities

11. Knowledge of how to effectively manage money

12. Willingness, strategies, and ability to continue learning.

How do curricular policies and curricular goals interrelate? In a sense, the policies establish the rules of the game ("take 3 years of health education") and the goals set the targets ("at the end of those 3 years, you will adopt constructive health habits"). In this sense, they should determine in a rational system the form and content of all the other components that follow. As will be evident throughout this work, however, educational organizations are usually not very rational. Typically, policies are not related to goals, and goals are not related to fields and programs of study.

Fields of Study

A **field of study** is an organized and clearly demarcated set of learning experiences typically offered over a multiyear period. In most school curricula, such fields of study are equivalent to the standard school subjects: English language arts, mathematics, social studies, science, and so on. At the college level, fields are more narrowly defined; thus, students pursue majors in history, or anthropology, or sociology—not "social studies."

Programs of Study

A program of study is the total set of learning experiences offered by a school for a particular group of learners, usually over a multiyear period and typically encompassing several fields of study. The program of study is often described in a policy statement that delineates which subjects are required and which are electives, with corresponding time allocations and credits. Here, for example, is a typical **program of studies** for an elementary school:

Reading and language arts: 8 hours a week

Social studies: 3 hours

Mathematics: 4 hours

Art: 1 hour

Music: 1 hour

Health and physical education: 1 hour

At the college level, a student's program of studies includes all the courses he or she will take or has taken.

Courses of Study

A course of study is a subset of both a program of study and a field of study. It is a set of organized learning experiences, within a field of study, offered over a specified period of time (such as a year, a semester, or a quarter) for which the student ordinarily receives academic credit. The course of study is usually given a title and a grade level or numerical designation. Thus, "third-grade science" and "English II" are courses of study. At the college level, courses of study seem to be the most salient component for both students and faculty: "I'm taking Economics I this term"; "I'm offering Elizabethan Literature this quarter."

Units of Study

A unit of study is a subset of a course of study. It is an organized set of related learning experiences offered as part of a course of study, usually lasting from 1 to 3 weeks. Many units are organized around a single overarching concept, such as "Mythical Creatures" or "The Nature of Conflict." Not all teachers think about units as they plan. Many high school teachers simply aggregate lessons: "I'll have a spelling lesson tomorrow and a grammar lesson on the next day." As college instructors conceptualize their courses, they often seem to think about a sequence of lectures rather than a unit of study.

Robert Marzano (as cited in Marzano, Pickering, & Pollock, 2001), noted author and researcher, believes that when developing units of study at any level it is best to view the process as a series of phases. The planning phases of unit development include the following:

- At the *beginning* of a unit, include strategies for setting learning goals.
- *During* a unit, include strategies
    - for monitoring progress toward learning goals
    - for introducing new knowledge
    - for practicing, reviewing, and applying knowledge
- At the *end* of a unit, include strategies for helping students determine how well they have achieved their goals.

Marzano's intent is for teachers to systematically utilize strategies that work. These are best-practice approaches. Basically, teachers should present students with the components and subcomponents of the unit process and then structure tasks to emphasize a specific component or subcomponent.

Lessons

A lesson is a set of related learning experiences typically lasting 20 to 60 minutes, focusing on a relatively small number of objectives. Ordinarily a lesson is a subset of a unit, although, as noted above, the unit level is sometimes omitted by teachers while planning for instruction.

These distinctions among the several components of curriculum have an importance that transcends the need for conceptual clarity. Each seems to involve some rather different planning processes. Thus, to speak generally about "curriculum planning," without differentiating between planning a program of studies and planning a course of studies, is to make a rather serious mistake.

Improving and enhancing lessons based on current brain research and curriculum design is becoming a critical component in the search for best practices. With that in mind, Marzano and his colleagues (2001) identified nine categories of strategies that have a strong effect on student achievement. They are as follows:

1. Identifying similarities and differences
2. Summarizing and note taking
3. Reinforcing effort and providing recognition
4. Homework and practice
5. Nonlinguistic representations
6. Cooperative learning
7. Setting objectives and providing feedback
8. Generating and testing hypotheses
9. Questions, cues, and advance organizers

As can be seen from analyzing these nine strategies, students need a fair amount of guidance when learning complex processes.

Classroom teachers therefore need to realize that curriculum planning should *emphasize metacognitive control* of all processes. These processes are similar to skills in that they often produce some form of product or new understanding. Teachers intuitively recognize the importance of metacognition but may not be aware of its many dimensions. Metacognitive ability is central to conceptions of what it means to be educated. The world is becoming more complex, more information-rich, more full of options, and more demanding of fresh thinking. With these changes, the importance of metacognitive ability as an educational outcome can only grow (Martinez, 2006).

THE MASTERY, THE ORGANIC, AND THE ENRICHMENT CURRICULA

One additional classification system first proposed by Glatthorn during the 1980s has proved useful, especially in developing and improving fields of study.

Curriculum Tip 1.7	Curriculum leaders should distinguish between the three types of learning in each field of study. The three types of learning are mastery, organic, and enrichment.

The three types of learning result from the following analytical steps. First, divide the learnings in that field between those that are basic and those that are enrichment.

Basic learnings are those that, in the views of knowledgeable educators, are essential for all students (all, in this use, refers to the top 90% of learners, excluding the least able and those with serious learning disabilities). Enrichment learnings are the knowledge and skills that are interesting and enriching but are not considered essential; they are simply "nice to know." Thus, in fifth-grade social studies, curriculum workers might decide that the early settling of the Vikings in Iceland would be interesting enrichment content.

Once the first division between basic and enrichment is made, then further divide the basic learnings into those that require structure and those that do not require structure. Structured learning, as the term is used here, has four characteristics:

1. Sequencing
2. Planning
3. Measurable outcomes
4. Clearly delineated content

Nonstructured learning, on the other hand, includes all those skills, knowledge, and attitudes that can be mastered without such careful sequencing, planning, testing, and delineation. Structured and nonstructured learning yield the three types of curricula depicted in Exhibit 1.4: mastery, organic, and enrichment.

EXHIBIT 1.4	The Three Types of Curricula	
	Basic	*Enrichment*
Structured	Mastery	Enrichment
Nonstructured	Organic	

Mastery learnings are those that are both basic and structured. An example of a mastery objective for language arts, Grade 2, is the following:

Use a capital letter for the first word in a sentence.

Organic learnings, however, are those that are basic but do not require structuring. They are the learnings that develop day by day, rather naturally, as the result of numerous interactions and exchanges. They tend not to be the focus of specific learnings. They are just as important as the mastery outcomes (if not more so), but they do not require sequencing, pacing, and articulation. Here is an example of organic learning for language arts, Grade 2:

Listen courteously while others speak.

The teacher might emphasize that learning on every occasion, not devote a specific lesson to it. And enrichment learnings, as noted above, are those learnings that simply extend the curriculum; they are not considered basic.

This tripartite division is more than an interesting intellectual exercise. It has significant implications for curriculum development. In general, district curriculum guides and scope-and-sequence charts should focus solely on the mastery elements. The nurturing of organic components can be enhanced through effective staff development; such outcomes do not need to be explicated fully and carefully in guides. The enrichment components can be included in a supplement for those teachers who want to share enrichment activities.

Curriculum-referenced tests should focus only on mastery elements; organic elements should not be tested. One district that ignored this important distinction wasted a great deal of time trying to develop a test for courteous listening before it was forced to give up in frustration. The distinction also has implications for the purchase of texts: Textbooks should focus on the mastery objectives; the teacher can nurture the organic without the aid of textbooks.

Finally, the distinction helps resolve the issue of district versus teacher control. In general, the district should determine the **mastery curriculum**, to the extent of specifying objectives. The district emphasizes the important outcomes but gives the teacher great latitude of choice in nurturing them. In addition, the enrichment curriculum is the teacher's own: Here the teacher can add whatever content he or she feels might be of interest to the students.

In addition to the discussion of basic versus organic structure of curriculum, it is also important that teachers be aware of brain research and how students learn. According to Patricia Wolfe (2001), an educational author and consultant, learning is a process of building neural networks. She notes that children construct networks in the cortex of the brain that contain information about an unbelievable variety of concepts. She lists three levels of learning: Concrete Experience, Representational or Symbolic Learning, and Abstract Learning.

Concrete Learning, according to Wolfe, is pretty much what the term implies. It is a combination of repeated experiences and visualizations that allow the brain to store, network, and recall when necessary.

The second level, Representational or Symbolic Learning, is based on the brain linking and cross-referencing information. All sensory data are linked through association and become part of memory. With concrete experiences available, sensory data can be "activated" when remembered. Without the concrete experience, the representation or symbol may have little meaning, no matter how much someone explains it to the student.

The third level, Abstract Learning, involves the brain using only abstract information, primarily words and numbers. With a strong neural network formed both by concrete experience and representations, it is possible for children to visualize in their "mind's eye." An understanding of terms, sets, and similarities depends on a child's developmental age and on a teacher's ability to give sufficient examples that relate to the student's experiences. It is also important for the teacher to involve students in experiences that make the abstract concepts understandable.

More research is helping educators grasp how students learn. For example, neuroimaging studies are revealing an under-activation in the brain region influencing fluency in struggling readers. According to Shaywitz and Shaywitz (2007), remarkable progress has been made in understanding the neural systems influencing reading and reading disability. Basically, this progress reflects the development of functional neuroimaging–functional magnetic resonance imaging (MRL), a technology that assesses increases in blood flow in brain regions while subjects carry out specific cognitive tasks. Such findings help educators select the most successful and evidence-based approaches to reading instruction. It is hoped that instruction using phonemic awareness, phonics, fluency, vocabulary and comprehension strategies will be enhanced with the feedback from neuroimaging research.

Curriculum Tip 1.8	The key to enriching curriculum is to involve students in real-life problem-solving scenarios.

Using real-life problem-solving scenarios assists in the process of developing the strongest brain networks that will be formed by actual experience. As a result, most schools are now using critical-thinking and problem-solving skills and strategies as a major part of the curriculum-development process.

THE HIDDEN CURRICULUM

The concept of hidden curriculum expresses the idea that schools do more than simply transmit knowledge. There are differences between written and hidden curriculums in that teachers teach and students learn implicit concepts and patterns (Deutsch, 2004). Hidden curriculum, which is sometimes called the "unstudied curriculum" or the "implicit curriculum," might best be defined in the following manner:

Those aspects of schooling, other than the intentional curriculum, that seem to produce changes in student values, perceptions, and behaviors.

As the definition suggests, students learn a great deal in school from sources other than the intentional curriculum. Although the term *hidden curriculum* is often used with negative connotations, those learnings can be both desirable and undesirable from the viewpoint of one aspiring to optimal human development. In examining the specific nature of the hidden curriculum, it seems useful at this point to distinguish between what might be termed the constants (those aspects of schooling that seem more or less impervious to change) and the variables (those aspects that seem susceptible to reform).

Curriculum Tip 1.9	Hidden curriculum might be seen as those aspects of the learned curriculum that lie outside the boundaries of the school's intentional efforts.

The Constants of the Hidden Curriculum

Certain important aspects of the hidden curriculum are so intrinsic to the nature of schools as a cultural institution that they might be seen as constants. Historically, the depiction of those constants presented below has been influenced by a close reading of several early curricular reconceptualists such as Apple (1979), Pinar (1978), and Giroux (1979); sociologists such as Dreeben (1968); and educational researchers such as Jackson (1968) and Goodlad (1984). One of the constants of the hidden curriculum is the ideology of the larger society, which permeates every aspect of schooling. Thus, schools in the United States inevitably reflect the ideology of democratic capitalism.

A key component of the school as an organization is the classroom, where the most salient aspects of the hidden curriculum come into play. The classroom is a crowded place, where issues of control often become dominant. Control is achieved through the differential use of power; the teacher uses several kinds of power to control the selection of content, the methods of learning, movement in the classroom, and the flow of classroom discourse. Control also is achieved by the skillful use of accountability measures; teachers spend much time evaluating and giving evaluative feedback. In such a classroom, students unconsciously learn the skills and traits required by the larger society; they learn how to be punctual, clean, docile, and conforming. They learn how to stand in line, take their turn, and wait.

Another example of the hidden curriculum, according to Butzin, Carroll, and Lutz (2006), is when a teacher works solo within a "grade," students lose instructional time at the beginning of each year while teachers get to know the students. Students also lose quality instructional time at the end of each school year after "The Test" because teachers back off from rigorous topics.

Even though the above features of the hidden curriculum are presented here as constants relatively impervious to change, it is important for curriculum leaders to be aware of their subtle and pervasive influence. Being aware of aspects and variables of hidden curriculum is crucial for the success of our future administrators and teacher–leaders.

The Variables of the Hidden Curriculum

Several other important aspects of the hidden curriculum can be more readily changed by educators. The most significant of these can be classified into three categories: organizational variables, social-system variables, and culture variables.

Organizational Variables

The term *organizational variables* is used here to designate all those decisions about how teachers will be assigned and students grouped for instruction. Here, four issues seem worthy of attention: team teaching, promotion and retention policies, ability grouping, and curriculum tracking. The evidence on the effects of team teaching on student achievement is somewhat inconclusive. Even though many school systems have implemented "promotional gates" policies that promoted students solely on the basis of achievement, several syntheses of the research indicate that social promotion results in better attitudes toward school, better self-image, and improved achievement.

Grouping practices in the schools have often been attacked by critics as one of the most baleful aspects of the hidden curriculum. Here the indictment of Giroux and Penna (1979) is perhaps typical of the era:

> The pedagogical foundation for democratic processes in the classroom can be established by eliminating the pernicious practice of "tracking" students. This tradition in schools of grouping students according to "abilities" and perceived performance is of dubious instructional value. (p. 223)

In an extensive review of literature, two problems surface with such an indictment. The first is that the authors seem to ignore a rather important distinction made by Rosenbaum (1980) between ability grouping (sorting students into ability-based groups for instruction, such as high, average, and low ability) and curriculum grouping (sorting students into such curricular tracks as vocational, general, and college preparatory). The other, more serious problem is that the empirical evidence available does not support their assertions.

The practice of curriculum grouping or tracking, in which students follow a predetermined career-oriented program such as college preparatory or vocational, seems to be a more complex matter. Here Rosenbaum's (1980) review of the research seems most enlightening. He first noted that there is no clear finding from the research on whether ability or social class is the primary determiner of track placement. According to several studies, the guidance counselor plays a key role in track selections. Many students, according to Rosenbaum, are in curricular tracks that are inconsistent with career choices. The lack of congruence is complicated by the fact that curricular tracking is relatively stable, and there is more movement from college preparatory to general and vocational than the other way around.

The chief problem with curriculum tracking, according to researchers, is the lack of challenge in the general curriculum. Many approaches to tracking have been developed to prevent an exodus of public school students to private schools as per NCLB. While tracking may have an uncertain effectiveness in achieving that goal, it creates considerable concerns about the potential for relegating the children "left behind" to mediocre schools and tracks and for increasing social stratification (Rotberg, 2007).

Secada (1992) concluded that tracking or ability grouping generally benefited only those students placed in high-end groups while having a detrimental effect on students placed in low-end groups. Evidence of other negative results exists due to tracking students based on ability:

- Minorities and low-income students are disproportionately represented. (Century, 1994)

- Experiences in mathematics and science differ between minorities and low-income students compared to their more advantaged and White peers during elementary school. (Oakes, Ormseth, Bell, & Camp, 1990)

- Students in low-ability tracks tend to receive lower-quality instruction. (Secada, 1992)

- Students in lower-ability tracks have difficulty in moving up to higher-ability tracks. (Century, 1994)

Another option in ability tracking is between-class grouping. Students participating in this arrangement find themselves grouped at different ability levels for each subject, depending on their ability in that subject area. Secada (1992) found the negative results plaguing full-time grouping also to be a problem here.

Most researchers agree that grouping is beneficial for gifted students. Advocates and opponents of grouping alike maintain the necessity to continue grouping gifted students together and that any reforms introduced to tracking in a school not necessarily affect gifted and talented programs (Century, 1994). Nevertheless, high-end grouping practices must include regular entry evaluations for students to ensure that these gifted tracks are open to all.

A better alternative to tracking would be the regular use of cooperative learning groups. According to Slavin, Chamberlain, and Daniels (2007), cooperative learning is effective at all grade levels, but it is particularly appropriate for the developmental needs of middle-school students. Cooperative learning allows students to be noisy, active, and social in the pursuit of academic excellence. Learning groups within a heterogeneous classroom have been shown to result in higher achievement, little or no psychological harm to the students, and reduced segregation. Students also gain experience in individual accountability and responsibility, as well as acquiring skills in working with others.

The weight of the research evidence suggests educational leaders interested in improving the organizational variables of the hidden curriculum might focus their attention on promotion policies and curriculum tracking as the key variables. They should ensure that the general curriculum is neither dull nor trivial.

Other organizational variables might include class size, breakfast and lunch, noncategorical special help, special programs like Reading Recovery, better libraries and better access to books, better assessment, as well as extended day and after-school programs (Cunningham & Allington, 1994).

Much discussion takes place regarding the impact of class size on curriculum planning and implementation. Many authors and researchers believe that smaller class sizes facilitate better teaching and more personalized instruction. Some authors and researchers do not. The key is that smaller class size may facilitate, but does not necessarily ensure, better teaching and learning. Most individuals do agree, however, that class size does affect how the curriculum is delivered, and thus the curriculum's nature can be implicit.

Breakfast and lunch may lie outside the boundary of curriculum, but they still may have an important impact on planning. For example, classes have to be scheduled around these activities, especially if the cafeteria is located in the gymnasium. Children having to eat late or not having proper nutrition may also influence when and how the curriculum is delivered.

Noncategorical special help has a substantial and yet hidden impact on a school's schedule in that staff may have to adjust classes to compensate for students' being out of the room. Teachers also have to adjust their classroom organization to accommodate students' arriving back into a classroom after receiving special help in another setting.

To increase the percentage of proficient readers, educators must increase the use of best reading practices (Carbo, 2007). Special programs such as Reading Recovery and Read Well are now important components of the classroom, since the passage of the NCLB Act in 2002. The hidden aspect of these special phonics-based programs is that primary teachers must now schedule their units and lessons around these intensive reading programs to accommodate high-risk children. There is little doubt about the impact of these special programs on how the curriculum in the classroom is being delivered.

Schools with better libraries and/or that provide students with better access to books may have an advantage over schools that do not. Getting reading and informational materials to students in a timely matter can be a key to learning. Albeit hidden, the ability of a teacher to have access to books and materials will make a big difference on how that teacher will teach.

Assessment and *accountability* are becoming bywords with the advent of the No Child Left Behind Act, and assessment and data analysis are now becoming major determiners of what is taught, when it is taught, and how it is taught. Entire curricula are being changed based on the collection of assessment data and student test scores.

Although the impact of assessment is not totally understood and often goes unnoticed, extended days and after-school programs appear to be having a major impact on curriculum planning and implementation. Teachers are now being paid extra for extended days to complete in-service and staff development requirements. Additional staff development opportunities often mean that teachers will be learning new material and trying different approaches in their classrooms. The impact of this change on curriculum may be obscure to some, but it is often immeasurable in scope.

Social-System Variables

Researchers are finding that the socioeconomic makeup of a school, rather than its racial makeup, drives student achievement (Kahlenberg, 2006). A small but growing number of school leaders are reviewing their *district's social system* and considering the integration of students by socioeconomic status.

The term *social system* as an aspect of school climate was first used by Tagiuri (1968) to refer to the social dimension concerned with the patterned relationships of persons and groups in the school. Anderson's (1982) review of the research on school climate indicated several social-system factors associated with positive student attitude and achievement. Several of these had to do with administrator–teacher relationships: The principal was actively involved in instruction; there was good rapport and communication between administrators and teachers; teachers shared in the decision-making process; and there were good relationships among teachers. Others were related to teacher–student relationships: Teacher–student interactions in general were positive and constructive; students shared in decision making; and there were extensive opportunities for student participation in activities. Obviously, all these factors can be influenced through effective leadership by both administrators and teachers.

Curriculum Tip 1.10	Social and economic issues can affect aspects of the hidden curriculum.

Social- and economic-related programs such as Head Start and Even Start are designed to assist economically challenged preschool children. Head Start is a federal program that has been around since the 1960s. Some school districts are designing their school operation to have Head Start on campus. This allows a good transition for the Head Start children to matriculate into a kindergarten program. Having Head Start on-site in a school district also enhances opportunities for staff development and offers a way to improve staff relations. Head Start teachers and administrators have an opportunity to plan their curricula so that it threads unnoticed into the district curriculum. On-site Head Start teachers are thus better able to understand the goals and objectives of the school district and are better able to correlate their program with district primary teachers.

There were two great achievements in the design of Head Start. First, the program emphasized social and emotional development—emphasizing health, comprehensive services, and social services to families. Second, Head Start introduced parent participation. Probably the most important single determinant of a child's growth is the behavior of parents (Perkins-Gough, 2007).

Even Start is a family literacy program that includes preschool children and their parents. Both children and parents go to school. Parents work to complete their high school education or receive adult literacy instruction. The implicit aspect of this program is that children are provided with an enriched preschool curriculum. Parents also learn more about parenting, including ways to involve their children in reading and writing (Cunningham & Allington, 1994).

Another social aspect of curriculum that may be hidden is the involvement of parents and community. Although parents may not directly create a change in curriculum, their approval or disapproval can have a tremendous impact on how a school is operated, what is taught, and how it is taught. An example might be the involvement of parents at the primary level and their support of technology. When parents are in the school at the primary level and see the impact that technology is having on their child, they often become major supporters of educational technology. This support is generated in the passage of special levies and bonds that affect the use of technology at all grade levels—even high school.

The involvement of the community can have an impact on curriculum development in much the same way. If members of the community feel positive about what is happening in their schools, they are much more apt to support the schools financially. This financial support might include more staff, improved facilities, materials, and/or staff development. The connection to the curriculum may not be readily apparent to some, but it is definitely a major factor in the success of the school.

Culture Variables

As noted by sociologist Arlie Hochschild, "we are call connected in chains of care, not only to friends and family around us, but also to other people whom we cannot see" (Hargreaves & Fink, 2006, p. 20). Sometimes in school settings it is the people of other cultures who are not seen and/or the people of other cultures who are not understood. Successfully teaching students from culturally and linguistically diverse backgrounds—especially students from historically marginalized groups—involves more than just applying specialized teaching techniques. It demands a new way of looking at teaching that is grounded in an understanding of the role of culture and language in learning (Villegas & Lucas, 2007).

Tagiuri (1968) defined *culture variables* as the social dimensions concerned with belief systems, values, cognitive structures, and meaning. According to Anderson's (1982) review, several key factors here play an important role in the hidden curriculum. All of the following are associated with either improved achievement or improved attitude:

- The school has clear goals that are understood by all; those goals are supported by a strong consensus among administrators and teachers.
- Administrators and teachers have high expectations for each other, and both groups are strongly committed to the importance of student achievement.
- Administrators and teachers have high expectations for students, and these high expectations are translated into an emphasis on academics.
- Rewards and praise are publicly given for student achievement; rewards and punishments are administered in a fair and consistent manner.
- The school emphasizes cooperation and group competition, rather than individual competition.
- Students value academic achievement; peer norms support the value of such achievement.

These aspects of the hidden curriculum also can be influenced by administrators and teachers working together.

To summarize, then, the hidden curriculum is seen here as both constant and variable aspects of schooling (other than the intentional curriculum) that produce changes in the student. The constants—the ideology of the larger society, the way in which certain knowledge is deemed important or unimportant, and the power relationships that seem necessary in large bureaucratic institutions—seem unlikely to change. However, the variables—those aspects of the organizational structure, the social systems, and the culture of the school that can be influenced—require the systematic attention of curriculum leaders.

In reviewing the intended and hidden curriculum, a coming together of the two can be observed. Exhibit 1.5 illustrates how the intentional curriculum and the hidden curriculum extend into the learned curriculum.

EXHIBIT 1.5 Relationships of Types of Curricula

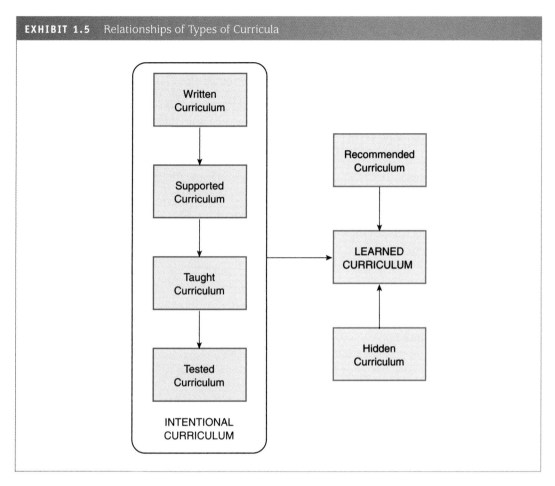

SOURCE: Developed by Mark A. Baron, Chairperson, Division of Educational Administration, School of Education, the University of South Dakota. Used with permission.

SUMMARY

This introductory chapter provides a general overview of the curriculum field and a set of concepts for analyzing that field. The chapter defines the concept of curriculum, examines the several types of curricula, describes the contrasting nature of curriculum components, and analyzes the hidden curriculum to provide some fundamental concepts essential for understanding the comprehensive field of curriculum. The chapter includes the topics of what curriculum is and why it is important; the types and components of curricula and how they have changed over the years; what mastery, organic, and enrichment curricula are and the roles they play in the development of curriculum; and why knowledge of the "hidden curriculum" is important to curriculum leaders.

APPLICATIONS

1. By reviewing the definitions of curriculum provided in this chapter and by reflecting on your own use of the term, write your own definition of *curriculum*.

2. Some educators have suggested that the profession should use simpler definitions for *curriculum* and *instruction*: Curriculum is what is taught; instruction is how it is taught. Do these definitions seem to suffice, from your perspective? If so, explain.

3. Descriptive curriculum has numerous definitions, which can be slightly confusing. Based on the general understanding by educators and their operational distinctions, rank the six examples provided on page 5 and explain why your selection meets the criteria.

4. Some leaders have argued for a very close fit between the written and the taught curriculum, suggesting that teachers should teach only what is in the prescribed curriculum. Others have suggested that some slippage is desirable—that teachers should have some autonomy and latitude, as long as they cover the essentials. What is your own position on this issue?

5. Although most curriculum texts do not make the distinctions noted here between programs of study, fields of study, and courses of study, those distinctions do seem to matter. To test this hypothesis, do the following: (a) List the steps you would follow in designing a program of studies for one level of schooling, such as elementary or middle school; and (b) list the steps you would follow in designing a field of study, such as social studies, K–12.

6. It has been suggested here that the "constants" of the hidden curriculum are not easily changed. Others would argue that they should be changed if we truly desire democratic and humanistic schools. As a school leader, would you attempt to change any of those "constants," or would you give more attention to the "variables"?

7. Outline a change strategy you would use in attempting to improve the "culture" variables that seem to be associated with improved attitude and achievement.

CASE STUDY   Bridging the Gap Between Theory and Practice

Dr. John Summers was hired to be the curriculum director to enhance the teaching and learning process for the Dover School District. Dr. Summers was the superintendent's choice for the position because he was highly qualified in the area of curriculum development, and his performance at a somewhat smaller school district with 5,000 students, in a neighboring state, was outstanding. The district John came from was known for its high academic achievement, which was attributed to a well-planned curriculum supported by the principals and teacher–leaders.

In contrast, the Dover School District was in curriculum disarray, and student achievement was low when compared to statewide achievement scores. As Dr. Summers soon discovered, some staff members and administrators in the Dover School District construed the curriculum as ideal because it met their standards. They also felt that if something was being taught, a curriculum existed. Others in the district, however, felt that a planned curriculum was vital for the district, but they were unable to generate the necessary leadership to bridge the gap between theory and practice.

The Challenge

Analyze the nature and concepts of curriculum in this chapter. As curriculum director of the Dover School District, how should Dr. Summers utilize administrators and teacher–leaders to help bridge the gap between curriculum theory and practice?

Key Issues/Questions

1. To what extent do you believe a written curriculum for the various disciplines plays a role in this case?

2. To what extent do you believe the supported, tested, and learned curricula for the various disciplines play a role in improving the intentional curriculum?

3. Do you think there is any hope of changing attitudes? If so, how would you attempt to do this? If not, why?

4. Do you feel that the intentional curriculum is prescriptive or descriptive, or a combination of both? Why?

5. What roles do the recommended curriculum and hidden curriculum play in developing the intentional curriculum?

6. In planning curricula, mastery curriculum should require from 60% to 75% of the time available. Do you agree that Dr. Summers should place an emphasis on mastery curriculum? Why?

WEBLIOGRAPHY

Association for Supervision and Curriculum Development
   www.ascd.org
   http://webserver3.ascd.org/handbook/demo/curricrenew/pocr/sectioni.html

Consortium on Chicago School Research
   http://ccsr.uchicago.edu

Education Trust
   www.edtrust.org

Education World
   www.educationworld.com

CHAPTER 2

Curriculum History

The Perspective of the Past

Understanding the history of curriculum development is useful for both scholars and practitioners. It results in a deeper awareness of the extent to which curricular changes are often influenced by and are a manifestation of larger social forces. It also offers a broader perspective from which to view so-called innovations and reforms, which often seem to reverberate with echoes of the past.

This understanding seems especially facilitated by a careful analysis of the past 100 plus years of that history. Such a demarcation results in a closer focus on the major developments affecting American schools, while still providing the broader perspective that is so essential. Those developments perhaps can be better grasped if analyzed as parts of specific periods of history. Of course, an obvious fallacy occurs in delineating such periods. Historical periods become an artifact of the historian's analysis: People do not live and events do not occur in neat chronological packages called "periods." Given that caution, an analysis of that century plus a decade of curriculum history seems to suggest that there were eight distinct eras, each with its own distinguishing features. Exhibit 2.1 is therefore suggested as a way of examining the past century plus a decade of curriculum theory and practice.

Although the verity of the eight eras may be accepted by most individuals, it follows that any attempt to understand or instigate educational reform would be based on an inquiry of what has occurred in the past.

As described by Sarason (1990),

> The significance of the historical stance is not only in what it tells us about the manifestations of a particular problem over time, or what one learns about the efficacy of remedial actions, but also in what one learns about the system quality—that is, the features of the system in which the problem arises and recurs, or remains constant but unremarked until it is seen [again] as destabilizing the system. (p. 34)

EXHIBIT 2.1 Educational Eras	
Date	*Period*
1890–1916	Academic Scientism
1917–1940	Progressive Functionalism
1941–1956	Developmental Conformism
1957–1967	Scholarly Structuralism
1968–1974	Romantic Radicalism
1975–1989	Privatistic Conservatism
1990–1999	Technological Constructionism
2000–Present	Modern Conservatism

Sarason also concluded that "one can write human history as a saga of the inability to recognize the obvious" (p. 146). Also, "public schools cannot exist as cocoons, isolated from a changing environment and climate" (Goens & Clover, 1991, p. 3).

Questions addressed in this chapter include the following:

- What were the periods of Academic Scientism, Progressive Functionalism, Developmental Conformism, Scholarly Structuralism, Romantic Radicalism, Privatistic Conservatism, Technological Constructionism, and Modern Conservatism, and why was each important in the development of curriculum?

- What were some of the predominant trends that transcended each major period of curriculum development?

Key to Leadership

In reviewing curriculum history, two general observations should be made. The first is to note the pace of change. The second is to note the rhythms and directions of that change.

ACADEMIC SCIENTISM

The term used here to identify the period from 1890 to 1916, Academic Scientism, derives from the two influences that seemed to predominate: the academic and the scientific. The academic influence was the result of systematic and somewhat effective efforts of the colleges to shape the curriculum for basic education; the scientific influence resulted from the attempts of educational theorists to use newly developed scientific knowledge in making decisions about the mission of the school and the content of the curriculum.

Curriculum Tip 2.1	There is a direct relationship between curriculum of the past and curriculum today.

The Temper of the Times

The educational trends of this period can perhaps best be discerned if viewed against the backdrop of societal changes. The turn of the century was characterized, first of all, by the post–Civil War growth of industry and the development of urban areas, stimulated primarily by the rapid growth of railroads.

The second distinguishing feature of the era was the impact of popular journalism. The linotype machine was introduced in 1890, the price of newspapers dropped to 1 cent, and the number of newspapers doubled. Magazines were also reaching larger audiences. Finally, it was a time when new immigrant waves were reaching these shores. The volume of immigrants increased, and their places of origin changed markedly. Whereas prior to the 1890s, immigrants came chiefly from the Western European countries, during the turn-of-the-century decades, they were more likely to come from the Eastern European countries.

The Predominant Trends

As noted above, the major educational influences of the period were both academic and scientific. The man who most clearly represented the academic influence of the colleges was Charles W. Eliot, president of Harvard University. In a perhaps immodest fashion, Eliot saw the entire curriculum as his purview, making specific recommendations for elementary, secondary, and higher education. In essence, Eliot's position was that a sound academic curriculum was best for all students, regardless of their college aspirations.

The scientific influence was perhaps stronger, even though less direct. One interesting sign of this scientific influence was the change of one of the major educational organizations: What had once been the Herbart Society changed its name in 1900 to the National Society for the Scientific Study of Education.

The scientific perspective seemed to influence educational thinkers in three important ways. First, science provided intellectual support for a rational and meliorist worldview, a view widely held by the educational thinkers of the period. Problems could be solved by the rational application of scientific processes: All that was needed was more knowledge and the ability to apply that knowledge.

Second, science provided a content focus for the curriculum. Flexner (1916) was one of several theoreticians who argued for the primacy of science. In his view, the central purpose of the school was to prepare children to cope in the real world—and that preparation would best be accomplished through a study of the physical and social world.

Finally, science provided a means for improving the schools. Scientific knowledge about the child yielded insights, proponents argued, about the desired nature of the curriculum—about what children could learn. Scientific knowledge also offered a rationale for the optimal methods of teaching.

The Exemplary Leaders

The major thrusts of this period were probably best represented by the careers and contributions of G. Stanley Hall and Francis W. Parker.

G. Stanley Hall

G. Stanley Hall (1904/1969) was an eminent psychologist who provided scientific support to the child-centered educators of the day. While earlier developmentalists had argued for the study of the child as the basis for curricular decision making, it was Hall who provided the charismatic leadership for the movement. As a social Darwinian, he believed in evolutionary social change, not radical transformation. The essential task of the school was to support this gradual change through the nurturing of the gifted, providing the gifted child with the opportunity to grow through individualized activities.

Francis W. Parker

Francis W. Parker seemed to have had even more influence than G. Stanley Hall; in fact, John Dewey (1964) himself called Parker "the father of progressive education." Parker is significant for his contributions to both pedagogy and curriculum development. The pedagogical methods he advocated could perhaps best be described as natural, child-centered methods.

His contributions to curriculum theory were similarly comprehensive. In his *Talks on Pedagogics* (1894), he argued for a child-centered curriculum that builds upon what the child instinctively knows.

In contrast to Hall's essentially conservative orientation, Parker was in almost every respect a progressive who believed that the common school was the key to human advancement.

In a chapter in his pedagogic work, he anticipated at least the rhetoric of more current social reformers: "This mingling, fusing, and blending [of children from all social classes] give personal power, and make the public school a tremendous force for the upbuilding of democracy" (p. 421).

The Major Publications

The major publications of the Academic Scientism period were perhaps the reports of two committees established by the NEA: the Committee of Ten, appointed to make recommendations for the high school curriculum, and the Committee of Fifteen, for the elementary curriculum.

The Committee of Ten

Although many educators cite the work of the Committee of Ten as an example of the attempt of colleges to dominate the curriculum, the committee was appointed by the NEA at the request of members. There was so much variation in college preparatory curricula in schools across the country that school administrators themselves desired more uniformity.

The major recommendation of the committee report (National Education Association, 1893) was that four separate programs of study be offered to high school students: classical,

Latin–scientific, modern languages, and English. In essence, the Committee of Ten said to the profession and to the public, "A sound academic curriculum is the best preparation for life—for all students."

The Committee of Fifteen

The other committee appointed by the NEA at almost the same time was given the charge of making recommendations for elementary curriculum and instruction. Eliot had some influence with this committee, which accepted two of his recommendations: that the number of elementary grades be reduced from ten to eight and that algebra be substituted for arithmetic in Grades 7 and 8. However, it rejected his recommendation that the time devoted to grammar and arithmetic be reduced so that the program could be diversified and enriched (the committee's recommendations were reported in the NEA's 1895 report).

In its curriculum recommendations, the Committee of Fifteen advocated a rather conservative approach. Grammar, literature, arithmetic, geography, and history were seen as the central subjects for training the mind, and clear separation of those subjects was essential. The following subjects were to be taught every year, from first to 8th: reading, English grammar (except in the 8th year), geography, natural science and hygiene, general history, physical culture, vocal music, and drawing. Handwriting was to be taught in the first 6 years, and spelling lists in Grades 4, 5, and 6. Latin was to be introduced in the 8th year, and manual training (for boys) and sewing and cooking (for girls) in the 7th and 8th. In mathematics, arithmetic was to be studied in the 1st through the 6th years, followed by algebra in the 7th and 8th.

In addition to the required oral lessons in general history for all grades, U.S. history was to be taught in the 7th year and the first half of the 8th; the Constitution was to be taught in the second half of the 8th year. Thus, a pupil in the 4th year would be studying 11 separate "branches" or subjects: reading, handwriting, spelling lists, English grammar, arithmetic, geography, natural science and hygiene, general history, physical culture, vocal music, and drawing.

The ultimate impact of the Committee of Fifteen report was to sustain a somewhat fragmented and subject-centered curriculum.

PROGRESSIVE FUNCTIONALISM

The era of Progressive Functionalism, which lasted approximately from 1917 to 1940, was characterized by the confluence of two seemingly disparate views: the progressive, child-centered orientation of the followers of John Dewey and the functional orientation of curriculum scientists.

The Temper of the Times

The decade of the 1920s was a time of seemingly unbridled optimism and growth in this country. Houses were being built at a record-making pace. By 1929, there were more than 26 million cars registered: one car for every five people.

All that optimism and growth was tragically destroyed in the Depression and the very slow recovery that followed. The human suffering of that period is difficult to exaggerate. At one point it was estimated that 28% of the population was without any income at all. Many school systems simply shut down because there was no money to pay teachers.

The international picture was no less depressing, for the 1930s was the decade marking the rise of Hitler in Germany and Stalin in the Soviet Union, both of whom were ultimately responsible for the mass genocide carried out in both nations. Confronted with the global rapacity of the dictators in Germany, Italy, the Soviet Union, and Japan, the Western democratic governments seemed for many years to be confused and impotent.

The Predominant Trends

As noted above, the term given this era derives from two forces—progressivism and functionalism—that, while seemingly antithetical in principle, often combined to influence both curriculum and instruction.

Progressivism in Education

It is obviously difficult in the brief space available to summarize a movement so complex and so often misunderstood as progressive education. Whereas in the prior decade the dominating influence of the curriculum was the academic subject, for progressive educators it was the child. The child-centered curriculum was based on a somewhat romantic and perhaps even naive view of child development: The child is innately curious and creative, with a thirst for learning and a need for self-expression. Such a view has clear implications for both the process and the content of the curriculum. In using a curriculum-development process, child-centered curriculum workers begin by determining the child's interests, assured that any desired content can be linked with those interests.

The content of the curriculum is similarly influenced. The arts are emphasized, because the nurturing of creativity is paramount. Subjects that have little immediate appeal to the child, such as mathematics and grammar, tend to be slighted.

Functionalism

Functionalism is the term given here to the educational theory of those whom Kliebard (1985) called "the social efficiency educators," who argued essentially that the curriculum should be derived from an analysis of the important functions or activities of adult life. As a curriculum theory, it was clearly influenced by two significant ideas current at the time: It was avowedly influenced by the stimulus response learning theory of Edward Thorndike that supported the importance of successful practice; and it reflected the concern for efficiency at the heart of the "scientific management" of Frederick Taylor (1911) and his followers. Taylor argued that any task could be analyzed for optimal efficiency by observing skilled workers, studying the operations they carried out, determining the time required, and eliminating wasted motion. Similarly, education could be made more efficient by analyzing learning tasks.

The Exemplary Leaders

Two figures seem to stand out in retrospect: John Dewey and Franklin Bobbitt. Although they espoused diametrically contrary views of the curriculum in particular, they both seemed to exert a strong influence on their contemporaries.

John Dewey

In a sense, of course, it is fallacious to identify Dewey as a leader of this period alone, because his career as a philosopher and an educator spanned the eras of both Academic Scientism and Progressive Functionalism (Dewey, 1964).

Dewey's (1900) beliefs about the relationship of school and society are, of course, fundamental to his theories of the curriculum and are best understood at the outset. For Dewey, democracy was the ideal society, and he believed that the society can prevail only as it enables diverse groups to form common interests, to interact freely, and to achieve a mutual adaptation. Dewey (1916) pointed out in his book *Democracy and Education* that such a society needed schools for more than the superficial reason of producing an educated electorate.

It was this concern for the social nature of schooling and learning, of course, that led him to place so much emphasis on experience. Yet he did not advocate a mindless activity-centered curriculum in which any activity is considered worthwhile as long as it is perceived by the learners as interesting and relevant. In *Experience and Education*, Dewey (1938) noted that experience and education cannot be directly equated; some experiences are "mis-educative," to use his term. Desirable learning experiences had to meet certain stringent criteria: They had to be democratic and humane, they had to be growth enhancing, they had to arouse curiosity and strengthen initiative, and they had to enable the individual to create meaning.

Franklin Bobbitt

Franklin Bobbitt was the other curriculum theorist who seemed to exert a profound influence on the schools of his time, and who still seems to affect indirectly even those who are not familiar with his work. The curriculum, in his view, was whatever was needed to process the raw material (the child) into the finished product (the model adult). He summarized in this early work the curriculum process as he saw it in the following manner:

1. We need first to draw up in detail for each social or vocational class of students in our charge a list of all of the abilities and aspects of personality for the training of which the school is responsible.

2. Next we need to determine scales of measurement in terms of which of these many different aspects of the personality can be measured.

3. We must determine the amount of training that is socially desirable for each of these different abilities and state these amounts in terms of the scales of measurement.

4. We must have progressive standards of attainment for each stage of advance in the normal development of each ability in question. When these four sets of

things are at hand for each differentiated social or vocational class, then we shall have for the first time a scientific curriculum for education worthy of our present age of science. (Bobbitt, 1913, p. 49)

Thus, while both Dewey and Bobbitt espoused a social meliorist view of the purpose of schooling, they differed sharply in their conception of the curriculum. From Dewey's (1902) perspective, the developing child was the beginning point for curriculum development; from Bobbitt's, the model adult was the starting point. Furthermore, while Dewey embraced an experience-centered program in which learnings emerged somewhat organically and informally from social interactions, Bobbitt seemed more concerned with a precise scientific matching of activity with outcome.

The Major Publications

Obviously, the writings of both Dewey and Bobbitt had an important influence on educational leaders of the time. However, two other works might be seen to have had a more direct impact: *Cardinal Principles of Secondary Education* (1918) and *The Foundation of Curriculum Making* (Rugg, 1927). While quite different in both their genesis and their intended audience, the two publications were surprisingly similar in their major emphases.

The Cardinal Principles of Secondary Education

In 1913, the National Education Association, perceiving a need to reconcile some important differences about the nature of secondary education, appointed the Commission on the Reorganization of Secondary Education. After 5 years of deliberation, the commission published its recommendations.

The seven cardinal principles emerged, therefore, from this rationale: health, command of fundamental processes (reading, writing, arithmetic, oral and written expression), worthy home membership, vocation, citizenship, worthy use of leisure time, and ethical character. These principles were seen as closely interrelated, not as separate goals. In achieving those goals, schools were encouraged to construct programs of study around three elements: constants (required courses), curriculum variables (specialized subjects chosen in relation to the student's goals), and free electives (subjects chosen to develop the special interests of the student).

In addition to providing a useful framework for the secondary school curriculum, the commission accomplished two other important goals: It attempted somewhat successfully to free the secondary schools from the domination of the colleges, and it articulated forcefully a rationale for the comprehensive high school. In the commission's view, the American high school should serve the needs of all youth, not just the college bound.

The Twenty-Sixth Yearbook

In the midst of all the ferment resulting from the attempts to reshape the schools, the National Society of Education (Rugg, 1927) decided to bring together in two volumes the thinking of all the major experts in the field—as the preface noted, "making a special effort to bring together, and as far as possible to unify or to reconcile, the varying and often seemingly divergent or even antagonistic philosophies of the curriculum that were being espoused by leading authorities" (p. 6). It is obviously difficult to summarize adequately these two volumes produced by men whom Tyler (1971) calls "pioneering leaders in curriculum development" (p. 28). Although the major weakness in the Rugg and Counts system, according to Tyler, was its failure to recognize the importance of the classroom teacher, the major contribution of the Twenty-Sixth Yearbook was its achievement of a consensus by the experts in the field on two of the major issues that divided the profession. First, the committee articulated a balanced position on whether studies of the child or the adult should provide the grounding of the curriculum: "We would stress the principle that in the selection and validation of curriculum materials expert analysis must be made both of the activities of adults and interests of children" (Rugg, 1927, pp. 12–13). The committee also recognized the importance of both individual and societal needs:

> The individual becomes an individual in the best sense only through participation in society. . . . The curriculum can prepare for effective participation in social life by providing a present life of experiences which increasingly indentifies the child with the aims and activities derived from an analysis of social life as a whole. (p. 14)

DEVELOPMENTAL CONFORMISM

The next period of educational history—the era of Developmental Conformism (1941–1956)—might be seen as a transition period, with the nation first embroiled in a cataclysmic war and then recovering from it to find a cold war on its hands.

The Temper of the Times

This period, of course, was in many ways a turbulent time. It was, first of all, a time of international conflict and tension. The United States entered World War II in 1941, and by 1945 the Allies had defeated the Axis nations. However, only 3 years after the war ended, tensions between the United States and the Soviet Union became critical with the Soviet blockade of Western Berlin—tensions that were to affect the nation for the next four decades.

It was also a time of racial unrest. For most of the period, this was a strongly segregated society, with deep-seated racial and ethnic biases. The U.S. Supreme Court outlawed school segregation in 1954, and in 1955 Rosa Parks refused to give her seat to a White man on a bus in Montgomery, Alabama.

Finally, it was the dawning of the atomic age. As several observers noted, the atom bomb profoundly changed the way the average person felt and thought about the world.

Most of the American people seemed to react to this societal turbulence by attempting to live lives of quiet conformity. As presidents, both Truman and Eisenhower seemed able to assure the American people that, despite these signs of unrest, the nation was essentially sound and its future was bright.

The Predominant Trends

Here again, two trends are singled out as shaping educational efforts: the interest in the developmental abilities and needs of youth, and a concern with conformity as an educational goal.

The Developmental Theorists

It was, first of all, a period marked by rather intensive interest in the educational implications of child and adolescent development. As noted above, Dewey had long been concerned with delineating and responding to the stages of growth in children and youth.

As will be discussed below, Piaget's work was just becoming known by educators who perhaps sensed its importance but could not yet discern fully its implications. Yet, it was the theories and research of Havighurst that during this period seemed to make the most immediate difference to educators. Havighurst (1972) conceptualized need as a "developmental task," which he defined as

> a task which arises at or about a certain period in the life of the individual, successful achievement of which leads to his happiness and to success with later tasks, while failure leads to unhappiness in the individual, disapproval by society, and difficulty with later tasks. (p. 2)

The importance of these developmental tasks for curriculum can be seen at once by examining just a few of the tasks that Havighurst identified for childhood and adolescence. Consider these examples:

Early Childhood

- Getting ready to read

- Learning to distinguish right from wrong

- Learning sex differences and sexual modesty

- Learning to talk

Middle Childhood

- Learning physical skills necessary for games

- Learning to get along with age-mates

- Learning an appropriate masculine or feminine social role

- Developing fundamental skills in reading, writing, and calculating

Adolescence

- Accepting one's physique and using the body effectively

- Preparing for marriage and family life

- Preparing for an economic career

- Desiring and achieving socially responsible behavior

- Developing intellectual skills and concepts necessary for civic competence

Conformity as an Educational Goal

Implicit in the conceptualization and language of Havighurst's developmental tasks is a strong sense of conforming to the status quo. Consider, for example, such tasks as these: "learning an appropriate masculine or feminine role," "accepting one's physique," "desiring and achieving socially responsible behaviors," and "accepting and adjusting to the physiological changes of middle age." It is perhaps not unfair to say that such a strong emphasis upon conformity was both a reflection of and a contribution to a prevailing educational view that held that one of the important responsibilities of the schools was to help children and youth conform to existing societal norms.

A second assumption was that the curriculum should emphasize functional outcomes—practical skills and knowledge that had immediate value for the student.

A concomitant assumption was that the disciplines themselves were not important as organizing bases for the curricula. Instead, schools were encouraged to develop "core curricula" that would minimize subject-matter distinctions and integrate learnings around major themes and issues. As Oliver (1977) noted, the primary objective of the core curriculum is "to develop unified studies based upon the common needs of the learners and organized without restriction by subject matter" (p. 246). Here, for example, are some of the "centers of experience" that Van Til, Vars, and Lounsbury (1961) recommended for structuring a core program: making and keeping friends, coming to terms with my body, money-magic or madness, meet your new school.

The recurring theme throughout much of this literature is that this is a good society that simply must be maintained. Also, the attempt to make education more relevant too often produced curricula that trivialized learning and overemphasized the needs of the present. Finally, in too many cases it provided a curricular excuse for tracking systems that imprisoned children from poor families in low-level programs that were banal and unimaginative and denied them the opportunity to pursue academic studies needed for success in college.

The Exemplary Leaders

Two curriculum theorists seem to have been important in this period: Ralph Tyler and Hollis Caswell. Although, like most exemplary leaders, their careers spanned several of the periods demarcated here, it seems most appropriate to examine their work within the framework of the period presently under discussion.

Ralph Tyler

Tyler first gained professional attention through his participation as research director of the Eight-Year Study sponsored by the Progressive Education Association to evaluate and systematize the efforts of progressive schools to free their curricula from the domination of the colleges. The curriculum results of the study were summarized by Giles,

McCutchen, and Zechiel (1942), who noted that curriculum development and evaluation involved attention to four basic issues: identifying objectives, selecting the means for attaining those objectives, organizing those means, and evaluating the outcomes. It seems apparent that their work influenced Tyler in his preparation of the syllabus for the graduate course he was offering at the University of Chicago. It is this syllabus for Education 305 (Tyler, 1950) that presents and explicates what has become known as the "Tyler rationale."

In the syllabus, Tyler noted that the first question that must be answered in developing any curriculum is, "What educational purposes should the school seek to attain?" These educational objectives can first be identified by examining three sources: studies of the learners themselves, studies of contemporary life outside of school, and suggestions from subject specialists.

The second question is, "How can learning experiences be selected that are likely to be useful in attaining these experiences?" Here he argued for several general principles that should guide curriculum workers in selecting objectives.

The third question is, "How can learning experiences be organized for effective instruction?" In making determinations about the organization of experiences, the curriculum developer should consider three criteria: continuity, sequence, and integration.

The final question is, "How can the effectiveness of learning experiences be evaluated?" Valid and reliable curriculum-based tests should be developed and the results used to improve the curriculum.

Tyler's publication has had a lasting impact on curriculum leaders. By 1985, more than 100,000 copies of the syllabus had been purchased. It made a significant contribution by systematizing in a sequential manner, and curriculum workers seemed to value its clearness, its comprehensiveness, and its simplicity.

Hollis Caswell

Caswell was one of the first to understand the importance of staff development as a necessary foundation for curriculum work. To that end, he developed excellent study materials and bibliographies helping teachers perceive the larger issues of child development and curriculum ends and using those materials in educating the teachers of Florida and other states who were working with him in a comprehensive curriculum-revision project.

Second, he put into practice on a major scale the widespread belief that teachers should be involved in curriculum development. In developing state curriculum for Virginia, he involved 10,000 Virginia teachers studying and discussing curricular issues.

Third, he developed a useful set of organizing structures that integrated the three determiners of curricula—child interests, social meaning, and subject matter. He began by reviewing what was known about child development to identify important child interests.

The Major Publications

Two quite different publications are singled out here for attention: one by the distinguished Swiss psychologist Jean Piaget, and one by a somewhat anonymous committee of American educators.

The Psychology of Intelligence

Because Piaget's publishing career spans several decades during which many seminal publications were produced, it is obviously difficult to select one work as most important. However, his 1950 book, *The Psychology of Intelligence*, seems to have been especially influential because it was one of the earliest to present in a systematic manner his comprehensive view of the nature of intelligence and the child's developmental stages.

Thus the developmental stages he identified are organized around this essential principle. Four such stages are usually discussed in the extensive literature on Piaget: sensorimotor, preoperational, concrete operations, and formal operations. While these stages, in his view, are invariant in their sequence, they are also hierarchically related: Early stages are integrated into later ones.

The sensorimotor stage, which begins with conception and lasts until about age 2, is a preverbal period in which the child relies on sensorimotor information to adapt to the environment and to acquire new behaviors. The child begins with simple reflex actions, then makes responses modified by experience.

During the next stage, the preoperational, which lasts until about age 6 or 7, language and symbolic thought have their beginnings. The learner reconstructs the developments of the sensorimotor stage, integrating prior knowledge into the new intellectual structures.

During the stage of concrete operations, between ages 7 and 11, the child develops the cognitive ability to classify, order, and handle numbers, spatial operations, and all the operations of classes and relations. In a sense, the concrete operations are similar to those of the prior stage, except for the fact that the child is able to use representational thought instead of direct action on the object. In this stage, the child seems to have a well-integrated cognitive system through which he or she can act on the environment. However, the child is still able to deal effectively in a cognitive sense only with concrete objects, not with symbolic representations of those objects.

During the final stage of formal operations, the adolescent can think about both the real and the possible. Educators who first learned of the Piagetian stages in the late 1950s and early 1960s were initially impressed with the research data supporting this stage theory.

Historically, however, other researchers have been more concerned with conducting research to verify or challenge Piaget's stage theory. After reviewing all the pertinent research, Gelman and Baillargeon (1983) reached this conclusion: "In our opinion there is little evidence to support the idea of major stages in cognitive development of the type described by Piaget. Over and over again the evidence is that the preoperational child has more competence than expected" (p. 214).

In substance, the report was essentially an argument for Developmental Conformism.

SCHOLARLY STRUCTURALISM

The Temper of the Times

In retrospect, the era of Scholarly Structuralism (1957–1967) seems to have been an interesting period of history. First, it was a time when the factors producing the turbulence of the previous period seemed to gather in strength. International tensions continued unabated.

The major event in education was the launching of *Sputnik* in 1957—an event that dramatized the need for strong programs in science and mathematics in American schools. Under the prodding of President Johnson, Congress responded with massive allocations of federal aid.

The Predominant Trends

The period under consideration was an interesting one from an educational perspective. This was the first time in American educational history that academic scholars decided that they had a key role to play in the development of specific curricula. Largely supported by federal funds channeled through the National Science Foundation, those scholars produced numerous curricula for every major discipline in both elementary and secondary education.

The Exemplary Leaders

During this interesting time, two curriculum theorists seem to have made major impacts—Jerome Bruner and Joseph Schwab.

Jerome Bruner

Bruner (1960) set forth rather cogently in *The Process of Education* a comprehensive rationale for Scholarly Structuralism. First, school curricula must be primarily concerned with effecting and facilitating the transfer of learning. Because school time is limited, educators must find the most efficient means of using the limited time available.

Understanding broad principles was especially important in the latter part of the 20th century. Bruner argued increased scientific knowledge was able to clarify those structures in a way that perhaps was not possible before. The explosion of knowledge made it impossible for the student to learn everything. Therefore, learning the structures of a discipline resulted in a kind of curricular parsimony.

Joseph Schwab

Schwab's (1969, 1971, 1973, 1978, 1983) writings on curriculum span a period of at least 20 years and have proved to be rather influential in the field of curriculum theory. Like Bruner, Schwab was early concerned with the structure of the disciplines; yet it seems fair to say that his writings on the matter demonstrate a complexity and sophistication missing from the Bruner work.

Rather than insisting that there is only one way of understanding the world, Schwab argues for a "permissive eclecticism," which enables the inquirer to use any valid approach to understand natural and human phenomena. He noted that few disciplines have a single structure and that the scientists in a field are too diverse in their preferences to be unanimous about one right mode of attack.

Schwab's later writings on curriculum seem much more concerned with process and much less concerned with the structure of the disciplines. The outcome, he hoped, would be incremental change, and the process would be an eclectic one, drawing from several bodies of knowledge and from several perspectives.

The Major Publications

Two publications seem worthy of note: the Conant Report and the Physical Science Study Committee (PSSC) curriculum project. One looked back; the other seemed to look ahead.

The Conant Report

In 1959, James Bryant Conant, former president of Harvard University and high commissioner for Germany after World War II, was invited by John Gardner, head of the Carnegie Corporation, to undertake a major study of the American high school. The result, known as the "Conant Report," put forth the following curricular recommendations, which were quite specific and somewhat conventional:

- All students should be required to complete 4 years of English, 3 years of social studies, 1 year of mathematics, and 1 year of science.

- Academically talented students should be required to take 3 additional years of mathematics, 4 years of one foreign language, and 2 additional years of science. If they wished, a second foreign language could be added.

- All students should be required to take a senior course in America problems, as part of their social studies requirement. In this course, students, heterogeneously grouped, would have free and open discussions of controversial issues.

Because the nation seemed to be searching for a new direction for its schools, the above recommendations were endorsed by most educators of the time. Principals and their faculties used the report as a set of criteria to judge their schools and changed their programs to bring them into line with Conant's recommendations.

PSSC Physics

This major curriculum project of the late 1950s and early 1960s (Physical Science Study Committee, 1961) claimed to involve students in discovery and inquiry as the basic pedagogical methods for identifying the structure of physics. Students "did physics" as physicists did, at least to the extent of their ability to do so. Although the implementation of the new course was supported by numerous federally funded teacher-training institutes, the developers had made a significant attempt to develop a "teacher-proof" curriculum that attempted to control all aspects of the instructional process.

ROMANTIC RADICALISM

The era of Romantic Radicalism (1968–1974) seemed to many observers to be a time of national fragmentation and upheaval, one in which the fabric of the society was stretched to its breaking point.

The Temper of the Times

It was, first of all, a time of rampant violence. It was also a time when youth seemed to be in the saddle. Popular writers trumpeted the glories of being young. A strongly vocal "counterculture" developed, espousing the virtues of drug-induced hallucinogenic visions, rock music, and spontaneous "openness" in all relationships—and at the same time rejecting the "bourgeois" values of work, punctuality, and bodily cleanliness.

The Predominant Trends

This period was obviously a time of experimentation in an attempt to develop child-centered schools and programs. The experimentation took three related but different forms: alternative schools, open classrooms, and elective programs.

Alternative Schools

The alternative schools were perhaps the most radical of all. While in later years alternative schools often seemed to be very similar to conventional schools, at the outset their faculties worked hard to make them different. Although these alternative schools ranged from completely unstructured "free schools" to mildly experimental schools that seemed different in only superficial ways, they did share certain characteristics (see Glatthorn, 1975, for a fuller account of the schools and their programs).

First, they were strongly teacher centered: Teachers often administered the schools without a principal, teachers determined the curriculum, and teachers offered many of the supportive services provided by specialists in the conventional schools. Second, the schools were in a real sense child centered: Curricula were shaped in response to the needs and interests of the children, and learning activities were selected primarily on the basis of their appeal to the children and parents. The most radical schools simply ignored the whole issue of evaluation; teachers in the more conventional alternative schools wrote anecdotal reports, basing their evaluations on students' self-assessments. Finally, of course, they were "schools of choice": Students elected to attend the alternative, rather than being assigned to it.

Open Classrooms

The open classroom was perhaps an attempt on the part of the educational establishment to respond to the mood of the times. Largely influenced by developments in the best British primary schools, the open classroom movement in the United States was to a great extent a revitalization of a moribund progressivism. Although the term *open classroom* was often simply an ill-defined slogan, there were certain important characteristics. There was, first of all, an emphasis on a rich learning environment. Teachers in the open classroom typically began by provisioning the classroom with stimulating learning materials and activities—centers of interest that would immediately appeal to the child and at the same time help the child learn. Children were free to move from center to center, to work together, and to engage each other in discussion. Thus, there was little concern for order in the conventional sense of the term: The best discipline was the self-discipline that came from learning on one's own.

Elective Programs

The elective programs were perhaps an attempt on the part of secondary schools to capture the vitality and excitement of the open classroom, which to a great extent had been limited to the primary grades. The basic concept of the elective program was a relatively simple one: Instead of a student taking a general "10th-grade English," the student should be able to choose from a variety of short-term courses, such as Women in Literature, The Romance of Sports, and War and Peace. In this sense, of course, such "electives" are different in organizational function from a subject such as music, which students elect to study or not to study.

The Exemplary Leaders

It is symbolic that the two figures selected as representing this exciting period of innovation and experimentation were not educators in the conventional sense of that term. Carl Rogers was a psychologist, and John Holt was perhaps a professional gadfly.

Carl Rogers

Rogers was a psychologist whose name came to be used to identify a school of counseling psychology: A Rogerian counselor is one who attempts to enter into the client's world, adopt the client's frame of reference, and listen empathically without advising.

Although Rogers (1969) worked with several college and school faculties that were interested in a Rogerian approach to organizational revitalization, his chief contribution seems to have been his ability to articulate clearly and to practice effectively what open educators and free-school advocates could only haltingly express and imperfectly implement.

John Holt

If Rogers was a counselor who did not believe in advising, then Holt might be characterized as a teacher who did not believe in teaching. In a sense, he is selected here as a representative figure of an influential group that included such other disenchanted teachers as Jonathan Kozol, James Herndon, and Herbert Kohl.

While it might seem surprising to identify a radical teacher as a major curriculum figure, Holt is selected because he and his associates represent a period of time when curriculum making itself was called into question. In Holt's (1964) view, the teacher *was* the curriculum. From his perspective, the schools did not need scope-and-sequence charts, clearly articulated objectives, or specified learning activities; the schools needed, instead, exciting and imaginative teachers who could provision a stimulating learning environment and who could involve learners in meaningful learning experiences.

The Major Publications

Two publications are selected here for quite different reasons: One heralded the promise of open education, and the other marked the end of federal involvement in curriculum making.

Crisis in the Classroom

In Ravitch's (1983) view, *Crisis in the Classroom* (1970) "projected open education into the public limelight as nothing previously had been done" (p. 245). Its author, Charles Silberman, was an experienced journalist who had been commissioned by the Carnegie Corporation to conduct a study of teacher education. Silberman, however, realized that a more important story was breaking—open education might be the one movement that would revolutionize education.

The answer, of course, was open education. Silberman was a highly skilled writer who knew how to personalize the dry stuff of educational change. He presented fascinating portraits of educators who seemed to be making a difference, and his own conviction made his message seem even more authentic.

Man: A Course of Study

This curriculum project (Curriculum Development Associates, 1972), usually identified by the acronym MACOS (*Man: A Course of Study*), had been developed at the Education Development Center with financial support from the National Science Foundation. As a social studies course designed for fifth- or sixth graders, MACOS seemed, in many ways, to represent the best of federally supported curriculum work. It drew heavily from Brunerian curriculum theory, taking pains to provide interesting "discovery" experiences that would help young children understand some of the basic structures of the social sciences.

PRIVATISTIC CONSERVATISM

The Temper of the Times

The period of Privatistic Conservatism (1975–1989) is generally recognized as the time when a strongly conservative philosophy permeated the national consciousness. It seemed that the American people were tired of violence, of experimentation, and of protest—and yearned for peace, stability, and traditional values.

It was also a time of increased religiosity. Fundamentalist groups especially became more active in the political arena, advancing their own candidates and giving large amounts of financial support to candidates who supported their agendas. Their agendas were concerned primarily with so-called family issues: elimination of abortion, restriction of the rights of homosexuals, and a return of Bible reading and prayer to the public schools. Interestingly enough, the resurgence of religiosity in this country seemed paralleled by an increase in religious fanaticism abroad.

This period was also a time when the information age fully arrived. More than 98% of American households owned one or more television sets—and most of those were color models.

Finally, it was a period of widespread immigration, especially of Hispanics and Asians. For the decade 1971–1980, more than 44% of all immigrants were from South American or Central American nations, and more than 35% were from Asian countries. Subsequently, many schools in the 70s had difficulty with the transition of multicultural populations. Some schools, however, eventually responded to the urban, multicultural student population by providing proactive support (Cuglietto, Burke, & Ocasio, 2007).

The Predominant Trends

As noted above, this period seems to have been a time when a conservative view of both society and its schools held sway. Those espousing such a conservative educational view essentially argued that the chief function of the school was to transmit the culture and to prepare students for their roles in a technological society; in accomplishing such a mission, the curriculum should emphasize the scholarly disciplines, should be characterized by intellectual rigor, and should be closely monitored for its effectiveness. Emanating from this broadly conservative view of the school and its curriculum were several specific trends.

School Effectiveness and School Reform

The first significant development was a broad-based research effort to identify the key elements in effective schools, with a concomitant attempt to translate those elements into a plan for reforming the schools. Following some groundbreaking research, one of the most useful was performed by Purkey and Smith (1983) who, after reviewing, critiquing, and synthesizing all the research, were able to identify the key factors shown in Exhibit 2.2.

A More Rigorous Curriculum

Central to this reform effort was an emphasis on "curriculum rigor." In general, this slogan seemed most useful simply as a rallying cry for those who believed that a more academically challenging curriculum would best serve the needs of American youth. The most common expressions of this concern for curricular rigor were state laws and district policies mandating additional graduation requirements.

The Critical Thinking Movement

This concern for a new rigor in the curriculum also took the form of widespread interest in teaching critical thinking. Most of those in the forefront of the movement argued for the importance of critical thinking by stressing the need for better thinking in a technologically oriented information age. Typical of these arguments was the conclusion reached by the Education Commission of the States (1982). After analyzing the needs of the society in an information age, the commission concluded in a special report that these were the "basics of tomorrow": evaluation and analysis skills, critical thinking, problem-solving strategies, organization and reference skills, synthesis, application, creativity, decision making given incomplete information, and communication skills.

Accountability

Allied with the concern for more rigor in the curriculum was a demand that teachers and students be held more accountable. First, school districts eagerly embraced several programs

---

EXHIBIT 2.2   Key Factors in Effective Schools

Organizational and Structural Variables

1. The leadership and staff of the school have considerable autonomy in determining the means they will use to improve academic performance.

2. The principal plays an active role as an instructional leader.

3. The staff remains relatively stable in order to maintain and promote further success.

4. The elementary curriculum focuses on basic and complex skills, with sufficient time provided and close coordination across grade levels and across disciplines; the secondary curriculum includes a planned and purposeful program without too many electives.

5. There is schoolwide staff development closely related to the instructional program of the school.

6. There is active parent involvement and support.

7. The school recognizes academic success, through symbols and ceremonies.

8. A greater portion of the day is devoted to academic subjects, with effective use made of academic time and with active involvement of students.

9. There is district support for school-based efforts.

Process Variables

1. There are collaborative planning and collegial relationships.

2. There is a pervasive sense of community.

3. Clear goals and high expectations are commonly shared.

4. There is order and discipline, with clear and reasonable rules fairly and consistently enforced.

SOURCE: Adapted from Purkey and Smith (1983).

that attempted to hold teachers more accountable for teaching and testing the prescribed curriculum. Such programs were usually identified as "curriculum alignment projects." Although they varied in detail, they attempted to align the written and the taught curriculum, usually by monitoring what was taught, and the written and the tested curriculum, ordinarily by matching the test with the instructional objectives.

These conservative responses noted some undesirable side effects: increased pressure on less able students, resulting in an unfavorable climate for growth, and the overemphasis on the knowledge-transmission function, resulting from mandates and competency tests.

Vouchers

Historians credit Adam Smith for giving birth to the voucher system in 1778 when he argued that parents are in the best position to decide how their children should be educated and that the state should give parents the money to hire suitable teachers. The intent of the voucher/choice schema was to provide opportunities, supported by tax monies, to target populations. Advocates of the voucher/choice concept believed that competition improves the marketplace and enhances educational effectiveness. Adversaries of the voucher/choice concept for public school, however, argued that:

- Choice is a notion that flies in the face of the basic mission of American public education.
- Choice is a means to circumvent laws governing due process, religious activities, and desegregation.
- Choice is a means to express personal biases and to construct and reform society through political/religious beliefs.
- Choice lowers the quality of some schools, and lessened enrollments can threaten equal educational opportunity for the majority of the students.
- The focus ought to be on improving schools rather than directing funds from one school district to another. (Boschee & Hunt, 1990, p. 75)

In the 1980s, states that endorsed the voucher/choice concept with varied and different requirements included Alaska, Arizona, California, Florida, Iowa, Louisiana, Massachusetts, Missouri, New York, Vermont, Virginia, Washington, and Wisconsin. Taking issue with where people stand on educational choice and vouchers, Boschee and Hunt (1990) wrote that

> people take sides without really knowing what impact the concepts will have on the economies of daily life in a competitive marketplace; the organization and regulation of educational systems related to teaching, learning, and financial accountability; professional employment; cultural, social-psychological, and racial issues; parental choice; the state and federal laws; and values. (p. 86)

Having said that, they developed an instrument titled "Pros/Cons of Vouchers/Choice" to help people determine whether they really endorsed the concept, were neutral, or were opposed. The instrument addressed seven areas: regulation versus deregulation; effectiveness/efficiency of schooling; legal/constitutional issues; roles: local, state, regional, federal, student, teacher, parent; accountability/instability factors; society, values, and schooling; and research on schooling. (The instrument and score key are published in the March 1990 *NASSP Bulletin*.)

Multicultural Education

The 1980s saw the emergence of a body of scholarship on multicultural education by progressive education activists and researchers who refused to allow schools to address their concerns by simply adding token programs and special units on famous women or famous people of color.

Today, the multicultural education activities for K–12 public schools among the states vary from having no requirements to **Monoethnic Courses (Phase 1)**, to **Multiethnic Studies Courses (Phase 2)**, to **Multiethnic Education (Phase 3)**, to **Multicultural Education (Phase 4)** (Banks, 1994). Several state mandates, models, and frameworks for multicultural education exist today. For example, Iowa references its requirements as "The Legal Authority: Multicultural, Nonsexist Education" (Iowa Code, Chapter 256.11). Tennessee requires that Black history and culture be taught in all public schools. Hawaii has a natural setting for multicultural education, and Indiana requires the public schools to incorporate world culture in the social studies curriculum. Nebraska compels all school districts to submit a multicultural education program for approval by the Nebraska Department of Education. From the survey results conducted by Boschee, Beyer, Engelking, and Boschee (1997) on K–12 multicultural education of the 50 states in the United States, a majority of the states did not mandate a multicultural education curriculum. Almost 20 years after the NCATE mandate, it appears that neither states nor teacher education programs have made substantial progress toward complying. Many, however, recommended that K–12 education be multicultural.

The National Education Goals 2000

In 1989, the president of the United States, George H. W. Bush, and the nation's 50 governors came together for a historic summit on one of the most important issues affecting America's future: the education of our nation's children. Born of an urgent realization that America's future prosperity was at stake, the first Education Summit, co-chaired by Governor Carroll Campbell and then-Governor Bill Clinton, produced six ambitious goals for the nation's performance in education:

By the year 2000,

1. All children in America will start school ready to learn.

2. The high school graduation rate will increase to at least 90%.

3. American students will leave Grades 4, 8, and 12 having demonstrated competency over challenging subject matter including English, mathematics, science, history, and geography, and every school in America will ensure that all students learn to use their minds well, so that they may be prepared for responsible citizenship, further learning, and productive employment in our modern economy.

4. United States students will be first in the world in mathematics and science achievement.

5. Every adult American will be literate and will possess the knowledge and skills necessary to compete in a global economy and exercise the rights and responsibilities of citizenship.

6. Every school in America will be free of drugs and violence and will offer a disciplined environment conducive to learning. (Archived information, n.d.)

With the passage of Goals 2000 legislation in 1994, the U.S. Congress added to Goal 3 the subjects of foreign languages, civics and government, economics, and the arts and added two additional goals:

By the year 2000,

1. The nation's teaching force will have access to programs for the continued improvement of their professional skills and the opportunity to acquire the

knowledge and skills needed to instruct and prepare all American students for the next century.

2. Every school will promote partnerships that will increase parental involvement and participation in promoting the social, emotional, and academic growth of children. (Archived information, n.d.)

Knudsen and Morrissette (1998) made an analysis and critique of Goals 2000 and concluded that "although a gallant effort, Goals 2000 will be remembered as a reform movement that funneled millions, perhaps billions, of dollars into American public schools with little to show in return" (n.p.). The concept for Goals 2000 lacked agreement. It was a vision that did not reach the grassroots level. It can be argued that America was built from the grassroots level, and it appeared that American public education needed to be built from the grassroots level as well.

The Exemplary Leaders

Three figures stand out in this period for their pervasive influence: Benjamin Bloom, John I. Goodlad, and James Banks. Each in his own way made major contributions and influenced both research and practice.

Benjamin Bloom

Bloom was a psychologist and professor of education at the University of Chicago. He first attracted widespread attention from the profession with the publication of what quickly became known as "Bloom's taxonomy" (see Bloom, 1956). Bloom's taxonomy includes his famous educational objectives: *Knowledge, Comprehension, Application, Analysis, Synthesis,* and *Evaluation.* Several interpretations of Bloom's taxonomy of educational objectives, in the cognitive domain, include sets of behavioral verbs that can be used to write higher-level reasoning tasks (O'Shea, 2005, p. 53).

While his work on the taxonomy was obviously influential, Bloom's theory of and research on mastery learning had perhaps an even greater impact. In discussing his work on mastery learning, it is important to make a sharp distinction between three understandings of "mastery learning": what he himself has advocated, how his students have applied his ideas in developing curricula, and what some publishers have done in commercializing mastery learning.

Despite the fact that some have distorted his theory, Bloom made a major contribution to curriculum—one whose effects will probably endure for some time.

John I. Goodlad

Goodlad is another leading figure in the curriculum field whose career spans several periods. For more than 25 years he conducted research, organized centers of educational change, and taught graduate courses in the field, publishing more than 20 books and some 200 articles. Educators tended to perceive him as a curriculum leader who understood schools, who had a clear vision of what those schools could become, and who had some tested ideas for helping them achieve their goals.

His analysis of the content of that balanced curriculum yielded a rather discouraging picture. By observing classes, interviewing teachers and students, analyzing texts and tests, and examining curriculum guides, he and his research team concluded that in all the academic areas—English language arts, mathematics, social studies, and science—the emphasis was on teaching basic skills and facts. Almost no attention in any grade was given to inquiry, critical thinking, or problem solving. The picture was especially dismal in lower-track classes.

James Banks

In *A Brief History of Multicultural Education*, Paul C. Gorski (1999), assistant professor in the Graduate School of Education at Hamline University and team member of *EdChange*, said,

> James Banks, one of the pioneers of multicultural education, was among the first multicultural education scholars to examine schools as social systems from a multicultural context. He grounded his conceptualization of multicultural education in the idea of "educational equality." According to Banks, in order to maintain a "multicultural school environment," all aspects of the school had to be examined and transformed, including policies, teachers' attitudes, instructional materials, assessment methods, counseling, and teaching styles.

The Major Publications

In 1983, nine national "school reform" reports were issued—so many that several educational publications saw fit to publish "scorecards" and "readers' guides" to help the profession make sense of the reform literature. Three of these reports seemed especially influential.

A Nation at Risk

This publication was produced by the National Commission on Excellence in Education (1983), appointed in 1981 by then–Secretary of Education Terrel H. Bell. The report presented what it termed the "indicators of risk," carefully selected statistics purporting to demonstrate the gravity of the risk and to warrant the dramatic language.

Perhaps because the language was so dramatic, the picture portrayed so dismal, and the recommendations so clear and simple, *A Nation at Risk* seemed to have a pervasive and widespread impact, especially on the public. It became the subject of television and radio broadcasts, it was discussed at parent and citizen meetings across the nation, and legislators often made reference to it as they drafted their own reform legislation. In retrospect, perhaps, the chief value of *A Nation at Risk* is that it dramatized the issue of educational reform and moved such reform into the arena of public debate. The report had a major impact in the continuing development of federal influence; however, in terms of curriculum, "the report's impact on schools and schooling is [an] illusion" (Hewitt, 2008, p. 579).

High School: A Report on Secondary Education in America

This book by Ernest Boyer (1983), while not getting the media attention of *A Nation at Risk*, was received much more favorably by educators and thus probably had a more pervasive impact. It was the result of a 2-year study of the American high school funded by the Carnegie Foundation for the Advancement of Teaching. The research staff reviewed the literature, consulted with numerous educational leaders, and spent 20 days in each of 15 high schools. While the study perhaps lacked the breadth and comprehensiveness of the Goodlad study mentioned above, it resulted in some recommendations that in many ways seemed more useful to the profession.

Several features of the Boyer report made it seem especially useful. First, it presented a balanced view of the achievement of American schools, eschewing the inflammatory rhetoric of *A Nation at Risk*. Second, it drew upon solid research and used the research in an illuminating and interesting manner, because the book was intended to reach a large audience. Next, it offered specific recommendations about the quality of the core curriculum that provided useful guidelines for local curriculum leaders. Finally, its recommendations for required service made great sense at a time when, according to some commentators, American youth seemed self-centered and materialistic.

Multiethnic Education: Theory and Practice

The five editions (1981, 1988, 1994, 2001, and 2006) of the book by James Banks help preservice and inservice educators clarify the philosophical and definitional issues related to pluralistic education, design and implement effective teaching strategies that reflect ethnic diversity, and prepare sound guidelines for multiethnic programs and practices. Each edition describes actions that educators can take to institutionalize educational programs and practices related to ethnic and cultural diversity.

What makes the book so relevant for multicultural education and implementation are the sequential parts. Part I discusses the history, goals, and practices in multiethnic education. Conceptual issues and problems related to education, ethnicity, and cultural diversity are the focus of Part II. The major research and programmatic paradigms related to ethnicity and education are described. The philosophical and ideological issues related to ethnicity, education, and citizenship are discussed in Part III. Part IV focuses on the curriculum, including efforts made in the last two decades to reform it, the nature and goals of a multiethnic curriculum, and how this curriculum can be reformed to reflect the ethnic characteristics of students. Planning units that focus on social issues, reducing prejudice in students, language diversity, and curriculum guidelines are discussed in Part V. The appendix, which enriches the book, consists of an inventory that will help educators to determine the extent to which their institutions reflect the ethnic diversity within their society. Figures and graphs illustrate the data.

TECHNOLOGICAL CONSTRUCTIONISM

The Temper of the Times

The era of Technological Constructionism (1990–1999) can be viewed as a time when the net was cast more widely. Along with digital opportunity, it was an era when state content standards came into being, the "school choice" movement was given an intellectual boost, voucher legislation allowed students to attend religious schools at taxpayers' expense, students being homeschooled increased from 10,000 in the 1970s to nearly 1,000,000 in the 1990s, and Goals 2000 was adopted.

The decade also saw increased prosperity for Americans as the Dow Jones and NASDAQ stock markets reached all-time highs. Due to the prevalence of computers and Internet use, "dot-commies" became a new type of upper-middle class. With that, 82% of the population had completed high school compared to 41% in 1960. Education subject guides appeared on the World Wide Web, and the Elementary and Secondary Education Act provided assistance to disadvantaged students and students with limited proficiency in English and improved instruction in math, science, and drug use prevention. The nation also experienced extreme violence in the form of school shootings; according to the National School Safety Center, 255 school-associated violent deaths occurred during this decade (Center on Juvenile and Criminal Justice, 2000).

The appointment of Lamar Alexander, a prominent former governor from Tennessee, as secretary of education brought the Department of Education closer to the president. Another former governor, Richard Riley, succeeded Alexander when Bill Clinton began his first term as president in 1993. During Riley's 8-year term, the longest of any secretary to that time, he weathered congressional attacks on the Department of Education. Nonetheless, he initiated substantive policies (e.g., higher standards, accountability, and increased investments) that helped to establish education as the key policy issue in the 2000 presidential election.

The Predominant Trends

This period followed an era, the 1980s, when the nation struggled mightily to improve public education. A report from InfoMedia (1993) titled *Educational Reform: A National Perspective* indicated that "ten years have passed since the hoopla surrounding *A Nation at Risk*. Ten years of speechmaking and of handwringing" (p. 3).

Charter Schools

The charter schools movement originated from a number of other educational reform ideas—namely, alternative schools, site-based management, magnet schools, public school choice, privatization, and community–parental choice (US Charter Schools, 2008). This idea was further refined in 1991 when Minnesota passed the first charter school law using the criteria of three basic values: opportunity, choice, and responsibility. California following suit in 1992, and by 1995, 19 states had signed laws allowing for the creation of charter schools. By 2003, that number increased to 40 states, Puerto Rico, and the District of Columbia. States in which a charter school law has still not been passed are Alabama, Kentucky, Maine, Montana, Nebraska, North Dakota, South Dakota, Vermont, Washington, and West Virginia. Charter schools are one of the quickest-growing developments in education policy, benefiting from extensive bipartisan support from governors, state legislators, and past and present secretaries of education (US Charter Schools, 2008).

Charter schools were publicly funded, publicly controlled, and privately run. As noted by US Charter Schools (2008), the intent of most charter school legislation is to do the following:

- Increase opportunities for learning and access to quality education for all students
- Create choice for parents and students within the public school system
- Provide a system of accountability for results in public education
- Encourage innovative teaching practices
- Create new professional opportunities for teachers
- Encourage community and parent involvement in public education
- Leverage improved public education broadly (n.p.)

Murphy and Shiffman (2002), however, analyzed the empirical evidence gathered over a period of time to determine the impact of charters—both on individual charter communities and on the larger educational system. They concluded that "by and large, the picture that emerges from the data . . . compiled was disappointing to charter purists—those who hold that the central goal of charters is to overhaul the extant system of education in the United States" (p. 216). Further, "the data on student achievement and school accountability . . . are not nearly as positive as charter advocates had hypothesized" (p. 216). To this day, charter schools have yet to show the kind of illumination hoped for by founders of the charter movement. Subsequently, many states today have turned to "alternative" charter authorizers outside the traditional structures of public school governance. Alternative authorizers include independent state-level charter boards, higher education institutions, city governments, and nonprofit groups (Palmer, 2007).

Technology

The stability of the core tool and the keystone of the educational system, the printed textbook yielded significant ground to the astonishing storage and retrieval capacities of the computer. A new educational future was no longer inhibited and shaped by the exigencies of print-/textbook-based education. It was during this era that we experienced the first stages of humankind's third major massive change in the way to communicate with each other and with future generations yet unborn. In the same manner that the alphabet and movable type changed everything about work and living in the decades after they were invented, the invention of the computer did change, and will continue to change, our lives and our children's lives dramatically.

The new technologies enabled a person with a computer and a phone line or cable in the remotest part of any state to connect to the equivalent of a million libraries worldwide. The use of an Internet browser and search engine allowed people to acquire within seconds the exact information they needed. Those same tools allowed those people to organize and analyze huge quantities of acquired information to use in solving problems and creating new opportunities. These technologies also enabled people to share information with one other person or with many millions of people worldwide (Whitehead, Jensen, & Boschee, 2003).

It was also during this decade that federal money was made available so that the country could go from a "digital divide" to a "digital opportunity" status. In 1994, President Clinton and Vice President Gore bridged the digital divide by setting the goal of connecting every classroom and library to the Internet. In 1996, President Clinton unveiled his Technology Literacy Challenge—and made a major commitment of resources to (a) connect every classroom to the Internet; (b) expand access to modern, multimedia computers; (c) make high-quality educational software an integral part of the curriculum; and (d) enable teachers to integrate technology effectively into their instruction. In retrospect, the 1990s provided a foundation for the unprecedented expansion and integration of technology in the classroom that we see today. Educational leaders can't afford to be intimidated by technology. Rather, as Vince Ferrandino (2007), former executive director of NAESP, indicated, it is important for leaders to realize that technology is a powerful instructional and management tool and to take the lead in emphasizing this belief to teachers, parents, and the wider community.

The Standards-Based Movement

The decade of the 1990s ushered in state educational standards. All the states, with the exception of Iowa, had adopted academic standards. Iowa requires each school district to develop its own standards. Although the research on the value of state standards is fairly new, and much of it is still in progress, the findings, according to Jones (2000), offer the following unfaltering guidelines:

1. *Make academic standards everybody's business.* Everybody—students, parents, teachers, business, everybody—needs to know what the standards are and why they're important. Research shows that when students and teachers better understand what is expected of them, they perform better.

2. *Focus, focus, focus.* Each state's standards are different, but they all have one thing in common: They're not perfect. Some state standards are so vague that teachers aren't sure what they mean. Others are so specific and so numerous that it's impossible to cover everything in the 13 years between kindergarten and high school graduation. Robert Marzano, senior fellow at the Mid-continent Regional Laboratory (McREL) in Aurora, Colorado, studied the standards around the country and found it would take 23 years of schooling to cover all of the benchmarks. "Teachers can't teach it all . . . and kids couldn't possibly learn it all."

3. *Make standards-based decisions.* If you want standards to work, researchers say, you have to work on standards. The simplistic-sounding advice means each decision, each program, each new hire should be examined with an eye toward its impact on helping students meet standards. Researchers say school districts should put their money where their standards are. If a district wants to improve students' performance in math, for instance, it should hire more qualified math teachers.

4. *Invest in teachers.* Numerous studies have identified the importance of teachers' credentials in determining students' academic achievement. . . . Teacher quality is so important that some researchers are beginning to suspect that low student achievement often seen in low-income communities just

might reflect the fact that the least qualified teachers are often assigned to schools in those communities.

5. *Demand helpful assessments that align with the curriculum.* If you want the curriculum to be taken seriously, you have to do something about assessments. In cases where there's concern about alignment between the test and the standards, districts ought to raise that with the state, and not assume that everything will work itself out. There can be real consequences if there's not good alignment.

6. *Approach accountability cautiously.* Most researchers recommend using test results and other standards-based data to make decisions about everything from textbooks to teachers.

7. *When students are in trouble, intervene.* Researchers have long touted the benefits of early intervention. Studies show . . . that a few weeks of one-on-one tutoring aimed at teaching first-graders to decode words can save many children from special education.

SOURCE: Reprinted with permission from "Making Standards Work: Researchers Report Effective Strategies for Implementing Standards," by R. Jones, September 2000, *American School Board Journal, 187*(9), 27–31. Copyright 2000 National School Boards Association. All rights reserved.

With the development of state educational standards, and if public education is to be improved, teachers will require better training and staff development. Moreover, curriculum, instructional materials, and parental attitudes will have to change. As a result of these initial reform actions, the 1990s helped set the tone for the unprecedented move to align standards in classrooms that we see today. Basically, over the last quarter century, a model for school standards and accountability has emerged in the United States that is now so locked into state and federal laws that its general shape seems here to stay. It can be said that where alignment between curriculum instruction and assessment is incomplete, the standards for validity are not being met (Barton, 2006).

The past quarter of a century also helped develop the long link between high school and college standards. High school administrators around the country are now modifying their curricula so that students desiring to go to college are better able to succeed academically. This is evidenced by the number of tech prep courses being offered in secondary schools today that help make the link easier between high schools and colleges. For example, Idaho high school students may register to complete an approved tech prep course at any high school, which allows them an opportunity to earn college class credit and move from their high school to North Idaho State College without having to repeat tech prep courses (North Idaho State College, 2007).

The Exemplary Leaders

Three figures stand out in this period of change: Elliot W. Eisner, Robert J. Marzano, and Joseph S. Renzulli. Each of these individuals contributed his own special influence to the field of curriculum development.

Elliot W. Eisner

Eisner is a professor of education and art at Stanford University. He is widely considered a leading theorist on art education. Eisner has won wide recognition for his work internationally. Among his many awards is the Palmer O. Johnson Award from the American Educational Research Association. He has been a John Simon Guggenheim Fellow and a Fulbright Scholar and has served as the president of the National Art Education Association, the International Society for Education Through Art, the American Educational Research Association, and the John Dewey Society (Provenzo, 2003).

Eisner works primarily in three fields: arts education, curriculum studies, and qualitative research methodology (identifying practical uses of critical qualitative methods from the arts in school settings and teaching processes). His research interests have focused on the development of aesthetic intelligence and on the use of methods from the arts to study and improve educational practice. Originally trained as a painter, Eisner teaches ways in which schools might improve by using the processes of the arts in all their programs. He is considered one of the foremost leaders in the field of arts in education.

Robert J. Marzano

Marzano is a senior fellow at the Mid-continent Research for Education and Learning (McREL) Institute in Aurora, Colorado, and has authored numerous books and articles. He is largely noted for translating research and theory into classroom practices. He heads a team of authors who developed *Dimensions in Learning* as well as *Tactics for Thinking*. Most recently, he is noted for his efforts in addressing standards and promoting leadership as evidenced in his book *School Leadership That Works* (Marzano, Waters, & McNulty, 2005). He has developed programs and practices used in K–12 classrooms that translate current research and theory in cognition into instructional methods.

Joseph S. Renzulli

A professor of educational psychology at the University of Connecticut, Renzulli also serves as director of the National Research Center on the Gifted and Talented. His research has focused on the identification and development of creativity and giftedness in young people and on organizational models and curricular strategies for total school improvement. He is a fellow in the American Psychological Association and was a consultant to the White House Task Force on Education of the Gifted and Talented. He was recently designated a Board of Trustees Distinguished Professor at the University of Connecticut (Tomlinson et al., 2001).

The Major Publications

Educators at this time began focusing on individualized instruction, technology, and data analysis. Although there were many outstanding works during this period, two publications are obvious for their pioneering and innovative approaches.

Classrooms That Work

Patricia Cunningham and Richard L. Allington's 1994 publication, *Classrooms That Work: They Can Read and Write*, compiled some of the best strategies that work effectively in classrooms. The book was one of the first to put an analytical emphasis on classroom instruction and focus on successful practices in schools from both research and teacher points of view. It is a positive resource containing practical ideas, activities, and organizational strategies. Five major components are noted in the book: engagement in real reading and writing, supported comprehension activities, supported writing activities, decoding and spelling activities, and knowledge-building activities. These components best describe the critical components of a balanced classroom program. In a supplement to the 1994 edition, Allington's 2005 book, *What Really Matters for Struggling Readers: Designing Research-Based Programs,* describes the characteristics of scientifically based reading research and some of its most significant subjects. He also discusses developing instruction for struggling readers, improving classroom instruction and access to intensive instruction, expanding available instruction time, and making support available for older struggling readers.

Data Analysis

The book *Data Analysis: For Comprehensive Schoolwide Improvement*, by Victoria Bernhardt (1998), had a vast impact on state officials, school district administrators, and teachers. As a result, it continues to play a major role in the school-improvement process nationally. It was written to help educators learn how to deal with data that will inform them of where they are, where they want to be, and how to get there. Bernhardt explained why data make the difference in quality school improvement. Also, depending on what data make the difference and how they are gathered, analyzed, and whether properly used, they make a difference in meeting the needs of every student in school. This book took data from schools and demonstrated how powerful data analyses emerge logically. It shows how to gain answers to questions and to understand current and future impacts.

MODERN CONSERVATISM

The Temper of the Times

The United States has undergone a period of modern conservative influence and control of its political system in the first decade of the 21st century. The range of persons identifying themselves as modern conservatives and the variety of sociopolitical beliefs that this group holds has increased in both number and diversity. Too, modern conservatism is an ideological shift that is due to the results of the 2004 presidential election.

Educational reform has become one of the most divisive issues in America, especially in the first decade of the 21st century. Concerns about our educational system are reverberating at the national, state, and local levels. A heated debate involving American education has raged in the press over time, but more since the passage of the No Child Left Behind Act. Politicians, business leaders, educators, and parents are just some of the diverse groups of people engaged in the educational reform controversy. The intensity of the issues is accentuated by proponents across the political spectrum.

In addition to the educational issues for America's public schools, Hardy (2004) reminded us that "over the past four years, the American electorate has been dealt a series of body blows, each capable of altering the political landscape" (p. 2). "The voting system broke down in a presidential election. A booming economy faltered, punctuated by revelation of one of the worst business scandals in U.S. history. And the country endured a devastating attack on its own soil" (p. 2). These events revealed a nation almost evenly divided politically and further apart in political values. The question looms: Where did this leave education?

The Predominant Trends

Americans increasingly recognize that the U.S. education system can and should do more to prepare our young people to succeed in the rapidly evolving 21st century. Skills such as global literacy, problem solving, innovation, and creativity have become critical in today's increasingly interconnected workforce and society.

No Child Left Behind Act

The biggest public school story in the 21st century thus far has been the 1,100-page No Child Left Behind Act signed into law by President George W. Bush in January 2002. Being it was bipartisan legislation, a congressional coalition formed around the ambitious federal education bill. However, that unity dissolved as Democrats blamed Republicans for withholding funding, and Republicans criticized Democrats for abandoning school reform.

Gerald Bracy (2003), in the "13th Bracy Report" for Phi Delta Kappa, referred to NCLB as "a weapon of mass destruction targeted at the public schools in a campaign of shock and awe" (pp. 148–149). Consequently, states across the nation are taking opposition to the law. For example, renewal of the oft-criticized No Child Left Behind federal law is supported by the nation's governors, but they want far more authority to carry out its mandates. Since the act has repeatedly come under fire, decried for such things as its focus on testing and punishments, it is set to be reauthorized. This time, however, the governors' voices could be included because they have a unique view about how this piece of legislation can be implemented. The recommendations for change by the National Governors' Association (NGA) would (a) allow states to decide the most appropriate way to test students, (b) have fewer restrictions to consider a teacher "highly qualified," and (c) make the federal government give states enough money to adhere to the act but not require any new tests (Vu, 2007).

According to Vince Ferrandino (2003, p. 3), executive director of the National Association of Elementary School Principals (NAESP), the intent of NCLB was to buttress education for all children. Is it accomplishing its intentions? Exhibit 2.3 is designed to explore your perceptions regarding the No Child Left Behind Act. Please place a check ✓ in the Agree, Disagree, or Don't Know columns to express your opinion on the success of NCLB.

Some other trends in education during the Modern Conservatism era besides the No Child Left Behind Act (NCLB) include global education, school vouchers, homeschooling, and P–16 education. The following sections highlight some of the trends.

EXHIBIT 2.3 Pros and Cons of No Child Left Behind Act			
NCLB successfully . . .	Agree	Disagree	Don't Know
set high standards and high expectations for all students, regardless of race, ethnicity, family, background, or disability.			
got all students to grade level or higher.			
emphasized reading and mathematics.			
got school districts to report test results separately for all different groups.			
got school districts to identify students most in need of assistance.			
required a state to set specific goals for student achievement.			
required that schools make Adequate Yearly Progress.			
required that every classroom have a highly qualified teacher.			
made paraprofessionals in Title I meet new requirements.			
Total			

Global Education

Secretary of State Colin Powell said in the aftermath of the September 11, 2001, terrorist attacks, "Americans must be engaged with the rest of the world more than ever before. Clearly our schools and institutions of higher education must play an important role" (Czarra, 2002–2003, p. 9). Since the tragic episode of September 11, Americans realize global literacy is important to live in a world that is made up of three elements: cultural literacy, scientific literacy, and multiple literacies. To bring about change in education via P–16 education, Gordon (Spud) Van de Water and Carl Krueger (2002) suggested the establishment of five central goals and recommend structural goals to achieve them:

1. Every child ready for school by age 6
2. Every child proficient in reading by age 8
3. Every child proficient in geometry and algebra by age 13
4. Every learner completing a rigorous core curriculum by age 17
5. Every learner expected to complete the first 2 years of college by age 21

To accomplish the recommended goals, structural goals include the following:

- Starting universal public education at age 3
- Smoothing transitions from one level of education to the next
- Moving from a Carnegie-unit system to a competency-based system
- Creating more flexible learning opportunities for adolescent learners
- Moving the accepted endpoint of public education from Grade 12 to Grade 14

To achieve these goals, a P–16 system stresses these factors: the use of research to guide decisions about when and how children learn, a clearly articulated set of high expectations, improvement of teaching quality, and the use of data to measure progress.

School Vouchers

Just as they have been in the past, **school vouchers** seem to find a way to maintain their position in education. With the advent of a new Republican administration in 2001, educational reform moved away from technological structuralism and returned to a more modern and conservative nature. This is especially the case with President George W. Bush's endorsement of vouchers.

One of the predominant trends, according to Joseph Bast (as cited in Bast, Harmer, & Dewey, 1997), has been the interest in school vouchers. He referenced Nobel Prize winner Milton Friedman's proposal to end the traditional model of schooling by giving parents tax-financed certificates or vouchers to pay tuition at schools, public or private, to which they chose to send their children. It was emphasized that school vouchers were to be considered a type of government grant that provides school tuition that can be used at both public and private schools and that could become a way to increase the option of school choice for low-income families. The concept behind school vouchers continues to focus on giving parents a wider choice of educational institutions and approaches.

The school voucher program has been controversial at best in that many individuals believe that such a program, if broadly applied, can destroy the American public education system. There is also debate over constitutional church–state issues when vouchers are used to allow students to attend religious schools. This continues to be a controversial issue, and a federal court held that when a voucher system resulted in almost all recipients attending religious schools instead of public schools, the system violated the Constitution.

Cook (2004) provided a sample of the voucher programs implemented or attempted at some cities and states:

- Milwaukee started in the 1990–1991 school year and served 12,950 students who attended 102 private and religious schools. Enrollment in the voucher program was capped at 15% of the public school population, or about 15,000 students. The cost exceeds $76 million.

- Cleveland started in the 1996–1997 school year and served 5,200 students in 50 private and religious schools in 2002–2003. The program is limited to K–3 students who live within the Cleveland school district; however, once a student qualifies, he or she can continue to receive a voucher through 10th grade. The Ohio legislature expanded the program in 2003 by 1,000 students and increased the funding for private schools by 44%.

- Florida started the voucher program in the 1999–2000 academic school year. The Opportunity Scholarships supported 663 students, the McKay Scholarship program supported 12,200 students, and Corporate Income Tax Scholarship supported between 14,000 and 16,000 students. The corporate tax credits provide $3,500 worth of vouchers to students from low-income families. These scholarship programs have been heavily criticized due to reports of financial corruption, lack of state oversight, and lax or nonexistent academic standards. For example, "the Department of Education provided tax credits to a Muslim school in Tampa that has been linked to terrorist activity" (p. 14).

School vouchers continue to be a controversial issue today. For example, noted author Jonathan Kozol (2007) indicated that while advocates argue that vouchers greatly benefit poor and disadvantaged children, the self-selectivity of the voucher process guarantees just the opposite. For many, and Kozol is an example, school vouchers continue to be controversial. He believes that vouchers represent the single worst, most dangerous idea to enter education discourse in decades.

Homeschooling

During the past 20 years, the general public's familiarity with homeschooling has evolved from a level of almost complete unawareness to one of widespread, if largely uninformed, awareness. Today, homeschooling parents are *reinventing* the ideas of school. Along with this movement, a growing body of literature on school choice has emerged. Despite legislative problems, regulatory hurdles, media attacks, and other affronts to the homeschooling movement, homeschooling has continued to gain in popularity and strength. As Thomas Jefferson alleged, the price of freedom is vigilance (Gilmore, 2005). That has never been truer than in the case of freedom to home school in the United States as in the 1980s and 1990s when battles were fought in the courtrooms and state legislatures.

In 1980, homeschooling was illegal in 30 states; however, it has been legal in all 50 states since 1993. Even though exact numbers are hard to come by, Ray (2006), an internationally known researcher, said "homeschooling may be the fastest growing form of education in the United States (at 7% to 12% per year)" (n.p.). In 2005–2006 there were an estimated 1.9 to 2.1 million children (grades K–12) home schooled. This represents an increase from the estimated 850,000 students who were home schooled in the spring of 1999 (National Center for Education Statistics, 2004).

Reasons for Homeschooling

Although each family has its own value system and its own reasons for homeschooling, researchers have identified several reasons why families choose to home school their children. Ray (2006) found that the most common reasons given for homeschooling are to

- Teach a particular set of values, beliefs, and worldview

- Accomplish more academically than in schools

- Customize or individualize the curriculum and learning environment of each child

- Use pedagogical approaches other than those typical in institutional schools

- Enhance family relationships between children and parents and among siblings

- Provide guided and reasoned social interactions with youthful peers and adults

- Provide a safer environment for children and youth, because of physical violence, drugs and alcohol, psychological abuse, and improper and unhealthy sexuality

Ray also disputes the position that adversaries of homeschooling have taken. His findings on homeschooling show there is better academic performance; above average social, emotional, and psychological development; and more success in the real world of adulthood.

P–16 Education

A wave of educational reform has swept the nation over the first decade of the 21st century. For example, school choice, charter schools, NCLB, and standards-based instruction, among others, are highly debatable because the landscape of education in the United States has not undergone major change (Chamberlain & Plucker, 2008). Although the jury is still out, Chamberlain and Plucker believe that P–16 education has potential because it is more responsive to society's needs.

There is widespread agreement that all students in our schools and colleges need to learn more to lead successful economic and civic lives as adults in the 21st century. Implicit in this consensus is the notion that the current system is not capable of bringing this about. Consider these data points:

- Fewer than 3 in 10 teenagers think their school is "very academically rigorous."

- "A" students in high-poverty schools score at the same level as "C" and "D" students in affluent schools.

- Seventy-two percent of high school graduates go on to some form of postsecondary education, yet only 44% have taken a college-prep curriculum.

- Twenty-nine percent of college freshmen take one or more remedial courses in reading, writing, or math.

- By age 24, 7% of young people from low-income families have graduated from college, versus 48% from high-income families. (Haycock & Huang, 2001, pp. 3–17)

The signs above would indicate that the educational system in the United States is under stress. A P–16 system could well smooth the needed transition from high school to college.

The Exemplary Leaders

Two major figures, Linda Darling-Hammond and Carol Ann Tomlinson, stand out from this unusual time of direct government involvement in individualized and differentiated learning, assessment, and school improvement. Never before has the federal government been so involved in making sure that schools apply standards and are accountable.

Linda Darling-Hammond

Darling-Hammond is a Charles E. Ducommun Professor of Education at Stanford University School of Education. She also served as executive director of the National Commission on Teaching and America's Future, which produced the widely cited 1996 blueprint for education reform, *What Matters Most: Teaching for America's Future.* Darling-Hammond's research, teaching, and policy work focus on teaching and teacher education, school restructuring, and educational equity. She has been active in the development of standards for teaching and served as a two-term member of the National Board for Professional Teaching Standards and as chair of the Interstate New Teacher Assessment and Support Consortium (INTASC) committee that drafted model standards for licensing beginning teachers. She is author of *The Right to Learn, A License to Teach*, and *Professional Development Schools: Schools for Developing a Profession*, along with six other books and more than 200 book chapters, journal articles, and monographs on education.

Darling-Hammond has served as the faculty sponsor for Stanford's Teacher Education Program (STEP). As a leader in the charge for enhanced teacher education and teacher preparedness, she has been instrumental in redesigning programs to better prepare teachers to teach diverse learners in the context of challenging new subject matter standards (Glass, 2003). It is evident that Darling-Hammond has made a major contribution to education and continues to work on issues of education policy and practice, including school reform, authentic assessment, professional development schools, and educational research.

Carol Ann Tomlinson

Tomlinson is a noted author whose work in the area of differentiated instruction is well known internationally. She is an associate professor of educational leadership, foundations, and policy at the Curry School of Education, University of Virginia. Her work has had a tremendous impact on the school-improvement process. Her books include information on curriculum and instruction for advanced learners and struggling learners, effective instruction in heterogeneous settings, and bridging the fields of general education and gifted education. She is the author of more than 100 articles, book chapters, and books. One of her best-known books is *The Differentiated Classroom: Responding to the Needs of All Learners.* Another is *Integrating Plus Differentiated Instruction and Understanding by Design* (2006) that she coauthored with Jay McTighe. Many school officials are turning to her work in their efforts to individualize classrooms and comply with the No Child Left Behind Act.

The Major Publications

No Child Left Behind Act

With the passage of the No Child Left Behind Act (2002), schools are continuing to turn to ways to enhance student achievement, align standards, and learn more about the brain and how children learn. There are five authors—Charlotte Danielson, Patricia Wolfe, Michael

Fullan, Rick Wormeli, and William Bender—whose works have dramatically helped build a foundation in these areas.

Enhancing Student Achievement

The book *Enhancing Student Achievement: A Framework for School Improvement* by Charlotte Danielson (2002) is fast becoming one of the most important books in education. Danielson's framework stresses the importance of aligning state and national standards and determining a means of assessing the school program as a whole. According to Danielson, when educators learn to "put it all together" to improve their schools, they will be bringing their entire expertise to bear on providing a first-rate education to all children.

Brain Matters

Brain Matters: Translating Research Into Classroom Practice by Patricia Wolfe (2001) has had a significant impact on classroom instructional strategies. Much of the research in this field confirms what experienced educators already know, and Wolfe's book helps to functionally understand the brain and how it operates. This allows teachers to critically analyze the vast amount of neuroscientific information arriving in the classroom daily. The book is divided into three parts. Part I is a mini-textbook on brain-imaging techniques and the anatomy and physiology of the brain. Part II introduces a model of how the brain processes information and explores some of the implications of this process for classroom practice. Part III presents examples of teaching strategies that match how the brain learns best: through projects, simulations, visuals, music writing, and mnemonics.

Wolfe's book continues to be important today in helping develop an awareness of brain research and connections to teaching. We now know that a combination of the art of teaching and the science of how the brain responds metabolically and electrically to stimuli can best guide educators in finding the most effective neuro-*logical* ways to promote learning (Willis, 2007).

Leading in a Culture of Change

Michael Fullan is the dean of the Ontario Institute for Studies in Education at the University of Toronto. An innovator and leader in teacher education, he has developed a number of partnerships designed to bring about major school improvement and educational reform. His powerful and pioneering book, *Leading in a Culture of Change* (2001), integrates theory, research, case studies, and anecdotes to flesh out the dynamics of effective leadership in this modern conservatism era. He identifies and elaborates on five components of leadership that can affect sustainable and systemic change: moral purpose, understanding change, relationship building, knowledgecreation, sharing, and coherence making. Fullan notes that in an increasingly complex and fast-changing world it is crucial that we cultivate leadership at all levels of organization, business, and education.

Fair Isn't Always Equal: Assessing & Grading in the Differentiated Classroom

Rick Wormeli's 2006 book is meant to do four things: (1) be a catalyst for serious reflection on current grading and assessment practices in differentiated classes, (2) affirm effective grading and assessment practices, (3) provide language and references for substantive conversations with colleagues and the public, and (4) provide coherent and effective grading practices in high-stakes, accountability world.

Response to Intervention: A Practical Guide for Every Teacher

William Bender's 2007 book addresses the issues and guidelines associated with Response to Intervention (RTI) key concepts and guidelines. RTI is now a mandated process. Bender's book assists educators with the basic and necessary steps to provide students with a Free and Appropriate Public Education (FAPE) in the Least Restrictive Environment.

The World Is Flat: A Brief History of the Twenty-First Century

Thomas L. Friedman's book, first released in 2005 and later as an "updated and expanded" edition in 2006 with additional updates in 2007, analyzes the progress of globalization with an emphasis on the early 21st century. The title is a metaphor for viewing the world as flat or level in terms of commerce and competition, as in a level playing field—or one where all competitors have an equal opportunity. As the first edition cover indicates, the title also alludes to the historic shifts in perception once people realized the world was not flat but round, and how a similar shift in perception—albeit figurative—is required if countries, companies, and individuals want to remain competitive in a global market where historical, regional and geographical divisions are becoming increasingly irrelevant. Thus, a major emphasis on global education is included in the school curriculum today.

A CENTURY OF CURRICULUM TRENDS IN RETROSPECT

In reviewing this century of curriculum history, two general observations might be made. The first is to note the pace of change. Observe that the first five periods become increasingly shorter, lasting 27 years, 24 years, 16 years, 11 years, and 7 years, respectively. The sixth and seventh periods—Privatistic Conservatism and Technological Constructionism—lasted about a decade each. The latest period, Modern Conservatism, seems to be determined by results of American presidential elections. Having said that, it would seem that futurists who have commented on the rapid pace of change in today's society are probably correct. One, therefore, might predict that future trends in curriculum will be relatively short-lived.

The second observation is to note the rhythms and directions of that change. Here it might be useful to search for the best metaphor describing those rhythms and directions. Currently, when most educators speak about the general directions of the curriculum past and present, they seize initially on the metaphor of the pendulum, which suggests short swings between extreme positions. Or they talk of cycles, a more abstract figure that suggests longer periods of recurring tendencies. Neither metaphor seems to portray the past century plus of curriculum history. Instead, it might be more appropriate and more insightful to speak of separate streams that continue to flow—at times swollen, at times almost dry; at times separate, at times almost joining.

In identifying such streams in our curricular history, some useful terms proposed by Eisner and Vallance as early as 1974 help delineate the five orientations in the curriculum: academic rationalism (foster intellectual growth in the subjects most worthy of study), personal relevance (emphasize the primacy of personal meaning), cognitive processes (help children acquire the

EXHIBIT 2.4   The Streams of Curricular History

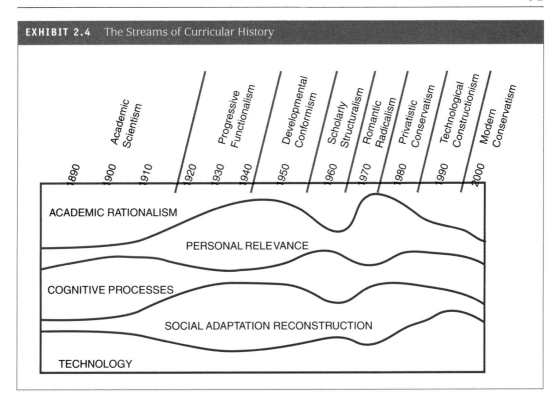

basic skills and learn how to think), social adaptation reconstruction (derive educational aims from an analysis of the society), and technology (operationalize curricular outcomes by technological analysis of the observable behaviors sought). The eight curricular orientations—Academic Scientism, Progressive Functionalism, Developmental Conformism, Scholarly Structuralism, Romantic Radicalism, Privatistic Conservatism, Technological Constructionism, and Modern Conservatism—are thus seen as streams that have always been present during the 20th century and the beginning of the 21st of curricular history.

Exhibit 2.4 shows how these streams seem to have ebbed and flowed throughout the separate periods. It reflects how their strength has varied and how, during a given period, one or two have predominated. It suggests that the strength of a given orientation at a particular time seems to have resulted from powerful social forces impinging upon the curriculum. It also makes clear that educators in general have typically espoused a pragmatic eclecticism, one in which all eight streams have at least some part to play.

SUMMARY

This chapter provides a useful understanding of the history of curriculum development for scholars and practitioners and a careful analysis of the past 110 years of curriculum development history. A historical understanding results in a deeper awareness of the extent to which curricular changes are often influenced by and are a manifestation of larger social forces. Chapter 2 offers an expansive perspective from which to view so-called innovations and reforms. This chapter focuses on the major developments affecting American schools and provides an essential broader perspective. Specifically, the chapter addresses the periods of Academic Scientism, Progressive Functionalism, Developmental Conformism, Scholarly Structuralism, Romantic Radicalism, Privatistic Conservatism, Technological Constructionism, and Modern Conservatism and why each was important in the development of curriculum. Finally, some of the predominant trends that transcended each major period of curriculum development are identified.

APPLICATIONS

1. Based on what you have learned about the history of curriculum and what you observe happening now, when do you think the period of Modern Conservatism will end, and what type of period will succeed it?

2. Some have argued that there are really no new ideas in education and that all so-called innovations are simply a refurbishing of old ideas. Based on your knowledge of curriculum history, would you agree or disagree? Please explain.

3. Most nationally disseminated reports recommending educational reform have very little impact. How, then, do you explain the seemingly profound impact made by the reform reports of the 1990s and the early years of the 21st century?

4. The No Child Left Behind Act (NCLB) has had a major impact on how schools plan and implement curriculum as well as on how students are assessed. What aspects of NCLB do you feel have been advantageous to the school-improvement process? What aspects, if any, do you feel have been detrimental, and why?

5. Charter schools, school vouchers, and homeschooling movements are becoming commonplace in American education. How do you feel about each of these practices, and do you believe that they will continue in the future? Why or why not?

6. According to Van de Water and Krueger (2002), much more evidence is needed concerning what works in a P–16 system. Which elements from the list below would be the most difficult to accomplish and which one would be the easiest to accomplish? Why?

   - *Inclusiveness*—everyone expected to meet rigorous learning standards
   - *Alignment*—of standards, curricula, expectations, assessments
   - *Support*—for all learners as they strive to meet learning standards
   - *Removal of artificial barriers*—especially those surrounding the transition from high school to college (for example, high school exit requirements, college entrance requirements, college placement assessments)
   - *Reductions in level of remediation*—high expectations, clear standards, and strong support services leading to better-prepared students able to meet postsecondary expectations upon entry (n.p.)

| CASE STUDY | **Curriculum Approaches Can Challenge Administrators** |

The new elementary school principal, Dr. Susan Davenport, was hired to replace Dr. Robert Edwards, who left Washington Elementary School for a professorship at a university in the same town. When she was hired, the superintendent told her that he expected the principal to get the school's staff onboard to bring the curriculum into compliance with district, state, and federal standards.

With the superintendent's edict to bring the staff onboard so that the standards could be met, Dr. Davenport felt that information was needed about the diverse faculty at Washington Elementary School. She arranged a meeting with the previous principal to get some insights about the faculty at the school. Dr. Edwards was pleased to meet with Susan and share some information about the teachers.

In describing the six fourth-grade faculty members at Washington Elementary School, Dr. Edwards made reference to Mr. Anderson, who was a 40-year veteran at the school. He noted that Mr. Anderson is very conservative in nature and a blend of Academic Scientism and Progressive Functionalism. He also does not believe in individualizing or having students work in groups. Another teacher, Mrs. Ferrell, is less conservative than Mr. Anderson; however, she is not a big fan of technology and focuses on the social aspects of the child, a type of Developmental Conformism.

Mrs. Bardwell, a close friend of Mrs. Ferrell, is a far more structured teacher who has the desks lined up in rows. She does focus on fundamentals but uses an inquiry approach to teaching at times, especially in science. Dr. Edwards felt that Bardwell fit nicely into the era of Scholarly Structuralism—curriculum should be focused on discipline-based principles, concepts, and inquiry processes. Tammy Rabine, another fourth-grade teacher, Dr. Edwards notes, is right out of the Romantic Radicalism period. She is an exciting and imaginative teacher but does not follow the district curriculum scope and sequence and is not interested in clear and articulated objectives. Her philosophy is that learning is about student discovery and student self-esteem. In contrast, Tammy's colleague, Jack Duringer, is very much into critical thinking and the development of an academically challenging curriculum. He is also a stickler for assessment and accountability, as well as technology, which places him in the Privatistic Conservatism and Technological Constructionism eras.

Juanita Sanchez, the last fourth-grade teacher that Dr. Edwards talked about, has taught for 2 two years and is a wiz with technology. Because she is interested in cultural diversity, she believes in teaching values through the curriculum. She is a strong proponent of standards for teaching and assessment and could well fit the Technological Constructionism and the Modern Conservatism eras.

The Challenge

Analyze the behavior of the fourth-grade teachers in this case. How can the new principal get the thinking of teacher–leaders and the fourth-grade faculty to work together to bring the curriculum into compliance with district, state, and federal standards?

Key Issues/Questions

1. Judging from your own experience, do you sense it was ethical for Dr. Edwards to discuss his former teachers with the new principal? Why or why not?

2. Curricular changes are often influenced by and are manifestations of larger social forces. What societal changes are influencing curricular changes today?

3. Is it possible to bring a school facing the problem of unsatisfactory levels of student achievement to meet the current standards set by the district, state government, and federal government with a diverse faculty? Why or why not?

4. One of the major problems of this school was the lack of incentive to change, a situation not unique to Washington Elementary School. Tradition and goal ambiguity tended to make this school sluggish. How can the new principal initiate change efforts and find ways of providing help instead of "managing" school-level programs?

5. How might the principal use the diversity of faculty as strength to improve the teaching and learning process?

WEBLIOGRAPHY

Center for Implementing Technology in Education
www.cited.org

Global Education
www.globaled.org/fianlcopy.pdf

International Society for Technology in Education's National Educational Technology Standards
www.cnets.iste.org

Kennedy School of Government report comparing data on public and private school achievement
www.ksg.harvard.edu/pepg/PDF/Papers/PEPG08-02-PetersonLlaudet.pdf

National Center for Education Statistics
http://nces.ed.gov

National Center for the Study of Privatization—US Charter Schools
www.uscharterschools.org/cs/r/view/uscs_sp/362

New Commission on the Skills of the American Workforce
www.skillscommission.org

P-K Education
http://eric.uoregon.edu/publications/digests/digest159.html

Research Room, EdChange Multicultural Pavilion
www.edchange.org/multicultural/papers/edchange_history.html

Thomas Fordham Foundation sponsorship of charter schools
www.edexcellence.net

U.S. Department of Education
www.ed.gov

CHAPTER 3
Curriculum Theory

Curriculum theory and research is growing increasingly important in policy debates. Fredrick Hess (2008), director of educational policy studies at the American Enterprise Institute, states, "Increased attention to educational research has primarily focused on the relative merits of various research methodologies, how to identify 'best practices' or 'scientifically based' methods, and how to encourage educators to make use of research findings" (p. 354).

While curriculum theory is usually esteemed by scholars in the field as an important component of curriculum studies, it seems to be held in low regard by most practitioners, who often dismiss it as completely unrelated to their day-to-day work. Although that impatience with the theoretical is quite understandable, the view advanced in this chapter is that sound theory can be of value to both the scholar and the practitioner. At its best, curriculum theory can provide a set of conceptual tools for analyzing curriculum proposals, for illuminating practice, and for guiding reform.

Questions addressed in this chapter include the following:

- What is the nature and function of curriculum theory?
- Why is it important to meld the theory and reality of school curriculum together as part of the planning process?
- What is the role of leadership in the development of curriculum theory?
- What are the major classifications of curriculum theory?
- How has technology been a catalyst for curriculum change?

Key to Leadership

Successful curriculum leaders realize educational theory serves as a catalyst for change.

75

Melding theory and the reality of school curriculum together is an important step in the educational planning process. Not all curriculum theories translate smoothly into real-world practice. Educators have found it difficult to use theoretical approaches to make continual analyses, reevaluations, and revisions of curriculum in light of such fields as informational technology and the sociology of knowledge. It is a daunting task to undertake the complexity of curriculum design given race, class, economic conditions, and cultural diversity—not to mention the continual changes evolving with technological advances in education. It is therefore essential to develop a fundamental understanding of curriculum theory by providing the tools necessary when analyzing curriculum proposals, illuminating practice, and guiding reform.

THE NATURE AND FUNCTION OF CURRICULUM THEORY

The concept of schooling and education has long been associated with the idea of curriculum and curriculum theory. With no definitive comprehensive theory that covers the field, a great deal of argument and discussion occurs in the field as to what curriculum theory is and what it is not. Today, with new intensity, educators, researchers, parents, and policymakers are working to create successful schools. In collaboration they are searching to blend philosophy and practice based on sound research that will result in a quality educational experience for every student (Swaim, 2003).

To understand the concept of theory, it is essential to understand the nature of theory in general. Much disagreement exists among philosophers of science. On the one hand, some espouse what has come to be known as the Received View of scientific theory.

Historically, the Received View holds that a theory is a formalized, deductively connected bundle of laws that are applicable in specifiable ways to their observable manifestations. In the Received View, a small number of concepts are selected as bases for the theory, axioms are introduced that specify the fundamental relationships among those concepts, and definitions are provided, specifying the remaining concepts of the theory in terms of the basic ones.

In reviewing the literature, Atkins (1982), noted that several criticisms of the Received View exist, even in its revised formulation. First, Suppe (1974) criticized it for its narrowness in requiring axiomatization, noting that several scientific theories are not and cannot be axiomated profitably. He argued instead for a broader view of theory that emphasizes the dynamic nature of all sound theory. Other critics, such as Hanson (1958), attacked the Received View for its posture of value neutrality; as Hanson and others have pointed out, every aspect of theory development is value laden. Scientists do not observe objectively; their observations are profoundly influenced by their worldviews and their values. Popper (1962) rejected the assumption of the Received View that scientific theories can be observationally verified; in his view, theories are conjectures that, although not verifiable, can be submitted to severe tests of falsifiability.

Those who reject the positivist assumptions of the Received View tend to be classified as either realists or instrumentalists, as Atkins (1982) noted. Realists see science as a rational and empirical endeavor, concerned primarily with explanatory and predictive outcomes. Thus, in the view of realists, theory is a description of those structures that generate observable phenomena.

In addition, the primary feature of scientific theory is the explanation of how underlying structures and mechanisms work to generate the phenomena being studied (Keat & Urry, 1975). Instrumentalists, on the other hand, concentrate on the function the theory performs. In this view, a theory is a tool of inquiry, rather than a picture or map of the world. In this sense, then, a theory is not judged in terms of its truth or falsity; instead, it is assessed on the basis of the quality of predictions it demonstrates (Kaplan, 1964).

Thus, current philosophers of science tend to take a more open view of the nature of theory, and it is this more open view that seems especially useful in a field such as education, where theory development seems still to be in a somewhat primitive stage. For the purposes of this chapter, therefore, this broader definition of curriculum theory is stipulated thusly:

> A curriculum theory is a set of related educational concepts that affords a systematic and illuminating perspective of curricular phenomena.

What are the functions of curriculum theory? Most philosophers of science argue that theory has only three legitimate purposes: to describe, to explain, and to predict. A review of curricular theory, however, suggests that many of those theories serve two additional functions. Some theorists, like Michael Apple, seem most concerned with providing educators with a critical perspective on the society and its schools. While Apple (1975) and others who share his viewpoint are concerned with describing and explaining curricular phenomena, their stance is an openly critical one. Some theorists, such as Ralph Tyler (1950), seem most concerned with guiding practice. While Tyler and others whom he has influenced attempt to describe and explain, the primary intent of their work is to help educators make more reasoned choices.

Educational experiences are selected based on their likelihood of attaining the educational goals. After educational experiences are selected, they are organized in a logical manner, with the intent of obtaining the maximum cumulative effect. The curriculum is then improved and refined by a process of evaluation. According to Tyler, curriculum development should be viewed as a cycle: The quality and impact of curricula functions are to be monitored by carefully observing the outcomes, and data from these observations are to be used to fine-tune the curricula (Burks, 1998).

The extent to which a particular theory is able to discharge its functions effectively seems to be influenced by the complexity and maturity of that theory. Here Faix's (1964) classification of the stages of theory development seems useful.

Basic theory, Stage 1, is an early speculative stage in which a theory has not yet been correlated with empirical data. Basic theory sets up untested hypotheses, involves few variables, and employs concepts that are not systematically refined and classified. Basic theory provides only descriptive explanations and directions for more meaningful theory. Glatthorn's (1980) analysis of the curriculum into mastery, organic, and enrichment elements might be described as a basic theory.

Middle-range theory, Stage 2, includes hypotheses that have been empirically tested. An effort has been made to eliminate unlikely variables and relations by the use of models and testing. Experimental laws and generalizations result, and theory can be used to illuminate, predict, and control events. Goodlad's (1979) delineation of what he called a "conceptual system" for guiding inquiry and practice is a good example of a middle-range theory.

General theory, Stage 3, is a general theoretical system or an inclusive conceptual scheme for explaining an entire universe of inquiry. General theory attempts to integrate the substantive knowledge produced from middle-range theories. Beauchamp's (1981) articulation of a comprehensive theory of curriculum might be seen as an attempt to present a general theory, although some would criticize the shallowness of its empirical foundation.

LEADERSHIP IN CURRICULUM THEORY

Teachers need to see their leaders as partners in education, learning with and from them (Hoerr, 2007–2008). The need for leadership and theoretical planning in school curriculum is a common thread running through education on a global level. Today's school administrators currently face one of the most challenging and exciting times in educational history. New curriculum leaders will need to be familiar with a broad spectrum of curriculum theory ranging from behavioral to critical. Leaders will need to fully understand the "mirrored" relationship between theory and practice and how each can be used to mold and define the other.

The role of leadership in reviewing the relationship between theory and practice will be a crucial element in the future success or failure of curriculum change and how it affects schools. It is therefore paramount for communities to encourage and recognize successful leaders who demonstrate an ability to make a difference in teaching and learning. No set rules or formulas exist for leaders to follow, only general guidelines, ideas, and generalities. In this age of technological reform, it is crucial that effective leaders formulate an understanding of curriculum theory if they are truly to evoke educational change in the future. Exercising leadership in these areas helps deepen a comprehension of "what works" and the "why" of curricula development.

Leaders also need to be aware of the cyclical nature of curriculum theory. This is especially true when reviewing needs analysis, methodologies, evaluation, processes, and assessment procedures. Areas of review for curriculum leaders of the future should include the following:

- Historical development of curriculum studies
- Current theory and practice in the field
- Macro and micro dimensions in curriculum
- Ethos and cultural considerations
- Process of curriculum change
- Impact of technology on curriculum
- Models and processes of instructional design
- Models and processes of developing learning strategies
- Identification and implementation of appropriate teaching methods
- Models and techniques of assessment and the evaluation process

- Staff development needs
- Practical application of curriculum design and product for student work programs

Quality leadership means having a thorough understanding of curriculum and being able to change administrative roles and responsibilities when needed to meet the new challenges of curriculum design. It is an art to know how and when to be flexible and yet at the same time to be able to make important curriculum decisions. It is an art to be able to change administratively by shifting from a focus on the system to a focus on the learner. Such shifts in leadership style allow teachers to have more input on curriculum changes that will allow for the greatest impact on learning. Having educational leaders who understand the curriculum review process, are supportive of change, and are willing to formulate new instructional strategies is a definite key to the success of schools in the future.

CLASSIFYING CURRICULUM THEORIES

Numerous attempts have been made to classify curriculum theories in terms of maturity and complexity as have numerous attempts at categorization. Curriculum, however, continues to remain dynamic. According to Kathy Christie (2007), senior vice president of knowledge management, "The 'basics' of tomorrow are skills considered to be of a high level today" (p. 165).

After reviewing attempts at classifying curriculum theories, McNeil (1985) set up what seems to be an unilluminating dichotomy: soft curricularists and hard curricularists. Soft curricularists, in his view, are those such as William Pinar and other reconceptualists who draw from the "soft" fields of religion, philosophy, and literary criticism; hard curricularists, such as Decker Walker and Mauritz Johnson, follow a rational approach and rely on empirical data. The difficulty with such a dichotomy seems obvious. It results in a grouping together of such disparate theorists as Elliot Eisner and Henry Giroux as "soft curricularists" simply because they draw from similar research perspectives.

A tripartite classification proposed by Pinar seems equally unsatisfactory. In his formulation, all curriculum theorists can be classified as traditionalists, conceptual empiricists, or reconceptualists. Traditionalists, in his formulation, are those such as Ralph Tyler, who are concerned with the most efficient means of transmitting a fixed body of knowledge in order to impart the cultural heritage and keep the existing society functioning (Pinar, 1978).

Traditionalists like Tyler view curriculum as notions of class, teacher, course, units, lessons, and so forth. For example, Hirsch (1995), in *What Your Fifth Grader Needs to Know: Fundamentals of Good Fifth-Grade Education*, one of his many books, revealed his commitment to the concept of basic knowledge and cultural literacy in school curricula. He founded the core knowledge series to promote excellence and fairness in early education. Proponents of formal education are generally very interested in the concept of schooling that emphasizes basic knowledge and a definitive structure of instruction that involves the classics. Common themes of formal education proponents might include the development of a syllabus, transmittal of data and knowledge via lecture, formulation of goals and objectives, assessment, and a focus on an end product.

Theorists who espouse an informal education reveal an entirely different perspective on how curriculum should be designed and implemented. Informal proponents such as conceptual empiricists and reconceptualists view education more as an existential experience. Conceptual empiricists, such as Robert Gagne, are those who derive their research methodologies from the physical sciences in attempting to produce generalizations that will enable educators to control and predict what happens in schools. The reconceptualists (a label Gagne applies to himself) emphasize subjectivity, existential experience, and the art of interpretation to reveal the class conflict and the unequal power relationships existing in the larger society. The basic difficulty with this tripartite formulation is that it mixes in a confusing fashion the theorists' research methodologies and their political stances as bases for categorizing theorists. Other theorists such as Elliot Eisner (1985) are equally informal in their approach and seem to be more interested in predicting what will happen in schools. Eisner, as a proponent of informal education, has been a leader in curriculum revision and new approaches for many years.

For example, one of the most widely cited classifications of curriculum theories was proposed by Eisner and Vallance (1974) in their *Conflicting Conceptions of Curriculum*. As they surveyed the field, they found five different conceptions of or orientations to the curriculum. A "cognitive-process" approach is concerned primarily with the development of intellectual operations and is less concerned with specific content. The "curriculum-as-technology" orientation conceptualizes the function of curriculum as finding the most efficient means of accomplishing predetermined ends. "Self-actualization" sees curriculum as a consummative experience designed to produce personal growth. "Social reconstruction–relevance" emphasizes societal needs over individual needs. Theorists with this orientation tend to believe that the primary role of the school is to relate to the larger society, with either an adaptive or a reformist stance. Finally, "academic rationalism" emphasizes the importance of the standard disciplines in helping the young participate in the Western cultural tradition.

While the Eisner and Vallance system seems to make more useful distinctions than either a dichotomy or tripartite system, it does seem to err in including "technology" as a basic orientation of the curriculum. All of the other four seem to designate the major sources for determining curriculum content—the cognitive processes, the person, the society, and the subject. A technological orientation is, on the other hand, concerned primarily with advocating one process for developing a curriculum—a process that could be used with any of the other four types.

The basic error of all three formulations (Eisner & Vallance, 1974; McNeil, 1985; Pinar, 1978) is that they do not sort out curricular theories in terms of their primary orientation or emphasis. Here, Huenecke's (1982) analysis of the domains of curricular inquiry seems most productive. She postulates three different types of curricular theorizing: structural, generic, and substantive. Structural theories, which she claimed dominated the first 50 years of the field, focus on identifying elements in curriculum and their interrelationships, as well as the structure of decision making. Generic theories center their interests on the outcomes of curriculum, concentrating on the assumptions, beliefs, and perceived truths underlying curriculum decisions. Sometimes referred to as critical theories, they tend to be highly critical of past and present conceptions of curriculum. They seek to liberate the individual from the constraints of society, using political and sociological frameworks to examine issues of power, control, and influences. The substantive theories speculate about what subject matter or content is most desirable, what knowledge is of the most worth.

While Huenecke's typology seems very useful, it seems to err in omitting one major domain—those theories such as Schwab's (1970) that are concerned primarily with the processes of curricular decision making. While Huenecke would probably argue that Schwab's work is primarily structural in its emphasis, the distinction between structure and process seems to be one worth maintaining.

It therefore seems most useful to divide curriculum theories into the following four categories, based on their domains of inquiry.

1. *Structure-oriented theories* are concerned primarily with analyzing the components of the curriculum and their interrelationships. Structure-oriented theories tend to be descriptive and explanatory in intent.

2. *Value-oriented theories* are concerned primarily with analyzing the values and assumptions of curriculum makers and their products. Value-oriented theories tend to be critical in nature.

3. *Content-oriented theories* are concerned primarily with determining the content of the curriculum. Content-oriented theories tend to be prescriptive in nature.

4. *Process-oriented theories* are concerned primarily with describing how curricula are developed or recommending how they should be developed. Some process-oriented theories are descriptive in nature; others are more prescriptive.

The rest of this chapter will use this categorization system for examining several major curriculum theories.

Structure-Oriented Theories

As indicated above, structure-oriented theorists of curriculum are concerned with the components of the curriculum and their interrelationships. Primarily analytical in their approach, they seek to describe and explain how curricular components interact within an educational environment. Structure-oriented theorists examine questions such as the following:

- What are the essential concepts of the curriculum field, and how may they most usefully be defined? For example, what does the term *curriculum* mean?

- What are the levels of curriculum decision making, and what forces seem to operate at each of those levels? For example, how do classroom teachers make decisions about the curriculum?

- How may the curriculum field be most validly analyzed into its component parts? For example, how does a program of study differ from a field of study?

- What principles seem to govern issues of content selection, organization, and sequencing? For example, how can curricular elements be articulated?

In seeking answers to such questions, structure-oriented theorists tend to rely on empirical research, using both quantitative and qualitative methodologies to inquire into curricular phenomena.

Structure-oriented theorists seem to operate at what might be termed either a macro level or a micro level. Macro-level theorists attempt to develop global theories that describe and explain the larger elements of curricular structure.

Here it is necessary to turn to the work of micro-level theorists who seem more concerned with describing and explaining curricular phenomena as they occur at the institutional instructional levels. George Posner seems most representative of the micro-level theorists. Over the course of several years, he identified and analyzed several microelements of curricular structure. Typical of his theoretical work is an article coauthored with Kenneth Strike in which they presented and explicated a "categorization scheme for principles of sequencing content" (Posner & Strike, 1976). By bringing to bear some useful epistemological distinctions and by analyzing the curriculum literature, Posner and Strike were able to identify five major types of content sequence.

They called the first principle for sequencing content "world related"—the content structure reflects the empirical relationships among events, people, and things. Subtypes here include sequences based on spatial relations, temporal relations, and physical attributes. The second principle is "concept related" in which sequences reflect the organization of the conceptual world. Thus one subtype of concept-related sequences is "logical prerequisite"—when it is logically necessary to understand the first concept in order to understand the second. "Inquiry-related" sequences are those that sequence the curriculum in relation to a particular method of inquiry, such as Dewey's analysis of the problem-solving process. "Learning-related" sequences draw from knowledge of the psychology of learning in making decisions about sequence; thus sequencing decisions based on such assumptions as "begin with content of intrinsic interest" or "start with the easiest skills" are learning related in nature. The final principle, "utilization related," sequences learning in relation to three possible contexts for utilization—social, personal, and career.

As Posner and Strike (1976) point out, these categories can be considered as a set of concepts that should be useful to the curriculum developer, the curriculum evaluator, and the curriculum researcher.

Value-Oriented Theories

Value-oriented theorists seem to be primarily engaged in what might be termed "educational consciousness-raising," attempting to sensitize educators to the values issues that lie at the hearts of both the hidden and the stated curricula. Their intent is primarily a critical one; thus they sometimes have been identified as "critical theorists." Because many have argued the need for reconceptualizing the field of curriculum, they often are labeled as reconceptualists.

In their inquiries, value-oriented theorists tend to examine issues such as the following:

- In what ways do the schools replicate the power differentials in the larger society?

- What is the nature of a truly liberated individual, and how does schooling inhibit such liberation?

- How do schools consciously or unwittingly mold children and youth to fit into societal roles predetermined by race and class?

- As curriculum leaders determine what constitutes legitimate knowledge, how do such decisions reflect their class biases and serve to inhibit the full development of children and youth?

- In what ways does the schools' treatment of controversial issues tend to minimize and conceal the conflicts endemic to the society?

In examining these issues, most value-oriented theorists draw eclectically from several inquiry methodologies, such as psychoanalysis, philosophical inquiry, historical analysis, and political theory.

The Major Value-Oriented Theorists

Because many critical theorists seem to focus on the person, and many others on the sociopolitical milieu, it seems appropriate to select for examination one person-oriented theorist, James Macdonald, and one milieu-oriented theorist, Michael Apple.

James Macdonald

For a period of almost two decades, James Macdonald seemed to serve as a respected gadfly for the curriculum profession, challenging educators to question their assumptions, to aspire to more worthy goals, and to reconceptualize the enterprise of curriculum making. A prolific writer, his work is so multifaceted that it is difficult to summarize.

Basic to all his work is his view of the human condition. Central to that human condition is a search for transcendence, the struggle of the individual to actualize the whole self. Much influenced toward the end of his career by the writings of Carl Jung, Macdonald (1974) used almost mystical metaphors in "A Transcendental Developmental Ideology of Education" to speak of this journey toward transcendence as the primary concern of all humans.

Although Macdonald has been criticized for being too mystical and vague, the cumulative effect of his work has been to challenge curriculum leaders to rethink their basic assumptions and to reconceptualize their field. In his view, the curriculum offered by most schools is seriously distorted in its emphasis. The goal of education should be to facilitate the development of autonomous and self-actualizing individuals. Macdonald (1977) put the matter cogently in this fashion:

> Any person concerned with curriculum must realize that he/she is engaged in a political activity. Curriculum talk and work are, in microcosm, a legislative function. We are concerned . . . with the goal of creating the good life, the good society, and the good person. . . . If we curriculum talkers are to understand what we ourselves are saying, and communicate to others, those values must be explicit. (p. 15)

Michael Apple

Michael Apple is a critical theorist who seems to be concerned primarily with the relationship between the society and the school. Central to Apple's (1975) critique of the society and its schools is his use of the term *hegemony* to mean "an organized assemblage of meanings and practices, the central effective and dominant system of meanings, values, and actions which are *lived*" (p. 113). Hegemony in this sense permeates the consciousness of the society as a body of practices and a set of meanings determined by the dominant culture.

One crucial way in which this cultural hegemony influences educators is in their perception of science. In this telling critique of what might be termed "educational pseudoscientism," Apple (1975) noted that almost all educators rely on a narrow and strict view of science, one that values only rationality and empirical data in the service of predictability and control and that ignores the close relationship between science and art, science and myth.

CONTENT-ORIENTED THEORIES

Content-oriented theorists are concerned primarily with specifying the major sources that should influence the selection and organization of the curriculum content. For the most part, their theories can be classified in terms of their views as to which source should predominate: child-centered theories, knowledge-centered theories, or society-centered theories.

Child-Centered Curricula

Those who espouse child-centered curricula argue that the child is the beginning point, the determiner, and the shaper of the curriculum. Although the developing child will at some point acquire knowledge of subject matter, the disciplines are seen as only one type of learning. While the child develops in and is influenced by a social environment, the needs of the society are not considered paramount; that society will best be served by the kind of mature and autonomous individual that child-centered curricula attempt to develop. As Francis Parker (1894) expressed it many decades ago, "The centre of all movement in education is the child."

During the past three decades, three major **child-centered curriculum** movements have occurred: affective education, open education, and developmental education.

Affective Education

The **affective education** movement emphasized the feelings and values of the child. While cognitive development was considered important, it was seen only as an adjunct to affective growth. Thus, curriculum leaders were concerned primarily with identifying teaching and learning activities that would help the child understand and express feelings and discern and clarify values. For example, Brown (1975), who advocated "confluent education" (a curriculum approach that attempted to synthesize physical, emotional, and intellectual growth), recommended a "fantasy body trip" as a learning activity. Students are asked to close their eyes and "move into themselves"; each person is asked to concentrate on different parts of the body, beginning with the toes, then all participants share their experiences.

Open Education

As previously noted, open education was a child-centered curriculum movement that emphasized the social and cognitive development of the child through informal exploration, activity, and discovery. Here the "whole child" was considered the beginning point and focus of curriculum work. As Lillian Weber (1971), one of the foremost exponents of open education, stated,

> These questions about children seem uppermost in developing plans for the classroom, for plans were not made from the vantage point of a syllabus of demand which a child had to meet, but with relevance to children in the most immediate way. A plan fitted itself to the child. (p. 169)

In fitting the plans to the child, the teacher provisioned a rich learning environment, one that emphasized the use of concrete and interactive materials organized in "learning centers."

The school day was not compartmentalized into subject periods, such as "language arts" and "mathematics." Instead, children experienced an "integrated day"; they were encouraged to solve problems that required the development of several skills and the acquisition of many kinds of knowledge.

Developmental Education

Developmental education. as the term is used here, refers to any curriculum theory that stresses the developmental stages of child growth as the primary determiners of placement and sequence.

Some current curriculum leaders use a Piagetian framework in selecting, placing, and structuring appropriate learning experiences. For example, Brooks (1986) described how the teachers in the Shoreham-Wading River (New York) schools first received extensive training in the theory and research on cognitive development. They then learned how to assess their students' cognitive development by using a variety of formal and informal measures. Finally, they were taught specific strategies for modifying and adapting predetermined curricula to match students' cognitive levels.

In the developmental perspective, curricula tend to be seen as instruments for facilitating child development. Certain general outcomes are postulated. The child's present developmental level is assessed. Then learning activities and content are selected that will challenge the student enough to produce growth, but without overwhelming the student with impossible demands. In all developmental curricula, the teacher is seen primarily as an adapter of curricula, one who learns to modify predetermined content to fit the developmental needs and capabilities of the learner.

While it seems useful to consider the child's development in selecting and placing content, no conclusive evidence exists suggesting that developmental curricula are more effective than those not embodying such a perspective.

Knowledge-Centered Curricula

Those leaders who advocate a **knowledge-centered curricula** approach argue essentially that the disciplines or bodies of knowledge should be the primary determiners of what is taught. While they acknowledge that child-development research should affect decisions about placement, they pay greater attention to the structure of the disciplines or the nature of knowledge, even in matters of sequence. While they admit that the child lives and grows in a social world, they see society as playing only a very minor role in developing curricula. In general, curricula based on a knowledge-centered approach might be divided into two groups: "structures of the disciplines" curricula and "ways of knowing" curricula.

Structures of the Disciplines

Two major attempts have been made to reform the curriculum so that it places greater emphasis on the subjects. During the period from 1890 to 1910, the concern of curriculum leaders was to standardize the school curriculum and to bring it into closer alignment with college requirements. During the period from 1958 to 1970, the curriculum-reform movement emphasized the updating of curriculum content by emphasizing the structures of the disciplines.

Ways of Knowing

This approach to the curriculum is of rather recent vintage. As Eisner (1985) noted, it grows out of several emerging research lines: cognitive science, human creativity, brain functioning, and conceptions of intelligence and knowledge. While Vallance (1985) saw this interest in **ways of knowing** as producing a radically different "curriculum map" that is quite distinct from the traditional disciplines, its emphasis on knowledge and knowing seems to warrant placing it in the broader category of knowledge-centered approaches.

Briefly, those espousing such a view argue that there are multiple ways of knowing, not just one or two. Further, these multiple ways of knowing should be given greater attention in the school's curriculum.

Society-Centered Curricula

Several curriculum theorists agree that the social order, a **society-centered curricula**, should be the starting point and the primary determiner of the curriculum. They differ sharply among themselves, however, about the stance the schools should take toward the existing social order; accordingly, they can best be understood by categorizing them on these bases: the conformists, the reformers, the futurists, and the radicals.

The Conformists

The **conformists** believe that the existing order is a good one—the best of all possible worlds. While problems obviously exist in that social order, in the eyes of the conformists those problems are of lesser consequence and can be handled by mature adults. Accordingly, the essential task of the curriculum is to indoctrinate the young: help them understand the history of this society, teach them to value it, and educate them to function successfully in it. Curriculum workers with a conformist intent begin curriculum development by identifying the needs of the existing society and its institutions; curriculum objectives are derived from those needs. The teacher is usually expected to serve as an advocate for the free-enterprise system, helping students understand why it is so much better than competing systems.

Curricula with a conformist thrust have been advocated in almost every period of curriculum history. Bobbitt (1918), in his basic work *The Curriculum*, argued for a social point of view, defining the curriculum as "that series of things which children and youth must do and experience by way of developing abilities to do the things well that make up the affairs of adult life; and to be in all respects what adults should be" (p. 42). In the eyes of many critics, the career education movement of the 1970s had a conformist thrust: Bowers (1977) saw its purpose as "designed to socialize students to accept the present organization of work and technology as the taken-for-granted reality" (p. 44). William Bennett, secretary of education during Ronald Reagan's second presidential term, advocated a brand of citizenship education that clearly had a conformist intent.

The Reformers

Those classified as reformers see society as essentially sound in its democratic structure but want to effect major reforms in the social order. The major vehicle is the curriculum: Courses should be developed that will sensitize students to emerging social issues and give students the intellectual tools they need to solve social problems. Thus, curriculum workers should begin the task of curriculum development by identifying social problems. Those social problems—such as racism, sexism, and environmental pollution—then become the center of classroom activity. The teacher is expected to play an active role in identifying the problems, in "raising the consciousness" of the young, and in helping students take actions to bring about the needed reforms.

The reformers seem most vocal during times of social unrest. During the 1930s, Counts (1932) challenged the schools to take a more active role in achieving his vision of a more liberal society: The title of his book—*Dare the School Build a New Social Order?*—conveys the tone of his work. During the late 1960s and early 1970s, liberal educators advocated curricula that would be responsive to what they perceived as a "cultural revolution." For example, Purpel and Belanger (1972) called for a curriculum that would institutionalize compassion and increase students' sense of social responsibility.

The Futurists

Rather than being attuned to the present problems of the society, futurists look to the coming age. They analyze present developments, extrapolate from available data, and posit alternative scenarios. They highlight the choices people have in shaping this coming age and encourage the schools to give students the tools to create a better future for them. In a sense, they might be described as reformers intent on solving the problems of the year 2020. In their view, the school curricula should have such a futurist orientation, focusing on the developments likely to occur and involving students in thinking about the choices they have and the consequences of the choices they make. Rapidly advancing and clear-cut new technologies will force schools to change rapidly. Gradual improvements of the educational process will not suffice. The education system of today will be completely transformed by 2020. Many factors will promote this change. The most important are the following:

- New management models from business will be applied to the educational system.
- Parents and students will promote change in the system.
- Private companies will play a larger role in the education process.
- Technology will influence the education landscape. (imagitrends, n.d.)

Technology can be used for learning. In an age of communication-rich technology environments, computers can be used for more than just communicating with other human beings (Foti, 2007).

Throughout the past few decades, technology has been viewed for improving student academic performance and for increasing the flexibility of public schools. As a result, computer availability and use have increased, and programs addressing educational technology have gained attention (Franklin, 2008). Our schools thrive on information. In the ever-changing world filled with new technology, our teachers and students require the right information, from the right sources, today. Having direct access to industry information gives the competitive edge needed to succeed.

The Radicals

Those who regard the society as critically flawed espouse curricula that would expose those flaws and empower the young to effect radical changes. Typically, reasoning from a neo-Marxist perspective, they believe the problems of the age are only symptoms of the pervasive structural inequities inherent in a technological capitalistic system. As a consequence, **radicals** want to reach the masses by revolutionizing education by "deschooling" the educational process.

One of the leading exponents of such an approach is Paulo Freire (1970), the Brazilian educator whose *Pedagogy of the Oppressed* made a significant impact on radical educators in this country. In Freire's view, the goal of education is *conscientization,* a process of enlightening the masses about the inequities inherent in their sociocultural reality and giving them the tools to make radical changes in that social order that restricts their freedom. He makes the process explicit in explaining how he teaches reading. Adults learn to read by identifying words with power—words such as *love* and *person* that have pragmatic value in communicating with others in the community. They create their own texts that express their perceptions of the world they live in and the world they want. They learn to read to become aware of the dehumanizing aspects of their lives, but they are helped to understand that learning to read will not guarantee them the jobs they need.

PROCESS-ORIENTED THEORIES

Over the past two decades, when curriculum theory seems to have reached its maturity as a systematic field of inquiry, several attempts have been made to develop conceptual systems for classifying curricular processes and products (see, e.g., Eisner & Vallance, 1974; Gay, 1980; Schiro, 1978). However, most of these categorization schemes are deficient on two grounds. First, they badly confuse what have been described above as value-oriented, content-oriented, and **process-oriented theories**. Second, they seem to give only scant attention to the curriculum-development process advocated by the theorist under consideration. Most suggest that there is some correspondence between the value or content orientation of the theory and the type of process espoused, although such connections do not seem apparent. Thus, one of Gay's (as cited in Eisner & Vallance, 1974) "conceptual models of the curriculum-planning process" is what she terms the "experimental model." Her description of the experiential model suggests that it gives predominant weight to the needs of the child as a determiner of content, is vaguely liberal in its value orientation, and emphasizes a planning process that she describes with such terms as *organic, evolving, situational*, and *inquiry centered,* but she does not provide much detail about the specifics of the planning process.

Thus, if we are asking about alternative planning models, we will have to turn to sources other than these widely known classification schemes. One source that offers some promise is Short's (1983) article "The Forms and Use of Alternative Curriculum Development Strategies." His work seems to build on previous efforts, it reflects a comprehensive knowledge of both the prescriptive and descriptive literature, and it seems to offer the greatest promise for analyzing and generating alternative systems.

Short's article has two explicit goals. One is to analyze what is known about the forms and use of alternative strategies of curriculum development, and the other is to organize this knowledge in a way that permits one to assess the policy implications of choosing and using one or the other of these strategies.

A System for Examining Curricular Processes

It would seem more pragmatic to both scholars and practitioners to have available for their use a systematic means for examining curricular processes. Such an analytic system should have the following characteristics: It would include all the process elements that the research would suggest are important, thus enabling curriculum researchers to make useful distinctions between sets of recommended and implemented processes; it would be open-ended in form, thus enabling practitioners to become aware of a comprehensive set of alternatives; and it would emphasize description and analysis, not evaluation, enabling both scholars and practitioners to reach their independent conclusions about desirability.

The set of descriptors presented in Exhibit 3.1 represents an initial attempt to formulate such an analytic system. Certain caveats should be noted here. First, the descriptors have been drawn from a preliminary analysis of the literature and the authors' personal experiences, but that analysis has not at this point been completely systematic and rigorous. Second, while there has been some initial success in using it to discriminate between development strategies that on the surface seem quite similar, it needs much more extensive testing and refinement. It is thus presented here as an initial formulation that invites criticism and improvement.

EXHIBIT 3.1   An Analytic System for Examining the Curriculum Process

1. What groups or constituencies should be represented in the developmental sessions?

2. What type of participation structure is recommended for the sessions—monologic, participatory, dialogic?

3. What shaping factors should receive significant consideration throughout the process?

4. Which curriculum element should be used as the starting point in the substantive deliberations?

5. Which curriculum elements should receive significant consideration—and in what sequence should such consideration occur?

6. Which organizing structures should receive significant consideration—and in what order: course structure, units, lessons, lesson components?

7. Should the progression from element to element or from structure to structure be predominantly linear or recursive?

8. What curriculum images and metaphors seem to influence the process?

9. What general type of problem-solving approach should be used throughout the process—technological, rational, intuitive, negotiating?

10. What recommendations are made about the form and content of the curriculum product?

11. What recommendations are made for implementing the curriculum product?

12. What recommendations are made for assessing the curriculum product?

13. What criteria should participants use to assess the quality and effectiveness of the process?

14. To what extent should developers be sensitive to the political aspects of curriculum development?

The first descriptor focuses on the participants in the process. As Short (1983) indicated, their competence and their perspective are so important that we need to have such information. The second descriptor is concerned with the general tenor of the discussions. A monologic discussion is one in which only one person participates or makes decisions, such as a college instructor developing a new course independently. In a participatory discussion, one individual clearly is in control but makes a genuine effort to solicit the input of others. A dialogic discussion is one in which there is much open discussion in an attempt to achieve consensus on key issues.

The third descriptor identifies those elements that influence curriculum decision making, even though they may not be explicitly referred to in the final document. As Exhibit 3.2 indicates, several factors variously affect curriculum decisions. Thus, nursing educators who have been observed developing courses seemed most conscious of the requirements of accrediting bodies. On the other hand, teachers in a large urban district seemed chiefly concerned about "accountability procedures."

The fourth descriptor is concerned with the starting point for the substantive deliberations. As indicated in Exhibit 3.3, several curricular elements are in this formulation, any one of which might conceivably be a starting point. The obvious intent here is to challenge the conventional wisdom that curriculum development must begin with a clear statement of objectives.

EXHIBIT 3.2   Shaping Factors in Curricular Deliberations

1. The developers: their espoused and practiced values; their knowledge and competence

2. The students: their values, abilities, goals, learning styles

3. The teachers: their values, knowledge, teaching styles, concerns

4. The organization: its ethos and structure

5. The administrators of that organization: their values and expectations

6. External individuals and groups (parents, employers, pressure groups): their values and expectations

7. Accrediting bodies: their requirements and recommendations

8. Scholars in the field: their recommendations, their reports of research; their perceptions of the structure of that discipline

9. The community and the larger society: what is required to maintain or change the social order

10. Other courses in that field of study, courses taken previously and subsequently

11. Courses in other fields that students are likely to take concurrent with the course being developed: their contents, impacts, and requirements

12. The schedule for the course: number of meetings, length of meetings, frequency

13. Accountability procedures: examinations, "curricular audits"

EXHIBIT 3.3   Curricular Elements

1. Rationale, philosophy, or statement of espoused values

2. Institutional goals or aims

3. Knowledge outcomes for the course, the units, the lessons: concepts, factual knowledge

4. Skill or process outcomes for the course, the units, the lessons

5. Affective outcomes for the course, the units, the lessons: values, attitudes

6. Content choices: elements of subject matter selected for their intrinsic worth (literary or artistic works, periods of history, important individuals, significant events, etc.)

7. Organizing elements: themes, recurring concepts, structures of linkage:
   a. Those used to link this course with courses previously or subsequently studied
   b. Those used to link this course with other courses studied concurrently
   c. Those used to link units in this course with each other
   d. Those used to organize units and relate lessons in a unit to each other

8. Teaching/learning activities

9. Instructional materials and media

10. Time allocations

11. Methods for assessing student learning

EXHIBIT 3.4   Analysis of Doll's (1986) Curriculum-Development Process

1. Groups represented: teachers, pupils, administrators, supervisors, school board, lay community

2. Participation structure: participatory

3. Shaping factors: organizational ethos; pupil needs; teachers' values, knowledge, teaching style, concerns

4. Starting point: institutional goals

5. Elements considered: goals, course objectives, evaluation means, type of design, learning content, interunit linkages, interlesson linkages

6. Organizing structures: not specified

7. Progression: linear

8. Images and metaphor: not used

9. Problem-solving approach: rational

10. Form and content of product: no specific recommendations

11. Implementation recommendations: no specific recommendations

12. Recommendations for evaluating product: extensive formative and summative assessments

13. Criteria in assessing process: 11 specific criteria offered

14. Political sensitivity: limited

As indicated in Exhibit 3.4, the fifth descriptor is concerned with those elements emphasized and the sequence in which they are considered.

The sixth descriptor focuses on the organizing structures of the course—the structural elements that give the course shape. Four structural components are included: the general structure and movement of the course itself, the units, the lessons, and the lesson components.

The seventh descriptor examines the progression of the discussion. A linear progression would move sequentially from element to element or from structure to structure; a recursive discussion would move back and forth in some systematic fashion. The eighth descriptor asks the researcher to be sensitive to the curricular images and metaphors that seem to influence the process. Does the developer seem to conceptualize a curriculum as a mosaic or a patchwork quilt, as a journey or series of travel experiences, as a set of steps moving from the basement to the top floor? The obvious point, of course, is that such images and metaphors reveal the pervasive belief systems of the developers with respect to that field of study—and such belief systems subtly but profoundly influence their decision making.

The ninth descriptor examines the type of problem-solving process at work. Contrary to what some deliberative theorists assert, it seems in many respects that all curriculum making is a type of problem solving. Four types of problem-solving processes have been recommended by theorists: technological, rational, intuitive, and negotiating. A technological approach to curriculum problem solving argues for a tightly controlled process assessing needs, deriving goals from those needs, performing a task analysis to identify learning objectives, determining the sequential or hierarchical relationship among the objectives, specifying instructional activities, and identifying evaluation procedures.

A rational approach to curriculum problem solving describes the somewhat looser but still logical approach advocated by Schwab (1970) and others: Deliberators collect and examine pertinent data, formulate the curriculum problem, generate alternative solutions, and evaluate those solutions to determine which is best.

In an intuitive approach, participants are encouraged to rely on their intuition and tacit knowledge, like Schon's (1983) "reflective practitioners" who make wise choices but cannot explain how they make those choices. Moreover, in some processes, the problem solving is more like a negotiating exchange in which bargaining and trading and making compromises seem to be the predominant activities.

The 10th descriptor examines the decisions about the form and content of the final product. Again, there might be much variation here. For example, Glatthorn (1980) recommended that the final product should be a loose-leaf notebook that contains only a summary of pertinent research and a list of the required and testable objectives. Teachers using the notebook thus have much latitude in how they organize the objectives and which methods and materials they use.

The 11th and 12th descriptors are concerned with the future—what plans are made for implementing and for testing the product. The 13th descriptor examines the criteria that the participants seem chiefly to rely on in assessing the quality of their work, and the last descriptor examines the extent to which the process is sensitive to the political aspects of curriculum work.

If such an analytic system is at all valid, then it suggests, of course, that the Tyler rationale is not the only system for developing curricula; in fact, the system has been used in initial trials to analyze the significant differences between several distinct models of curriculum development. Exhibit 3.4 shows how the descriptors were used to analyze Doll's (1986)

EXHIBIT 3.5   Analysis of Glatthorn's (1987) Curriculum-Development Process

1. Groups represented: teachers

2. Participation structure: dialogic

3. Shaping factors: students, teachers, administrators, scholars, other courses, schedule

4. Starting point: knowledge and skill outcomes for course; starting point for unit planning varies

5. Elements considered: knowledge and skill outcomes for units and lessons, unit themes, teaching/learning activities, instructional materials and media, time allocations, student assessment

6. Organizing structures: units, lessons

7. Progression: recursive

8. Images and metaphors: not used

9. Problem-solving approach: intuitive

10. Form and content of product: open-ended "scenarios"

11. Implementation recommendations: no specific recommendations

12. Recommendations for evaluating product: emphasis on quality of learning experiences

13. Criteria in assessing process: none provided

14. Political sensitivity: extensive

process, and Exhibit 3.5 shows how they describe the "naturalistic" process reviewed in Chapter 8 in this book.

Alternative Curriculum Approaches

Glatthorn's four curriculum categories still hold up to scrutiny today and continue to help provide a road map for curriculum theory. Nonetheless, Smith (1996, 2000) developed his own categories for understanding curriculum development:

- *Transmission of Information:* Curriculum as a body of knowledge to be transmitted via a syllabus
- *End Product:* Curriculum as an attempt to achieve certain ends (products)
- *Process:* Curriculum as a process
- *Praxis:* Curriculum as praxis (action that is committed)

Smith's categories reflect and synthesize the essence of curriculum theory into four easily understood approaches. With this in mind, the authors have taken the liberty of combining Smith's ideas into a figure that also includes categories noted by Glatthorn. Exhibit 3.6 is modified to reveal some clear links between Glatthorn and Smith. Areas of consideration include the body of knowledge and content to be transmitted, the process and value models to be conveyed, the focus on an end product, and the practical and technical deliberation. Most interestingly, Smith's categories mirror elements of Aristotle's characterization of the productive.

When reviewing the model using ideas from Smith and Glatthorn, it is important to note change results from several different perspectives. The model blends together the substantive nature of curriculum theory as well as the development of awareness and

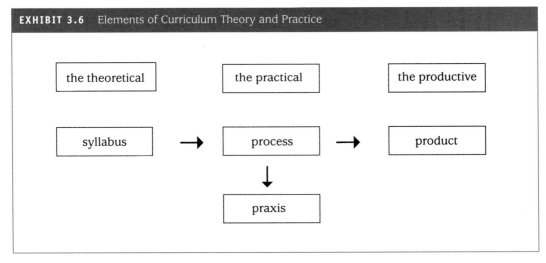

EXHIBIT 3.6   Elements of Curriculum Theory and Practice

SOURCE: Adapted from Smith (1996, 2000).

understanding. Below, we expand on and compare the similarities between Smith's categories of transmitter of knowledge, end product, process, and praxis as they relate to Glatthorn's typology of structure-oriented theories, **value-oriented theories**, **content-oriented theories**, and process-oriented theories.

Curriculum as Transmission of Information

Smith views curriculum as a body of knowledge to be transmitted and equates it with the use of a syllabus. Some theorists believe that an overemphasis on the use of a syllabus as the sole foundation of curriculum is a dependence on content as well as an overdependence on a particular way of organizing a body of knowledge, content, and/or subjects.

The syllabus and transmitter-of-knowledge approach seems to follow closely with Glatthorn's *structured-oriented theories*. Structure-oriented theorists generally wish to transmit the body of knowledge but tend to rely on empirical research, using both quantitative and qualitative methodologies to inquire into curricular phenomena.

For example, macrostructural theorists are now more globally oriented and use technology to transmit information about curriculum. The use of e-mail and the Internet is becoming a larger part of developing curriculum at this level. Educators are using the World Wide Web to share curriculum designs and syllabi. Larger, global forces of polity, economics, common cultures, and classics are becoming points of interest and are more evident when transmitting and sharing basic information. The transmitter-of-knowledge approach is often determined and manipulated to agree with the local interests, values, needs, and wants of the controlling agency, such as a state government educational agency, community, or school.

Curriculum as End Product

A second fundamental aspect of Smith's curriculum theory is that of *achieving an end product*. Goals and objectives become the common focus of theorists using this approach. Educators using this approach are less concerned with how curriculum is taught than what the end product is and what the goals and objectives are that are used to achieve that product or result—for example, a science report, multimedia math project, piece of literature, poetry, or a speech. This follows with the concept of expanding and explaining curriculum. Themes often center on preparing the student for life, developing abilities, attitudes, habits, and appreciations. The focus of curriculum is generally that of systemic study, needs assessment, training, implementation, and evaluation with an emphasis on students' producing tangible results that reflect their potential.

End product approaches seem to follow closely with Glatthorn's *content-oriented theories*. As mentioned previously, content-oriented theorists are often concerned with determining and specifying the major sources as well as the details that influence the selection and organization of curriculum content.

Proponents of product-based curriculum usually focus on the following:

- *Real problems*—Real and relevant to the student and the activity

- *Real audiences*—Utilizing an "audience" that is appropriate for the product, which could include another student or group of students, a teacher (not necessarily the class teacher), an assembly, a mentor, a community or specific interest group

- *Real deadlines*—Encouraging time management skills and realistic planning

- *Transformations*—Involving original manipulation of information rather than regurgitation

- *Appropriate evaluation*—With the product and the process of its development being both self-evaluated and evaluated by the product's audience using previously established "real world" criteria that are appropriate for such products (Farmer, 1996)

An example of a product-based approach is Understanding by Design. Understanding by Design proponents Grant Wiggins and Jay McTighe (2005) noted that this approach often looks at instruction from a "results" orientation. They believe that Understanding by Design is a recursive process, not a prescriptive program. It targets achievement through a "backward design" process that focuses on assessment first and relevant instructional activities last. The design also uses a spiral of learning where students use and reconsider ideas and skills versus a linear scope and sequence. Individuals using the Understanding by Design approach have a tendency to view curriculum in terms of desired "performances of understanding" and then "plan backwards" to identify needed concepts and skills (Tomlinson & McTighe, 2006).

Researchers who espouse product-based curriculum commonly place an emphasis on case studies. Case studies help curriculum designers focus on the realities of classroom life. Teachers have long been aware of the increasing gap between the principles of education taught in university preservice programs and the classroom. The current burgeoning interest in educational case methods is testimony to the promise of case-based teaching as a way of bridging that gap and of easing the novice teacher's entry into the classroom. A case study holds attributes of both theory and practice, enabling teachers and students alike to examine real-life situations under a laboratory microscope. Case studies provide a piece of controllable reality, more vivid and contextual than a textbook discussion, yet more disciplined and manageable than observing or doing work in the world itself (Wiggins & McTighe, 2005).

Curriculum as Process

A third fundamental aspect of current curriculum theory noted by Smith focuses on *curriculum as process*. Viewing curriculum as process places the emphasis on the interaction among teacher, student, parent, and knowledge rather than on a syllabus and/or on an end product. The focus is on what is actually taking place in the classroom as well as the learning process itself. Critical thinking, listening, and communication are important components of process curriculum. Often an emphasis is placed on thinking about planning, justifications of procedures, and actual interventions, as well as providing feedback and changes during the curriculum process.

One of the earlier curriculum planning approaches involved the *instructional design process*. The instructional design process, often referred to as ISD, emerged from psychology laboratories and helped establish the first systematic approach to the development of instructional materials and teaching strategies. Instructional design is the systematic development of instructional specifications using learning and instructional theory to ensure the quality of instruction. It is the entire process of analysis of learning needs and goals and the development of a delivery system to meet those needs. It includes development of instructional materials and activities and tryout and evaluation of all instruction and learner activities (Shulman, 2003). Robert Gagne's (1985) *The Conditions of Learning and Theory of Instruction* and *Principles of Instructional Design* (Gagne, Briggs, & Wager, 1992) describe this approach. Gagne (as cited in Willwerth, 2003) once said,

> To know, to understand, to gain insight into, and so on are not useful as descriptions of relatively observable behavior; nor are their intended meanings easily agreed upon by individuals. . . . The action verbs which are used in the construction of the behavioral objectives for *Science: A Process Approach* are: identify, construct, name, order, describe, demonstrate, state a rule, and apply a rule. (n.p.)

The instructional design process continues to be an important part of the planning, implementation, and evaluation of curriculum.

Allan Glatthorn's concept of *value-oriented theorists* relates well to Smith's process and end product approach. It is primarily engaged in what might be termed "educational consciousness raising," attempting to sensitize educators to the values and issues that lie at the heart of the stated curriculum. Advances in technology and the World Wide Web have provided value-oriented theorists with a global platform to access electronically to share information on social reform, culture, and economics.

Value-oriented theorists draw heavily and eclectically from several inquiry methodologies, such as psychoanalysis, philosophical inquiry, historical analysis, and political theory. For example, A. N. Maheshwari (2003), chairperson of the National Council for Teacher Education, states,

> As the world enters the Information Age another dimension to value education concerns information itself. This is to do with the nature of information. (¶ 4)
>
> Information is received by human beings through five senses—the senses of seeing, hearing, touch, taste and smell. Information as any one of us receives it is value neutral. Information of seeing is carried by ElectroMagnetic [*sic*] waves, which consist of vibrations of electric and magnetic fields. These vibrations when received by our eyes are transmitted as signals to the brain. The response of brain to information that is received by it is determined by its sub-conscious [*sic*] mind. (¶ 5)

"Therefore," according to Maheshwari, "teachers of the future will have to provide learning experiences for holistic development of mind, body intellect and emotions" (¶ 7), and this will require value-oriented teacher education. Maheshwari goes on to state, "There are two challenges that may have to be faced in providing value orientation to teacher education—stability and change. Stability demands preservation of culture and change demands technology" (¶ 10).

Curriculum as Praxis/Awareness

The fourth aspect of Smith's curriculum model is *praxis*. Praxis models deal primarily with practical deliberation and differentiated curriculum. Through the use of technological advances, curriculum leaders can now access a body of knowledge, formulate content that is interdisciplinary, and provide a process of electronic communication that helps cut across cultural, economic, and social boundaries worldwide. The praxis concept encourages the student and teacher to reach a higher level of awareness through curriculum differentiation and with the use of technology to speed up the process.

Curriculum differentiation focuses on maximizing the potential of each student in their classrooms, including students who come to the class with defined disabilities (Carolan & Guinn, 2007). Differentiation is a broad term referring to the need to tailor teaching environments and practices to create appropriately different learning experiences for different students. Keirouz (as cited in Maheshwari, 2003) suggests the following procedures for enhancing differentiation:

- Deleting already mastered material from existing curriculum
- Adding new content, process, or product expectations to existing curriculum
- Extending existing curriculum to provide enrichment activities
- Providing coursework for able students at an earlier age than usual
- Writing new units or courses that meet the needs of gifted students

The focus here is to create a differentiated learning environment that encourages students to engage their abilities to the greatest extent possible, including taking risks and building knowledge and skills, in what they perceive as a safe, flexible environment. In that regard, a differentiated learning environment should do the following:

1. assess students before a unit of instruction to determine what they already know.
2. adjust the core curriculum by content (below to above grade level), process (concrete to abstract), and product (simple to complex).
3. provide assignments tailored for students of different levels of achievement.
4. have HIGH expectations for ALL students.
5. provide educational experiences which extend, replace, or supplement standard curriculum.
6. structure class assignments so they require high levels of critical thinking and allow for a range of responses.
7. have students participate in respectful work.
8. have students and teachers collaborate in learning.
9. put students in situations where they don't know the answer—often.

10. differ the pace of instruction.

11. provide a blend of whole class, group, and independent learning. (*Principles of differentiation*, n.d. Used with permission from the Manteno C.U.S.D. #5, Manteno, Illinois.)

Differentiated curriculum in enriched learning environments follows closely with a constructivist philosophy and focuses on making meaning of one's environment and becoming aware of the interaction between the enacted curriculum and the experienced curriculum. For example, Seymour Papert (1993) used the term *constructionism* to brand his favored approach to learning. He stated,

> Constructionism is built on the assumption that children will do best by finding ("fishing") for themselves the specific knowledge they need. Organized or informal education can help most by making sure they are supported morally, psychologically, materially, and intellectually in their efforts. As such, the goal is to teach in such a way as to produce the most learning for the least teaching. (¶ 4)

Constructionism differs from constructivism in that it looks more closely than other educational-isms at the idea of mental construction. According to Racer (2007):

> constructivist teachers too often skip the foundation, the discipline and practice of a subject. Because of the failings of the constructivist philosophy, educators have had to endure the back-to-basics movement, the accountability and standards movements, and now the imposition of NCLB. (p. 95)

Constructionism teachers, however, attach special importance to the role of constructions in the world as a support for those in the head, thereby becoming less of a purely mentalist doctrine. As historical examples of constructionist learning activities, Papert (1993) referred, amongst others, "to measuring quantities while making a cake, building LEGO or working with the computer programming language LOGO developed specifically . . . for educational use" (¶ 5). As scientists study learning, they are realizing that a constructivist model reflects their best understanding of the brain's natural way of making sense of the world (Papert, 1993). Some educators in the field, however, become confused as to who are constructivists and who are behaviorists. In a behaviorist class, one focuses on the answers desired and tries to shape the responses until they resemble a prototype. In a constructivist classroom, students continually try out ideas and practice for themselves to see where the ideas will work and where they prove to be inadequate (Abbot & Ryan, 1999).

Constructivists and differentiated instruction do, however, require that teachers study differences in understanding, learning modalities, and interests. This can be a problem in that it requires a great deal of time and requires the complexity of keeping track of different approaches (Perkins, 1999). Critics of differentiated instruction and constructivist approaches also note that is too permissive and that it lacks rigor. The concern is that the teacher may cast aside the information, facts, and basic skills embedded in the curriculum (Scherer, 1999). There is an additional fear concerning how it will fare with a continuing emphasis on curriculum based on standards and high-stakes testing. With the advent of state and national assessments and a focus on the alignment of standards, some construc-tivists are concerned that students are losing out on special instructional practices that fos-ter meaningful learning (Brooks & Brooks, 1999).

Conflicts between constructivists and those who favor high-stakes testing may be soft-ened by the advent of technology. Advances in technology may hold the promise of pro-viding a means to ameliorate the situation by allowing students to have an active, social, and creative learning environment as well as enable educators to align the curriculum to state and national standards and assessments.

Through actual practice and activities in the classroom, students will be able to negoti-ate problems and analyze strategies on a case-by-case, situation-by-situation basis. This approach not only allows for description and explanation but also emphasizes prediction and problem solving at higher levels. It is a curriculum that makes teachers and students more introspective on a global level and allows teachers and students to see through each other's eyes. Learning involves exploration and is based on reflection, exploration, and physical experience. The praxis model becomes more metacognitively and activity-centered and more personal in nature, allowing the development of real-life experiences to unfold. A greater chance exists for the dynamic interaction and reflection between student and teacher that drives the learning process. With the assistance of technological advances, a teacher today can be more involved in the process and is better able to capture the coveted "teachable moment."

CURRICULUM AS CHANGE

Feedback from the field suggests that a gap between research and practice persists while bridges between them remain tenuous and unsteady (Davis, 2007). Curriculum, whether it is hidden or apparent, seems to be changing even more to meet today's needs and realities. Current instructional design based on brain research is becoming more common.

For example, processes involved in learning to read are now being found to occur dur-ing dynamic states of brain development. According to Willis (2007), "In this pioneering age of neuroimaging research, neuroscientists and educators must collaborate for the benefit of all students" (p. 80).

In reviewing the literature, brain research completed by D'Arcangelo revealed that the brain changes physiologically as a result of experience and that an individual's environment may determine to a large extent the functioning ability of the brain (Brooks & Brooks, 1999). Work in the field of brain research is helping to suggest strategies for teachers in the class-room. Research is helping teachers know how students learn and how students receive, process, and interpret information (Caulfield, Kidd, & Kocher, 2000). The importance of a student's emotional intelligence is also being considered. Daniel Goleman's *Emotional Intelligence* and Joseph LeDoux's *The Emotional Brain* are books that have advanced our understanding of the role of emotions in learning. In addition, Howard Gardner's work in multiple intelligences and the dimensions of learning reveals that human intelligence encompasses a far wider and more universal set of competencies than a single general intel-ligence (Given, 2000). Bransford, Brown, and Cocking (2001), in *How People Learn: Brain,*

Mind, Experience, and School, note that it is important for students to organize their knowledge around important ideas and concepts—that students "learn how to see" a problem like an expert and understand the "why?" and "when?" as well as the "what?" and "how?" They state that it is important that students integrate their new knowledge with existing knowledge (constructivism) and for students to monitor their learning and problem solving (*metacognition*) (Caulfield et al., 2000).

Metacognitive ability appears now to be central to conceptions of what it means to be educated. Martinez (2006) states, "Metacognition is usually presented as a conscious and deliberate mental activity—*we become aware that we don't understand a paragraph we read or a statement we hear* [italics added]" (p. 697).

With the advent of recent research and clinical observations, educators no longer have to apply a "one size fits all" approach in helping struggling students. Brain-based research is providing new strategies for identifying and treating the many causes of slow learning.

Problems in reading and writing often originate from underlying neurodevelopmental dysfunctions. Levine and Barringer (2008) note, "to better understand how students' neurodevelopmental profiles affect student learning and performance, eight constructs—groups of related functions—help organize thinking and communication about learning differences were developed" (p. 17).

These constructs are as follows:

- *Attention*—This includes the ability to concentrate, focus on one thing rather than another, finish tasks, and control what one says and does.

- *Temporal-Sequential Ordering*—Whether it's being able to recite the alphabet or pushing a response button on Jeopardy [*sic*], being able to understand the time and sequence of pieces of information is a key component to learning.

- *Spatial Ordering*—The ability, for instance, to distinguish between a circle and a square, or to use images to remember related information.

- *Memory*—Even if people are able to understand, organize, and interpret complex information at the moment, their inability to store and later recall that information can dramatically affect their performance.

- *Language*—Developing language functions involves elaborate interactions between various parts of the brain that control such abilities as pronouncing words, understanding different sounds, and comprehending written symbols.

- *Neuromotor Functions*—The brain's ability to coordinate motor or muscle functions is key to many areas of learning, including writing and keyboarding.

- *Social Cognition*—One of the most overlooked components of learning is the ability to succeed in social relationships with peers, parents, and teachers. Students strong in other areas may have academic difficulties because of an inability to make friends, work in groups, or cope with peer pressure.

- *Higher-order Cognition*—This involves the ability to understand and implement the steps necessary to solve problems, attack new areas of learning, and to think creatively. (Levine & Barringer, 2008, pp. 14–18)

With the advent of more innovative ideas and with the advancement of understanding and technology, curriculum is becoming more comprehensive and differential in nature. It is forcing change in order to meet new challenges and changes. Educational content and teaching–learning materials now appear to be more functional, diversified, and operational in nature. An increased emphasis is placed on relevance, flexibility, needs, and speed. Demographics, population, health, nutrition, and environment are becoming dominant factors in what appears to be a value-oriented instructional design process focused on the global community.

A case can be made that the very nature of educational structure and educational methodologies is undergoing a significant change. Web-based programs, educational technologies, multimedia capability, and distance education are changing the face of educational curriculum worldwide. Electronic media on a global level appear to be evolving their own pedagogical methodologies and strategies. These advancements in technology are leading to a multitude of approaches that are blending a milieu of curriculum that caters to the needs of interested, disinterested, and remedial learners worldwide.

Technology as Catalyst of Curriculum Change

Educational instructional practices and skills are currently blending with new developments in technology to help create the global classroom of the future. Little doubt is evidenced that technology is serving as the catalyst for change. Data-driven instruction no longer is requiring teacher buy-in. Schools often develop data binders containing analyses and action plans based on the previous round of assessments and keep a copy in the main office or in each classroom (Bambrick-Santoyo, 2007/2008).

As part of the global change process, further advances in technology are now utilizing the cooperative learning and differentiated curriculum strategies and combining them with the use of wireless handheld computing devices. Currently, a movement is underway toward low-cost, portable handheld devices for student use in all schools that can be connected through global networks and tailored for specific tasks or applications. Some classroom teachers now have the capability of communicating and exchanging information worldwide with students via classroom workstations and district servers.

THE THEORETICAL SCHOOL OF THE FUTURE

Patricia Patterson (2007), a practicing principal, envisions schools of the future as learning communities in which teachers and students succeed in infusing technology seamlessly into classroom practice. Her goal is to have, *first*, every teacher becoming proficient in using technology in all aspects of instruction, and *second*, creating a technological infrastructure that is self-sustaining and self-renewing.

Patterson believes that curriculum and teacher leaders should be responsible for determining needs at every grade level and developing a Web-based system that will address those needs. Through self-evaluation and assessment tools, future leaders can identify hardware and software needs, teacher proficiency levels, and teacher interest in integrating technology into the curriculum.

Professional training and staff development programs of the future will build a scaffold supporting plans of technology integration. Improvement plans will reflect professional development and technology models.

Funding sources in the future will be redirected to support a school's need for ongoing technology infusion. From those plans each teacher will develop a personal growth plan indicating the training he or she will need.

Integration of technology will increase the emphasis on project-based learning. Students are now using technology in student-centered learning environments for research, collaboration, communication, presentation of knowledge, and multimedia production. With this infusion of technology, the areas of greatest impact will be student and teacher interest, motivation, improved student behavior, increased technology skills for both student and teachers, and the developing of high-order thinking skills in students.

It will be the global mission for tomorrow's curriculum and teacher leaders to support the implementation of technologies for high-quality and safe learning environments that will allow all students to achieve at their highest potential for future years to come.

Along these same lines, the National Association of Elementary School Principals commissioned the Institute for Alternative Futures (IAF) to explore areas of uncertainty and opportunity for schools as part of its Vision 2021 Project. The IAF crafted nine forecasts to start a dialogue with school principals, other educators, and the public about a preferred future:

1. Schools become the learning portals to a global workplace. This forecast explores what schools must become to align with the new requirements of a global society.

2. Free-market forces favor school choice over educational equity. This forecast probes social preferences for choice and the possibility for recommitting to educational equity.

3. Hyperlinked learning explores meaning through multimedia. This forecast examines new capabilities to enrich and transform the learning experience.

4. Scientific knowledge brings new understanding to child development. This forecast anticipates scientific research that clarifies individual differences and defines appropriate learning approaches for different students.

5. Holistic standards expand expectations for achieving student potential. This forecast explains how today's proficiency standards will necessarily morph into standards that support educating the whole child.

6. Networks of learning innovation experiment with new learning strategies for children. This forecast anticipates networks of research and development that link schools to centers of innovation in collaborating research and knowledge sharing.

7. Surveillance society links schoolhouses into electronic safety network. This forecast projects today's concerns about school safety into a future where surveillance is ubiquitous and welcome.

8. Society's mounting debts compromise future investments in education. This forecast takes a hard look at the limitations schools face and asks what it would take to create a tipping point where education is a priority.

9. Principals set the standard for chief learning officers. This forecast acknowledges that principals will be using continuous learning processes to engage students, teachers, parents, and the community in achieving learning outcomes for students.

As can be seen from NAESP's Vision 2021, the implications of *new theoretical constructs* embracing technology and schools on a global scale will be staggering. The implications of educational change in the future seem to be limitless.

SUMMARY

Chapter 3 explains that sound theory can be of value to both the scholar and the practitioner because curriculum theory can provide a set of conceptual tools for analyzing curriculum proposals, for illuminating practice, and for guiding reform. This chapter shows how melding theory and the reality of school curriculum is an important step in the educational planning process. Because it is difficult to use theoretical approaches to make continual analyses, reevaluations, and revisions of curriculum, especially in such fields as informational technology and the sociology of knowledge, this chapter explains the necessity of developing a fundamental understanding of curriculum theory by providing the tools necessary when analyzing curriculum proposals, illuminating practice, and guiding reform. This chapter addresses the nature and function of curriculum theory. It also addresses why it is important to meld the theory and reality of school curriculum together as part of the planning process. This chapter explains the role of leadership in the development of curriculum theory and the major classifications of curriculum theory. Finally, it addresses how technology has been a catalyst for curriculum change.

APPLICATIONS

1. As noted in this chapter, much debate occurs in the field about the value of curriculum theory. As you understand the nature of curriculum theory, how much professional value does it seem to have for you?

2. Most of the theoretical work in the field would be subsumed under the headings of value-centered and content-centered theories. How do you explain the fact that structure and process matters have received much less attention from curriculum theorists?

3. Several experts who have analyzed process theories claim that all attempts to develop new process approaches turn out to be simply variations of the Tyler rationale. To what extent do you agree with this assessment?

4. Use the proposed descriptive system to analyze any article or book that describes a curriculum-development process.

5. As noted in this chapter, very little work has been done in applying ways-of-knowing approaches to curriculum-development projects. What do you think a school curriculum would look like, in general, if it attempted to embody a ways-of-knowing approach to the curriculum?

6. Looking at your school system, how have advancements in technology changed the roles of the education process?

CASE STUDY   Integrating Curriculum Theory

Bruce Novac has been a PK–5 elementary school principal in the Plentywood School District for the past 2 years. This is the beginning of his 3rd year and the year in the district in which he will be up for tenure. He has a meeting scheduled with the school superintendent, Dr. Robert Kerr, and the curriculum director, Dr. Karla Johnson, to review test score data of the third-grade students in his school. The results revealed that the third-grade students' scores were well below state and federal guidelines for proficiency. In fact, second-grade students had higher achievement scores than the third-grade students in his school.

Mr. Novac was told by the two central office administrators that his theory of curriculum implementation was not working. In fact, what he was doing was held in low regard by the teachers in his school. In a panic, Novac begins to search for some answers on curriculum theories espoused by authors of curriculum textbooks and in educational journals. His focus is captured by structure-oriented, value-oriented, content-oriented, and process-oriented curriculum theories, which he hopes will provide answers to the third-grade low-achievement dilemma in his school.

The Challenge

Student achievement is often thought to be the result of curriculum theory that teachers support. How can Mr. Novac educate and motivate the third-grade teachers to integrate sound curriculum theory into their day-to-day work with students?

Key Issues/Questions

1. What are your impressions of the superintendent and curriculum director? Did they adequately address Mr. Novac's responsibilities in this incident? Why or why not?

2. What are your impressions of the third-grade teachers in this elementary school in the Plentywood School District?

3. If the principal meets with the third-grade teachers, what should be discussed?

4. What are some possible reasons why third-grade students in Mr. Novac's school are low achievers?

5. What are some theoretical curriculum approaches that Mr. Novac might use to increase student achievement scores? Identify the strategies and explain why you think they might be effective.

WEBLIOGRAPHY

Curriculum Theory: Understanding by Design/Grant Wiggins
www.arps.org/grant170/170a/curriculum_theory.htm

Educational Theory Journal
www.ed.uiuc.edu/EPS/educational-theory

Education Week's Research Center
www.edweek.org

Education World article on Multiple Intelligences
www.education-world.com/a_curr/curr054.shtml

Guide to active research
www.infed.org/research/b-actres.htm

Guide to educational research
www.eric.ed.gov

Media and Policy Center Foundation
www.mediapolicycenter.org

National Association of Elementary School Principals Vision 2021
www.vision2021.org

University of Maryland, Department of Education: Educational Policy and Leadership
www.education.umd.edu/EDPL/areas/curriculum.html

CHAPTER 4

The Politics of Curriculum

According to Margaret Evans (2008), associate executive director of Diverse Learning Communities, "Schools are in a prime position to model the many benefits of successfully developing diverse communities because they reflect the changing demographics of the 21st Century" (p. 63). What actually is taught in the classroom results from a confluence of several often conflicting factors. Federal and state governments, professional organizations, local school boards, textbook publishers, accrediting organizations, parent and community groups, school administrators, and classroom teachers all seem to make a difference. Those conflicting influences seem to change in their strength from time to time, and their particular impact on a given classroom is often difficult to trace. However, any curriculum leader who wishes to develop or improve curricula needs to understand the politics of curriculum, the way those organizations and individuals attempt to influence what is taught in the schools. For example, many reform books have been on the market, like William Bender and Cara Shore's *Response to Intervention: A Practical Guide for Every Teacher* (2007), Tomlinson and McTighe's *Integrating Differentiated Instruction & Understanding by Design* (2006), Ruby Payne's *Understanding Learning* (2002), John Holt's *How Children Fail* (1964), and Ivan Illich's *Deschooling Society* (1972). Jonathan Kozol's *Savage Inequalities: Children in America's Schools* (1991) and Grace Llewellyn's *Teenage Liberation Handbook: How to Quit School and Get a Real Life and Education* (1997) are also examples of reform books that are still popular. As a result, this chapter presents an overview of the way influences are brought to bear and then examines in greater detail those agencies that seem to have the greatest influence.

Questions addressed in this chapter include the following:

- What has been the role of the federal government in curriculum development, and how has this changed over the years?
- What is the general role of state governments in curriculum development today? How has this changed over the years?
- What are the roles of educational organizations, courts, educational leaders, and classroom teachers on current curriculum development?

Key to Leadership

Curriculum leaders are now realizing that we have entered a political era of global knowledge exchange and application.

AN OVERVIEW OF THE CURRICULUM-INFLUENCE PROCESS

Simply gathering and analyzing data will not solve entrenched problems in education policy; some rethinking on the part of policymakers is also necessary (Ingersoll, 2008). In understanding how several groups and individuals influence curriculum policy and curriculum development, it is important at the outset to realize that such influences do not take place in a vacuum. They occur in a complex social and cultural environment—an environment that significantly determines which belief systems and practices will gain the widest audience.

As Henig (2008) notes,

> Historically, K–12 education has been among the most localized of government functions. It is too soon to declare localism a thing of the past—its political roots are strong and resilient—but it is equally clear that changes are under way [*sic*]. The states began asserting themselves both as sources of funding and as promoters of academic standards during the 1980's [*sic*] and the advent of NCLB marks a new era of regulatory aggressiveness from Washington, D.C. (p. 360)

Conners (2007) adds, "If we have learned anything about history, it was that those who formulate these plans always retain, for a time anyway, exclusive control of the measurement of their effectiveness" (p. 520).

In reviewing the literature, Schon (1971) is most illuminating. As he sees it, ideas "in good currency" flow into the mainstream, mediated by certain roles. New ideas incompatible with the prevailing conceptions are suppressed within the social system but kept alive by people in vanguard roles until a crisis occurs. At that time those new ideas might be released and spread by information networks and the mass media. Before they are accepted, however, these new ideas become issues in power struggles. As Schon sees it, only a limited number of "slots" are available for new ideas, because these new ideas are attached to advocates competing for power positions. In this manner, inquiry around the ideas becomes politicized. Those that have the most powerful support become legitimated by approval from powerful people. Only then can the new ideas become public policy.

On July 1, 1954, the National Council for Accreditation of Teacher Education (NCATE) was founded. Five groups were instrumental in the creation of NCATE: the American Association of Colleges for Teacher Education, the National Association of State Directors of Teacher Education and Certification, the National Education Association, the Council of Chief State School Officers, and the National School Boards Association. When NCATE was founded as an independent accrediting body, it replaced the American Association of Colleges for Teacher Education as the agency responsible for accreditation in teacher education. Although membership is voluntary, NCATE is the accrediting body for colleges and universities that prepare teachers and other professional specialists for work in elementary and secondary schools. The goal of the NCATE accreditation process aims to ensure that accredited institutions produce competent, caring, and qualified teachers and other professional school personnel who can help all students learn (NCATE, 2007).

Curriculum Tip 4.1	This struggle for power in the curriculum-making process seems to occur most stridently at the federal, state, and local district levels and differentially, in some cases positively, affects the recommended, the written, and the taught curricula.

The end of the 1970s signaled a dramatic change in the form and purpose of public schools. From an economical standpoint, individual income and state financial resources were falling and costs were spiraling upward. School enrollments were declining with parents moving their children into private schools or into the suburbs. Financial problems of public schools, especially large urban public schools, continued to be a problem. Budgets reflected a drop in local support from 60% to 30%, while the role of the state increased. Federal government educational assistance continued at around 10%. With an increase in state contributions to education, the role of politics intensified.

At the same time that states were gaining a firmer foothold in education, Ronald Reagan was elected to the presidency. This began a new era of conservative government at the federal level. Between a decline of enrollment and rising costs, school boards were in difficulty and began to take a more conservative stand. The code phrase of the conservative movement became "Back to the Basics," and accountability became the norm.

At the federal level, the struggle for power occurs chiefly behind the scenes, as several influence groups and individuals attempt to persuade members of both the executive and legislative branches. Bell (1986) described how the decision not to abolish the Department of Education during President Reagan's second term came about as the result of such behind-the-scenes maneuvering. First, the platform-drafting committee for the 1984 Republican National Convention decided to ignore pressures to abolish the department that came mainly from individuals whom Bell called movement conservatives, "ideologues of the far right." As Bell pointed out, key members of the platform committee were House Republicans running for office in 1984. They had read *A Nation at Risk*, they had sensed the grassroots interest in education, and they did not want to be perceived by voters as being antieducation. Although the "movement conservatives" continued to attempt to persuade Reagan to exert leadership on the issue, Reagan was, in Bell's view, a pragmatist with different priorities. He cared deeply about tuition tax credits, vouchers, and prayer in the schools, but he saw the fate of the Department of Education as a matter of lesser consequence. Knowing there was no broad-based support to abolish the department and not caring enough to spend his political capital in fighting the battle, Reagan quietly put the proposal on the back burner and never again raised the matter with Bell.

Lobbying groups can play an important role in this hidden power struggle at the federal level. Levine and Wexler (1981) documented clearly how the Council for Exceptional Children and other interest groups representing the handicapped played a determining role in the passage of Public Law 94-142, the most important national legislation affecting the handicapped. These lobbyists had developed close relationships with the staff and members of the congressional education committees, had formed close alliances with leaders in the Bureau of Education for the Handicapped, and spoke authoritatively at every congressional hearing on the bill.

The same picture of policy being made in a highly charged and politicized environment with much behind-the-scenes lobbying is seen at the state level. A case in point is the way

Pennsylvania adopted its new curriculum regulations. In 1981, a forward-looking secretary of education proposed a radical restructuring of the state's curriculum regulations, replacing lists of required courses with the specification of student competencies that could be developed in a variety of ways. For 2 years these changes were discussed and debated by lobbyists (chiefly those from professional organizations), by the state board of education, and by Department of Education officials. No action was taken; state legislators were indifferent. One legislative leader expressed it this way:

> The reaction of the legislature when they were talking about these learning outcomes—the competency-based curriculum proposal—was pretty much a hands-off thing. They realized it was an issue they didn't want to get involved in. . . . Then all the reports came out in the intervening time, and there was a kind of a rush to judgment to see who was going to address this serious problem . . . all of a sudden the national environment was "let's do these things," and so everyone wanted to have their stamp on them. (Lynch, 1986, p. 74)

The governor published his own recommendations for "turning the tide," the House passed legislation mandating increased curriculum rigor and an emphasis on traditional subjects (not competencies), the Senate passed a resolution directing the state Board of Education to take action, and the state board adopted revised curriculum regulations—all within 6 months' time.

In such a politicized environment at the state level, numerous groups and individuals have a differential impact. In her study of policymaking in one of the eastern states, Marshall (1985) identified 15 influence groups. The strongest of those include the governor and his or her executive staff, the chief state school officer, individual members of the state legislature, the legislature as a whole, the legislative staff, and education interest groups. Those with moderate influence are the teachers' association, the state board of education, and the administrators' organization. The courts, the federal government, the school boards' association, non-educator groups, and researchers had much less influence.

It was during this time that an attempt was made to introduce "international" achievement testing as a measure of excellence. There was concern that American children were somehow behind the children in other countries. Berliner and Biddle's book *The Manufactured Crisis* (1997) soon put this argument to rest by noting that the top 10% of children in countries like Germany were being compared to the upper 50% of American children. Berliner and Biddle contended that America's best and brightest children could compete with Europe's top children on any testing measure.

Nonetheless, this assault on progressive education continues today. Hess (2008), director of education policy studies at the American Enterprise Institute, states, "In recent years, the rigor and quality of educational research have drawn much attention. This increased interest has been driven by state efforts to collect student achievement data" (p. 354). Phillips (2007), professor of education at San Francisco State University, adds, "Within the policy sphere, education has been dominated by the No Child Left Behind Act (NCLB) and its closely related state-level mandates. The focus has been on standards, test scores and accountability" (p. 712). As such, it can be seen that education across the country is clearly being directed by state agencies as well as mandated programs such as NCLB and Response to Intervention (RTI).

At the local level, there is the same interplay of conflicting and coalescing influences; only the key actors are different. As the local school board sets general curriculum policy, it too is sensitive to prevailing trends in the society; in this context, it makes general decisions that have been strongly influenced by the superintendent, who is responding to his or her own perception of the larger educational scene and local needs. At the same time, local pressure groups, often acting in concert with nationally organized lobbies, will attempt to influence the board's curriculum policy as it involves such specific controversial issues as sex education, evolution, creationism, and values education.

Once general policy has been determined at the district level, key decisions are made about the written curriculum by curriculum leaders, school administrators, and teachers. At the district level, the assistant superintendent for curriculum and instruction and several subject matter supervisors usually provide leadership in developing and improving a field of study, such as mathematics K–12. Typically, the assistant superintendent or a supervisor will appoint a committee made up of representatives of the major constituencies: a principal, department chair, two to five teacher–leaders, and perhaps a token parent. In making decisions about the scope and sequence of that field, the committee typically uses a variety of professional sources: It consults state guidelines and standards, checks mandated tests, reviews available texts, confers with consultants, reviews guides from other districts and from professional associations, and surveys classroom teachers. When conflicts arise in their deliberations, committee members typically resolve them through political processes—negotiating, compromising, and deferring to the most powerful.

The picture changes somewhat at the school level. In elementary schools, the principal as well as teacher–leaders seem to play a key role in determining curricular priorities and in monitoring the curriculum. If conflict arises, it will usually occur between the principal and a small group of teacher–leaders who are jealous of their curricular autonomy. At the secondary level, the principal will usually delegate that responsibility to a team leader or department chair, because subject matter expertise is more important at this level. In secondary schools, curricular battles are usually waged between departments as they compete for scarce resources.

It should be noted that in the past, when the classroom door closes, the teacher can, at times, become the curriculum. It used to be behind closed doors, a teacher would make decisions based on a somewhat unconscious response to several sources: the district guide, the textbook, curriculum-referenced and standardized tests, the teacher's knowledge of and perception of the subject matter, and the teacher's assessment of pupil interest and readiness. Teachers' of today, however, are not as independent. With new technologies, data-driven curricula, as well as charts and graphs of students' achievement, it is far less easy for teachers to dictate their own curricula from behind closed doors.

Thus, at different levels of curriculum decision making, the major sources of influence vary considerably, yet at every level the process seems to be a highly politicized one in which issues of power and control are resolved in curriculum decision making. At this juncture, a closer examination of certain key elements might be useful.

THE ROLE OF THE FEDERAL GOVERNMENT

The role of the federal government in schools is increasing. According to Fugate (2007),

In the 1950s and 1960s when many of our lawmakers were in school themselves, not every child remained in school until graduation. Many students dropped out to go to work, to join the service, or to get married. Most of the students who remained in school were college-bound or had a clear vocational interest. Today, all students are expected to have the same education, whether they want it or not, whether they need it or not. (p. 72)

It therefore seems abundantly clear to many government leaders that it is imperative that schools in the 21st century be held accountable for high standards, for providing well-trained teachers, and for creating a safe environment.

A review of the literature shows that since 1970, in the United States the business sector has been invading schools with the objective of replacing public schools with something else. As early as the first Nixon administration (1968–1972), the federal government promoted "performance contracts" to enable business to compete with schools for tax dollars. More recently, the George W. Bush administration has promoted testing and vouchers as a means of discrediting public schools (Wiles & Lundt, 2004).

The discussion below, therefore, examines that role in the three most recent periods discussed in Chapter 2 of this work: **Scholarly Structuralism**, 1957–1967; **Romantic Radicalism,** 1968–1974; and **Privatistic Conservatism**, 1975–1989. Prior to 1957, there was almost no federal involvement in curriculum; before the 1950s, as Kliebard (1979) noted, the activities of the federal government in education were limited to convening prestigious groups, creating professional societies, and disseminating the recommendations of prominent individuals.

Curriculum Tip 4.2	In examining the role of the federal government in influencing the school curriculum, it is useful to bring to bear a historical perspective, because patterns of influence have changed over the past few decades.

1957–1967: Scholarly Structuralism

This was the period of the national frenzy to "catch up with the Russians." Largely instigated by the launching of *Sputnik*, it was a time of intensive and extensive federal intervention in curriculum. During this period, education seemed to be dominated by what Atkin and House (1981) called a "technological" perspective. Educational leaders were convinced that rational, technological approaches could solve the schools' problems. Teaching was seen as a technological endeavor: The essential skills of teaching could be identified and taught through a step-by-step approach. Curriculum development similarly was viewed as a rational technological enterprise: The right content could be identified by the scholars and then delivered in tested packages. Even the change process was seen from this perspective: The agricultural model of conducting research and disseminating its results through "change agents" was viewed as the only proper means for changing the schools.

The primary intervention strategy adopted by the federal government was the development and dissemination of generic curricula. To use the constructs explicated in Chapter 1, the developers of the "alphabet soup curricula" attempted to fuse the recommended, the written, and the taught curricula; they sincerely believed that their idealistic recommendations would be embodied into district curriculum guides and that teachers would willingly and faithfully implement what they had produced.

The developers of these generic curricula seemed most concerned with course content: The National Science Foundation developed and supported the Course Content Improvement Program, which in turn strongly influenced a similar program adopted by the U.S. Office of Education, called the Curriculum Improvement Program. In the view of these leaders, curriculum and content were synonymous. That content, in their view, should be determined only by the scholars in the disciplines—not by "educationists." It was the scholars alone who understood the structures of the disciplines, who could identify the critical concepts, and who knew how to organize and sequence that content.

Once the scholars had developed these ideal curricula, the dissemination effort began. Large-scale publicity efforts were undertaken: Articles appeared in the professional journals touting the high quality of the products, and sessions were held at the major professional conferences advocating the adoption of the materials. Teachers were trained in summer institutes with rather generous stipends provided. More than 30 regional laboratories were funded to aid in the development and dissemination efforts, and the curriculum was translated into marketable packages—either textbooks produced by commercial entities or sold by the developers themselves.

Initially these federally funded generic curricula seemed successful. The materials produced were significantly different from what had been developed before, especially in science and mathematics. Even the conventional textbooks produced by mainline publishing houses included concepts introduced by the scholarly curriculum projects. Early users, the most committed and knowledgeable of teachers, seemed enthusiastic.

However, resistance to these federal efforts to transform the curriculum through direct intervention began to increase at the end of this period. First of all, concern surfaced about what some termed the *federal curriculum*, a fear that these federally supported curriculum projects would reduce local curricular autonomy. Others pointed out, of course, that in some fields, at least, the effect was quite the opposite. Until Project Social Studies came along, there was in effect a nationally standardized curriculum in social studies—a curriculum that was limited almost solely to recurring courses in U.S. history, a little geography in elementary schools, and a smattering of civics in junior high schools and "Problems of Democracy" in senior high schools. Project Social Studies offered more alternatives: Schools could now teach economics, anthropology, and sociology, using materials that had a scholarly cachet.

Objections also mounted as to the specifics of the content. Many teachers complained that the materials were too difficult for their students. Parents and lay critics argued that the "basics" were being slighted: Not enough attention was paid to computational skills in the mathematics curriculum projects or to spelling and grammar in the English curricula. There were also numerous protests about the values issues embedded in many of the social studies and science curricula; many individuals and organizations felt that these nationally disseminated projects espoused values they considered too liberal and permissive. As noted in Chapter 2, these complaints reached a crescendo in the bitter controversy over *Man: A Course of Study* (MACOS; Curriculum Development Associates, 1972).

Finally, it was obvious that these so-called teacher-proof curricula were doomed to fail, because they were put in the hands of "curriculum-proof" teachers. The developers of these curricula seemed totally oblivious to the nature of schools as organizations and to the complexities of classroom life. They somewhat naively believed that their curricula would be adopted uniformly and implemented as designed. They foolishly expected teachers to acquire, internalize, and use teaching strategies that were radically different from those they already used and that were quite demanding in their complexity.

1968–1974: Romantic Radicalism

During this period, the national agenda changed. While international issues such as the war in Vietnam continued to dominate the headlines, at the grassroots level people seemed more concerned with their own individual freedoms. It was a time when "rights," not responsibilities, was the dominant slogan: Black people, handicapped individuals, homosexuals, women, and nonnative groups all asserted their rights to liberation and to greater power.

In this 7-year period, educational thinking at the policymaking level seemed to be dominated by what Atkin and House (1981) called a political perspective, in contradistinction to the technological perspective that had dominated the previous period. A political perspective views educational reform essentially as a political process. The legitimacy of several conflicting views is recognized. Decisions are made primarily through a process of compromise and negotiation.

It was this political perspective that seemed to influence both Congress and the several federal agencies empowered to enforce compliance with federal legislation. Their intervention strategy seemed to be a "carrot and stick" approach: Develop specific policies mandating changes in the operation of schools and offer financial rewards to those who comply. Their impact on school curricula is best seen perhaps in an analysis of their response to pressures from two groups: those insisting on the need for bilingual education and those arguing for the educational rights of the handicapped.

Bilingual Education

From a historical perspective, Ravitch (1983) pointed out, the demand for bilingual education seemed to result from a surge of new ethnocentrism that argued for ethnicity as a basis for public policy. Initially, the demand seemed modest enough. As Ravitch noted, those advocating bilingual education in the congressional hearings of 1967 desired funding only for demonstration projects that would meet the special educational needs of Hispanic children; in their view, the aim of bilingual education was to help the Hispanic child master the English language. The Bilingual Education Act of 1968, which ultimately became Title VII of the Elementary and Secondary Education Act, covered not just Hispanic children but all children of limited English-speaking ability, especially those from low-income families. The act was intentionally vague in key particulars: Bilingual education was not defined, and the purpose of the act was never made explicit.

Although the act itself did not require districts to provide bilingual programs, in 1970 the Office of Civil Rights (OCR) informed every school district with more than 5% "national origin–minority group children" that it had to take "affirmative steps" to rectify the language deficiency of such children or be in violation of Title VI of the Civil Rights Act. The OCR guidelines were sustained and supported by the Supreme Court in its *Lau v. Nichols* (1974) decision, which directed the schools to create special language programs for "non–English-speaking children," to correct what it called "language deficiency."

Also in 1974, Congress renewed and extended the 1968 act, making several important changes in response to pressures from lobbying groups representing ethnic minorities. First, the provisions of the act covered all children, not just those from low-income homes. Instead of being primarily concerned with teaching these children how to speak English, the act recognized the importance of maintaining the native language and cultural heritage. Ravitch (1983) added that the 1974 act was a landmark in that it marked the first time the Congress had dictated a specific pedagogical approach to local districts.

What had started out as a modest demonstration program to aid Hispanic students had become a mammoth program that funded the teaching of 68 languages, including 7 Eskimo languages and a score of Native American languages.

Educating the Handicapped

In many ways, federal intervention in the education of the handicapped seemed to parallel its activities on behalf of nonnative children. What began as a relatively small effort became a major establishment supported with federal funds. Prior to 1965, there seemed to be almost no concerted effort to secure federal funds to aid the education of the handicapped. The leaders of organizations such as the National Association for Retarded Citizens and the Council for Exceptional Children, however, viewing the success of the civil rights movement, began to coordinate their lobbying efforts. Their efforts quickly paid off: In 1966, Congress established the Bureau of Education for the Handicapped, within the Office of Education, and in 1970 passed new legislation increasing the amount of aid for the education of the handicapped and expanding the definition of the term to include the learning disabled and the socially and emotionally disturbed.

Two important court decisions provided strong impetus for further efforts. In 1971 the federal courts issued a consent decree requiring Pennsylvania to provide a free public education to all exceptional children between the ages of 6 and 21; and in 1972 the federal court in the District of Columbia held that every school-age child in the district had to be provided with a "free and suitable publicly supported education regardless of the degree of a child's mental, physical, or emotional disability or impairment" (*Mills v. Board of Education*, 1972).

Congress then responded by enacting the Rehabilitation Act of 1973, including Section 504, which Ravitch (1983) termed "the handicapped person's equivalent of Title VI of the Civil Rights Act of 1964" (p. 307). The enactment of that legislation was quickly followed by the passage in 1975 of Public Law 94-142. In many ways this particular law was the most prescriptive educational legislation ever passed by Congress. The law not only required that every child receive an Individualized Educational Program (IEP), but it even specified the content of these plans. They had to include a statement of present levels of performance, a statement of annual goals and short-term objectives, a statement of the educational services to be provided, and the extent to which the child would be able to participate in regular programs. Projected dates for initiation and duration, objective criteria and evaluation procedures, and schedules also determined whether the objectives were being achieved. Finally, the law required the mainstreaming of the handicapped: Such children were to be educated with the nonhandicapped "to the maximum extent appropriate."

Whereas the development of generic content-oriented courses did not seem to have a lasting impact, the carrot-and-stick approach of passing and enforcing legislation had a pervasive impact, to the extent that many educational leaders of the time expressed grave concern about the intrusion of the federal government and the courts into matters that they believed were better left to local control.

1975–1989: Privatistic Conservatism

This period, of course, was dominated by President Ronald Reagan, who was elected on a conservative platform and who used his considerable leadership skills to implement that platform. As perceived by Terrel H. Bell (1986), then secretary of education, Reagan had in mind six goals relating to education: substantially reduce federal spending, strengthen local and state control, maintain a limited federal role in assisting states in carrying out their educational responsibilities, expand parental choice, reduce federal judicial activity in education, and abolish the Department of Education.

Certain of the Reagan administration's initiatives had clear implications for curriculum. To strengthen the state role in education and to provide equitable services for private school students, Congress adopted under Reagan's prodding a program to award block grants to the states: Chapter 2 of the Education Consolidation and Improvement Act of 1981 consolidated more than 30 categorical programs into a single block grant to each state. An initial study by Hertling (1986) of the effects of this block-grant program indicated that, in general, the Chapter 2 money had been used to support computer-based education, curriculum development, staff development, and pilot development of new programs. Although inner-city districts tended to lose the largest amount of money under the block-grant approach, 75% of the districts gained funds under Chapter 2, and per-pupil spending for nonpublic schools increased.

Much of this curriculum development undertaken by the states seems to have responded to secretary of education William J. Bennett's agenda of "choice, content, character, and citizenship." In his initial distribution of more than $2.5 million in discretionary grants to 34 organizations, Bennett made 11 awards to organizations desiring to develop materials in character education and seven to those interested in strengthening the academic content of the curriculum.

The most controversial of Bennett's initiatives was his attempt to modify the federal government's approach to bilingual education. He proposed several changes in the regulations governing the distribution of bilingual education funds: Allow districts to increase the English-language component of bilingual programs, encourage them to mainstream limited-English-proficiency students more rapidly, and require districts to assume increased financial responsibility for the programs. His proposals were hailed by many who criticized the practice of teaching such students in their native language and attacked by those who saw the new proposals as jeopardizing the educational rights and opportunities of such students.

1990–1999: Technological Constructionism

Throughout much of the 1990s, conservatives would address their concerns with education via teacher certification (National Board certification), standards-based curriculum (America's Choice), as well as other similar programs. The standards-based and technological reform movement continued to gain support at the national, state, and local levels. This was especially true with regard to having chief state officers (politically elected) state commissioners of education) disseminate and enforce tests and measures of educational competency. With more interest focused on standards and student achievement, the U.S. Department of Education and Congress began looking at more effective ways to close the achievement gap between students in wealthy and poor communities.

It was during this era that Jonathan Kozol's (1991) publication of *Savage Inequalities* exposed the gross disparities existing between public school districts serving the poorest of the poor and the most affluent sectors of American society. Kozol's work shed light on overlapping inequalities emergent in public education. Such disparities merely reflected the growing gap between rich and poor exacerbated by the Reaganomics of the previous decade (Schugurensky, 2003).

On March 26, 1994, President Clinton's Goals 2000: Educate America Act, was passed by the U.S. Congress. This bill was intended to

improve learning and teaching by providing a national framework for education reform; to promote the research, consensus building, and systemic changes needed to ensure equitable educational opportunities and high levels of educational achievement for all American students; . . . [and] to promote the development and adoption of a voluntary national system of skill standards and certifications. (Schugurensky, 2003, ¶1)

Part A of the legislation outlined national goals for education, to be achieved by the year 2000. The goals were organized in eight categories: (1) school readiness; (2) school completion; (3) student achievement and citizenship (including access to physical and health education); (4) teacher education and professional development; (5) mathematics and science; (6) adult literacy and lifelong learning; (7) safe, disciplined, and drug-free schools; and (8) school and home partnership.

The Goals 2000 Technology Plan, built on local, state, and regional initiatives in technology and telecommunications, was a major part of the technological constructionism reform movement. Goals 2000 included such programs as the Star Schools project as well as the growing demand for and use of the Internet. The planning and implementation efforts of the Goals 2000 Technology Plan greatly helped the enhancement of telecommunications in education.

To help schools and communities, especially those with high concentrations of poor children, meet higher education standards, Congress and the U.S. Department of Education in 1997 also developed the Comprehensive School Reform Demonstration (CSRD) program (*Partnerships 1990–2000: Ten Years of Supporting Education*, 2003). The CSRD program was designed to give schools more flexible funding to adopt research-based models that focused on improving the whole school, not just specific students or subject areas. CSRD grants created a wave of interest among schools and districts, all seeking to improve teaching and learning and to meet higher education standards. The grants allowed schools to choose among a new and wider range of research-based models, many of which provided both strategies and technical assistance for school improvement and student achievement.

More and more communities began to realize the pressing needs and challenges of public schools as the nation increased its focus on new education reform strategies. School systems were being asked to aim higher academically and to do more for students and families, but many lacked the resources (financial, human, and administrative) needed to accomplish these ambitious goals. In light of this situation, partnerships emerged as a powerful strategy for strengthening and improving schools. For many communities, meeting higher education standards and special education needs was often dependent on finding more resources to apply to the task.

For example, new legislation in the 1990s restructured IDEA (Individuals with Disabilities Education Act) into four parts: Part A, General Provisions; Part B, Assistance for Education of All Children With Disabilities; Part C, Infants and Toddlers With Disabilities; and Part D, National Activities to Improve Education of Children With Disabilities (Summary of the Individuals with Disabilities Education Act [IDEA], 2003). Affirmative-action programs were also becoming more prevalent during this time of technological constructionism. A new focus on children's rights and school safety emerged following the aftermath of such tragedies as the Columbine High School shooting. A move toward homeschooling was on the rise as well.

School leaders searched for new ways to use local resources to meet education goals and current challenges. Building on new coalitions of schools and communities forced a move away from individualism and toward partnerships at the end of the century. With the assistance of university and college programs, schools began providing much-needed training and professional development to teachers. In addition, partnerships with small and large businesses emerged to help school officials learn how better to leverage their human and financial resources. Through successful collaborations with community agencies, public schools started blending resources and offering a continuum of comprehensive and preventive services. A transition to a new, more federal conservative privatistic movement could be seen in the offing.

2000–Present: Modern Conservatism

With a modern conservative agenda, there is a fundamental belief that under our system of governance, education is necessary for democracy (Garrison, 2008). Interventions are now based on an economic theory that contends that people, including students and their parents, will make rational choices, such as choosing to work hard, if opportunities are offered and rewards are available (Lewis, 2007a).

Unfortunately, under this system of governance, there appears to be a move in making all students perform alike. Competency testing and standardizing the curriculum have become the norm. It is as if an interest in students and their emotional state has been pushed to the background overnight. With a new move to standardization and testing, the "education industry" has quickly become a major financial entity (Wiles & Lundt, 2004).

In 2001, educational reform moved away from technological constructionism and returned to a more privatistic and conservative nature. This is especially the case with President George W. Bush's move toward charter schools, vouchers, and tax credits. Supporters for charter schools, vouchers, and tax credits believed that the government should not be in the business of running schools. State-funded vouchers should pay for privately run education at private schools, parochial schools, charter schools, homeschooling, or whatever schools parents choose. Charter schools were generally considered publicly funded and publicly controlled schools that were privately run. They were usually required to adhere to fewer district rules than regular public schools. Vouchers, on the other hand, were considered by the administration as a means of implementing school choice—parents were to be given a "voucher" by the school district, which entitled them to choose their public school or private school ("Parents Choose," 2003). This same movement was initially called the School Choice Movement. "School choice" referred to a school district allowing parents to decide in which school within the district to enroll their children. The underlying philosophy of school choice appeared to be that parents should have the right to choose how their children were educated, regardless of income level. The political issue became whether to allow the choice to include private schools, parochial schools, and homeschooling at taxpayer expense ("Parents Choose," 2003).

Another aspect of the modern conservative approach linked vouchers and charter schools to a move toward standards, assessment, and accountability of public schools. This came with the passage of the No Child Left Behind Act (NCLB) in 2002. According to the 2003 Education Commission of the States, NCLB and the revised Elementary and

Secondary Education Act are blends of new requirements, incentives, and resources, and they pose significant challenges for states. The law sets deadlines for states to expand the scope and frequency of student testing, revamp their accountability systems, and guarantee that every teacher is qualified in his or her subject area. NCLB requires states to make demonstrable annual progress in raising the percentage of students' proficiency in reading and math and in narrowing the test-score gap between advantaged and disadvantaged students.

Basically, NCLB called for quality education and accountability for all children in U.S. schools. This approach opened the doors for a great deal of speculation. For example, Hill and Flynn (2006) took the word *all* to mean *all*. They stated, "if the rhetoric of NCLB is to become a reality, the phrase 'all means all' must be applied to include ELLs [English language learners], as well as other populations of U.S. students" (p. vii).

> The No Child Left Behind Act (NCLB) calls for quality education and accountability for all children in U.S. schools. If the rhetoric of NCLB is to become a reality, the phrase "all means all" must be applied to include to include ELLs [English language learners] as well as other populations of U.S. students. (p. vii)

In reviewing the legacy of NCLB, Jay Mathews, *Washington Post* staff writer, noted as early as 2003 that NCLB is an ambitious law and forces states to move faster and further to improve the achievement of every student. Mathews further stated, "Rarely has such a gulf existed between the authors of a major piece of federal legislation and its executors—in this case, the 90,000 public schools across the country" (p. A12).

More recently, Anne Lewis noted (2007b) that NCLB would likely become irrelevant. She believes its influence will continue to dwindle unless its policies and purse are directed toward supporting changes in teaching and learning that are more aligned with what is best for kids and society.

Obviously there will be changes. The focus on annual yearly progress, narrow standards, and NCLB's political grip on education cannot reflect the shared vision that is needed for the future. Jon Wiles and John Lundt (2004) noted that we have entered an era of global knowledge exchange and application, and yet schools have not been able to make the conversion. They state that for our schools even to begin to respond to the kind of political paradigm shift needed, they would first have to develop the following:

- New avenues for learning and communicating would have to be designed.
- Standardization of the curriculum would have to be deemphasized.
- Human differences and capabilities would have to be acknowledged.
- New facilities would have to be envisioned and constructed.
- Huge sums of startup capital for technology would have to be expended.
- Large investments in technological training would have to be allocated.
- A new kind of teacher would have to recruited.
- Teachers and students would have to be networked and allowed freedom.
- Knowledge would have to be valued for its application, not acquisition.

Education reform, therefore, continues to be a major problem facing political administrations seeking to limit the role of the federal government in education in the coming years. States and localities continue to grapple with ways to improve their education systems. Whatever the outcome, the reform process presents difficult challenges to this modern conservative movement.

At present, it appears that standards-based teaching and high-stakes testing are going to be with educators for a while. Time will tell whether teaching to the standards will succeed or if the standards approach will die under its own weight. According to Marge Scherer (2007–2008), "When our students understand that we value their learning more than their test scores, then, maybe—just maybe—they will stop asking the sort-sighted question and embark on their own learning journeys" (p. 7).

STATE ROLE IN CURRICULUM

The Education Commission of the States convened in November 2007 to review the states' role in curriculum. Governors, legislators, state board members, chief state school officers, and other state education leaders representing 34 states, the District of Columbia, and Puerto Rico met to discuss the critical education issues (Christie, 2008). Many educators are not holding their breath and expecting much in the way of resolution. The only thing not tried is changing the basic system for elementary and secondary education (Hubbard, 2007).

When examining the role of the states in curriculum, two problems present themselves. The *first* is the fact that the states differ significantly in the extent to which they are centralized, retaining authority at the state level, or decentralized, delegating authority to the local districts.

The *second* difficulty is that the patterns of state influence have shifted in response to the federal No Child Left Behind Act (NCLB). Most state departments of education are now playing their own expanded roles in ensuring compliance with federal mandates including Response to Intervention (RTI) models.

Curriculum Tip 4.3	Forty-nine of the 50 states have adopted state standards.

What has caused such an increase in the influence of the states? In continuing to review the literature we find that Doyle and Hartle, as early as 1985, posited several important reasons: the increased quality and competence of state governments, the concern over school quality stimulated by reports of declining SAT scores and by the reform publications, a growing body of research on school effectiveness, an insistent public demand to make schools more accountable, and a conviction that high-quality education would ensure economic growth.

While these problems of differences persist from state to state with variations over time, some constants prevail about the nature of the states' influence over curricula. In general, most states have adopted policies and procedures regulating the following matters:

1. Specifying time requirements for the school year, for the school day, and for particular subjects

2. Mandating specific subjects, such as English and mathematics, and requiring instruction in such specific areas as alcohol and drug abuse, driver safety, and the American economic system

3. Setting graduation requirements

4. Developing programs for such special groups as the handicapped and those for whom English is a second language

5. Mandating procedures for the adoption of textbooks and other instructional materials

6. Specifying the scope and sequence of topics to be covered in various subjects and grades

7. Mandating a testing program at specific grades in certain critical areas

The last three matters listed—the adoption of textbooks, the scope and sequence of the curriculum, and the assessment/testing program—perhaps deserve some careful attention here. First, many states have strong textbook-adoption laws. Perhaps the strongest and most restrictive of these are found in Texas. In Texas, the state periodically adopts a small number of approved textbooks in a given field, such as secondary English grammar and composition. School districts that select their texts from that approved list receive those texts without charge from the state textbook depository. If a district wishes to adopt a text not on the approved list, then it must use its own funds. Obviously, in a time of limited educational funding, few districts bother to adopt books other than those on the approved list.

> **Education Is a State Function**
>
> "The courts have consistently held that the power over education is an essential attribute of state sovereignty." (Alexander & Alexander, 2005, p. 99)

Because many teachers still rely greatly on the textbook in making their own curricular choices, strong adoption laws like those of Texas have the effect of standardizing the curriculum. In a sense, the state controls the curriculum by selecting the texts, and the issue of textbook quality becomes a major curriculum concern in such states. This issue was dramatized as early as 1985 when William Honig, commissioner of education for the state of California, announced that the state board of education had rejected all the science books recommended by its committee because none of those books adequately dealt with the subject of evolution.

In dealing with the scope and sequence of the curriculum, most state offices of education seem to be at an intermediate position between centralization and decentralization. The predominant pattern is for a given subject matter office, such as the Division of Mathematics Education, to develop and disseminate general guidelines, not to prescribe specific content and placement. These general guidelines, often called "frameworks," typically indicate the goals to be achieved in that subject area, summarize present theory and research dealing with that subject, and recommend two or three alternative curricular patterns for achieving the goals. Local districts can then use the state frameworks in developing their own more specific curricula.

Many educators today believe the emphasis of curriculum should be more on student learning and assessment than on textbooks. For example, James Popham (2007), Professor Emeritus at the UCLA Graduate School of Education and Information Studies, believes individual states in the future need to establish challenging, but realistic, expectations for what constitutes grade-level performance. This would include an annual increasing percentage of students who will need to earn grade-level or better test scores—in schools, districts, or the entire state.

This approach could be used to determine adequate yearly progress for students as a whole as well as for various subgroups of students if necessary. Using a different, more appropriate accountability yardstick would give educators an opportunity to establish demanding improvement targets that are both realistic and attainable.

THE ROLE OF PROFESSIONAL ORGANIZATIONS

When gauging the impact of professional organizations, many educators wonder at times who is really controlling public schools. According to Chris Gallagher (2008), professor of English at the University of Nebraska, "We never learned Dewey's lesson. In fact, public schools today are less in the direct control of those who spend their days in them, or those immediately affected by them, than ever before" (p. 341).

It is therefore important to review the roles of international, national, and state professional organizations and their impact on public schools. The way professional organizations come together to influence schools often differs from the formalized and regulated procedures involved with governmental agencies.

The role of many *international* professional organizations today should be to improve excellence in education. Participants in the 2007 Phi Delta Kappan Summit shared ideas for ensuring that a global perspective becomes an integral part of teaching and learning. Erin Young (2008) lists some of the ideas that originated from that panel:

- Acknowledge different learning styles
- Celebrate and respect diversity
- Instill a desire for continual, lifelong learning
- Build partnerships with organizations such as Rotary and UNICEF
- Develop students' skills in other languages at an early age
- Develop proficiency in one other language
- Develop a teacher education corps to work in other countries and communities
- Model empathy and intercultural understanding
- Crate a heightened sense of cultural awareness
- Provide cross-cultural experiences for students and teachers
- Prepare students to live and work in a digital world
- Overlay globalization on every course
- Expand the diversity of the teacher education pool
- Set standards for cultural competency to be integrated into curricula
- Help students understand geography
- Use popular media to highlight positive features of linguistic and cultural diversity, at home and abroad

- Integrate language learning and intercultural communication into business, technology, science, and arts programs
- Model open-mindedness
- Teach students to be strong communicators who can connect with others around the world
- Prepare students to use technology effectively and responsibly
- Make international awareness and understanding a focus
- Promote international sister-school projects
- Use video conferencing to cross borders (pp. 349–353)

With such an emphasis on worldwide issues, American educators today believe the best way to improve excellence in education is by studying excellence on a global scale. This means studying what other countries are doing well. Trends in International Mathematics and Science Study (TIMSS) shares teaching methods internationally. A study of other countries has revealed what we should do differently (Waskiewicz, 2007).

At a national level, the role of professional organizations takes three forms. First, professional groups such as the Council for Exceptional Children, the National Education Association, and the National Council for Accreditation of Teacher Education are at times highly effective in lobbying for or against curriculum-related legislation. Second, several professional organizations, such as the National Council of Teachers of Mathematics, attempt to influence the written curriculum by publishing curricular guidelines or model scope and sequence charts. These professional publications seem to be effective in reaching only a limited audience of subject-matter curriculum specialists. School administrators and classroom teachers for the most part do not give them much attention: They are usually perceived as too "idealistic," insensitive to the realities of the classroom. Finally, they attempt to influence local practice by sponsoring institutes and workshops in which new programs and approaches are explained and demonstrated. Such show-and-tell sessions seem to have an impact on participants; they return to their schools often eager to share what they have learned.

Curriculum Tip 4.3	Professional organizations exercise their influence at the national, state, and local levels.

At a state level, the role of professional organizations seems most influential as per large memberships and strong lobbyists—the teachers' and administrators' associations that fight to protect the interests of their constituencies. In many states, the state teachers' association is so active politically that it can be the determining factor in close elections and thus has significant influence with both office holders and candidates. At the local level, professional associations' attempts to influence curricula have been curtailed with the passing of the No Child Left Behind Act (NCLB). Many states are following explicit directives from their state boards of education or legislatures. Also, because the Education Commission of the States began tracking states' progress toward meeting the components of NCLB, local school districts across the nation, and especially teachers, are less influential in determining curriculum than in the past (Christie, 2005).

National Council for Accreditation of Teacher Education

Regarding teacher preparation programs, the National Council for Accreditation of Teacher Education (NCATE) is the accrediting body for colleges and universities that prepare teachers and other professional specialists for work in elementary and secondary schools. It is a nongovernmental coalition of more than 30 national associations representing the education profession at large. There is widespread support because membership on policy boards includes representatives from organizations of (a) teacher educators, (b) teachers, (c) state and local policymakers, and (d) professional specialists. These boards develop standards, policies, and procedures for the teacher preparation programs. In essence, accountability and improvement are central to NCATE's mission. Subsequently, the NCATE accreditation process determines whether schools, colleges, and departments of education meet demanding standards for the preparation of teachers and other school specialists. Through this process, NCATE seeks to provide assurance to the public that graduates of accredited institutions have acquired the knowledge, skills, and dispositions necessary to help all students learn. The standards that teacher preparation must meet to be accredited are shown in Exhibit 4.1.

Although the U.S. Department of Education and the Council for Higher Education Accreditation recognize NCATE as an accrediting body for schools, colleges, and departments of education, only 623 of approximately 1,363 institutions are NCATE accredited. Some of the pros and cons expressed regarding NCATE accreditation are shown in Exhibit 4.2.

THE COURTS

Increasingly, the courts seem to play an active role in curriculum. Both federal and state courts have become so active in this area that some educators now speak of the "court-ordered curriculum." Perry Zirkel (2007), a professor of education and law at Pennsylvania's Lehigh University, noted that in terms of legal principle, it appears that public school authorities rather than parents determine curriculum. This position, of course, is still highly debatable.

From a historical standpoint, Van Geel (1979) examined school programs and noted programs that might be termed constitutionally required. Many of his points are still applicable today. Based on his analysis of the major decisions by federal courts in the area of curriculum and program, certain salient features of such a required program emerge. First, it must be secular, but not militantly secular. The schools cannot establish a religion of secularism. Second, English may be the chief language of instruction, as long as non–English-speaking students are assisted in learning it. Third, the program must be minimally adequate for all students, even those with serious limitations of ability and capacity. Antiquated notions of sex roles may not be imposed on students by segregating them for instruction in such courses as industrial arts and home economics. Instructional materials and courses may be politically biased in favor of the free-enterprise system, but teachers and students who hold views favoring some other system of government may not be excluded from the school. As Van Geel suggested, the courts in general have determined that students have a constitutional right to receive information and ideas, no matter how distasteful those ideas might seem to the local community.

State courts have taken positions similar to those supported by the federal courts. Several state courts have held that state plans for the financing of education may be unconstitutional

EXHIBIT 4.1 NCATE Standards for Teacher Preparation

Standard 1: Candidate Knowledge, Skills, and Dispositions expects that candidates preparing to be teachers or other school professionals know and can demonstrate the content, pedagogical, and professional knowledge, skills, and dispositions necessary to help all students learn. Candidates should know the subject matter they plan to teach and have knowledge of instructional strategies to help all students learn. They are expected to be able to assess student learning and create meaningful learning experiences for all students. Candidates for other school personnel roles are expected to have the professional knowledge expected in their field and to be able to create positive environments that support student learning. Also, the rubrics for the standard expect candidates to use technology in their practice and facilitate student learning through the integration of technology.

Standard 2: Assessment System and Unit Evaluation expects that the professional education unit has an assessment system that collects and analyzes data on applicant qualifications and candidate and graduate performance. It is expected that the teacher preparation institution assesses a candidate's competence before admission to a program, during the course of the preparation program, including assessment of field-based and clinical experiences, and before the completion of the program and/or recommendation for licensure. Multiple assessments should be used and must include performance-based assessments.

Standard 3: Field Experiences and Clinical Practice expects the professional education unit and school partners to design and implement field and clinical experiences so that candidates develop and demonstrate the knowledge, skills and dispositions so that all students learn. Rubrics for this standard expect that "Clinical practice is sufficiently extensive and intensive for candidates to demonstrate competence in the professional roles for which they are preparing." It is also expected that "All candidates participate in field experiences or clinical practice that include students with exceptionalities and students from diverse ethnic, racial, gender, and socioeconomic groups." Also the rubrics expect that candidates have the opportunity in their field and clinical experiences to use technology to support teaching and learning.

Standard 4: Diversity expects that the unit designs, implements, and evaluates curriculum and experiences for candidates to acquire and apply knowledge, skills, and dispositions necessary to help all students learn. It includes the expectation that candidates have the opportunity to interact with candidates, faculty, and P–12 students from diverse groups.

Standard 5: Faculty Qualifications, Performance, and Development require that faculty model best professional practices in scholarship, service, and teaching. Higher education faculty are expected to be engaged in scholarship and to be involved in the world of practice by providing education-related services at the local, state ,or national levels. Faculty who supervise clinical experiences are expected to have contemporary professional experience in the areas they supervise. Also, the rubrics expect that faculty integrate technology into their teaching.

Standard 6: Unit Governance and Resources expects the unit to have the budget, personnel, and facilities, including information technology resources to prepare candidates to meet professional, state, and institutional standards. The rubrics expect that the budget allocations are at least proportional to other units on campus, that there are sufficient numbers of full-time faculty and support personnel to support programs, that faculty workloads allow faculty to be effectively engaged in teaching, scholarship, and service. It is also expected that facilities support the use of information technology by candidates and faculty, and that faculty and candidates have access to current and sufficient curricular and library resources and electronic information.

SOURCE: Reprinted with permission of the National Council for Accreditation of Teacher Education.

EXHIBIT 4.2 NCATE Institutional Accreditation Pros and Cons	
Pros	*Cons*
The institution is subjected to external scrutiny by educators outside the college or university.	Preparation for NCATE accreditation costs too much.
A teaching license earned in one state will be treated reciprocally by another state.	The language of the NCATE standards is political.
The institution meets the highest current national standards in the field of teacher education.	Admitting the American Federation of Teachers to join the group and allowing the teachers' union to appoint members to NCATE's governing boards.
The institution is responsive to standards that are central to the pursuit of excellence in teacher education.	NCATE is an external organization attempting to dictate curriculum and internal policy.
NCATE accreditation assures programmatic quality.	There is a danger that common standards may reflect the preferences of a particular group rather than the American population as a whole.

NOTE: The pros and cons for NCATE accreditation are samples that the authors experienced as chairs and/or members of NCATE teams and from the literature.

if they result in significant differences among local districts in the level of expenditures for education; such differences, the courts have held, violate the equal-protection clause of state constitutions. As Van Geel (1979) posited, a doctrine of a "state-created right to an education" has emerged from the decisions of state courts. This continues to have profound implications for school programs today: Education is no longer seen as a privilege, but as a right for all. He also pointed out that as state legislatures become more active in adopting complex and often ambiguous educational codes, state courts will have increased influence as they resolve issues of the rights, duties, and discretionary authority allocated by those codes. This has certainly been the case with NCLB and mandated testing.

LOCAL EDUCATIONAL LEADERS

At the local district level, central office administrators, school building principals, and teachers continue to play key roles in influencing curriculum. First, the typical school superintendent perceives himself or herself as relatively weak in the curriculum area and appoints a generalist as an assistant superintendent for curriculum and instruction, who then serves as the district leader in the area of curriculum. Several factors complicate the assistant superintendent's role. First, such individuals are usually assigned an array of responsibilities that always seem to have a higher day-to-day priority—meeting with unhappy parents, conferring with principals about the budget, planning an in-service program. Second, the assistant superintendent for curriculum in even some larger districts is expected to supervise the curriculum with little or no staff support;

districts faced with budget problems typically begin to reduce personnel by reducing the size of the central office supervisory staff. Finally, the emphasis on the school as the locus of educational improvement has created confusion in the minds of many assistant superintendents about the importance of their roles in curriculum development and improvement.

> **Leadership Tip**
>
> "To make a successful, sustainable school [district], we need to allow all participants to bring their gifts to the table." (Shorr, 2006, p. 24)

Despite such complicating factors, the assistant superintendent for curriculum and instruction in most districts is the sole individual exercising general supervision over the entire curriculum.

As noted above, the role of the principal in curriculum leadership seems to vary with the level of schooling. Thomas Hoerr (2007–2008), a school administrator in New York City, believes principals should be instructional leaders. The title "principal," according to Hoerr, emanated from the term "principal teacher." The assumption behind the title was that the principal had more skill and knowledge than anyone in the building and would guide others on how to teach.

It is now commonplace that elementary principals in the most effective schools are taking a very active role in curriculum leadership. They play the central role in articulating educational goals and curricular priorities, in influencing teacher perceptions about curricular emphases and approaches, in helping teachers use test results, and in aligning the curriculum. At the secondary level (especially in larger schools), however, the effective principal is more likely to delegate these roles to department heads, whose subject-matter expertise enables them to influence the curricular decision making of secondary teachers.

Just as the roles of elementary and secondary school principals are changing, the role of teacher–leaders in curriculum development is becoming more evident. Considering changes in technology and the need for curriculum alignment, teacher–leaders are now playing an ever greater role in changing the makeup of schools. With higher stakes placed on the performance of all students, teachers must play an increasingly vital role in curricular and instructional leadership. Through the development of effective collaborative teacher teams, teacher–leaders gain deeper understandings of standards, curriculum, and best instructional practices (Gregory & Kuzmich, 2008).

THE CLASSROOM TEACHER

As discussed in Chapter 1, to a great extent the teacher is the curriculum. Developing teacher learning communities is one of the best ways for teachers to develop their skills (Wiliam, 2007–2008). The key is to handle both internal and external pressures.

The Internal Pressures

As per internal pressures, teachers assume a wide range of roles to support school and student success. Whether these roles are assigned formally or shared informally, they build the entire school's capacity to improve (Harrison & Killion, 2007). For example,

First, teachers need to satisfy strong personal ambitions.

Second, they need a sense of independence, an understanding they have the power to make decisions.

Third, they need to feel that they are valued—that students need them, that they are important to the school.

Fourth, teachers have a strong need for success, a need to feel that they are a part in helping students succeed.

The External Pressures

Besides responding to personal and professional needs, the teacher is also susceptible to numerous external pressures. According to Gordon Donaldson (2007), professor of education at the University of Maine, administrators, school boards, and state and federal policymakers should do the following:

First, identify and support those clusters of teachers in which professional relationships and commitments are fostering instructional innovation.

Second, respect the judgment of the teachers and be willing to adjust strategies to complement teacher innovations.

Third, put resources behind the efforts of teacher–leaders by supporting shared practice, planning, and professional learning focused on improvement of practice.

Fourth, acknowledge that goals and initiatives can best be addressed by treating teacher–leaders as vital and powerful partners.

Regardless of internal or external pressures, great schools grow because of great teachers. It is the classroom teacher who basically holds the power to improve student learning. The bottom line is that there will have to be major changes in our educational system to accommodate societal and political pressures in the classroom in this new global age.

Power and Responsibility

"Accountability without commensurate power is unfair and can be harmful." (Ingersol, 2007, p. 25)

Wiles and Lundt noted as early as 2004 that the future of education in the United States will require five things in order to construct this global perspective of learning: (1) a rationale for learning, (2) a learning place, (3) learning mediums, (4) validation of learning, and (5) informed teachers. By contrast, the new vision of education promises the following:

- Instead of linear learning, it promises multimedia convergent learning.
- Instead of instruction, it promises construction and discovery.
- Instead of teacher centeredness, it promises student centeredness.
- Instead of memorization, it promises exploration and navigation.
- Instead of place-bound learning, it promises learning anywhere, anytime.
- Instead of promoting learning as work, it promises learning as natural and motivating.
- Instead of the teacher as transmitter, it promises the teacher as a facilitator.

As can be seen, the challenges of the past can help lead the way to tomorrow's success. According to Deborah Harvest (2008), NAESP Foundation board member, achieving success is possible. She believes it takes a school environment that lets all children know that they can succeed, as well as strategies to help them. The greatest challenge, therefore, is to politically accommodate effective change.

The rationale for learning in the past has been politically dominated by the desire of government and educators to have students acquire content or knowledge. The new rationale will have to be that of students' developing a value of knowing as well as requiring a belief that learning is a continuous process that is defined by individual needs and experiences. Therefore, the key to improving education is having a *shared vision* of teaching and learning, and having a shared vision results from the participation of many people, each helping and leading in their own way.

SUMMARY

Federal and state governments, professional organizations, local school boards, textbook publishers, accrediting organizations, parent and community groups, school administrators, teacher–leaders, and classroom teachers all pose conflicting influences that seem to change in their strength from time to time, and in their particular impact on a given classroom. This chapter provides curriculum leaders who wish to develop or improve curricula an understanding of the politics of curriculum and the way organizations and individuals attempt to influence what is taught in the schools. This chapter presents an overview of the way influences are brought to bear and then examines in greater detail those agencies that seem to have the greatest influence. This chapter addresses the role of the federal government in curriculum development and how it has changed over the years. Chapter 4 gives an overview of the general role of state governments in curriculum development today and how this has changed over the years. Finally, this chapter explains the roles of educational organizations, courts, educational leaders, and classroom teachers on current curriculum development.

APPLICATIONS

1. Some experts have argued that the difficulty of finding sufficient fiscal resources will shortly reduce state activity in the curriculum field. If that development does occur, and if the federal government continues to take a less active role, which sources of influence do you believe will increase in power?

2. Based on what you now know about the sources of curriculum influence, what advice would you give a superintendent who posed this question to you: "Does our district really need central office curriculum specialists?"

3. Some analysts have reached this conclusion: "All curriculum making is essentially a political process." Would you agree or disagree? Prepare a well-thought-out response to the question.

4. As the conclusion in Application 3 suggests, the federal government has for the most part abandoned the change strategy of funding the development of exemplary generic curricula. Some have argued that such abandonment was premature—that given greater

insight into the change process, such a strategy might be effective. Consider two related issues: Under what circumstances would you recommend that this strategy be reintroduced? What modifications in the approach would you recommend?

5. What advice would you give this fourth-grade teacher: "My principal and the district science supervisor do not agree about what I should emphasize in teaching science. The principal wants me to spend more time on practical applications; the supervisor, on science processes."

6. Less than one half of the institutions of higher education are NCATE accredited, but they prepare two thirds of new teachers yearly. Should school administrators hiring 1st-year teachers give preference to applicants who graduated from NCATE accredited institutions? Defend your answer.

7. Various individuals and groups influence curriculum in our states. Complete the chart below to identify the relative influence that you feel individuals or groups have on curriculum.

Perceptions Regarding Curriculum Influence in Your State

The chart below is designed to explore your perceptions regarding the relative influence exerted by various individuals and groups on the curriculum process within the state in which you work. Please identify the state in which you work and rate the relative influence you feel that each individual or group within the state exerts by placing a check in the most appropriate columns.

	Level of Influence				
State:	None	Little	Some	Great	Don't Know
1. Governor					
2. State Department of Education					
3. State Board of Education					
4. Chief State School Officer					
5. State and Local Courts					
6. State Legislature					
7. Local Board of Education					
8. Local Superintendent					
9. Local Principal(s)					
10. Local Teachers					
11. Local Community Members					

State:	Level of Influence				
	None	Little	Some	Great	Don't Know
12. State Administrators' Organization(s)					
13. State Teachers' Association(s)					
14. State Special Interest Groups					
15. Local Teachers' Organization(s)					
16. National Professional (Subject Area) Organizations					
17. Federal Government					
18. National Council for Accreditation of Teacher Education					
19. Other					

CASE STUDY   Being Politically Correct

Richard F. Elmore (1997) wrote that "U.S. elementary and secondary education is a vast and extraordinarily complex enterprise that seems to defy simple generalizations. However, the two central imperatives of U.S. educational governance are dispersed control and political pluralism" (p. 1). He believes that control of education is not decentralized in the United States and that "local control of schools is largely inaccurate and outmoded, especially in the light of the direction education reform has taken in the past decade" (p. 2). In essence, "the idea of political pluralism is more straightforward. It captures a fundamental principle of U.S. politics—that political decisions and actions are the result of competing groups with different resources and capacities vying for influence" (p. 2).

According to Elmore (1997), "the story of U.S. education reform since the 1980s is worthy of either a Gilbert and Sullivan operetta or theater of the absurd, depending upon your tastes" (p. 2). Consider the following, which called for major educational reform: *A Nation at Risk* in 1983, Goals 2000 in 1989, and the No Child Left Behind Act in 2002. Intermittent interventions resembled a "horse trade—greater flexibility and less regulation for schools and school systems in return for tangible evidence of results, reckoned mostly in terms of student achievement" (p. 2). Subsequently,

> control of education . . . is only local when schools and school systems appear to be doing the right thing; when they're not, they are fair game for elected officials, at whatever level of government, with a political interest in their performance. (p. 3)

The Challenge

How can educators, especially curriculum specialists looking for the cutting edge of curriculum and instructional practice, deal with the virtual blizzard of leading-edge advice on curriculum and pedagogy?

Key Issues/Questions

1. Various groups compete for resources and thus require school districts to prioritize their needs to gain political influence and resources. How do politics influence what is included or excluded in curriculum and determine what is funded?

2. What measures can a school district take to leverage resources to enable the district to achieve higher curriculum standards?

3. If the federal government allocates 6% of a district's budget, but mandates a specified curriculum, how do you justify the discrepancy?

4. What questions should curriculum leaders ask before addressing state and federal mandates and embarking on a course of major change within their school districts?

5. What role does politics play in the development of state and national education regulations?

6. What are the differences between internal political pressures and external political pressures?

WEBLIOGRAPHY

NAESP Federal Legislative Action Center
http://capwiz.com/naesp/mlm/signup

National Conference of State Legislatures
www.ncsl.org

National Educator Training and Leadership Center & Counsel of Chief State Officers
www.ccsso.org/projects/national_educator_training_and_leadership_center

Organisation for Economic Co-operation and Development
www.oecd.org

United Nations Children's Fund
www.unicef.org

United Nations Educational, Scientific, and Cultural Organization
http://unesco.org

U.S. Department of Education
www.ed.gov

U.S. House Committee on Education and Labor
http://edworkforce.house.gov

PART II

Curriculum Processes

Understanding the history and process of curriculum development is useful for both scholars and practitioners. The purpose of Part II is to help curriculum leaders acquire the skills needed to bring about major curricular change. Curriculum change is often based on specific details involved in improving and developing three levels of curricula—programs of study, fields of study, and courses and units of study.

CHAPTER 5

Curriculum Planning

Curriculum planning is at the heart of school reform. The accountability movement has put responsibility of student achievement squarely on schools. As part of this process, district policies and programs provide a framework that can help or hinder a school or school district's efforts to provide a high-quality learning environment for its students (Protheroe, 2008).

The specific details of the curriculum-planning process are determined by the level and nature of curriculum work; designing a field of studies, improving a program of studies, and developing a course of study involve quite different processes, as the following chapters indicate. Nevertheless, some general planning processes are useful in all curriculum work.

Questions addressed in this chapter include the following:

- What is a goal-based model of **curriculum planning**, and how does one determine the locus of planning decisions and organizational structures that are needed?

- How can we identify and allocate leadership functions as well as align goals with curricular fields?

- How do we organize, evaluate, change, and provide curriculum resources?

Before answering these questions in detail, it might be useful at the outset to define curriculum planning: *Curriculum planning* is the specification and sequencing of major decisions to be made in the future with regard to the curriculum.

Key to Leadership

Successful curriculum leaders know that a goal-based model of curriculum planning provides organizing strategies to determine the locus of control in decision making and what organizational structures are needed.

A GOAL-BASED MODEL OF CURRICULUM PLANNING

The use of standards-based teaching as part of the goal-based process is becoming common practice. Thorough preparation for effective standards-based teaching goes beyond the simple curriculum alignment and materials-adoption strategies that are popular throughout the United States (O'Shea, 2005). Although several planning models are available to educators, one that seems very effective for curriculum planning is the goal-based model delineated in Exhibit 5.1. The rest of this chapter then clarifies the steps in the model more fully.

EXHIBIT 5.1 A Goal-Based Curriculum Planning Model

Organize for Planning

1. Determine the locus of planning decisions: Differentiate between district and school planning responsibilities.
2. Determine the organizational structures needed to facilitate planning, and set up those structures.
3. Identify leadership functions, and allocate those functions appropriately.

Establish the Planning Framework

1. Align the district's educational goals with appropriate curricular fields as well as recommended standards by the learned societies and mandated state standards.
2. Develop a curriculum database.
3. Develop a planning calendar based on leaders' assessments of organizational priorities.

Carry Out Specific Planning Activities

1. Conduct **needs assessment** in high-productivity areas by using standardized tests, curriculum-referenced tests, and other measures and data sources; use assessment results to determine the need for curriculum development or improvement.
2. Organize task forces to carry out development or improvement projects, and monitor the work of the task forces.
3. Evaluate development or improvement projects.
4. Make necessary organizational changes and provisions for effective implementation.
5. Secure resources needed for new or revised curricula.
6. Provide staff development needed for effective implementation.

Curriculum Tip 5.1

People will support what they help create.

The model begins with three organizing strategies. First, the leaders distinguish between district- and school-based responsibilities to clarify the locus of decision making. They then decide what organizational structures are needed, appointing the needed advisory groups and task forces. Finally, they allocate specific leadership functions to district and school staff.

With those organizational moves accomplished, leaders take steps to establish a framework for planning. First, leaders align the broad educational goals of the district with the several fields of study, so that each field of study has a clear set of curricular goals for which it is responsible. Then the district develops a computerized knowledge base for curriculum, systematizing the information needed for good curriculum work. Leaders then assess general district priorities and develop a 5-year planning calendar, showing the major events and foci of the curriculum-improvement process. With the framework established, the specific planning activities are undertaken. With the goals thus stipulated, a needs assessment is conducted, using standardized and curriculum-referenced tests and other appropriate measures, as well as data in the knowledge base.

As for the larger building or districtwide curricular projects, task forces are appointed to carry out the development and improvement suggested by the needs assessment. Their work is evaluated, and appropriate plans are made to implement the new or revised programs effectively.

This goal-based model has several features that recommend it. It is goal based, ensuring that curriculum revisions are made with general outcomes clearly in mind. It emphasizes feasibility: It assists the district in undertaking only priority projects that leaders believe can be accomplished effectively. It is systematic: Planning decisions are cast in a rational framework that emphasizes orderly progression.

Curriculum Tip 5.2	Sharing common goals is key to making curriculum changes in a classroom, school, or district.

Leading change and implementing a goal-based approach often go hand in hand. The key to success in both is a thorough, inclusive curriculum-planning process. The process described and tools provided in this book will assist you in leading change and help guide you through the curriculum-planning process.

DETERMINE THE LOCUS OF PLANNING DECISIONS

Curriculum planning obviously occurs at several levels: at the federal level, when policy decisions and their implementation are planned; at the state level, when state offices of education plan for major changes in graduation requirements; at the district level, when the district plans to revise a field of study; at the school level, when the school revises its program of studies or adds a new course; and at the classroom level, when the teacher plans a unit of study. Because most of the important alterable decisions are made at the district and school levels, the discussion that follows focuses on these two critical levels of planning.

The central question is the balance between district-based and school-based curricular decision making. On the one hand, there are those who argue for strong district control. According to Douglas Reeves (2007–2008), founder of the Leadership and Learning Center, "every program, initiative, and strategy in the school is subjected to the relentless question, Is it working?" (p. 87).

Just as Fenwick English advocated in 1980, there should, realistically, only be two levels of curriculum management: the state and the district. In such a curriculum-management system, district policies and curriculum documents completely control what occurs at the school and classroom levels. These views seem to be shared by the leaders of many large school districts, who have attempted in recent years to standardize the curriculum throughout the entire district. For example, curriculum guides issued by the Vermillion School District 13-1, Vermillion, South Dakota, in 2004 not only specified what was to be taught and what materials were to be used but even indicated when it was to be taught. Here is a sample entry from the district's secondary mathematics curriculum guide (Vermillion School District, 2004):

Grade 7: September 24–October 19. Whole numbers. 3.5 weeks.

The rationale for such standardization speaks in terms of achievement, equity, and efficiency. The first argument is that standardized curricula will result in higher achievement. The second is that standardization ensures equity: Every student gets the same curriculum, regardless of school and teacher assignment. Critics would point out that equity does not equal uniformity. The final argument is that the standardized curriculum is more efficient and thus more economical: The district can offer the same type of staff development, order large quantities of the same materials, and develop a single set of curriculum-referenced tests. This claim of efficiency is probably a reasonable one; the issue is whether other considerations are more important.

On the other hand, some argue just as persuasively for school-based curriculum development. Zmuda, Kuklis, and Kline (2004) wrote that teachers desire to have a more active role in curriculum development—and it is more likely that school-based processes will provide for such active participation. However, several reservations might be noted about granting schools too much curricular autonomy. The resulting collection of different curricula would be difficult to coordinate and manage; the process would result in much inefficiency and duplication of effort; and quality might be adversely affected, because the school-based curriculum team would probably not have as many resources as district teams.

Because no conclusive research exists on this issue, it would seem wise for each local district to resolve the matter through a clear analysis of the options, weighing such factors as the size of the district, the competence of district and school leaders, and the degree of heterogeneity throughout the district. The major issues involved here, as listed in Exhibit 5.2, should be discussed and resolved by the superintendent and the district leadership team; those decisions can then be used as policy guidelines for future curriculum planning.

EXHIBIT 5.2 Issues in District/School Curriculum Decision Making

1. May the school modify district goals so that those goals are more appropriate for the students of that school?

2. May the school reconceptualize and reorganize fields of study, using such approaches as interdisciplinary courses and "broad fields" curricula?

3. May the school develop its own instructional objectives or modify district objectives, as long as those objectives are consonant with district goals?

4. May the school recommend which instructional processes and activities are to be used?

5. May the school make its own recommendations about the pacing of instruction?

6. May the school develop and select its own tests for evaluating student achievement?

7. May the school select its own instructional materials, as long as the materials meet district guidelines?

8. May the school evaluate its own program of studies and make needed changes, including the addition or elimination of specific courses?

One of the areas most affected by the school-based versus the district-based approach to curriculum planning is the area of technology. To assess the impact of technology use on students and staff, it is important to establish achievable outcomes for the use of technology. In developing curricular outcomes, it is wise to consult local, state, or national technology use standards. Districts or states that have no adopted standards should consider reviewing International Society for Technology in Education (ISTE) standards at www.iste.org.

DETERMINE THE ORGANIZATIONAL STRUCTURES NEEDED

With those district and school delineations made, the district leadership team should next determine which organizational structures are needed to provide ongoing curriculum leadership. Many school districts seem to err here by appointing too many standing curriculum committees. Such a mistake results in a cumbersome bureaucratic structure that only complicates curriculum planning. It is more desirable to have a simple and flexible organizational structure that can provide the continuity required and also respond quickly to changing needs. An examination of both the research and reports of effective practice suggest that the following structures would accomplish those goals.

District Curriculum Advisory Council

The District Curriculum Advisory Council is a standing committee, with members appointed by the superintendent of schools. Its membership will vary with the size of the school district, but the following members or constituencies should be represented:

- The school superintendent or assistant superintendent

- The school district curriculum directors or supervisors

- Secondary-school principals

- Elementary-school principals

- Teachers

- Parents and other community representatives

- Secondary-school students

The advisory council, as its name suggests, serves in an advisory capacity only, recommending to the superintendent what problems require systematic attention and what processes might be used to solve those problems. Typically it would meet four times during the school year to identify problems, review planning calendars, receive evaluation reports, and review curriculum proposals. Its members would serve for a stated period of time; a rotating 3-year term of office would ensure both continuity and fresh ideas.

Larger districts may wish to establish a separate community advisory council composed of parents and representatives of the business and professional community. Most superintendents, however, seem to feel that such separate councils complicate the work of the curriculum advisory group and may even attempt to usurp certain board functions.

School Curriculum Advisory Council

Each school should also have a standing advisory group, especially if individual schools are to have a large measure of curricular autonomy. Its members should be nominated by the faculty and appointed by the principal. The school advisory council would include the principal, subject-matter specialists or grade-level leaders, teachers, and parents. Students from upper grade levels might also be included. One of the teachers and one of the parents on the school advisory council should represent the school on the district council to ensure good communication between the two advisory groups. The school advisory council advises the principal on school-based curricular issues, in a manner similar to the district advisory council. Its members would also serve for a specified term, like those on the district council.

In smaller school districts, there might not be a need for separate school councils; the district council could be composed so that it had representatives from each school. In either case, these standing groups provide the continuity required for effective planning.

Curriculum Task Forces

In addition to these two standing committees, the superintendent would appoint a number of task forces to deal with any major issues that might need attention. These task forces would be seen as working groups, numbering from perhaps 6 to 12 members, depending on the nature of the problem. Members would be appointed on the basis of the technical skills required for the job; at the same time, the superintendent should be sure that the membership is generally representative of the types of professional roles that exist in the district. Thus, most task forces would include a curriculum specialist, a principal, and several knowledgeable teachers. If a task force needed additional technical assistance, it would request approval from the superintendent to secure a qualified consultant.

Each task force would be given a specific problem to solve, a deadline for developing and implementing the solution, and the resources required to do the job. Ordinarily, a task force would continue in existence only until the problem had been solved. These ad hoc groups give the school system the flexibility it needs and in this sense complement the standing bodies.

An example might be the formation of a technology task force committee. A technology task force committee can be made up of administrators, teachers, parents, and community members. At least six of the members of this larger committee can be asked to form a special steering committee.

Curriculum Tip 5.3	Giving the task force a special title is an important part of the process. For example, some school districts call their Task Force Council "The Vision Alive Committee."

This select committee can assist with the development of the district's vision and curricula mission statements as well as assist with the development of guidelines for technological infrastructure. The committee can also help to formulate guidelines for equipment use and programs designed to enhance communication and technological awareness. This type of task force committee is representative of how a school district special committee might be organized. Developing an effective task force or select committee can be a crucial part of the process of curriculum planning.

IDENTIFY AND ALLOCATE LEADERSHIP FUNCTIONS

Today, principals are expected to be experts in all aspects of administration, leadership, and instruction. As instructional leaders they are often, and should be, heavily involved in curriculum planning and staffing. In the past, however, principals were only expected to be organized with good management skills and have a deep understanding of the school and community (Fleck, 2007). Historically, during the period from 1980 to 2003, this was a somewhat common pattern of curriculum staffing developed in larger districts across the nation.

Typically, an assistant superintendent for curriculum and instruction was expected to provide systemwide leadership. The central office staff also included several subject-matter coordinators, who usually were responsible for coordinating the K–12 curriculum in a designated content area. At the school level, the building principal was expected to provide leadership; in larger secondary schools, the curriculum responsibility was usually delegated to an assistant principal for curriculum and instruction. In large elementary schools, either grade-level leaders or teacher specialists, especially in reading and mathematics, assisted the principal. All high school–level department chairs were appointed to provide subject-matter leadership. Some middle-school principals relied on grade-level team leaders; others used department heads.

In recent years, this prevailing pattern has been seriously altered. Three factors seem to be at work here. The first, of course, is money. Many districts, forced to economize by tax caps, considered central office staff the most expendable and dismissed all central office curriculum supervisors. The second factor is dissatisfaction with the prevailing pattern. Much of this dissatisfaction focused on the performance of district coordinators and school department heads; in many cases, they seemed not to be providing the leadership needed. The final factor is the widespread conviction, supported by some research, that the principal should be the instructional leader. If that is the case, then, it is reasoned, district coordinators and department heads are not needed.

These interacting forces seem to have decimated the ranks of curriculum leadership and, in many districts, have led to a state of uncertainty and confusion in which no curricular leadership exists. A busy assistant superintendent, suffering from role overload, attempts to respond to curricular crises, and building principals, overwhelmed by administrative responsibilities, wonder what it means to provide curriculum leadership.

The response to this crisis, it would seem, would not be to return to the previous pattern and simply hire additional personnel to fill these old positions. A more useful answer is to analyze the leadership functions required at both the district and school levels, allocate these functions to those best able to perform them, and then decide what additional staff, if any, are needed—in some cases, creating new kinds of positions. This specification and allocation process can begin by having the district curriculum advisory council develop a form like the one shown in Exhibit 5.3. It lists all the leadership functions relating to curriculum, organizing them into four categories based on the level and the focus of the responsibility. The intention here is to describe these functions as clearly as possible, because too many curriculum workers have only a vague understanding of their responsibilities.

The advisory council should first review the form to ensure that it includes all the functions they consider important and that it uses language that communicates clearly to the educators in that district. At that point, the superintendent or the assistant superintendent, with input from central office staff and the building principals, should take over the complex and sensitive task of reallocating and reassigning those functions for maximum effectiveness. The leaders should first analyze which individuals in the district are presently responsible for those functions, entering role designations in the "Now" column. In many instances, they will indicate that no one is presently performing those functions.

After assessing how effectively those functions are being performed and how equitably they are distributed, the advisory council should next determine where changes should be made in present assignments, entering those decisions in the "Assign" column. The entries in this column yield a clear picture of which functions can best be discharged by reassigning them to present role incumbents. In some cases, however, it will be apparent that a new role is needed: Several important functions are not being performed successfully, and no one among the present staff is available and competent to assume those critical functions. The allocation of functions to a newly conceived role is reflected by placing the new role title in the "New" column. The first few entries on the form have been completed to show how the form can be used to record and analyze those decisions.

EXHIBIT 5.3 Functions of Curriculum Leadership			
Function	Now	Assign	New
At the district level—for all areas of the curriculum			
1. Articulate district curriculum goals and priorities.	Supt.	Supt.	
2. Chair district advisory council.	Supt.	Asst.	
3. Develop and monitor curriculum budget.	Supt.	Supt.	
4. Develop and implement plans to evaluate curricula and use evaluative data.			Dir. of Curr.
5. Identify and prioritize curricular problems to be solved.			
6. Develop curriculum planning calendar.			
7. Appoint task forces, and review their reports, proposals, and products.			
8. Develop and monitor processes for materials selection and evaluation.			
9. Plan districtwide staff-development programs required by curricular changes.			
10. Represent district on curricular matters in relationships with state and intermediate unit curriculum offices.			
11. Evaluate district-level curriculum staff.			
12. Develop general district guideline for aligning curricula at the school level.			
At the district level—for special areas of the curriculum			
1. Develop and implement plans to evaluate curriculum, as specified in district planning calendar.			
2. Use evaluative data to identify specific curricular problems, and develop proposals to remedy them.			
3. Evaluate articulation of the curriculum between elementary and middle schools and between middle and high schools.			

Function	Now	Assign	New
4. Provide leadership in developing and improving K–12 curriculum materials in that special area.			
5. Implement district guidelines in selecting and evaluating texts and other instructional materials.			
6. Provide leadership in implementing K–12 staff-development programs for that specific area.			
At the school level—for all areas of the curriculum			
1. Implement plans to monitor and align the curriculum.			
2. Evaluate curricula at the school level, and use evaluative data to identify school-level problems.			
3. Ensure that important skills that cut across the disciplines are appropriately taught and reinforced in those disciplines.			
4. Monitor coordination of the curriculum between those content areas where close coordination is important.			
5. Develop school-based budget for curriculum needs, reflecting school priorities.			
At the school level—for special areas of the curriculum			
1. Supervise teachers with respect to curriculum implementation.			
2. Assist teachers in developing instructional plans based on curriculum guides.			
3. Implement school-based staff development required by curriculum change.			
4. Select instructional materials.			
5. Help teachers use student-evaluation results to make needed modifications in curriculum.			

The preliminary decisions are first reviewed by central office staff and school principals and then by the district advisory council to secure their input and keep them informed. The final allocations then become the basis for reconceptualizing present roles and creating any new positions needed. This process thus enables a local district to develop its own staffing pattern, one that reflects its special needs and resources.

Leadership and planning appear to be common threads invariably found in the curricula design of any successful K–12 program. Today's school administrators, teacher–leaders, and teachers face one of the most challenging and exciting times in the educational history of this nation. The changes in curriculum that schools are being asked to accommodate can be both academically threatening and liberating for teachers and administrators.

To exercise the level of leadership required to ensure the successful integration of planning into the curriculum, principals, curriculum coordinators, and superintendents must reach clear answers to four basic questions:

1. What is required to make the improvements we wish to see in the student-centered learning environments of our schools?

2. Why do we want to commit a great deal of time and money to a curriculum initiative for change, and how are our motives focused on improving student learning?

3. Who is the best person to lead the curriculum initiative we are considering?

4. Who will be best suited to assess and maintain the quality of curricular programs after the initial stages of implementation are completed?

The ability of the school administrator to shift leadership styles can provide a supportive climate for broad-based discussions between administrators and teachers. Such discussions can also build a platform for shared decision making when opportunities are appropriate. Involving teachers in curricular deliberations may well take a good deal of courage on the part of the administrator, but that courage enables real benefits for student learning.

ALIGN EDUCATIONAL GOALS WITH CURRICULAR FIELDS

Determining the goals for each field of study remains the key step in the goal-based model. Several methods are available to accomplish this task. This chapter explains one method for allocating goals to curriculum fields as an aspect of the planning process; the next chapter explains a somewhat different process for aligning and assessing the several fields for goal conformance as part of the program-improvement process. However, when creating an alignment of educational goals with curricular fields, the following guidelines will be helpful:

1. *Specify district educational goals.* An educational goal is a general long-term outcome to be accomplished through the total educational program. Most states have developed lists of such goals to be used in all school districts. Facing competition through the development of goals should bring us around to what's most important about our public schools: that they are vital community centers for teaching and learning. Determining what is important is the key to setting district educational goals (Ferrandino, 2007).

For example, the Nebraska Department of Education specified early on that "for a school building or school district to meet federal accountability, each group of students must meet all target goals for reading, mathematics, writing, high school graduation rate, assessment quality, and student participation" (Christensen, 2004). The state goal for proficiency has a starting point between 61% and 66%, while other states have proficiency goals ranging from 14% to 80%. School districts that have the freedom and wish to develop their own goal statements might well consult Goodlad's (2004) book *A Place Called School*. This work includes an excellent set of goal statements that he developed after reviewing a large number of state and district statements.

In addition to the core curriculum, educators today are not just focusing on district and state curriculum issues. They are also focusing, to a larger extent than previously, on a global perspective as well. Generating a clear narrative of a school district's basic mission and fostering a shared sense of purpose among students and school personnel can be a major factor in generating a positive school climate and an engaging academic curriculum. As Suarez-Orozco and Sattin (2007) proclaimed, "The world needs young people who are culturally sophisticated and prepared to work in an international environment" (p. 58).

2. *Determine which of the educational goals should be accomplished primarily through the courses of study.* Many educational leaders neglect this important step; they assume that every educational goal is a curricular goal. Thus, Pennsylvania educators, noting that the state board specifies the development of self-esteem as an educational goal, mistakenly assume that they need to develop courses and units in self-esteem. Many educational goals, like this one, can better be accomplished through other means, such as instructional methods or programs, the organizational climate, the activity program, or through the guidance program.

For this reason, the leadership team and school faculties should carefully analyze each educational goal and make a preliminary determination of whether that goal will be accomplished primarily through organized courses of study or through some other means. In this manner, they identify a shorter list of curriculum goals—those general long-term outcomes that are to be accomplished primarily through the organized curriculum. Advisory councils should review their tentative decisions. The input from those groups should then be used to make any needed modifications so that the resulting list represents a broad consensus.

3. *Allocate the curricular goals to the several fields of study.* Once the curricular goals have been identified, the leadership team, with faculty input, should allocate those goals to appropriate fields of study. A system like this one seems to work.

This is a "top-down" process—one that begins with the district's educational goals and ends with curricular goals for each field. The process can be reversed: Each field can develop its own list of curricular goals, and these can be synthesized into one comprehensive district list. The outcome, not the process, is important: Each field should have a clear list of curricular goals.

Curriculum Tip 5.4	A good example of a "top-down" process is the alignment of technology goals into curricular fields.

A school district technology task force often establishes district-level technology goals, but the teachers at a grade level or subject areas generally align these goals with their lessons. Teachers often use this template to create a more detailed plan for how they are going to incorporate technology into their individual classrooms. Once created, this document can be shared with the principal and a school-site technology support person.

Technology Planning Goals

- Align technology resources with district curricula programs and planning.

- Facilitate integration of technology with the instructional program as to be consistent with the district's curriculum.

- Implement technologies that support a high-quality and safe learning environment and allows all students to achieve at their highest potential.

- Develop teacher and student interest and motivation in utilizing technology to develop higher-order thinking skills.

- Teachers work to create technology standards and share best practices.

- Develop authentic, problem-based use of technology that becomes self-renewing for teachers.

- Transform every classroom into a digital learning environment. (Patterson, 2007, pp. 22–25)

DEVELOP A CURRICULUM DATABASE

A second key aspect of the planning framework is the development of a comprehensive curriculum database. Using a system's instructional tools, teachers can search for a particular theme or standard, click on items addressing that area, and incorporate them into their lesson plans. Having resources available at the click of a mouse means that teachers no longer have to spend hours scouring the Internet and libraries for age-appropriate resources for students (Mills, 2007). The argument here is that good curriculum work requires extensive knowledge about resources, inputs, and constraints. To that end, each district should develop a computerized knowledge base that can be used in assessing needs and developing curricula. What should be included? The temptation is to collect too much information, just because it is available or seems interesting. It makes more sense to collect and organize only that information likely to be used. Exhibit 5.4 lists the kinds of information that seem most essential in the needs-assessment process; as will be explained in Chapter 8, a shorter list of information needs can be useful in the course-planning process.

EXHIBIT 5.4 Information for the Curriculum Database

Community Resources

1. People with knowledge, expertise, and influence

2. Organizations and places useful as resources

Students

1. Date of birth, sex, and ethnic identity

2. Eligibility for federal or state assistance programs

3. Parents' occupations and marital status

4. Verbal and mathematical abilities and IQ score

5. Talents, skills, and special interests

6. School achievement: standardized test scores and curriculum-referenced test scores

7. English proficiency; native language if other than English

8. Limitations: physical, emotional, and learning disabilities

9. Learning styles and cognitive levels

10. School record: subjects studied, grades, and attendance

11. Career and educational plans

12. Extracurricular activities

13. Community activities

Faculty

1. Subjects and grades certified to teach

2. Present assignment

3. Special interests and competencies

4. Recent professional development: courses, workshops, etc.

School

1. Courses offered and enrollments

2. Extracurricular activities and student participation

Other Resources

1. State curriculum guides

2. Curriculum guides from other districts

3. Other sources of learning objectives

4. Professional materials and resources for teachers

Such information stored in database will greatly facilitate the work of the several task forces. Consider, for example, how the database would be used by a task force appointed to develop a new Personal Well-Being course for middle-school students that would combine health and physical education. They would first get comprehensive data about the students likely to take the course, to become aware of students' needs, limitations, and capacities: "About 15% of the students will have limited English proficiency; we may need a separate section or special materials for them." Next, they would get data on student participation in extracurricular activities and note that very few students participate in activities that require a high level of physical exercise: "We should include a unit that deals explicitly with the value of and opportunities for in-school aerobic activities." They then would retrieve information about other professional resources available—state curriculum guides, guides from other districts, banks of learning objectives: "A nearby district has just started a pilot program similar to the one we're planning; let's see how it's going." Then they would take a look at faculty data: "The teachers we plan to use do not seem to have an up-to-date knowledge of nutrition; we had better plan some special staff development here and beef up the teacher's guide for that unit." Finally, they would examine community resources: "The hospital dietitian has offered to share her media on good nutrition for the young." For the task force, the curriculum database is invaluable.

Having a curriculum database team can be very beneficial in aiding the process. The team would have the task of translating national and state content standards into academic performance indicators from prekindergarten to Grade 12, which can then be adopted as official achievement targets for the district. Assessments can be administered every 8 weeks, and the tests would measure every standard that had been taught up to that date. Thus the first step on the path to high student achievement is to establish transparent, common, rigorous assessments. This enables teachers to make solid, root-cause analyses from data, which in turn facilitates far more effective action plans. Even with high-quality interim assessments and effective analysis of data, student achievement will not improve without targeted follow-through. The key is to provide a seamless connection between assessment analysis and teaching. The seamless coherence among assessments, data analysis, and action creates the ideal classroom (Bambrick-Santoyo, 2007–2008).

Developing an effective data-analysis program to improve curriculum is therefore a vitally important component. When planning change, school leaders will find that a technology database and a system of data analysis can be used to facilitate systemic curriculum changes regarding issues between teachers and administrative personnel, between administrators and parents, and among administrators within the same district or throughout a region. For example, databases in the area of curriculum can be used to determine professional development interests and needs, develop a background of skills and usage, and identify individuals willing to share ideas and techniques as well as to inventory the type and level of materials and resources used in the classroom. Conducting an in-depth analysis of your curricular needs is, therefore, a crucial part of any program.

DEVELOP A PLANNING CALENDAR

One of the central leadership functions is to develop and monitor the district's curriculum planning calendar, a master schedule that assists district leaders in making systematic plans for curriculum evaluation and development.

As Exhibit 5.5 suggests, the planning calendar should include the six steps listed as "specific planning activities" in Exhibit 5.1. Note that a distinction is made between major and other fields, simply to assist in the planning process, not to depreciate the importance of such areas as art and industrial arts. Provision is also made for evaluating the several programs of study. Note that, in this example, the district has chosen to do a needs assessment each year of one major and one other field and one program level. With such a schedule, the district would be able in a 5-year period to assess all major fields, five other fields, and every program level.

EXHIBIT 5.5 Curriculum-Planning Calendar

Major Projects	2009–2010	2010–2011	2011–2012
1. Needs assessment, major fields	Lang. arts	Math	Science
2. Needs assessment, other fields	Ind. arts	Art	
3. Needs assessment, programs	**Middle**	**Elem.**	**High**
4. Task forces appointed, at work		Lang. arts Ind. arts	Math Art
5. Evaluate projects		Lang. arts Ind. arts	Math Art
6. Organizational provisions		Lang. arts Ind. arts	Math Art
7. Resources selected and provided		Lang. arts Ind. arts	Math Art
8. Staff development			Lang. arts Ind. arts

The superintendent and the district leadership team should begin by tentatively mapping out a 5-year plan that would indicate year by year the major projects to be undertaken. They should make these decisions based on their own analysis of district needs and their own priorities for improvement. The decision about how many projects should be initiated will, of course, be influenced by their perception of district needs and resources. A large school district with well-staffed curriculum and evaluation offices could obviously plan for many more projects than a smaller district with an overextended staff. A newly appointed superintendent given a mandate by the board to improve the curriculum would want to plan for a more ambitious and comprehensive development program than a superintendent who has been presiding for several years over a district that seems to be making excellent progress.

Those tentative decisions should be reviewed by district and school administrators and supervisors and then be shared with the district advisory council for its input before a final form of the calendar is developed. The final form of the calendar can then be used by leaders to develop budget requests, appoint task forces, and monitor their progress.

Curriculum Tip 5.5	The planning calendar should mark important reference points for the planning committee to reach in order to keep the project on schedule.

Administrators and curriculum committee members must work closely together to construct a practical calendar for any curriculum project. Realistic target dates are a key ingredient, and committee members should be included, as this is really the only way to ensure a workable schedule of events. In this respect, it is important to remember that committee members are usually chosen because they know how to get tasks done, and they are also the ones who usually have the best idea of how long it will take to accomplish these tasks.

CONDUCT NEEDS ASSESSMENT

The next major step in the model is to conduct a needs assessment. An example of a classroom needs assessment might include the following questions (Pollock, 2007).

- Do I have just-right learning targets?

- Do I use a functional planning schema?

- Do I vary assessment to elicit useful data?

- Does my feedback improve student performance?

The term *needs assessment* seems to be used often in the profession without much understanding of what is involved. A definition developed by Kaufman back in 1982 seems most useful even today. He defined a needs assessment as a process of identifying gaps between what is and what should be. In his comprehensive review, he identified and analyzed 17 needs-assessment models. His analysis of these 17 models led him to conclude that they share several major shortcomings: They focus on internal elements, ignoring the societal impact and payoffs; they shy away from empirical data, relying too much on people's perceptions; they place too much emphasis on such "middle level" concerns as learner characteristics, methods, and test scores, slighting long-term outcomes; most are really status surveys and thus give too much attention to "what is"; and most are not sufficiently comprehensive, limiting attention to only a few components (see Exhibit 5.6).

EXHIBIT 5.6   Establishing a Data-Driven School Culture Checklist

What does the district want to know?
Where to look:

- Current district goals
- Patterns in data
- Upcoming district decisions
- Questions raised by teachers, administrators, or the community

How will the district find out?
What to do:

- Form data team.

- Conduct inventory of data currently compiled in the district and determine format (electronic or paper).

- Assess technological capacity of the district to manage and analyze data.

- Determine the extent to which personnel in the district have time, skills, and willingness to engage in data-driven projects.

- Identify indicators of input, process, and outcome variables related to goals.

- Determine which additional data are reasonable to collect.

- Train staff to collect and use data.

- Analyze and disaggregate data.

What does the district do next?
How to proceed:

- Establish benchmarks and measure progress toward goals over time.

- Develop action or school improvement plans.

- Communicate findings.

SOURCE: From "Creating Data-Driven Schools," by P. Noyce, D. Perda, and R. Traver, 2000, *Educational Leadership*, *57*(5), pp. 52–57.

To deal with these deficiencies, Kaufman advocated a rather complex and sophisticated model that would use multiple data about inputs, processes, products, outputs, and outcomes and would be sensitive to both the internal organization and the external society. The major drawback of the model he advocated is that it would seem to be too complicated, time-consuming, and expensive for most districts to implement.

A simpler needs-assessment model that avoids many of the pitfalls noted in Kaufman's review could be built on several of the elements explained in this chapter and in Chapter 12 (note that this section explains the needs-assessment process in developing a field of study; Chapter 6 explains how to assess needs in improving a program of studies). First, the district would develop a comprehensive curriculum database, as noted above. This would provide information about what Kaufman and others call the two major "inputs"—the teachers and the learners. Next, the district would develop for each field a clear set of curricular goals, using the processes described above. These specify the ends to be accomplished. Then the district would evaluate selected fields of study, assessing the major components of the field explained in Chapter 1: the written curriculum, the supported curriculum, the taught curriculum, the tested curriculum, and the learned curriculum. Thus, if a district is concerned with assessing curricular needs in a single field of study, the process is a rather straightforward one.

On the other hand, if a district wishes to make a needs assessment that focuses on a general curriculum goal (not a single field), then the process is slightly more complex. This process is explained below, using as an example the general goal of "enhancing creativity."

The process begins with a vague sense of deficiency. Some individual or group asks, "Are we doing all we can in the curriculum to enhance creativity?" (Note that the question focuses on the curriculum; if a broader assessment of an educational goal is desired, then other components, such as the guidance and activity programs, would also be included.) A task force is appointed to answer the question; it begins its work by identifying those fields of study that emphasize or contribute to this goal. In this case, it would be likely that these fields would make such a claim: English language arts, home economics, art, music, and science.

The task force would then proceed to examine the written curriculum in those fields: Do the written guides give sufficient and explicit attention to the goal of enhancing creativity? They then would turn to the supported curriculum, examining budgets, schedules, and materials: Does the district provide sufficient funds for creative materials? Do texts and other instructional materials emphasize creativity in their approach and content? Are these fields of study allocated sufficient time to include creative activities?

Members of the task force can then consider a multitiered or more complicated approach of the taught curriculum. Here they would focus on critical issues: Do teachers actually teach those units in the written guide that were designed to enhance creativity? Do the teachers teach in a manner that fosters creative thinking? Obviously these questions would require evaluators to observe a representative sample of classrooms.

The tested curriculum would next warrant scrutiny: Do curriculum-referenced and teacher-made tests make adequate provisions for assessing creativity? Finally, they would attend to the learned curriculum: Are the students actually learning to think creatively and to produce creative works? This question could be answered through several data sources: results from tests of creativity; results from surveys of teachers, parents, and students; and an evaluation of a representative sample of student creative products.

The results of these several processes would then be used to determine which elements of the curriculum need strengthening or to suggest that perhaps a new course should be added to the curriculum.

As can be seen, a curriculum needs-assessment format can be used for a series of multilevel purposes. Through the use of a needs-assessment program, the district curriculum specialist along with staff members can examine curriculum goals and objectives to best identify instructional opportunities. Information derived from a quality needs-assessment program can be used to infuse change directly into the classroom. The result is a major improvement in the teaching and learning process and a major improvement in the learning environment. Effective curriculum planning, therefore, should always include some type of needs assessment. It is through the development of quality needs-assessment programs that administrators, curriculum leaders, and teachers can best facilitate systemic educational change and reform in our schools and in our classrooms.

ORGANIZE, EVALUATE, CHANGE, PROVIDE RESOURCES

The next steps in the planning process involve development and implementation strategies more fully explained in subsequent chapters. After determining whether to strengthen existing elements or add new ones, the leaders appoint another task force to take over the responsibility of developing the recommended solution. The original task force's work is evaluated by expert review and systematic field testing. Any necessary organizational elements are changed, such as the school schedule, teacher assignments, or grouping practices. Then plans are made to secure the necessary material resources required by the new or improved program.

Curriculum Tip 5.6	It is critical to avoid implementing change for change's sake.

Implementing change without regard for how resources and materials will be integrated into the curriculum has usually not been successful. It is important to make sure that the curriculum process is based on curricular goals and available resources. Available resources include not only materials but also the capacity to provide training and staff development. The curriculum-planning committee along with administration should decide, based on their goals and resources, the extent to which staff development will be infused into the daily operation of the curriculum, classroom, or school.

The entire school system must be evaluated in the curriculum-planning process. Legislation increasingly requires that schools establish objectives, develop plans, drive instruction, and prescribe assessment. Evaluating curriculum systemwide is based on the premise that school systems must set objectives and provide the means for administrator and teacher performance to enable students to meet those objectives. Decisions to guide school personnel performance need to be provided by board of education policy.

PROVIDE STAFF DEVELOPMENT

Teachers will live up to their potential as leaders only when the school environment supports their efforts. For example, they can mentor new faculty members, contribute deep knowledge of their school and community to the decision-making process, provide examples of outstanding teaching to colleagues, and support school improvement (Lattimer, 2007).

One of the most effective means of ensuring successful implementation of new curricula is to integrate effective staff-development programs with any major curricular change. Many curriculum projects of excellent quality have not been implemented successfully because they were not supported with the right kind of staff development. The discussion that follows focuses on the planning of staff-development programs as they relate to the general curriculum-planning process; Chapter 9 examines staff development as a means of supervising the taught curriculum, and Chapter 10 offers detailed suggestions for using staff in the development and implementation stages.

Curriculum Tip 5.7	The strength of a staff-development model relies not only on the model's guiding principles but also on its flexible implementation.

One of the major planning issues is the timing of staff development as it relates to curricular change. Although there are many variations in the specifics of this issue, we will address several models that have been used successfully: Staff development precedes and leads to curricular change, staff development follows and supports curricular change, and community-based learning provides for the needs of the community.

In the *first* model, staff-development sessions are held prior to any major curriculum change. The intent here is to update teachers' knowledge about new developments in the field, to give them the skills they need for writing curriculum and instructional materials, and to provide an opportunity for them to exchange and try out such materials. In general, this is the planning model used in the highly successful National Writing Project (see Keech, Stahlecker, Thomas, & Watson [1979] for a comprehensive evaluation of this approach). Although this model was developed in the 1970s, it certainly seems to be applicable today. James Gray, the individual chiefly responsible for the Bay Area Writing Project, the precursor of the National Writing Project, explicitly rejected curriculum change as the major intervention strategy. His knowledge of the research on the change process led him and his colleagues to begin with a highly effective staff-development model that showed teachers new ways of teaching writing. As teachers explored the new process approach and developed instructional materials, they began gradually to change the curriculum.

The chief advantage of this approach is that it tends to result in a teacher-produced curriculum of high quality. The teachers involved in the staff-development program become local experts who have a better understanding of the field, and the materials they produce have usually stood the test of rigorous trials in the classrooms. The chief drawback to this model is that it can result in piecemeal change; the curriculum becomes a collection of interesting exercises and lacks an integrating conceptual framework.

In the *second* model, staff-development sessions are held subsequent to the curriculum change. The new curriculum is developed, then those who developed the curriculum identify the new knowledge, skills, and attitudes required for successful implementation. Those new learnings then become the basis for a series of staff-development programs offered immediately prior to the introduction of the new program and during its implementation stage. This essentially is the model used in most curriculum development and implementation projects.

The chief advantage of this model is the close fit between curricular change and staff development. If planned carefully, the staff-development program equips the teachers with the skills they need to implement the new curriculum. The chief drawback is that it can place the teacher in a passive role: "Here is your new curriculum, and this is how you teach it."

The *third*, and more contemporary, is the **community-based learning model**. An example might be Teacher Leaders Network (TLN). These are community-based independent networks, both physical and virtual, that make it possible for teachers to draw on external communities that promote divergent thinking. Such networks support the view that teachers have unique insights that can improve education and accelerate student achievement. These networks are especially important because they enable some of the best teaching minds in a state, region, or nation to bond together into influential professional learning communities. Independent teacher networks have the potential to transform traditional concepts of teacher input and staff development (Berry, Norton, & Byrd, 2007).

The community-based learning model is a broad framework that includes service learning, experiential learning, school-to-work, youth apprenticeship, lifelong learning, and other types of learning experiences that are beneficial to the local community. A problem with these individual approaches is that each focuses on only a portion of the learning outcomes that potentially can be achieved through community-based learning.

Community-based learning may be better described as the broad set of teaching/learning strategies that enable youth and adults to learn what they want to learn from any segment of the community. This definition provides for learners of all ages to identify what they wish to learn and opens up an unlimited set of resources to support them. By *community*, we are including the schools, formal and informal institutions in one's neighborhood, and the entire world through such resources as the Internet (Owens & Wang, 1996).

While the principles of staff-development models provide a firm pedagogical foundation, each model requires somewhat different schedules and support arrangements. Each model should be somewhat responsive to the needs and challenges of different teachers, schools, and school systems.

SUMMARY

Curriculum planning is the specification and sequencing of major decisions to be made in the future with regard to the curriculum. Some general planning processes are useful in all curriculum work. A goal-based model of curriculum planning provides organizing strategies to determine the locus of control in decision making and what organizational structures are needed and enables a targeted allocation of functions to staff. Curriculum planning provides a district with the opportunity to identify and allocate leadership functions and align goals with curricular fields. Curriculum planning also entails organizing, evaluating, changing, and providing curriculum resources as an integrated process. Long-range curriculum planning combined with strong leadership, a shared vision, and a successful staff development model can be a powerful tool to support student learning and increase staff productivity. It remains, therefore, vitally important that educational leaders realize the importance of implementing and enforcing a successful curriculum plan. By doing so, our future educational leaders will help ensure that all teachers will be able to teach and that all students will be able to learn.

APPLICATIONS

1. In the school district about which you are most knowledgeable, would you recommend a separate community advisory council, rather than appointing representatives to a general council? Explain the reasons behind your decision to set up a separate council or to appoint a general one.

2. In the school district you know best, how would you balance the need for school autonomy? Use the questions in Exhibit 5.2 as guidelines for resolving this issue.

3. How would you allocate leadership functions in that same district? Use the form shown in Exhibit 5.3 to answer this question, indicating how you think functions should be allocated.

4. Develop a planning calendar you would use in a district you know well. Use the form shown in Exhibit 5.5.

5. Some experts in the field have recommended a more complex needs-assessment model, one that would make extensive use of such measures and processes as parent interviews, community surveys, student interviews, and futures forecasting techniques. If you were in a district leadership position, would you recommend using one of these more complex processes instead of the more sharply focused model described here? Justify your answer.

6. Superintendent Goodloe-Johnson praised the Seattle School Board for adopting arithmetic textbooks and lesson plans to be used for all students through eighth grade (Blanchard, 2007). However, this move was controversial in a district where schools operated independently for years. Why is it important to have a standard curriculum to improve the district's lagging math test scores?

CASE STUDY Involving Community Leaders

A Kentucky school district superintendent appoints David Smith, local businessman, to the district's curriculum committee. The businessman is viewed as an influential person who can get things done in the community—an individual who is called a "mover and shaker."

"Thanks for being able to attend our meeting, Mr. Smith," says Principal Powers.

"Glad to be here. What are some things you want to do with the curriculum?" he asks.

"Well, we were just discussing some options—but the concern is that a number of committee members don't have a good understanding of what is needed. That means that we should develop an extensive needs-assessment component as well as draft some surveys as part of the process."

"I understand," says the businessman. "Education is changing pretty rapidly these days. I happen to be on the boards of several banks here in town—perhaps I can bring a business as well as community perspective to some of the questions on some of the needs-assessment surveys."

"That would be great!" says the superintendent enthusiastically.

Principal Powers can feel the excitement in the room. "We really appreciate your help, Mr. Smith," he says, smiling. "We want to involve the community in our decision-making process. I'll talk to the superintendent and begin setting up a meeting and check on surveys as soon as possible. This will make it a lot easier for the committee to have a better understanding of how our community feels about the school and about our curriculum."

The Challenge

Reaching out to the community and developing a school-to-community connection is becoming a vital component of the curriculum-planning process. What are some possible criteria that Principal Powers can use to select other community members who are similar to Mr. Smith and who can lend their expertise to his school?

Key Issues/Questions

1. In planning curricula, most administrators agree that determining the locus of planning is crucial. To what extent should Principal Powers involve community member David Smith?

2. Do you think the decision to involve businessman David Smith in the curriculum-planning process should have been made by the district superintendent? Why or why not?

3. What are some other strategies that the district superintendent and/or Principal Powers can use to involve more community members in the curriculum-planning process?

4. Do you think there might have been any resistance from staff or teachers unions in having community members like David Smith on the curriculum committee? Why or why not?

5. How might a businessman like David Smith help in developing a curriculum planning calendar?

6. What roles might David Smith play in organizing, evaluating, and providing resources for curriculum programs?

WEBLIOGRAPHY

Curriculum planning resource for administrators and teachers

http://teacher.pathfinder.org/School/school.html

Parent Institute

www.parentinstitute.com

Quia online educational plans, activities, and Web-based workbooks and textbooks

www.quia.com

Southwest Educational Development Laboratory

www.sedl.org

CHAPTER 6

Improving the Program of Studies

$\mathbf{A}$s explained in previous chapters, the program of studies is the total set of organized learning experiences at a given level of schooling—all the courses offered at the elementary, middle, or high school level. From time to time, it is useful for educational leaders to implement a systematic process to assess and to improve the program of studies offered at one or more of these levels. This chapter suggests such a process, after reviewing some recent attempts to reconceptualize programs of study. It should be noted here that the chapter focuses on improving an existing program, rather than developing a completely new program, because few educators have the opportunity to develop new programs of study.

Questions addressed in this chapter include the following:

- What basic attempts have been made in the past to reconceptualize programs of study?
- What can current curriculum leaders do to best improve programs of study?

Key to Leadership

Successful curriculum leaders know that improving school studies should involve the interaction of teachers, students, and instructional materials with an integrated knowledge base.

RECONCEPTUALIZING PROGRAMS OF STUDY

Before discussing the assessment and improvement strategies, it might be useful to examine briefly some widespread attempts to reconceptualize schools' programs of study. Those attempts have mostly been motivated by dissatisfaction with the discipline-based curriculum, which uses the standard disciplines as the fields or organizing centers of learning.

It is therefore important to build a diverse intellectual climate within the school. Giving teachers opportunities to engage in intellectual discussions not immediately related to their teaching can have surprising benefits that translate directly into the classroom (Bunting, 2007).

In reviewing the literature there are those who argue that the traditional disciplines, such as science and mathematics, are rigid boxes that fragment knowledge unduly (see Cawelti [1982] for a statement of this position). As a consequence, there have been several attempts to break away from the standard academic disciplines as ways of organizing knowledge. Such attempts have a long history. In fact, one of the byproducts of the progressive era was widespread interest in developing a curricular mode that transcended or ignored the traditional disciplines. One of the most pervasive models of this period was the **core curriculum movement**, which flourished in the 1940s and still persists as a curricular model for many middle schools. In one widely disseminated model of the core curriculum, ninth-grade student would have two periods a day of learning experiences related to personal interests, three periods a day of "common learnings" (one continuous course that would help students develop life competencies), and one period of health and physical education (Educational Policies Commission, 1952). The organizing center of the common-learnings course was not the disciplines, but the needs of youth.

Some of the basic principles of the core curriculum still influence current attempts to reconceptualize the curriculum. While there are many possible ways of categorizing those attempts, most can be classified as attempts either to develop interdisciplinary courses or to achieve a total restructuring of the program of studies.

Interdisciplinary Courses

Interdisciplinary courses are courses of study that either integrate content from two or more disciplines (such as English and social studies) or ignore the disciplines totally when organizing learning experiences. According to author Rick Wormeli (2005), students enjoy the variety, creativity, and structure and teachers enjoy their students' diverse and substantive responses. Integrated approaches often take the form of "humanities" courses that include content from literature, history, art, and music. Such humanities courses can be organized in terms of cultural epochs (The Renaissance), area studies (American Studies), ethnic identity (The Black Experience), or themes (The Utopian Vision). While such courses include material from several disciplines, there is still a strong sense of the disciplines' informing the decisions about content and sequence. At the elementary level, while not concerned with "humanities courses," innovative teachers have always developed interdisciplinary units, such as Our Animal Friends, that draw from such subject areas as language arts, social studies, science, and art.

Courses or units that ignore or transcend the disciplines are almost always thematically structured. Thus, a team of teachers might develop a course called The Nature of Conflict, which would embody concepts from literature, biology, anthropology, philosophy, and psychology. The planning focuses on key concepts and skills, with no regard for their disciplinary sources. Or an elementary team might cooperatively develop an integrated unit called Families First, which would integrate content from social studies, reading, and language arts. In reality, interdisciplinary courses usually begin when one or two people get a good idea and then seek the appropriate ways and means to carry it out.

Interdisciplinary courses of both types can be offered either as a substitute for the standard required courses ("take American Studies instead of junior English and American history") or as enrichment electives ("take our new humanities course in addition to junior English and American history").

The research on interdisciplinary courses has been neither extensive nor deep. However, the few well-designed studies available suggest that such interdisciplinary courses are as effective as the standard courses in teaching basic skills.

Restructured Programs of Study

Reformers who have been critical of the standard discipline-based curriculum have expressed impatience with modest attempts to reform it by adding interdisciplinary courses. They have advocated instead a total restructuring of the curriculum, arguing that only a completely fresh reconceptualization can bring about meaningful change. Historically, such an advocate is Mortimer Adler (1982), creator of the *Paideia* proposal, recommended that the school curriculum be perceived as "three columns of learning"—column one, the acquisition of organized knowledge (language, literature, fine arts, mathematics, natural science, history, geography, and social studies); column two, the development of intellectual skills (reading, writing, speaking, listening, calculating, problem solving, observing, measuring, estimating, and exercising critical judgment); and column three, the enlarged understanding of ideas and values (through discussion of books and other works of art and involvement in artistic activities).

Despite the attractiveness of such proposals, most educators believe that the disciplines will persist. One reason for such persistence, of course, is the force of tradition: Curricula have been discipline based for several hundred years, and such time-honored educational traditions are difficult to change. There are the practical arguments: Teachers are trained and certified in the disciplines, and textbooks are written for the disciplines. With the implementation of the No Child Left Behind Act (NCLB), those who advocate continuing the emphasis on the disciplines gained national support. NCLB emphasizes the use of "highly qualified teachers" in each school and requires "new teachers" to have full state certification, a bachelor's degree, and have taken a state test. In lieu of the state test, middle school and high school teachers can meet the requirement by having a major or a graduate degree in the content area. For experienced teachers, NCLB again requires the three basic parts for meeting the criteria of a "highly qualified teacher" with the option of substituting subject-specific requirements for the state test. School districts will be very cautious in their hiring practices because poor results in the standardized tests will require more and more accountability by schools. Districts who hire teachers outside their major field of study would be hard pressed to explain to the constituents why their children were not given a highly qualified teacher, as NCLB defines it. This trend will keep the disciplines as the driving force for programs of study.

Finally, there is an intellectual basis for continuing discipline-based curricula. As several writers have pointed out, each discipline has its own special way of knowing its own syntax of inquiry; consequently, they assert, attempts to ignore the disciplines might produce students who do not know how to think mathematically or artistically.

According to Douglas Reeves (2006–2007), founder of the Center for Performance Assessment, there is a series of steps that are needed to accommodate change and yet be able to preserve what works. *First*, one has to define what you will not change. Effective change leaders identify and build on traditions rather than compete with them. *Second*, recognize the importance of actions. To lead challenging reform efforts, you must be willing to make personal changes in decision-making policies. *Third*, use the right change tools for your school or district. Leaders must choose the appropriate change tools on the basis of a combination of factors, including the extent to which staff members agree on what they want and how to get there. *Fourth*, be willing to do whatever it takes to make change happen and yet be able to value what has worked traditionally.

IMPROVING THE PROGRAM OF STUDIES

While it is unlikely that there will be widespread interest in these total reconceptualizations, there is a continuing concern for improving the program of studies. Some of that concern results from external pressures. Accrediting bodies, such as the Middle States Association of Secondary Schools, are scheduled to conduct an evaluation. The federal government, under the auspices of NCLB and state departments of education, continues to issue new requirements for all schools. Local school boards decide to increase graduation requirements, or the superintendent asks each principal to determine where reductions in the instructional budget might be made with the least damage to the educational program. In a sense, all these mandates are external demands for assessing and improving the program of studies. While such externally mandated reviews are useful and necessary, they are no substitute for an internally motivated assessment that responds to the special concerns of those directly involved with that school— its administrators and faculty. This section, therefore, explains a process that a school district can use on a systematic basis to assess and improve the program of studies in its schools.

Improving Low-Performing Schools

Many schools are facing major challenges in making school-improvement changes as mandated by such programs as the NCLB. According to University of Montana research professor Conrad W. Snyder (2004), this situation is particularly a problem for many schools trying to achieve AYP (annual yearly progress) per NCLB regulations. Low-performing schools with a large number of nonproficient and novice students are now facing several formidable tasks: to change and improve their curriculum process, streamline their political institutions, and reform their education systems. Schooling, in these settings, is often dominated by memorization and lecture. In addition, educators are confronting serious problems such as low salaries, uncomfortable or unsuitable classroom conditions, lack of books, apathetic teachers, and disinterested students. All too often, students only memorize, without having to think and develop knowledge on their own.

Curriculum Tip 6.1	Two major factors for school improvement are cooperation and buy-in of state and local educational agencies and the development of some type of specialized district curriculum planning team.

For any project involving curriculum improvement to succeed, several factors need to be addressed. One is the cooperation of state and local educational agencies as we have seen in the case of NCLB and, most recently, Response to Intervention (RTI). Another is the development of some type of specialized district curriculum team that is dedicated to combining the best of the school's current curriculum with enhancements based on modern approaches to knowledge development, curriculum design, and teacher education. The development of a **Curriculum Development Team** (CDT) is an example of how some school districts are helping to improve the program of studies.

A model CDT is often made up of approximately six CDT members who are highly interested in helping schools to improve curricular programs. If the model is to be successful, team members selected must be creative, innovative, contemporary, and visionary. All participants on the team should have prior experience in teaching and in writing instructional materials. School districts can recruit a combination of specialists and educators as well as a member of the community for this important committee.

A major purpose of the CDT is to provide briefings on the status of curriculum within the district. It is best if these briefings and meetings are held with organizations working in the education arena, the state educational agency, teachers, students, and so forth. Members of the CDT can then visit various schools and begin the process of assessing all relevant documents.

An early goal of any curriculum team is to visit selected schools, interview teachers and students, and review materials. This is necessary to conduct preliminary needs assessments. Schools selected for participation in the CDT process should have a means of providing data collection and Internet accessibility. Having access to digitized survey data will be important when noting differences between teaching methods, student involvement, and the like, at schools where only traditional teaching methods are utilized. It is best if CDT members are linked via interactive Internet connections to maintain communication throughout the process.

After data have been collected and analyzed by the CDT, the role of the committee is to select specific topics or subtopics for which curriculum materials and accompanying units in the teacher's manual can be developed or enhanced. The CDT then has the ability to send different examples of textbooks, supplemental materials, visual aids, curriculum guides, teacher's manuals, video media, evaluation forms, and more to individual schools and to individual teachers.

Topics to be covered might include examples of other school curriculum, contemporary approaches to knowledge development, new approaches to curriculum design and development, evaluation and assessment, and educational leadership, as well as hands-on training in computers and Internet use and new technologies for classrooms. Interviews with students, teachers, and administrators can be arranged throughout the process. Meetings and interviews with specialists in state agencies and other educational organizations can be organized as well.

The process for developing a draft of curricular materials and a teacher's manual is primarily the responsibility of the committee. CDT members can meet with each selected school's principal and teacher(s) to review new concepts and programs to be introduced. They can also reaffirm CDT's readiness to provide support throughout the school year and emphasize its need for feedback, and they can reaffirm that CDT members will regularly visit the schools to talk with teachers and sit in on classes to view progress, reaction, interaction, receptivity, and so forth. Information collected and shared with participating schools and individuals is often invaluable. Intensive interactions among all members often lead to strong mentoring relationships and personal ties between the individual administrators and teachers. These ties can be sustained throughout the project, and into future years as well, assisted by communications via the Internet.

Common Findings at Low-Performing Schools

In many low-performing schools, especially in many large public urban schools, CDT committees are finding that the most common form of instruction is the development of declarative knowledge, facts, and concepts. Trained teachers and relevant curriculum materials serve as the key resources for knowledge development of this kind. Memorization is an enabling goal so that the information is useful in the development and application of procedural knowledge. Without effective teachers and materials, students have no external framework to structure the activities of their schooling experience, and given the wealth of information in textbooks and other learning materials, the most obvious way to learn facts is to memorize them through rote practice. This limits the development of procedural knowledge and devotes instruction to factual memory.

More effective methods, such as those labeled "elaboration," can be used to enhance memorization and help the student develop semantic or graphic representations of information so that more mental links enable efficient recall, or analogical thought. The links also help provide clues for application with knowledge already acquired at other times, thus increasing the complexity of the schemas that engage the world and laying the groundwork for the development of procedural knowledge. A trained teacher, a textbook, and other instructional materials can present declarative information in ways that aid the process of memorization and encourage application, but they can also assist in the development of dynamic knowledge.

Developing Dynamic Knowledge

Dynamic knowledge refers to metacognitive strategies, cognitive processes, thinking skills, and content-area procedural knowledge. In dynamic knowledge, curricula and teachers no longer serve solely as static knowledge options but assist in the development of a knowledge base that is student centered and enhances effective thinking on the part of the individual learner. Lessons are comprehensively planned and developed, and both the teacher and the materials become key resources in the instructional strategy menu to build the cognitive base for greater student understanding and application.

| **Curriculum Tip 6.2** | A goal of curriculum planning is to increase the knowledge and levels of understanding that students take from the instructional events embedded in learning and instructional materials. |

Developing Learner Interaction and Curriculum Integration

Improving school studies involves the interaction of teachers, students, and instructional materials with an integrated knowledge base, an extended understanding of that knowledge in the ability to use the knowledge meaningfully, and the proper development of attitudes, perceptions, and effective habits of cognition that enable complex reasoning and effective applications of that reasoning. These processes are embedded in declarative knowledge but enable the student to extend that base and operate successfully in an increasingly complex world where learning is a lifelong endeavor. The problem is that dynamic knowledge is often absent from education in low-performing schools. Many teachers require their students simply to repeat verbatim the lessons assigned. The key to effective thinking about problems of history, civics, and government (including law and constitutions) is the development of deep understanding, in terms of both declarative and procedural knowledge.

The goal is not to define intelligence in terms of the apprehension of truths or fact in these areas but to explicate instead the apprehension of truths in terms of intelligence. Under this type of approach, students develop the capacity to find and organize facts and to exploit them in application. Understanding, then, is more than mere knowledge.

Operationalizing Change and Reform

When curriculum questions are operationalized in an effective package, the roles of a teacher, textbook, and other instructional materials are changed from the articulated, comprehensive curriculum framework to an outline of possibilities. Both the teacher and the materials are more of a resource and reference book that lies in the background of the instructional program. Lecturing teachers and printed materials, by their very nature, provide linear presentations, and due to the inherent development limitations, both time and finance, they reflect the sequential perspective of one or a few people (and not that of the student). For this reason, a lot is not covered in textbooks and other materials that are part of a content area. A successful classroom can add the richness that is needed to build deeper understanding and encourage effective habits of the mind by including important and uncovered aspects as an intentional part of the instructional strategy.

The attention caused by Thomas L. Friedman's book *The World Is Flat* (2005) has intensified the thought for changing to a different education model for the 21st century. The changes that have been forecast by Ohio's career and technical educators and incorporated by the Miami Valley Career Technical Center (MVCTC) strategic planning unit include the New Three Rs—rigor, relevance, and relationship, as shown in Exhibit 6.1—that elevate the teaching and learning process.

Developing the Assessment Agenda

The first step is to develop the program of studies assessment agenda. District administrators, school administrators, key faculty members, and parent leaders should meet to discuss these issues:

- How often should program assessment be undertaken?
- Which program-assessment issues should be addressed?
- What levels of schooling should be examined?
- What resources are available?

These questions should be answered, of course, by weighing assessment priorities ("Are we most concerned with our middle school?"), by noting any forthcoming external reviews

EXHIBIT 6.1 The New Three Rs	
Application	*Definition*
Rigor	The definition of rigor is "complicatedness." In academic terms, rigor is where students are given the opportunity to display an in-depth mastery of exigent concepts using Bloom's higher order of thinking skills, namely analysis, synthesis, and evaluation. It is the quality of thinking, not the quantity that defines academic rigor. Therefore, merely adding extra assignments or asking questions that require simple recall answers is not academic rigor.
Relevance	Relevance and rigor should run parallel in learning. Relevance is where students apply the core knowledge, concepts, and skills to solve real-world problems. Contrarily, students may do well academically, but without relevance fail in the real world if their higher level thought processes were not developed.
Relationship	Relationship can be defined as interrelated. In the New Three Rs, relationship is the element that keeps students engaged in learning. Students who have developed a connection with a teacher are more engaged in school. Therefore, by providing social, and academic support, teachers can motivate students to make a stronger academic effort.

SOURCE: Adapted from "The Three Rs Redefined for a Flat World (The World Is Flat)," by J. A. Boggess, May 1, 2007, *Techniques*. Retrieved from http://goliath.ecnext.com/coms2/gi_0199-6694070/The-three-Rs-redefined-for.html

("When is the high school scheduled for its next accreditation visit?"), and by reflecting on the importance of program assessment ("How much time and effort should we really be putting into this process?").

One of the key components of the assessment agenda is the set of assessment issues. The five major issues that might be considered are listed briefly here and then discussed at length in the following sections:

1. Goal–curriculum alignment: To what extent does the program of studies reflect and respond to the school district's goals?

2. Curriculum correlation: To what extent do learning experiences in the various subjects correlate with each other at a given grade level?

3. Resource allocation: To what extent does the district's allocation of resources to the program of studies reflect district priorities and provide for equity of opportunity?

4. Learner needs: To what extent does the program of studies respond to present and future needs of the students?

5. Constituent satisfaction: To what extent are teachers, students, and parents satisfied with the program of studies?

The decisions about the assessment agenda can be formalized in a program-assessment calendar, such as the one shown in Exhibit 6.2.

EXHIBIT 6.2	Program-Assessment Calendar	
Year	Level	Assessment Issues
2009–2010	Middle schools	Goal–curriculum alignment; Resource allocation; Learner needs
2010–2011	Elementary schools	Goal–curriculum alignment; Resource allocation; Constituent satisfaction
2011–2012	High schools	Goal–curriculum alignment; Resource allocation; Curriculum correlation

Using Standards and Outcome Statements

Practically speaking, this approach involves turning content **standards and outcome statements** into question form and then designing assignments and assessments that evoke possible answers. Only by framing our teaching around valued questions and worthy performances can we overcome activity-based and coverage-oriented instruction and the resulting rote learning that produces formulaic answers and surface-level knowledge. The benefit of a modern curriculum development training model is that it serves as the core of the content coverage for topics while tending to uncover concerns. Reinterpreting textbook information within the same instructional objectives will add to instructional effectiveness by taking students into the realm of cognitive understanding. The curriculum materials and teacher's manual will help structure learning episodes that include both declarative and procedural knowledge and that enable students to think thoroughly and deeply about enduring and changing schemas. What is learned in the classroom will relate to life and enhance individual students' understanding of their world. Interactive learning and the incorporation of standards, outcome statements, and data-based forms of assessment will give students the ability to think for themselves and generate a better understanding of how what has been learned relates to their lives.

Aligning District Goals and the Curriculum

In the previous chapter, the process of aligning goals with specific fields of study was explained as a critical step in the goal-based planning model. This chapter suggests a slightly different procedure to use when the focus is on improving a program of studies.

The first step is to identify the school's curriculum goals—those educational goals to which the curriculum is expected to make a major contribution. As indicated in Chapter 5, too often educators assume that all educational goals are curriculum goals. Such an assumption ignores the fact that some goals might best be met through noncurricular means. Consider this goal, one found in many goal statements: *The student will develop a positive self-image.*

When teachers collaborate to find ways to improve instruction, they create a community of learners and leaders (Goldys, Kruft, & Subrizi, 2007). In general, the research suggests that self-image is chiefly affected by the expectations of others, such as peers, parents, and teachers, and by the role one chooses for oneself. Because the curriculum makes only a relatively minor contribution, this educational goal probably should not be identified as a curriculum goal.

One useful way of making such a determination is to survey the faculty, using a form such as the one shown in Exhibit 6.3. Rather than simply distributing and collecting the

---

EXHIBIT 6.3   Identification of Curriculum Goals

To the Faculty: Listed below are the educational goals of the school. In your opinion, to which of these educational goals should the school's curriculum make a major contribution? Write the letter *C* after each educational goal to which you think the curriculum should make a major contribution. We should note here that not all these educational goals necessarily have to be curriculum goals. Some goals, for example, might be achieved primarily through the extracurricular program, with the curriculum making only a minor contribution.

1. Develop a positive self-image.   _____

2. Value own ethnic identity and accept
   people of other ethnic groups.   _____

---

forms without discussion, it makes more sense to provide time at a faculty meeting for a general discussion of the issues, to let teachers meet in small groups for fuller discussion, and then to ask them to complete the survey after such analysis and reflection. After the surveys have been completed, the faculty should meet again to discuss the results in an attempt to achieve a consensus. In general, any educational goal that at least half the faculty believes should be met primarily through the curriculum should be considered a curriculum goal for the school.

The next step is to determine to what extent and in what subjects these curriculum goals are being met. The objective here is to develop a matrix that shows in graphic form each goal and the contributions of each subject, grade by grade.

Part of such a matrix is shown in Exhibit 6.4 to illustrate the format and content desired here. The curriculum goals are listed down the left-hand side. Across the top are the required subjects offered by the school (note that only required subjects are listed; because not all students take electives, the contributions of electives should not be assessed here). Each subject column is further subdivided into grade levels, because it is important to analyze grade-level progression. The entries note major curriculum units, which make a major contribution to each goal.

How can the data for this matrix best be obtained? Two ways are possible. One method is to do a goal analysis of the curriculum guides for all major subjects. A member of the leadership team can go through a guide systematically, entering in the matrix the titles of units that relate to a particular goal and listing any units that do not seem directly related to any of the goals. One drawback to this process is that the matrix reflects only what is in the written guides, not what is actually taught. For that reason, districts may

---

EXHIBIT 6.4   Curriculum Goals and Subject Contributions

Goal	Grade 4	Grade 5
Think critically and solve problems creatively	Solving personal problems	Solving school problems

prefer to build the matrix by surveying teachers. The form can be a simple one, with these directions:

> Listed above is a sample of our school's curriculum goals. Consider each goal. If you teach a unit of study that relates directly to or makes a major contribution to that goal, enter the title of the unit. Please keep in mind that we are trying to identify only major units of the curriculum that make major contributions; therefore, you should not note any incidental attention you give to this goal.

Because the objective is to get valid data from individual teachers, individuals should probably complete this survey without consultation or discussion with colleagues. Teachers working in groups often claim to be teaching a particular unit because they sense pressure from colleagues to be doing so.

The results collated in the matrix should then be reviewed by the leadership team, keeping these questions in mind:

- Is each curriculum goal adequately addressed in at least one of our required subjects? This question examines the basic goal–curriculum relationship to ensure that every goal is dealt with in at least one subject.

- Are complex curriculum goals reinforced appropriately in two or more subjects? This question is concerned with reinforcement across the curriculum. A complex goal, such as the development of critical thinking, should appear as a focus in several subject areas.

- Is each goal appropriately developed and reinforced from grade to grade? This question examines the developmental sequence from grade to grade to be sure that each goal is sufficiently reinforced.

- Are we avoiding unnecessary duplication and overlap from subject to subject and from grade to grade? This question focuses on the particular units to be sure that unnecessary duplication is avoided.

- Does each required subject seem to be making an adequate contribution to the curriculum goals of the school? This question focuses on a given subject and examines its contributions to all the goals.

The results of the alignment process can lead to several responses. One response is to reconsider the set of curriculum goals. If it turns out that a curriculum goal is not adequately treated in at least one of the required subjects, then perhaps that goal might better be assigned to some other aspect of the educational program, such as the activity program. A second response is to add a new required course or sequence of courses specifically designed to address a particular goal. Thus, if it appears that critical thinking is not sufficiently stressed in any of the subjects, a required course could be developed that students would have to take at some point in their program. The third response to a perceived deficiency—and perhaps the most effective—would be to determine with teachers in each department how they could develop new units in their courses that would specifically relate to goals not receiving adequate treatment.

Curriculum Tip 6.3	**Correlating curricula** is a process of aligning the contents of two or more subjects.

Correlating Curricula

Correlation of curriculum is most essential in schools with a departmentalized structure. An elementary teacher in a self-contained classroom is probably able to achieve whatever correlation is necessary without special intervention. In the same way, a group of teachers working closely together in an interdisciplinary team are probably able in their own way to effect the correlation they consider desirable. In departmentalized schools, however, teachers in each subject often go their own separate ways, so that what is taught in one subject has no relationship to what is taught in the rest of the program.

Some good reasons exist for a closely correlated curriculum, as long as the integrity of individual disciplines is not violated. Teachers in one subject can call upon and develop the skills students have learned in another discipline, without having to take the time to teach those skills themselves. So the chemistry teachers know that they can expect students to be able to handle quadratic equations. Important skills that transcend a given discipline, such as retrieving and evaluating information, can be reinforced from subject to subject without excessive repetition. The sense of isolation that seems endemic to departmentalized teaching can be reduced as teachers discuss their curricula and develop correlated units of study. Consequently, students begin to see more clearly how their learning is interrelated.

There are some obvious drawbacks, however, to excessive or misdirected correlation. In some cases, misdirected efforts to correlate can impose unduly restrictive constraints upon teachers. Consider, for example, the problems in trying to correlate American history and American literature. The period of the American Revolution is vitally important in American history, deserving intensive treatment from a historical perspective, but the literature of that period is considered by most experts to be insignificant as literature and merits only brief consideration. A second drawback is that some attempts to impose correlation can result in a situation in which one is perceived as a "service" subject that exists chiefly to serve the needs of other disciplines. English often suffers this fate: "That's the English teacher's job" is the common cry across the disciplines.

For these reasons, a problem-solving approach to correlation is emphasized, where school leaders work with classroom teachers in determining subject by subject how much correlation is needed. The process begins with a survey, using a form such as that shown in Exhibit 6.5. Notice that it first asks about five general sets of skills and concepts that seem to have applicability across the curriculum: library and study skills; reading skills other than basic comprehension; academic writing skills, such as summarizing an article; mathematics skills; and English grammar. The data from this section of the survey can be collated and shared with the faculty to help them determine how to proceed.

These data will usually indicate two sorts of problems in correlation. One problem occurs when one or more departments indicate that the curriculum requires the intensive development of one of the basic skills. Suppose it happens, for example, that several departments indicate that their students should know certain basic library skills. There are essentially three options available to administrators. One would be to develop a new course that would

EXHIBIT 6.5 Curriculum-Correlation Analysis

Department/Team

Directions: Our school has decided to undertake a study of curriculum correlation to determine what is taught in the various subjects that can be mutually reinforcing. Consider the subject that you teach, and answer the following questions based on your knowledge of your own subject.

1. What library/study skills do you think your students should have in order to perform more successfully in your subject?

    Grade 10 _____

    Grade 11 _____

    Grade 12 _____

2. What special reading skills (other than comprehension skills) do you think your students should have?

    Grade 10 _____

    Grade 11 _____

    Grade 12 _____

3. What academic writing skills do you think your students should have?

    Grade 10 _____

    Grade 11 _____

    Grade 12 _____

4. What mathematics skills do you think your students should have?

    Grade 10 _____

    Grade 11 _____

    Grade 12 _____

5. What knowledge of English grammar (parts of speech, parts of the sentence) do you think your students should have?

    Grade 10 _____

    Grade 11 _____

    Grade 12 _____

6. List below any units of study you presently teach that you think could profitably be correlated with units in other subjects, or any new units with a correlated approach that you might be interested in developing.

    Grade 10 _____

    Grade 11 _____

    Grade 12 _____

teach the required skills; such a new course would serve the needs of all departments. A second option would be to ask one department (in this case reading/language arts) to assume primary responsibility, with each department then adding its own special content. The third option would be to decide that each department should teach in its own way the library skills its students need. A fuller discussion of these options as they relate to academic writing and critical thinking is presented in Chapter 14.

In some cases, the problem is misalignment of content: The 9th-grade science curriculum requires a mathematics skill that the mathematics curriculum places in 10th grade. In such instances, the two departments should confer to determine which adjustment seems more feasible—to change the science curriculum so that the skill is not required until the later grade, or to change the mathematics curriculum so that the skill is taught in the earlier grade.

In the same manner, the responses to the last question, dealing with the possibilities of developing correlated units, can be shared with the appropriate departments or teams to see if such units might be cooperatively planned. It might happen, for example, that the mathematics teachers, learning about a unit in logical thinking taught by the English teachers, would suggest a correlated unit that would include an analysis of valid and invalid uses of statistics in reasoning.

Thus correlation is achieved through a problem-solving process of determining need, assessing the options, and making decisions that seem best for the students.

Analyzing Resources Allocated to Curricula

The third process for assessing and improving the program of studies is to analyze the resources allocated to the several curricula. The resource allocation analysis provides data relevant to these related issues:

- Does the school's allocation of resources reflect its educational priorities? The assumption here is that the manner in which resources are allocated should reflect the system's priorities.

- Does the school's allocation of resources seem adequate for achieving the outcomes desired? If certain important educational outcomes are desired, then those classes will need adequate time, appropriate staffing, and suitable class size.

- Does the allocation of resources seem to be cost-effective? This question essentially examines the relationship between the number of students served and the resources required to serve them.

- Is the allocation of resources equitable? This question is concerned with whether the needs of all students are being met in an equitable fashion. In too many instances, less able students receive less than their share.

The examples shown in Exhibit 6.6 illustrate the types of data that might be analyzed in answering those questions. Obviously, additional data could be included, such as classroom space, instructional costs, noninstructional costs, and overhead and indirect costs. However,

EXHIBIT 6.6	Analysis of Curriculum Resources				
Subject	Required or Elective	Enrollment	Number of Sections	Faculty Assigned	Minutes per Week
Art	Elective	250	14	1.0	80
Phys. Ed.	Required	1,500	50	6.0	120
Russian	Elective	36	3	0.6	200

that additional information would contribute only some refinements to the basic data presented in Exhibit 6.6 and therefore might be omitted without harm to the analysis.

A special note might be made about the importance of analyzing time allocations. The intrusion on classroom time and continuity of instruction cannot be underscored enough (Zellmer, Frontier, & Pheifer, 2006).

Several studies both old and new (see, e.g., Stallings, 1980) indicate quite clearly that the time allocated to a particular area of the curriculum is directly related to student achievement in that area. One useful standard for assessing time allocations has been provided by John Goodlad (2004). After reviewing the time allocations in the numerous schools he studied and assessing his own extensive experience in curriculum development, he concluded that the following allocations would be desirable for the three upper grades of elementary school:

- Language arts, 1.5 hours a day

- Mathematics, 1 hour a day

- Social studies, 2.5 hours a week

- Science, 2.5 hours a week

- Health and physical education, 2.5 hours a week

- Arts, 3.5 hours a week

In many states, of course, minimum time allocations are stated in the school code; where the district has some flexibility, however, allocations should be closely examined.

In examining those data in relationship to the questions noted above, the leadership team might decide that certain reallocations would strengthen the overall program. Such reallocations might take several forms: increasing or decreasing time allotments, increasing or decreasing section size, or increasing or decreasing the number of teachers assigned.

Curriculum Tip 6.4	In the current world of technology and education, data analysis is fast becoming one of the most important aspects of assessment and of improving programs of study.

Importance of Data Analysis in Assessment

When comparing groups, it's important to make sure the groups are comparable (Bracey, 2006). Victoria L. Bernhardt's book *Data Analysis for Comprehensive Schoolwide Improvement* (1998) helps school leaders learn how to deal with curricular data that will inform them of where they are, where they want to be, and how to get there. Her pioneering work reveals that data analysis is a major help in identifying and uncovering powerful curriculum solutions to some of our schools' biggest problems. Data analysis, however, has not always been well received in the study of school improvement. Some of the reasons that schools may not use data regularly include the following:

- Work culture does not focus on data.
- Gathering data is difficult and often perceived as a waste of time.
- Teachers are trained to be subject oriented, not data oriented.
- Data are often not used systematically.

Supporters of data analysis, however, note that data collection and analysis provide curriculum leaders with the power to make good decisions, work intelligently, work effectively and efficiently, change in better ways, understand the impact of hard work, help prepare for the future, and know how to make work benefit children. The collection of data can make a major difference in school reform by accomplishing the following tasks:

- Replacing hunches and hypotheses with facts concerning changes that are needed
- Identifying root causes of problems
- Assessing needs to target curriculum services and issues
- Determining if goals are accomplished

The key is that schools gather data correctly and use the data appropriately. According to Lynn Olson (2004), writer for *Education Week*, officials should inventory the data currently stored by their district, assess the quality of that information, and estimate the cost of correcting or "cleaning" the data. Schools also need to evaluate their data and analytical needs and must weigh how much outside or third-party help they require to set up the system, including inventorying the initial data, cleaning the data, merging data sets, and housing the data over time. Districts also need to consider how long it will take to get the system up and running, as well as its cost. Olson went on to state that schools and districts would be well advised to contact other schools using the software, query them thoroughly, and visit as many as possible to get practical feedback on the types of products and levels of services each vendor offers.

Assessing Learner Needs

One of the most important analyses of the program of studies involves the extent to which the curriculum seems to respond to both present and future needs of the learners. However, to argue for the importance of such an analysis is not to assert that learner needs must always be the primary determiner of curriculum. As explained in Chapter 3, other sources might be just as or more important, depending on the orientation of curriculum planners. Yet even curricula that have been influenced primarily by other sources should give some attention to present learner needs if they are to be successful in eliciting student interest. In addition, all curricular orientations seem to accept the importance of preparing students for the future, even though they construe that preparation differently.

If such an assessment is therefore important, it must be done carefully and conscientiously; it should not be perceived as a meaningless exercise undertaken just to satisfy administrators or some external group. The process should begin by involving the faculty in a systematic study that results in an explicit statement of present and future learner needs. How this is done will obviously vary with the local situation; however, the process explained below is one that should work well in most systems.

Begin by setting up a small task force or committee composed of one district administrator, one or more school administrators, and several key faculty members. Their first task should be to develop a tentative draft of present learner needs. Two points should be stressed about this needs analysis. First, it should focus on the developmental needs of the age group enrolled in that school, not on the needs of all children and youth. The assumption is that the district's goals speak to the broader needs of all students; the needs analysis is concerned solely with the age group served by that school. Second, it should be concerned primarily with those needs that might best be served through the curriculum, because the emphasis is on assessing the educational program, not other aspects of schooling.

The task force should use two general sources of information: publications and people. First, task force members should undertake a systematic examination of current publications dealing with that age group. For each age level—the children in elementary schools, the preadolescents, early adolescents in middle schools, and the youth in high schools—numerous sources synthesize the research on the psychological, physical, social, and intellectual needs of that population. The task force would be wiser, perhaps, to limit themselves to a careful study of a smaller number of the best sources (perhaps no more than five or six), rather than attempting a comprehensive survey. They should also use whatever expert advice they can get from both district personnel (such as school nurses, counselors, social workers, and psychologists) as well as from professionals in the community.

Their draft report might take the form of the one shown in Exhibit 6.7. This document synthesizes the most current and reliable information about middle-school learners. Observe that it first states the need and then suggests a curricular response.

Their second major task is to identify future needs of the learners. Here, the intent is not to play the role of futurist and attempt to develop elaborate scenarios; instead, the goal is to identify rather predictable features of the next 20 years that should influence the kind of education provided for today's students. Here a task force can turn to two types of documents for assistance. First, there were several commission reports written during early 2000 that both examined the present performance of schools and addressed specifically the issue of future curricular needs. Two that seem worth checking are the National Science Board report *U.S. Losing Ground in Science Education* (Ashton, 2004) and the Education Commission of the States (American Association of Colleges for Teacher Education [AACTE], 2004) study of the No Child Left Behind Act. Second, several reports are available that look more broadly at the issue of planning for the future. While some of these seem unduly speculative, one that seems especially worthwhile is the Secretary's Commission on Achieving Necessary Skills (SCANS) report (Northwest Mississippi Community College, 2004), which defines competencies.

EXHIBIT 6.7 Adolescent Needs and Curricular Responses	
The research suggests that young adolescents have these needs:	*The program of studies for young adolescents should provide the following to meet their needs:*
1. Understanding the physical changes occurring and the special nutritional needs that result	1. Health education units and science units emphasizing that these physical changes are normal and stressing the importance of good nutrition
2. Developing greater physical coordination in a nonthreatening environment	2. Physical education experiences that build coordination without overemphasizing competition
3. Increasing level of cognitive development, moving from semiformal to formal operations	3. Units in all appropriate subjects that include a mix of concrete and abstract learnings
4. Becoming more supplicated in their political reasoning	4. Units in social studies that help students examine complexities of current political issues
5. Increasing level of moral development	5. Units in social studies, science, and English that help students examine complex moral issues
6. Developing clear sense of personal identity	6. Units in English that explore issues of personal identity and self-awareness
7. Maintaining balance between growing sense of autonomy and continuing need for peer approval	7. Units in social studies that explore the nature of peer influence from a sociological perspective

Most recently the focus has been on federal mandates. According to Sally McConnell, (2007), National Association of Elementary School Principals associate executive director,

> As Federal mandates have increased in recent years, public schools have been hampered by the lack of resources to implement them. The reauthorization of the Elementary and Secondary Education Act (ESEA) should hopefully provide an opportunity to move away from the shortcomings of its present version, the No Child Left Behind Act. (p. 16)

Improving the Program of Studies

This section of the draft report might take the form shown in Exhibit 6.8. Again, a future development is indicated and then a curricular response is suggested. The draft report on present and future needs should then be analyzed and discussed by the faculty, meeting in small groups, with perhaps a member of the task force leading each group. Out of these discussions should emerge a final draft reflecting a faculty consensus. That process results in a final document that can then be used in assessing the programs of study. The process obviously is a time-consuming one, but the commitment of large amounts of time seems warranted. Not only will the faculty have produced a highly useful document, but teachers will also have had an opportunity to analyze and discuss some very critical issues.

EXHIBIT 6.8 The Future and the Curriculum	
The experts predict that the future will be marked by these developments:	*The curriculum should respond to future developments by offering the following:*
1. The world becomes a "global village."	1. Units in social studies and English that increase students' awareness of national interdependence; foreign language study made available to all students
2. New immigrant groups continue to arrive in this country in large numbers.	2. Units in English and social studies that emphasize our immigrant past and the contributions of immigrants
3. The information age arrives: a glut of information made available by computers.	3. Units in all appropriate subjects on information retrieval, evaluation, and application
4. Digital television becomes increasingly dominant as a medium of communication and entertainment.	4. Units in English that emphasize critical viewing
5. The family continues to change; more family instability, more one-parent families.	5. Units in social studies that put such changes in perspective
6. The technology continues to change, with the job market changing frequently and unpredictably.	6. Units in English and social studies that emphasize career-mobility skills, rather than examining particular careers

How can this document be used in assessing the program of studies? Two processes might be considered. The first is a mapping of what may be called the "needs-responsive curriculum"—those aspects of the curriculum that specifically respond to the needs that have been identified. A form similar to the one shown in Exhibit 6.9 should be distributed to departments or teams of teachers, who should meet in small groups to discuss the questions and respond to the survey. The results can then be reviewed by the leadership team to determine areas of strength and weakness.

It might be useful here to distinguish between the goal–curriculum alignment process and the mapping of the needs-responsive curriculum. Goals are usually very general statements that apply to all levels of schooling and are ordinarily produced at the state or district level.

EXHIBIT 6.9 The Needs-Responsive Curriculum	
Directions: The following curriculum characteristics have been suggested by our analysis of our students' present and future needs. Consider each characteristic. If you feel that the curriculum in your subject in some way reflects that characteristic, then indicate specifically how it does.	
Department: English language arts	
A needs-responsive curriculum should have these characteristics:	Our curriculum reflects these characteristics with the following guidelines:
1. Helps students develop a global perspective	1. Students read some contemporary literature written by European and Asian writers.

The goal–curriculum alignment process attempts to align larger curriculum entities, such as units of study, with these very general outcomes. The statement of needs is produced at the school level and focuses on the more specific needs of a given age level, and the mapping process seeks detailed evidence of how a given curriculum responds to those needs. Because the alignment and mapping processes are somewhat similar in approach, however, it might be desirable to use only one, not both, during a given assessment project.

The other process for assessing the needs-responsive curriculum takes an entirely different approach. Each homeroom or adviser/room teacher is asked to identify three students from that homeroom and conduct an in-depth interview with them to ascertain the students' perceptions of how well the program of studies responds to the needs identified. If the homeroom group is heterogeneous in abilities, the teacher should choose one student from each ability level. The interview might open with a statement of this sort:

> The teachers in our school have been thinking about students your age and the kinds of things they should be learning. We'd like to find out from some of our students how they feel about what they are learning. You've been selected because I think you have some good ideas about what you're studying. I'm going to read a statement about what our faculty believes you should be learning. I would then like you to answer in two ways. First, tell me if you agree that those things are important to learn. Then tell me in which subjects, if any, you are learning those things.

The teacher, of course, should caution students not to be critical of particular teachers, because the intent is not to evaluate teachers but to examine the program of studies.

Each teacher should then be asked to prepare a written summary of results of the interviews. Time should also be provided for small groups of homeroom advisers to meet together to discuss their findings. The written summaries should be reviewed by the leadership team to identify specific ways in which the program of studies does not seem sufficiently responsive to learner needs.

Both these processes will have identified certain needs-based deficiencies in the existing program of studies. The leadership team can then decide how to respond to those deficiencies. One response, obviously, is to determine that a particular need should not be addressed in the curriculum. Upon further reflection, the leaders might determine that a particular need can better be satisfied through some other educational means or through some other agency. The more likely response is to suggest to appropriate teams or departments that they spend more time deciding how they could make the curricula more responsive. Thus, if it is apparent that none of the school's courses is concerned with, for example, the need to develop a global perspective, several departments might be asked to examine how their curricula might be suitably modified. The social studies, English, music, art, and family and consumer science (formerly home economics) departments would need to be involved in this instance.

| **Curriculum Tip 6.5** | Curriculum leadership teams should be aware that instructional knowledge, not content knowledge, is a more frequent cause of instructional ineffectiveness. |

Assessing Constituent Satisfaction

The last assessment process involves measuring constituent satisfaction; *constituent* is used here as an umbrella term that includes students, teachers, and parents as constituents whom the curriculum serves. This is not to suggest that all groups need to be surveyed, especially at the elementary level. Measures of pupil perceptions tend not to yield valid results. Curriculum leaders might decide to survey all teachers, a stratified sample of 20% of the students, and all parents.

Ordinarily, the survey should focus on the entire program of studies, not on individual subjects or the instructional processes; a faculty committee should be charged with the responsibility of developing the specific items to be included. The items shown in Exhibit 6.10

EXHIBIT 6.10   Student Survey

To the Student: Below you will find several statements about the subjects you are studying this year. Consider each statement and decide how much you agree with it. Circle one of these responses to show how much you agree or disagree with that statement:

SA = strongly agree   D = disagree
A = agree   SD = strongly disagree
? = uncertain

Remember also to read the question at the end of this survey.

Statement		*Your Response*			
1. I am learning things that seem useful to me now.	SA	A	?	D	SD
2. I am learning things that will be helpful to me in the future.	SA	A	?	D	SD
3. I am learning things that seem interesting to me.	SA	A	?	D	SD
4. I think I should have a chance to take more electives.	SA	A	?	D	SD
5. The things I am studying seem much too difficult for me.	SA	A	?	D	SD
6. The courses I am taking make me think and develop my abilities.	SA	A	?	D	SD
7. The courses I am taking seem connected with each other; what I learn in one course ties in with what I learn in the other courses.	SA	A	?	D	SD
8. The bright students in our school have better courses than students who are not so bright.	SA	A	?	D	SD

Is there some course not offered by our school that you would like to see offered? If so, list it below. You may list more than one course if you wish.

_____   _____

_____   _____

_____   _____

_____   _____

suggest types of items that might make up the survey. Observe that the survey shown in Exhibit 6.10 attempts to assess satisfaction with several dimensions of the program of studies: present relevance, future value, interest, the required/elective balance, difficulty and challenge, subject correlation, and curricular equity. These seem to be the aspects where constituent satisfaction is most salient.

The results of these surveys require careful analysis before steps are taken to improve the program of studies, and the leadership team should examine the data with these questions in mind:

- Do major discrepancies exist in the extent to which teachers, parents, and students seem satisfied with the program of studies? If so, what do those discrepancies mean?

- Where general dissatisfaction is expressed with some dimension of the program of studies, what changes might best be made?

It should be stressed here that constituent satisfaction is only one standard by which a program of studies should be assessed. The leadership team and the faculty should use one or more of the measures discussed above to supplement this particular analysis.

Taken together, then, these five assessment processes—developing the assessment agenda, aligning district goals and the curriculum, analyzing resources allocated to curricula, assessing learner needs, and assessing constituent satisfaction—can yield some highly useful data that the leadership team and the faculty can use in improving the program of studies.

SUMMARY

Educational leaders periodically need to implement a systematic process to assess and to improve each program of studies. The process usually involves improving an existing program rather than investing in developing new programs of study. Value is gained from examining past attempts to reconceptualize programs of study. Curriculum leaders can improve existing programs of study by developing an assessment agenda, aligning district goals and the curriculum, correlating curricula, analyzing resources allocated to curricula, and finally assessing constituent satisfaction.

APPLICATIONS

1. Compare a process from this chapter with a process recommended by one of the accrediting bodies. What do you perceive to be the advantages and disadvantages of each? List at least two advantages and two disadvantages. What local factors might affect the one you would recommend to a school district?

2. Some argue that speculating about the future is a futile pursuit, because the future is so unpredictable. Many also point out that if we teach students how to think, how to communicate, how to read, and how to solve problems, there is no need to worry about the future. How would you respond to such arguments? What are some specific recommendations you would give curriculum leaders when speculating about future educational events?

3. Try your hand at reconceptualizing the curriculum. Choose a level of schooling you know best (elementary, middle, high). Identify the way you would organize learning (using some of the disciplines, if you wish), and indicate what percentage of time would be devoted to each broad field.

4. Develop a detailed program-assessment calendar for a school that you know. Include the following: the program-assessment issues to be analyzed, the individuals primarily responsible, and the dates by which the final assessments should be made.

5. As you look at the future and the curriculum, what developments would you add to the items in Exhibit 6.8, and how should the curriculum respond?

6. Regarding the student survey in Exhibit 6.10, what can be learned from the responses by the students?

CASE STUDY   Mapping Out New Ways to Improve Programs

A Pennsylvania principal talks to her fifth-grade teacher–leader about ways to teach difficult material that will help improve student achievement.

"Ron, I know that you use a lot of high-level math curriculum in your classroom, and your student test scores are always high. Is there a way we can use some of your strategies with other fifth-grade teachers?" asks Susan Neal, principal of Cecilia Hazelton Intermediate School. "I had a few of the other fifth-grade teachers in my office, and they are very upset about the standards and what is expected. They think the material is too difficult. As you know, many of our students are far below the math proficiency standard set by the state. I sure hope that you can help me with this problem."

"I'll be glad to help," says Ron. "I'm in the process of meeting with our fifth-grade teaching team this afternoon. I know that they're concerned, but I can share what I'm doing with a Web-based curriculum-mapping project that improves students' scores in the area of Number Sense and Operations. The teachers have been pretty frustrated with student test results in that area. For example, our textbooks emphasize 'Standard Estimation,' while the test items call for 'Front End Estimation.'"

"That sounds like just what we need," notes Principal Neal. "I'm sure that the teachers will respond better to your suggestions rather than just hearing from me all the time."

The Challenge

Utilizing Web-based curriculum mapping for each grade level as a way to improve programs of studies is becoming an important component of the school curriculum. Analyze this process and propose other strategies that Principal Neal could use to get more teachers involved.

Key Issues/Questions

1. Judging from your own experience, how do you feel about Ron's classroom Web-based curriculum-mapping project being used to help develop interdisciplinary courses?

2. Restructuring curriculum may involve a great deal of resistance. What types of problems might Principal Neal experience when she proposes that all teachers should be using Web-based curriculum mapping?

3. What are some ways that Principal Neal can use technology and Web-based curriculum mapping to enhance program assessment?

4. How do you think the parents of Cecilia Hazelton Intermediate School might react to their children using Web-based information? How might Principal Neal deal with this safety concern?

5. How can Principal Neal use Ron's Web-based curriculum-mapping approach to help develop and assess constituent satisfaction of her school?

WEBLIOGRAPHY

Annenberg Media—Free video course and workshops for teachers
www.learner.org

Educational Research Service—Instructional strategies
www.ers.org

Teachers.net—Teaching strategies and lesson plans
www.teachers.net

Trilemma Solutions educational consulting—Information on teacher improvement
www.trilemmasolutions.com

CHAPTER 7

Improving a Field of Study

Whena school district decides to improve a field of study, it usually is concerned with strengthening one subject area, such as English language arts, across several grade levels. Such a decision typically emerges from an awareness of a deficiency: Poor articulation exists between the various levels of schooling, teachers are no longer using existing guides, or the present curriculum has become outdated. This chapter describes a process for effecting such improvements, after noting some attempts to reconceptualize fields of study.

Questions addressed in this chapter include the following:

- What basic attempts have been made in the past to reconceptualize fields of study?
- What can current curriculum leaders do to best improve fields of study?

Key to Leadership

School district leaders need and deserve accurate measures that align with standards and produce timely results.

RECONCEPTUALIZING FIELDS OF STUDY

Whereas attempts to reconceptualize programs of study usually are concerned with proposals for minimizing the rigid demarcations between the disciplines, those involving fields of study ordinarily focus on eliminating the rigidity imposed by graded curricula. Curriculum leaders have long contended that what schools teach must reflect the needs of society, the needs of the learner, and the recommendations of scholars in various academic fields (Cawelti, 2006).

Proponents of reconceptualization of programs of study argue that curricula organized by grade level (Grade 10 English, Grade 6 mathematics) militate against individualization and result in "batch processing" that ignores individual differences. They argue for curricula that are not bound to grade levels but that are instead mapped for individual progress. According to Heidi Jacobs (2004), curriculum mapping addresses some of the most critical questions for any teacher work team:

- Who is doing what?

- How does our work align with our goals?

- Are we operating efficiently and effectively?

Curriculum mapping is thus an invaluable tool that can be used to help teachers and students cross imposed grade levels and reach students at their levels of interest.

The idea of minimizing the importance of grade levels in designing curricula is not new, of course. As early as 1919, Carleton Washburne, working in the Winnetka (Illinois) schools, developed an individualized program that emphasized self-paced progress. The pupils worked as long as they needed on self-instructional and self-correcting materials, progressing to subsequent units on the basis of teacher-administered tests (see Washburne & Marland [1963] for a fuller discussion).

While several current models for a nongraded curriculum are available, most seem to be varieties of two basic ones: the diagnostic–prescriptive model and the elective model.

Diagnostic–Prescriptive Models

Diagnostic–prescriptive models of the curriculum begin by structuring the field of study as a series of sequential nongraded levels of learning. These models may or may not use differentiated instruction.

According to Rick Wormeli (2006),

> Differentiated instruction is a collection of best practices strategically employed to maximize students' learning at every turn, including giving them the tools to handle anything that is undifferentiated. It requires teachers to do different things for different students, some, or a lot, of the time in order for them to learn when the general classroom approach does not meet student needs. It is not individualized instruction, though that may happen from time to time as warranted. It's whatever works to advance the students. It's highly effective teaching. (p. 3)

The diagnostic–prescriptive approach, therefore, can be labeled as an approach to instruction of students on an individual basis, with attention to strengths or weaknesses, followed by teaching prescriptives to remediate the weaknesses and develop strengths. This approach complements and is often used with the Response to Intervention (RTI) model (Bender & Shores, 2007).

Thus, elementary mathematics might be organized into 18 levels instead of six grades. Each level, in turn, comprises several sequential modules or units. Thus, in Level 3 mathematics, 16 modules might be arranged in a developmental sequence so that Module 2 builds on Module 1 and leads to Module 3. The curriculum is thus conceptualized as a linear series of tightly sequenced learning experiences, ordered without respect to grade level. The student moves through this linear sequence at an individualized pace. The teacher diagnoses the student's present level of achievement, prescribes the appropriate placement ("begin with Module 4, Level 3"), and monitors the student's progress through a series of formative and summative tests. When determining the performance of a student, a school, or an entire school district, multiple measures of assessment are used to provide more accountability and clarity than performance on any single test can provide (Guilfoyle, 2006).

How effective are the diagnostic–prescriptive models? The answer is difficult to determine, because it is almost impossible to sort out the effects of the curricular structure itself from those of the instructional system. However, studies by Jim Ysseldyke and Steven P. Tardrew (2003) show implementing a computer-based math management system with a school's existing curriculum improved scores in a short time. The difference in gains in just one semester for students in Grades 3–10 ranged from 7 percentile points in Grade 6 to 14 percentile points in Grades 3 and 5.

Elective Models

Elective models are quite different in concept from diagnostic–prescriptive models. Whereas developers of diagnostic prescriptive models conceptualize the curriculum as a linearly ordered sequence, those advocating elective models view the curriculum as a multipath network It is believed that the more aware teachers become of their capacity to drive change, the more likely it is that deep change will occur (Reason & Reason, 2007). The contrast is illustrated in Exhibit 7.1. The elective curriculum is usually delivered as an array of mini-courses typically lasting 6, 9, 12, or 18 weeks (see Oliver, 1978, for a useful description of the various elective options). Because those mini-courses usually are offered to students from several grade levels, they achieve nongrading in their own way.

EXHIBIT 7.1   Individualized and Elective Systems Contrasted

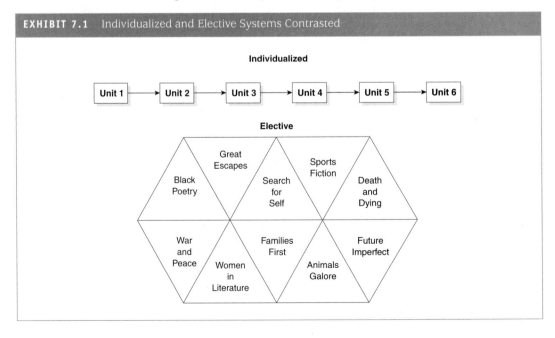

The content of a given elective course is usually determined by an individual teacher or a team of teachers who draw on their own special interests and perceptions of student interest. Thus, an English department might offer electives with titles such as the following:

The Black Experience

Hispanic Literature

The Dialects of the South

Conflict: Literature of Battle

Looking at Television With a Critical Eye

Communicating With Computers

Utopias, Real and Imagined

The historical review of research on the effectiveness of the elective model is even less conclusive than assessing the diagnostic–prescriptive models. Although several writers have blamed the elective program for the "educational crisis" of the early 1980s, no hard evidence supports such a conclusion (see Copperman [1978] for one such attack). In fact, only a handful of studies have even attempted to assess electives systematically. Hillocks's (1972) study of English electives is one of those few. After reviewing more than 100 such programs, he concluded on a rather optimistic note:

> Given the time to study, plan, and evaluate their work, English teachers, with their newly awakened sense of professional dignity, may manage to revolutionize the teaching of English. . . . For that reason alone, elective programs will have been worth the effort. (p. 123)

While most objective observers tend to agree that electives were often poorly designed, the issue of whether well-designed programs could be as effective as the standard curriculum must still be considered unresolved.

What of the future of diagnostic–prescriptive and elective models? First, the diagnostic–prescriptive model has been enhanced in the past few years, mainly because of the extensive use of technology in the classroom. Technology integration facilitates diagnosis, prescription, and assessment. Therefore, computer-based programs help the teacher modify curriculum for each student's individual needs. An example of this is Accelerated Math by Renaissance Learning. Implementation of Accelerated Math resulted in improved performance for students at multiple points on the ability/disability spectrum. Accelerated Math has a significant effect in all respects for students who are gifted and talented, low achieving, English-language learners, and for students in the Title I programs (Ysseldyke & Tardrew, 2003). The elective model at this time seems to have been a short-lived fad; its openness and lack of structure are considered suspect by those concerned with standards and rigor. Most leaders in the field seem to take for granted that the graded curriculum will persist because it is so deeply entrenched in the ways in which schools are organized, teachers are assigned, students are grouped, and materials are written. However, the process described below for improving the field of study can be applied in a way that will permit nongrading, if local administrators and teachers decide that such an option is desirable.

IMPROVING THE FIELD OF STUDY

The process described below is a teacher-centered process that relies on teacher input; a rationale for such an approach is presented in the next section. It is only one of many ways that a field of study might be improved; however, it has been used successfully by several school districts and seems to achieve the results desired without requiring excessive time or money. The phases in the process include the following:

1. Establish project parameters.
2. Orient for mastery.
3. Map the desired curriculum.
4. Refine the map.
5. Develop curriculum materials.
6. Suggest time allocations.
7. Select and develop tests.
8. Select instructional materials.
9. Provide for staff development.

Each of these steps will be explained in detail in the sections following the rationale. Although the English language arts curriculum is used for most of the examples, the process has worked equally well with several other fields of study.

Curriculum Tip 7.1	Teacher-centered planning should reflect the formal, perceived, or operational curriculum.

A RATIONALE FOR A TEACHER-CENTERED PROCESS

A great unfinished task in U.S. education is to create conditions to better support teachers. It is not enough to just pay teachers more; the conditions have to be in place to give them a chance to succeed (Darling-Hammond & Berry, 2006). This concept is not new. Teachers have been long viewed as the key. This teacher-centered process has been developed as a solution to a problem and was perhaps first identified by Goodlad (1977). As discussed in Chapter 1, his studies of school curricula indicate that there are in fact five different curricula that exist almost as separate entities: the *ideal* curriculum (in this work termed the **recommended curriculum**), that set of recommendations proposed by the scholars and experts in the field; the formal curriculum (identified in this work as the **written curriculum**), the curriculum embodied in the school district's curriculum guides; the perceived curriculum (in this work called the **taught curriculum**), the curriculum that the teachers believe they are teaching; the **operational curriculum**, which an observer would observe; and the experiential curriculum (in this work called the **learned curriculum**), the curriculum that students are learning.

According to Goodlad, the ideal curriculum rarely influences either the written or the taught curriculum: The written curriculum often is completely ignored by the classroom teacher, the teacher and an observer do not agree as to what the teacher actually taught, and students do not learn all that the teacher attempts to teach. His conclusions have been supported by several subsequent studies focusing on the teacher as curriculum maker (see, e.g., Cusick, 1983). Those studies present this general picture: Classroom teachers (especially secondary teachers) in making decisions about what to teach rely primarily on their knowledge of the subject, their teaching experience, and their perceptions of their students, giving only cursory attention to the district curriculum guide. In studies by Homan (as cited in Schmidt, 2004) of fifth graders and high school algebra students, teachers who were engaged in curriculum planning had strong classroom-management skills and were able to teach the curriculum they planned with specific teaching strategies produced the highest achievement among their students.

A process is needed that will at least bring the recommended, the written, and the taught curricula into closer alignment. The recommended curriculum should not be ignored: What teachers teach should reflect the best current knowledge about that subject, tempered by the realities of the classroom. Moreover, the written and the taught curricula should be more congruent. Each teacher doing what he or she wants to do can result in curricular anarchy.

The process described below attempts to accomplish these objectives. It begins with the teachers' determining what they think should be taught. It reviews their decisions in light of the best current knowledge, and it produces written guides that reflect that synthesis of the recommended and the taught. Observe that this improvement process, therefore, is not concerned primarily with improving the written materials; it is concerned with the much larger issue of improving teaching and learning in that field throughout the district. When discussing curriculum that is recommended, written, and taught, it is best perhaps to view the process of improving curriculum as a series of steps.

Curriculum Tip 7.2	Curriculum plans are often set up as content matrices, and the lessons or units are described in terms of key content.

According to University of Montana research professor Conrad W. Snyder (2004), the first step in determining the development of a desirable curriculum for schools entails identifying and specifying understanding that is enduring and needed and what is important to know and what would be good to be familiar with (for students to encounter). This information may already exist in the curriculum created by a state educational agency or local school district, but it needs to be checked for comprehensiveness and expansiveness. Four criteria are often used to sort content listings and begin the development of generative questions around which the instructional events of materials can operate:

1. To what extent does the idea, topic, or process represent a big idea that has enduring value beyond the classroom in everyday life and reality?
2. To what extent does the idea, topic, or process reside at the heart of the discipline?
3. To what extent does the idea, topic, or process require coverage through other instructional events in the classroom, extending the textbook?
4. To what extent does the idea, topic, or process offer potential for engaging students, keeping their attention, and encouraging their interest in the topic?

In the second step, it is important to develop each unit framed around the enduring understandings and essential questions. Once a unit is established, then the question to ask is, What evidence exists to accept this as an understanding? The design criteria or filters at this point for the assessments are (a) validity, (b) reliability, (c) sufficiency, (d) authenticity, (e) feasibility, and (f) friendliness. These criteria are instructional events, with the difference that the student produces all the required responses in order to diagnose or check the status of the student in the areas of importance. Standard measurement criteria apply, but we make allowances because the effects are only remediation, which probably doesn't hurt as continuing thoughtful practice. The better the evidence, however, the better the decisions made for instructional strategies. Quality of measurement is an essential feature of quality instruction.

It is here that one should introduce technology to enhance the process, enable continuous connection among the educational colleagues, and allow substantive work to be ongoing and sustainable. For example, a program that can be utilized is Microsoft's Live Meeting (software for online/Internet meetings). This is available online, and the operational cost is low. This program enables continuing dialogue and frequent contact. Online editing and review routines also enable interchange and interaction within the curriculum-development process. The curriculum is available for update and revision without expensive printing and publishing requirements, and the distribution of materials can be carried out efficiently.

In the third step, it is important to attend to research-based teaching strategies to implement an intended curriculum. These strategies are guides to effective approaches; the problem with modern instructional design for school improvement lies in the level of teacher training and practicing expertise. The ideal project requires a teaching cadre that is trained in modern approaches to knowledge development, as well as mandated programs such as RTI and corresponding teaching methods. Teachers do not always know how to use instructional material to provide a rich classroom learning experience. This requires considerable expertise. Therefore, it is important to combine the curriculum in understandable terms with the structure of more didactic approaches (i.e., improving on the direct instruction methods already in place) with structured instructions to teachers in the newer teaching strategies. At first, teachers may find this restrictive, because every step in the process is standardized and fixed. As inquiry methods are explored, there should be adequate structure to assist the lesser-trained and unsophisticated teachers. This occurs in the third step: planning of the teaching strategies. In typical curriculum development, the teacher is given only the barest of instructions, and the final enactments are creative products of the teacher, not the designer. In the approach to teacher education under this project, the designer would provide complete strategic scaffolding for teacher enactments. Student instructional materials, whether textbooks or otherwise, will reflect an inquiry approach, but the teacher's guide will spell out the specific instructional events and behaviors. Because many teachers have not been trained in modern technological methods, they have no examples from their own school or that they learned during training at their previous university or college to fall back on. Various teacher manuals developed by current curriculum publishing companies should help in providing teachers with some new ideas and strategies that can be used as beginning building blocks.

Preparation of curricular materials and teacher's manuals seeking to combine the best parts of a district's current curriculum with modern approaches will require many steps to complete. Each step needs to be negotiated in terms of progress and effectiveness as the process continues from initial selection of curriculum development team members to review of existing materials and methods, to training, preparation of first and final drafts, pilot testing, and evaluation. Each step also constitutes professional development on the part of the team members themselves. The steps we envision are as follows (based on Snyder, 2004):

1. Study local school district's curriculum. The local school district may have special needs and emphases different from those of other schools, so it is important to be sure that these are given attention and appreciation in the design process.

2. Select certain topics or subtopics in the school's curriculum and match with both state and federal standards to ascertain areas of coverage and uncoverage.

3. Merge these plans to look for emphases and gaps.

4. Identify text and other printed material from a wide range of sources to serve as exemplars of good instructional content and approaches in terms of the selected essential questions.

5. Review of content by teachers in consultation with team members. Create collaborative teams to work through development details, using interactive international video and special curriculum links to provide for simultaneous connection to the materials.

6. Enhance materials and write the text for selected curriculum portions and teacher's manual.

7. Identify educational assessments from a wide range of sources.

8. Study assessments provided by state educational agencies at relevant grade levels that have proven to be effective guides to instruction.

9. Compare/contrast the school's assessment material to other assessment material. Enhance and rewrite using various methods for demonstration and creating an item bank of assessments for reference.

10. Prepare initial drafts of written materials; obtain feedback from other curriculum members, trainers, and mentors; revise and prepare final draft versions.

11. Select pilot test and assessment sites in the school district (with current classes) to ascertain level of difficulty and usefulness of responses.

12. Check to see that material exists for those areas where deficits are apparent in the current school district instructional program. (Use a small sample evaluation.)

13. Create pictures/illustration used in the curriculum subtopics. Identify new pictures or retain old ones as appropriate. Work again with the collaborative teams.

14. Identify other media resources needed for each topic.

15. Create enhancement and revision materials using multimedia and Web-based materials. Pictures and media will be drawn from many sources of materials and resources.

16. Develop student and teacher assessment instruments for pilot pre- and posttests: evaluate and incorporate feedback into preparation of final versions; print and distribute school district sample copies of curriculum and teacher's manual as required.

SOURCE: From *Calendar of Activities/Itinerary Narrative*, by C. W. Snyder, 2004, an unpublished paper completed for the University of Montana International Studies Program. Used with permission.

Curriculum Tip 7.3	Defining the scope of a project and setting budget parameters is crucial to the success of curriculum planning.

Establish Project Parameters

The first task is to define the scope of the project. In addition to providing for the necessary budget support, administrators need to answer several questions.

What Grade Levels Will Be Included?

The usual answer here is to improve the entire field, from prekindergarten to Grade 12. However, other options might be considered: Improve elementary, and then add middle and high school levels; improve the middle and then add elementary and high; improve the high school and then build backward to middle and elementary.

What Ability Levels Will Be Included?

If the schools group by ability levels, then the district has to decide whether it will produce a different guide for each level or produce one basic guide that will then be supplemented with other materials. The mastery-curriculum theory posits a curriculum that can be mastered by most students. It makes more sense to produce one basic mastery guide, which is then supplemented with special materials for more able students.

Who Will Direct the Improvement Project?

Nearly all districts have found that a small task force is most efficient and effective. It should include one district administrator, one or two school administrators, the district supervisor for that field, at least one teacher–leader from each level to be included, and one parent representative. The task force should probably be led by one of the district administrators or the district supervisor.

How Much Time Will Be Needed?

Although the answer will vary with the size of the district, the scope of the project, and the resources available, most districts have found that one school year is sufficient for the entire project.

Orient for Mastery

Once the project parameters are set, the process begins with an orientation for all teachers who will be affected by the improvement program. The project leader should prepare materials summarizing the project and stressing two basic features: The improvement program will rely heavily on teacher input; and the improvement program will focus on the mastery curriculum only. As explained in Chapter 1, the mastery curriculum is that part of a field of study that meets two criteria: It is considered essential for all students, and it requires careful structuring and organization for optimal learning. District curriculum efforts should focus on the mastery curriculum; the organic curriculum and the enrichment curriculum can be strengthened at the school level, chiefly through staff development.

Map the Desired Curriculum

With that orientation accomplished, the next phase is mapping the desired curriculum, or finding out what teachers think *should* be taught in that field of study at their grade level. Note that the intent is to determine what teachers believe should be taught, not what they actually teach. Although several experts (see English, 1980; Jacobs, 2004) advocate mapping to determine what teachers actually teach, several studies indicate quite clearly that teachers in effect know better than they teach. For a variety of reasons, they do not teach what they think should be taught: They lack materials, they believe they are constrained by administrators' or parents' preferences, and they are not sure that colleagues would approve. Therefore, it seems desirable to find out what they think they should be teaching, rather than simply formalizing the unnecessary compromises they have made. The process attempts to tap the classroom teacher's perception of the "ideal," as well as that of the scholars.

The best way to map the desired curriculum is to survey the teachers grade by grade. The survey instrument is a crucial element here, because the content and structure of the instrument will very much affect the kinds of data elicited. An expert in the field (either someone from the district or an external consultant) should develop a draft of the form by considering several crucial issues (Exhibit 7.2 shows a portion of a form used to map the social studies curriculum in a suburban school district):

- What elements of the mastery curriculum will be mapped? The objective is to elicit only essential information, not to clutter up the process with unnecessary detail. English teachers, for example, might decide that they do not want to get specific data about punctuation or usage items, because those matters are extensively covered in most English textbooks.

- What strands will be used for the mapping process? The strands are the elements that make up a given field of study—the divisions of that field. Any given field of study could be analyzed differently in terms of its strands. Some, for example, would argue that English language arts comprises only three strands: language, literature, and composition. The objective is to identify strands that make sense to the teachers—to conceptualize the field as they do, not as the experts do.

- How detailed should the mapping data be? Some who use mapping prefer to get very detailed data—long lists of specific objectives. Extensive experience with mapping suggests that more general data at this stage of the process are desirable. The specific objectives can be produced at a later stage of the process.

- Will the survey form include a summary of the recommendations of experts, so that teachers can make more informed decisions? One advantage of including such information is that the process of completing the mapping form also serves to educate teachers about recommended practice. A remaining concern is that summaries might influence teachers to recommend content they would probably not really want to include. Someone who knows the teachers well should make this decision.

EXHIBIT 7.2 Mapping the Social Studies Curriculum: Skills

The Experts Recommend That . . .

1. Skill development is an important aspect of social studies goals. A skill is the ability to do something well—"knowing how."

2. Social studies skills are best developed through sequential instruction and practice, from prekindergarten through Grade 12.

3. The social studies curriculum should emphasize the important skills of acquiring information: reading skills, study skills, reference and information searching skills, and the use of the computer in acquiring information.

4. The social studies curriculum should emphasize the skills of organizing and using information: critical thinking and decision-making skills.

5. The social studies curriculum should emphasize the skills needed for effective interpersonal relationships and social participation: personal skills, group skills, and social and political participation skills.

What information-acquiring skills do you think should be taught for mastery at your grade level?

1.

2.

3.

What information-organizing skills do you think should be taught for mastery at your grade level?

1.

2.

3.

What interpersonal and social skills do you think should be taught for mastery at your grade level?

1.

2.

3.

That draft of the survey form should be tested with a small group of teachers to be sure that the directions are clear, that the strands seem appropriate, and that the structure of the form will elicit the kinds of information desired.

Teachers should then have an opportunity to complete the form during an in-service day or a faculty meeting. They should be notified in advance about the mapping process in case they wish to bring along textbooks, lesson-plan books, or existing curriculum guides. Should the teachers complete the form together in small teams, or should they work alone? Either approach can be used. The team approach provokes good discussion; the individual approach prevents assertive teachers from dominating too much. The principal should make the decision, because he or she probably best understands faculty work habits.

The returns should then be collated on a large scope-and-sequence chart, which shows the strands, the grade levels, and the teachers' responses. Exhibit 7.3 shows a portion of such a chart. Note in this example that the chart also shows responses school by school, because such information can help leaders identify special staff-development needs.

EXHIBIT 7.3   Results of the Mapping Process: Grade 7 English

The following chart shows how the English language arts teachers in our three middle schools responded in indicating where they believe the parts of speech should be taught for mastery. The tallies indicate the number of teachers so responding for each part of speech.

Grammar: Parts of Speech

North	*South*	*Central*
Noun-2	Noun-3	Do not wish to teach parts of speech in Grade 7
Verb-2	Verb-3	
Adjective-2	Adjective-3	
Adverb-2	Adverb-3	
	Determiner-3	
	Conjunction-3	
	Pronoun-3	
	Preposition-3	

Curriculum Tip 7.4   Teachers should have an opportunity to critique curriculum revisions.

Refine the Map

The next phase of the process is refining the map—reviewing the first version of the scope-and-sequence chart and making the necessary modifications. Here the advice of an expert in the field might be needed, unless there are local leaders who have a deep and current knowledge of that field. The results should be reviewed with these questions in mind:

- What important skills and concepts have been omitted and should be included? Have the teachers ignored some important recommendations of the experts?

- What less-important content has been included that might be dropped to reduce the overall content load? Have teachers tried to accomplish too much?

- What skills and concepts seem to be misplaced by level and might better be taught at some lower or higher level? Does placement reflect current knowledge about cognitive development?

- Where is there unnecessary duplication and repetition? Should some concepts and skills be taught for mastery at more than one grade level?

- Does each strand show a desirable development from grade to grade? What does the data indicate? Is there good progression in relation to difficulty and complexity?

- Is there good balance from grade to grade? Are some grades overloaded?

- Does the scope-and-sequence chart respond adequately to state and district mandates concerning student competencies?

It is this phase especially where the influence of the ideal curriculum is paramount: The recommendations of the teachers are checked against the best judgment of the scholars and the experts.

The results of that critique are then reflected in a revised scope-and-sequence chart, which should be distributed to all administrators and classroom teachers involved. If a majority of the teachers object to the inclusion or placement of any specific item, then that item should be changed to reflect majority wishes. The intent is to develop a consensus curriculum, one that teachers will support.

Develop Curriculum Materials

The revised scope-and-sequence chart shows the grade-level placement of the major skills and concepts, strand by strand. The task force now needs to resolve this important issue: What curriculum materials are needed to help teachers implement the improved curriculum?

Three likely options are available for the curriculum materials: a curriculum guide, a curriculum-objectives notebook, and a curriculum-scenario book.

The standard curriculum guide, described in detail in Chapter 8, is perhaps used most often by districts. Its main components are the specific learning objectives and the activities suggested for each objective. If it is decided that a standard curriculum guide is needed, then a team of teachers should first use the general skills and concepts identified in the scope-and-sequence chart to develop the specific objectives. Thus, if the scope-and-sequence chart includes "nouns" as a concept in the grammar strand for Grade 8, then the team might develop this list of objectives:

- Define *noun*.

- Identify nouns in sentences.

- Define *concrete noun* and *abstract noun*.

- Identify concrete and abstract nouns in sentences.

- Use concrete and abstract nouns appropriately in sentences.

- Define *proper noun* and *common noun*.

- Identify proper and common nouns in sentences.

- Use proper nouns in sentences, capitalizing correctly.

That list of specific objectives is developed by analyzing the general skill or concept and determining what specific knowledge would be most appropriate for a given grade level. For each objective or set of objectives, the team would then identify the necessary learning activities.

The distinguishing feature of the curriculum guide is its comprehensiveness. It ordinarily covers every grade level. It not only details objectives and activities but also contains a statement of the philosophy, suggestions for evaluation, and lists of materials.

The second option is to produce a **curriculum-objectives notebook** (or *Web-based data notebook*). The curriculum-objectives notebook is a loose-leaf notebook that contains the following: a summary of the research on how to teach a given subject, a copy of the scope-and-sequence chart in reduced form, and a list of the objectives for those grade levels taught by the teacher to whom the guide is issued. Thus, a seventh-grade teacher would have a copy of the seventh-grade objectives only. The objectives are developed through the process described above.

The distinguishing features of the curriculum-objectives notebook are its simplicity and flexibility. Only the essentials are included for only the grade level needed. Learning activities are not suggested; it is assumed that teachers can develop their own activities or be trained how to use varied educational activities from staff-development programs. An important message is implied by this format: "Achieve these mastery objectives in any reasonable way you wish." The flexibility is of two sorts. First, the loose-leaf format (or data-entry format) makes it easy for teachers to add, delete, and modify. They are encouraged to make the notebook their own: to include their own learning materials, to insert their lesson plans, to add professional articles they find useful. The second type of flexibility results from listing only the objectives. Teachers thus have a great deal of freedom both in how they organize those objectives for teaching and in how they teach. If some teachers wish to teach integrated units, they may; if some wish to focus on discrete skills, they may do so.

The **curriculum-scenario book** is the term given here to describe a collection of learning scenarios. The team takes each general concept or skill and asks, "What mix of learning activities, learning materials, and learning objectives can result in quality learning experiences?" Thus the team working on the concept "noun" might produce these scenarios, among others:

- Have students read the section from Helen Keller's autobiography where she first learns that things have names? Introduce the concept of nouns as names. Discuss the importance of naming as an aspect of using language. Discuss as well the danger of reification—of believing that whatever is named is real.

- Have students write noun poems—poems made of lists of very specific nouns. Discuss the importance of specificity. Ask students to think about the usefulness of general nouns. Advanced students may be interested in the "abstraction ladder" of the general semanticists.

Notice that the scenarios emphasize the holistic nature of the learning experience; the objectives are there, but they are implicit and do not dictate what occurs. In addition to the learning scenarios, the scenario book would also include a copy of the scope-and-sequence chart and a summary of the research.

Which of these three choices is best? The answer depends on the needs of the system and the maturity and competence of the teachers. The curriculum guide probably best serves the needs of a school district in which administrative control is important and in which teacher experience is limited. The curriculum-objectives notebook is perhaps best in a district wishing to give mature and competent teachers a great deal of freedom while still emphasizing the importance of the mastery learning objectives. The scenario book perhaps best serves the needs of those districts whose leaders feel they can be more concerned with the quality of the learning experiences and less concerned with the specification of objectives.

Curriculum Tip 7.5	Time allocated to a particular area of the curriculum often relates directly to student achievement in that area.

Suggest Time Allocations

At some point in the improvement process, the leadership team should suggest time allocations to be used in teaching that subject. Time allocations for teaching should not be encroached upon by testing. One huge consequence is that testing shifts the focus, for at least a month, from learning to testing (Zellmer, Frontier, & Pheifer, 2006).

Time allocations can be set several ways. One method uses the several strands as the basis for establishing time allocations at a district level. The curriculum-improvement task force reviews the recommendations of experts, reflects on district curricular goals, and recommends time allocations for each strand of the curriculum. These recommendations are made part of the final curriculum report.

A variation of this method relies more on teacher input about time and strands and sets allocations level by level. A district supervisor poses the question to all teachers in the district who teach that subject at a given level of schooling: "As you think about the students in our middle schools, what percentage of time do you think we should allocate to each strand of this curriculum?" The supervisor helps the teachers agree on time allocations that reflect their perceptions and at the same time are responsive to district priorities. Here is how one group of middle-school social studies teachers answered the question:

History: 50%

Map and study skills: 20%

Geography: 15%

Civics: 10%

Other: 5%

A third method focuses on unit planning at the school level. At every grade level in each school, teachers are asked to submit at the start of every marking period a unit-planning proposal, indicating for each unit the unit objective, the important concepts and skills emphasized, and the number of instructional periods allocated. The principal reviews these plans and discusses with the teachers any proposals that seem to reflect unwise allocations of time.

A fourth method relies on staff development. Rather than specifying district guidelines or checking on unit plans, a member of the leadership team uses staff-development sessions to raise with the teachers issues of time allocation and achievement, to encourage teachers to discuss openly with each other how they allocate time, and to assist teachers in making decisions about time that reflect their knowledge of the learners and the district's curricular priorities.

Obviously, these methods can be used together, because in effect they complement each other.

Select and Develop Tests

The testing aspect of curriculum improvement involves both selection of the appropriate standardized tests and development of curriculum-based tests (electronic or paper). First, the task force should consult with measurement specialists in the district to select standardized tests that adequately reflect the improved curriculum. This is an important consideration, because performance on standardized tests is often used as a measure of school success. While the issue is most critical in reading and mathematics, it also needs careful consideration in any area of the curriculum where standardized tests are used.

Curriculum-based or curriculum-referenced tests are also needed. These are locally developed examinations (albeit can be Web-based, such as Exam View format) that are based solely on the district's curriculum. They can be used both to assess student achievement and to ensure that teachers are implementing the mastery curriculum. If teachers know that their students will be tested on specific content, they are more likely to emphasize that content.

How many curriculum-based tests are needed at each grade level? The answer seems to vary with the district and the level. In many high schools, curriculum-based tests are usually administered as semester and final examinations. The key is balance. It is important to understand that one size does not fit all. One high-stakes test does not accurately measure individual achievement (Fugate, 2007).

Because tests are often used as measures of student progress, school success, and even teacher performance, it is essential that they be developed with the utmost care, to ensure reliability and validity. It is crucial to keep testing and assessment in perspective. State accountability requirements, correlated closely with needs and wishes of the corporate community, are gaining control of the ethos and the aims of education that are offered to the students at some schools (Kozol, 2007). The advice of measurement specialists should be required, and every form of the tests should be used in pilot studies before the tests are administered throughout the district.

Curriculum Tip 7.6	Computerized testing, as well as Web-based assessments, can provide quick and accurate measures that can be aligned with state and national standards.

Electronic Testing

School districts need and deserve accurate measures that align with standards and produce timely results. Districts also need scores that have meaningful references, for example:

- Norms for public accountability

- Curriculum references to focus instruction

- Prior scores to assess growth individually and collectively

- Benchmarks to measure yearly adequate progress

The Northwest Evaluation Association (NWEA) (Olson, 2004) is one of a few organizations providing computerized achievement-level tests, aligned with local curriculum and state standards, that provide accurate information about academic performance. Computerized or Web-based adapted tests combine the benefit of technology with the integrity of level tests. Those tests draw from a bank of more than 15,000 calibrated test items. When students use the computerized adaptive test, the difficulty of the test is adjusted to the student's performance. The difficulty of each question is based on how well the student has answered the questions up to that point. As the student answers correctly, the questions become more difficult. If the student answers incorrectly, the questions become easier. Each student then receives a personalized test. Schools using NWEA's Measures of Academic Progress (MAP) system find that it reduces test anxiety and is very accurate. Students can stop at any point and go to lunch or recess and come back to start where they left off.

When a student completes the computerized adaptive test, the MAP system reports the student's score on the screen, allowing for immediate feedback. A student's score should show growth from year to year and can be correlated longitudinally to scores from previous years. NWEA prepares tests for the district around local standards and curriculum or an already prepared state version. Within 24 hours, test administrators can download information about students and classes to a local server and print them off for individual teachers or parents. Administrative printouts can also be obtained for data-analysis purposes. Teachers can assess individual students at any time throughout the year to obtain gains made in certain areas. Curriculum and teaching strategies can be altered, depending on immediate feedback. This type of computerized adaptive test has proven to be one of the fastest and easiest ways to assess student learning and learner needs.

Select Instructional Materials

The improved curriculum will probably require new instructional materials. The task force should develop guidelines for evaluating materials, pointing out any special features that the improved curriculum might require ("All language arts texts must give special attention to the composing process."). An instructional materials committee should then use those guidelines in reviewing and selecting materials that will provide the best support for teachers implementing the improved curriculum.

It should be stressed here that the textbooks, and Web-based learning approaches, should serve the curriculum, not dictate it. In too many instances, districts reverse the process. They purchase a basic text and then use the publisher's scope-and-sequence chart as the basis of their own curriculum. The folly of such an approach is apparent to anyone who understands how school textbooks are designed. To sell well, they must appeal to a mass market; as a consequence, textbook authors often include content that they know is inappropriate, for no other reason than because they believe the market demands it. Thus, almost every elementary language arts series includes a great deal of grammar, even though most experts in the field believe that such content is totally inappropriate at the elementary level.

Curriculum Tip 7.7	Staff development is the key to successful curriculum implementation.

Provide for Staff Development

Consider two major issues in planning for staff development: timing and content. Because resources are limited, staff-development sessions must be held at a time when they will be most effective. As explained in Chapter 5, two approaches seem to be successful in the timing of staff development. In the first approach, teachers in a given field of study meet for several sessions to review the research, to reflect on the recommendations of experts, to exchange ideas about teaching that subject, and to develop and share materials. The materials they produce—units of study, sample lessons, and student learning materials—in a sense become the improved curriculum. All that is needed is some work at the end to systematize and formalize what they have produced. Many new composition curricula, for example, have been developed in this way.

The second approach provides staff development at the crucial implementation stage. Once the improved project has been completed, instructional leaders conduct a series of staff-development sessions to help teachers understand the new program, to assist teachers in acquiring the new skills they will need, and to work with teachers in fleshing out the details of the improved program. In this manner, staff development is seen as supportive of the curriculum. Either of these approaches can work well. The important consideration is to provide good staff development at a time when teachers seem to need it.

What is good staff development? Here the answer is clear. Over the past decade there have been numerous studies whose results have yielded a clear picture of what staff development should be. Those results are summarized in Exhibit 7.4. While it may not be possible for a district to offer staff-development programs that meet all those guidelines, they

---

EXHIBIT 7.4 Summary of Research on Effective Staff Development

Duration

1. The program should be ongoing and continuous.

Management

1. The principal should participate actively but should not dominate.
2. Teachers and administrators should plan the program jointly.
3. There should be regular project meetings in which participants review progress and discuss substantive concerns.

Content

1. The program should provide a necessary theoretical base for the new skills.
2. The program should give primary attention to the specific skills teachers believe they need.
3. The content should be timely, directly related to job needs.

Learning Activities

1. The program should make extensive use of hands-on activities and demonstrations of new skills.
2. The program should provide for the trial of those new skills in simulated or real settings.
3. The program should make it possible for teachers to get structured feedback about their use of those skills.
4. The program should provide opportunities for observation in other classrooms and schools.

Site

1. The program should be school based, not university based.

Instructors

1. Local teachers should be the instructors, with minimal use of outside consultants.

should be given serious consideration whenever staff-development programs are planned. (The guidelines have been synthesized from the following reviews of the research: Corcoran, McVay, & Riordan, 2003; Education Commission of the States, 2005; National Staff Development Council, 2001; Snow-Renner & Lauer, 2005.)

The steps for staff development presented in this chapter can help a district improve any field of study. Obviously they are time-consuming, but there are no shortcuts to educational quality.

Set Staff Development as Priority

The key to providing staff in-service is to make staff development a priority from the onset (Whitehead, Jenson, & Boschee, 2003). For example, being able to integrate multimedia and Web-based technology as a tool along with the traditional resources is now one of the essential elements of any classroom curriculum experience. Instituting the appropriate professional development for faculty, staff, and students is critical to the success of linking technology to the curriculum. It is essential to remember that technology is a tool, and like any educational tool, teachers need to be trained in its appropriate use.

Curriculum Tip 7.8	It is the creation of a vision, formation of a sound plan, and the implementation of the plan at a local level that will determine the success or failure of any quality staff-development program.

Creative Staff-Development Strategies

A creative and innovative use of physical and human resources for staff development at the local level is going to make the real difference as to whether curriculum change will be successful. Most schools have been fortunate to have a number of educators and community members who have used this sense of creativity and innovation to provide quality staff development in their schools. A partial list of creative staff in-service ideas that have proven successful with limited resources include the following:

The Rule of Three

Teachers and staff are encouraged to help each other before going to a principal, supervisor, curriculum leader, or technology coordinator. *The simple rule is: Ask three and then me.* This little rule helps take pressure off of supervisors and coordinators and improves staff development and cooperation. Teachers can also use the rule with their students. If students ask three other students for help before going to the teacher, the teacher will have more time for curriculum-related instruction.

Early-Out Time for Students

Numerous schools have found ways to adjust schedules and provide planning and/or in-service time for teachers while maintaining state requirements for student contact time. Teachers have agreed to start earlier and end later each day as well as give up some recess time in order to develop blocks of time per week, or every other week, for in-service and planning. A key is to make sure part of that earned block of time is devoted to in-service. It is also important to make sure that state requirements for student contact time are met.

Sending Pairs of Individuals to Workshops and Seminars

A minimum of two individuals should attend workshops, seminars, and conferences. Teachers feel more comfortable working and training in a cooperative and supportive environment. Having at least two teachers (preferably from the same grade level) obtain the same in-service background is a tremendous way to increase the success of the curricular programs. Many programs have failed because only one teacher received the training and did not have the time or energy to carry the program through all of the implementation stages.

Substitute Rotation

School leaders have developed blocks of time by having a set of substitutes rotate through the schedule. For example, a set of five substitutes could release five teachers in the morning while the same five substitutes could release another set of teachers in the afternoon. Because this procedure diminishes regular teacher/student contact time, it is recommended that it should be used sparingly. It is beneficial when scheduling a special consultant for a certain period of time.

Free Consulting Services

Innovative school districts have collaborated to obtain the services of free national consultants during textbook-adoption processes. Some textbook companies are often happy to provide consultants without obligation on the hopes that their book series or materials will be selected. Naturally, some publishers do not provide such services. It is up to the creative administrator to contact publishing companies for possible services. A key here is to work with company representatives and collaborate, if possible or necessary, with several adjoining school districts to bring a consultant into a certain area.

Schedule Adjustment

Creative school leaders have found ways to adjust and align scheduled prep times—such as music, art, library, and physical education classes—to provide in-service to new teachers. For example, it is beneficial to align an experienced teacher's prep times with a new teacher's so they can visit and share ideas. The experienced teacher can assist and model effective uses of technology during these times.

College and University Preservice Programs

Higher education is always looking for ways to extend learning on campus as well as beyond campus. Recent restructuring efforts have led to major changes in preservice and student teaching programs. Additional core classes now address curricular change as well as professional leadership projects. An innovative program now being used by a number of universities includes the use of online staff-development opportunities. Another involves the development of a collaborative master's degree in educational leadership to be delivered via interactive video from regional sites.

School/University/College Partnerships

Both college and university faculty are always looking for ways to integrate their students into local schools, whether they are small or large. Many schools are using college and university students to help in-service faculty on technological innovations and/or model teaching strategies involving technology in the classroom. Local school faculty members learn new ideas, and the university student receives a grade and credit for the experience.

Curriculum and Technology Cooperatives

More small and rural school districts are now realizing the benefits of developing cooperatives. What cannot be achieved singly can be achieved through a collaboration of resources. School districts have banded together and have hired curriculum and technical coordinators who can provide the training and staff development needed at a local level. Some school district cooperatives have joined with colleges and universities to provide credit to experienced teachers acting as instructors, as well as credit for participants.

Community Resources

Both small and large school districts across the country have found valuable resource people within their communities. Individual community members who have a great deal of technical experience can provide both equipment and knowledge to school districts. Many individuals in the private sector are especially good at providing in-service in the area of word processing, e-mail, satellite, multimedia, cable, and other technical applications. The key is that school leaders seek out and involve community members who can make these types of contributions in the area of technology to the district.

Management Planning Matrix

The Management Planning Matrix has been one of the most successful tools used by school leaders in designing effective staff-development programs in the country. The Northwest Regional Educational Laboratory in Portland, Oregon, has developed a Management Planning Matrix that can be used to plan, implement, and evaluate an effective staff-development program. The matrix design encourages planners not only to develop technology staff-development goals but also to formulate measurable indicators of successful in-service. The matrix also forces planners to detail activities, leadership roles, and to set implementation and evaluation dates (Whitehead et al., 2003; see also Exhibit 11.4, Management and Monitoring Matrix, in this volume).

It is therefore apparent that staff development is becoming an increasingly integral and critical part of our schools. Our nation's schools cannot address the problem of educational equity without first talking about substantial teacher preparation linking technology, pedagogy, and curriculum development. If teachers are to make the most effective use of new teaching strategies and technology applications available for classrooms, then state leaders will have to focus on providing adequate funding for staff development. Currently, many school districts are investing thousands of dollars in technological equipment and software but very little toward in-service programs. It is now time to establish an equitable balance between technology and staff development.

SUMMARY

This chapter describes a process for reconceptualizing fields of study and emphasizes that staff development is becoming an increasingly integral and critical part of our schools. The chapter illustrates how basic attempts have been made in the past to reconceptualize fields of study, and it outlines what current curriculum leaders can do to best improve fields of study. School districts usually decide to improve a field of study by strengthening one subject area over several grade levels. The decision to reconceptualize a field of study typically emerges from an awareness of a deficiency, such as when poor articulation across the various levels of schooling exists, when teachers are no longer using existing guides, or when the present curriculum for a particular field of study has become outdated. Substantial teacher preparation is necessary to improve a field of study so that teachers are equipped to make the most effective use of technology, pedagogy, and curriculum development in our nation's classrooms.

APPLICATIONS

1. If you wanted to develop a series of elective English courses for high school students, how could you ensure that all students would develop their reading and writing skills, regardless of the electives they chose?

2. Design a mapping form for a subject you know well. In designing the form, consider the issues presented in this chapter's discussion of such forms.

3. Develop a detailed planning schedule that you could follow in improving a field of study in a local school district. Note strengths and weaknesses of the planning schedule and why you chose this approach.

4. How do you account for the fact that the ideal curricula of scholars and experts have had such little impact on the written or the taught curriculum? As an administrator, how would you counteract this problem?

5. Suppose you are part of a Grade 5 team of teachers. You decide that you would like to give the pupils some choices about the social studies content by offering elective units. How would you ensure that all pupils mastered the requisite skills, regardless of the content emphasis? How would you incorporate technology to achieve this goal?

6. Based on the synthesis of research by Snow-Renner and Lauer (2005), professional development that is most likely to affect teacher instruction positively is

   - Of considerable duration

   - Focused on specific content and/or instructional strategies rather then general

   - Characterized by collective participation of educators (in the form of grade-level teams or school-level teams)

   - Infused with active learning, rather than a stand-and-deliver model (p. 6)

   Using the above criteria, analyze the professional-development activities in your school district, and compare them to the research findings. How does your district compare?

CASE STUDY   Providing Diverse Teaching Strategies

The following case study is an example of how an Ohio principal is able to use staff development and differentiated instruction strategies to improve school curriculum.

"We have a situation whereby the fourth-grade teachers are fearful of meeting NCLB guidelines, and feel they are restricted to teaching only the basics," says the principal, Art Mandel. "Parents of the higher-level students are grumbling."

Susan Gibbons, a fourth-grade teacher–leader, listens and nods her head in agreement. "Yes, you are right," she says. "Martha and Bob are concerned their students will not make AYP."

Principal Mandel is frustrated. "How can we help them?"

"Well," says Susan, smiling. "Why don't you arrange for some staff development on compacting and differentiated instruction? That way, Martha and Bob can see some different ways to align their teaching with state standards and still reach all their students."

"That sounds like a great idea," says Principal Mandel approvingly. "I'll contact the district office as well as the local university to see if we can get some help in setting up an inservice on differentiated instruction as well as some other strategies."

The Challenge

Formulating strategies to improve fields of study and enhance staff development is a major goal for many school administrators. What can Principal Mandel do to get more teachers like Susan Gibbons involved in leadership roles?

Key Issues/Questions

1. What are your impressions of how Principal Mandel handled the situation involving Martha and Bob at his school?

2. Do you feel that Principal Mandel might have used or manipulated teacher Susan Gibbons to solve his problem?

3. How do you think other teachers will react when they find out that Susan Gibbons is providing staff development suggestions to the principal? What should be discussed?

4. What are some other possible ways that Principal Mandel can enhance staff development and improve fields of study at his school?

5. How would you feel about Principal Mandel asking Susan Gibbons and Martha as well as Bob to attend a differentiated instruction conference together? Do you think this would be useful? Why or why not?

WEBLIOGRAPHY

McREL—Professional staff development
www.mcrel.org/PDF/ProfessionalDevelopment

Schools Attuned Program
www.allkindsofminds.org

U.S. Department of Education's What Works Clearinghouse
www.whatworksclearinghouse.org

CHAPTER 8

Processes for Developing New Courses and Units

From time to time, administrators, supervisors, or teacher–leaders and teachers will decide that a new course and new strategies are needed. In some cases, they will determine that an existing course should be completely redeveloped with a fresh perspective: "Let's rewrite our American history course—the old course just isn't working anymore." In some instances, they will see the need for a new course to fill a gap newly perceived in the existing program: "We need a course in career planning."

This chapter explains how to develop a new course or unit using two contrasting processes: the standard *technological* process and what is termed here a *naturalistic* process. The intent is not to suggest that one process is better than the other but only to contrast two divergent processes that might be used in different subject areas, at different grade levels.

Questions addressed in this chapter include the following:

- What is the technological process of curriculum planning?
- What is the naturalistic process of curriculum planning?
- How can curriculum leaders develop new courses that involve both the technological and naturalistic processes of curriculum planning?

Key to Leadership

Successful curriculum leaders realize that curriculum planning should drive technology rather than having technology drive curriculum.

THE TECHNOLOGICAL PROCESS OF CURRICULUM PLANNING

While the technological process has many variations, it tends to be a rational, systematic, ends-oriented model. It is the process that is important.

Curriculum Tip 8.1	The term *technological process* describes any curriculum development model that emphasizes the importance of defining terminal learning objectives early in the process and then identifies the steps needed to accomplish those objectives.

Historically, basic principles were perhaps most clearly articulated by Tyler (1949), and the model's details are probably most clearly explained in manuals written for industrial training. Its systematic nature and its efficiency make it the preferred process in most industrial and military training. While details of the process will vary from specialist to specialist, in general it moves in an orderly sequence through certain specified steps (for a useful explication of the technological process, see Wulf & Schave, 1984):

1. Determine the course parameters—a rationale for the course, its general goals, and its probable time schedule.
2. Assess the needs of the learners.
3. On the basis of those needs and the goals previously specified, identify the course objectives, the terminal outcomes desired.
4. Determine the optimal sequence for those course objectives and cluster related objectives into unified learning experiences.
5. For each objective, identify learning activities that will enable the learners to achieve those objectives.
6. Select instructional materials that will support the learning activities.
7. Identify methods by which the attainment of those objectives will be assessed.
8. Systematize all these decisions in a curriculum guide. (Wulf & Schave, 1984, cited in Glatthorn, 1987, p. 198)

It should be noted that the steps identified above are usually followed in that sequence; the most competent technological developers use them in a recursive, iterative fashion and do not apply them in a mechanistic, unthinking manner.

Each of these steps will be described in detail, using as an example a course for high school students in career planning.

Curriculum Tip 8.2	A statement of principles guiding curriculum development and an argument for any new course is an important step in developing parameters of curriculum projects.

Determine Course Parameters

It is significant to note that the core concepts employed by schools are diverse and yet surprisingly similar (Schmoker, 2001). The first step is to determine course parameters by establishing a rationale for the course—a statement of the principles guiding the developers and an argument for the course. With the rationale established, the curriculum specialist then makes a determination about the goals of the course—the general outcomes desired (the term curriculum specialist is used here to designate any administrator or supervisor with responsibility for and training in curriculum development; he or she may organize a team of colleagues to assist in the process). A course goal is a very general statement of the intended outcomes; typically, a one-semester course would have no more than three goals. Thus, the goal for the career course might be stated in this fashion:

This course will help students develop their career-planning skills.

A new integrated unit for fourth grade might have this as its goal:

This unit will help the pupils understand that there are many different kinds of careers and that each career has value to society.

With the course or unit goal established, the developers then consider the matter of the course schedule—how long will it last, how often will it meet, and for how many minutes per session.

Assess the Needs of the Learners

The next step is needs assessment; a need is perceived as a gap between a present and a desired state. Thus, the needs-assessment process evaluates the present state of the learners in relation to the general outcomes expected. The data for the needs assessment can come from several sources: achievement scores, surveys, observations, interviews, and measures of performance.

The key is to link needs assessment with analysis. In this regard it is best if teachers develop action plans to design targeted tutoring sessions and differentiated small groups. The seamless coherence among assessments, analysis, and action creates the ideal classroom environment for significant gains in student learning (Bambrick-Santoyo, 2007–2008).

Curriculum Tip 8.3	The purpose of data collection is not to judge people's performances or to profile underachieving students. Rather, school leaders need to regard data as a tool for continuous improvement.

In addition, school districts can begin by making better use of existing data and by choosing a specific area of focus. With clearly defined objectives in place, schools will garner the support and cooperation needed to meet their goals and objectives (Johnson, 2000).

Identify Course Objectives

The curriculum specialist would next take the critical step of identifying the course objectives. This is usually accomplished by first doing a task analysis of the outcome desired. In the case of the career-planning course, the specialist would ask, "Given what is known about how career choices are best made, what specific skills must be mastered?" The results of the task analysis are then checked against the needs-assessment data as a means of determining which of those skills should be stressed for the intended population. The result would be a comprehensive list of course objectives, stated in measurable terms. Exhibit 8.1 shows a list that might be developed for this course in career planning.

Sequence and Cluster Course Objectives

With the objectives determined, the next step is to determine the optimal sequence in which those objectives should be mastered. Curriculum specialists who use the technological process usually opt for a learning-relaxed sequence, determining the optimal sequence by examining the relationships among the objectives and then assessing the entry-level skills, knowledge, and attitudes of the learners. In the case of the career-planning course, the order

---

EXHIBIT 8.1   Course Objectives for Career Planning

1. Define these three terms in a way that distinguishes them from each other: job, career, vocation.
2. Define these terms correctly: talent, skill, value.
3. Describe two career-related talents that you believe you possess to a high degree.
4. List four career-related skills that you possess.
5. Explain three ways in which you might acquire additional career-related skills.
6. Explain the two career values that seem most important to you.
7. In a well-organized essay, explain at least two factors that have influenced your career values.
8. In a well-organized paragraph, explain how you would distinguish between a highly reliable source and a less reliable source of career information.
9. Identify three reliable sources that provide current information about career opportunities and requirements.
10. Using those sources, identify three careers for which you possess the necessary talents and that would adequately respond to your career values.
11. Identify the education and experience you would need for securing an entry-level position in each of those three careers.
12. Describe the processes by which you would obtain the required education and experience.
13. Explain three sources of information you would use in locating an entry-level vacancy in one of the three careers selected.
14. Write a career resume that you could use in applying for one of those positions.
15. Demonstrate that you know how to handle a job interview by role-playing such an interview.
16. In a well-organized essay, explain three factors that might cause you to change careers.

in which the objectives are listed in Exhibit 8.1 is one that many curriculum specialists would use as the optimal sequence in a course of this sort. The sequence establishes a conceptual basis, moves to the student's awareness of self, and orders the rest of the objectives in what seems chiefly to be a temporal sequence.

Once the specific objectives are sequenced appropriately, the next step is to cluster related objectives into unified learning experiences, such as units of study or instructional modules. The specialist examines the entire list, assesses the constraints of the schedule, reflects on student interest and attention span, and determines which objectives should be placed together in a unified set of learning experiences. Thus, the specialist may determine that Objectives 1 and 2 in Exhibit 8.1 might make a good, brief introductory unit, which would establish the conceptual base for what follows.

Identify Learning Activities

The curriculum specialist would identify one or more learning activities for each objective stated that would be specifically shaped to help the learners master the objective. The learning activities are usually seen as an ordered set of learning experiences that move the learner step by step to the objective. Consider, for example, Objective 7 in Exhibit 8.1:

> In a well-organized essay, explain at least two factors that have influenced your career values.

The following learning activities could be prescribed:

- Identify several possible factors that might influence career values: culture, ethnic group, family, peers, gender, region in which you were reared, school experiences, physiological factors.
- By reflecting about yourself and your values, identify two of those having the greatest influence.
- Check your perceptions and gather supporting information by discussing the question with parents and friends.
- Develop a plan for your essay; have the preliminary plan reviewed by your teacher and a classmate.
- Use the revised plan to write the first draft of the essay.
- Ask a classmate to edit your essay and give you feedback about the essay.
- Write a revised draft of the essay.

Note that learning activities are chosen primarily on the basis of their fit with the objective; only those activities that move the student step by step to the objective are prescribed.

Select Instructional Materials

With the objectives and activities identified, the next step is to select the instructional materials that will help accomplish the objectives and support the learning activities. A systematic search would be made for texts, computer software, video media, and other instructional media.

Curriculum Tip 8.4	Selecting instructional materials that help accomplish the objectives and support the learning activities is key to the process.

Identify Assessment Methods

The specialist would next determine which assessment methods are needed. Some assessment is done to evaluate readiness for a unit and to diagnose learner needs; some is done to provide the student and teacher with formative feedback to determine whether remediation is needed; and some is done to make summative judgments for grading purposes. In addition to the usual written tests, the specialist might decide to make use of other assessment methods, such as interviews, observations, or performance tests.

The specialist planning the career course, after consultation with measurement specialists, might decide on the following tests: one diagnostic test to determine specific learning needs of each student, one short formative test for each lesson, one longer formative test for each group of five lessons, and one final summative test covering the entire course.

Carol Ann Tomlinson (2007–2008) stated, "From judging performance to guiding students to shaping instruction to informing learning, coming to grips with informative assessment is one insightful journey" (p. 8). Giving student feedback now seems to be more productive than giving grades. The greatest power of assessment appears to be in its capacity to help individuals become better teachers.

Stiggins (2002) stated that we need to use assessments for learning. "If assessments of learning provide evidence of achievement for public reporting, then assessments for learning serve to help students learn more. The crucial distinction is between assessment to determine the status of learning and assessment to promote greater learning" (p. 4).

The term *assessment for learning* was coined by the Assessment Reform Group (1999) in their *Assessment for Learning: Beyond the Black Box*. Whatever assessment teachers decide to use, the following guidelines should be considered even today. They are as follows:

- Understanding and articulating in advance of teaching, the achievement targets that their students are to reach

- Informing their students about those learning goals, in terms that students understand, from the very beginning of the teaching and learning process

- Becoming assessment literate and thus able to transform their expectations into assessment exercises and scoring procedures that accurately reflect student achievement

- Using classroom assessments to build students' confidence in themselves as learners and help them take responsibility for their own learning, so as to lay a foundation for lifelong learning

- Translating classroom assessment results into frequent descriptive feedback (versus judgmental feedback) for students, providing them with specific insights as to how to improve

- Continuously adjusting instruction based on the results of classroom assessments

- Engaging students in regular self-assessment, with standards held constant so that students can watch themselves grow over time and thus feel in charge of their own success

- Actively involving students in communicating with their teacher and their families about their achievement status and improvement (Stiggins, 2002, p. 5)

Curriculum Tip 8.5	An important step in developing new courses is to systematize decisions into a curriculum guide.

Develop the Curriculum Guide

While formats vary from district to district, most guides developed from the processes described above include the following components:

- A rationale for the course or a statement of the philosophy that guided the course planners

- A list of the objectives, ordered in the desired sequence

- The recommended learning activities, displayed graphically so that their relationship to the objectives is very clear—in some cases, activities are described under each objective; in some guides, the objectives and activities are arranged in parallel columns

- A list of recommended instructional materials

- Copies of tests and suggestions for other assessment activities

The Technological Process Summarized

Observe certain key features of the technological approach. The basic flow of the decision-making process might be described as progressing from specific to general or as "bottom up." Specific outcomes are identified and then clustered into related sets of learning experiences. Objectives play a central role: They are specified early in the design process and control the selection of learning activities and instructional materials. The process is thus essentially ends oriented. Methods are determined on the basis of the extent to which they accomplish specified outcomes, and the process is primarily linear.

This technological approach has several advantages when used by an expert or a team of knowledgeable people. It seems orderly and systematic and thus might be more readily mastered by those less skilled in curriculum work.

However, it has several significant limitations: It seems insensitive to the politics of curriculum making. Most curricular decisions in schools are inherently political, because they involve issues of power and "turf." The new course in career planning, for example, might be opposed by any teachers who include career units in the courses they already teach; they would see the new course as dealing with content they believed they owned.

THE NATURALISTIC PROCESS OF CURRICULUM PLANNING

An awareness of the limitations of the technological process and extensive work with curriculum specialists and teachers have led to the development of a special version of the naturalistic process.

	The naturalistic process attempts to embody the following characteristics:
Curriculum Tip 8.6	• Attempts to be sensitive to the political aspects of curriculum making • Places greater emphasis on the quality of the learning activities • Attempts to reflect more accurately the way curricula have actually been developed • Is cognizant of the way teachers really plan for instruction

In the following discussion, the steps in the process are described in the order in which courses ordinarily would be taken, although other sequences could just as well be followed. The process has been conceptualized as an interactive and recursive one, in which flexibility is emphasized. To illustrate these steps and to highlight comparisons with the technological approach, the discussion again uses the development of a new course for high school students in career planning. It then shows how an elementary team would use the same process in developing an integrated unit.

Assess the Alternatives

Before developing a new course, the naturalistic process begins with a systematic examination of the alternatives to a new course. Although many of those using a technological approach begin in the same manner, some technological developers seem to move too quickly from the identification of need to the development of the course.

To understand why this assessment of alternatives is important, consider how the initiative for a new course usually develops. Someone with a stake in the outcome, such as a principal, department head, teacher–leader, or teacher, assumes that a new course is needed.

Only in rare instances does the conviction emerge from a rational analysis of the data available. Even though most experts urge curriculum supervisors to use such information sources as test scores, parent surveys, and student interviews, such data are often sought to justify a predetermined solution, not to establish the need for a given response.

For this reason it is important for someone in authority—such as the director of curriculum or the principal—to examine the alternatives before allowing the decision to offer a new course to move ahead too quickly. Any new course is costly. It involves what economists call "opportunity cost"—every student who takes the new course loses in the process the opportunity for some other educational experience. It also involves substantial development cost—the time and efforts of those responsible for planning it. Finally, it involves significant implementation costs—the funds needed to staff the course, provide facilities, and secure the necessary equipment and materials.

What are the alternatives to offering a new course? Several alternatives are available for those interested in a new course in career planning:

- Ignore the need, based on the assumption that somehow adolescents will acquire the career-planning skills they need without organizational intervention.

- Ask some other agency to respond to the need. Decide that helping adolescents make wise career choices is the responsibility of the family, the business community, or the YMCA—not the school.

- Provide for the need through the activities program. Arrange for assemblies, career-planning days, or career clubs; develop programs for the homeroom.

- Use noncurricular methods of responding to the need. Put career materials in the library; buy computer software on career planning and make it available in the guidance suite; increase the guidance staff, adding specialists in career planning.

- Integrate the skills into existing courses. In each existing subject, include units in the careers that emphasize career-planning skills.

It is not suggested here that any of these alternatives is necessarily better than offering a new course. The point is simply that the alternatives should be examined before finally deciding that a new course is needed.

Curriculum Tip 8.7	The process of staking out territory is very similar to that of identifying course parameters.

Stake Out the Territory

If it still appears that a new course is the most desirable option, then the next step is to stake out the territory. The planning team considers the students for whom the course is intended, makes some initial determinations about the schedule, and tentatively identifies the coverage of the course. Note that the active parties in the naturalistic process are identified as a planning team, in contradistinction to the curriculum specialist, because teams of teachers more typically are involved in using the naturalistic process.

However, there is an important difference between identifying the course parameters and staking out the territory—a difference connoted by the metaphors used. The identification of course parameters tends to be more definitive and final; the staking out of territory is a more tentative and open-ended boundary-setting process.

To assist in further development, the course territory should be described in a course prospectus. The course prospectus presents the answers to possible questions—and does so in a manner that will both guide planners and inform others. In the case of the career course, the prospectus might read as follows:

> We're thinking about offering a new course tentatively titled "Thinking About Careers." As we see the course now, it would be an elective offered to all juniors and seniors, although our hunch is that it would probably appeal most of all to those not presently interested in higher education. It would probably run for one term and meet three times a week for a total of about 40 classroom hours. As we presently conceptualize the course, it would help students examine their career values, assess career skills, learn how to retrieve career information, and do some systematic career planning. It would probably deemphasize the study of particular careers and focus on processes instead. Our written materials will include only the mastery component, not enrichment or organic content. All of these notions are very tentative; we need the advice of anyone competent and interested.

Observe that the description is general and the language tentative. The intent is to identify broad boundaries that will be flexible enough to accommodate the ideas of all those who will later be involved in the more detailed planning.

Develop a Constituency

As noted above, all curriculum making has a political aspect. Those developing the new course wield power to advance their own interests. While genuinely concerned with improving the education of students, they are also motivated by personal interests: to enhance their reputations, to make their positions more secure, to win the attention of superiors. For this reason, it is important throughout the naturalistic process for course planners to build a constituency for the new course—to mobilize support and neutralize likely opposition. How much time and energy are devoted to such politicking will depend, of course, on the likely impact of the proposed change and the extent to which the course seems to have broad-based support.

Win the Support of the Powerful

Early in the process, course planners should try to secure the endorsement of those with power. Sally McConnell (2007), associate executive director of NAESP, stated, "It is important for schools and other state and local agencies to work together to help students to succeed in school and to lay a strong foundation for success in later life" (p. 20).

Basically, a system of coordinated services should be established in every state, funded by state and federal resources. From a historical view point, several studies (see, e.g., Leithwood & Montgomery's 1982 review) indicate that in many schools the principal has played a key role as the curriculum gatekeeper. If the principal supports a curriculum change and works closely with governmental agencies, the process moves along well. If the principal opposes the change, major problems develop: Meetings are canceled, requisitions are delayed, and space is unavailable. Central office supervisors who try to impose curricular changes on resistant principals soon discover the folly of such attempts.

Curriculum Tip 8.8	Opening up the planning process to all those who want to participate is an important component of the process.

Share the Power and the Glory

It is important to make the new course "our course," not "my course." Make a special effort to involve the undecided. Spread the credit around in all public discussions.

For example, Ohio's statewide system for supporting school improvement emphasizes a collaborative partnership in which members of regional school-improvement teams engage with district instructional leaders. Each team works with districts using a Tri-Tier Model of service delivery (Christie, 2007). If curriculum development is to respond adequately to regional differences, including sociocultural and ethnic diversity, school districts must allow the stakeholders the opportunity to participate in the curriculum-development process. This decentralization, or school-based curriculum development, provides the advantages of greater teacher involvement in the selection of textbooks, designing of lesson plans, and implementation of teaching practices. However, such involvement also calls for proper in-service training programs for those teachers.

Be Prepared to Negotiate

The process of getting a new course approved often requires the art of negotiating. Especially when the opposition seems strong, course planners should give themselves room to bargain, by asking publicly for more than they hope to get: asking for four periods, hoping to get three; asking for two classrooms in the expectation of getting one.

All these strategies will require time. For that reason, the process of developing a constituency is not initiated and then dropped; instead, it should continue throughout both the planning and implementation stages.

Curriculum Tip 8.9	Course planners should begin with a cursory "data-driven needs assessment" of the students.

Build the Knowledge Base

As noted in Chapter 5, another fundamental step that should be initiated early is building the knowledge base—retrieving and systematizing information about the students, assessing faculty readiness, analyzing the relevant research, and identifying available materials and programs. Too often those using the technological process slight this crucial step: Course planners often ignore those who will be teaching the course, slight the research, and act as if nothing else has ever been done in the field before.

The questions listed in Exhibit 8.2 can guide the development of the knowledge base as it relates to course development. Note that the questions here are not as comprehensive as those suggested in Chapter 5; because local course planners usually have limited resources, only the most important questions are listed.

EXHIBIT 8.2   Questions to Answer in Building the Knowledge Base

The Students
Consider the students likely to take the course and find out . . .

1. What is the students' IQ range?

2. What levels of cognitive development are represented?

3. What is known about their academic achievement?

4. What are their predominant values and attitudes?

5. What similar learning experiences have they already had?

The Teachers
Consider the teachers likely to be assigned to the course and find out . . .

1. How interested are they in teaching the course?

2. How much do they know about the content likely to be covered by the course?

3. How effective are they as teachers?

The Research
Consider the course territory and find out . . .

1. What research is available that will help planners determine course content?

2. What research is available that will help planners select teaching/learning activities?

What's Available
Consider the course territory and find out . . .

1. Have similar courses been developed by national curriculum centers?

2. Have similar courses been offered by other schools?

3. What materials (texts, multimedia, software, Web-based resources) are readily available in the field?

The student questions are designed to help planners understand the constraints imposed by the characteristics of those likely to take the course. In contrast to the usual "needs assessment," which often turns out to be a useless documentation of the obvious ("Students need to reflect about their career values"), this component of the knowledge base reminds developers of the reality they face in implementing the course successfully. Will the course attract less able, unmotivated students? Will many of them have serious reading problems? Will they have trouble understanding abstract concepts?

The teacher questions are intended to guide the developers in deciding how detailed the course planning should be and how much staff development will be required. Comments of the following sort illustrate how the answers might impinge on the planning process:

- We'll have to use teachers not too interested in teaching the course, so we can't expect too much extra time from them.

- This is a new field for most teachers; we'd better be rather explicit as to where to find materials.

- The course will be taught by a few of our most competent people, so we don't need to go into a lot of detail about teaching methods.

The research questions focus on course content and teaching/learning methods. Stated generally here so that they can apply to any new course, they should be rephrased more specifically by the planners so that they can be answered more readily. For example, individuals developing the career-planning course might seek answers to these more specific questions:

- What do we know about the career values of adolescents?

- What do we know about the Career and Technical Education Improvement Act of 2006 or the New Commission on the Skills of the American Workforce? (see Tucker, 2007).

- What do we know about general patterns of career choice? How stable are career decisions?

- What do we know about changing occupational trends?

- What do we know about the skills needed for career decision making?

- What instructional methods seem to be most effective in developing decision-making skills?

Finally, the questions on "what's available?" help the planners profit from the experience and work of others. If they locate an excellent program developed by a major curriculum center, they may decide to adopt it with modifications.

Block in the Unit

With the knowledge base developed, the next step that usually should be taken is to block in the units—to determine the number and focus of each unit of study that will make up the new course. Note that while the recommended direction is top-down (from general to specific, from unit to lesson), in some cases it might be desirable to reverse the flow—to identify lessons and then cluster lessons into units.

In blocking in the units, planners make tentative decisions about these issues:

- How many units of study are planned?

- How many lessons will there probably be in each unit?

- What is the general objective of each unit?

- What is the optimal sequence of the units?

One unit-blocking process that seems to work well in most disciplines is the following one. First, identify the probable number of units by reviewing the course territory and assessing the interest span of the learners: "We're planning a one-semester course that will meet three times a week, and many of the learners will probably have a short attention span, so maybe we need about seven to nine units—some 2 weeks long, some 3 weeks long."

Then tentatively identify the general objective of each unit. The *unit objective,* as the term is used here, is the one general outcome desired at the end of the unit. How can the tentative unit objectives be produced? One method that seems to work well is to convene the planning team, review with them the course prospectus and the knowledge base, and then ask, "What do we really want the students to learn?"

Here is a list of tentative unit objectives that might be produced by those developing the career course:

- Understanding your career values

- Learning about your skills and aptitudes

- Thinking about the education you need

- Retrieving and using career information

- Career-mobility skills

Once the tentative list of unit objectives has been developed, the planning team should review the list in order to refine it. The refining process attempts to reduce the number of unit objectives to match the number of units previously identified and to ensure that the final list closely matches the course territory. Questions of the following sort should be asked:

- Which unit objectives might be combined?

- Which unit objectives are of low priority and might be eliminated?

- Which unit objectives are tangential to the central thrust of the course and might be eliminated?

The refining stage is also the best time to make a tentative decision about the number of lessons. In making this decision, the team should reflect on the complexity and importance of the unit and the attention span of the learners, realizing, of course, that the decision is only preliminary.

Thus, the team planning the career course might produce a final list such as the following one, in which both the unit objectives and the probable numbers of lessons are indicated:

- Careers, jobs, and vocations: 6
- Looking at yourself—skills, aptitudes, values: 6
- Changing occupational needs: 6
- Retrieving and using career information: 9

The final step in this stage of blocking out the units is determining the optimal sequence. Again, as with the technological process, course planners would have several types of sequences available to them. However, those using the naturalistic process ordinarily combine several types of sequence, giving considerable weight to student interest and the rhythms of the school year.

Plan Quality Learning Experiences

With the units blocked out, the next stage in the process is planning quality learning experiences—designing a set of learning experiences that together will lead to the unit objective. It is perhaps at this stage that the naturalistic process differs most significantly from the standard model; it therefore might be useful at this point to clarify the distinction.

Curriculum Tip 8.10	In the technological model, objectives drive the planning process. In the naturalistic model, objectives are set to produce desirable student experiences or outcomes.

In the technological model, the objectives determine the activities and influence the choice of materials. The intent is to control the learning process to ensure that a predetermined end is achieved. The process is linear and unidirectional, as Exhibit 8.3 suggests.

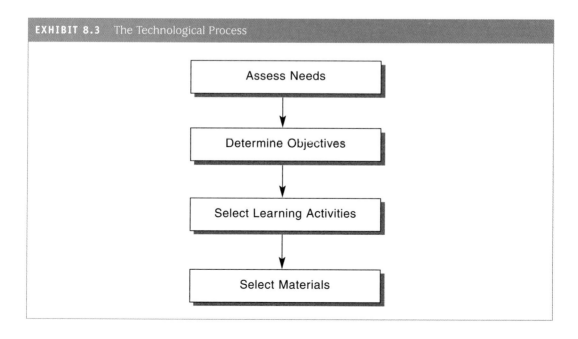

EXHIBIT 8.3   The Technological Process

In the naturalistic process, the planners attempt to design quality learning experiences—stimulating teaching/learning transactions that will produce several desirable outcomes, some of which might occur serendipitously. They think about the learners—their learning styles, their motivations, and their abilities. They keep in mind the unit objective, as the general outcome to be attained, and reflect on the more specific objectives it comprises. They search for excellent materials that will have high interest value and good instructional payoff. They reflect on learning activities that will appeal to the learners, will challenge them to think, and will give them an opportunity to be creative.

Sometimes the specific objectives will dominate their thinking, as in the technological approach. Sometimes, however, planners will begin by thinking about materials and will derive an objective from a particular text or Web-based application.

In the naturalistic model, objectives, materials, and activities are all examined in an interactive and recursive manner as components of a quality learning experience. Exhibit 8.4 illustrates this process.

The intent is to develop plans for quality learning experiences—meaningful learning transactions mediated by the teacher. Some learning requires hard work and, occasionally, drudgery—such as writing a story or solving a math problem. Some learning can be facilitated by a clear and well-organized lecture that derives from the subject content, not the child.

Observe, finally, that this process of identifying quality learning experiences does not preclude objectives-based planning. If, because of the nature of the discipline or their own curricular orientation, planners prefer to start with objectives, they may do so.

EXHIBIT 8.4 The Naturalistic Model

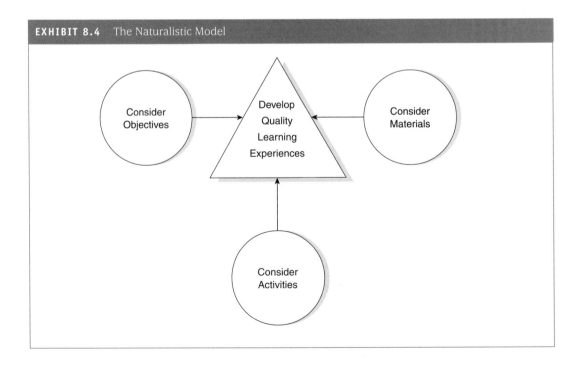

Develop the Course Examination

The naturalistic process places less emphasis on assessment. Rather than developing in advance several detailed assessment devices, course planners ensure that teachers are given the staff development needed to make their own ongoing assessments.

Develop the Learning Scenarios

Instead of using the standard curriculum guide, the naturalistic process culminates in the production and dissemination of learning scenarios for each unit of study.

Curriculum Tip 8.11	A **learning scenario** is a more flexible and open-ended guide that assists the teacher in implementing a new course of study.

Learning scenarios usually include these components:

- A clear and detailed statement of the unit objective

- A suggested number of lessons

- A list of recommended quality learning experiences, phrased in a way that integrates objectives, activities, and materials

- Reprints of articles, maps, photographs, and/or online Web-based resources that teachers could use in making lesson plans; observe that materials are not just listed—they are included (the copyright law allows such professional use in a teacher's guide if three conditions are met: proper credit is given, the guide is not sold for profit, and the articles are not reproduced for student use)

An example of a learning scenario is shown in Exhibit 8.5.

EXHIBIT 8.5   Learning Scenario: Self-Understanding and Career Planning

Course: Career Planning
Unit objective: At the end of the unit it is hoped that the students will have a clearer sense of their talents, skills, and values as they relate to the career-planning process. The goal is to help students become somewhat more realistic as they think about careers—but not to box themselves in or aim too low. Keep reminding them that weak talents can be developed, that new skills can be acquired, that values change with age and experience.

(Continued)

EXHIBIT 8.5 (Continued)

Suggested number of lessons: 6 to 8
Quality learning experiences: (These are listed in what seems to be a desirable sequence, but you should feel free to modify the order as you see fit.)

1. Have students write a paper that they could share with peers, parents, and counselors on "My Ideal Career." Provide some good prewriting discussion and allow time for revision. This is a good initiating activity; the paper will provide you and the student with some baseline data—how the student thinks about self and careers before the unit starts.

2. Conduct a discussion of the nature of talents (the general aptitudes that we possess, such as a talent for music), skills (specific career-related behaviors we have mastered, such as being able to use a word processor), and values (those aspects of life we consider worthwhile, such as liking to be outdoors). Emphasize: People have multiple talents and skills; the strengths of those talents and skills vary for each individual; while all talents and skills have intrinsic worth, our culture accords them varying merit; all of us have different values as they relate to careers.

3. Help students analyze test scores and grades as a way of understanding themselves. If possible, ask the guidance counselor to prepare a test-and-grade profile for each student and to discuss the uses and limitations of test scores and school grades in assessing talents, skills, and values.

4. Have each student develop a talent profile. Identify the range of talents people possess—mechanical, verbal, mathematical, scientific, musical, physical, artistic, interpersonal, and managerial. Chart your own highs and lows on the profile to illustrate that talents are differentially strong in one individual.

5. Help each student develop a skills inventory. Most students will probably believe that they have few career-related skills. Help them reflect on their part-time jobs, their school experiences, and their community experiences as sources of skills that can be used in a job.

6. Ask students to interview one or both parents about parental career values. Emphasize that the goal here is not to intrude on parents' privacy (the results will not be shared with classmates or the teacher) but to get a broader understanding of parents and to see whether parent values have influenced student values. Stress that most studies show similarities between core values of parents and of children. Teach students how to conduct a supportive interview, one that helps the interviewee be reflective about self. The students should probably summarize the results of the interviews in their journals, only to systematize what they know—but these summaries need not be shared with the teacher. You may wish to check just to be sure that they were written.

7. Arrange for students to take the values section of the program called SIGI (System of Interactive Guidance and Information). This is a software program produced by Educational Testing Services and is available in the guidance office that gives students some useful information on their career values. The results will need some discussion in class.

8. As a culminating activity, ask students to write a final paper on the topic, "Seeing Myself in Relation to Careers." They'll probably need some prewriting help in organizing all the information they have collected. This will also provide a good opportunity for teaching students how to present information in a table or a figure and how to integrate tables, figures, and text.

9. As an enrichment activity for those with special interest in the subject, discuss how culture shapes career values. Ask them to speculate about the career values of an Eskimo and those of an urban factory worker.

Adapting the Naturalistic Model for Elementary Grades

Curriculum Tip 8.12	The naturalistic model can be used effectively, especially at the elementary level.

By making some simple modifications in the naturalistic model, it can become quite effective at lower instructional levels. Assume that a fourth-grade team of teachers, teaching in self-contained classrooms, decides to plan together a unit on "communication," using the naturalistic model. The steps they would take are as follows.

Stake Out the Territory

They begin by defining the boundaries of the unit, considering the pupils, the schedule, the general content of the unit, and the length. They would produce a prospectus for themselves and the principal.

Develop the Knowledge Base

They begin this phase by getting good information about their pupils, reviewing their abilities, and checking with second- and third-grade teachers to determine what was taught in earlier grades about communication in general. They discuss their own expertise and background in the field. They review the research on the cognitive development and communication interests of the age group. They take some time to see what is available, checking especially on instructional materials.

Block in the Unit

Now they proceed to block in the unit. They have tentatively considered the general content and think they can spend 3 weeks on the unit before pupil interest wanes. They then move on to consider the general outcomes that they hope to achieve.

Develop Quality Learning Experiences

With those general topics listed and sequenced, they then brainstorm the quality learning experiences they need. Again, as with the career unit, they begin with an activity, with learning materials, or with an objective.

Develop the Unit Test

The team would cooperate in developing the end-of-unit test, assessing all the learnings they considered important.

Develop the Learning Scenarios

As with the career unit, the teachers would systematize and package their work in a learning scenario.

The Naturalistic Model Summarized

The naturalistic model is characterized by several features that set it off from the technological model. It is looser, more flexible, and less rational. It is more responsive to the political realities of curriculum making. It tends to be a "top-down" process, moving from the larger unit to the smaller lesson. It seems to be more in accord with the way teachers actually plan, and it gives equal weight to objectives, activities, and materials, rather than giving primary attention to objectives.

Its advantages seem clear. It should result in curricula that are more likely to be implemented, rather than shelved. Because it addresses the political reality of schools and because it is in accord with teachers' actual planning styles, it should have greater appeal to both principals and teachers. It should also result in more interesting and challenging learning experiences, because it emphasizes the intrinsic quality of the experience.

Its main drawback is its looseness. Especially in the hands of the inexperienced, it can result in a seemingly random collection of entertaining activities that appear unrelated to the intended outcomes.

The Technological Model Summarized

Integrating technology into instruction has made good schools even better. Many schools are now characterized by the seamless use of technology at all levels of the curriculum (Patterson, 2007). Students must be successful in employing technological advances to facilitate processing of information in meaningful ways. Teachers planning new courses can now do Web-based research to locate current technological applications available to enable students to better collect and analyze "real-time, virtual, real-world" data in the field. For example, teachers could design an action plan for an ecosystem field trip that incorporates current technological equipment for gathering, analyzing, and sharing data.

Many curriculum planners now believe that it is important to get as many people on board as possible when developing new courses via the use of technology. They note that opinions can be dangerous if they are not buttressed by facts and believe that technology should be a learning aid or it will become an educational barrier. The bottom line is that new courses need to be developed on the basis of fact, not fiction. It is therefore crucial to get accurate data before making generalizations as to what is needed in the curriculum and before developing new courses.

Researcher Conrad Wesley Snyder (2004) noted advancements in educational technology that were helping to transcend both the technological curriculum planning model as well as the naturalistic planning model. Snyder's research is still applicable today. He states that there are six objectives for understanding that can also serve as criteria for lesson development using technology:

1. Explanation: knowledgeable and justified accounts of events, actions, and ideas

2. Interpretation: narratives and translations that provide meaning

3. Application: using knowledge effectively in new situations and diverse contexts

4. Perspective: critical and insightful points of view

5. Empathy: identification with another person's feelings and worldview

6. Self-knowledge: wisdom to know one's ignorance and one's patterns of thought and action

These criteria help ensure that understanding is not trained explicitly but is "awakened more than trained by design, not exhortation." The goal is for students to come to the realization that they are responsible for making meaning of ideas rather than waiting for teacher explanations. The "design" part is similar to a highly structured curriculum approach (sometimes referred to as Instructional Systems Design), and it includes didactic or direct instruction while emphasizing coaching and reflective or facilitative instruction. The latter are fostered by explicit attention to the creation of generative instructional events, created from what can be called an "inverse design" from basic understandings and essential or generative questions.

Inverse Design Process

Inverse design entails three steps: (1) identify the desired results in terms of understandings and questions—that is, develop the essential questions; (2) determine the acceptable evidence to meet the standards specified in the desired results—that is, specify how learning will be assessed; and (3) plan learning experiences and instruction. This includes the following questions:

- What enabling activities will lead to the needed knowledge and skills?

- What needs to be taught and coached, and how should it best be taught, in light of the performance goals?

- What materials and resources are needed?

- Is the overall design coherent and effective?

Each of these steps reflects an important aspect of both the technological and naturalistic approaches. More and more administrators and teachers are currently embodying each of the characteristics listed above.

| **Curriculum Tip 8.13** | An alternative for addressing NCLB and RTI concerns and formulating new courses can be the development of a distance learning component. |

Develop Distance Learning Courses as an Alternative

The Internet and related communications technologies, along with political, social, and economic changes in our society, have spawned unprecedented growth of interest in distance education and in the number of courses and programs available through distance learning.

Research findings increasingly show that high school students who take college coursework while in high school (dual enrollment) are more likely to go to college. Dual enrollment provides high school students with significant opportunities to challenge themselves academically as well as to explore career and academic options not available in high school. When the distance-delivered course is provided for high school students only, it is important for the teacher to know and be able to meet the instructional, curricular, and legal expectations for teaching in that setting. When the distance-delivered course is a college course made available to high school students, it is important that the course be taught like any other course at the college level (Montana State University, 2007).

Develop Technology as a Classroom Learning Scenario

The use of the Internet, electronic white boards, videoconferencing, and other novel technological applications has brought about not only technological innovations but also provides new ways of approaching learning and instruction. From the Read/Write Web: blogs, wikis, podcasts, social bookmarking, online photo galleries, as well as RSS (Real Simple Syndication), technology continues to change the structure of traditional education. According to Richardson and Mancabelli (2007), advancements in educational technology change have been coming in shifts.

> *First:* There is the shift from traditional education to open learning. Traditional education was built on the idea that knowledge is a scare commodity. Now, through the Web, students have the potential to access more content than we can teach them. Learning no longer has to stop at the end of the school day.
>
> *Second:* There is a shift from teachers no longer being the sole arbiters of knowledge in the classroom. There new role is one of being connectors. Interactive exchanges are possible because of the Read/Write Web. Social networking sites like MySpace (www.myspace.com) have over 100 million accounts. Sites such as del.icio.us, Furl, Digg.com and Flickr.com are being joined by new sites. The ability for students to connect to others creates new communities of communication.
>
> *Third:* A major shift is occurring in how literacy changes the new environment. In the past, printed material was often edited and proofread before publication. Now, readers have to weigh the veracity of the material instead of simply believing what they read. Students now need to be guided on how to use technologies effectively and safely. (pp. 12–17)

The bottom line is that technology is leveling the field of learning and knowledge acquisition. With today's infusion of technology in the classroom, the Web is now a powerful, global learning space for all students.

Answer the What and Why

Why do you want to put course materials online, and what are the materials you want to include? For example, you may want to have lecture notes or presentation materials accessible to your students. You may want to provide an online resource directory to assist your students' research or information gathering. Or it may be simply to have a course syllabus available for your students. Whatever the reason, you should start small. Online forms, video or animation clips, and many other types of interactive feedback are not something to tackle until you have more experience.

Learn the How

How are you going to take what you have—printed material, computer documents, slides, transparencies, graphics—and get it on the Web? Plus, how do you present it so your students can easily find what they are looking for?

Determine the Where

Where will you publish your course materials? You have more than one choice here as well. There are specialized companies that faculty members can use for their Web sites.

Distribute Your Web Address

How will your students find your site? You might want to consider posting your Web address (URL) in the classroom, on class handouts, and on a specialized Web site.

Curriculum Tip 8.14	Use of WebQuests is one way that the Internet can be meaningfully incorporated into the curriculum.

Use Alternatives to Identify Learning Activities

Locating quality information on the Internet presents a variety of challenges. Users need to be able to sort through the multitude of information to locate the most relevant pieces. Some teachers avoid using the Web as a resource in their classrooms because students have not acquired the skills needed to use the Internet effectively. In addition to the Web-based ideas provided earlier, teachers can also design a WebQuest to enhance a classroom unit or a particular curriculum area and engage their students in meaningful research. WebQuest is located at http://webquest.org/index.php.

As tempting as it is to develop learning applications that make use of Web-based technologies and distance learning, educators remind us again and again that learning must be developed around learner needs. While this may be self-evident to many, it is a message that is ignored with surprising frequency. To some extent, this is because our established postsecondary institutions have evolved as teacher- and subject-centered institutions with little emphasis on the students' needs and interests. It is also because—just as anyone can be a publisher on the Internet—on the Internet, anyone can also be a distance educator. Many educators and subject specialists are newly involved in distance education with little or no awareness of some of the important principles that have been developed over the years for developing new online distance courses.

Develop Acceptable Use Policy

With the arrival of Internet connections and distance learning at schools comes the question of safety for children. Educators are rightfully concerned about giving students free rein to "browse" the Web for fear that they might access inappropriate material (Sholten, 2003). At the same time, parents are concerned about the potential of those on the outside gaining access to children. Teachers need to learn how schools guarantee the safe implementation of a technically enriched curriculum through Acceptable Use Policies (AUP) and design a policy for their own schools.

In review, it is important to view curriculum as a way to safely empower students and to develop creativity and enhance problem solving when developing new courses of study. Teachers using both technological and naturalistic approaches must make sure that the curriculum is relevant and meaningful to all. It is critical that educators of the future be empowered in every way possible to maximize their opportunities and to make the necessary changes needed to deepen and to improve our global understanding of others and of our world.

Our schools today are under the microscope of increased accountability, and many "have been identified as underperforming on the basis of their low test scores" (Chrisman, 2005, p. 6). Realistically, schools and students need an accountability system that combines commonsense flexibility with shared responsibility and also provides the resources to actually help close the achievement gap (Packer, 2007). Subsequently, the search continues for how schools can improve student achievement and sustain it year after year.

Valerie Chrisman (2005), director of district and school support services at the Ventura County Superintendent of Schools Office, Ventura, California, conducted a study of California's primary and secondary reform programs. Chrisman's study, using "three criteria: analyses of test scores and school characteristics; interview responses from teachers and principals; and questionnaire responses from 356 principals whose schools experienced growth in at least one of the two years of the reform program" (p. 16), revealed the following results for successful schools:

- Strong teacher leadership was apparent in each of the four successful sample schools.
- Teachers [at the successful schools] engaged in various forms of informal action research.
- Teachers [at the successful schools] developed their own internal leadership structures—such as team teaching, mentoring new teachers, and collaborating to share lesson designs—support one another's resolve to improve student achievement.
- Teacher leaders at the successful schools also made policy decisions. (p. 16)

Principal Leadership

- The successful schools in the study, as opposed to the unsuccessful ones, more often had the same principal for the last 3 years.

- Principals at the successful schools were more likely to create time for teachers to collaborate and to provide them with structured support.

- Principals [at the successful schools] were comfortable using data and making changes when the data demonstrated that student achievement had not risen.

- Principals from the unsuccessful schools were far less comfortable with data. (Chrisman, 2005, p. 18)

District Office Leadership

- District leaders in successful schools provided more services than their counterparts. The successful schools benefited from focused district-wide professional development on pedagogy.

- At the start of each school term, successful schools more often received assessment data disaggregated by teacher and by individual student than did unsuccessful schools. Teachers and principals also received training on how to use these data to improve instruction and academic achievement.

- New principals were placed in schools in which parent demands and conflicts were expected to be fewer. These schools tended to be in the lowest socioeconomic areas of the district. That assignment . . . was either an entry-level position for new principals or a way of penalizing them for being unable to effectively handle parent conflicts.

- Principals from the successful schools said that their districts scheduled monthly cohort meetings with all the district's state improvement program schools. (Chrisman, 2005, pp. 18–19)

Programs and Practices

- Students who are learning English as a second language and students who are academically below grade level attending the successful schools had quite different experiences from those of comparable students who attended unsuccessful schools.

- At the successful schools, teachers presented instruction that directly reinforced the students' understanding of how the English language works instead of teaching students conversational English.

- Teachers from the successful schools reported that students were grouped by their English language levels.

- In the successful schools, principals and district office personnel were instrumental in supporting all newly adopted district programs. (Chrisman, 2005, pp. 19–20)

Remarkably, Chrisman's study and suggestions continue to reflect what is needed in schools today. The key is for curriculum leaders at all levels to find and develop planned corrective activities to meet state and national requirements. According to Thomas Guskey (2007–2008), effective corrective activities possess three essential characteristics:

First, corrective activities present the concepts differently. The best corrective activities involve a change in format, organization, or method of presentation.

Second, effective corrective activities engage students differently in learning. To make corrective strategy effective, students engagement in learning must be qualitatively different from what took place during the initial instruction.

Third, effective corrective activities provide students with successful learning experiences. The best ideas for effective corrective activities generally come from fellow colleagues. (pp. 28–34)

As noted above and mentioned throughout this chapter, the authors of this book believe that school districts can improve student achievement *if* they are willing to examine their practices and to embrace change. In fact, most all schools can replicate the strategies mentioned and improve education for everyone.

SUMMARY

This chapter compares and explains how to develop a new course or unit using two contrasting processes: the standard technological process and what is termed here a *naturalistic* process. The chapter also explores how curriculum leaders can develop new courses that involve both the technological as well as naturalistic processes of curriculum planning. How to improve academic achievement and sustain it is covered as well.

APPLICATIONS

1. Consider this issue: Should the choice of the technological or naturalistic process be influenced by the nature of the educational organization? If so, in what types of organizations should each be used?

2. To test your ability to use the technological model, do the following:
   a. Identify the parameters of a new course you might develop.
   b. Describe the purpose of data in regard to assessing the needs of the learner.
   c. List the learning objectives for the course.
   d. Identify the learning activities you would recommend for one of the objectives.

3. To test your ability to use the naturalistic model, do the following:
   a. Describe the territory of a new course.
   b. Describe the advantages of school-based curriculum development.

    c. List all unit objectives.

    d. Write at least four quality learning experiences for one of the units.

4. Some who have used the naturalistic process have suggested that it is more suitable for elementary grades than for secondary. If you were an elementary school principal, would you recommend that your teachers use the naturalistic process? Discuss in detail your rationale for using the naturalistic process rather than a technological process approach.

CASE STUDY   The Importance of Using Data Analysis

A sixth-grade teacher in Florida discusses with her principal the problem of her students not meeting NCLB standards in the area of reading.

"I'm pleased you were able to drop by my office," says Principal Woodward. "As I recall from a previous conversation, you are interested in individualizing reading instruction and addressing specific skills."

"That is correct, Mr. Woodward," states sixth-grade teacher Nita Caterlin. "I'm looking for ways to identify student strengths and weaknesses in reading as well as determine what strategies I should use to address identified weaknesses."

"How about using a Web-based data-analysis program?" he asks. "We just purchased rights to a program, and it has been helping a number of other teachers."

"Is this one of those Internet-based programs that gives you a detailed analysis of student academic strengths and weaknesses?" she asks.

"Yes," says Principal Woodward. "You will have to go through the training online, but that shouldn't be a problem. Mrs. Hall uses it and has found it to be very helpful." The principal can see that Mrs. Caterlin is interested in the possibility of using an Internet-based assessment program.

"How does it work?"

"Well, Mrs. Hall had all of her students go to the lab and go online to take a pretest. The results were immediate in that the students were assessed electronically. She found that her children were having difficulty with the concept of 'main idea,' which is one of the state reading standards."

"That's sounds like a great program!"

"Yes, online assessment programs are becoming quite popular," says the principal. "What is especially important is that the program not only provides pre- and posttests but also provides teaching strategies and links to other resources."

"I would really like to get started," says Mrs. Caterlin enthusiastically.

"No problem!" says the principal. "I'll contact the district testing coordinator and have you up and running very soon."

The Challenge

Analyze the importance of online data analysis as it relates to developing the technological process of curriculum planning and enhancing student achievement. How can Principal

Woodward educate and motivate other teachers to use online data analysis strategies to improve test scores and raise student achievement in his school?

Key Issues/Questions

1. What questions should principals ask before incorporating or committing to an online assessment program?

2. What role will politics play, and what needs to be done by Principal Woodward to make sure that he develops a constituency of support before embarking on this project?

3. Making sure that an online assessment program is aligned with district, state, and national standards is crucial to the curriculum process. What are some steps that Principal Woodward needs to take to make sure that his online assessment program is aligned with the district's curricula?

4. The expense of online assessment programs can be prohibitive for many school districts. How can superintendents and principals justify such costs to teachers and to the community?

5. Conversion to online assessment programs can be a daunting task. Such changes often affect the development of new courses and units. What measures can be taken to reduce opposition by teachers to such radical curriculum changes?

WEBLIOGRAPHY

James Madison University—Steps for developing new courses and/or units
www.jmu.edu/registrar/Course%20Approval/stepsnewcourse.html

Teachers.net—Online strategies and lesson plans
www.teachers.net

PART III

Curriculum Management

Many curriculum leaders focus unduly on the written curriculum, neglecting the taught curriculum and the supported curriculum. The purpose of Part III is to incorporate ways to supervise instructional processes and the selection of materials, recommend specific processes for developing and implementing curriculum, provide a rationale for curricular alignment, and make specific suggestions for developing and implementing a comprehensive evaluation plan.

CHAPTER 9

Supervising the Curriculum

Teachers and Materials

"The direction of leadership and development of schoolwide instructional change is a shift of responsibility for growth from supervisor to supervisee, from master teacher to mentee, from teacher to student" (Glickman, 2001, p. 104). Too many curriculum leaders focus unduly on the written curriculum, neglecting the taught curriculum and the supported curriculum. Obviously such neglect is unwise and counterproductive.

An excellent written curriculum will have little impact if it is not taught well and supported with appropriate materials. This chapter, therefore, examines the problems and issues in supervision as well as how to improve these two often-slighted aspects of curriculum.

Questions addressed in this chapter include the following:

- Who are some of the major leaders who have been concerned with supervision, and what are some of the current approaches to curriculum supervision?

- What are some of the issues and problems that relate to supervision that are facing curriculum leaders today?

- What are some of the major roles associated with curriculum supervision?

- Why is motivating staff an important component of supervision?

- Why are some of Abraham Maslow's theories on supervision still relevant today?

- What are the elements that make up supportive curriculum, and why is the supportive curriculum important?

Key to Leadership

One of the most important aspects of a quality supervision program is the area of assessment. No program can be significantly improved without assessment of both teacher and instructional programs.

SUPERVISING THE TAUGHT CURRICULUM: CURRENT APPROACHES

Principals can benefit from knowing which of their behaviors or attitudes are the most valued (Richards, 2007). According to Cheryl Riggins-Newby (2003), NAESP's associate executive director for urban alliances, principals in all schools must be instructional leaders. Curriculum and instruction are at the heart of any school-improvement program. Principals need to work with teachers to supervise and coordinate decisions within and between grade levels. Doing so will help align the school's curriculum both horizontally and vertically. A well-aligned and supervised curriculum ensures that students are taught the necessary skills and standards that will be tested on statewide exams.

Curriculum Tip 9.1	Real leadership challenges the leader before it challenges others. Real leadership is often the key to developing a successful supervision program (Glover, 2007).

Teachers will live up to their potential as leaders only when the school environment supports their efforts (Lattimer, 2007). Leaders concerned with supervising the taught curriculum have available to them a number of approaches to supervision. In reviewing the literature, four seem to have had the greatest impact. These are Hunter's (1984) "Knowing, Teaching, and Supervising"; Glickman, Gordon, and Ross-Gordon's (2003) *Supervision and Instructional Leadership: A Developmental Approach*; Costa and Garmston's (2002) *Cognitive Coaching: A Foundation for Renaissance Schools*; and Glatthorn's (1984) *Differentiated Supervision*. The first three are reviewed in this section; the last is explained more fully in the next section.

Hunter's "Essential Elements"

During the middle of the 1980s, the work of Madeline Hunter seemed to be the dominant mode of supervision: Several state offices of education, in fact, had given the Hunter approach their official blessing and encouraged its adoption through workshops for administrators, supervisors, and teachers. Although Hunter herself advocated a number of "templates" that could be used to analyze and improve teaching, her "**elements of lesson design**" attracted the most attention. By reviewing the theory of and research on learning, Hunter was able to identify the following elements of good lesson design:

Anticipatory set: A set that helps students develop a mental set that allows them to focus on what will be learned

Objective and purpose: Stating what is to be learned and how it will be useful

Input: Giving students information about the knowledge, skill, or process they are to achieve

Modeling: Demonstrating the process or skill

Guided practice: Directing the student practice of the new process or skill

Independent practice: Assigning independent practice of the process or skill (cited in Glatthorn, 1987, p. 222)

What made the Hunter "elements" so popular with practitioners? First, they were based on sound theory, even though the research base seemed thin to some critics. Second, they gave educators a common vocabulary to discuss teaching: Everyone could talk about "anticipatory set" and know what was meant. Finally, they seemed "teacher friendly": They did not require teachers to adopt new behaviors but instead helped teachers systematize what they had already been doing.

Hunter's approach, however, was not without its critics, most of whom were university professors, not practitioners. Those critics faulted the model, first of all, because it offered a narrowly constricted view of teaching. Sergiovanni (1985) made the point that Hunter conceived teaching and learning only as an instructional delivery system, a conception that saw teaching as sending information through a pipeline to passive students. Others were unhappy because the elements seemed to be derived from the direct instruction model of teaching and slighted other models, although Hunter argued that the elements could be used flexibly in any model of teaching.

Although many administrators who had adopted the Hunter "elements" approach reported enthusiastic reception on the part of teachers and noted many positive effects, the early research on its impact on achievement indicated that it was not more effective than standard approaches to supervision (see Stallings, 1986).

Glickman's Developmental Supervision

Carl Glickman, Stephen P. Gordon, and Jovita M. Ross-Gordon's (2003) "developmental supervision" is characterized by two important features that set it off from Hunter's work. First, Glickman and colleagues argue that the development of teacher thought should be the focus of supervisors' work with teachers—helping teachers increase their conceptual level of development. They posit three levels of development: low abstract (the teacher is confused, lacks ideas, wants to be shown, gives habitual responses to varying decisions), moderate abstract (depends on authority, identifies one dimension of instructional problem, generates one to three ideas about solutions, needs assistance from experts), and high abstract (uses various sources to identify problems, generates multiple ideas, chooses for self the action to be taken).

This "thought-oriented" approach permeates the four ways supervisors can help teachers grow: by offering direct assistance (what is usually called "clinical supervision"), by providing in-service education, by working with teachers in curriculum development, and by helping them carry out action research.

Although Glickman et al. admit that the results on developmental supervision have been "predictably mixed," both features make the model seem very useful for curriculum leaders. They recognize the fact that teachers are different and require different approaches. They also broaden the prevailing understanding of supervision by emphasizing the importance of in-service, curriculum-development, and action research.

Costa and Garmston's Cognitive Coaching

Like Glickman, Costa and Garmston (2002) emphasized the importance of teacher thinking, although their approach seems quite different. Rather than using all the approaches that Glickman advocated, they gave their attention exclusively to direct assistance or clinical supervision. However, it is clinical supervision with a profound difference. They were not concerned initially with skills; they believed it more productive to emphasize teacher thinking. As the supervisor works with teachers in this cognitive coaching mode, the supervisor has these goals: to create and manage a trusting relationship, to facilitate teacher learning by restructuring teacher thinking, and to develop teacher autonomy. Those goals are achieved primarily through in-depth conferences in which the supervisor listens actively, questions insightfully, and responds congruently.

Although the authors indicated that their approach was based on current theory and sound research on adult development, they did not offer any empirical evidence about its effectiveness. Its emphasis on teacher thinking and its concern for teacher autonomy both seem to be useful from the standpoint of curriculum leaders.

PROBLEMS AND ISSUES IN SUPERVISION

Many unsolved problems are associated with the development of curriculum and the formation of an effective instructional program. Hours can be spent organizing personnel, material resources, and activities of the school.

Curriculum Tip 9.2	Three main areas that appear to thread their way through the supervised curriculum are students, classroom climate, and informational resources.

A major problem facing educators, historically, has been the inability of our instructional programs to reach students and meet their needs (Weeks, 2001). This situation has led to the passage of the No Child Left Behind Act, which is responsible for holding schools more accountable for student learning levels and student achievement. Unfortunately, according to author Tom Allen (2004), there is something wrong with a law that brands good schools with "failing" labels.

Nevertheless, a growing concern over skills and school climate is revolutionizing the way schools are developing curriculum from preschool years through high school. The lack of real understanding in subject areas such as mathematics and reading has led to a series of mandates from the federal government requiring strict proficiency levels and adequate yearly progress goals. School leaders are realizing the need for well-written curriculum with quality supportive materials (Gilman & Gilman, 2003).

In the quest to provide well-written curriculum and supportive materials, technology is quickly becoming a major aspect of how classrooms are designed, instruction is planned, and information is delivered. Curriculum planners, administrators, and classroom teachers are finding new and innovative ways to deliver subsequent stages of educational development for students. Schools are learning the importance of becoming part of the communication age as well as becoming a part of a global learning network (Harmon, 2004).

THE ROLE OF THE CURRICULUM SUPERVISOR

Developing ways to get to the heart of curriculum programming and bringing about educationally significant change lies with curriculum leaders as well as school principals.

Curriculum Tip 9.3	The role of the principal has grown from that of a manager to that of a change agent, an administrative–organizational specialist.

Principals need to become aware and knowledgeable about new approaches to curriculum supervision. They have to know how to write and direct curriculum as well as have the ability to find needed supportive materials during a time of declining budgets. Principals and school supervisors are now learning how information is best acquired by children and how it relates to their overall growth and development (Merrow, 2004). A crucial part of that process is providing a quality learning environment based on effective staff development. An important part of this process, therefore, is the development of a quality differentiated professional-development program.

DIFFERENTIATED PROFESSIONAL DEVELOPMENT

Each school possesses its own traditions, values, culture, and willingness to accept change. There is no universal model of school reform that will work in all settings (Piltch & Quinn, 2007). It is in this light of multiple variables affecting school climate that differentiated professional development should be considered. Differentiated professional development (Glatthorn, 1984) is essentially a reconceptualization of the supervisory function, one that attempts to broaden the practitioner's view of supervision. Glatthorn argues that one of the reasons educational leaders neglect the taught curriculum is that they hold a very narrow view of supervision. Too often it is equated with clinical supervision—the intensive process of observing a teacher, analyzing observational data, and giving the teacher feedback about such data. Such a narrow view is unproductive for several reasons. First, clinical supervision is so time-consuming that principals especially find it impossible to provide it for everyone.

Second, clinical supervision is only one of several means of facilitating the professional development of teachers; other processes, as Glickman notes, should be used, too. Also, not all teachers need clinical supervision; experienced, competent teachers need some options. Finally, most models of clinical supervision do not give sufficient attention to major aspects of curriculum.

Curriculum Tip 9.4	Leaders who wish to improve the taught curriculum need to reconceptualize the supervisory process—to see it more broadly and to differentiate its use in relation to teacher need.

Such a reconceptualization can make a modest contribution to what Sergiovanni (2005) referred to as "leading and learning together"—a theory that takes account of the complex messiness of classrooms and teaching, that uses the practical language of classroom life, that is sensitive to the way teachers and supervisors construe classroom meanings, and that is explicitly designed to improve teaching and learning. In this attempt to reconceptualize supervision, it seems useful to substitute the term *professional development* for those activities ordinarily subsumed under the heading of *supervision*. The advantage of using new terminology is that it facilitates the task of reconceptualizing the field by distancing users from the restrictive assumptions implicit in the old language. In this reconceptualization, *professional development* is used in this sense: All those systematic processes used by school administrators, supervisors, and teachers to help teachers grow professionally. Those professional development processes are divided into four distinct yet related tasks: staff development, informal observations, rating, and individual development.

Staff Development

The term *staff development* is used here to designate all those district- and school-sponsored programs, both formal and informal, offered to groups of teachers in response to organizational needs. Elevating teachers from isolated assembly-line workers to collaborative professionals requires a major change in today's school culture (Boles & Toen, 2007). The importance of staff development has been noted in Chapter 5, as an aspect of the planning process, and in Chapter 7, as a critical ingredient in improving a field of study.

The ability of teachers to develop and guide curriculum requires a sophisticated set of judgments about the content, students, learning, and teaching. Creating a network of educators (colleagues, parents, students, and experts in the community) is one way to increase professional sophistication (Tomlinson et al., 2002). Several issues seem important here in examining staff development as an aspect of broader professional development.

First, staff development can be both formal and informal. Formal staff-development programs have a specific agenda, a set schedule, and a structured set of experiences. Typically, such formal programs are skill focused. The research on such skill-focused programs suggests that they will be more effective if they embody the tested practices recommended in Chapter 7.

As noted in previous chapters, staff development of both the formal and informal type is essential throughout the curriculum development and improvement process. If staff development has helped teachers change their perceptions of a subject, develop the materials to be used in implementing the new curriculum, and acquire the skills needed to deliver it, then it is quite likely that the written, the taught, the tested, and the learned curricula will be in much closer congruence.

Informal Observations

Informal observations are brief, unannounced classroom visits, lasting from perhaps 5 to 15 minutes. Some term these informal visits "**walkthroughs**"; some experts in the corporate world call such informal observations "management by walking around." The key to making accurate decisions based on short observations in the walkthrough, principals should ask six questions posed and defined in Exhibit 9.1.

EXHIBIT 9.1 Seeing the Trees and the Forest	
Questions to Ask Oneself	*Answers*
1. Are teachers using research-based teaching strategies?	1. It is important to look for teachers' use of instructional strategies. No single "right way" to teach exists, but great teachers use myriad teaching strategies, understand the instructional purposes of each, and use each strategy intentionally.
2. Do student grouping patterns support learning?	2. "Cooperative learning" is one of the nine categories of effective instruction in *Classroom Instruction That Works*. It includes supporting student learning using large groups, small groups, pairs, cooperative groups (each member has an assigned role), or working individually. Determining whether teachers are intentional in their use of grouping patterns is key.
3. Are teachers and students using technology to support student learning?	3. Educational technology is more prevalent in today's classrooms, but many teachers still do not put these tools to their best use. During walkthroughs, principals should note the technology being used and how it is being used.
4. Do students understand their goals for learning?	4. While conducting a walkthrough, principals should go beyond conducting a checklist of teacher practices; they also should observe what students are doing and learning. Are students able to explain what they are doing in terms of their learning goals? Are students involved in true learning objectives, or are they just focused on activities? Over time, student responses will tell how well teachers are communicating these goals and whether students are engaged and deliberate about their own learning.

Questions to Ask Oneself	Answers
5. Are students learning both basic and higher-order levels of knowledge?	5. Classroom observation also should reveal if students are learning at the lower rungs of Bloom's Taxonomy (e.g., remembering, understanding, and applying) or at the higher levels (analyzing, evaluating, and creating). All of these forms are necessary and appropriate in different contexts. If the majority of student learning, however, is focused on lower-level learning, principals should have conversations with teachers about the levels of student learning they observed.
6. Do student achievement data correlate with walkthrough data?	6. Principals should also view classrooms through the lens of student achievement data. When principals conduct their classroom observations within the context of student achievement data, they can dramatically increase the acuity of their observations and discover ways to improve teaching and learning.

SOURCE: Adapted from "Classroom Walkthroughs: Learning to See the Trees and the Forest," by H. Pitler & B. Goodwin, 2008, Summer, *Changing Schools, 58*, pp. 9–11. Reprinted by permission of McREL.

There are a number of misconceptions on how to use the data generated from classroom walkthroughs. Likewise, some teachers' resistance to walkthroughs is because they or their principals, or both, are unclear about how observation data is or should be used. The walkthrough data should be used in the following ways:

Coaching, not evaluating. The purpose of a walkthrough is not to pass judgment on teachers, but to coach them to higher levels of performance. Walkthroughs are not teacher evaluations; they are a method for identifying opportunities for improvement and supporting the sharing of best practices across the school.

Measuring the impact of staff development efforts. In its best use, the walkthrough process will provide strong data to schools and districts regarding the extent to which their professional development initiatives are actually making it into the classroom. By systematically collecting and analyzing data from classroom observation, school leaders can determine whether staff development efforts are making a difference and guide real-time adjustments to the professional development they are offering teachers.

Supporting professional learning communities with walkthrough data. Savvy principals also understand the power of sharing their aggregated observation data with school staff to support professional learning communities. (Pitler & Goodwin, 2008, p. 11)

For walkthroughs to be highly successful, the data collected must be aggregated over a period of time. "One or two, or even 10 observations of an individual teacher, do not provide a clear picture of the quality of instruction within a school. But 10 visits each to 40 teachers' classrooms does provide a more accurate picture" (Pitler & Goodwin, 2008, p. 11). Pitler and Goodwin see the walkthroughs as a mosaic. "Looking at one tile in isolation tells you almost nothing. But when you see 400 of those tiles laid out in an orderly manner, a picture begins to emerge" (p. 11). Thus, when principals or supervisors know what to look for and understand the purpose of their observations, "the power of walkthroughs lies not only in seeing the trees, but also the forest" (p. 11).

Rating

Specific, accurate, and timely feedback is often a missing element in most leadership encounters (Reeves, 2007). This is especially significant when relating to decision making. In the reconceptualization, the term **rating** is used in this sense: The process of making formative and summative assessments of teacher performance for purposes of administrative decision making. The term is chosen to distinguish this formal assessment function from a more general act of evaluation, which is often construed to mean a judgment about the quality of performance made on any occasion for a variety of purposes. This distinction between rating and evaluation is intended to clarify the conceptual confusion that is so prevalent in our professional discourse. In reviewing the literature, one an interesting example of the conceptual confusion is McGreal's (1983) monograph titled *Successful Teacher Evaluation*, which really seems to be a treatise on teacher supervision.

Perhaps some examples of the two concepts would provide more clarity. You make an informal observation of a teacher with a disorderly class. You make a judgment: You do not like what you see. You observe a teacher for the purpose of diagnosing teaching style. You try your best to be objective, but you find yourself smiling in approval. You conduct a staff-development session and ask one of the teachers to demonstrate a particular skill. You are not happy with the demonstration. In each instance you have made an evaluation—a judgment about quality. Despite all attempts to be objective, it is probably impossible to observe the act of teaching without making judgments. Most teachers would not want an observer to pretend that he or she had not made any judgments about their performance. In addition, there is some evidence that supervisors who are candid about their assessments are judged to be more effective than those who do not provide evaluative feedback (see Gersten, Green, & Davis, 1985).

Now consider a contrary example. You visit a teacher's class in September with a rating form in hand in which very explicit criteria are stated along with the standards of performance. You observe the class and complete the rating form. You confer with the teacher and say, "Your performance in that class was not satisfactory; I hope your supervisor will be able to help you improve before the next rating observation." You have made a formative rating. You make several more formative rating observations throughout the year. Then, in May, you make a summative assessment based on all your data and say to the teacher, "Your performance this year was unsatisfactory; your contract will not be renewed."

Perhaps one more analogy will help. The gymnast performs a set of exercises at a meet. The coach watches and says, "Your approach was faulty; we'll have to work on that." The coach has made an evaluation. The judges were also watching. They hold up their score-cards with numerical scores on each. The judges have made a rating.

What rating systems are most effective? After studying 32 school districts reported to have effective rating systems, Wise, Darling-Hammond, McLaughlin, and Bernstein (as cited in Glatthorn, 1987) reached five conclusions (their term *teacher evaluation* is used below instead of the narrower term *rating*, because many of the systems included processes that in the reconceptualization are considered primarily developmental):

1. To succeed, the teacher-evaluation system must suit the goals, management style, conception of teaching, and community values of the school district.

2. Top-level commitment to and resources for evaluation are more important than the particular kind of checklist or procedures used.

3. The school district should decide about the main purpose of the rating system and then match the process to the purpose.

4. The evaluation process must be seen to have utility: It is cost effective, fair, valid, and reliable.

5. Teacher involvement in and responsibility for the process improves the quality of teacher evaluation. (Glatthorn, 1987, p. 229)

Obviously, these conclusions suggest that several types of rating systems can be effective. However, if the purpose is administrative decision making, then a criterion-based system using multiple observations seems preferable. One process that has been used effectively in several districts is described below.

Together, administrators, supervisors, and teachers analyze the job of teaching and the research on effective teaching. From those reviews, they develop a comprehensive set of criteria dealing with the three important aspects of the teacher's role. First, they define the non-instructional aspects of the teacher's role. In most cases, a short list of noninstructional responsibilities is all that is necessary: Supervise students in noninstructional settings, communicate with parents, attend faculty meetings and staff-development sessions as required, carry out other assigned duties.

Curriculum Tip 9.5	The research-based list of the "essential observables" and the "essential non-observables" plays a crucial role in both rating teachers and helping them grow professionally.

By reviewing the research, supervisors can identify the essential instructional skills that can be directly observed, such as providing a clear lesson structure. Finally, they identify the essential instructional skills that are probably not always directly observable, such as making valid tests. Therefore, care should be taken to ensure that the list includes only those skills well supported by the research. One formulation of these skills is shown in Exhibit 9.2.

EXHIBIT 9.2 Essential Skills of Teaching

The following list of essential skills is intended to provide general guidelines for administrators, supervisors, and teachers. While based on a careful review of the literature and a reflective analysis of shared experience, it is not intended as a definitive prescription of the "best way to teach." Other cautions need to be noted:

1. The list focuses on the instructional role of the teacher; it does not address the important non-instructional responsibilities.

2. The list does not speak directly to the skills of lesson planning and communicating. As will be noted below, effective planning and clear communication lie behind several of the skills listed below.

ESSENTIAL SKILLS OBSERVABLE IN CLASSROOM INSTRUCTION

Skills relating to lesson content and pace might include:

1. Chooses content for the lesson that relates directly to curriculum goals, is at an appropriate level of difficulty, and corresponds with assessment measures

2. Presents content of lesson in a way that demonstrates mastery of subject matter

3. Paces instruction appropriately

Climate

4. Creates a desirable environment that reflects appropriate discipline and supports the instructional function

5. Communicates realistically high expectations for students

6. Uses instructional time efficiently, allocating most of the time to curriculum-related instruction

7. Keeps students on task

8. Provides organizing structure for classroom work: reviews, gives overview, specifies objectives, gives clear directions, summarizes, makes relevant assignments

9. Uses instructional strategies, learning activities, and group structures that are appropriate to objectives, respond to student needs, and reflect sound learning theory

10. Ensures active participation of students in learning activities

Assessment

11. Monitors student learning and uses evaluative data to adjust instruction

12. Questions effectively: asks clear questions, asks questions at appropriate level of difficulty, varies types of questions

13. Responds effectively to student answers: allows sufficient wait time, gives prompt and corrective feedback, praises appropriately

ESSENTIAL SKILLS NOT DIRECTLY OBSERVABLE IN CLASSROOM INSTRUCTION

1. Develops long-term plans that reflect curricular priorities and adequately deal with all aspects of written curriculum

2. Uses tests that are consistent with instructional objectives

3. Grades student learning fairly, objectively, and validly

NOTE: The above list of skills has been synthesized from several reviews of the research on teaching effectiveness. Three sources have been especially useful:

Berliner, D. C. (1984). The half-full glass: A review of the research on teaching. In P. Hosford (Ed.), *Using what we know about teaching* (pp. 51–85). Alexandria, VA: Association for Supervision and Curriculum Development.

Brophy, J. E., & Good, T. L. (1986). Teacher behavior and student achievement. In M. C. Wittrock (Ed.), *Handbook of research on teaching* (3rd ed., pp. 328–375). New York: Macmillan.

Rosenshine, B., & Stevens, R. (1986). Teaching functions. In M. C. Wittrock (Ed.), *Handbook of research on teaching* (3rd ed., pp. 376–391). New York: Macmillan.

The essential observable skills become the basis of a Rating Observation form, which identifies each skill and for each one specifies several indicators of performance. A portion of one such form is shown in Exhibit 9.3. That form is then used in making a rating observation. The rater tells the teacher that he or she will be observing the class some time next week to rate performance. The teacher is familiar with both the criteria and the indicators and understands clearly that the purpose of the observation is to rate, not to improve instruction. The rater arrives with the rating observation form in hand. The rater observes solely to rate: He or she makes careful notes throughout the lesson about the teacher's performance in relation to each of the criteria and then makes a holistic rating of the entire class. Then the rater holds a rating observation conference, informs the teacher of the general rating, reviews the specific strengths and weaknesses, and in conjunction with the teacher lays out a professional development plan for remedying any perceived deficiencies.

All these formative data are drawn together in a summative rating conference: The rater reviews with the teacher the teacher's performance of the noninstructional responsibilities, summarizes the results of all the rating observations, synthesizes the results of the conferences at which the nonobservable skills were assessed, and provides a final holistic rating of the teacher's performance for that year. The conference ends with a view to the future: How will the teacher build upon strengths and remedy any deficiencies?

Obviously, such a rating system will require a great amount of administrator and supervisor time if it is to be thorough—much more time than is perhaps warranted in relation to the value of the process for teachers who are known to be highly competent. Therefore, the reconceptualized model proposes two rating tracks: standard rating and intensive rating. The standard rating is used for career teachers whose performance is clearly satisfactory; it is a pro forma compliance with the state school code, usually involving one observation and one final conference. An intensive rating is used for all probationary teachers, for any teachers being considered for special promotion, and for teachers whose level of performance

---

EXHIBIT 9.3 Portion of Rating Observation Form

Teacher's Name_____   Rater_____
Class _____   Date and Time _____

Rating Code:

1, unsatisfactory; 2, satisfactory; 3, more than satisfactory; NA, not able to make a judgment.

1. Chooses content that relates directly to curriculum goals and assessment measures, at appropriate level of difficulty

  1. Chooses unrelated content, too difficult or too easy
  2. Chooses related content, with appropriate difficulty
  3. Chooses related content, with appropriate difficulty, relates content to student needs and interests

Rating

Observations Supporting Rating
Teacher Comments

Overall Rating for This Class:
1. Which essential teaching skill(s) does this teacher seem to use most successfully?
2. Which essential teaching skill(s) does this teacher need to improve?

---

is questionable. The intensive rating involves several observations by two or more observers, with a conference following each observation.

Individual Development

In contrast to staff development, individual work is with a single person, not the group; and the needs of the individual, not the needs of the organization, predominate.

Curriculum Tip 9.6	Individual development includes all the processes used by and with individual teachers to help them grow professionally.

For two reasons, a differentiated system of professional development is recommended— one that gives teachers some options in the type of developmental processes used. First, as noted above, most principals are too busy to provide clinical supervision to all teachers. Second, teachers vary significantly in their conceptual development, in their learning styles, and in their professional needs; they thus should be provided with different types of developmental services. Accordingly, the differentiated system offers three options for individual development: intensive, cooperative, and self-directed.

Intensive development is what is ordinarily called "clinical supervision," although it is more broadly construed. It is an intensive and systematic process in which a supervisor, an administrator, or an expert teacher works closely with an individual teacher in an attempt to effect significant improvement in the essential skills of teaching. While the intensive development is most needed by inexperienced and struggling teachers, it can be provided for any teacher who wants to work with a skilled educational leader to bring about significant improvement in teaching performance. In providing intensive development, the leader works closely with the teacher in determining which of several processes will be used. Rather than relying solely on planning conferences, observations, and debriefing conferences, they examine together a wide array of commonsense processes to determine which ones might be most effectively employed:

- Planning conferences: conferring with the teacher on yearly planning, semester planning, unit planning, and daily planning

- Student-assessment conferences: conferring with the teacher about assessing student progress, testing, grading, and record keeping

- Diagnostic observations and diagnostic feedback: observing all significant transactions in a classroom to diagnose priority developmental needs and providing appropriate feedback

- Focused observations and feedback: observing one particular aspect of teaching and learning (such as classroom management) and providing appropriate feedback

- Video analysis: making a video of teaching and analyzing it with the teacher to complement direct observation

- Coaching: developing a particular teaching skill by providing a rationale, explaining the steps, demonstrating those steps, providing a supportive environment in which the teacher can use the skill, and giving the teacher feedback

- Directed observation of a colleague: structuring and guiding an opportunity for the teacher to observe a colleague using a specific skill

Although some administrators would say that certain teachers do not need mentoring, they need firing—intensive development does provide a variety of supportive services; to be most effective, those services should be provided in a systematic manner. First, after an initial orientation session, the supervisor makes a diagnostic observation, one in which all important classroom interactions are recorded and analyzed to determine patterns of behavior. The supervisor analyzes those diagnostic data and tentatively identifies which skills can best be developed over the next 2 to 3 months. The supervisor and the teacher then confer about the observation. They review together those observational data and any other information they have and decide together on the skill-development agenda for the months ahead. They formalize this decision in a professional development plan, which lists the skills to be developed, the resources to be used, and the deadlines to be met.

They then begin to work together on the first skill. The supervisor coaches the teacher in the use of that skill. Then the supervisor makes a focused observation of one of the teacher's classes, gathering data on only the skill being developed. They confer again to decide whether more coaching and observing for that skill are needed or whether they should move to the next skill. It is an intensive process of diagnosing, developing a growth plan, coaching, holding a focused observation, and then assessing the next move. Obviously, it takes a great deal of time to implement effectively; the hope is, however, that only a few teachers in each school will be involved in such intensive development.

Cooperative development is an option usually provided only to experienced and competent teachers; it enables small groups of teachers to work together in a collegial relationship for mutual growth. It is intended to be a teacher-centered, teacher-directed process that respects the professionalism of competent teachers. While it requires administrative support, it does not require inordinate amounts of administrator or supervisor time; the expectation is that the cooperative groups can direct their own growth. In doing so, they may decide to use a variety of processes: observing and conferring about each other's classes, exchanging classes, collaborating on action research, and developing curricular and instructional materials.

Self-directed development is an option usually provided to experienced and competent teachers who wish to work on their own, rather than as part of a cooperative team. Teachers who choose this option identify a small number of professional-growth goals for the year and work independently in attempting to accomplish those goals. In a sense, the self-directed model is akin to the management-by-objectives assessment process, except that it is completely nonevaluative. The administrator or supervisor simply acts as a supportive resource for the teacher in the self-directed mode.

Albeit many school districts mandate evaluative policy as dictated by state boards of education or state departments of education, teachers should be able to choose which of these options they prefer, with the understanding that all probationary teachers will be involved in the intensive mode and that the principal will be able to identify tenured teachers who should also be involved in this mode. A form facilitating these choices is shown in Exhibit 9.4. These three individual development options provide teachers with a choice and enable

---

EXHIBIT 9.4   Options for Professional Development

Teacher's Name _____ School _____ Date _____

Basic Assumptions:

1. All teachers will participate in system-based and school-based staff development.
2. All teachers will be observed informally several times during the year.
3. All teachers will be rated by an administrator.

Teacher's Preferred Option (check one):

_____ For this year I prefer not to participate in any special professional development activities other than those outlined above.

_____ For this year I prefer to work cooperatively with colleagues using the processes identified below.

_____ For this year I prefer to work in a self-directed mode using the processes identified below.

Preferred Developmental Processes (check all those that at this point seem desirable):

_____ Observe a colleague and confer about observation.

_____ Exchange classes with a colleague and confer about exchange. Develop new course of study.

_____ Develop and try out new instructional materials. Improve an advanced teaching skill.

_____ Conduct action research.

_____ View and analyze videotapes of own teaching.

_____ Plan and implement an independent study program.

_____ Enroll in graduate course or special workshops.

_____ Other _____

supervisors and administrators to focus their supervisory efforts on those teachers in the intensive mode who most need their skilled services.

MOTIVATING STAFF

As can be seen, staff development, informal observations, rating, and individual development are all crucial parts of the supervision component.

The more aware teachers become of their capacity to drive change, the more likely it is that deep change will occur (Reason & Reason, 2007). Motivated teachers require less supervision and are willing to accomplish teaching and learning goals. They accept teaching goals as personal goals. They have a sense of confidence, enjoy teaching, are loyal, and are more committed to education as a whole. In contrast, unmotivated teachers are less apt to achieve their curricular goals, have more student discipline problems, and are less interested in change. With strict evaluation strategies, prodding, clear instructions, and close supervision, they often do a satisfactory job at best (Weis & Pasley, 2004).

Curriculum Tip 9.7	A primary factor for curriculum success is motivating teachers to work.

Effective supervisors, therefore, should focus on the interrelationship of the four processes with an interest in motivating teachers to invest themselves in their work to obtain desired returns and rewards. Taking an interest in teachers, helping to build their confidence, assisting in preparing unique lesson plans, and providing new learning programs can make the difference between a good teacher and a great teacher. Greatness in teaching has always been a result of a mentor helping an individual teacher to go the extra mile. The key is to motivate teachers and show them how to exceed normal expectations when developing an interrelationship among the four processes of staff development, informal observations, rating, and individual development.

The Interrelationship of Processes

How do processes for professional development interrelate? Obviously they are closely related.

Curriculum Tip 9.8	Data derived from informal observations can be used to supplement the information derived from rating other observations and can play an important part in assessing staff-development needs.

The rating process can help the supervisor or administrator identify those teachers who need intensive development. The activities undertaken in all the options for individual development can be linked with ongoing staff-development programs. In addition, the staff-development program can provide needed support for the individual development. All the processes obviously play key roles in improving the taught curriculum.

Having administrators and supervisors examine these processes separately and analytically has clear advantages, because each requires different skills, provides different kinds of information, and employs different processes. In such an examination, it is most useful to work with individual school districts to assist them in developing their own model, rather than presenting them with a formulaic solution. Thus, some districts link rating and individual development rather closely; others keep them quite distinct. Some emphasize curriculum alignment in the informal observations; others focus on instructional processes. Some offer teachers only the cooperative and intensive options; others provide the full array. Because such matters are much affected by district size, administrative philosophy, and available resources, they are best resolved at the district level.

One particular local option needs to be emphasized here. As each district develops its own model, it determines who will be primarily responsible for each of the four approaches. Some districts limit the informal observations to administrators; others expect supervisors to be involved. Some require that rating be done only by administrators; others expect input from the supervisory staff. Some districts use assistant principals for the intensive development; others use supervisors or expert teachers. Some expect administrators to direct staff development; others see this as a supervisory function. Rather than beginning with a set of foreordained conclusions about these important matters, the professional-development approach suggested here enables local districts to resolve these issues in a way that makes most sense to their administrators, supervisors, and teachers.

Although the differentiated model has been found to be feasible and acceptable to teachers (see Glatthorn, 1984), again no empirical research proves it to be more effective than other approaches. Curriculum leaders, therefore, would be well advised to study all four approaches carefully (as well as any others that seem useful) and choose or develop a model that seems to respond best to their own district's needs.

MASLOW'S THEORY OF HUMAN NEEDS

Any discussion of supervision, staff development, and/or teacher motivation would not be complete without noting the work of Abraham Maslow.

Maslow's need hierarchy is arranged in pyramidal form with physiological needs at the bottom of the pyramid and self-actualization at the top. Curriculum and instructional leaders need to interact with teachers and others, whose support will be needed to accomplish the objectives for the school district. To gain support, curriculum or instructional leaders must be able to understand and motivate them. To understand and motivate people, you must know human nature. Human nature is the common quality in all human beings. People behave according to certain principles of human nature. These principles, as noted in Exhibit 9.5, govern our behavior.

Maslow's taxonomy specifies that needs at the lower levels of the hierarchy are to be reasonably satisfied before one is interested in needs at the next higher level. For example, teachers who are working at a lower-based need, such as the social-need level, are primarily concerned with obtaining acceptance by administrators, other teachers, and parents. These teachers are less apt to be concerned with self-esteem, autonomy, and/or self-actualization. They could, however, abandon the need for social acceptance if a lower need, such as security or safety, presented itself.

EXHIBIT 9.5 Maslow's Higher Hierarchy of Needs	
Needs for Self-Actualization	The needs for self-actualization are activated when all the preceding needs are satisfied.
Needs for Self-Esteem	The needs for self-esteem can become dominant when the first three needs are satisfied.
Needs of Love, Affection, and Belongingness	When the needs for safety and for physiological well-being are satisfied, the needs for love, affection, and belongingness can emerge. The key word is *belonging*: "People will support what they help create."
Safety Needs	When the physiological needs are satisfied and no longer control thoughts and behaviors, the needs for security can become active.
Physiological Needs	These are biological needs—oxygen, food, water, and a relatively constant body temperature—that come first in a person's search for satisfaction.

SOURCE: Adapted from *The Search for Understanding*, by J. A. Simons, D. B. Irwin, and B. A. Drinnien, 1987, New York: West Publishing.

Critics argue as to whether Maslow was practicing a rigorous scientific study of personality and whether it relied too heavily on case studies and not enough on experimental work. Another common criticism is that Maslow's classification of self-actualized individuals related only to highly educated White males. Regardless of these criticisms, it is important for students of curriculum supervision to have some basic understanding of his taxonomy as a historical reference when reviewing curriculum development.

SUPERVISING THE SUPPORTED CURRICULUM

Because time and personnel allocations have been discussed in Chapter 6, this chapter focuses on the commonsense application of instructional materials as a central aspect of the supported curriculum.

Curriculum Tip 9.9	Supported curriculum is defined as all the resources provided to ensure the effective implementation of the curriculum: the time allocated, the personnel assigned to plan and implement the curriculum, and the instructional materials required.

The importance of developing an effective system for selecting and using instructional materials cannot be overemphasized. As noted in Chapter 4, the textbook plays a central role in influencing what teachers select to teach and how they teach it. For most teachers in the United States, textbooks are their single most widely used teaching resource

(Komoski, 1985). Textbooks are often used to provide structure for the course of study and the sequence of instruction. Many studies have shown that teachers adhere closely to texts, especially in mathematics, science, and reading instruction (Elliot & Woodward, 1990). Studies of teacher planning in these subjects have indicated that texts are the source of 85% to 95% of instructional activities.

Given that importance, it is especially discouraging to note how little systematic attention is given to the textbook-selection process. One survey by the Educational Products Information Exchange as early as 1978 determined that nearly half the teachers surveyed had no role at all in choosing the instructional materials they were using and that those who were involved reported spending only 1 hour a year in reviewing and selecting texts. What is needed, obviously, is a sound process for supervising the selection and use of materials— one that recognizes the central importance of the supported curriculum. The procedures outlined below, drawn from a review of the literature on textbook selection, should provide a useful beginning for local leaders who wish to review their current selection and adoption procedures. (The discussion that follows uses the term *text* to refer in general to any instructional material that plays a central role in the curriculum; Chapter 14 discusses some current developments in computer software.)

Develop a Statement of Board Policy and Administrative Procedures

The board policy should delineate the functions of instructional materials and specify the roles of the board, school administrators, and teachers in selecting particular materials. That policy should be supplemented with a more specific set of administrative procedures for implementing those policies. The administrative procedures should specify how materials will be selected, how citizens can register complaints, and how administrators should respond to such complaints.

Appoint the Textbook Adoption Committee

The Textbook Adoption Committee should be representative—large enough to include broad representation and small enough to work efficiently. At a minimum, the committee should be composed of one school principal, a supervisor in that field, one teacher from each school who will be using the text, an instructional materials specialist, and a parent.

Textbook Adoption Committee Involving Distance Learning

Distance education is a formal educational process in which the instruction occurs when student and instructor are not in the same place and audio, video, or computer technologies are employed. When distance education is used by a group of schools that receive special services through a central cooperative office, a teacher representing each school needs to be involved in the process. If the cooperative has a curriculum director, he or she needs to be on the committee. If this position does not exist, a school principal needs to be on the committee and in charge of the organization of the committee. Committee membership will be limited to the number of schools involved in the cooperative. Most, if not all, of the meetings could be held over the distance-learning video equipment in distance-learning conferencing labs of the individual schools.

Prepare the Committee

Because the committee will play such a central role in the adoption process, the committee should be trained in the following skills: understanding board policy and district procedures, maintaining ethical and professional relationships with publishers, understanding current research in the field, assessing district and teacher needs, evaluating instructional materials, and monitoring the implementation and use of instructional materials.

Provide the Committee With Selection Resources

The committee should also have easy access to selection resources. Two types of resources are especially needed. First, the committee should have access to catalogs of available materials and media. Several catalogs of print materials are now available as computerized catalogs, making it possible to conduct sharply focused searches for materials. Second, the committee should have access to objective reviews of materials. The journals published by the several subject-centered professional groups (such as the National Council of Teachers of English) often include such reviews. Two other excellent sources of a more general sort are the journal *Curriculum Review*, which includes reviews of materials and articles about current developments, and the Educational Products Information Exchange (EPIE), which publishes evaluative profiles of textbook materials.

Determine How Teachers Will Probably Use the New Materials

To make a wise decision, the adoption committee needs good information about how teachers will probably make use of the materials. Here the committee should survey, interview, and observe teachers to secure answers to these questions:

- For which groups of students will the text be used?

- Will the text be used primarily in class or outside of class?

- Will the text be used chiefly to teach skills and concepts or to provide guided and independent practice?

To understand the importance of this information, contrast two groups of teachers teaching mathematics in elementary school. One team comprises specialists in a departmentalized setting; they have been well trained in modern approaches to mathematics and are highly skilled in explaining concepts. They want a mathematics text to be used primarily as a source of problems for pupils to work on in class and at home. The other teachers are teaching several subjects in a self-contained classroom. They do not have a deep or current understanding of mathematics. They want a mathematics text that can explain concepts clearly and that can reduce their preparation time. Those two contrasting uses of the text require quite different textbooks.

Determine How Teachers Will Allocate Space

Different opportunities for teachers to work together not only expand their perspectives but also allow them to learn who is expert in subject matter, in curriculum, and in teaching strategies (Penuel & Riel, 2007). Teachers working collaboratively are able to generate a series of questions that help facilitate learning. For example, how are students and teachers assigned to space in the school in relation to the implementation of new materials? Where will materials be stored? Is it possible to situate instructional teams adjacent to one another? (Teams may actually be created because of space restrictions.) Which classrooms are nearest to the library (Danielson, 2002)? Is there a learning support center and, if so, where is it located? Some of these decisions are essentially arbitrary, but others are more purposeful and can further the goals of the selection process.

Develop a Sharply Focused and Weighted Set of Criteria for Selection

Historically, textbook selection practices have been criticized for several reasons, including lack of inadequate criteria for evaluation, lack of time devoted to the review process, politics, and inadequate or nonexistent training for those charged with making textbook recommendations (Allington, 2002).

One useful way of summarizing all these matters is to record them in a set of specifications similar to those shown in Exhibit 9.6. Also, an example of a textbook selection guide to be used by a textbook review committee is illustrated in Chapter 10.

EXHIBIT 9.6 Specifications for Elementary Language Arts Texts

For Which Pupils:
All pupils (except those with limited English proficiency) in Grades 1–6.

How Texts Will Probably Be Used:
Most teachers will use them in class, as the primary source for language arts instruction. Pupils will frequently read the text independently, discuss what they have read, and then do practice exercises.

Basic Requirements:

1. Texts should be free of racial, ethnic, and sexist stereotyping.

2. Texts should be written so that they can be read by all pupils who will use them but should not be too simple or childish.

Major Selection Criteria (listed in order of importance):

1. The texts emphasize a process approach to writing, giving special attention to prewriting and revision.

2. The texts include a number of integrated units that show the interrelationships of writing, speaking, listening, and reading.

3. The texts reflect an informed view of language learning: Good form is stressed as an aid to clarity, not as a set of rigid rules; pupils are encouraged to value their own language and to accept the languages of others; grammar is presented as a system of language structures, not a collection of abstract terms and rules.

Ancillary Materials Required:

1. Testing program

Basing Selection on Research

Even though the educational community seems to know much about effective instruction, researchers are concerned that educators have generally not based their selections on research. Realistically, school districts should review selections based on scientific research. Other national educational organizations and panels are moving in the same direction as well. For example, in the area of reading, the National Reading Panel concluded that all students must be taught alphabetics (phonemic awareness and phonics), reading fluency, vocabulary, and strategies for reading comprehension. The panel also endorses systematic phonics instruction for all students and one-to-one tutoring for struggling readers. Not everyone agrees, however, in that a number of educators believe that the National Reading Panel and other organizations rule out too many reliable studies before making their decisions. As a result, the debate continues to create controversy. Nevertheless, there is little doubt that more schools are currently selecting their textbook materials based on scientific research ("Perspectives," 2004).

Identify Five Texts That Best Meet the Requirements and the Criteria

The committee should then use the set of specifications to identify five texts or series that meet the criteria and then rank these five in order of merit.

Get Teacher Input on the Top Three Texts

At this point, all teachers who will be using the text should be given an opportunity to review the top three identified by the committee and give their own input. Perhaps the best way to do this is for the committee member representing that school to meet with the teachers from that building, explain the requirements and criteria, and discuss the five texts that have passed the initial screening. The teachers should be encouraged to discuss the merits of each of the texts and then to express their own preferences, with the understanding that the final decision will be made by the committee, not by a majority vote.

Select the Best Text

The committee should then meet, review teacher input, take a fresh look at the three texts, and make their final choice. One of the authors of this book successfully used the following process to select the proper textbook in his school district. The textbook selection committee essentially was formed in a manner similar to the one previously mentioned. However, the final selection of the textbook differed slightly. The major difference in this selection process came in the final stage, and before a service contract was developed with the publisher. The committee selected three (not five) companies whose textbooks most closely matched the requirements and criteria the committee had identified. The companies were asked to send a representative to the school district to demonstrate how their company's textbook correlated with the requirements and criteria of the school district. The committee members attended the presentation, but only those members who attended all three presentations were allowed to vote on the selection of the final textbook. The presentations served to affirm the committee's confidence in the company's ability to meet the needs of their school district and curriculum. The committee used this presentation along with teacher input to make their final choice.

Develop a Service Contract With the Publisher

Muther (1985) and other specialists in the field of text adoption have recommended that before an order is placed, the district should develop a service contract indicating what services it expects the publisher to provide. Services that can be requested include the following: giving the district the right to photocopy certain portions, training teachers in use of the materials, helping teachers place pupils appropriately in the program, correlating the text with the district curriculum, assisting schools in ordering materials, and providing follow-up assistance when problems develop. Obviously, such services will be costly to the publisher, and the amount of service provided will likely be contingent on the size of the order.

Train the Teachers in the Use of the Textbooks and Provide Materials to Correlate the Texts With the Curriculum

Teachers will need assistance before school begins on how to use the texts most effectively. They also should receive correlation charts showing how the text correlates with the district curriculum. Chapter 11 explains this matter more fully.

Monitor the Use of the Texts

Too many districts purchase expensive textbooks and then consider the matter closed. Experts in the field point out the necessity of monitoring closely the use of the texts to be sure that they are being used appropriately and to identify problems with them. The selection committee can be given this responsibility, although Muther recommended that a separate monitoring committee be established. Once problems have been identified, corrective action should be taken. The loss of books as well as student misuse of texts also needs to be addressed. Replacement copies are expensive. Many districts have policies in place requiring students to pay for damaged or lost texts.

If these steps are taken, it is likely that the supported curriculum will be more effective.

SUMMARY

This chapter examines problems and issues in supervision as well as how to improve two often-slighted aspects of curriculum: the taught curriculum and the supported curriculum. The chapter addresses major leaders who have been concerned with supervision and some current approaches to curriculum supervision. Major roles associated with curriculum supervision are discussed, including an important component of supervision, motivating staff. It is perhaps important to note that regardless of democracy in the selection process, final decisions are often made based on people's judgments and biases. It is the hope of the authors that educational leaders will make every attempt possible to eliminate arbitrary judgments and biases when selecting and developing supportive curriculum.

APPLICATIONS

1. On the basis of your experience in schools, do you believe that teachers should have some options regarding the types of supervisory services they receive? Give examples and support your position with well-reasoned arguments.

2. Glatthorn (1984) recommends that each district develop its own differentiated system of professional development. Sketch out the main components of a system that you think would work well in a district with which you are acquainted. Which components would you emphasize (staff development, rating, informal observations, individual development), which options would you provide to teachers, and who would be responsible for the several components?

3. The list of essential teaching skills presented in this chapter is only one way of describing and analyzing effective teaching. Review the research on teacher effectiveness and develop your own list of essential teaching skills, one that you could use in supervising teachers. Discuss in detail your list of skills and why you chose them.

4. Using a textbook evaluation form like the one shown in Chapter 10, evaluate a textbook in a subject field you know well and discuss your findings.

5. One of the issues that confront larger districts is whether all the elementary schools in that district should use the same basal reading series. What position would you take on this issue? What reasons would you advance in support of your position?

6. With more and more small schools consolidating, give examples of how distance-learning technology can improve your curriculum.

CASE STUDY   Improving Staff Development

An Illinois school district superintendent is looking for ways to make sure that all of his teachers are using the same textbook series. He decides to meet with a group of principals for ideas.

"I need to find a way to make sure our staff follows the text in each of our curriculum subject areas," says Superintendent Stanford.

Karen Carpenter, principal of a K–5 elementary school, offers an example of what she is doing in her school. "I found that my teacher–leaders do best if they receive staff development in smaller bands of time using the same textbook series rather than trying to learn everything at once. Whenever I've tried to take a 'one long in-service fits all' approach, I find that the staff begins to wander away from the text."

"So how do we change our in-service schedule?" asks the superintendent.

"I try to set up in-service by grade level, for only half of a day. I do a substitute rotation plan," says Carpenter. "I also schedule a lot of my early outs for in-service relating to the text. Whenever I have a series of short in-services spread out over the year, the staff seems to stick with the text. I find that shorter and more frequent staff-development programs keep the basal fresh and the material interesting."

Principal Carpenter continues, "I like to use this format because the teachers don't become so overwhelmed with information. It is also great because it is a better use of their time. My staff has been very happy with the whole process."

"Well, let's take a look at this as an option for our staff-development program," says Superintendent Stanford with a smile. "I'll schedule another meeting to discuss it in more detail."

The Challenge

Substitute rotation plans proved to be very effective for Principal Carpenter. What are some other supervisory strategies that she can use to support curriculum and free up teachers for staff development?

Key Issues/Questions

1. What are some supervisory steps to consider before adopting any staff-development program?

2. How do you feel about Principal Carpenter's use of a substitute rotation to enhance in-service? Is this something you might use in your school? Why or why not?

3. To what extent could Principal Carpenter's substitution rotation plan lend itself to differentiated professional development?

4. What other innovative supervision strategies can be used to aid the supported curricula?

5. How do you think Principal Carpenter's substitute plan would lend itself to the selection and adoption of textbooks for a school district? What other strategies could be used in the selection and adoption of textbooks as well?

WEBLIOGRAPHY

Supervising the Curriculum
www.ascd.org
www.mcrel.org/powerwalkthrough
www.eyeoneducation.com/prodinfo.asp?number = 679-9

Curriculum Change Process
www.mcrel.org
http://policy.osba.org/fernridg/I/IFA_IFB % 20R % 20D1.PDF

CHAPTER 10

Curriculum Development and Implementation

DEVELOPING A PROGRAM PHILOSOPHY AND RATIONALE STATEMENT

Previous chapters have discussed the processes used in developing new courses and in improving programs and fields of study. Each of these processes represents a type of curriculum change, and the literature on educational change suggests that to be successful those new and improved curricula will require careful support throughout several stages.

The dialogue that follows examines several questions as well as the critical stages for curriculum development and implementation.

Questions addressed in this chapter include the following:

- What is the procedure for developing a program philosophy and rationale statement?
- What is the procedure for developing a program scope and sequence, goals, objectives, learning outcomes, and authentic tasks?
- What methods can be used for choosing teacher representation?
- What procedures should be followed for developing program elements?

Key to Leadership

Today's school administrators face one of the most challenging and exciting times in the educational history of this nation. Setting priorities and formulating curriculum change continues to be an important role of any successful leader.

SOURCE: Excerpts from *Performance-Based Education: Developing Programs Through Strategic Planning* (pp. 57–88), by M. Baron, F. Boschee, and M. Jacobson, 2008, were used for most of the content in Chapter 10. Permission was granted by Rowman & Littlefield Education, Lanham, Maryland.

The philosophy and rationale statement for a school program, also known as a subject area curriculum or discipline, must augment a school district's philosophy, vision, mission, and exit (graduation) outcomes. The school administrator in charge of curriculum holds the responsibility of providing the destination and/or direction for the development and implementing a comprehensive school curriculum. Curriculum development for all disciplines necessitates the establishment of a districtwide curriculum council that meets on a monthly basis during the school year.

The curriculum council should consist of professional staff in leadership positions— that is, the curriculum director, building principals, department heads, team leaders, and others in leadership positions. Council members should be cognizant of the school district's mission, vision, philosophy, exit outcomes, program philosophies and rationale statements, program goals, program objectives, learning outcomes, learning activities, assessment, textbooks used (including publication year, edition, and condition), and so on.

A major function of the curriculum council is to develop a sequence and review cycle for districtwide curriculum development. For example, a typical 5-year cycle is illustrated in Exhibit 10.1.

EXHIBIT 10.1 Typical 5-Year Curriculum Development Cycle		
2009–2010	English Language Arts	2014–2015
2010–2011	Science and Social Studies	2015–2016
2011–2012	Fine Arts	2016–2017
2012–2013	Mathematics and Health	2017–2018
2013–2014	All Others	2018–2019

NOTE: Technology and business/vocational subjects may need a shorter development cycle.

The curriculum council should also select teacher representation for curriculum development. The representatives should be chosen using one of five methods: voluntary, rotation, evolvement, peer selection, or administrative selection.

The procedure for developing a districtwide English language arts (ELA) program philosophy and rationale statement and examples of the declarations follow.

Procedure

To develop a sound philosophy for an ELA program (or any school program), an ELA program committee (also known as a subject-area committee) must be established for the initial phase. The steps for structuring, along with responsibilities for the committee, are as follows:

Step 1

- The school district superintendent and board of education must approve the process for districtwide curriculum development. *Special note*: J. Timothy Waters, CEO of McREL, and Robert J. Marzano, a senior scholar at McREL (2006), found a statistically significant relationship (a positive correlation of .24) between district leadership and student achievement.

- The curriculum council should form an ELA program committee composed of ELA teachers representing all grade levels (K–12), preferably two teachers from each grade level. In smaller districts, however, one teacher per three grade/course levels is satisfactory (with feedback from those teaching the other grade/course levels). In smaller districts, a curriculum director could be hired by their cooperative (if such a co-op exists) to lead this process (a cooperative is a consortium of school districts cooperatively working together toward common goals). Co-op superintendents would need to support this approach to curriculum development. The superintendents, building principals, and content-area teachers would need to see the value of receiving input from other teachers in the cooperative and embrace the idea of a similar curriculum in cooperative schools. Although there may be resistance to adopting a first-grade curriculum throughout the co-op, there would be some classes that would benefit from a standard curriculum. Distance learning classes (e.g., foreign languages) would benefit from having a co-op curriculum coordinator help the schools set up a common curriculum. This common curriculum (including the textbook) would give the co-op schools much more flexibility in creating a schedule. Schools would not be tied to one school in the co-op. If school A could not fit its students into the schedule of the school that usually offered the class, the students could receive the same class from another school in the cooperative and be confident that the materials and content would be the same. In their process, the curriculum coordinator could use the distance learning equipment to facilitate meetings. Each school could have staff sit in their own distance learning rooms and share with the other members of the co-op. They would eliminate travel and make the possibility of having meetings more often realistic.

- Building principals (or designees) from the elementary, middle level or junior high school, and senior high school must be members of the committee as well (preferably with one principal or designee from each level).

- The school district curriculum director (or designee) should serve as chairperson and be responsible for organizing and directing the activities of the ELA program committee.

- The school district's board of education should be informed by the board curriculum committee about the process used for program (curriculum) development.

- All ELA program committee members must have a thorough understanding of the school district's philosophy, vision, mission, and exit (graduation) outcomes to enable committee members to blend them into the ELA program philosophy and rational statement.

- The Dialogue Technique, the Delphi Technique, the Fishbowl Technique, the Telstar Technique, or the Nominal Group Technique could be used to guide the ELA program committee in developing a program philosophy.

- The number of meetings to complete the task of writing a program philosophy by the ELA program committee should be limited to three or four during the school year.

- The curriculum meetings should be held in a comfortable environment; in other words, comfortable work seats, circular seating arrangement, tables with room for participants to spread their papers out, and good acoustics. Name tents for the participants should be made by folding a piece of paper so it will stand on its own.

Step 2

- Immediately after completion of the ELA program philosophy, disseminate it to the ELA staff and building administrators throughout the school district for their input. Grade- and department-level meetings should be organized by the building principals to peruse the program philosophy developed by the committee.

- A timeline for return of the program philosophy with additions, corrections, or deletions from noncommittee ELA staff and administrators is 1 week.

Step 3

- After the ELA program philosophy is returned to the curriculum director, the original ELA program committee should reassemble to consider the additions, corrections, and/or deletions that are suggested by noncommittee ELA staff and administrators.

Step 4

- The completed ELA program philosophy is now ready to be given to the school superintendent and board of education for approval.

- After approval by the school superintendent and board of education, the ELA program philosophy is given to the ELA writing committee responsible for writing the ELA program scope and sequence, program goals, objectives, learning outcomes, and authentic tasks.

The step-by-step process should be used to develop a program philosophy, followed by the same procedure to develop a program rationale statement (see Exhibit 10.2, which represents this top-down as well as bottom-up process).

The process heightens commitment by the district ELA staff, building administrators, central administration, and the board of education to the ELA program.

EXHIBIT 10.2 Process for Developing a Program Philosophy and Rationale Statement

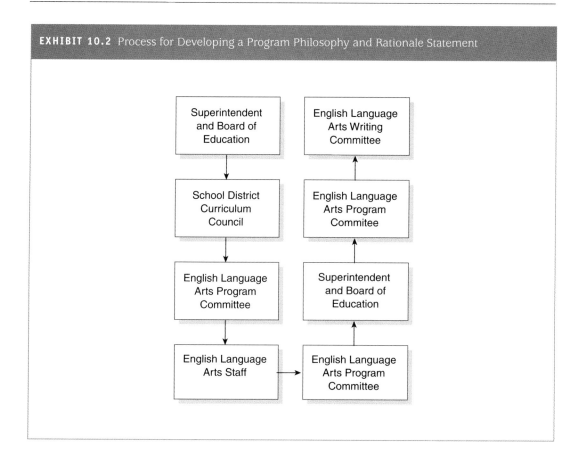

Sample English Language Arts Program Philosophy

Learning is a complex process of discovery, cooperation, and inquiry and is facilitated by the ELA program. The language processes of listening, speaking, reading, writing, viewing, and representing are interrelated and interdependent. Language is not only systematic and rule governed but is also dynamic and evolving, facilitating communication with others and flexibility of meaning. Through interaction with the social, cultural, intellectual, emotional, and physical components of the environment, the learner acquires language developmentally along a continuum.

Language learning thrives when learners are engaged in meaningful use of language. The process of constructing meaning is influenced by the learners' previous knowledge, attitudes, experiences, and abilities. All forms of communication, oral and written, expressive and receptive, are equally valuable. The ELA program utilizes an integrated approach that treats skills as part of all subject areas. Through the study of language, literature, and media, students broaden their experience, weigh personal values against those of others, become appreciative of the past, sensitive to the present, and inquisitive about the future.

The ELA program accommodates each learner's abilities, interests, and background by allowing for a range of learning styles, teaching styles, instructional strategies, and resources. The program supports a classroom environment that encourages mutual respect, risk taking, and experimentation. Effective evaluation is an integral part of the learning process. Continual evaluation that encompasses both process and product and both cognitive and affective domains allows each learner to take ownership of and responsibility for learning. The learner is already processing information and constructing meaning when formal schooling begins and continues to refine the processes of communication throughout the years of formal education and beyond.

SOURCE: The English language arts rationale statement was excerpted from the *Language Arts English Primary–Graduation Curriculum Guide*, by Canadian Ministry of Education, 1992, Victoria, BC: Author, p. 13.

Sample English Language Arts Program Rationale Statement

The language skills and processes developed through the ELA program are central to successful achievement in all subject areas and equip students with skills necessary to pursue learning throughout life. Students who read, write, speak, represent, view, and listen with intelligence, empathy, respect, and discrimination will develop the skills in thinking and communication, as well as the attitudes and knowledge that will prepare them for active participation in a complex society.

The ELA program allows students to better understand themselves and others. The reading and study of literature enhance the aesthetic, imaginative, creative, and affective aspects of a person's development. Literature preserves and extends the imaginative power of individuals. It allows young people to explore imaginatively the places where they live and provides them with an understanding of cultural heritage and a historical perspective, exposing them to points of view other than the present and personal.

- Through fiction, the reader has the power to be transported in time and place, to experience vicariously places, people, and events otherwise unavailable.

- Through poems, the reader may achieve heightened perceptions of the world, sharpened senses, clarified thoughts, and broadened emotions.

- Through drama, the participant continually renews a sense of the vitality and complexity of human actions.

- Through nonfiction, the reader accesses a wide range of possibilities, opinions, and interpretations.

The electronic media provide a similar range of possibilities and furnish material for experience and study. In addition, the study of literature and of media provides models of effective and varied language use for students to draw on in their own compositions.

The ELA program encourages students to develop meaning, both through active response to others' work and through their own speaking and writing. Through speaking and writing, students learn to clarify thought, emotion, and experience and to share these ideas, emotions, and experiences with others. Like reading, writing is a source or pleasure, enjoyment, and knowledge. It is a way to experience the delight and wonder of everyday life.

Curriculum Tip 10.1	"Preparing students for tomorrow requires that we thoughtfully reexamine and rethink the curriculum." (Perkins-Gough, 2003/2004, p. 12)

Writing proves the opportunity for careful organization of one's picture of reality and stimulates development of the precision, clarity, and imagination required for effective communication. In this way, writing is socially valuable, one of the ways individuals engage in and contribute to the activities and knowledge of society. Writing is personally valuable and is also an important means of learning within this program and all other subject areas. It allows students to create personal meaning out of the information offered in and out of school.

Education today increasingly emphasizes evaluation and analysis skills, critical thinking, problem-solving strategies, organizing and reference skills, synthesis, application of ideas, creativity, decision making, and communication skills through a variety of modes. All these skills and processes are based in language use; all are the material of a language program; all are developed through the ELA program at Anytown School District, U.S.A.

SOURCE: The English language arts program philosophy statement was excerpted from the *Language Arts English Primary–Graduation Curriculum Guide*, by Canadian Ministry of Education, 1992, Victoria, BC: Author, pp. 18–30.

Methods for Choosing Teacher Representation

The five methods for choosing teacher representation for curriculum development have advantages and disadvantages. Discussion of each method of selection and recommendations as to when it should be used are shown in Exhibit 10.3.

EXHIBIT 10.3 Methods for Choosing Teacher Representation for Curriculum Development		
Method	*Advantages*	*Disadvantages*
Voluntary	• People who volunteer are interested in the program. • The use of volunteers is an open, democratic process.	• Incompetents may volunteer. • Calling for volunteers may indicate unimportance of the task.
Recommended use: When everyone is acceptable.		
Rotation	• All possible participants can eventually be involved. • Rotating eliminates the need for selection.	• There is little or no continuity. • There is an assumption that all eligible participants have equal ability.
Recommended use: When the rotating membership will not hinder the development of an acceptable process or product.		

(Continued)

EXHIBIT 10.3 (Continued)

Method	Advantages	Disadvantages
Evolvement	• It provides leadership from the group. • Cooperation from committee is high because they choose the leader or representative through their own process.	• The evolvement process is feasible only in a long-term situation. • Emerged leaders exist without recognized authority.
	Recommended use: When determining who the most competent teachers are in curriculumdevelopment.	
Peer selection	• Committee members feel that they have control over their own destiny. • Cooperation is more likely.	• Committee representatives may be chosen for the wrong reasons. • Groups do not always know the kind of leadership or representation they need.
	Recommended use: When the group has maturity and experience.	
Administrative selection	• It tends to legitimize a committee member's position. • Administrators generally know who the best qualified people are.	• Administrators may not know who the best qualified are for curriculum development. • It can have negative implications if the selections were based on politics rather than reason.
	Recommended use: When peer selection is not practical.	

The five group techniques shown below can be described for sensitizing school-focused issues by enabling each practitioner's perspective to be uncovered and systematically, if relevant, incorporated into curriculum development and implementation. The procedure is based on small group discussions but involves specific procedures, sampling, timing, and methods of recording. The techniques not only permit teachers and administrators to articulate their views and practice in a manner that is relatively undistorted by received rhetoric but also results in data which readily inform the design of a working curriculum aimed at enhancing the teaching and learning process for a school district.

The main characteristic of the Dialogue Technique is that participants in the process are expected to rely more on dialogue to make decisions and less on individual preparation.

• Participants do not deal with content decision making until they are in the actual development process with other participants.

- The dialogue approach gives participants the opportunity to listen to other views that will either contradict or support their positions.

- The dialogue approach gives participants the opportunity to acquire ownership of a group product.

The Delphi Technique is a method for reaching consensus without the need for face-to-face meetings of all participants.

- Each member of the program committee writes a philosophy statement that they submit to the curriculum director.

- The philosophy statement written by each committee member is copied and distributed to all members on the program committee.

- Each committee member reviews the written philosophy statements and indicates which ones are germane.

- The curriculum director places the philosophy statements into two columns, one for those that are mostly agreed upon and one for those for which general agreement was not found.

- The most-agreed-upon philosophy statements are resubmitted to committee members and the process repeated until consensus is reached.

The Fishbowl Technique is one in which representatives from each of a large number of subgroups meet to reach consensus on a list of philosophy statements.

- Subgroups of six to eight participants meet and develop a philosophy statement.

- One elected representative from each subgroup meets with representatives from the other groups, who will bring their own group's philosophy statement.

- The representatives sit in a circle facing each other while all others remain seated outside the circle.

- Representatives within the circle discuss each of the subgroup's philosophy statements until consensus is reached.

The Telstar Technique is similar to the Fishbowl Technique but differs in its method of involving all committee members and their degree of involvement.

- The large group is divided into subgroups with each group representing specific grade level groupings (e.g., primary grades, intermediate grades, middle level or junior high school, and senior high school).

- Two representatives are elected from each group to represent that group and bring their respective group's completed philosophy statement to the group of all representatives.

- Each two-member delegation may be joined by a small advisory committee from its constituency.

- Any member of an advisory committee can stop the discussion at any time to meet with her or her representatives regarding the issue at hand.

- This procedure continues until a general consensus among all representatives is reached.

The Nominal Group Technique is a process that encourages divergence by individuals.

- A small group convenes to focus on a program philosophy. Members of the group work on an identified task, which is to develop a program philosophy, in the presence of each other but without any immediate interaction.

- Once the task of developing a program philosophy is explained by the curriculum director, group members are given time (20 to 30 minutes), during which each individual will write a program philosophy.

- After the time has expired, the committee members present the program philosophies one at a time. The program philosophies are posted. No discussion of alternative philosophies takes place until all program philosophies have been disclosed.

- Following disclosure, committee members rank the program philosophies presented and start the process over, considering the top three program philosophies.

- After individual committee members have chosen and modified one of the three program philosophies, one is selected by the committee to be adopted as the program philosophy.

- A disadvantage of the process is that during the initial brainstorming no interaction exists for one's idea to inspire another. However, because committee members know that each member is developing a program philosophy and that everyone's philosophy will be displayed, the competitive pressure establishes impetus.

DEVELOPING A SCOPE AND SEQUENCE, PROGRAM GOALS, OBJECTIVES, LEARNING OUTCOMES, AND AUTHENTIC TASKS

To make a scope and sequence for a program, program goals, objectives for the program goals, learning outcomes for the objectives, and authentic tasks for the learning outcomes practical and results-centered for students, they must be correlated with the district's philosophy, vision, mission, and exit (graduation) outcomes and with the program's philosophy and rationale statement.

Curriculum Tip 10.2	A writing committee should be selected to assume primary responsibility for writing the ELA curriculum.

The following presents procedures for developing these program elements.

The Committee Structure

To develop a scope and sequence, program goals, objectives, learning outcomes, and authentic tasks for any school program, a subject area writing committee must be established. The steps for structuring the committee, along with responsibilities, follow.

Step 1

- The writing committee is selected by and from the program committee members. It must be made up of teachers representing all grade levels (K–12) and preferably two staff members from each grade grouping: primary, intermediate, middle level or junior high school, and high school. In smaller school districts, one teacher per three-grades/course level is satisfactory as long as there is feedback from those teaching the other grade/course levels.

- A building principal or designee from the elementary, middle level or junior high school, and senior high school must be represented on the committee.

- The school district curriculum director or designee should serve as chairperson and be responsible for organizing and directing the activities of the writing committee.

- The school district's board of education must be apprised by the board curriculum committee about the process used to write curricula.

- The writing committee work space must be in a comfortable environment: comfortable work seats, tables to spread their papers out on, good acoustics, access to the district's curriculum lab containing sample courses of study and program textbooks, and clerical assistance.

- The ideal time to develop and write the program scope and sequence, program goals, objectives, learning outcomes, and authentic tasks is after the school year is completed. One week to 10 days is a normal timeline for a writing committee to complete the writing exercise for a program or subject area.

- Reasonable stipends or an extended contract should be given to members of the writing committee.

- All writing committee members must understand and be able to write meaningful program goals and objectives.

- The writing committee must be informed that the process for developing a course of study—the English language arts program, for example—entails the following sequential tasks.

1. Review and use the school district's philosophy, vision, mission, and exit (graduation) outcomes for developing a course of study for the specified program.

2. Review and use the specified program philosophy and rationale statement developed by the ELA program committee for developing a course of study for the ELA program.

3. Develop an ELA program scope-and-sequence matrix for the K–12 grade levels (for an example, see Sample Scope-and-Sequence Matrix for the Objectives of an ELA program in this chapter).

4. Develop ELA program goals (usually seven to nine) that are driven by the exit (graduation) outcomes (see this chapter).

5. Develop ELA program objectives (usually six to nine) for each program goal (see this chapter).

6. Develop ELA program learning outcomes for the objectives (i.e., primary, elementary intermediate, middle level or junior high, and high school; see this chapter).

7. Develop ELA program authentic tasks for the learning outcomes (see this chapter).

8. Develop criterion-referenced test items for the developed program (curriculum). If this is not possible, an item analysis of the standardized tests used should be made.

9. Correlate the program scope and sequence, program goals, objectives, learning outcomes, and authentic tasks with textbooks and learning materials.

10. Include learning materials for each learning outcome and authentic task.

The Dialogue Technique should be used to guide the ELA writing committee. Also, a taxonomy-of-thinking guide is useful in developing new programs (see Exhibit 10.4 for categories and cue words).

EXHIBIT 10.4 Taxonomy of Thinking

CATEGORIES	CUE WORDS	
KNOWLEDGE		
Recall Remembering previously learned information	Cluster Define Label List Match Memorize Name	Observe Outline Recall Recognize Record Recount State

CATEGORIES	CUE WORDS	
COMPREHENSION		
Translate Grasping the meaning	Cite Describe Document Explain Express Give examples Identify	Locate Paraphrase Recognize Report Review Summarize Tell
APPLICATION		
Generalize Using learning in new and concrete situations	Analyze Dramatize Frame How to Illustrate Imagine Imitate	Manipulate Organize Sequence Show/Demonstrate Solve Use
ANALYSIS		
Break Down/Discover Breaking down an idea into component parts so that it may be more easily understood	Analyze Characterize Classify/Categories Compare/Contrast Dissect Distinguish/Differentiate Examine	Infer Map Outline/No Format Given Relates to Select Survey
SYNTHESIS		
Compose Putting together to form a new whole	Combine Compose Construct Design Develop Emulate Formulate	Hypothesize Imagine/Speculate Invent Plan Produce Propose Revise
EVALUATION		
Judge Judging value for a given purpose	Appraise Argue Assess Compare/Pros/Cons Consider Criticize Evaluate	Justify Judge Prioritize/Rank Recommend Support Value

Step 2

- After the program scope and sequence, program goals, objectives, learning outcomes, and authentic tasks have been written, they must be distributed to all ELA teachers and building administrators throughout the school district for additions, corrections, and/or deletions during the school year. Teachers and administrators should be given 4 to 6 weeks to return the document to the curriculum director or designee.

- During the 4- to 6-week districtwide review period for the program scope and sequence, program goals, objectives, learning outcomes, and authentic tasks, grade-level, and department meetings at the building level must be utilized to peruse the document. Members of the writing committee should be used as consultants (to provide clarification) at the grade level and department meetings.

Step 3

- After receiving the corrected program documents from districtwide non-committee ELA grade- and course-level teachers and administrators, the curriculum director (or designee) must reassemble the writing committee to consider the additions, corrections, and/or deletions suggested.

Step 4

- After the ELA program course of study (curriculum resource guide) is completed with suitable additions, corrections, and/or deletions suggested, the document should be given to the school superintendent and the school board curriculum committee for presentation to the board of education for districtwide adoption and implementation.

Step 5

- Once the ELA program course of study (curriculum resource guide) is adopted, a textbook-review committee, encompassing members from the ELA writing committee, is selected by that committee. Membership must include one person representing each grade and course level.

- Members of the textbook review committee must evaluate and rank each ELA series using a similar textbook-selection guide (see Exhibit 10.5) from the various publishing companies for their grade level.

- The entire ELA staff should consider for review the three highest ranked textbook series selected by the textbook-review committee.

- The ELA program scope and sequence, program goals, objectives, learning outcomes, and authentic tasks should be submitted to the three highest ranked publishing companies selected by the textbook-review committee for their review and presentation to the districtwide ELA staff.

- The presentations by the three selected publishing company representatives should be scheduled during the school year, preferably with no more than one presentation each day.

EXHIBIT 10.5 Textbook Selection Guide

ANY SCHOOL DISTRICT NO. 3
Any Town, USA
TEXTBOOK SELECTION GUIDE

_____   _____   _____
(Textbook)   (Publishing Company)   (Grade Level)

Reading level: _____ (should be at or above grade level)

Rate each characteristic listed for the textbook on a scale from 1 to 5. Circle your choice and total your ratings to obtain a single overall measure for each textbook reviewed.

Content	Low				High
1. Matches the program objectives	1	2	3	4	5
2. Presents up-to-date, accurate information	1	2	3	4	5
3. Avoids stereotyping by race, ethnicity, and gender	1	2	3	4	5
4. Stimulates student interest	1	2	3	4	5

Organization and Style					
1. Is clearly written	1	2	3	4	5
2. Uses language and style appropriate for students	1	2	3	4	5
3. Develops a logical sequence	1	2	3	4	5
4. Contains useful practice exercises	1	2	3	4	5
5. Provides thorough reviews and summaries	1	2	3	4	5
6. Includes clearly outlined table of contents and index	1	2	3	4	5
7. Includes helpful student aids such as illustrations, charts, etc.	1	2	3	4	5
8. Provides practical teacher aids such as lesson plans, test questions, etc.	1	2	3	4	5

Physical Features					
1. Has attractive cover	1	2	3	4	5
2. Presents up-to-date, interesting illustrations and photographs	1	2	3	4	5
3. Has well-designed page layout	1	2	3	4	5
4. Uses clear type appropriate for students	1	2	3	4	5
5. Has durable binding	1	2	3	4	5

Subtotals =

TOTAL   =   _____

Evaluator _____   Grade Level/Subject _____

- All ELA staff and school principals must be invited to attend. Voting rights are granted to only those who attend all three presentations by the publishing company representatives.

- The textbook series preferred by a majority of staff for the ELA program must be submitted, with rationale for the selection and cost to the district, to the school superintendent and the school board curriculum committee for presentation to the school board for adoption.

Step 6

- Appropriate in-service activities must be planned for the ELA staff to accommodate the newly developed ELA course of study (curriculum resource guide). Some in-service activities may need to take place before the program is implemented and some should take place after teachers have implemented the program.

Step 7

- Evaluation of the ELA program must be an ongoing process and in-flight corrections should be made until the next 5-year cycle. The curriculum director should have expertise in program (curriculum) evaluation.

The step-by-step process should be used to develop a course of study (curriculum resource guide) for all programs in the public schools. As illustrated in Exhibit 10.6, this top-down, bottom-up model will engage the process of planning, implementing, and evaluating in such a way that the work of content experts—the teachers—is facilitated.

EXHIBIT 10.6 A Process for Developing a Course of Study for the ELA Program

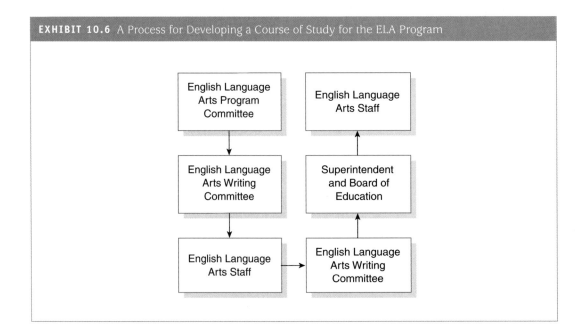

The process described will consolidate the efforts of staff, district administrators, and the board of education. Teachers, especially, will be advocates of a program if the process permits them to be the decision makers.

Samples of Program Scope and Sequence, Program Goal, Exit Outcomes Met, Objectives, Learning Outcomes, and Authentic Tasks

The following are examples of a scope-and-sequence matrix, a program goal, objectives for the program goal, learning outcomes for the objectives, and authentic tasks for the learning outcomes of an ELA curriculum (see Exhibits 10.7 and 10.8 and the pages that follow). The program goal is driven by exit (graduation) outcomes, and the objectives, which constitute the program goal illustrated, are given specific implementation direction (scope and sequence) at the proposed groupings of primary, elementary intermediate, middle level or junior high, and high school.

EXHIBIT 10.7 Sample Scope-and-Sequence Matrix for the Objectives of an ELA Program

P EI ML/JH HS	These indicate the proposed groupings, which are primary, elementary intermediate, middle level/junior high, and high school.
0	Indicates an orientation stage. Preparatory activities are undertaken prior to the explicit teaching and learning activities suggested in the learning outcomes related to the objective. Refer to learning outcomes at the next stage if appropriate.
E	Indicates an emphasis stage. Learning outcomes are suggestions in this course of study (curriculum resource guide) as examples of appropriate authentic tasks (activities) and observable behaviors. Explicit teaching and learning activities are expected.
M	Indicates a maintenance stage. Provisions are made to reinforce learning outcomes and authentic tasks related to the objective.

Continue on to the program goal and outcomes that follow.[1]

Program Goal 1

To develop the knowledge, skills, and processes needed to communicate effectively by listening, speaking, reading, writing, viewing, and representing.

Exit Outcomes Met

1. A purposeful thinker

   • Uses strategies to form concepts, make decisions, and solve problems

   • Applies a variety of integrated processes including critical and creative thinking to accomplish complex tasks

- Evaluates the effectiveness of mental strategies through meaningful reflection
- Demonstrates flexibility, persistence, and a sense of ethical considerations

2. A self-directed learner
   - Directs own learning
   - Sets well-defined goals and manages the process of achieving them
   - Acquires, organizes, and uses information
   - Initiates learning activities in the pursuit of individual interests
   - Applies technology to specific tasks
   - Applies realistic self-appraisal in selecting the content, method, and pace for learning
   - Integrates knowledge and skills in both familiar and new situations

3. An effective communicator
   - Conveys messages through a variety of methods and materials
   - Adapts messages to various audiences and purposes
   - Engages the intended audience to understand and respond
   - Receives and interprets the communication of others

4. A responsible citizen
   - Understands diversity and the interdependence of people in local and global communities
   - Demonstrates a respect for human differences
   - Makes informed decisions
   - Exercises leadership on behalf of the common good

EXHIBIT 10.8 Objectives Chart

Objectives	P	EI	ML/JH	SH
Students will be able to				
1.1 Identify reasons for communicating	E	E	E	E
1.2 Communicate ideas with clarity and precision	E	E	E	E
1.3 Experience satisfaction and confidence in the communication skills and processes	E	E	E	E
1.4 Produce, explore, and extend ideas and information	E	E	E	E
1.5 Read and examine independently, by choosing appropriate strategies and processes	O	E	E	E
1.6 Comprehend that the communication skills and processes are interrelated avenues for constructing meaning	E	E	M	M

Learning Outcomes and Authentic Tasks for an ELA Program

Curriculum Tip 10.3	"Consistent use of defined behavioral verbs in composing, rewriting or selecting learning objectives can lead to improvement in efforts to change and reform education in general and curriculum in particular." (Kizlik, 2008, n.p.)

Objective 1.1: Students will be able to identify reasons for communicating.

Primary Grades

Students will be able to

1.1.1 Recognize why they are communicating

Authentic task: Students will express feelings, solve problems, or confirm the meaning of a message.

1.1.2 Discuss the purposes of communicating

Authentic task: Students will make a classroom chart on "Why We Read."

1.1.3 Plan and lead classroom activities

Authentic task: Students will chair news time, act as spokesperson for a small group, or introduce a visitor.

1.1.4 Listen to and follow directions to perform a new activity

Authentic task: Students will playact a new game.

1.1.5 Choose to read for a variety of purposes

Authentic task: Students will read for enjoyment, to find new ideas, or to confirm ideas.

1.1.6 Choose to write for a variety of purposes

Authentic task: Students will write to request information, to express gratitude, or for entertainment.

1.1.7 Compose notes and lists to themselves

Authentic task: Students will write a list of telephone numbers or a reminder note to return library books.

1.1.8 Engage in prewriting discussion

Authentic task: Students will choose a topic, focus ideas, or clarify purpose.

1.1.9 Use a grid, chart, graph, cluster, or web to organize information

Authentic task: Students will organize collected facts from researching an animal.

Elementary Intermediate Grades

Students will be able to

1.1.10 Describe the broad purposes that are common to communication skills and processes

Authentic task: Students will advise, command, direct, entertain, inform, persuade, or socialize.

1.1.11 Arrange their own specific purposes that identify the desired result and focus attention

Authentic task: Students will tune in to the radio news to get information on a specific item.

1.1.12 Arrange their own purposes for listening

Authentic task: Students will listen attentively to a poem to form sensory images.

1.1.13 Organize their own purposes for speaking

Authentic task: Students will make a speech to express a personal point of view.

1.1.14 Determine their own purposes for reading

Authentic task: Students will read a selection to answer specific questions.

1.1.15 Determine their own purposes for writing

Authentic task: Students will record observations to write a science report.

1.1.16 Arrange their own purposes for viewing

Authentic task: Students will analyze TV commercials to identify persuasive techniques.

1.1.17 Determine their own purposes for representing

Authentic task: Students will develop a diagram to organize similarities when comparing two opinions.

1.1.18 Identify the purposes of other people's communication

Authentic task: Students will recognize propaganda and the desire to convince in a biased presentation.

1.1.19 Recognize the purposes of various media

Authentic task: Students will infer that television aims to entertain, to inform, and to persuade.

Middle Level/Junior High

Students will be able to

1.1.20 Recognize the broad purposes that are common to communication skills and processes

Authentic task: Students will do controlling, imaging, informing, and socializing.

1.1.21 Identify the audience to which communication is addressed

Authentic task: Students will communicate with adults, friends, or relatives.

1.1.22 Recognize and focus attention on the desired result of communication

Authentic task: Students will write a letter of complaint or speak to a group in order to raise funds for a project.

1.1.23 Engage in preparatory activities for listening, speaking, and viewing

Authentic task: Students will recall prior knowledge of the topic or predict what could be learned about a topic.

1.1.24 Establish a purpose for speaking

Authentic task: Students will give a formal speech to persuade a group to accept a personal point of view.

1.1.25 Create a purpose for representing

Authentic task: Students will use a chart to show similarities of themes in American literature.

1.1.26 Recognize persuasive techniques

Authentic task: Students will recognize bias, propaganda, use of connotation, and use of emotive language.

High School

Students will be able to

1.1.27 Employ language strategies and processes that are most likely to elicit the desired results

Authentic task: Students will choose between a telephone call and a letter to deal with business.

1.1.28 Identify the audience to which a communication is to be directed

Authentic task: Students will choose peers, adults, or special-interest groups as the appropriate audience.

1.1.29 Select the desired result of a communication

Authentic task: Students will write a letter of application or a student council letter of request to the principal.

1.1.30 Appraise the difference between active and passive listening by discussing which activities require no effort on the part of the listener and which will demand full attention

Authentic task: Students will decide that background music is passive listening, and listening for a main idea is active listening.

1.1.31 Develop and apply criteria to evaluate what is heard

Authentic task: Students will utilize criteria agreed to by the class, such as the main idea, details, and examples to be applied to class speeches.

1.1.32 Identify main ideas

Authentic task. Students will write down the main ideas after hearing a passage read or will paraphrase a speaker's message orally or in written form.

1.1.33 Distinguish fact from opinion

Authentic task: Students will, after listening to a reading, list orally or in writing what is fact and what is opinion.

1.1.34 Recognize the influence of the listener's bias or perception

Authentic task: Students will examine possible preconceived ideas on a topic before the class hears a speech.

1.1.35 Recognize a speaker's purpose and bias

Authentic task: Students will peruse differences between speeches from the opposing sides on an issue such as capital punishment.

SOURCE: The ELA program scope and sequence, program goal, objectives, and learning outcomes were excerpted from *Language Arts English Primary–Graduation Curriculum Guide*, by Canadian Ministry of Education, 1992, Victoria, BC: Author, pp. 18–30.

Each program goal should also list a wide variety of resources, accessible to the staff, to help students accomplish the exit outcomes. Examples of resources include textbooks, textbook activities, novels, nonfiction books, anthologies, collections, handbooks, dramas, selected readings from reserved material in the library or classroom, printed handouts, kits, periodicals, transparency sets, video recordings, audio recordings, and computer software. The ELA staff should have an updated inventory of materials available that lists where each is located, such as in the classroom, departmental media center, school media center, district media center, regional media center, or state media center.

The program (curriculum) development process described is a design-down, deliver-up model (see Exhibit 10.9). Samples of scope and sequence, program goal, objectives for the

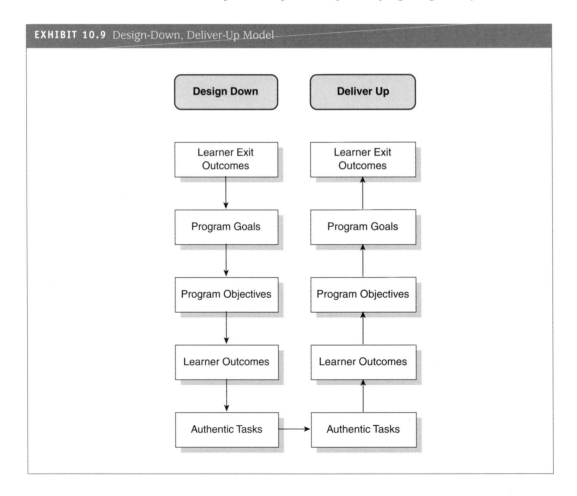

EXHIBIT 10.9 Design-Down, Deliver-Up Model

program goal, learning outcomes, and authentic tasks provided should enable a school district to develop a performance-based education program. Once a program is developed, teachers can easily develop unit plans and daily lesson plans for their students.

Developing a program's course of study assures continuity of instruction across grade levels and subsequently allows a smoother transition from one grade level to the next. It is a road map for staff and students in a district.

Indicators of Effective Curriculum Development

How can a developed and implemented curriculum be measured for effectiveness? The 10 indicators that follow should be considered when measuring curriculum effectiveness.

1. *Vertical curriculum continuity:* The course of study reflects a K–12 format that enables teachers to have quick and constant access to what is being taught in the grade levels below and above them. Also, upward spiraling prevents undue or useless curricular repetition.

2. *Horizontal curriculum continuity:* The course of study developed provides content and objectives that are common to all classrooms of the same grade level. Also, daily lesson plans reflect a commonality for the same grade level.

3. *Instruction based on curriculum:* Lesson plans are derived from the course of study, and curriculum materials used are correlated with the content, objectives, and authentic tasks developed.

4. *Curriculum priority:* Philosophical and financial commitments are evident. Clerical assistance is provided and reasonable stipends are paid to teachers for work during the summer months. In addition, curriculum topics appear on school board agendas, administrative meeting agendas, and building-staff meeting agendas.

5. *Broad involvement:* Buildings in the district have teacher representatives on the curricular committees; elementary, middle level or junior high, and high school principals (or designees) are represented; and school board members are apprised of and approve the course of study.

6. *Long-range planning:* Each program in the district is included in the 5-year sequence and review cycle. Also, a philosophy of education and theory of curriculum permeate the entire school district.

7. *Decision-making clarity:* Controversies that occur during the development of a program center on the nature of the decision, and not on who makes the decision.

8. *Positive human relations:* All participating members are willing to risk disagreeing with anyone else; however, communication lines are not allowed to break down. Also, the initial thoughts about the curriculum come from teachers, principals, and the curriculum leader.

9. *Theory-into-practice approach:* The district philosophy, vision, mission, exit (graduation) outcomes, program philosophy, rationale statement, program goals, program objectives, learning outcomes, and authentic tasks are consistent and recognizable.

10. *Planned change:* Tangible evidence shows that the internal and external publics accept the developed program course of study for the school district. The process of developing a course of study for each program or discipline in a school district is no longer one of determining how to do it, but one of determining how to do it better.

SOURCE: The 10 indicators of effective curriculum development were excerpted from *Curriculum Leadership and Development Handbook*, by L. H. Bradley, 1985, Englewood Cliffs, NJ: Prentice Hall.

SUMMARY

The chapter provides an example of the necessary steps for curriculum development and implementation. The role of each of the constituents (board of education, superintendent, school administrators, and teachers) is displayed in the schematics presented. As well, the chapter illustrates how to assemble an actualized and effective curriculum that utilizes the key elements shown below.

Recommended → Written → Supported → Taught → Tested → Learned

The actual results of the curriculum development and implementation process are shown in Chapter 11, Exhibit 11.7.

APPLICATIONS

1. Why must a curriculum council and program committee have a thorough understanding of the school district's philosophy, vision, mission, and exit outcomes?

2. What characterizes a program philosophy? What characterizes a program rationale statement?

3. What advantages do the Dialogue Technique, the Delphi Technique, the Fishbowl Technique, the Telstar Technique, and the Nominal Group Technique have over other ways groups make decisions?

4. Identify interrelationships that exist between scope and sequence, program goals, objectives, learning outcomes, and authentic tasks.

5. Explain how developing a course of study (curriculum resource guide) facilitates the teacher as content expert.

6. Outline responsibilities for the program committee.

7. Distinguish the responsibilities of the subject writing committee from those of the program committee.

8. Should the course of study be written by the writing committee during the school year or during the summer months with stipends? Defend your answer.

9. Plan an inservice activity for the staff to accommodate a newly developed course of study.

CASE STUDY Building Consensus by Committee

Phillip Wright, a 1st-year curriculum director of a large school district, meets with the superintendent, Dr. Roberta Ellis, to discuss ways to develop an ELA program procedure for adoption.

Searching for some feedback, Wright states, "I need to explore how and when you want me to organize a curriculum committee or committees for the ELA program because the current program is due in the district's 5-year curriculum development cycle. For example, I'm thinking of formulating an adoption committee or committees this fall. Do you have any concerns in that regard?"

Dr. Ellis nods her head. "Well, yes, actually, I do have some concerns about organizing committees, especially writing committees, during the school year." Folding her arms across her chest, the superintendent gives a sigh. "I've found hiring substitutes for staff during the year is quite costly—but more important, instructional time lost due to teachers being out of their classrooms is a huge concern because students learn only one third as much with a substitute teacher as they do with their own classroom teacher."

The new curriculum director's eyes widen. "Oh, I didn't realize that," he says demurely. "I'll be happy to establish a writing committee for the summer months. However, the district must pay stipends to teachers participating in committee work."

"Good," says Dr. Ellis and asks, "What process are you using to select teacher representation?"

"Well, my plan is to use the administrative selection method, choosing some strong experienced teachers from each instructional level—you know, primary, intermediate, middle, and high school," shares Wright, continuing to observe his boss for approval, or at least for direction.

Dr. Ellis leans back in her chair. "Well, that's a possibility, but you want to be very careful about whom you select—especially when it comes to strong personalities." The superintendent now focuses her gaze on her new curriculum director and adds, "What sometimes happens is the creation of four armed camps—you know what I mean: no consensus, strife between teachers—basically a lack of cooperation between each other."

"Oh, yeah. Good point."

The superintendent smiles and then decides to share some last words of wisdom. "As effective leaders *we need to anticipate the need for consensus* and pick some folks who not only know their subject material but who are also flexible and committed to the district's vision and core curriculum beliefs."

"Great idea!" extols Wright, now aware of several crucial points critical to formulating curriculum-development committees. After thanking Superintendent Ellis for her input, the curriculum director, with a valise full of notes, begins heading for the door, realizing he has another appointment waiting in his office.

The Challenge

Choosing teacher representation for committees and anticipating the importance of consensus building are both crucial steps toward successful curriculum development. Analyze each of the methods of choosing teacher representation—voluntary, rotation, evolvement, peer selection, and/or administrative selection—and discuss what challenges a curriculum director might face. Which method do you think is best? What strategies might Phillip Wright use in helping to select members for the ELA program committees?

Key Issues/Questions

1. What questions does Phillip Wright need to ask before formulating curriculum committees for the ELA program?
2. What measures does one need to take during the *early planning* phase of committee development?
3. What procedures does one need to take during the planning phase of curriculum development?
4. What actions does one need to take *after* a curriculum program has been adopted?
5. What is the best method of choosing teacher representation for curriculum committees? Why?

WEBLIOGRAPHY

Effective schools research
www.mcrel.org

Missouri Department of Elementary and Secondary Education sample career ladder plan
http://dese.mo.gov/divteachqual/careerladder

Ten Common Denominators of Effective Schools
www.spotsylvania.k12.va.us/tms/ktower/schoolresearch.htm

National Association of Elementary School Principals
www.naesp.org

National Association of Elementary School Principals Leadership Compass
www.naesp.org/ContentLoad.do?contentId = 323

National Association of Secondary School Principals
www.nassp.org

Principals' Office—NAESP blog for members to connect with colleagues on educational issues
http://naesp.typepad.com

NOTE

1. The program goal listed (p. 300) was excerpted from the *Language Arts English Primary–Graduation Curriculum Guide*, by Canadian Ministry of Education, 1992, Victoria, BC: Author, pp. 19–27. The nine goals for the ELA program are as follows:

    *   Program Goal 1 develops the knowledge, skills, and processes needed to communicate effectively by listening, speaking, reading, writing, and representing.
    *   Program Goal 2 develops knowledge, understanding, and appreciation of language and how it is used.
    *   Program Goal 3 develops knowledge, understanding, and appreciation of a wide variety of literary genres and media forms.
    *   Program Goal 4 develops knowledge, understanding, and appreciation of American and other world literature.
    *   Program Goal 5 develops and extends knowledge of self, the world, and our multicultural heritage through language, literature, and media.
    *   Program Goal 6 extends capacity for creative thought and expression within the context of language, literature, and media.
    *   Program Goal 7 extends capacity for critical thought and expression within the context of language, literature, and media.
    *   Program Goal 8 develops the wide variety of strategies for learning.
    *   Program Goal 9 develops attributes of wonder, curiosity, independence, and interdependence necessary for lifelong learning.

CHAPTER 11

Aligning the Curriculum

Curriculum alignment is a process of ensuring that the written, the taught, and the tested curricula are closely congruent. This is not always the case notes Lance Fusarelli (2008), associate professor of educational leadership and policy studies at North Carolina State University, Raleigh. He stated, "There is the common perception that educational leaders ignore research when they make decisions about school improvement" (p. 365).

Ignoring important research can be a major roadblock toward formulating congruency between the written, taught, and tested curricula. In too many schools, little correspondence exists between the district curriculum guides, the teacher's instructional plans, and the assessment measures. This problem, however, can be easily addressed by school leaders developing a consistent program of curriculum alignment. Curriculum alignment, based on research and with a focus on a standards-based curriculum, can provide a way to remedy this situation in order to improve achievement for all students.

Questions addressed in this chapter include the following:

- What are the essential elements for curriculum alignment?
- How does one organize a curriculum alignment project?
- What organizational strategies should be used for curriculum alignment?
- What are mastery objectives and curriculum-based tests?
- What is the value of using scientific research in curriculum management?
- How important is staff development in curriculum alignment?
- How can the curriculum alignment project be monitored and evaluated?

Key to Leadership

It is important that curriculum leaders provide curriculum alignment and teacher professional-development activities that reflect the elements of high-quality instruction with clear, explicit learning goals.

A RATIONALE FOR CURRICULUM ALIGNMENT

The argument for curriculum alignment is clear in that school leaders should begin by asserting the need for a close fit between the written curriculum and the taught curriculum. The written curriculum, it is assumed, represents a districtwide consensus about instructional objectives and their relative importance for a given group of learners. If developed in the manner outlined in previous chapters, it reflects the input of curriculum experts, subject-matter specialists, district administrators and supervisors, and classroom teachers. Because it thus represents an informed consensus, it should be the determining element in what is taught day by day.

If the district does not take reasonable steps to ensure that the guides are followed, the evidence suggests that many teachers may make unwise choices of content.

The real question to ask here is whether teachers should feel free to adapt the practices they learn rather than comply strictly with expert guidance. Developing effectiveness requires more than just giving teachers a guide or telling teachers about research-based practices. It requires teachers understanding they must assume executive control of instructional practices, That is, when the needs of particular students or particular instruction situations require it, teachers must take charge modifying practices to make them fit.

Gerald Duffy, a Distinguished Professor of Literacy, and Kathryn Kear, a doctoral student, both from the University of North Carolina (2007), noted that recent research on adaptive aspects of effective teaching has spurred a move away from just training models and toward "educative" models of professional development. Four characteristics of Duffy and Kear's professional development model include:

1. Adaptive teaching is promoted when in-service sessions help teachers develop a "moral compass" to guide them.

2. The presenter's attitude should promote adaptive thinking rather than be authoritative.

3. Adapted thinking is promoted when profession development is longitudinal, rather than a one-shot session.

4. Adaptive thinking is promoted when professional development is "case based" or "problem based."

The key to Duffy and Kear's model is to have teachers refine the selection and alignment of materials to meet district goals as well as meet state standards. Marzano (2005) suggested the following to evoke change:

1. Consciously challenge the status quo

2. Be willing to lead change initiatives with uncertain outcomes

3. Systematically consider new and better ways of doing things

4. Consistently attempt to operate at the edge versus the center of the school's competence (Marzano, Waters, & McNulty, p. 45)

An obvious need exists for a close fit between what is taught and what is tested. Whatever the theoretical underpinnings of a program, no single test can tell all there is to know. As the directors of the National Center for Research on Evaluation, Standards, and

Student Testing emphasized (Herman, Baker, & Linn, 2004), "Multiple measures are needed to address the full depth and breadth of our expectations for student learning" (p. 2). Beyond the multiple-choice and short-answer items that are typical of current assessments, "other types of performance measures—essays, applied projects, portfolios, demonstrations, oral presentations, etc.—are needed to represent and guide students' progress" (p. 2).

In addition, valid and fair assessment systems require curriculum-based tests that correspond adequately with what was taught. Standardized tests will not suffice, because the content of standardized tests does not correspond closely with what is usually taught in the classroom. These arguments for curriculum alignment have not totally persuaded the profession. Some educators and researchers are concerned that administrative attempts to align closely the written and the taught curricula will reduce teacher autonomy and creativity. Others have pointed out the dangers of making the test too important: The test becomes the curriculum, and teachers focus all their efforts on preparing students for that test even though "there is no convincing evidence that high-stakes testing has the intended effect of increasing learning. By contrast, there is growing literature suggesting that the unintended consequences are damaging to the education of students" (Nichols & Berliner, 2008, p. 672).

Such reservations, it should be noted, support the principles of the mastery curriculum articulated in Chapter 7. As explained there, district curriculum guides should encompass only the mastery curriculum—those aspects of the curriculum that are both essential and structured. District guides should not deal with the organic elements—those that do not require structuring; or the enrichment elements—those not essential for all students. Obviously, then, the alignment process should focus only on the mastery curriculum. Because neither organic nor enrichment components are assessed or monitored, the teacher will thus have an important measure of autonomy.

CURRICULUM DESIGN

Curriculum leaders often formulate a top-down curriculum design model. Curriculum is often designed from an outcome perspective or end-in-mind approach, which is generally inverse in nature. This is usually a standards-based alignment, which often accompanies high-stakes testing. Clearly defined steps are followed, and there is a continual link to content standards. Curriculum work is usually coordinated by a district administrator and enhanced by outside experts, such as a professor from a local university, but the teachers make the essential curriculum decisions. This process usually falls into the categories of goal development, defining courses, dividing courses in units, planning units, and formulating lessons (Danielson, 2002).

Goal-Based Design

Improved public awareness of how alignment and standards can enhance curriculum development is crucial. This often leads to a greater understanding of how curriculum can benefit teachers, students, and citizens. Community appreciation leads to the creation of shared vision and mission statements, joint curriculum committees, appropriate financing programs, infrastructure development, staff development, maintenance and service arrangements, favorable program evaluation, and, finally, successful public relations programs.

A key standard for school jurisdictions to consider is goal-based design—the setting of clear and practical goals that will expand the curriculum. Along this line, curriculum leaders need to coordinate school-based services and resources to best integrate curriculum for students in their schools. Envision helping participants to become change agents in the teaching–learning process of incorporating new strategies into the classroom curriculum. Questions that might be asked include the following:

- What is the mission of my school?
- What should students be learning?
- What role does activity-based learning play in the curriculum?
- What strategies and tools are we using to achieve our curricular objectives?

Successful guiding principles for curriculum planning might include the following:

- Community involvement in planning and implementing the use of an integrated curriculum should be a high priority for school leaders.
- Developing quality leadership and planning for effective teaching strategies must receive considerable attention.
- Emphasis should be placed on incorporating learning centers into classrooms.
- Curriculum should use technology but not be driven by it.
- Staff development involving integrated learning should be made highly practical by having "teachers instruct teachers."
- Planning and implementation phases for the inclusion of new instructional strategies should include assessment and evaluation standards.

Successful curriculum mission statements involving technology might include the following:

- To enhance student learning in all curriculum areas from basic skills through higher thinking skills using state and national standards
- To enhance student global understanding
- To stay abreast of new curricula developments
- To assist the staff in completing routine tasks involving curriculum
- To provide staff in-service on curriculum
- To build student competency in using technology to access and process curriculum information

Unit and Lesson Design

An 18-month study titled "Inside the Classroom" reviewed more than 350 lessons that included accurate, significant, and worthwhile content, yet many of the lessons were generally not intellectually rigorous, did not include effective teacher questioning, and did not guide students appropriately (Weiss & Pasley, 2004). One of the purposes of the study was to find high-level lessons that invited students to interact purposefully with content. These types of lessons involve students and try to build on previous knowledge, often using real-world examples or engaging students in firsthand experiences.

Developing quality lessons is an important part of curriculum design. As part of a curriculum alignment process, it is important that teachers have a vision of effective instruction to guide the design and implementation of their lessons. Activities should engage students. The classroom curriculum should support and challenge students with appropriate questioning and sense-making strategies. Questioning strategies should enhance the development of students' problem solving, with the teacher emphasizing higher-order thinking skills.

It is important that curriculum leaders provide workshops and other teacher professional development activities that reflect the elements of high-quality instruction with clear, explicit learning goals. It is critical that schools also provide supportive and yet challenging learning environments. The findings of the Inside the Classroom study (Weiss & Pasley, 2004) included a number of interventions that will help teachers improve instruction.

Interventions

- Skilled, knowledgeable facilitators who provide teachers with helpful learning opportunities

- Support materials accompanying textbooks and other instructional materials

- Workshops and professional-development activities that focus on high-quality instruction

- Policymakers who explore the apparent inequities in quality of instruction and who take steps to resolve them

- Administrators who ensure that teachers receive a coherent set of messages

As can be seen, it is crucial that teachers have assistance in formulating and delivering highly effective lesson plans that relate directly to mastery objectives. This will require the alliance of curriculum leaders who share a vision of quality instruction at district and state school levels.

ORGANIZING THE ALIGNMENT PROJECT

The first important step is to organize the alignment project and to allocate responsibilities. The project is a complex one, involving several critical steps, and it will probably operate most effectively if it systematically involves all those who can contribute. Each district, of course, will develop its own organization and management system for the project; the system outlined below has been derived from an analysis of several successful alignment projects.

One effective way to begin is to appoint a curriculum-alignment task force, a representative group that will be responsible for planning and coordinating the project. The task force should include an appropriate number of representatives from the following constituencies: district administrators, district supervisors, school administrators, teachers, and parents. At the outset, the task force should develop its own planning guide, indicating the steps to be taken, the deadline for each step, and those responsible for each step. A special point should be made here about the allocation of leadership responsibilities. Rather than simply assuming that the principal will play the key leadership role at the school level, the task force should attempt to identify and develop a leadership team at each school, so that the talents of many individuals are utilized and responsibility is shared. Exhibit 11.1 shows a form that can be used to assist in such planning. It lists all the steps in the alignment project and provides space for deadlines and the names of those responsible for each step.

EXHIBIT 11.1 Alignment Project Planning Guide

Project Step	Deadline	Primarily Responsible	Assists
1. Determine scope of project.			
2. Orient school administrators.			
3. Orient teachers.			
4. Orient students and parents.			
5. Revise curriculum guides.			
6. Identify mastery objectives.			
7. Develop curriculum-based tests.			
8. Correlate mastery objectives with instructional materials.			
9. Develop planning aids.			
10. Help teachers use planning aids.			
11. Monitor teacher use of planning aids.			
12. Develop test-reporting materials.			
13. Help teachers use test reports.			
14. Help school administrators use test reports.			
15. Use test reports in evaluating curriculum.			
16. Provide staff development for school administrators.			
17. Provide staff development for teachers.			
18. Monitor and evaluate the alignment project.			

In the discussion that follows, certain assumptions will be made about those providing leadership simply for purposes of illustration; however, each district should develop its own system for allocating leadership responsibilities.

One of the initial decisions the task force should make is the scope of the alignment project. For example, the question that should be asked is, which subjects at which grade levels will be included? The decision will, of course, be affected by such considerations as the size of the district, the resources available, and administrators' perceptions of needs.

The task force should then make plans to orient all the key groups that will be involved in and affected by the alignment project. The first group to be oriented should probably be the school principals. They should have in-depth preparation to enable them both to discharge their own responsibilities and to explain the project to others. The principals can then, at the school level, orient both their own faculties and parent groups.

ORGANIZATIONAL STRATEGIES

A major focus of the curriculum alignment task force is to determine whether the curriculum will be standards-based or integrated or a blend of both. The task force will then need to determine a sequence, formulate requirements and electives, and eventually coordinate the entire curriculum.

Standards-Based Versus Curriculum Integration

The past decade has witnessed considerable interest in curriculum integration and yet, paradoxically, schools at the same time are being required to move to an "accountability" and "standards-based" subject-centered curriculum. How can curriculum integration survive under such circumstances? One deterrent to curriculum integration is the fact that most state standards and proficiency tests are set up in terms of conventional subject areas, such as reading, mathematics, science, or social studies. Another problem is the sheer number of competencies specified in the standards. According to Vars and Beane (2000),

> It is still too early to obtain reliable data on how students in integrative programs fare on state proficiency tests. However, in reviewing the literature of earlier studies by Arhar (1997), the National Association for Core Curriculum (2000), and Vars (1996, 1997), they came to the same general conclusion: Almost without exception, students in any type of interdisciplinary or integrative curriculum do as well as, and often better than, students in a conventional departmentalized program.
>
> For the most part, these results were obtained using standardized achievement tests designed for a conventional separate subjects program. Most standardized tests are normed—scores of individual students are compared with the mean or average of whatever group is considered "normal." In contrast, current state tests may have arbitrary cut-off scores that all students must meet in order to "pass" or be considered "competent." In other words, the rules of the assessment game have been changed radically. Furthermore, the quality of many statewide

assessment measures has been widely criticized, raising serious questions about the morality of using them to determine a student's grade promotion or high school graduation.

It will probably be many years before problems in the assessment of student performance are solved. In the meantime, educators considering curriculum integration will need to proceed carefully and take full advantage of the decades of research and experience with this potentially powerful way of designing and carrying out education (Beane, 1997; Vars, 1993). It also is important to keep all stakeholders—students, teachers, families, and the general public—both informed and involved in continuing efforts to provide every student with meaningful learning experiences. (p. 3)

In support of Vars and Beane, Charlotte Danielson (2002) believes curriculum integration can be done by considering the following design issues: *sequence, required versus elective,* and *coordination and integration* of subject matter.

Sequence

A well-organized curriculum will have goals stated in a clear and concise manner. Complex ideas and skills will follow simpler ones. Student abilities will be considered when determining teaching strategies. Topics are addressed and then covered again in a spiraling curriculum approach with the learning level advancing with each reteaching. Students develop a richer understanding of the subject area, and there is an appreciation of nuances within the material.

Required Versus Elective

Elements of consistency within the curriculum begin to change as students move from elementary to middle to high school levels. The distinction between mandatory and optional is more evident at high school levels. Students at higher levels are able to pick and choose courses as they relate to graduation and college requirements.

Coordination and Integration

Some curriculum specialists consider subjects as distinct bodies of knowledge to be aligned as standards throughout the curriculum. Other curriculum specialists see subject areas as bodies of knowledge that are to be interwoven in a thematic scheme. In the latter, information can be covered through methods of inquiry, and topics can be coordinated and integrated across disciplines. Regardless of which approach is used, there is the need for the educational task force to *identify mastery objectives* within the curriculum.

IDENTIFYING THE MASTERY OBJECTIVES

According to Rick Stiggins (2001), sound assessments should reflect clear achievement targets. Educational task forces should turn their attention to the critical task of identifying the mastery objectives (as explained in Chapter 1, the mastery objectives are those objectives that are essential for all and require careful structuring). Because that list of mastery objectives will be used in developing both the curriculum-based tests and the teachers' alignment materials, it is essential that the task be done with care and due deliberation. If the district has developed a curriculum that focuses only on mastery objectives, then the task is a very simple one: The objectives have already been identified for each grade level. If the district is basing the alignment project on existing guides that do not embody the mastery approach, then subject-matter committees should be assigned the task of identifying the key objectives.

The subject-matter committees should begin by reviewing and revising the guides, if revision seems indicated. Even the best guides become outdated; it is obviously unwise to base an alignment project on an inadequate curriculum. Once necessary revisions have been made, the committee should identify for each grade the mastery objectives—the key skills, concepts, and information that students are expected to master (a sample list is shown in Exhibit 11.2).

EXHIBIT 11.2 Sample Mastery-Objectives List

GRADE 5. SOCIAL STUDIES: PEOPLE OF AMERICA

Maps, Globes, and Graphics Skills

1. Locate Canada on globe.

2. On an outline map of Canada, identify each province.

3. On an outline map of Canada, with locations of cities indicated, identify Montreal, Vancouver, Toronto, Winnipeg, and Calgary.

4. Use scale on map to estimate distance between two Canadian cities.

5. Identify major ethnic groups and their relative sizes from bar graph.

Three types of objectives should probably not be included in the mastery list:

1. Objectives too difficult to assess with district-made tests. Most districts, for example, would probably choose not to assess listening skills, because valid listening tests are very difficult to develop, administer, and score. Similarly, most affective outcomes (such as "appreciating poetry") are difficult to measure validly with objectives.

2. Objectives that are not considered essential for all students. Many district guides include content that has been identified in this text as enrichment material: objectives that are not really basic for all students but simply broaden the curriculum or challenge the more able.

3. Objectives that have been emphasized at some previous grade level or that will be emphasized at some future grade level. While many district guides include

objectives that are to be "reviewed" or "introduced," only those objectives to be emphasized at that particular grade level should be identified in the alignment project. It is expected that teachers will review as necessary and will feel free to introduce skills and concepts as the occasion arises.

These preliminary lists of grade-level mastery objectives should then be reviewed by classroom teachers. At the elementary level, the reviews should be made by grade-level teams; third-grade teachers, for example, should have an opportunity to review the mastery lists for all areas for which they are responsible. At the secondary level, the review should be conducted departmentally. This teacher review is essential, because teachers will be expected to teach and test for the objectives on the final list.

The task force should then undertake a final review of the mastery lists. One of the important questions to be raised at this juncture is whether the skills and concepts can be taught for mastery within the time allotted. How much time should be allotted to mastery objectives? The Pittsburgh alignment project suggests a figure of 60% of the total instructional time available; the remaining time is provided for remediation and enrichment.

DEVELOPING CURRICULUM-BASED TESTS

That graded list of mastery objectives should then be used to develop curriculum-based tests. Because these tests play such a key role in the alignment project, they should be developed with the advice of measurement experts who can guide the development of the tests and also assess the tests for reliability and validity. Test development is a highly complex process that requires very specialized technical skills. If districts do not have their own evaluation experts, they may wish to use the services of professional and commercial organizations that will develop such tests on a contractual basis.

Glatthorn (1987) attested that measurement experts usually recommend that a process like the following one be used in developing and assessing the curriculum-based tests:

1. Determine test scope and frequency. Will curriculum-based tests be administered at the conclusion of each unit, at the end of each semester, or at the end of the school year? More frequent testing provides administrators and teachers with formative data that can be used to monitor student progress and take corrective actions; however, frequent testing reduces instructional time and seems to increase teacher resistance to the project.

2. Determine how many forms of each test will be required. Larger school systems may require several alternative forms for each test in order to ensure test security. For smaller systems, two forms for each test will probably suffice.

3. For each objective, develop a pool of test items. Be sure that the test items validly assess the objective. Do not use "comprehension" items, for example, to assess "application" objectives.

4. Construct the pilot forms of the tests by selecting a sample of test items, grouping the items in some logical manner, and preparing clear instructions.

5. Develop a scoring system that will provide administrators, teachers, and students with the information they require in order to understand and use test results. Administrators will need information about overall achievement; teachers will need diagnostic information about classes and individual students; and students will want grades.

6. Have content specialists review the tests to ensure that items are valid, that the answers are correct, and that the sampling reflects curricular priorities. Administer the pilot forms of the test to groups of students in order to measure test reliability. (p. 260)

Those requiring more information about the development of curriculum-based tests can consult one of the standard references: Gallagher and Ratzlaff's (2007–2008) article on how Nebraska is developing its own system of local assessments; Baron and Boschee's (1995) text provides insightful thoughts on the purposes of evaluation; Bloom, Hastings, and Madaus's (1971) text provides a comprehensive treatment of evaluation.

The process outlined above obviously describes the development of objective tests, the type most commonly used in alignment projects. Many districts, however, have seen fit to supplement those objective tests with certain performance tests, especially in the area of written composition. Those performance tests will require quite different methods of development and assessment.

Obviously the process of developing curriculum-referenced tests is a complex and time-consuming one. These tests are so important, however, that such an expenditure of time and effort is fully warranted.

CORRELATING THE MASTERY LIST AND INSTRUCTIONAL MATERIALS

With the tests prepared, the subject-matter committees should turn their attention to the instructional materials. By reviewing texts currently in use and checking their content against the mastery list, the committees should first establish whether new basal texts would be required. Quite often the development of the mastery-objectives list will highlight deficiencies in existing texts—deficiencies that were not apparent when teachers alone determined what they would teach.

The committees should then develop objectives—materials-correlation charts for each grade to assist teachers in using instructional materials. On the left of the chart are listed the mastery objectives; across the top are the titles of both basal and supplementary texts, including, of course, any new texts that will be ordered. Each mastery objective is then keyed to specific pages in the texts. A sample correlation chart is shown in Exhibit 11.3. Although many publishers make such correlation charts available to districts that have purchased their texts, such publisher-produced charts are not sufficiently reliable for use in the alignment project.

The correlation process thus accomplishes two important goals: It provides a means for the district to ensure that adequate instructional materials are available, and it helps teachers make their instructional plans.

EXHIBIT 11.3 Sample Objectives: Text Correlation Chart

GRADE 10. SCIENCE: BIOLOGY		
Mastery Objective	Life Sciences	Modern Biology
1. Define ecosystem.	pp. 75–78	pp. 14–18
2. Identify three common air pollutants.	pp. 78–79	pp. 19–20
3. Explain probable causes of acid rain.	pp. 82–83	

DEVELOPING INSTRUCTIONAL PLANNING AIDS

The next important component of the alignment project is the instructional-planning aids. These are materials that will assist teachers in developing and implementing instructional plans. Besides helping teachers plan, they also can facilitate discussions between administrators (or supervisors) and teachers about the planning process. Major types of planning aids that play an important role include a Yearly Planning Matrix, a Management and Monitoring Matrix (see Exhibit 11.4), and Unit-Planning Guides.

Yearly Planning Matrix

Teachers will first need help in making tentative plans for the school year, to ensure that all mastery objectives are taught and reinforced and that adequate time has been provided. One way of helping them accomplish these goals is by providing a yearly planning matrix, like the one shown in Exhibit 11.5. The teachers first list the mastery objectives, grouped according to subject-matter subdivisions. They then indicate the report or marking period when they plan to teach this objective for mastery and when they expect to reinforce that objective. They then estimate the total number of instructional periods required.

One effective way of using the yearly matrix is as follows:

- The teacher submits the yearly matrix to an instructional leader. The initial entries reflect the teacher's tentative decisions about yearly planning.

- The instructional leader and the teacher confer about the yearly plan, discussing issues of sequencing and time allocation and making any changes they both agree are necessary.

- The yearly matrix is posted in the classroom so that students and classroom visitors can be informed. As the teacher teaches or reinforces a mastery objective, the appropriate entry is marked.

- The teacher is expected to bring the yearly matrix to any supervisory or evaluation conferences.

EXHIBIT 11.4 Management and Monitoring Matrix

Target Area _____   Product _____

1. GOAL _____   End Point _____

3. STATUS TODAY What is the situation today?	4. ACTIVITIES What must be done to get from 4 to 3?	5. LEADERSHIP Who is responsible to initiate/follow through with activities?	6. SCHEDULE What is the timeframe for accomplishing each activity being monitored?	2. INDICATORS If the goal were attained, what would really be happening? What would the target area look or be like? List 8 to 10 indicators.
A.				A.
B.				B.
C.				C.
D.				D.

EXHIBIT 11.5 Sample Yearly Planning Guide

Grade 8. English Language Arts (Literature)

Mastery Objective	Report Period				
	First	*Second*	*Third*	*Fourth*	*Total Time Required*
1. Define *character*.	T		R		2 periods
2. Identify three means of character.	T		R		2 periods
3. Infer character's motivations.	T	R	R		4 periods

Code: T = teach for mastery; R = reinforce.

Management Planning Matrix

Another design tool is the Management Planning Matrix, which has been developed to help curriculum leaders plan, implement, and evaluate an effective staff-development program (Whitehead, Jensen, & Boschee, 2003). The matrix design encourages planners not only to develop technology staff development goals but also to formulate measurable indicators of successful in-service. The matrix additionally forces planners to detail activities and leadership roles and to set implementation and evaluation dates. This has been one of the most successful tools used by school leaders in designing effective staff-development programs. A Management and Monitoring Matrix can be found in Exhibit 11.4. The example of a yearly matrix thus serves several important purposes.

Unit-Planning Guide

Teachers will also need help with their unit planning. Two approaches can be used in deriving unit plans from the yearly matrix. In fields such as mathematics and science, where units are built from closely related objectives, the teacher can begin with the yearly matrix, list related objectives in unit clusters, and check to see that the time allocations seem appropriate for that grade level. In this approach the objectives shape the unit.

In fields such as English and social studies, where several types of objectives are often included in one unit, teachers will need special help in learning how to integrate mastery objectives into thematic units. Most teachers will find it helpful to begin by "roughing in" the unit—identifying the unit theme, determining the approximate length of the unit, specifying the major unit generalizations, and identifying the key resources. Next they turn to the yearly matrix and select appropriate objectives for that unit, checking off each objective as it is included in a particular unit. They then make a final check to be sure that all objectives have been included in at least one unit. Exhibit 11.6 shows one form that can be used in integrating mastery objectives into a thematic unit. In this approach, the unit theme influences the selection of the objectives.

EXHIBIT 11.6 Sample Unit-Planning Chart

Grade 10. English. Second Report Period
UNIT THEME: The Changing American Family
LENGTH OF UNIT: 10 periods

Thematic Generalizations

1. Understand how American family is changing
2. Understand reasons for changes

Common Readings

1. *My Antonia*
2. *Life With Father*
3. *Kramer vs. Kramer*
4. Selected articles from current magazines

Mastery Objectives to Be Emphasized

1. Write expository essay of causal analysis
2. Identify author's bias in an essay of opinion
3. Identify three means of character portrayal
4. Infer character's motivations

These unit-planning guides should also play an important role in the supervision process. They can assist the supervisor and the teacher in discussing curricular priorities, in reflecting on planning approaches, in determining instructional methods, and in examining issues of individualization and remediation.

In addition to the yearly and unit-planning aids, some school districts expect teachers to indicate in their daily lesson plans which mastery objectives will be covered. Others feel that teachers should have more flexibility and autonomy in daily planning. The research does not provide any clear guidance here. Although well-structured lessons are usually associated with increased achievement, there is no evidence that the quality of written lesson plans is related to student achievement. Some teachers can write good plans but cannot deliver them effectively; other teachers can deliver well-structured lessons without committing plans to paper (for an excellent review of the research on planning and achievement, see *Performance-Based Education: Developing Programs Through Strategic Planning* by Baron, Boschee, and Jacobson, 2008).

Also, some districts provide pacing charts that indicate when a given set of objectives should be taught and approximately how much time should be devoted to each group of outcomes. While such charts can be helpful to teachers who need assistance with pacing, most teachers seem to view the pacing charts as too controlling. Their use would seem to reduce teacher autonomy in planning, teaching, and providing remediation. The purposes of such pacing charts can perhaps be better realized through discussions between supervisor and teacher about yearly and unit planning and by team or departmental discussions of time allocation and instructional pacing.

The intent of all the instructional-planning aids should be to help teachers plan more effectively, not to control their classroom decision making.

IMPORTANCE OF SCIENTIFIC RESEARCH

Any alignment of reading curriculum at the elementary level should involve understanding of scientific research. This has been especially the case with the No Child Left Behind Act and Response to Intervention requirements. In a recent research study, principals in both high- and low-performing schools indicated that instructional knowledge, not content knowledge, was the more frequent cause of teacher ineffectiveness (Torff & Fusco, 2007–2008). According to G. Reid Lyon and Vinita Chhabra (2004), research reveals that a majority of students can learn to read irrespective of their backgrounds, and yet many elementary students are not having success in reading. The problem is that many elementary teachers do not have the background or training in scientific-based reading research. Teachers frequently rely on experience and anecdotal information to guide their teaching. As a result, it is more important that educators have a basic understanding of scientific knowledge as it relates to reading and what needs to be done to guide instruction.

Two major questions that should be asked by curriculum leaders selecting reading programs should be these:

1. Does the program comprehensively cover each of the evidence-based skills that students need to read proficiently?

2. Has the program or approach been proven scientifically to work with students?

Asking these types of questions is important for curriculum leaders. Research obtained should include information on appropriate methodologies, peer review, converging evidence, and practical application. For example, Lyon (Lyon & Chhabra, 2004) noted that the National Reading Panel (NRP) found that systematic phonics instruction produced significant benefits for K–6 students and for those having difficulty learning to read. The NRP also found that systematic phonics instruction was most effective when provided within the context of a comprehensive reading program that addressed phonemic awareness, fluency, vocabulary, and comprehension strategies. This is the type of detailed scientific research that curriculum leaders need before selecting, planning, or implementing a reading program.

The U.S. Department of Education is in the process of developing the What Works Clearinghouse as a resource that will provide curriculum leaders with central and independent scientific evidence of what works in class. For more information, contact the clearinghouse (see www.w-w-c.org).

DEVELOPING REPORTING MATERIALS

The task force should also determine, in consultation with administrators, supervisors, and teachers, what reporting materials will be required in the alignment project. As Victoria Bernhardt noted her 1998 classic book, *Data Analysis for Comprehensive Schoolwide Improvement*, data reports help curriculum leaders in initializing needed change as well as allowing them to monitor instructional practices successfully. The following types of materials have been used in numerous projects:

- The **planning report** summarizes student performance for each class on the previous year's summative examination. The report is distributed to teachers in workshops that precede the opening of school; teachers use the report to determine which objectives need additional review and which students require special attention.

- The **class diagnostic summary** is provided to teachers after each test administration. It gives information about the test results of all the students in the class, objective by objective. The teacher uses this report to plan posttest remediation and to make adjustments in the yearly and unit forms.

- The **individual student report** provides comprehensive information for each student; it also is distributed after each major testing. It gives the student's name and indicates for all objectives the number correct and incorrect. The individual student report is made available to teachers, the student, and the student's parents.

- **Data analysis reports** are also very helpful. They often provide a practical tool to help educators make better decisions based on information collected over a period of time. School leaders can use data to analyze and utilize information about their curriculum and their school communities. (Bernhardt, 1998)

These reports, which provide a great deal of useful information, can be produced at relatively little cost through the use of technology. With the proper interplay among interim assessments, analysis, action, and data-driven culture, schools can be transformed, and a new standard can be set for student learning (Bambrick-Santoyo, 2007–2008).

PROVIDING STAFF DEVELOPMENT FOR THE ALIGNMENT PROJECT

Once all these decisions have been made and materials have been developed, the school administrators and teachers should be provided with the in-depth training they will need to make the project successful. Part of this staff development should occur, of course, before the project begins, to prepare both groups for the requirements of the alignment project. Much of it, however, should be made available on a continuing basis throughout the year as problems develop. The specific content of the staff development will certainly depend on local needs. In general, the following topics might be included in staff development for principals:

- A rationale for curriculum alignment
- Orienting teachers and parents about alignment
- Helping teachers use test reports

- Helping teachers make yearly and unit plans
- Monitoring teacher planning and instruction
- Using test reports to evaluate the school's program of studies
- Using the alignment project to make supervision more effective
- Evaluating the alignment project

The staff development for teachers will include some similar topics, with a different emphasis. The following topics would probably be helpful:

- A rationale for curriculum alignment
- Identifying mastery objectives
- Using mastery objectives in yearly and unit planning
- Using test reports to plan instruction and monitor progress
- Locating and using instructional materials
- Teaching for mastery objectives
- Communicating test results to students and parents

The staff-development workshops for both administrators and teachers should also be used to get participants' input about improving the project. Even well-planned projects will need refinement and revision, and the staff-development sessions provide an excellent opportunity for groups to raise problems and suggest solutions.

MONITORING AND EVALUATING THE ALIGNMENT PROJECT

Throughout its operation, the alignment project should be monitored to be sure it is working as planned and then evaluated to assess its overall effectiveness. Two types of monitoring are required. First, district administrators should be responsible for monitoring project management, seeking answers to the following questions:

- Have all necessary instructional materials been provided, and are correlation charts accurate?
- Are tests being administered and scored on schedule?
- Are staff-development sessions being conducted as planned, and are they judged by participants to be helpful?
- Are principals and supervisors helping teachers plan effectively, teach to mastery objectives, and use test results to modify instruction?

Several methods can be used to answer these questions. First, those responsible for carrying out the steps identified in the planning guide should be expected to submit periodic reports, noting dates when key steps were carried out and identifying any problems that developed. Second, as noted above, some time during each staff-development session should be used to identify problems and assess progress. Regularly scheduled administrative and faculty meetings can also be used, of course, to assess the progress of the project. Finally, a representative sample of administrators and teachers should be interviewed, perhaps once every 2 months, to survey their perceptions and probe their concerns.

The second type of monitoring focuses on the teachers' implementation of the project at the classroom level. The intent here is for school administrators to ensure that teachers are carrying out their responsibilities but to do so in a professional manner that does not create an atmosphere of distrust. This goal can be accomplished if principals present the project as a means of helping teachers, not as a method of controlling them. All of the following activities should therefore be carried out in that spirit. First, of course, the submission of the yearly planning matrix will enable the principal and the teacher to discuss together such essential matters as the organizing of objectives, the optimal sequencing of instruction, and the allocation of instructional time as a reflection of curricular priorities.

Also, the unit plans should facilitate professional discussions between supervisors and teachers. The review of those plans will enable the supervisor and the teacher to discuss issues of unit planning, time allocation, instructional methods, assessment of student learning, and remediation strategies. Because these unit plans are so important, some districts require teachers to submit them for review; others simply expect teachers to develop such plans and review them with colleagues and supervisors, without requiring the plans to be submitted.

Finally, the alignment project can support an objectives-focused supervisory process. Instead of being concerned primarily with instructional methods, supervisors can focus on outcomes. In preobservation conferences they can help the teacher assess what progress has already been made and determine what mastery objectives should be emphasized in the week ahead. The preobservation conference should also provide both with an opportunity to reflect on assessment concerns: How will student learning be assessed? What will be an acceptable level of student achievement for a given lesson and a series of lessons? In their observations, they can focus on the clarity of objectives and the evidence of student mastery. In the postobservation conference, they can help the teacher use student-achievement data as a means of diagnosing instruction.

Such outcomes-focused supervision enables the supervisor and the teacher to examine data objectively and to concern themselves with the essential issue of student learning, rather than emphasizing instructional methods. Issues of method are raised only if the data suggest that students did not achieve at the agreed-upon level.

The summative evaluation of the alignment project can make use of two measures. First, the perceptions of administrators, supervisors, and teachers should be surveyed at the end of each school year. Exhibit 11.7 shows one type of survey form that can be used. The more important measure, of course, is student achievement. School districts should maintain and carefully analyze the results of both curriculum-based and standardized tests, noting trends over a multiple-year period of time. If the project has been designed carefully and implemented professionally, districts should find that student achievement increases. Using the curriculum development and implementation procedures illustrated in Chapter 10, one of this text's authors oversaw composite scores in his school district rise more than 10 percentiles for each grade level in 1 year due to curricular alignment (see Exhibit 11.8).

EXHIBIT 11.7 Survey of Perceptions of Alignment Project

Directions: Listed below are several statements about our alignment project and its components. Circle the symbol that best represents the extent to which you agree or disagree with the statement:

SA = strongly agree	D = disagree
A = agree	SD = strongly disagree

Statement   *Your Perception*

1. The list of mastery objectives helped teachers plan, teach, and assess learning.	SA	A	D	SD
2. The objectives-materials correlation charts helped teachers plan and use materials.	SA	A	D	SD
3. The yearly planning matrix helped teachers make effective plans for the year.	SA	A	D	SD
4. The unit-planning guides helped teachers develop and implement unit plans.	SA	A	D	SD
5. The curriculum-based tests provided useful information to administrators and teachers.	SA	A	D	SD
6. The alignment project improved the professional climate of the school.	SA	A	D	SD
7. The alignment project seemed successful in improving student learning.	SA	A	D	SD

Please provide brief responses to the two items below.

8. The main advantage of the alignment project was _____

_____

9. The alignment project could be improved by _____

_____

Please check below to indicate your professional role; there is no need to sign your name.

_____ District administrator   _____ District supervisor

_____ School administrator   _____ Team or department leader

_____ Classroom teacher

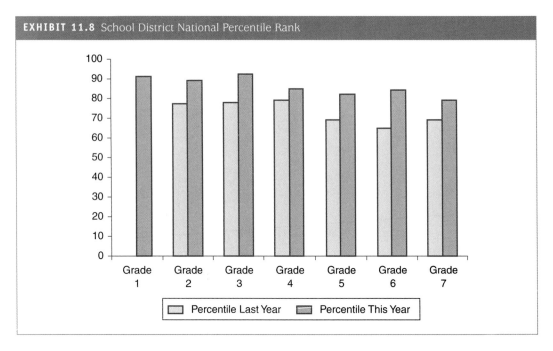

EXHIBIT 11.8 School District National Percentile Rank

A summative evaluation of curriculum can also be attained through a reflection on the following questions adapted from Carol Tomlinson and colleagues' (2002) *The Parallel Curriculum: A Design to Develop High Potential and Challenge High-Ability Learners.* Does the curriculum do the following:

- Guide students in mastering key information, ideas, and the fundamental skills of the disciplines?
- Help students grapple with complex and ambiguous issues and problems?
- Move students from novice toward proficient and expert levels of performance?
- Provide students with opportunities for original work in the disciplines?
- Allow students to encounter, accept, and ultimately embrace challenges in learning?
- Prepare students for a world in which knowledge expands and changes at increasingly rapid rates?
- Allow students to develop a sense of themselves as well as of their possibilities in the world in which they live?
- Provide sufficient challenges to encourage students to develop to the fullest of their capabilities?

UNDERSTANDING THE IMPORTANCE OF CURRICULUM

With the advent of the communication age, a globally shared vision of educational curriculum is not far in the future. Changing societies can change students. Students with knowledge and vision can change societies. Cultural diversity is an important aspect of our world, but cultural understanding is equally as important. While effective curriculum and instruction worldwide contain many diverse elements, curriculum also needs to be responsive to individual students globally. An appreciation of contemporary learners necessitates a need to maximize the capacity of each learner and to guide and align the process through a myriad of opinions and perceptions.

SUMMARY

This chapter provides a rationale and process for curriculum alignment. This process ensures that the written, the taught, and the tested curricula are closely congruent. Curriculum alignment attempts to improve student achievement by remedying the discrepancy that often exists in too many schools between the district curriculum guides, the teacher's instructional plans, and the assessment measures.

APPLICATIONS

1. Be prepared to discuss or write about your views on this statement: Curriculum-alignment projects are unnecessary attempts by administrators to control teachers and damage the climate of trust essential in effective schools.

2. Using the form shown in Exhibit 11.1 (or your own modification of it), develop an alignment-project planning guide that could be used in a school district with which you are acquainted.

3. One of the issues raised in this chapter is the need for pacing charts. Based on your knowledge of classroom teachers, would you consider such charts helpful or intrusive?

4. "Since our competency is being judged by students' test scores, due to high-stakes testing, do you feel teaching to the test is necessary?" How would you respond to this statement?

5. Why are multiple measures needed to address the full depth and breadth of our expectations for student learning?

CASE STUDY   Making Adjustments via Alignment

A group of third-grade teachers in Portland, Oregon, meet after school to review student achievement test data. The principal happens to arrive at the door of the classroom as the teachers are reviewing the results.

"I think this whole standards movement and emphasis on tests is a way for administrators to control the faculty," says teacher Melody Taylor, revealing anger in her voice.

Principal Barbara Bevington enters the room. "I understand your frustration, Melody," she says calmly. "Nonetheless, I can assure you that I'm not interested in controlling anyone. I'm interested in our school doing the best it can for our students."

Melody looks on disapprovingly, as if she is not buying the principal's sincerity.

Bevington decides to address the group. "What I don't understand is why our students are falling behind in the area of measurement in mathematics. It can't be because of our teachers—we have some of the best teachers in the state," declares the principal, looking approvingly over at Melody who blushes, embarrassed.

The principal continues, "Math measurement is noted in our district standards as well as being addressed in our textbook, and yet the test data reveal that our students are really struggling in this area." Four of the other teachers are nodding their heads in agreement as they study the data.

Sue Cockrill, another third-grade teacher adds, "I think I know why our students are doing poorly on measurement. The chapter on measurement is one of the last chapters in our math book, and we usually never get there."

"You're right!" says Melody. "Why don't we move the chapter on measurement up on our schedule? That will ensure that we will cover it."

"Great idea!" says another third-grade teacher, penciling in the change. Everyone smiles.

The principal is beaming. "I am really proud of all of you as a third-grade team. You are really doing some great work in analyzing the test results and adjusting the curriculum accordingly." She then turns and walks back down the hall to her office. Principal Bevington is very impressed that through data analysis her teachers were able to identify an area in the standards that is not being met by the local curriculum. She is also very proud that Melody Taylor is part of that important team.

The Challenge

Getting teachers to align curriculum to state and federal standards and regulations is a major challenge for school administrators. Analyze the problems and hurdles that Principal Bevington had to overcome. What other strategies can she use to get her teachers to accept mandated changes and to align her school's curriculum?

Key Issues/Questions

1. What are your impressions of Principal Bevington? Did she adequately handle the issue of data analysis and aligning curriculum? Why or why not?

2. What are your impressions of the third-grade teachers in this elementary school?

3. If the principal has another meeting with the third-grade teachers, what should be discussed?

4. What are some possible reasons that Principal Bevington's third-grade curriculum is out of alignment with state and national standards?

5. What are some other innovative approaches that Principal Bevington might use to increase student achievement scores? Identify the strategies and explain why you think they might be effective.

WEBLIOGRAPHY

High-stakes testing
www.apa.org/pubinfo/testing.html

Institute for Educational Leadership
www.iel.org

Curriculum alignment
www.mcrel.org
www.ascd.org

CHAPTER 12
Curriculum Evaluation

Evaluation has a long history. As Guba and Lincoln (1981) pointed out, a Chinese emperor in 2200 B.C. required that his public officials demonstrate their proficiency in formal competency tests. In the United States, the concern for evaluating schools can be traced at least as far back as the recommendations of the Committee of Ten, which at the end of the 19th century set perhaps the first example of "evaluative standards" for the nation's secondary schools (National Education Association, 1969). In recent years, however, the interest in curriculum evaluation in particular has seemed to increase markedly. The public's insistence on educational accountability, the experts' demands for educational reform, and the educators' concomitant need for evidence of results have all contributed to the current interest in theories and methods of curriculum evaluation. Unfortunately, much of this interest seems to have resulted in an ill-conceived obsession with test results. A broader perspective and more diversified approaches seem necessary.

This desired breadth and diversification have been reflected throughout this work. Chapter 6 described a comprehensive assessment model that can be used in improving a program of studies. Chapter 8 emphasized the importance of evaluating new courses of study. Chapter 10 explicated an approach especially useful during the implementation stage, and Chapter 11 described the importance of curriculum alignment. The intent of this chapter is to bring all these approaches into focus and to provide for greater understanding of the evaluation process. To that end, it begins by proposing a broad definition of the term curriculum evaluation. It then describes several current evaluation models. It concludes by proposing a comprehensive and eclectic process that can be used to evaluate a field of study, which is perhaps the most difficult curricular element that evaluators face.

Questions addressed in this chapter include the following:

- What principles best define curriculum evaluation?
- What curriculum evaluation models are most effective?
- What criteria should be used to develop a curriculum evaluation model?
- How can a field of study be evaluated?
- How can effective teaching be identified?

Key to Leadership

Successful curriculum leaders realize that evaluation in education is to help the educational process better relate to individual learners.

CURRICULUM EVALUATION DEFINED

That broader perspective mentioned above requires a less constricting view of both the purposes and foci of curriculum evaluation. In reviewing the literature and acquiring a broader understanding of purpose, two concepts delineated by Guba and Lincoln (1981) seem especially useful: *merit* and *worth*. Merit, as they use the term, refers to the intrinsic value of an entity—value that is implicit, inherent, and independent of any applications. Merit is established without reference to a context. Worth, on the other hand, is the value of an entity in reference to a particular context or a specific application. It is the "payoff" value for a given institution or group of people. Thus, a given English course may seem to have a great deal of merit in the eyes of experts: It may reflect sound theory, be built on current research, and embody content that experts deem desirable. The same course, however, may have relatively little worth for a teacher instructing unmotivated working-class youth in an urban school: It may require teaching skills that the teacher has not mastered and learning materials that the students cannot read. In this sense, then, curriculum evaluation should be concerned with assessing both merit and worth.

The foci of curriculum evaluation also need to be expanded. To use the concepts of this present work, curriculum evaluation should be concerned with assessing the value of a **program of studies** (all the planned learning experiences over a multiyear period for a given group of learners), a **field of study** (all the planned learning experiences over a multiyear period in a given discipline or area of study), and a **course of study** (all the planned learning experiences for a period of 1 year or less in a given field of study). All three levels of curriculum work are important. Substantive differences exist between evaluating a program of studies and a field of study and differences of scope between evaluating a field of study and a course of study.

Assessment Leadership Tip

"Any responsible conversation about assessment must attend to the quality of the curriculum." (Kohn, 1994, p. 40)

The foregoing analysis yields this stipulative definition of *curriculum evaluation*: *The assessment of the merit and worth of a program of studies, a field of study, or a course of study.*

EVALUATION MODELS

How can the merit and worth of such aspects of curriculum be determined? Evaluation specialists have proposed an array of models, an examination of which can provide useful background for the process presented in this work.

Tyler's Objectives-Centered Model

One of the earliest curriculum evaluation models, which continues to influence many assessment projects, was that proposed by Ralph Tyler (1950) in his monograph, *Basic Principles of Curriculum and Instruction*. As explained in this work and used in numerous large-scale assessment efforts, the Tyler approach moved rationally and systematically through several related steps:

1. Begin with the behavioral objectives that have been previously determined. Those objectives should specify both the content of learning and the student behavior expected: "Demonstrate familiarity with dependable sources of information on questions relating to nutrition."

2. Identify the situations that will give the student the opportunity to express the behavior embodied in the objective and that evoke or encourage this behavior. Thus, if you wish to assess oral language use, identify situations that evoke oral language.

3. Select, modify, or construct suitable evaluation instruments, and check the instruments for objectivity, reliability, and validity.

4. Use the instruments to obtain summarized or appraised results.

5. Compare the results obtained from several instruments before and after given periods in order to estimate the amount of change taking place.

6. Analyze the results in order to determine strengths and weaknesses of the curriculum and to identify possible explanations about the reason for this particular pattern of strengths and weaknesses.

7. Use the results to make the necessary modifications in the curriculum. (as cited in Glatthorn, 1987, p. 273)

The Tyler model has several advantages: It is relatively easy to understand and apply. It is rational and systematic. It focuses attention on curricular strengths and weaknesses, rather than being concerned solely with the performance of individual students. It also emphasizes the importance of a continuing cycle of assessment, analysis, and improvement. As Guba and

Lincoln (1981) pointed out, however, it suffers from several deficiencies. It does not suggest how the objectives themselves should be evaluated. It does not provide standards or suggest how standards should be developed. Its emphasis on the prior statement of objectives may restrict creativity in curriculum development, and it seems to place undue emphasis on the preassessment and postassessment, ignoring completely the need for formative assessment.

Stufflebeam's Context–Input–Process–Product Model

These obvious weaknesses in the Tyler model led several evaluation experts in the late 1960s and early 1970s to attack the Tyler model and to offer their own alternatives. The alternative that had the greatest impact was that developed by a Phi Delta Kappa committee chaired by Daniel Stufflebeam (1971). This model seemed to appeal to educational leaders because it emphasized the importance of producing evaluative data for decision making; in fact, decision making was the sole justification for evaluation, in the view of the Phi Delta Kappa committee.

To service the needs of decision makers, the Stufflebeam model provides a means for generating data relating to four stages of program operation: **context evaluation,** which continuously assesses needs and problems in the context to help decision makers determine goals and objectives; **input evaluation,** which assesses alternative means for achieving those goals to help decision makers choose optimal means; **process evaluation,** which monitors the processes both to ensure that the means are actually being implemented and to make the necessary modifications; and **product evaluation,** which compares actual ends with intended ends and leads to a series of recycling decisions.

During each of these four stages, specific steps are taken:

- The kinds of decisions are identified.

- The kinds of data needed to make those decisions are identified.

- Those data are collected.

- The criteria for determining quality are established.

- The data are analyzed on the basis of those criteria.

- The needed information is provided to decision makers. (as cited in Glatthorn, 1987, pp. 273–274)

The context–input–process–product (CIPP) model, as it has come to be called, has several attractive features for those interested in curriculum evaluation. Its emphasis on decision making seems appropriate for administrators concerned with improving curricula. Its concern for the formative aspects of evaluation remedies a serious deficiency in the Tyler model. Finally, the very detailed guidelines and forms provided by the committee provide step-by-step guidance for users.

The CIPP model, however, has some serious drawbacks associated with it. Its main weakness seems to be its failure to recognize the complexity of the decision-making process in organizations. It assumes more rationality than exists in such situations and ignores the political factors that play a large part in these decisions. Also, as Guba and Lincoln (1981) noted, it seems very difficult to implement and expensive to maintain.

Scriven's Goal-Free Model

Michael Scriven (1972) was the first to question the assumption that goals or objectives are crucial in the evaluation process. After his involvement in several evaluation projects where so-called side effects seemed more significant than the original objectives, he began to question the seemingly arbitrary distinction between intended and unintended effects. His goal-free model was the outcome of his dissatisfaction.

In conducting a goal-free evaluation, the evaluator functions as an unbiased observer who begins by generating a profile of needs for the group served by a given program (Scriven is somewhat vague as to how this needs profile is to be derived). Then, by using methods that are primarily qualitative in nature, the evaluator assesses the actual effects of the program. If a program has an effect that is responsive to one of the identified needs, then the program is perceived as useful.

Scriven's main contribution, obviously, was to redirect the attention of evaluators and administrators to the importance of unintended effects—a redirection that seems especially useful in education. If a mathematics program achieves its objectives of improving computational skills but has the unintended effect of diminishing interest in mathematics, then it cannot be judged completely successful. Scriven's emphasis on qualitative methods also seemed to come at an opportune moment, when there was increasing dissatisfaction among the research community with the dominance of quantitative methodologies.

As Scriven himself notes, however, goal-free evaluation should be used to complement, not supplant, goal-based assessments. Used alone, it cannot provide sufficient information for the decision maker. Some critics have faulted Scriven for not providing more explicit directions for developing and implementing the goal-free model; as a consequence, it probably can be used only by experts who do not require explicit guidance in assessing needs and detecting effects.

Stake's Responsive Model

Robert Stake (1975) made a major contribution to curriculum evaluation in his development of the responsive model, because the responsive model is based explicitly on the assumption that the concerns of the stakeholders—those for whom the evaluation is done—should be paramount in determining the evaluation issues. He made the point this way:

> To emphasize evaluation issues that are important for each particular program, I recommend the responsive evaluation approach. It is an approach that trades off some measurement precision in order to increase the usefulness of the findings to persons in and around the program. . . . An educational evaluation is a responsive evaluation if it orients more directly to program activities than to program intents; responds to audience requirements for information; and if the different value perspectives present are referred to in reporting the success and failure of the program. (p. 14)

Stake recommends an interactive and recursive evaluation process that embodies these steps:

- The evaluator meets with clients, staff, and audiences, to gain a sense of their perspectives on and intentions regarding the evaluation.

- The evaluator draws upon such discussions and the analysis of any documents to determine the scope of the evaluation project.

- The evaluator observes the program closely to get a sense of its operation and to note any unintended deviations from announced intents.

- The evaluator discovers the stated and real purposes of the project and the concerns that various audiences have about it and the evaluation.

- The evaluator identifies the issues and problems with which the evaluation should be concerned. For each issue and problem, the evaluator develops an evaluation design, specifying the kinds of data needed.

- The evaluator selects the means needed to acquire the data desired. Most often the means will be human observers or judges.

- The evaluator implements the data-collection procedures.

- The evaluator organizes the information into themes and prepares "portrayals" that communicate in natural ways the thematic reports. The portrayals may involve videotapes, artifacts, case studies, or other "faithful representations."

- By again being sensitive to the concerns of the stakeholders, the evaluator decides which audiences require which reports and chooses formats most appropriate for given audiences. (as cited by Glatthorn, 1987, pp. 275–276)

Clearly, the chief advantage of the responsive model is its sensitivity to clients. By identifying their concerns and being sensitive to their values, by involving them closely throughout the evaluation, and by adapting the form of reports to meet their needs, the model, if effectively used, should result in evaluations of high utility to clients. The responsive model also has the virtue of flexibility: The evaluator is able to choose from a variety of methodologies once client concerns have been identified. Its chief weakness would seem to be its susceptibility to manipulation by clients, who in expressing their concerns might attempt to draw attention away from weaknesses they did not want exposed.

Eisner's Connoisseurship Model

Elliot Eisner (1979) drew from his background in aesthetics and art education in developing his "connoisseurship" model, an approach to evaluation that emphasizes qualitative appreciation. The Eisner model is built on two closely related constructs: connoisseurship and criticism. Connoisseurship, in Eisner's terms, is the art of appreciation—recognizing and appreciating through perceptual memory, drawing from experience to appreciate what is significant. It is the ability both to perceive the particulars of educational life and to understand how those particulars form part of a classroom structure. Criticism, to

Eisner, is the art of disclosing qualities of an entity that connoisseurship perceives. In such a disclosure, the educational critic is more likely to use what Eisner calls "nondiscursive"— a language that is metaphorical, connotative, and symbolic. It uses linguistic forms to present, rather than represent, conception or feeling.

Educational criticism, in Eisner's formulation, has three aspects. The descriptive aspect is an attempt to characterize and portray the relevant qualities of educational life—the rules, the regularities, the underlying architecture. The interpretive aspect uses ideas from the social sciences to explore meanings and to develop alternative explanations—to explicate social phenomena. The evaluative aspect makes judgments to improve the educational processes and provides grounds for the value choices made, so that others might better disagree.

The chief contribution of the Eisner model is that it breaks sharply with the traditional scientific models and offers a radically different view of what evaluation might be. In doing so, it broadens the evaluator's perspective and enriches his or her repertoire by drawing from a rich tradition of artistic criticism. Its critics have faulted it for its lack of methodological rigor, although Eisner has attempted to refute such charges. Critics have also argued that use of the model requires a great deal of expertise, noting the seeming elitism implied in the term *connoisseurship*.

DEVELOPING AN ECLECTIC APPROACH

The innovative practices to which many educators aspire can accommodate and build on more traditional mandates (Ferrero, 2006). Although the models above seem sharply distinct from each other, some evidence of congruence exists in current theories of evaluation. This congruence is quite evident in the Association for Supervision and Curriculum Development monograph *Applied Strategies for Curriculum Evaluation* (Brandt, 1981) in which seven experts in evaluation were asked to explain how their "evaluation model" would be used in evaluating a secondary humanities course. While the models proposed by the experts (Stake, Scriven, Eisner, and Worthen) differed in many of their details, several common emphases emerged in the approaches: Study the context, determine client concerns, use qualitative methods, assess opportunity cost (what other opportunities the student is missing by taking this course), be sensitive to unintended effects, and develop different reports for different audiences.

By using these common emphases along with insights generated from analyzing other models, it is possible to develop a list of criteria that can be used in both assessing and developing evaluation models. Such a list is shown in Exhibit 12.1. Districts with sufficient resources to employ an expert consultant can use the criteria to assess the model proposed by the consultant; districts developing a homegrown process can use the criteria to direct their own work.

The criteria will obviously result in an eclectic approach to evaluation, one that draws from the strengths of several different models. Such an eclectic process has been used successfully in evaluating a field of study; this same process can be used as well to evaluate a course of study with the scope of the evaluation reduced.

EXHIBIT 12.1 Criteria for a Curriculum Evaluation Model

An effective curriculum evaluation model . . .

1. Can be implemented without making inordinate demands upon district resources
2. Can be applied to all levels of curriculum—programs of study, fields of study, courses of study
3. Makes provisions for assessing all significant aspects of curriculum—the written, the taught, the supported, the tested, and the learned curricula
4. Makes useful distinctions between merit (intrinsic value) and worth (value for a given context)
5. Is responsive to the special concerns of district stakeholders and is able to provide them with the data they need for decision making
6. Is goal oriented, emphasizing objectives and outcomes
7. Is sensitive to and makes appropriate provisions for assessing unintended effects
8. Pays due attention to and makes provisions for assessing formative aspects of evaluation
9. Is sensitive to and makes provisions for assessing the special context for the curriculum
10. Is sensitive to and makes provisions for assessing the aesthetic or qualitative aspects of the curriculum
11. Makes provisions for assessing opportunity cost—the opportunities lost by those studying this curriculum
12. Uses both quantitative and qualitative methods for gathering and analyzing data
13. Presents findings in reports responsive to the special needs of several audiences

---

Challenges to Program Evaluation

The single largest barrier to effective curriculum implementation continues to be basic awareness of the measurable benefits. Unprecedented assessment of public schools is spurring an investment of billions of dollars, but the lack of research and quality measurement has led to unclear results. The key issues are the establishment of more effective and accurate ways with which we can measure the real benefits of education and measure the true associated costs in money and time spent learning about curriculum and instruction. Sociological acceptance and adoption of new communications technologies continue to represent a challenge as well. Another concern is the lack of leadership in establishing strong evaluation and assessment agendas and programs.

Leadership and Evaluation

Quality leadership is a key component in the success of any evaluation process. One of the most important aspects of that leadership role is for educational planners to understand the process of evaluation and how it should be administered. Understanding the evaluation process means leaders will have to convey knowledge of curriculum as well as instructional strategies. They will also have to convey their expectations of how teaching and learning can be enhanced via the curriculum. There is a special need for leadership and more understanding as to the process of evaluation and how it relates to the development of effective curriculum.

Technology and Evaluation

The rapid changes occurring in computer technology also pose a challenge to establishing effective evaluation programs. Technology capabilities have continued to change faster than educational researchers can sustain. For example, initial evidence on the use of computers in the classroom showed that "drill and practice" activities were successful in reinforcing skills. Now, with continued advances in software and technology, teachers are using computers in classrooms in entirely different ways. It has therefore been difficult for researchers to complete large-scale, controlled studies that lead to solid conclusions because by the time their research is published, new technologies are providing new opportunities for teachers and students. With the exception of National Educational Technology Standards and the International Society for Technology in Education, the lack of correlated state technology standards and guidelines at times creates a barrier to providing quality assessment. Currently, a limited number of districts in the country have established formal guidelines for evaluating the effectiveness of technology in their schools.

Strong evidence of technology's effectiveness will surely further strengthen public and political support. Richard Mayer (Mayer, Schustack, & Blanton, n.d.), professor of psychology at the University of California, stated,

> Our research provides encouraging evidence that appropriate experience with educational technology can promote important cognitive changes in children, including improvements in content knowledge about computing, strategies for comprehending written instruction, strategies for devising problem-solving plans and even in basic academic skills. (p. 6)

As the demand for technology in the classroom increases, the need for evaluation also increases. Administrators, teachers, and parents want to know and understand the impact that technology has made on district goals relating to student learning, staff development, and program content.

EVALUATING A FIELD OF STUDY

"How good is our K–12 science curriculum?" The answer to this question comes from evaluating a field of study—a multigrade sequence of learning experiences in one discipline, subject area, or field. Such evaluations are almost always made for a single purpose—to identify strengths and weaknesses in order to plan for improvements. The process of evaluating a field of study includes five important phases: preparing for the evaluation, assessing the context, identifying the evaluation issues, developing the evaluation design, and implementing the evaluation design.

Preparing for the Evaluation

Preparations for the evaluation include three major steps: setting the project parameters, selecting the project director and the evaluation task force, and preparing the evaluation documents.

In setting the project parameters, district administrators in consultation with the school board should determine both the purpose and the limits of the project. They should, first of all, be clear about the central purpose of the review, because purpose will affect both issues to be examined and methods to be used. In identifying the limits of the project, they should develop answers to the following questions:

- How much time will be allocated, and by what date should the evaluation be completed?
- What human, fiscal, and material resources will be provided?
- Which fields will be evaluated?
- What constituencies will be asked for input? Specifically, will parents, community representatives, and students be involved?

With those parameters set, the project director and evaluation task force should be selected. The project director should be a consultant or a member of the district staff who has considerable technical expertise in curriculum evaluation. The task force should function as an advisory and planning group, making recommendations to and monitoring the performance of the project director. It should probably include a total of 10 to 20 individuals, depending on the size of the district, and have adequate representation from these constituencies: school board, school administrators, teachers and other faculty members, and parents and community organizations. If administrators wish, and if it is felt that their input can be useful, secondary students can be included.

The project director and the task force can then begin to assemble the documents necessary for the program review. The following documents would typically be needed:

- A statement of the curriculum goals for that field
- A comprehensive description of the community and the student body
- A list of all required courses in that field, with time allocations and brief descriptions of each course
- A list of all elective courses in the field, including time allocations, course descriptions, and most recent enrollment figures
- A random selection of student schedules
- Syllabi or course guides for all courses offered
- Faculty schedules, showing class enrollments

Other materials, of course, will be required as the review gets underway, but the above-listed materials are important at the outset.

Assessing the Context

The next stage in a comprehensive evaluation of a field of study is to assess the context. While this stage is obviously of critical importance for an outside evaluator, it is also essential in district-directed projects. The context assessment stage enables the evaluators to identify both the salient aspects of the educational environment that impinge upon the field of studies and the critical needs of the learners. In assessing the context, the evaluators typically should seek answers to the following questions:

1. What are the prevailing attitudes, values, and expectations of the community?

2. What significant aspects of the school district impinge upon the field of study: size, leadership, organizational structure, fiscal resources?

3. What are the special characteristics of school facilities that impinge upon or constrain this field of study?

4. What are the special characteristics of the student body: scholastic aptitude, achievement, home background, ethnic identity, social and physical development?

5. What are the special characteristics of the faculty: experience, educational values, overall competence, educational background?

6. What is special about the school organization: nature of leadership, organizational structure?

The context assessment should result in a report that calls attention to the salient aspects affecting the field of study and identifies the special needs of the learners.

Identifying the Evaluation Issues

The next step in the process is to identify the evaluation issues, to be sure that the evaluation is sensitive to the special concern of the stakeholders and will provide the information needed. Here the distinctions between the several aspects of the curriculum are essential: the written, the supported, the taught, the tested, and the learned curricula all subsume quite different assessment issues.

Also, each of these five must be assessed if the results are to be at all valid. In too many curriculum evaluations, the team evaluates only the written curriculum (the official course guides) and the learned curriculum (the results on achievement tests). No valid inferences can be drawn from such an assessment, because the other three important components have been ignored. Suppose, for example, that the students in a particular district do not perform well on measures of critical thinking in social studies, even though district guides include such units. District administrators cannot be sure about the causes of the problem. It might well be that teachers have chosen not to teach those units because they lack the training and materials necessary. Only a comprehensive assessment can yield the information needed to make improvements.

As shown in Exhibit 12.2, those five components subsume more than 50 different issues. Obviously, not all these issues will be used in every evaluation. Here it is essential for the evaluation team to identify the issues by surveying and interviewing stakeholders. That list of issues can be used to survey such constituencies as board members, school administrators, faculty, and parents, using a form similar to the one shown in Exhibit 12.3. The responses can then be analyzed to determine which issues should be evaluated, given the

EXHIBIT 12.2 Evaluation Issues: Field of Study

THE WRITTEN CURRICULUM

Goals

1. Are the goals of this subject clearly and explicitly stated and readily accessible to those who need to refer to them?
2. Are those goals congruent with relevant curricular goals of the school district?
3. Are the goals in accord with the recommendations of experts in the field?
4. Are the goals understood and supported by parents?
5. Are the goals understood and supported by school administrators?
6. Are the goals understood and supported by classroom teachers?
7. Are the goals understood and supported by students?

Scope and Sequence of Level Objectives

1. Have the goals of this field been analyzed into a set of grade-level (or achievement level) objectives that identify the important concepts, skills, and attitudes to be attained?
2. Are those level objectives sufficiently comprehensive so that they adequately reflect the goals of this field?
3. Are those level objectives clearly displayed in some form (such as a scope-and-sequence chart) that facilitates understanding and use?
4. Are the level objectives in accord with and do they reflect the recommendations of experts in the field?
5. Does the grade placement of objectives reflect the best current knowledge of child development?
6. Does the grade placement of objectives provide for sufficient reinforcement without undue repetition?
7. Is the grade placement of objectives appropriate in relation to their difficulty for learners at that level?
8. Are the objectives appropriately distributed over the grades so that there is balance between the grades?

Written Course Guides

1. Are there written course guides for this field covering all grade levels?
2. Are those guides readily available to administrators, teachers, and parents?
3. Does the format of the guides facilitate revision and amplification?
4. Do the guides clearly specify grade-level objectives in a format and manner that facilitate use?
5. Do the guides make appropriate distinctions between mastery, organic, and enrichment outcomes and focus primarily on the mastery outcomes?
6. Do the guides indicate clearly the relative importance of the mastery outcomes and suggest time allocations that reflect their importance?
7. Do the guides suggest ways of organizing the objectives into learning units, without requiring a particular type of unit organization?
8. Do the guides recommend (but not mandate) teaching/learning activities that seem likely to lead to the attainment of the relevant objectives?
9. Do the teaching and learning activities recommended reflect the best current knowledge about teaching and learning, and are they qualitatively excellent?
10. Do the guides suggest appropriate evaluation processes and instruments?
11. Do the guides recommend appropriate instructional materials and other resources?

THE SUPPORTED CURRICULUM

Time

1. Has the school district clearly specified time to be allocated to this field of study at each level of schooling?
2. Does the time allocated to this field seem appropriate in relation to the district's goals, the goals of the field of study, and the recommendations of experts?
3. Do school master schedules and administrative guidelines on time allocation appropriately reflect district allocations?

Materials

1. Is the quantity of instructional materials adequate in relation to student enrollments?
2. Are the learning objectives of the instructional materials consonant with the objectives of the written course guides?
3. Do the instructional materials reflect the best current knowledge in this field of study?
4. Are the instructional materials free of gender bias and ethnic stereotyping?
5. Are the instructional materials written at an appropriate level of difficulty?
6. Are the instructional materials designed and organized in a manner that facilitates teacher use?
7. Do the instructional materials reflect sound learning principles, providing adequately for motivation, explanation, application, reinforcement, and enrichment?

Staff Development

1. Does the district provide ongoing staff-development programs that help the teachers use the curriculum guides effectively and involve teachers in improving the guides?

THE TAUGHT CURRICULUM

1. Do the teachers allocate time to this field of study in accordance with district and school guidelines?
2. Do the teachers allocate time to the several components of this field of study in a way that reflects curricular priorities?
3. Do the teachers teach for the objectives specified for that grade?
4. Do the instructional methods used by the teachers reflect the best current knowledge about teaching that field of study and are they qualitatively excellent?
5. What unintended effects does this curriculum have on teaching?

THE TESTED CURRICULUM

1. Does the district provide curriculum-based tests that adequately reflect and correspond with the objectives stated in the course guides?
2. Are such tests valid and reliable measures of performance?
3. Does the district make use of standardized tests that provide norm-referenced data on achievement in this field of study?
4. Do any standardized tests used by the district adequately reflect and correspond with the objectives stated in the course guides?

(Continued)

EXHIBIT 12.2 (Continued)

THE LEARNED CURRICULUM

1. Do pupils believe that what they are learning is useful and meaningful?
2. Do pupils achieve the specified objectives at a satisfactory level?
3. What unintended learning outcomes are evidenced?
4. What are the opportunity costs for pupils involved in this field of study?

FORMATIVE ASPECTS

1. By what processes was this field of study developed, and did those processes provide for appropriate input from all constituencies?
2. What specific provisions are there for continuing input from those constituencies?
3. What specific provisions are there for revising and modifying the program of studies?

EXHIBIT 12.3 Survey Form—Evaluation Issues: Mathematics

Directions: As you probably are aware, our school district will soon begin to evaluate the mathematics curriculum in our district. Listed below are the questions we might ask in such an evaluation. Tell us how important you think each question is. Read each question and then circle one of the following symbols:

VI: I think this question is very important.

 I: I think this question is important.

LI: I think this question is less important.

Your responses will help us decide which questions to study.

Question	*Your Response*		
1. Are the goals of this subject clearly and explicitly stated	VI	I	LI

constraints previously identified. The surveys, of course, should be supplemented with interviews of key individuals to provide supplementary data.

Developing the Evaluation Design

With the evaluation issues identified, the project director and the task force should cooperatively develop the evaluation design. One historical and yet very useful framework for such a design was proposed by Worthen (1981). For each evaluative question (or evaluation issue, to use the terminology employed here), identify the information required, the sources of information, and the methods for collecting that information. Thus, in an example used by Worthen, if the evaluation proposes to answer the question, "Do student attitudes demonstrate that the curriculum is producing the desired results?" the attitudes of students with regard to the values and concepts taught constitute the information required. Students are the source of information, and the methods employed might include a comparative design using attitude scales and simulated situations requiring an attitudinal response.

In identifying the methods for collecting information, evaluators should be certain to include qualitative approaches. As noted above, current evaluation theory gives strong emphasis to such qualitative methods as interviews and observations in assessing curriculum impact.

Those decisions—about the issues, the information required, the sources of information, and the methods for collecting information—should form the basis of a detailed evaluation plan, which would include as well the specific tasks to be undertaken, the names of those responsible for each task, and the deadline for accomplishing the task.

Focusing on Student Performance

According to Thomas Guskey (2007–2008), many teachers use computers and other forms of technology—including videodiscs, laser discs, interactive video, various forms of hypermedia, and a variety of powerful online resources—as a primary means of corrective activities. The highly versatile, user-friendly nature of technology makes it appropriate for almost any subject area and grade level. Computer activities enable students to work alone or in collaboration with classmates.

It is therefore essential that the direction for the technology initiative remain focused on student performance. The key behind computer assessment is to create a more symbiotic relationship between Web-based learning and the curriculum. In doing so, correlations between student performance and the use of technology in the classrooms will become more evident. Thus, appropriate mechanisms and administrative structures will need to be made so that student performance can be measured and assessed in relevant ways. The key here is that teachers, students, administrators, and the external community see that technology is having a positive effect on student achievement and that students are performing better because of the technological changes enacted within your school.

Electronic Testing

According to Allan Olson (2004), president and executive director of Northwest Evaluation Association (NWEA), schools in the future will not be grouped by age but by instructional needs, and it will be done electronically. Students will not be assigned one teacher and will not be in a closed-door classroom but will have multiple teachers and be in a more open and collaborative environment. Students will be matched with teachers who have the skills and proficiency to best instruct them. To arrive at this future, schools must use cutting-edge evaluation tools such as adaptive electronic testing that provides a comprehensive assessment of a student's needs.

The ultimate indicator of an effective school is the measure of academic growth of its students. Without sufficient data, schools cannot fine-tune programs or respond to students' individual needs quickly enough to meet local, state, or federal guidelines. This is a major problem with the states and the federal government mandating that schools attain a high proficiency rate of student achievement.

New developments in technology are allowing schools to use Internet-enabled assessment tools that adjust in difficulty to the individual students' ability. Because electronic tests are customized on demand, each student is engaged and the results are more accurate. Electronic results are also instantaneous. This allows teachers to see quickly whether students are succeeding or falling behind. Curriculum and instruction can then be modified to address the results. Electronic adaptive tests can be given any time: fall, winter, or spring. Tests can be tailored to meet federal, state, and district mandates.

Unlike conventional evaluative tests, computerized adaptive tests measure achievement status and academic growth for every child. Schools and curriculum leaders can assess a program's effectiveness for children with different instructional needs. Timely, accurate data provide school leaders with information to adjust instruction and/or programs as needed during the school year to ensure individual learning and to improve program effectiveness. Using up-to-date Internet-enabled assessments, curriculum leaders and teachers will have a chance to shape tomorrow's schools today.

Value-Added Assessment

Value-added assessment is a technique of using test data to determine the value that teachers add to the learning of each student. It focuses on how test data can help each child academically. This type of assessment makes it possible to isolate the impact of the individual teacher and to respond with appropriate rewards or corrective training. Former University of Tennessee statistician William Sanders, who helped pioneer value-added research, noted that this method offers a way to ensure that as few children as possible suffer a disadvantage in learning. Sanders (as cited in Holland, 2001) believed that "under effective teachers, students could make gains no matter what their ability or achievement levels were when they started" (p. 3).

Value-Added Assessment Format:

- Each spring, students take a norm-referenced state test in five core subjects (math, science, reading, language, and social studies). Nonredundant test items are added each year in an attempt to discourage blatant "teaching to the test."

- Each fall, districts receive a report card broken down by school and grade showing progress in each subject in the context of 3-year averages. The system records student achievement gains in scale score points and in the form of comparisons to local, state, and national averages. School and district reports are reported to the public.

- Each teacher receives a report card—one that is not released to the general public—showing the year-to-year progress of his or her students. Supervisors also receive these reports. It is this application of these data that holds the greatest promise for building a better teacher.

Evaluation of the Curriculum Using Student Achievement and Effective Instruction

The increased involvement of the state and federal government in education and curriculum has had a definite impact on the development of curriculum. With the implementation of the No Child Left Behind Act (NCLB) and Response to Intervention, states have increasingly become involved in setting standards for course curricula. These standards are the basis for state testing and for meeting the regulations set forth by NCLB. However, according to James Popham (2001), many teachers fail to take advantage of the instructional benefits that properly constructed tests can bring to themselves and students. Therefore, the written curriculum of schools needs to closely follow state standards. With this in mind, the evaluation of the written curriculum and its effectiveness is ever more dependent on the taught curriculum. To be effective, the written curriculum needs to be the "taught curriculum."

Ineffective and Effective Teaching

In a study by Pam Homan (2003), in the Sioux Falls, South Dakota, school district, the importance of teaching and testing the "written curriculum" was reinforced. Dr. Homan looked at all fifth-grade teachers in the district. By studying 3 consecutive years of test results and by using a multiple regression analysis, Dr. Homan was able to identify the fifth-grade teachers whose children always scored higher on the standardized tests administered by the school district. She also identified the teachers whose students performed below expectations on the same tests. Through a process of observations, Dr. Homan and other district administrators were able to identify effective instruction as the major contributing factor in student achievement.

Results. Homan's (2003) observational analysis, detailed in Exhibit 12.4a, found a difference in the presence of 12 of the 14 categories of effective teaching between teachers with high student achievement and teachers with low student achievement. No difference existed in the presence of Re-teaches and Positive Self-Concept. The greatest differences between the two groups were in Instructional Planning, Instructional Techniques, Provides Feedback, Communicates Expectations, Manages Behavior, and Maximizes Instructional Time. Exhibit 12.4a shows the difference in percentages of the indicator traits demonstrated between the two groups. Exhibit 12.4b lists the specific indicators within each category of effective teaching.

Summary. The results indicate that specific indicators of effective teaching do exist to a greater degree in classrooms with high overall student achievement versus classrooms with low overall student achievement. Given the implications of the No Child Left Behind Act and the expectation that all students be proficient by 2013–2014, it is very important that effective teaching be maximized for each student. The findings of this study confirm the need for both identification and follow-up of targeted interventions to help classroom teachers maximize effective teaching.

The district will develop a training model to assist building principals in observing and providing specific feedback to teachers regarding the presence or lack of indicators of

EXHIBIT 12.4a Teachers and Student Achievement Levels		
	Teachers With Low Student Achievement	*Teachers With High Student Achievement*
Categories of Effective Teaching	*Percentage of Indicator Traits Demonstrated*	
Instructional Planning	46	100
District Curriculum	93	100
Effective Lesson	83	100
Instructional Techniques	68	97
Enhances Self-Concept	92	96
Assesses Students	80	100
Provides Feedback	77	100
Communicates Expectations	60	100
Re-Teaches	100	100
Checks Understanding	80	100
Organizes Classroom	92	95
Manages Behavior	75	100
Maximizes Instructional Time	70	100
Positive Self-Concept	100	100

SOURCE: From *Sioux Falls School District 2002–2003 Value Added Analysis of Student Achievement and Effective Instruction* by P. Homan, 2003, unpublished manuscript. Printed with permission.

effective teaching in their classrooms. In addition, this model will provide principals a vehicle for training teachers within their building to self-assess the presence or lack of indicators of effective teaching in relationship to student achievement.

Evaluation Checklist

Evaluation checklists are helpful to educational planners trying to gauge the success of their classroom curricular program. The checklist for the curricular program components chart (Exhibit 12.5) is easy to administer and provides a quick assessment of program components.

Evaluation tools such as the checklist do not have to be complicated. These instruments help determine whether key components are present in the classroom program.

EXHIBIT 12.4b Effective and Unavailing Teachers	
Teachers With High Student Achievement	*Teachers With Low Student Achievement*
• Strong instructional focus—knew the curriculum and where he/she was headed	• Low expectations not directly related to grade appropriate curriculum • Lacked clear, purposeful instruction
• Smooth and quick transitions	• Spent excessive time telling students what they would be doing • Transitions were chaotic
• Maximized time on purposeful instructional tasks—all aspects of the lesson were clearly connected to a district learning standard	• Lost time on task with noninstructional tasks—parts of the lesson included activities not related to grade appropriate learning standards
• Naturally and positively redirected students without disrupting instruction for others	• Redirection disrupted learning for others and did not maintain dignity of students
• Naturally and immediately included students returning from pull-outs	• Did not attend to students returning from pull-outs
• Established routines known by all students	• Constant low-key commotion in the room

SOURCE: From *Sioux Falls School District 2002–2003 Value Added Analysis of Student Achievement and Effective Instruction* by P. Homan, 2003, unpublished manuscript. Printed with permission.

EXHIBIT 12.5 Evaluation Checklist	
Check ✓ if yes	*Curricular Program Components*
	Does the curriculum provide evidence of administrative and school board support?
	Does the curriculum plan incorporate a mission statement?
	Does the curriculum plan establish a task force or advisory committee?
	Does the curriculum plan facilitate the involvement of parents and the community?
	Does the curriculum design allow for research development?
	Does the curriculum plan utilize student learner outcomes as a measure?
	Does the curriculum plan have an evaluation tool that provides for the collection of qualitative data?

Evaluation Strategies

The following are strategies that successful administrators use in developing assessment and evaluation programs.

Setting Goals and Indicators

The evaluation and assessment process must be linked back to the original mission statement and objectives of the district. Indicators of successful curriculum integration for the purposes of evaluation should be established during the early planning stages of the program.

Identifying Target Populations

Successful evaluation and assessment procedures should focus on targeting specific external and internal population groups. Parents and community represent external groups. Trustees, administrators, teachers, and students represent internal target groups. Data collection needs to focus specifically on these target areas and how they relate to school and curriculum.

Evaluation Centers

The National Study for School Evaluation, located in Schaumburg, Illinois, provides a wealth of information on technology evaluation and assessment.

Regional Technology Training Centers

The Northwest Regional Educational Laboratory and other regional technology centers across the United States provide a plethora of information on best practices involving assessment and evaluation. They also provide conferences and workshops on evaluation strategies. Regardless of the process used to evaluate a program, planners need to be willing to utilize data and to make changes and adjustments where necessary. They must understand that curriculum improvement and instructional improvement are interconnected and that a change in one area will probably elicit a change in another area. Problems and concerns can cloud issues at hand, making evaluation an important tool. With higher quality and more detailed information at our disposal, curriculum leaders will be able to focus more on how technology can help teachers with student achievement in the future.

Implementing the Evaluation Design

With the design developed, the evaluation team can move expeditiously to implement the design and report the results. Two matters should be stressed here: First, the implementation process should be flexible. If new issues develop or if additional data sources become apparent, they should be built into a revised design and incorporated into the implementation process. Second, the results should be reported in ways that will accommodate the special needs of the several audiences. Thus, several reports might be envisioned: a summary written in plain language for the public, an action plan presented to the board and school administrators, a detailed technical report for the broader educational community.

Once people know, firsthand, and are able to measure the benefits of effective curriculum planning and evaluation, the public support for funding will become viable. Indicators of success used to measure the impact of student achievement in schools will be a determining factor. It is hoped that future research will be based on these indicators to give educational planners a more complete picture as to the impact of technology on teaching and learning in our nation's classrooms. A key to the success of any curricular program in the future is the ability of school leaders to develop awareness and understanding through the implementation of an effective evaluation program. Throughout the entire evaluation process, the focus for administrators should be on combining appropriate strategies with measurable results indicating positive correlations on teaching and learning.

SUMMARY

This chapter brings approaches of curriculum leadership into a global focus and provides for greater understanding of the evaluation process. To that end, it proposes a broad definition of the term *curriculum evaluation*. It also describes several current evaluation models. The chapter proposes a comprehensive and eclectic process that can be used to evaluate a field of study as well as technological applications. In addition, challenges to curriculum leadership are addressed.

APPLICATIONS

1. Choose one of the issues identified for the field of study evaluation. Use the Worthen (1981) framework in developing a design for that issue.

2. Select one of the models described and write a detailed explication and critique of that model.

3. Suppose a classroom teacher posed this question to you: "I want to evaluate my own course. I don't know much about statistics. Can you tell me how to evaluate it in a way that won't take too much time?" Write the answer you would give that teacher.

4. Examine Homan's (2003) study on effective teaching and its importance in relationship to student success. Develop an in-service presentation for teachers in your school district in which you could effectively use this study to enhance teaching and improve student performance.

5. Using the evaluation checklist in Exhibit 12.5, evaluate a classroom curricular program in your school.

CASE STUDY   Teaching to the Test

A school trustee shares with Kathy Peterson, district superintendent, that one of the school district teachers is teaching to the test.

"I understand that one of our sixth-grade teachers is teaching to the test in Principal Harris's building," says board trustee Ron Dawson.

Superintendent Peterson smiles. "It would be a problem if we are talking about a norm-referenced standardized test as the evaluative tool. Fortunately, it is my understanding that the sixth-grade teacher is referring to our criterion-referenced test that is currently based on state standards. In this case, we want the teachers to analyze the items and adjust their curriculum to benchmarks on the test—so in effect, she is teaching to the test."

Trustee Dawson looks as if he is slightly confused.

Peterson continues, "Not only is she teaching to the test, but she has also developed a computerized grading system that has the capability of providing e-mail reports to parents. This way, the parents can also help address the acquisition of certain basic skills. The result is that we have basically wrapped the testing process into our curriculum evaluation process."

"And how is that?" Ron Dawson asks.

"Well, at a push of a button, your sixth-grade teacher can average and total any student's grade at any time. If parents walk through the door, she can tell them exactly how their child is doing. She also has an electronic portfolio of every student as part of the evaluative process."

Trustee Dawson likes the idea of having the district's teachers addressing basic skills that are on the state test. "This concept of teaching to the test—a criterion-referenced test—is what we should have been doing all along," he says enthusiastically.

The Challenge

Using electronic testing and setting benchmarks is proving to be a very successful evaluation strategy for Principal Harris. What are some other novel or innovative ways that Principal Harris can use to evaluate and assess student achievement as well as his overall school curricula?

Key Issues/Questions

1. What are some major differences between electronic testing and regular testing? Do you feel that electronic online testing is worth the cost? Why or why not?

2. How might Principal Harris deal with resistance from teachers who oppose the use of electronic testing and data analysis?

3. If the principal meets with other teachers about using a data analysis approach, what should be discussed?

4. What future role will online electronic testing have in evaluating a field of study?

5. What are some other technological approaches that Principal Harris might use to assess student achievement? Identify the strategies and explain why you think they might be effective.

WEBLIOGRAPHY

Curriculum evaluation
   www.mcrel.org
   www.ascd.org

National Center for Educational Accountability
   www.nc4ea.org

National Center for Education Statistics
   http://nces.ed.gov

Research Center for Leadership
   http://wagner.nyu.edu/leadership

PART IV

Current Trends in the Curriculum

One of the best ways to understand general developments in the curriculum is to examine trends in the specific subject areas. The purpose of Part IV is to examine trends in the subject fields and across the curriculum, as well as to focus on trends linking individualizing the curriculum and needs of special students and global and multicultural education.

CHAPTER 13

Current Developments in the Subject Fields

O ne of the best ways to understand general developments in the curriculum is to examine trends in the specific subject areas. While certain innovations transcend the discipline, most of the important changes take place and are worked out in the subject areas themselves. Recently, with the passing of the No Child Left Behind legislation, standards (state and national) have driven curriculum to look first at the standards and then mold curriculum decisions around those standards.

Many developments and trends in K–12 education are altering the landscape for curriculum work. Although history shows that it is often hard to predict which changes will have a substantial impact on schools and which will turn out to be nothing more than fads, it is worthwhile to assess current trends as part of curriculum renewal. This chapter will examine those developments in the subject areas that ordinarily constitute the common curriculum: English/language arts/reading, social studies; mathematics, science, foreign language, physical education and health, technology, vocational education, and the arts. In each case, the discussion begins with a review of the recent history of that field, starting with the curricular reform movement of the post-*Sputnik* era, and concludes with a description of current trends along with standards.

Questions addressed in this chapter include the following:

- What are some of the trends and issues involved in the subject area of English?
- What are some of the trends and issues involved in the subject area of language arts?
- What are some of the trends and issues involved in the subject area of reading?
- What are some of the trends and issues involved in the subject area of mathematics?

- What are some of the trends and issues involved in the subject area of social studies?
- What are some of the trends and issues involved in the subject area of science?
- What are some of the trends and issues involved in the subject area of foreign language?
- What are some of the trends and issues involved in the subject area of arts education?
- What is the current role of brain research in curriculum planning for subject areas?
- How is technology affecting the delivery and implementation of curriculum in subject areas?

Key to Leadership

Successful curriculum leaders are finding that a multitiered approach involving high-quality classroom instruction combined with targeted, small-group interventions enhances learning.

DEVELOPMENTS IN ENGLISH/LANGUAGE ARTS/READING

"Cognitive demands are not just rising; they are changing as well," according to Andreas Schleicher (2008), head of Indicators and Analysis Division of the OECD Directorate for Education. "It's no longer enough to memorize content-area knowledge. Now people need to manage, evaluate, reflect upon, and act on information. At every level, literacy skills are becoming the foundation for success" (p. 4).

According to Thomas Armstrong (2003), author of *The Multiple Intelligences of Reading and Writing,*

> we need to reconnect literacy to all that has come before it, and all that is still connected to it in the brain, by creating environments where reading and writing skills are nourished and supported with music, art, nature experiences, logical analyses, dramatic performances, oral recitations, emotional expression, social interaction, and a wide range of other creative nutrients. (p. 136)

All across the United States, literacy has become a high priority. During this new millennium, public attention is being sharply focused on education and particularly on language arts instruction. Policymakers and parents see direct evidence that our country's future depends on the education of its workforce, and they worry that schools are not as effective as they need to be. With the global economy increasingly demanding high levels of literacy from both workers and managers, a series of questions has become part of a national conversation: How can we break the cycle of failure? What will it take to help all children achieve academically? What kinds of changes in curriculum and instruction will increase student achievement? How can schools ensure that every child learns to read and write well?

As Linda Darling-Hammond and Barnett Berry explained in *Highly Qualified Teachers for All* (2006),

> To meet the laudable goals of teacher-quality, we need more than mandates and regulations. We need a far-reaching national plan. Studies show that well prepared and well-supported teachers are important for all students, but especially for students who come to school with great needs. (pp. 14–15)

The National Institute of Child Health and Human Development (2000) published the *Report of the National Reading Panel, Teaching Children to Read: An Evidence-Based Assessment of the Scientific Research Literature on Reading and Its Implications for Reading Instruction.* From a historical perspective, taking into account the foundational work of the National Research Council Committee, *Preventing Reading Difficulties in Young Children* (Snow, Burns, & Griffin, 1998), the report has identified and summarized research literature relevant to the acquisition of beginning reading skills. The report highlights the importance of teacher preparation and emphasizes both phonics and comprehension as critical skills for young readers. These reports illustrate that consensus is emerging on the components of a successful reading program.

Curriculum Tip 13.1	Things are not always as they appear. In regards to reading, an important step for curriculum leaders is to draw valuable lessons from the relationship between current educational research and practice in general.

Being able to read to learn is more important today than ever before. The U.S. workforce is changing. Professional and related occupations and service occupations will be the fastest-growing sectors for the foreseeable future. Both demand strong communication skills for sharing complex ideas across diverse communities (Gomez & Gomez, 2007). *Excellent Reading Teachers,* a position statement issued in 2000 by the International Reading Association (2004), urges that "every child deserves excellent reading teachers because teachers make a difference in children's reading achievement and motivation to read" (p. 15). According to the IRA (2000), excellent reading teachers share several critical qualities of knowledge and practice:

- They understand reading and writing development and believe all children can learn to read and write.

- They continually assess children's individual progress and relate reading instruction to children's previous experiences.

- They know a variety of ways to teach reading, when to use each method, and how to combine the methods into an effective instructional program.

- They offer a variety of materials and texts for children to read.

- They use flexible grouping strategies to tailor instruction to individual students.

- They are good *reading* "coaches" (that is, they provide help strategically). (p. 235)

In addition, the IRA statement stated, excellent reading teachers share many of the characteristics of good teachers in general. They have strong content and pedagogical knowledge, manage classrooms so that there is a high rate of engagement, use strong motivation strategies that encourage independent learning, have high expectations for children's achievement, and help children who are having difficulty.

Issues Facing K–12 English Language Arts

Many issues confront K–12 English language arts teachers, administrators, and curriculum specialists. Some of the most pressing issues include the following:

- The ongoing debate over best practices in the teaching of reading

- The influence of standards on curriculum and instruction

- The increasing attention being paid to assessment and student results

International comparisons of student achievement have persuaded the public that education in general, and literacy in particular, is the key to personal happiness and financial security. Every politician has a stand on the subject and a plan for "fixing" schools. The American public wants more say in what happens in its schools and wants clear evidence that schools are producing measurable results.

Slavin, Chamberlain, and Daniels (2007) believe there is a literacy crisis in U.S. secondary schools. Too many students enter high school reading far below grade level. With the development of strong standards and through intensive reading instruction, however, new reading programs are giving adolescents the boost they need to become successful readers.

The standards movement continues to drive curriculum and instruction. Every state but Iowa has established standards in language arts, and most are in the process of developing standards-based assessment instruments, many with high-stakes consequences for students. There is a growing commitment to the idea that clear and shared goals for students are the foundational pieces upon which effective teaching and powerful learning occur. Standards provide direction for curricular improvement. As James W. Stigler and James Hiebert (1999) explained in *The Teaching Gap: Best Ideas From the World's Teachers for Improving Education in the Classroom*, "Standards set the course, and assessments provide the benchmarks [bold added], but it is teaching that must be improved to push us along the path to success" (p. 2). The impetus to hold students, teachers, schools, and districts accountable for results gains momentum daily.

Standards for English Language Arts

The vision guiding these standards is that all students must have the opportunities and resources to develop the language skills they need to pursue life's goals and to participate fully as informed productive members of society. These standards assume that literacy growth begins before children enter school as they experience and experiment with literacy activities— reading and writing and associating spoken words with their graphic representations. Recognizing this fact, these standards encourage the development of curriculum and instruction that make productive use of the emerging literacy abilities that children bring to school. Furthermore, the standards provide ample room for the innovation and creativity essential to teaching and learning. They are not prescriptions for particular curriculum or instruction. Although we present these standards in Exhibit 13.1, we want to emphasize that they are not distinct and separable; they are, in fact, interrelated and should be considered as a whole.

ENGLISH/LANGUAGE ARTS

The discussion that follows focuses on all the language arts except reading; reading is considered so important that it is given special attention in the subsequent section.

Trends in English and Language Arts

Four developments in English curricula seem to be significant. The first is a widespread interest in the composing process and a concomitant attention to diverse types of writing. Motivated primarily by the widely disseminated National Writing Project, the developers of English curriculum guides are stressing the importance of an inclusive writing process that gives due attention to prewriting and revision, rather than focusing solely on the final product, and are emphasizing varied forms of writing for real audiences and purposes, rather than limiting writing to standard school essays written to satisfy the demands of a teacher.

The second development is a more comprehensive and diversified view of the student's response to literature. While previous curriculum guides stressed the interpretive and evaluative responses, more enlightened approaches encourage students to respond personally and creatively to the work studied. The intent is to help students find personal meaning in literature, not to develop young literary critics.

The third gives specific attention to the teaching of critical thinking in English. As part of a general nationwide interest in teaching thinking (see Chapter 14), curriculum leaders and experts have been urging English teachers to see thinking as central to all classroom uses of language.

Finally, there is renewed interest in integrating the English language arts. While such interest can be traced back to *English for Social Living* by Roberts, Kaulfers, and Kefaurer (1943), the present emphasis on *IRA/NCTE Standards for the English Language Arts: The 12 Standards*, by the National Council of Teachers of English (2005), seems to have resulted in the development of measures to "develop the language skills [students] need to pursue life's goals and to participate fully as informed, productive members of society" (n.p.). The "standards assume that literacy growth begins before children enter school as they experience and experiment with literacy activities—reading and writing, and associating spoken words with their graphic representations" (n.p.).

How are these developments to be translated into effective curricula? Two publications seem to offer guidance to curriculum workers. The first, *Language Arts English Primary–Graduation Curriculum Guide* (Canadian Ministry of Education, 1992), is illustrated in Chapter 10. It illustrates a philosophy and rationale, scope and sequence, program goal, exit outcomes, objectives, learning outcomes, and authentic tasks for the English language arts program.

The second publication is the *IRA/NCTE Standards for the English Language Arts: The 12 Standards* referred to above (National Council of Teachers of English, 2005). Exhibit 13.1 summarizes the outcomes recommended by the council. As is apparent, the goals are broad based and comprehensive and would provide a useful beginning point for curriculum leaders.

EXHIBIT 13.1 The 12 Essential Goals of English

1. Students read a wide range of print and non-print texts to build an understanding of texts, of themselves, and of the cultures of the United States and the world; to acquire new information; to respond to the needs and demands of society and the workplace; and for personal fulfillment. Among these texts are fiction and nonfiction, classic, and contemporary works.

2. Students read a wide range of literature from many periods in many genres to build an understanding of the many dimensions (e.g., philosophical, ethical, aesthetic) of human experience.

3. Students apply a wide range of strategies to comprehend, interpret, evaluate, and appreciate texts. They draw on their prior experience, their interactions with other readers and writers, their knowledge of word meaning and of other texts, their word identification strategies, and their understanding of textual features (e.g., sound–letter correspondence, sentence structure, context, graphics).

4. Students adjust their use of spoken, written, and visual language (e.g., conventions, style, vocabulary) to communicate effectively with a variety of audiences and for different purposes.

5. Students employ a wide range of strategies as they write and use different writing process elements appropriately to communicate with different audiences for a variety of purposes.

6. Students apply knowledge of language structure, language conventions (e.g., spelling and punctuation), media techniques, figurative language, and genre to create, critique, and discuss print and non-print texts.

7. Students conduct research on issues and interests by generating ideas and questions and by posing problems. They gather, evaluate, and synthesize data from a variety of sources (e.g., print and non-print texts, artifacts, people) to communicate their discoveries in ways that suit their purpose and audience.

8. Students use a variety of technological and information resources (e.g., libraries, databases, computer networks, video) to gather and synthesize information and to create and communicate knowledge.

(Continued)

EXHIBIT 13.1 (Continued)

9. Students develop an understanding of and respect for diversity in language use, patterns, and dialects across cultures, ethnic groups, geographic regions, and social roles.

10. Students whose first language is not English make use of their first language to develop competency in the English language arts and to develop understanding of content across the curriculum.

11. Students participate as knowledgeable, reflective, creative, and critical members of a variety of literacy communities.

12. Students use spoken, written, and visual language to accomplish their own purposes (e.g., for learning, enjoyment, persuasion, and the exchange of information).

SOURCE: From *Standards for the English Language Arts*, by the International Reading Association and the National Council of Teachers of English. Copyright 1996 by the International Reading Association and the National Council of Teachers of English. Reprinted with permission.

These volumes together should provide sufficient guidance for local curriculum workers interested in both substantive and process guidelines for the English curriculum.

Differentiating Curriculum

Teachers of English are currently focusing on differentiated instruction to help energize and expand learning. According to Nancy Protheroe (2007), director of special research projects at the Educational Research Service, there is no single formula for making differentiated instruction work in schools. The standards-based expectations for today's schools seem to mandate a cookie-cutter approach to education. All students, regardless of abilities, background, and interests, are expected to learn a common set of standards. However, both research and the experiences of educators make it clear that a significant number of students will fail to learn the specified knowledge and skills, unless focused attention is paid to the instructional needs of individual students. Dialectical journals, expository writing, critical analysis, analytical writing skills, and evaluation are some current topics teachers can use help differentiate instruction. Students can write stories about single authors, about alienation and hardship, and about adulthood.

Curriculum Tip 13.2	Students should research and write from a multitude of perspectives and approaches.

Central to teaching is *what* we ought to teach—what we want students to know, understand, and be able to do. To be an expert teacher is to continually seek a deeper understanding of the essence of a subject, to increasingly grasps its wisdom. That understanding is key to a teacher's role in curriculum planning (Tomlinson & McTighe, 2006).

Teachers of English continue to use the Backward Curriculum Design Process developed by Grant Wiggins as well as an Understanding by Design Process by Jay McTighe (Schneider, 2000). A form of Socratic seminar is in effect throughout our nation's language arts classrooms. Teachers are beginning and ending the year with discussion and writing prompts. Think-and-write sessions are providing challenging activities. A form of cognitive coaching and student mentorship is becoming commonplace. According to Evelyn Schneider (2000), director of Educational Associates, English teachers find useful such strategies as circle writing, sketch to stretch, literature roles, as well as literature circles as ways to teach language arts.

Circle Writing

Circle writing involves students in groups of three reviewing photos from a multitude of aspects, including historical background, prediction, five senses, comparison, classification, and evaluation. The group creates a template for designing opening questions for discussion. The opening question becomes a starting point for circle writing. Each student adds his or her perspective as the paper is shared around the classroom.

Sketch to Stretch

Using a novel with controversial themes such as racism, homelessness, or literacy, students develop questions relating to community and humanity. A paper is folded into four sections so that students can sketch the most important theme from each reading segment. Ideas emerge about varied choices, visual representations, titles, or sentence summaries.

Differentiated Roles

Students develop short biographies using strips of paper containing information about an important person. The strips of paper are passed around the classroom. Students classify the strips into reader-friendly labels, patterns of the subject's life, or metaphors and then compare these aspects to other well-known individuals.

Literature Circles

Students review literature as part of a group of four individuals. One student is the reader while another finds quotable quotes. The other two students become either the illustrator or the "vocabulary enricher," who looks for unfamiliar words.

These are just a few strategies being used by English teachers to revitalize their classrooms. In actuality, there is a plethora of ways that teachers can change their language arts curriculum. One of the fastest growing and most popular approaches is the incorporation of a critical literacy component.

Critical Literacy

According to Gerald Bracey (2006), an associate for the High/Scope Foundation, researchers, such as Whitehurst, are finding substantial declines in reading for pleasure, and it's showing up in literacy levels. As a result, there is a strong trend toward the implementation of a critical literacy component in classrooms today. Language arts teachers are looking for ways to capture children's imaginations in and out of the classroom. This is being done by immersing students in rich, provocative literature—a literature that has the potential to challenge, arouse interest, and awaken in students a passion for reading, writing, and imaging (Long & Gove, 2004).

Critical literacy is questioning the stance and possibility of change in the teaching of language arts. Historically this trend is rooted in the work of Paulo Freire (1921–1997), the Brazilian educationalist, who left a significant mark on thinking about progressive practice (McDaniel, 2004). Critical literacy has developed into a way to encourage English teachers and their students to adopt a questioning stance and to work toward changing themselves and their worlds. The approach goes beyond **critical thinking skills**. It promotes a certain version of reality for both teacher and student.

READING

Although reading in the strictest sense is one of the language arts (usually construed to cover reading, writing, speaking, and listening), it has so much importance, especially in the early grades, that it is given separate consideration as a curriculum field.

Trends in Reading

Research studies on reading have generated much controversy and confusion among educators. According to Marie Carbo (2007), to increase the percentage of proficient readers, educators must increase the use of best reading practices. A trend is that teachers need to be more and more creative to interest students in reading and in books (Glendening, 2004). The focus is now on a statistical procedure called meta-analysis that synthesizes data from a number of studies as to "what works" in classrooms (Camilli & Wolfe, 2004). Evidence from many successful schools and from multiple research studies seems to show that a *multitiered approach* involving high-quality classroom instruction and in combination with targeted, small-group interventions can substantially reduce the proportion of students who struggle to read (Lyon, Fletcher, Torgeson, Shaywitz, & Chhabra, 2004). According to Reid Lyon, a recent classroom Title I study reveals that effective instruction alone can reduce reading failure to approximately 6%. Other studies noted by Lyon et al. seem to substantiate that a combination of effective classroom instruction and targeted small-group instruction can reduce the number of students having a problem in reading.

Curriculum Tip 13.3	Regardless of expert tutoring or the use of small-group instruction, most reading researchers seem to agree that a strong exposure of teachers to a variety of approaches and different types of instruction is highly beneficial.

No one secret formula emerges for reading, albeit most studies seem to concur that a balance of methods that incorporate both direct instruction and means-based approaches appear to be prevalent in successful schools (Camilli & Wolfe, 2004, p. 28). According to noted researcher and author Richard Allington (2001), the goal of all students reading on grade level will be achieved only with an expansion of expert tutoring, which has repeatedly been shown to be the most effective intervention. Allington said, however, that this will require much more funding than anyone has imagined. Recent classroom studies are underscoring the importance and cost-effectiveness of allocating resources to improving teacher knowledge.

Brain Research

A major trend in the study of reading continues to be a renewed interest in brain research and how the brain functions. In this pioneering age of neuroimaging research, neuroscientists and educators must collaborate for the benefit of all students (Willis, 2007). Some scientists are concerned about an emphasis on brain research and how it is related to the field of reading. Others, such as Patricia Wolfe (2001), say that it would be foolish not to discuss the implications and applications of this field. Wolfe believes that it is like saying that physicians need not understand the body in order to treat it. Wolfe believes that the more we understand the brain, the better we will be able to design instruction to match how it learns best.

Marge Scherer (2004) noted that brain research using MRI technology has yielded fascinating information about how the brain works—especially how brain images of struggling readers and proficient readers differ. According to Scherer, studies show that intensive, expert tutoring changes the signature of dyslexia and helps struggling readers.

Professors of pediatrics at Yale University, Sally and Bennett Shaywitz (2004), share Scherer's views on brain research. They concluded that all children must be taught alphabetics, comprising phonemic awareness and phonics, reading fluency, vocabulary, and strategies for reading comprehension. In addition, according to professors Sally and Bennett Shaywitz, these elements must be taught systematically, comprehensively, and explicitly. It is inadequate to present the foundational skills of phonemic awareness and phonics incidentally, casually, or fragmentally.

But not everyone agrees with recent events in brain research. Psychologist Gerald Coles (2004) is concerned about "brain glitch" research and how it might be misinterpreted. He feels that it is crucial that any such research address the following questions:

- Will alternative teaching approaches configure brain activity in alternative ways?

- Will children's differing assumptions about what it means to "read" correspond to differing brain activity and organization?

- How do different aspects of reading, such as comprehension, syntax, and word analysis, interact in certain reading tasks, and what kinds of brain activity do the interactions produce?

- How does the knowledge children bring to literacy learning affect brain activity?

Technology and Reading Improvement

The Read/Write Web, with its ability to connect users around online content, is beginning to have a profound impact on curriculum, classroom instruction, and professional practice (Richardson & Mancabelli, 2007). Electronic classroom networks can enhance student participation and achievement in reading. Classroom networks facilitate learner-centered environments because they require every student to think actively during class (Roschelle, Penuel, & Abrahamson, 2004). The rapid accumulation of student feedback enables the teacher to adjust instruction as needed. The integration and success of classroom technology is attracting the attention of professional researchers.

For more information on the reading research community, browse through a few of the following Internet sites (Perkins-Gough, 2004):

- *The International Reading Association (IRA).* This is a professional membership organization with members and affiliates in 99 countries. The organization's mission is to promote high levels of literacy by improving the quality of reading instruction, disseminating research and information about reading, and encouraging the lifetime reading habit. At the IRA Web site (www.reading.org) you can find sample archives of selected articles from *Reading Teacher, Journal of Adolescent & Adult Literacy*, and *Reading Research Quarterly* as well as IRA's peer-reviewed online journal *Reading Online*.

- *Education Commission of the States.* See Reading/Literacy section at www.ecs.org. This site includes links to *Common Strategies to Improve Student Reading, A Consumer's Guide to Evaluating a Core Reading Program*, and *Preventing Reading Difficulties in Young Children*.

- *Council for Learning Disabilities (CLD).* This organization's Web site contains a collection of InfoSheets designed to support the translation of research into practice. Go to www.cldinternational.org.

Recommendations for Curriculum Leaders

According to noted researcher Marie Carbo (2003), founder and executive director of the National Reading Styles Institute in Syosset, New York, curriculum leaders and principals should refer to the following recommendations to improve reading in their schools.

- *Help students become familiar with rich, well-written language.* Have teachers read a variety of literature aloud to their classes.

- *Help students associate reading with pleasure.* Encourage teachers and parent-support groups to provide cozy reading areas with lots of high-interest books.

- *Support the development of a library of specially recorded books* (slow paced, special phrasing). Encourage struggling readers to listen to an audiotape and follow along with the text a few times before reading aloud.

- *Provide recorded textbooks.* This tactic enables struggling readers to become familiar with the content and can raise reading levels substantially.

- *Become familiar with a variety of reading methods.* When one method isn't working, teachers need to try an alternate method.

- *Encourage teachers to allow students choices.* Allow students to decide with whom they wish to read.

- *Make skill practice fun.* Allow students to work with peers, and provide some skill practice in the form of hands-on games.

The role of the school library is also important in improving reading scores. Curry Lance Keith (2004) noted that researchers are showing more and more evidence that a well-stocked and well-staffed library plays a key role in student achievement. This is largely due to school libraries' offering students resources for both conducting research and for reading for fun. Well-stocked school libraries can therefore do much to help nonproficient readers.

Predominant reading styles of nonproficient readers are global, tactile, and kinesthetic. The gap between our poor and excellent readers is widening. It is therefore important for school administrators and curriculum leaders to provide as many intervention strategies as possible. The International Reading Association's Exemplary Reading Program Award Committee found three common characteristics necessary for developing quality reading programs: a focus on reading throughout the curriculum, strong administrative leadership, and an emphasis on encouraging students to read for pleasure (International Reading Association, 2004). Whether it is through a focus on reading throughout the curriculum, small-group instruction, expert tutoring, a multitiered approach, staff development, or just an awareness of the problem, leaders need to address the issue of improving reading.

SOCIAL STUDIES

Elementary teachers, who are responsible for all subjects in the curriculum, rarely have extensive preparation in either history or geography (Thornton, 2007). This has caused some concern among curriculum leaders. As the following discussion will reveal, early attempts at reform resulted in seemingly little change, and the current period seems marked by some confusion of aims.

Historically, the post-*Sputnik* curriculum reform movement, which first affected science, mathematics, and foreign languages, seemed initially to make a major impact on the field of social studies as well. More than 40 curriculum development projects of national scope were initiated under the aegis of the U.S. Office of Education's (USOE) Project Social Studies and the National Science Foundation. All the USOE project centers were located at universities, and the curriculum efforts clearly reflected an academic orientation.

The period following the curriculum-reform era was characterized by Jarolimek (1981) as a time when social studies was in disarray. The projects had run their courses, and there were no funds available in significant amounts for new projects.

The backlash was perhaps predictable. In what seemed to many to be a well-orchestrated response, several conservative organizations and local parent groups attacked any course that raised questions of values and morality. *Man: A Course of Study*, a course that attempted to involve fifth graders in an examination of values from an anthropological point of view, seemed to be a favorite target; the furor even resulted in congressional hearings, because federal funds had been used to produce that particular curriculum package.

Several studies of the past status of the field suggested a somewhat discouraging picture at the time of the present work (the following synthesis is drawn from Ponder, 1979; Shaver, Davis, & Helburn, 1979; Superka, Hawke, & Morrissett, 1980). First, the discipline-centered projects of the post-*Sputnik* era do not seem to have made a lasting impact; even generous estimates suggest that they were being used in only 20% of the school districts of the nation. Second, despite a widely held belief that there was little uniformity in the social studies, a standard organizational pattern had firmly taken hold. Exhibit 13.2 shows the sequence of what Superka and colleagues called "a virtual nationwide curriculum held rather firmly in place by state laws, district requirements, textbook offerings, and tradition" (p. 365).

EXHIBIT 13.2 Dominant Organizational Patterns for Social Studies

K—Self, school, community, home

1—Families

2—Neighborhoods

3—Communities

4—State history, geographic regions

5—American history

6—World cultures, Western hemisphere

7—World geography or history

8—American history

9—Civics or world cultures

10—World history

11—American history

12—American government

Despite improvements in texts, the taught curriculum had changed very little. The whole class lecture–recitation method dominated, and students were tested primarily on their ability to remember and reproduce information. Experience-based curricula and inquiry learning were rare. Teachers were the final arbiters of the curriculum actually delivered, and those teachers tended to support a somewhat traditional view of the field.

While the National Council for the Social Studies (1984) recommended a scope and sequence that very closely resembles the dominant patterns noted in Exhibit 13.2, they also sketched in three optional structures for Grades 6 to 12 that they believed would afford local districts greater flexibility. Thus, in Grade 8, these optional frameworks were offered:

Option 1—U.S. history with emphasis on social history and economic developments

Option 2—Economics and law-related studies

Option 3—Interdisciplinary study of the local region

Trends in Social Studies

In the face of today's pressures to focus on literacy and mathematics, schools and textbook publishers are attempting to "integrate" social studies into the teaching of reading. Beyond ensuring a superficial treatment of the subject matter, this practice threatens the continuing development of reflective, engaged citizens (McGuire, 2007).

As a result, new trends in teaching social studies appear to be focusing on a technique that engages students. The new century is bringing a broadening scope to the teaching and learning of history. For example, concept mapping, clustering, brainstorming, mind maps, and other types of graphic organizers are all being used in social studies classes today. Chandler (2003) noted these visual learning symbols, pictures, and other representational techniques allow students to go deeper into ideas and concepts. New perspectives are causing social studies and history teachers to rethink their approach to teaching. Teachers are now finding that achieving a high standard in the learning of history goes well beyond the basics. Students are no longer just focusing on "learned facts" but are learning how to think in a different and deeper way. An important influence on social studies curriculum and teaching has to do with the differences between traditional and restructured schools (Crocco & Thornton, 2002). There is now an interest in not just giving dates, places, and names but giving students an opportunity to question, to investigate, and to make a personal connection to the lives of people they are studying. Students are now using historical thinking skills to examine rich content. "Inspired history" is allowing students to make a connection to the past as well as to open ideas and thinking about how to address the future.

| **Curriculum Tip 13.4** | Social studies and history need to come alive for students. Finding ways to engage students appears to be the key to successful curriculum planning. |

According to Alan Stoskopf (2001), associate program director for professional development at Facing History and Ourselves, a national nonprofit educational foundation in Brookline, Massachusetts, a set of historical thinking skills helps students learn about history. These skills include point of view, credibility of evidence, historical context, causality, and multiple perspectives.

Point of View: Relates to how an author's personal background and status influence what is written. How is the point of view of the author being interpreted?

Credibility of Evidence: Is the source reliable? Where did it originate, and for what purpose was it used at the time?

Historical Context: How does one see the past on its own terms? Are current values obscuring what really happened?

Causality: How does one avoid seeing past events as caused by one factor? Complex history should not be reduced to a single driving force.

Multiple Perspectives: How does one weigh different interpretations of the same event? There is a need to search for the ideas and opinions of different historical individuals to gain a more sophisticated understanding of the past.

Building understanding is a major factor in revolutionizing how social studies and history are taught. For example, students learn that they can view texts as "just someone's ideas written down"—ideas that may not always be clear or complete (Beck & McKeown, 2002). They can ask questions such as, "What is the author trying to say?" or "What did the author say to make you think that?" As students read a text or material, the teacher can intervene at selected points and pose queries to prompt students to consider new information. Student queries can drive discussion and keep it focused on meaning. This helps build understanding as the students read.

The skills noted above are being integrated into social studies and history units all across the United States. The role of technology is also important. For example,

Worker Education and Training Program (WETP) advocates using geographical, mapping, and history-based software applications, as well as age-appropriate simulations with elementary students who are expanding their understanding of the world beyond themselves and their families. Simulations offer students the opportunity to participate in historical events or major decision-making events by virtue of role playing. Whether studying the 50 states or debating the pros and cons of declaring American's independence from England, students will find a wealth of excellent technology-based applications to make exploring social studies themes exciting. (North Central Educational Regional Laboratory, n.d.)

Students are now turning in their presentations in the form of WebQuests (Chandler, 2003). A WebQuest is an inquiry-oriented activity in which most or all of the information used by learners is drawn from the Web. WebQuests allow students to use selected Internet resources to find specific information about their topic. Resources are previously organized by either a student or a teacher into subject-based Web sites.

These new ways of addressing social studies and history are forcing teachers to rethink how they should teach. They are forcing a rethinking of dominant assumptions of how history is written and how it is taught. Pedagogy is broadening and expanding to include narratives relating to such fields as social, economic, and cultural histories.

MATHEMATICS

Math wars continue to rage. Currently the back-to-basics faction seems to dominate the National Mathematics Advisory Panel, whose recommendations have as much effect on curriculum and instruction as those of the National Reading Panel (O'Brien, 2007). The question on everyone's mind is, "Can this generation of American students add, subtract, multiply, and divide better than previous generations?" According to Tom Loveless and John Coughlan (2004), researchers have pointed to causes for optimism. Scores on the main math test of the National Assessment of Educational Progress (NAEP) have risen steadily over the past decade. From the 1990s to 2003, eighth graders picked up 15 scale score points and fourth graders increased their results by a whopping 22 scale score points, which is equal to almost 2 years of knowledge. These data suggest that the Untied States' future in math achievement looks bright.

Except for the short-lived reform movement of the post-*Sputnik* era, the mathematics curriculum has perhaps undergone less change than other disciplines. However, as the discussion below will note, greater change seems likely to occur during the coming decades.

Trends in Mathematics

If trends in the subject areas are strongly influenced by the widely disseminated pronouncements of professional associations, then trends in mathematics are relatively easy to identify. Here, the National Council of Teachers of Mathematics (NCTM) has played a very active role. First, the NCTM (1980) published a very useful set of guidelines for the teaching of mathematics titled *An Agenda for Action: Recommendations for School Mathematics of the 1980s*. Then, with support from the National Science Foundation, their Priorities in School Mathematics Project (PRISM) surveyed several thousand classroom teachers, college instructors and mathematics teacher–educators, supervisors of mathematics, principals, and school-board and parent-organization presidents about most of the issues covered in the agenda's recommendations. The focal points, as shown in Exhibit 13.3, are the recommended content emphases for mathematics for prekindergarten through Grade 8 by the National Council of Teachers of Mathematics.

The teaching of mathematics is a cultural activity: learned implicitly, hard to see from within the culture, and hard to change. Local Systemic Change Projects, funded by the National Science Foundation, were designed to help teachers of mathematics and science deepen their content

EXHIBIT 13.3 Mathematics Curriculum Focal Points

Prekindergarten Focal Points (student age: 4 or 5 years old)

Focal Points	Related Content Standard	Example
Developing an understanding of whole numbers	Number and Operations	How many blue pencils are on the table?
Identifying shapes and describing spatial relationships	Geometry	What is the name of this shape?
Identifying measurable attributes and comparing objects by using these attributes	Measurement	Which one is bigger?

Fourth Grade Focal Points (student age: 9 or 10 years old)

Focal Points	Related Content Standard	Example
Developing quick recall of multiplication facts and related division facts and fluency with whole number multiplication	Number and Operations, Algebra	Fluently multiply 26 by 89.
Developing an understanding of decimals, including the connections between fractions and decimals	Number and Operations	Write 0.25 as a fraction.
Developing an understanding of area and determining the areas of two-dimensional shapes	Measurement	What is the area of a rectangular room that measures 8 feet by 10 feet?

Eighth Grade Focal Points (student age: 13 or 14 years old)

Focal Points	Related Content Standard	Example
Analyzing and representing linear functions and solving linear equations and systems of linear equations	Algebra	Solve simple linear algebra equations, such as $12 = 4x + 4$.
Analyzing two- and three-dimensional space and figures by using distance and angle	Geometry, Measurement	Use the Pythagorean theorem to determine the length of one side of a right triangle.
Analyzing and summarizing data sets	Data Analysis, Number and Operations, Algebra	What is the median price in this list?

SOURCE: From http://en.wikipedia.org/wiki/Principles_and_Standards_for_School_Mathematics, adapted from National Council of Teachers of Mathematics, www.nctm.org/standards/focalpoints.aspx?id = 298.

knowledge and improve their instructional practices (Weiss & Pasley, 2007). Stigler and Hiebert (2004) stated that the key to change will be teachers and students working on problems as lessons unfold. New lesson study will not be about just improving a single lesson—it will be about building pathways for ongoing improvement of instruction. Observers may focus on one student who struggles with math concepts, one who quickly finds the correct answer and becomes bored, or one who is an English language learner. Information about what students are actually learning is essential to instructional improvement (Lewis, Perry, & Hurd, 2004). The result will be a common, coherent, and challenging curriculum that can transform mathematics education in the United States (Schmidt, 2004). Teachers will be changing the way they teach mathematics. The National Council of Teachers of Mathematics (NCTM) is now emphasizing the important role of communication in helping children construct understanding of mathematical concepts and develop connections between their informal knowledge and the abstract symbolism of mathematical concepts (Hunsader, 2004). Teachers are becoming more guided about learning as well as developing a common continuum of goals that relates to mathematics standards (Boss, 2001). As a result, the learning process is becoming more seamless from grade to grade. The focus is now on developing a rich math curriculum, built on a deep understanding.

Curriculum Tip 13.5	Mathematics teachers are now asking the questions: What do my students understand? How do I know they understand?

We live in a mathematical world. Whenever we decide on a purchase, choose an insurance or health plan, or use a spreadsheet, we rely on mathematical understanding. The Web and other technological media disseminate vast quantities of quantitative information. The level of mathematical thinking and problem solving needed in the workplace has increased dramatically.

In such a world, those who understand and can do mathematics will have opportunities that others do not. Mathematical competence opens doors to productive futures. A lack of mathematical competence closes those doors. For example, the choice of textbook often determines what teachers will teach, how they will teach it, and how their math students will learn (Reys, Reys, & Chavez, 2004).

Students have different abilities, needs, and interests. Yet everyone needs to be able to use mathematics in his or her personal life, in the workplace, and in further study. All students deserve an opportunity to understand the power and beauty of mathematics. Students need to learn a new set of mathematics basics that enables them to compute fluently and to solve problems creatively and resourcefully. According to Strong, Thomas, Perini, and Silver (2004), recognizing different mathematical learning styles and adapting differentiated teaching strategies can facilitate student learning. As Rita Dunn and Shirley Griggs (2007) said in *What If? Promising Practices for Improving Schools* (as reviewed by Christopher Hammill [2008]), "What if we taught elementary school students the way they learned?" (p. 57).

The Standards 2000 Project

With the release of *Curriculum and Evaluation Standards for School Mathematics* in 1989, the National Council of Teachers of Mathematics (NCTM) moved to the forefront of efforts to improve mathematics education in the United States and Canada. The document marked a historically important first step by a professional organization to articulate extensive goals for teachers and policymakers in a school discipline. Since its release, the *Curriculum and Evaluation Standards* has provided focus, coherence, and new ideas to mathematics education.

Educational decisions made by teachers, school administrators, and other professionals have important consequences for students and for society, and the principles for school mathematics provide guidance in making these decisions.

The Equity Principle

Excellence in mathematics education requires an **equity principle**—*high expectations and strong support for all students.*

All students, regardless of their personal characteristics, backgrounds, or physical challenges, must have opportunities to study—and support to learn—mathematics. This does not mean that every student should be treated the same, but all students need access each year they are in school to a coherent, challenging mathematics curriculum that is taught by competent and well-supported mathematics teachers.

Too many students, especially students who are poor, not native speakers of English, disabled, female, or members of minority groups, are victims of low expectations in mathematics. For example, tracking has consistently consigned disadvantaged groups of students to mathematics classes that concentrate on remediation or do not offer significant mathematical substance. The equity principle demands that high expectations for mathematics learning be communicated in words and deeds to all students.

Some students may need more than an ambitious curriculum and excellent teaching to meet high expectations. Students who are having difficulty may benefit from such resources as after-school programs, peer mentoring, or cross-age tutoring. Students with special learning needs in mathematics should be supported by both their classroom teachers and special education staff. An excellent resource for understanding mathematical standards can be found at http://standards.nctm.org (National Council of Teachers of Mathematics, 2004).

SCIENCE

The recent history of science curricula perhaps provides a paradigmatic example of federal influence in curricular matters and therefore deserves a close examination. One of the pervading questions in schools is, what is the best way to teach science? (Padgett, 2007).

Trends in Science

In analyzing trends in science, three sources are especially useful for the curriculum leader. First, the National Science Teachers Association (NSTA) has adopted and promulgated a position statement that, while somewhat general in nature, does indicate some important curricular emphases. As the summary in Exhibit 13.4 indicates, this professional association places strong emphasis on laboratory and field experiences, inquiry and problem solving, a comprehensive concept-based curriculum, and on science-related societal issues.

EXHIBIT 13.4 National Science Standards

Physical Science

Levels K–4	Levels 5–8	Levels 9–12
Properties of objects and materials Position and motion of objects Light, heat, electricity, and magnetism	Changes of properties in matter Motions and forces Transfer of energy	Structure of atoms and properties of matter Chemical reactions Structure of atoms Motions and forces Conservation of energy and increase in disorder Interactions of energy and matter

Life Science

Levels K–4	Levels 5–8	Levels 9–12
Characteristics of organisms Life cycles of organisms Organisms and environments	Structure and function in living systems Reproduction and heredity Regulation and behavior Populations and ecosystems Diversity and adaptations of organisms	The cell Molecular basis of heredity Behavior of organisms Interdependence of organisms Matter, energy, and organization of organisms Biological evolution

Earth and Space Science

Levels K–4	Levels 5–8	Levels 9–12
Properties of earth materials Objects in the sky Changes in Earth and sky	Structure of the Earth system Earth's history Earth in the solar system	Energy in the Earth system Origin and evolution of the Earth system Origin and evolution of the universe Geochemical cycles

Science and Technology

Levels K–4	Levels 5–8	Levels 9–12
Abilities of technological design Understanding about science and technology Abilities to distinguish between natural objects and objects made by humans	Abilities of technological design Understanding about science and technology	Abilities of technological design Understanding about science and technology

SOURCE: *National Science Education Standards*. Reprinted with permission of National Academy Press.

How such a curriculum might be achieved is the focus of a second valuable study. Historically, NSTA's Search for Excellence in Science Education project has identified 54 exemplary science programs throughout the nation and has examined their common characteristics (see Yager, Aldridge, & Penick, 1983).

The curricular order of high school science is also currently being examined. Since the recommendation by the 1893 Committee of Ten education task force, high school science curriculum has been traditionally taught in the sequence of biology first, then chemistry, followed by physics. Only the top 25% of high school students continued taking science classes through physics (Allen, 2004). The *National Science Education Standards* endorses students' taking physics first, then chemistry and biology, reversing the traditional order of physics and biology. Changing the order holds many curricular implications. The aim of this curricular reversal is to allow students a more in-depth understanding of the concepts and connections across the three science disciplines. A different curriculum approach will require major pedagogical adjustment, as physics has been taught to older students, who have a strong grounding in abstract math. In lieu of math skills, students will need to be taught physics from a hands-on and inquiry approach (Allen, 2004). However, students who have studied physics build a stronger understanding of atoms and molecules, which will enable them to better understand the complexities and interrelationship with chemistry and biology. In addition, proponents of the curricular order change advocate that by students' taking physics first, they will be motivated to take more advanced science courses. Nobel Prize–winning physicist Leon Lederman stated,

> I'm mostly interested in improving science literacy. By the end of high school, a student should be ready for all possible futures, whether at work, in the military, in engineering school, college, or family life. A good science and math education prepares students for life. (Allen, 2004, p. 8)

According to Ingrid Chalufour, Cindy Hoisington, Robin Moriarty, Jeff Winokur, and Karen Worth (2004), more teachers are now engaging science students in the rich process of inquiry. There can be seen a strong focus in current reform documents on increasing student understanding in the area of science processes and the nature of science, in addition to gains in content knowledge (Melber, 2003). For example, the two most current trends in science education continue to be constructivism and inquiry-based learning. Studies by Piaget and others since the 1970s have led to the constructivist philosophy, which focuses on the framework that students carry into learning situations. Constructivism says that learners bring their personal experiences into the classroom, and these experiences have a tremendous impact on their views of how the world works. Students come to learning situations with a variety of knowledge, feelings, and skills, and this is where learning should begin. This knowledge exists within the student and is developed as individuals interact with their peers, teachers, and the environment. For example, hands-on activities help students understand the concepts and reveal differences in understanding levels (Robertson, Gallagher, & Miller, 2004). Learners construct understanding or meaning by making sense of their experiences and fitting their own ideas into reality. Children construct thoughts, expectations, and explanations about natural phenomena to make sense of their everyday experiences. Schulte (1996) noted that constructivists believe that actual learning takes place through accommodation, which occurs when students change their existing ideas in response to new information. Constructivism allows students to learn by asking questions and forming their own opinions.

Inquiry-based learning is not a new technique—in fact, it goes back to John Dewey—but it does stand in contrast to the more structured, traditional framework of today's school. Asking questions is at the heart of inquiry-based learning. The goal is not to ask just any questions but to ask ones that children honestly care about.

Teachers using an inquiry approach find that it melds easily with technology. But finding ways to use technology to facilitate the inquiry approach takes time. Faculty and staff need time to consider how best to adapt science content and pedagogy to an online format. They also need time to experiment and share their work with others to evaluate its effectiveness and to make necessary adjustments. Staff members also need ongoing access to technology and to professional development that meets their individual needs. The bottom line is that schools can increase access to science expertise by providing technical support and time to highly qualified science teachers if they are to create text, podcasts, and vodcasts (Colombo & Colombo, 2007).

As can be seen, technology provides powerful tools to help teachers lead their students through the inquiry process. Inquiry-based instructional strategies lead to student investigations that in turn can lead to great conceptual understanding. Direct instruction alone cannot replace the in-depth experience with science concepts that inquiry-based strategies provide (Hubbell & Kuhn, 2007).

Implementing and sustaining this type of new science curriculum is not without great challenges. As with any meaningful change, it will need dedicated leaders. Districts need to make considerable investments in materials and ongoing professional development, along with an infrastructure to facilitate the scheduling of materials for classrooms and professional development. Districts also need to keep track of which teachers need more science training and to recruit and prepare teacher–leaders to model professional development activities, using the discover and inquiry methods (Young, 2007). Finding new and improved ways of teaching science is important, but what is equally important is making a connection between the science curriculum and standards.

Stepanek (2001) noted that standards help provide students with meaningful and engaging science learning. They not only outline content that students study but also define high expectations for students. Standards can be an effective tool for selecting specific areas from the textbook. They also help teachers focus on the information that students really need and make the content much more manageable.

Curriculum Tip 13.6	Standards provide a guideline for curriculum development and implementation.

FOREIGN LANGUAGE

There seems to be a growing realization that we live in a "global village" where the price of oil from the Middle East affects employment levels in Texas. In such a global village, competence in a foreign language would seem to be a vital necessity.

In relation to a statement of philosophy, the recommendations in Education for Global Leadership (2007) are:

- Teaching international content across the curriculum and at all levels of learning to expand American students' knowledge of other countries and cultures.

- Expanding training at every level of education as well as addressing the paucity of Americans fluent in foreign languages, especially critical, less commonly taught languages.

- National leaders—political leaders as well as the business and philanthropic communities and the media—should educate the public about the importance of improving education in languages other than English and international studies.

Recent studies indicate, however, that only about one fourth of the nation's students are studying a foreign language. The discussion that follows examines some current trends in language study.

Trends in Foreign-Language Education

Trends in foreign-language education can perhaps best be analyzed by dividing them into curricular approaches and instructional approaches, although such a division is in some ways misleading, especially with respect to foreign language.

Curricular Approaches

Several new approaches to the design and development of curricula have appeared in recent years.

The first approach is termed *problem-posing education*, a foreign-language curriculum with an existentialist emphasis.

The second curricular approach gaining attention, at least from leaders in the profession, is the functional–notional syllabus. Influenced greatly by the theories of psycho- and sociolinguistics, the functional–notional syllabus is predicated on the importance of two closely related aspects of language: the functions of language (such as requesting information, giving instructions, clarifying the order of events) and the notions or semantic meanings (concepts such as time, quantification, possession, modality). Thus, the functional–notional syllabus stresses the purposes for which learners need the language and the notions or concepts involved with those purposes.

A third approach to curriculum development might be termed the *proficiency approach*. These are curricula developed around the proficiencies identified by the American Council of Teachers of Foreign Languages (1982). The ACTFL guidelines describe in very specific terms six proficiency levels in speaking, reading, listening, and writing: Level 0, no functional ability; Level 1, elementary survival-level proficiency; Level 2, limited working proficiency; Level 3, professional working proficiency; Level 4, full professional proficiency; Level 5, the proficiency of a native speaker.

Instructional Approaches

Two quite different instructional approaches have attracted the attention of foreign-language specialists: immersion programs and "Suggestopedia."

Immersion programs were first developed in Canada in response to the concerns of English-speaking parents in Quebec. Teachers use the target language to teach regular school subjects: The second language is not another subject but is instead the medium of instruction. In early total-immersion programs, all instruction for the first three or four grades is presented in the target language; the native language is not introduced until second or third grade. By the end of elementary school, each language is used to teach about half of the curriculum.

Suggestopedia, first developed by Lozanov (1978), is an instructional method that attempts to involve both conscious and unconscious faculties by using intensive time periods (3- or 4- hour sessions for 5 days a week), a secure group atmosphere (ideally, six males and six females with a highly skilled teacher), rhythmic breathing exercises, and baroque music. Its instructional procedure consists of three parts: a review of the previous day's work through conversation, games, and skits; new material introduced using dialogue in familiar situations; and a "seance" that aims at unconscious memorization using yogic breathing and baroque music.

Students in U.S. classrooms are culturally, linguistically, ethnically, and socioeconomically diverse (Hammerberg, 2004), and it is important that educators understand the current methods of comprehension instruction taught to students from diverse backgrounds. Professionals need to deepen their understanding of the impact of culture and language on the instructional and assessment process (Santos, 2004). In any educational field, a close relationship exists between assessment and instruction. In light of current brain-based research and the current educational climate, policymakers and national organizations often initiate new trends in standards and assessment to bring about changes in instructional objectives and approaches at the classroom level. As these instructional objectives and approaches change, updated assessment practices are needed to reflect the changes. This interactive relationship between assessment and instruction, in which each influences the other, has characterized the foreign-language field during the past two decades (Santos, 2004). Since the early 1980s, the focus of foreign-language instruction has moved away from the mastery of discrete language skills, such as grammar, vocabulary, and pronunciation, to the development of communicative proficiency—that is, the ability to communicate about real-world topics with native speakers of the target language. Widely termed the "proficiency movement," this change has developed in tandem with changes in how students' foreign language skills are assessed.

The traditional assessment tools of earlier decades—usually discrete-point tests that focused on individual skills—evaluated students' knowledge *about* the language, not what they could *do with* the language. Although discrete-point tests are still used in many circumstances, particularly for large-scale standardized assessments, many of the newer assessment measures and techniques are performance based; that is, they require students to demonstrate knowledge and skills by carrying out challenging tasks. This enables teachers to measure what the students can actually do in various communicative contexts using the target language.

Current trends are finding that in teaching foreign languages it is most effective to use drama, art, music, and physical movement as well as reading, writing, and grammar usage. Students, for the most part, should have the opportunity to teach some aspect of what they learn. For example, many schools have developed "little buddy" programs. These programs are designed for older students to teach an aspect of the weekly theme or what the younger students (buddies) are learning in English.

Because of these principles of instruction as well as types of teaching strategies, leaders in the field, such as Stephen Krashen (Comprehensible Input) and Blaine Ray (Total Physical Response–Storytelling, TPR), are changing the face of foreign-language instruction in schools (Schutz, 2007). Many believe the TPR approach is making pure book memorization less useful.

Changes in foreign-language assessment in recent years can be divided into two main categories based on their catalysts: National assessment initiatives have widely influenced classroom instruction in a top-down approach; local assessment initiatives, which have appeared in response to curricular and instructional changes, may be seen as bottom-up initiatives. Top-down and bottom-up influences on foreign-language assessment will undoubtedly continue. The publication of the national foreign language standards (National Standards in Foreign Language Education Project, 1996) means that attainment of these standards will need to be assessed (see Exhibit 13.5).

EXHIBIT 13.5 Standards in Foreign-Language Education

Statement of Philosophy
Language and communication are at the heart of the human experience. The United States must educate students who are linguistically and culturally equipped to communicate successfully in a pluralistic American society and abroad. This imperative envisions a future in which ALL students will develop and maintain proficiency in English and at least one other language, modern or classical. Children who come to school from non-English backgrounds should also have opportunities to develop further proficiencies in their first language.

Standards for Foreign Language Learning

COMMUNICATION
Communicate in Languages Other Than English
Standard 1.1: Students engage in conversations, provide and obtain information, express feelings and emotions, and exchange opinions
Standard 1.2: Students understand and interpret written and spoken language on a variety of topics
Standard 1.3: Students present information, concepts, and ideas to an audience of listeners or readers on a variety of topics

CULTURES+
Gain Knowledge and Understanding of Other Cultures
Standard 2.1: Students demonstrate an understanding of the relationship between the practices and perspectives of the culture studied
Standard 2.2: Students demonstrate an understanding of the relationship between the products and perspectives of the culture studied

---

CONNECTIONS
Connect with Other Disciplines and Acquire Information
Standard 3.1: Students reinforce and further their knowledge of other disciplines through the foreign language
Standard 3.2: Students acquire information and recognize the distinctive viewpoints that are only available through the foreign language and its cultures

COMPARISONS
Develop Insight into the Nature of Language and Culture
Standard 4.1: Students demonstrate understanding of the nature of language through comparisons of the language studied and their own
Standard 4.2: Students demonstrate understanding of the concept of culture through comparisons of the cultures studied and their own

COMMUNITIES
Participate in Multilingual Communities at Home and Around the World
Standard 5.1: Students use the language both within and beyond the school setting
Standard 5.2: Students show evidence of becoming life-long learners by using the language for personal enjoyment and enrichment

---

SOURCE: From American Council on the Teaching of Foreign Languages (ACTFL).

It will take time before the real extent of the impact of the enforceable curriculum standards on multicultural education and/or foreign language is known (Bohn & Sleeter, 2000). To many curriculum leaders, standards make visible the expectations for learning that otherwise might be implicit. At the same time, teachers of foreign language or multicultural education are not looking for a quick fix.

Curriculum Tip 13.7	Teachers must be given time to examine their own views on foreign language and multicultural education as well as be able to relate those views to standards that are adopted.

The best way to face the challenge of assessing attainment of national goals may be by using alternative assessments that are developed in specific instructional contexts. English-language learners (ELL) are capable of high levels of conceptual understanding. While many ELL students have difficulty writing in English, they can speak with a level of sophistication not reflected on written assignments (Cox-Petersen & Olson, 2007). Given the wide variation among foreign-language students, teachers, courses, and contexts, an assessment tool or procedure that works well in one situation may be totally inappropriate in another. To evaluate students' progress and proficiency effectively, teachers need to learn about and gain competence in the use of a variety of assessment measures and procedures to discover what works best for them in each of the changing contexts in which they teach and with the full range of students in their classes.

The Internet can also be a valuable tool in aiding assessment and instruction of foreign languages in U.S. classrooms. Diane Vitaska (2002), a French teacher, uses the Internet to research cultural aspects of France in her classroom. Students can create a PowerPoint presentation, a brochure, or a newsletter as a Web page. LCD projectors are used to help students view computer images on a screen. Digital cameras can be used to help students develop personalized notebooks or practice language skills. Some teachers of foreign languages are using mobile videoconferencing labs with a webcam and speaker microphone to connect U.S. classrooms to classrooms in Europe. As can be seen, technology can be used in a plethora of ways to aid the teaching and assessing of students in foreign-language classes.

EDUCATION IN THE ARTS

Over the years, the arts have had to struggle for a place in the school's curriculum. Ever since the Committee of Fifteen's report (National Education Association, 1895/1969), the arts have usually been defined as "minor" subjects taught only an hour or two a week up to Grade 8 and then offered as electives at the high school level. As the survey below notes, this situation seems unlikely to change in the near future.

Trends in Art Education

During the 1950s and 1960s, art education was conceived rather narrowly as including only the visual arts and music. Children in the elementary grades were assisted by art and music specialists who emphasized performance (drawing and singing, primarily) as a way of making those subjects interesting. At the junior high level, units and courses in art appreciation and music appreciation were introduced, usually emphasizing the study of the great masters as a means of teaching students some elementary aesthetic principles. At the high school level, students majoring in art spent five or more periods a week in art studies. The emphasis on performance continued: Many suburban high schools offered courses called band, orchestra, and chorus in which students spent most of their time preparing for public performances.

This patchwork arts curriculum, which seemed to lack any organizing principle or governing theory, was the target of two major reform efforts during the 1970s, both supported with the federal funds that seemed so abundant in that decade. When federal funds were no longer available, the local districts found it possible to support these exemplary projects for only a few more years.

The lack of continued federal funding for projects in the past decade has not deterred leaders in the field from their continued efforts to strengthen education in the arts and to reassert the importance of the arts at a time when the rest of the profession seems obsessed with the academic curriculum.

Those efforts seemed to have found expression in three related developments. The first is an attempt to broaden the field. Rather than limiting the arts to the visual arts and music, current thinking stresses the multiple nature of aesthetic expression. While such an expanded understanding of the nature of the arts seems theoretically desirable, practitioners have expressed reservations about the difficulties of finding the time, money, and staff to support such a diversified and comprehensive program.

The second development is an attempt to formulate and promulgate a new rationale for the arts. In previous years, those advocating the arts tended to speak in terms that connoted a subtle elitism: The arts refine the aesthetic sensibilities and help people appreciate the finer things in life. The tendency in the current period is to defend the arts as an essential and unique way of knowing—one that is basic for all students.

Finally, there seems to be a resurgence of interest in interdisciplinary humanities courses in which the arts play a central role. Such courses enjoyed a period of brief popularity in the early 1960s; during that period, these courses tended to emphasize literature and history and gave only scant attention to the fine arts. After this, there seemed to be a concerted effort, through the development of standards, to position the arts more centrally in such interdisciplinary courses.

For example, National Standards for Arts Education were developed in 1994 by experts in education and the arts. These standards describe what a child with a complete, sequential education in the arts should know and be able to do at various grade levels in each artistic discipline. The 1997 National Assessment for Educational Progress was developed in coordination with these national standards.

Standards in the arts (dance, music, theater, visual arts) continue to be developed to provide a guide and resource to states and school districts that want to develop their art programs. Most states have standards in place for arts education, and still other states are in the process of developing arts standards. State-by-state summaries of arts education standards and other policies are available from each state educational agency (Americans for the Arts, 2008).

As Reeves (2007) aptly noted, the stark choice between academics and the arts is a false dichotomy. Teachers need to regard literacy not as a diversion from their primary subjects but as a useful way of helping students think about their subjects. We write in music and art class because those subjects are worth writing about.

Curriculum leaders need to encourage content-area teachers to integrate the arts into their classes. This will ensure that every student receives opportunities to excel not only academically but also in the arts.

Curriculum Tip 13.8	Curriculum leaders are urging the approach to the teaching of art along three broad avenues: universals, the community, and the individual.

In reviewing the literature, Donovan Walling (2001), director of publications and research at Phi Delta Kappa, stated that the changing priorities of schools, coupled with high standards, high-stakes testing, and the ascendancy of math and science is pushing art education back to the heart of education.

The arts have had a long struggle finding an appropriate place in the school curriculum. The arts did not figure in the America 2000 program but were included in President Clinton's 2000 bill. The published standards were discipline specific to dance, music, theater, and the visual arts. The five general standards shown below for the visual arts illustrate their placement.

1. The student understands and applies media, techniques, and processes related to the visual arts.

2. The student knows how to use the structures—sensory qualities, organizational principles, expressive features—as a function of art.

3. The student knows a range of subject matter, symbols, and potential ideas in the visual arts.

4. The student understands the visual arts in relation to history and cultures.

5. The student understands the characteristics and merits of one's own artwork and the artwork of others.

These standards primarily addressed general principles and are open to interpretation. Discipline Based Art Education (DBAE) follows these standards and is often found in school curriculum today. One of the originators of discipline-based art was Dwaine Greer, whose aim was to develop mature students who are both comfortable and familiar with major aspects of the disciplines of art (Walling, 2001, p. 628).

New trends in educational art are favoring aesthetics, art history, and art criticism. Complementary interest in extending art education through interdisciplinary studies—across all disciplines—appears to be currently driving the process. Walling (2001) notes several questions that pertain to this movement:

- How should we define "universals," and who should have a say in the definition?

- What traditions characterize the "community," and how can they be incorporated into the art curriculum?

- How will the "individual" be recognized, and how will individual differences be accommodated, validated, and valued?

No matter how art educators address the questions above, a move continues today to incorporate technology into the art curriculum. Two themes appear here: The first incorporates creating art by using the computer to create and manipulate images, and the second is using the computer to investigate the visual arts. Teachers and students are finding a plethora of ways to use the computer and Internet in the field of visual arts. So many Web sites about art exist that it takes a considerable amount of time to review them. There is little doubt that technology is fast becoming a major factor in how art is both viewed and integrated into the local school curriculum.

PHYSICAL EDUCATION AND HEALTH

Today, schools are continuing to take an important step toward helping children become healthy. Daily physical activity does not replace, but rather is one important component of, a complete, quality health and physical-education curriculum. Encouraging vigorous physical activity is helping to complement the health and physical-education programming that already exists in schools (Canadian Association for Health, Physical Education, Recreation and Dance, 2008). Cutting-edge research is currently helping to tackle the obesity epidemic, motivating children and their families to maintain a physically active lifestyle. As a result, physical educators are assuming a key role in leading school wellness initiatives and physical-education programs (National Association for Sport and Physical Education, 2008).

Trends in Physical Education

Schools today can expect increasing numbers of students who are both poor and overweight in what is being called the childhood obesity epidemic (Daniels, Queen, & Schumacher, 2007). This is one of the many reasons our physical-education programs in schools are so vital. Physical education teaches students to add physical activity to their daily lives and exposes students to content and learning experiences that develop the skills and desire to be active for life (see Exhibit 13.6). In addition to physical activity's improving muscular strength and endurance, flexibility, and cardiovascular endurance, physical activity helps children establish self-esteem and set and achieve goals.

The American Heart Association (Department of Health and Human Services, 1995) recommended that all children aged 5 years and older should engage in at least 30 minutes of daily physical activity at a moderate intensity and in vigorous activity for 30 minutes at least 3 days per week. Supporting the recommendation by the American Heart Association, the research on brain-based education reported in the *Journal of Exercise, Pediatric Exercise Science*, and the *Journal of Exercise Physiology Online* suggested "that exercise is strongly correlated with increased brain mass, better cognition, mood regulation, and new cell production" (Jensen, 2008, p. 412). Because this information is relatively new, an active physical-education curriculum should be implemented in our schools.

The Centers for Disease Control and Prevention finds that most major health problems in the United States today are caused by six categories of behavior: behaviors that lead to intentional and unintentional injuries; smoking; alcohol and other drug use; sexual behaviors leading to sexually transmitted diseases, HIV infection, and unintended pregnancy; poor nutrition; and lack of physical activity (Kolbe, 1993b). According to Kolbe (1993b), behaviors and attitudes about health that are initiated during childhood are responsible for most of the leading causes of death, illness, and disability in the United States today.

Comprehensive school health education programs represent one effective way of providing students with the knowledge and skills to prevent health-impairing behaviors.

EXHIBIT 13.6 Physical Education Standards

Standard 1: Demonstrates competency in motor skills and movement patterns needed to perform a variety of physical activities.

Standard 2: Demonstrates understanding of movement concepts, principles, strategies, and tactics as they apply to the learning and performance of physical activities.

Standard 3: Participates regularly in physical activity.

Standard 4: Achieves and maintains a health-enhancing level of physical fitness.

Standard 5: Exhibits responsible personal and social behavior that respects self and others in physical activity settings.

Standard 6: Values physical activity for health, enjoyment, challenge, self-expression, and/or social interaction.

SOURCE: From *Moving Into the Future: National Standards for Physical Education*, 2nd Edition (2004). Reprinted with permission from the National Association for Sport and Physical Education (NASPE), 1900 Association Drive, Reston, VA 20191–1599.

Health education works. Hundreds of studies have evaluated health education and concluded that education effectively reduces the number of teenage pregnancies, decreases smoking rates among young people, and prevents many high-risk behaviors. Nevertheless, its effectiveness depends on factors such as teacher training, comprehensiveness of the health program, time available for instruction, family involvement, and community support (Gold, 1994; Seffrin, 1990). Sequential school health education programs for K–12 students have been found to be more effective in changing health behaviors than occasional programs on single health topics (Kolbe, 1993a).

The Louis Harris survey of more than 4,700 students in Grades 3 through 12 who were attending 199 public schools found that health knowledge, attitudes, and behaviors improved with increasing years of health instruction (Harris & Associates, 1989). The School Health Education Evaluation (Connell, Turner, & Mason, 1985), which looked at four different health curricula for 30,000 fourth through seventh graders in 20 states, found the following:

- Students receiving health instruction had higher knowledge scores than students with no health instruction, with the greatest differences seen in knowledge of substance use and abuse.

- Knowledge, attitudes, and skills improved even with minimal instruction, but gains were most apparent when students received at least 50 hours of health instruction per school year.

- More hours were needed to improve attitudes than to enhance health knowledge and practices.

In addition to the subject field standards, educators need to incorporate global education and multicultural education into the subject fields. To do this, curriculum leaders "must consider actions that have the greatest impact and those that make no difference" (Whyte, 2008, n.p.).

GLOBAL EDUCATION

To prepare American students for the 21st century, educators must make them globally literate. Many of the state educational standards contain some global and international components; however, there are many issues related to global and international studies that are missing (Czarra, 2002–2003). As secretary of state Colin Powell said in the aftermath of the September 11, 2001, terrorist attacks, "Americans must be engaged with the rest of the world more than ever before. Clearly our schools and institutions of higher education must play an important role" (Czarra, 2002–2003, p. 9).

The American Forum on Global Education provides a "Global Education Checklist for Teachers, Schools, School Systems, and State Education Agencies." The document is a complete self-assessment tool to measure the degree of success in the different areas in question in your school or school district about global education. It is retrievable at www.globaled.org/fianlcopy.pdf and should be used to ensure that the international dimension receives attention.

MULTICULTURAL EDUCATION

Geneva Gay (2003/2004), a professor of education at the University of Washington, Seattle, stated that "multicultural education is more than a few lessons about ethnically diverse individuals and events or a component that operates on the periphery of the education enterprise" (p. 33). Multicultural education, according to Gay, "has not yet become a central part of the curriculum regularly offered to all students" (p. 31). Rather, "educators have relegated it to primarily to social studies, language arts, and the fine arts" (p. 31).

Clearly, there is no template of actions at the present time that can be placed on an educational system to make multicultural education compatible with the many diverse groups. However, the following guidelines, not prescriptive in nature, allow for the ever-accelerating demands our society is making to evolutionize curriculum.

Tips for improving multicultural education, which is a process, are shown in Exhibit 13.7.

As Boschee, Beyer, Engelking, and Boschee (1997) stated,

EXHIBIT 13.7 Tips for Improving Multicultural Education

Tips	Descriptors
An understanding of groupness	Students should learn that while all groups have unifying elements, they also reflect internal diversity, and that group cultures are constantly changing.
An understanding of both objective and subjective culture	To avoid superficiality it is important that multicultural education address subjective culture-a group's values, norms, expectations, and beliefs.
An ability to see the perspectives of others	To become multicultural persons, students must be given the opportunity
An understanding of our E Pluribus Unum heritage	Students should be given the opportunity to learn the nature and significance of the critical formative experiences of the various ethnic groups. Pluribus experiences of individual groups and the Unum experiences of Americans as a whole.
An understanding of the potential contribution that pluribus can make to society	If done, the multicultural person will have the wherewithal to recognize the positive power of Pluribus that can function hand-in-hand with cohering Unum.
The capacity to use, and not be used by, the media	Critical thinking activities will help students become more "media literate." After all, school learning does come to an end, but media learning does continue for a lifetime.
A deeper civic commitment	Schools should try to develop in students a greater dedication to building a better, more equitable society. The process includes the hidden curriculum such as teacher attitudes and expectations, grouping of students and instructional strategies, school disciplinary problems and practices, school and community relations, and classroom climates.

SOURCE: Excerpts from *Special and Compensatory Programs: The Administrators' Role*, by F. Boschee, B. M. Beyer, J. L. Engelking, & M. A. Boschee, 1997, Lanham, MD: Rowman & Littlefield, pp. 229–232.

multicultural education should be integrated into the curriculum in every school or school district. As such, multicultural education should operate continuously, not sporadically; it should span the curriculum from preschool through twelfth grade; it should cut across subject areas; and it should be implemented throughout the school year. (pp. 232–233)

SUMMARY

This chapter examines general developments in the curriculum by examining trends in specific subject areas, because even though innovations transcend the discipline, most of the important changes take place and are worked out in the subject areas themselves. Many current developments and trends in K–12 education are altering the landscape for curriculum work, and it is worthwhile to assess current trends as part of curriculum renewal. This chapter includes some of the trends and issues involved in the subject areas of English, language arts, reading, mathematics, social studies, science, foreign language, arts education, and physical education. This chapter also addresses the current role of brain research in curriculum planning for subject areas. Finally, the chapter includes some ways that technology is impacting the delivery and implementation of curriculum in subject areas as well as global education and multicultural education.

Other areas in education that are currently developing standards are vocational studies and technology/computers. Vocational studies such as shop, family and consumer science, and mechanics are important to career opportunities for today's students. Technology and computers are constantly changing. Curriculum should be developed for these areas and updated on a regular basis. Computer curriculum and education is discussed in greater depth in the next chapter.

APPLICATIONS

1. An analysis of the curriculum trends suggests quite clearly that the ideal curriculum proposed by national commissions is always far ahead of the taught curriculum delivered in the classroom. In a well-organized essay that draws from your own experience and your knowledge of the research, explain why it seems to be difficult to change the taught curriculum.

2. Select one of the fields discussed. By analyzing how it has changed and is changing now, project the major changes that might occur during the next 10 years. Write a summary of your projections.

3. Based on a close reading of this chapter and your own observations, determine which of the fields seems to have experienced the greatest changes. Write a brief essay in which you explain why this particular field seems to have changed more than the others.

4. Knowing that constructivism is linked to the higher achievement of students in science, how can this strategy be implemented into other areas of the curriculum?

5. Access the Global Education Checklist Web site at www.globaled.org/fianlcopy.pdf and complete the self-assessment instrument to measure the degree of success in the different

areas in question in your school or school district on global education. Based on the needs assessment, develop some action plans for the development of specific goals, resources needed, and time and participation required.

Note: If the Web site is inactive, contact the American Forum for Global Education via email (info@globaled.org) or telephone (212-624-1412) to secure the self-assessment instrument.

6. From the "Tips" provided for multicultural education, identify those that exist in your school or school district. If some Tips are missing in your school or school district, what should be done to make them a reality?

CASE STUDY   What Is Taught vs. What Should Be Taught

When planning and developing curriculum, it sometimes happens that what is taught in the classroom is not always what is proposed as the district's curriculum. As an example, a south-western school principal has been having differences with several teachers who do not want to follow the district's proposed curriculum, which matches national recommendations. This situation is a major concern for Dave Anon, the superintendent in charge of a number of small southwestern rural schools, who has principal Bob Huerta on the phone.

"Bob, I asked for curriculum surveys from your teachers, and I found that what they are teaching in their classrooms does not follow our district's curriculum scope and sequence," says Dave Anon. "For example, I noted on the surveys that the teachers are not covering geometry in the fourth grade. Our district math curriculum is based on national recommendations and specifically requires that geometry be taught at that level."

"Yes, I know," states Principal Huerta. "I have several fourth-grade teachers who feel the previous series is better than the newly adopted series." There is silence on the phone. Bob Huerta can sense that the superintendent is upset.

"Bob, I e-mailed you a month ago that our math scores are down and we need to align our elementary curriculum with state standards. I specifically noted that your fourth-grade students are not doing well on math test items related to geometry."

"It is a concern," says Principal Huerta. "I am trying my best to get this resolved."

"Well, you need to get this situation under control. It is crucial that our teachers follow the curriculum that we have outlined and that the national commission recommends," notes the superintendent. "How do you plan to address this problem?"

The Challenge

Good communication and an understanding of curriculum applications between the district office and a local school is a critical issue. What else can Superintendent Anon do to improve communication with his principals . . . as well as with his teachers and with local parents?

Key Issues/Questions

1. What are your impressions of Superintendent Anon and Principal Huerta? Do you think the issue of communication will be resolved? Why or why not?

2. How do you feel about technology and its impact on communication in schools?

3. What are some areas in language arts and reading that have changed dramatically with the advent of technology? Explain your answer.

4. What are some areas in mathematics and science that have changed dramatically with the advent of technology? Explain your answer.

5. What are some areas in social studies and art that have changed dramatically with the advent of technology? Explain your answer.

WEBLIOGRAPHY

Annenberg Media–sponsored real-life math applications
www.learner.org/interactives/dailymath

Fort Worth Museum of Science and History online inquiry-based strategies for teachers
www.fwmuseum.org/educate/prof_dev_tci.html

Institute for Inquiry online professional development activities
www.exploratorium.edu/ifi

International Reading Association
www.reading.org

Intervention program for primary children
www.readingrecovery.org

K–12 Mathematics Curriculum Center
www2.edc.org/mcc

Learning First Alliance
www.learningfirst.org

Multicultural education
www.ascd.org
www.pdkintl.org

National Academy of Sciences—Provides guide for teaching and learning
www.nasonline.org

National Council of Teachers of Mathematics Focal Points information
www.nctm.org/focalpoints

National Reading Styles Institute
www.nrsi.com

National Science Resources Center
www.nsrconline.org

National Science Teachers Association
www.nsta.org

Public domain books available for free download
www.authorama.com

Reading Recovery Council of North America
www.readingrecovery.org

Science activities collection
www.kineticcity.com

U.S. Department of Education's free site of science resources
www.free.ed.gov/subjects.cfm?subject_id = 41

Web-based manipulatives for K–12 Mathematics
http://nlvm.usu.edu/en/nav/vlibrary.html

CHAPTER 14

Current Developments Across the Curriculum

Ordinarily, most curricular change takes place within a given discipline, because the discipline tends to be the beginning point of curriculum work. In recent years, however, curriculum workers have become concerned with changes transcending a single discipline, such as using writing to learn, improving thinking skills, speaking, listening, and the integration of technology in the curriculum. Such changes require both a different perspective on curriculum change and different processes for planning and implementation.

Questions addressed in this chapter include the following:

- What are some of the curriculum changes that are improving writing skills?
- What are some of the curriculum changes that are improving thinking skills?
- What are some of the curriculum changes that are improving speaking skills?
- What are some of the curriculum changes that are improving listening skills?

Key to Leadership

Successful curriculum leaders realize that the writing process is itself made up of a number of processes. As an act of making meaning, it assumes recursive movement through five major processes: prewriting, drafting, revising, editing, and publishing.

USING WRITING TO LEARN

State academic standards broadly support the writing process, including the planning (prewriting), drafting, revising, editing, and publishing (sharing) stages. As advocated by the Massachusetts Institute of Technology (MIT) Online Writing and Communications Center (1999), "Writing is a process that involves at least five distinct steps: prewriting, drafting, revising, editing, and publishing. It is known as a recursive process. While you are revising, you might have to return to the prewriting step to develop and expand your ideas" (n.p.). Exhibit 14.1 provides descriptors for each step to be used in writing and teaching the writing process.

EXHIBIT 14.1 The Writing Process	
Steps	*Descriptors*
Prewriting	Prewriting is anything you do before you write a draft of your document. It includes thinking, taking notes, talking to others, brainstorming, outlining, and gathering information (e.g., interviewing people, researching in the library, assessing data).
	Although prewriting is the first activity you engage in, generating ideas is an activity that occurs throughout the writing process.
Drafting	Drafting occurs when you put your ideas into sentences and paragraphs. Here you concentrate upon explaining and supporting your ideas fully. You also begin to connect your ideas. Regardless of how much thinking and planning you do, the process of putting your ideas in words changes them; often the very words you select evoke additional ideas or implications.
	Don't pay attention to such things as spelling at this stage.
	This draft tends to be *writer-centered*: it is you telling yourself what you know and think about the topic.
Revising	Revision is the key to effective documents. Here you think more deeply about your readers' needs and expectations. The document becomes *reader-centered*. How much support will each idea need to convince your readers? Which terms should be defined for these particular readers? Is your organization effective? Do readers need to know X before they can understand Y?
	At this stage you also refine your prose, making each sentence as concise and accurate as possible. Make connections between ideas explicit and clear.
Editing	Check for such things as grammar, mechanics, and spelling. The last thing you should do before printing your document is to spell check it.
	Don't edit your writing until the other steps in the writing process are complete.
Publishing	The writer shares what has been written with the intended audience. [Added by the authors.]

SOURCE: Steps and descriptors adapted from "The Writing Process," by MIT Online Writing and Communication Center, 1999, Boston: Massachusetts Institute of Technology.

Learning to Write by Writing

The National Council of Teachers of English (NCTE) guidelines (2008) stated,

> as is the case with many other things people do, getting better at writing requires doing it—a lot. This means actual writing, not merely listening to lectures about writing, doing grammar drills, or discussing readings. The more people write, the easier it gets and the more they are motivated to do it. (n.p.)

Recognizing that writing is an increasingly multifaceted activity, as shown in Exhibit 14.2, NCTE offers several principles that should guide effective teaching practice.

EXHIBIT 14.2 NCTE Principles for Effective Writing Instruction

Writing Principles	Descriptors
1. Everyone has the capacity to write, writing can be taught, and teachers can help students become better writers.	Though poets and novelists may enjoy debating whether or not writing can be taught, teachers of writing have more pragmatic aims. Setting aside the question of whether one can learn to be an artistic genius, there is ample empirical evidence that anyone can get better at writing, and that what teachers do makes a difference in how much students are capable of achieving as writers.
2. People learn to write by writing.	Writing instruction must include ample in-class and out-of-class opportunities for writing and should include writing for a variety of purposes and audiences.
3. Writing is a process.	Whenever possible, teachers should attend to the process that students might follow to produce texts—and not only specify criteria for evaluating finished products, in form or content.
4. Writing is a tool for thinking.	In any writing classroom, some of the writing is for others and some of the writing is for the writer. Regardless of the age, ability, or experience of the writer, the use of writing to generate thought is still valuable; therefore, forms of writing such as personal narrative, journals, written reflections, observations, and writing-to-learn strategies are important.
5. Writing grows out of many different purposes.	Often, in school, students write only to prove that they did something they were asked to do, in order to get credit for it. Or, students are taught a single type of writing and are led to believe this type will suffice in all situations. Writers outside of school have many different purposes beyond demonstrating accountability, and they practice myriad types and genres. In order to make sure students are learning how writing differs when the purpose and the audience differ, it is important that teachers create opportunities for students to be in different kinds of writing situations, where the relationships and agendas are varied.

(Continued)

EXHIBIT 14.2 (Continued)	
Writing Principles	*Descriptors*
6. Conventions of finished and edited texts are important to readers and therefore to writers.	Though poets and novelists may enjoy debating whether or not writing can be taught, teachers of writing have more pragmatic aims. Setting aside the question of whether one can learn to be an artistic genius, there is ample empirical evidence that anyone can get better at writing, and that what teachers do makes a difference in how much students are capable of achieving as writers.
7. Writing and reading are related.	One way to help students become better writers is to make sure they have lots of extended time to read, in school and out. Most research indicates that the easiest way to tap motivation to read is to teach students to choose books and other texts they understand and enjoy, and then to give them time in school to read them. In addition to making students stronger readers, this practice makes them stronger writers.
8. Writing has a complex relationship to talk.	In early writing, we can expect lots of talk to surround writing, since what children are doing is figuring out how to get speech onto paper. Early teaching in composition should also attend to helping children get used to producing language orally, through telling stories, explaining how things work, predicting what will happen, and guessing about why things and people are the way they are. Early writing experiences will include students explaining orally what is in a text, whether it is printed or drawn.
9. Literate practices are embedded in complicated social relationships.	The teaching of writing should assume students will begin with the sort of language with which they are most at home and most fluent in their speech. That language may be a dialect of English, or even a different language altogether. The goal is not to leave students where they are, however, but to move them toward greater flexibility, so that they can write not just for their own intimates but for wider audiences. Even as they move toward more widely used English, it is not necessary or desirable to wipe out the ways their family and neighborhood of origin use words. The teaching of excellence in writing means adding language to what already exists, not subtracting. The goal is to make more relationships available, not fewer.
10. Composing occurs in different modalities and technologies.	Writing instruction must accommodate the explosion in technology from the world around us. From the use of basic word processing to support drafting, revision, and editing to the use of hypertext and the infusion of visual components in writing, the definition of what writing instruction includes must evolve to embrace new requirements.

Writing Principles	Descriptors
11. Assessment of writing involves complex, informed, human judgment.	Instructors of composition should know about various methods of assessment of student writing. Instructors must recognize the difference between formative and summative evaluation and be prepared to evaluate students' writing from both perspectives. By formative evaluation here, we mean provisional, ongoing, in-process judgments about what students know and what to teach next. By summative evaluation, we mean final judgments about the quality of student work. Teachers of writing must also be able to recognize the developmental aspects of writing ability and devise appropriate lessons for students at all levels of expertise.

SOURCE: Guidelines from "NCTE Beliefs About the Teaching of Writing," by the Writing Study Group of the NCTE Executive Committee, November 2004. Copyright 2004 by the National Council of Teachers of English. Reprinted with permission. http://www.ncte.org/about/over/positions

It has become commonplace to talk about how globalization is changing both the skills required to thrive in the modern economy and education in the United States. As a result, teachers in the National Writing Project believe there is a need for conviction and community in fostering change (Lieberman & Friedrich, 2007).

Students often use multiple writing strategies that differ across developmental stages (Dahl et al., 2003–2004). It is important that students use writing as a way of learning. The 6 + 1 Trait Writing Program was developed 20 years ago and has been consistently refined by teachers. The six-trait writing process analytical model is centered on these six traits of writing: ideas, organization, voice, word choice, sentence fluency, and conventions. A study conducted in Portland, Oregon, by the Northwest Regional Educational Laboratory indicated that using the six-trait writing process resulted in considerable gains in students' writing ability. This writing process is used in every state in the Union (Northwest Regional Educational Laboratory, 2001).

Regardless of the perspective and processes of writing, concern continues over plagiarism. This has been a major problem with the development and accessibility to the Internet. According to Doug Johnson (2004), the director of media and technology for Mankato Area Public Schools, educators are expending much effort trying to catch plagiarism in student work. Teachers and library media specialists use various Web services and Internet search techniques to detect student work that is lifted from online sources. Hopefully, educators will find effective ways to curb the problem of plagiarism.

Curriculum Tip 14.1	"To be a writer is to throw away a great deal, not to be satisfied, to type again, and then again, and once more, and over and over...." —John Hersey

According to Henk and colleagues (2003–2004), curriculum leaders have seen a major shift in the basic way writing is taught within the past three decades. The focus has changed from evaluating students' written product to examining the processes that writers employ during writing.

Given cogent theoretical reasons, what response should local curriculum leaders make? According to educational consultants David and Meredith Liben (2004), students need to be aware not only of how to write but also of how they learned to write. Glatthorn (1984) recommended a teacher-centered process that he found useful in staff-development workshops. This process asks teachers in each department to develop their own **writing-to-learn** framework. Teachers need first to identify what Glatthorn called the *continuing* uses of writing in their discipline. These continuing uses are ways that teachers use writing in an ongoing manner, without making special assignments or giving special instructions; they include such uses as taking notes from lectures, taking notes from the text, writing essay answers, doing written exercises at home or in class, keeping a journal for that subject, and writing responses in class to clarify and fix learning.

Glatthorn (1984) next turned to what he called *special* uses—writing tasks in that discipline that require special assignments and focused instruction. These special uses include the following: writing a report citing several sources, reporting on one's own investigations, describing one's problem-solving processes, translating from one symbol system to another, writing a creative paper based on that subject, writing about one's response to a work, explaining how that subject relates to one's personal life, explaining to other students how to do some process related to that subject, persuading students about some issue relating to that subject, and doing an exercise that teaches a thinking skill important in that subject.

Through discussion and analysis, therefore, each department identifies the special and continuing uses of writing that teachers consider appropriate for that subject, also known as **writing across the curriculum.** The final task in developing the framework is for the teachers in each department to identify the essential qualities they want evidenced in all longer pieces of writing in that discipline. Thus, science teachers might note the importance of objectivity and accuracy in reporting experiments, social studies teachers might recognize the careful use of historical evidence in supporting conclusions, English teachers might ascertain the value of creative personal responses in interpreting literature, and mathematics teachers might determine the need for precision in writing verbal translations of mathematical equations.

A sample framework summarizing all three types of information is shown in Exhibit 14.3.

With that framework established, each department would then develop instructional materials to support both the special and continuing uses. These instructional materials would typically include the following resources:

- A description of the composing process and a summary of the pertinent research

- A reproduction of the framework

- Suggestions for implementing the "continuing uses" proficiently

- Suggestions for making the "special uses" assignments more productive

- Sample assignment sheets for the "special uses" assignments

- Suggestions to the teachers on responding to and grading student writing

- Handouts for the students, clarifying matters of format and style and explaining the special qualities desired

Because writing is primarily learned rather than taught, the role of the teacher shifts from instructor to facilitator. Instead of telling students what and how to write, teachers help students find their own topics and voices, model the processes and strategies, and foster an accepting and dynamic communication environment.

EXHIBIT 14.3 Framework for Writing-to-Learn Project

Department: Family and Consumer Science

The following *continuing uses* of writing are important in family and consumer science:

1. Taking notes from lectures and class discussions

2. Taking notes from texts and other resources

3. Keeping a home economics journal

The following *special uses* of writing are important in home economics:

1. Writing recipes

2. Writing directions for craft and decorating projects

The following qualities are considered essential to writing in home economics:

1. Precision in measurements and quantities

2. Clarity in giving directions

Thinking

The second major movement to effect improvements across the curriculum is the concerted effort to improve critical thinking. Critical thinking, cultural awareness, and impassioned writing are not just for the college bound. There is a hope to provide all students with an intellectually challenging education that fosters critical thinking and understanding of domestic and global realities and exposes students to important cultural touchstones (Schmoker, 2007).

A major focus area for improving thinking is the engagement of students with content (Weiss & Pasley, 2004). High-quality lessons involving thinking skills generally invite students to interact purposefully with the content. Various strategies are used to involve students and to build on their previous knowledge using real-world examples or engaging students in firsthand experiences. This is one of the best ways to get students to think.

Curriculum Tip 14.2	Critical thinking is the skillful application of a repertoire of validated general techniques for deciding the level of confidence you should have in a proposition in the light of the available evidence. (Francis Bacon, 1605)

In reviewing the literature, another major strategy involving the integration of thinking skills is the concept of metacognition, or thinking about thinking. In the research literature, metacognition is usually presented as a conscious and deliberate mental activity—we become aware that we don't understand a paragraph we read or a statement we hear (Martinez, 2006). Studies in metacognition have led to a number of applications in teacher-directed learning. Some of these focus on teaching students to relate academic success to personal effort rather than to chance. Other applications emphasize the teaching of self-regulation. Students learn the efficient management of their own participation, studies, and assignments. Other applications emphasize teaching students learning strategies, processes, and systems that they can apply to a range of tasks and situations—in other words, teaching students how to think and learn. Some individual teachers believe engaging students is not enough—they must be involved in a critical thinking process as well.

Bruce Smith (2004), editor of the *Phi Delta Kappan*, noted that it is important for students to exchange ideas. Smith stated that "there will be no give and take, no working out of differences, as long as 'memorize and test' is the dominant pedagogy and as long as test scores are the sole legal tender." He believes that "it is important for young people to be introduced to the marketplace of ideas and made to feel comfortable and competent there" (p. 482).

Many educators ask, "Can students learn to think critically if they are not asked to engage with critical issues?" According to Nel Noddings (2004), Lee Jacks Professor of Education Emerita, Stanford University, fostering critical thinking is frequently stated as a fundamental aim of education. Nevertheless, many teachers report that they have been forbidden to discuss such critical issues as wars, religion, and cultural differences in styles of parenting.

A second question that seems to divide the profession is whether thinking skills are more usefully perceived as a set of general processes that transcend the disciplines or as content-specific skills that should be anchored in a discipline. If thinking is a set of general processes, then these processes can best be taught in separate thinking courses. If thinking is subject specific, then it is best taught within the context of a discipline.

Researchers are now finding that it is crucial to engage students in the process. Research results indicate that student success depends on three qualities of teaching: teachers' content knowledge, pedagogy, and strong relationships with students (Lewis, 2004). Studies, reports, and initiatives affirm that engagement in learning, environments that value trust, and integrity in relationships between teachers and students and their families work together to make a critical difference in learning as it relates to subject-centered curriculum.

Curriculum Tip 14.3	"When we teach only for facts, rather than how to go beyond facts, we teach students how to get out-of-date." (Sternberg, 2008, p. 25)

Both the general approaches and the subject-anchored materials suffer from perhaps the same weakness: They attempt to change the curriculum through a top-down process, asking teachers to use materials developed by central office staff. Others in the field are placing more emphasis on staff-development programs that teach teachers how to think critically and how to use their own curriculum as a means for improving student thinking.

Glatthorn (1985) had some success in using such an approach. After reviewing current theory and research on thinking, teachers in each secondary department are first asked to select one of the following units of study as being most appropriate for each grade level they teach: controlled problem solving (using algorithms and heuristic strategies for solving convergent problems with one right answer), open-ended problem solving (using systematic strategies to find the optimal solution to an open-ended problem), information processing (storing, retrieving, and evaluating information), reasoning (the systematic application of logic), evaluating (using critical thinking processes to evaluate products and individuals), analyzing persuasive messages (including critical analysis of the mass media), mastering disciplinary inquiry (learning the special inquiry processes and truth tests used in a discipline), making moral choices (making ethical judgments), and using thinking in making other life choices (especially college and careers). These particular unit topics, focusing as they do on more general processes that are relatively simple to link to a given discipline, seem to appeal to most teachers as both important and subject relevant. After each departmental team reaches a consensus on the units to be developed, the team works together to develop discipline-based instructional materials focusing on the general processes identified. They are thus able to produce a graded series of units that, while lacking professional sophistication, are likely to be used.

Curriculum Tip 14.4	The most basic premise in the current thinking skills movement is the notion that students CAN learn to think better if schools concentrate on teaching them HOW to do so.

With that phase of the project accomplished, they turn their attention to specific thinking skills that were not incorporated into the units. They review a comprehensive list of such specific skills as classifying and making inferences and identify those that they think should be taught. In teams, they decide whether each skill so identified would be better taught in an "integrated" or a "focused" lesson (see Exhibit 14.4 for a form that can be used to assist teachers in making these decisions). In an *integrated* lesson, as the term is used here, a content objective (such as being able to describe Cortez's first meeting with Native Americans) is the focus of the lesson; the thinking skill (in this case, perhaps, contrasting) is taught as part of that lesson. In a "focused" lesson, a thinking skill, such as evaluating sources for bias, is the focus of the lesson. Subject content is merely the carrier.

Also worth noting are the Six Correlates of Effective Schools developed by Ronald Edmonds and John Frederickson (Taylor, 2002):

1. Clearly stated and focused school mission

2. Safe and orderly climate for learning

3. High expectations for students, teachers, and administrators

4. Opportunity to learn and student time-on-task

5. Instructional leadership by all administrators and staff members

6. Positive home-school relations

The **effective schools process** is considered by many a tried-and-true process of school change that can create schools in which all children make progress and are ready for study at the next grade level. To complement the effective schools process, a number of schools are developing and using instructional design as well (March & Peters, 2002). The instructional design process can help schools to restructure the delivery and assessment of classroom instruction and to integrate thinking skills into the curriculum. If school leaders are to formulate an instructional design process to enhance the use of thinking skills, it is also important to involve three thinking skills strategies: independent thinking, self-managed learning, and self-directed learning (Gibbons, 2004, p. 466).

EXHIBIT 14.4 Identifying Specific Thinking Skills

The following critical-thinking skills are often taught in school subjects. Consider that skill and its importance in the subject and grade level you teach. Indicate your preference for teaching that subject by putting an X in the appropriate column. A focused lesson is one in which the thinking skill represents the main objective of that lesson. An integrated lesson is one in which a subject matter concept or skill represents the main objective; the thinking skill is taught in the process of teaching that concept or skill. "Not Appropriate" means that you do not think that particular skill is appropriate for your subject or grade level.

Skill	Focused	Integrated	Not Appropriate
1. Finding and defining problems			
2. Representing problems in an appropriate symbol system			
3. Organizing facts and concepts in a systematic way			
4. Inferring a conclusion from what is stated			
5. Locating and evaluating sources			
6. Synthesizing information to reach a conclusion			
7. Distinguishing between observations, assumptions, and inferences			
8. Classifying logically			
9. Making predictions			
10. Interpreting nonliteral material			
11. Identifying persuasive messages and techniques			
12. Applying logical operations of negation, disjunction, and conjunction			
13. Making and using analogies			
14. Determining likely causes			
15. Explaining cause-and-effect relationships			
16. Avoiding misleading use of language			
17. Avoiding statistical fallacies			
18. Other:			

Independent thinking requires students to address subsets of related questions and to develop essential skills outlined in the curriculum. Requirements include inquiry into essential questions that students pose for themselves. These pursuits are supported by a number of excellent instruments, practices, and services.

Self-managed learning requires that students have outcomes to achieve. Students make their own timetables; work alone; work with others; attend seminars, workshops, and labs; work online; and use other resources to help them in their self-regulated efforts.

Self-directed learning requires that each day of the week is set aside for independent activities, regular education, trips, or challenging exercises. This may include the Walkabout program, logical inquiry, creativity, practical applications, or community activities. Students present their accomplishments to their peers, teachers, parents, and other adults at graduation. Individual work is supported by an adviser. According to Dave Brown (2002), professor of education at West Chester University, Pennsylvania, educational researchers dream about such a classroom, write about the possibilities, and encourage teachers and administrators to use such approaches as student choice, curriculum integration, differentiated learning, and self-assessment to engage students deeply into learning.

When focusing on the classroom restructuring process, it is important to place an emphasis on the integration of thinking skills. As part of this process, we find the development of activities in processing information, inventing and expanding upon ideas, and examining and evaluating facts and processes to be an essential part of every discipline. Similarly, thinking skills should be deeply embedded in all strands of the communication arts. Students must think to respond to literature, to write, to speak, to use media, to listen, and to read. In short, thinking skills provide students with the means to make the most effective use of all areas of their education.

Curriculum Tip 14.5	While critical thinking can be thought of as more left-brain and creative thinking more right brain, they both involve "thinking." The "higher-order thinking skills" (HOTS) concentrate on the top three levels of Bloom's Taxonomy: analysis, synthesis, and evaluation (see Bloom's Taxonomy in Chapter 10).

It is important, in planning curricular strategies, to introduce thinking skills, to reinforce them throughout the content levels, and to build more complex processes on the foundation of skills introduced earlier. Students should be encouraged to "think about their thinking," examining the thinking skills and strategies they apply to interpret literature and media, to choose language, to make an appeal in advertising, or to follow directions.

Speaking

Children enter school with some basic competence in speaking, but without social contact and modeling, speech may not develop as it should. A child's self-concept is largely formed through interaction with significant people in the child's environment. The role of the teacher is to help students improve and refine their speaking skills in a variety of situations. Good speaking skills are important to students for their success in school and in the workplace. Employers frequently identify oral communication skills as the most important skills considered for initial employment, retention, and promotion. An average of 30% of our communication is spoken, and speech is second only to listening in frequency of use in everyday life. Speech has an important place in the curriculum.

Speaking is developmental. Instruction should be direct, frequent, and sequenced as the individual grows in proficiency. However, districts often see speech as limited to public speaking rather than intrapersonal, interpersonal, group, and mass communication. While speech instruction at the secondary level is often relegated to a speech elective, at other grade levels students often give speeches without receiving instruction on how to become better oral communicators.

Given the importance of speech and the position it has often had in the curriculum, districts developing speaking curricula should keep in mind the following statements. Instruction in speaking should (a) address the communication needs of students that arise from everyday situations; (b) provide direct instruction, supervised practice, constructive feedback, and more practice in a variety of situations rather than offering only opportunities to speak; (c) include all communication contexts, (e.g., intrapersonal, interpersonal, group, public, and mass communication); (d) be integrated with the teaching of all of the other communication arts strands; (e) be interdisciplinary and across the curriculum; (f) offer opportunities for co-curricular programs that aid students in refining their speaking skills; and (g) be sensitive to the diversity of culturally appropriate speaking behaviors.

Listening

Listening is the first source of communication. By developing competent listening skills, one expands vocabulary, develops sentence structures, and begins to discriminate what is heard. Speaking, reading, and writing are built upon this foundation. Students come to school with some degree of competence in listening, acquired "naturally" in the developmental process. Consequently, listening is often the most neglected area of instruction in the communication arts curriculum.

Many educators have assumed that listening skills can be developed by telling the students to listen and periodically reminding them they are not listening. Also, teacher education programs, textbooks, communication research, and assessments give little assistance in listening instruction. In spite of this neglect, the importance of listening has been documented. For example, McCaulley (1992) conducted a study on the effects of a semester-long listening skills program on listening comprehension and reading comprehension with elementary school students. Using meta-analysis, practical significant differences were noted between the treatment and control groups in the comprehension modes of listening and reading. The effect size in reading (.9953) was considered a large difference, while the effect size for listening (.3747) was considered a small difference. The effect size data indicate that treatment of listening-skills training had an effect of improving listening comprehension and reading comprehension. This is consistent with research on the benefits derived from expertise in one comprehension mode carrying over to another language arts strand. The overall conclusion of the study revealed that more time should be spent on listening-skills development.

Listening is a skill that can be improved through direct instruction and practice. Students learn to hear accurately and evaluate what is said so they may respond in conversation and discussion.

Instruction in listening should do the following:

- Address communication needs of students that arise from real-life situations
- Involve direct teaching of listening strategies and practice of those strategies in a variety of listening situations
- Include listening in all communication contexts including interpersonal, small group, public communication, and mass communication
- Integrate with the teaching of all of the other communication arts strands
- Be interdisciplinary and across the curriculum
- Be incorporated in co-curricular programs that aid students in refining their listening skills
- Be sensitive to the diversity of culturally appropriate listening behaviors

TECHNOLOGY AND THE CURRICULUM

Interim assessments, defined standards, and data-driven instruction clearly mark the benefits of technology and curriculum. Action plans must be connected to lesson plans, which need to translate to changes in teaching (Bambrick-Santoyo, 2007/2008).

While technology promises to make many facts of our work easier to understand and analyze, getting up to speed and staying there represents a step and formidable learning curve. It is important for principals to realize that technology is a powerful instructional management tool. It is therefore important to take the lead in emphasizing this belief to teachers, parents, and the wider community (Ferrandino, 2007).

After several decades of having computers in public education, it is amazing that questions still abound regarding their usefulness and purpose in the classrooms of the nation (Whitehead, Jensen, & Boschee, 2003). It is also interesting that governments, public businesses, and private enterprise are not asking these questions regarding implementing technology in their sectors, albeit this is getting better. Schools have access to the same hardware that the external community does. They also have access to a plethora of software programs designed specifically to meet educational needs. For example, the Internet and Web-based applications allow students to access real-world research in a variety of fields. Unlike the external community, many school districts have the ability to access a variety of means of financial support to implement technology in the classrooms. So why has business succeeded, and in what areas has education failed?

Changing Contexts

Layton (2000), in an article on digital learning, noted that administrative leaders have misdirected planning efforts by envisioning technological direction around where educators are and how to move forward. Instead, he suggested that we envision where we want to be and then work backward to design the appropriate frameworks to get us there.

With an increase in interest in how technology can change schools, a continuing widespread introduction of computers and multimedia into the schools has taken place. As shown in Exhibit 14.5, Internet access in U.S. public schools and classrooms increased from 35% in 1994 to 100% in 2003.

EXHIBIT 14.5 Internet Access in U.S. Public Schools and Classrooms: 1994–2003

School characteristic	1994	1995	1996	1997	1998	1999	2000	2001	2002	2003
All public schools	35	50	65	78	89	95	98	99	99	100[2]
Instructional level[1]										
Elementary	30	46	61	75	88	94	97	99	99	100[2]
Secondary	49	65	77	89	94	98	100[2]	100[2]	100[2]	100
School size										
Less than 300	30	39	57	75	87	96	96	99	96	100
300 to 999	35	52	66	78	89	94	98	99	100[2]	100[2]
1,000 or more	58	69	80	89	95	96	99	100	100	100
Locale										
City	40	47	64	74	92	93	96	97	99	100
Urban fringe	38	59	75	78	85	96	98	99	100	100[2]
Town	29	47	61	84	90	94	98	100	98	100
Rural	35	48	60	79	92	96	99	100[2]	98	100
Percent minority enrollment[3]										
Less than 6 percent	38	52	65	84	91	95	98	97	99	100
6 to 20 percent	38	58	72	87	93	97	100	100	100	100
21 to 49 percent	38	55	65	73	91	96	98	100	99	99
50 percent or more	27	39	56	63	82	92	96	98	99	100
Percent of students eligible for free or reduced-price lunch[4]										
Less that 35 percent	39	60	74	86	92	95	99	99	98	100
35 to 49 percent	35	48	59	81	93	98	99	100	100	100
50 to 74 percent	32	41	53	71	88	96	97	99	100	100
75 percent or more	18	31	53	62	79	89	94	97	99	99

1. Data for combined schools are included in the totals and in analyses by other school characteristics but are not shown separately.
2. Estimate is rounded to 100% for presentation in table.
3. Percentage of minority enrollment was not available for some schools. In 1994, this information was missing for 100 schools. In subsequent years, the missing information ranged from 0 schools to 46 schools. In 2003, this information was missing for 28 schools. The weighted response rate was 97.5%.

4. Percentage of students eligible for free or reduced-price lunch was not available for some schools. In the 1994 survey, free and reduced-price lunch data came from the Common Core of Data (CCD) only and were missing for 430 schools (percentages presented in this table are based on cases for which data were available). In reports prior to 1998, free and reduced-price lunch data were not reported for 1994. In 1998, a decision was made to include the data for 1994 for comparison purposes. In subsequent years, free and reduced-price lunch information was obtained on the questionnaire, supplemented, if necessary, with CCD data. Missing data ranged from 0 schools (2002 and 2003) to 10 schools (1999).

SOURCE: From *Fast Response Survey System, Internet Access in Public Schools and Classrooms (1994–2003)*, by U.S. Department of Education, National Center for Education Statistics, Washington, DC: U.S Government Printing Office.

According to Simkins, Cole, Tavalin, and Means (2002), project-based multimedia learning was becoming prevalent as early as 2002. Multimedia at that time had seven key dimensions: core curriculum, real-world connection, extended timeframe, student decision making, collaboration, assessment, and multimedia. As can be seen, the use of multimedia as well as the integration of technology into our nation's classrooms has been an ongoing process.

The important realization in this process is that students in the 21st century are different and require different learning styles. This is especially true when applying new developments in distance learning. When examining the qualities of targeted distance-learner groups, schools need to adapt technology applications to meet local demands and constraints. Attempts to apply outdated models of technology use to current realities highlight why we are having a hard time realizing the full potential that technology can offer to learning environments of today.

The dilemma is that when implementing technology in the schools of the United States, we still have not fully connected technology to the changing learning contexts needed by students. For example, there is the unwritten rule that schools should not buy technology unless the school can fully fund the technology-implementation process. Under the existing structures, various entities concerned with technology and education have spent significant dollars in establishing school computer labs, but no one is managing them or assisting students in many schools. The problem with this approach is that computer labs counter the notions of time, relationships, flexibility, and learning style on which students rely. As the president's Panel on Educational Technology (1997) indicated, the difficulty about technology and education is that people think about technology first and education later. In response to the changing student context, boards of education and school administrators should consider adding technology classroom designs to their existing school infrastructures.

Current technology has the capability of significantly reshaping education in the United States. Many schools are now exploding with new technological innovations and a host of educational changes. Interested and knowledgeable teachers and administrators are now becoming media specialists, and students are finally stepping into a learning environment that was unimaginable only a decade or two ago.

School Technology Realities

A careful look around the country reveals that some schools are making giant steps in their use of technology while a vast majority of schools and teachers remain tied to past educational strategies. As a result of limited funding for technology, many schools continue to locate the majority of their computers not within the individual classrooms but in specialized computer labs that are shared by all classes. This makes student computer use with small groups impractical in most classrooms. Knowledgeable school principals and superintendents are beginning to express concern over this state of affairs. These administrators feel a strong need to refocus district and state efforts to continue challenging school technology infrastructures so that they more appropriately address students' academic and social needs. With their help, a movement is now underway to bring the benefits of electronic information gathering and other technological advances to classrooms across America.

When school administrators and teachers begin to analyze the academic and social needs of their students carefully, they quickly see the value of putting technology into the hands of teachers and students. For example, some schools are now providing handheld devices and other high end Web-based devices for students. However, many schools have not been able to achieve this goal.

On a basic level, some schools are using portable word processors or computers on wheels (COWs). These function well for basic word-processing applications in the classroom.

On a higher level of technology integration, schools are providing classroom sets of individual wireless laptops, which are especially beneficial. The Internet-accessible wireless laptops can be accompanied with an electronic board, scanner, and access to a color printer. This model appears to be one of the most pedagogically sound ways to create connections between the curriculum and technology. Nonetheless, sets of traveling or fixed laptops can be expensive due to replacement cost.

Another model being used by schools involves providing a ratio of one to four classroom computers along with a high-speed Internet-accessible teacher computer, LCD projector, electronic board, scanner, and a printer in each classroom. The downside of having multiple computers in each classroom is again replacement cost. Banks of outdated computers can become a budget albatross for administrators if a school is not well funded.

Still other schools are utilizing a classroom model that does not involve student computers, only a single high-speed, Internet-accessible teacher computer and an LCD projector, electronic board, scanner, and access to a color printer. This last model seems to help in reducing the cost of replacing banks of student computers and still allows a teacher to deliver Web-based technology to the class. The major replacement cost is one computer and one electronic board per classroom. The key naturally is keeping all the equipment upgraded.

The success of state-of-the-art classroom technology centers is causing school administrators, board members or trustees, and teachers to shift their ideas of how technology best works in schools. Within this alternative structure, school administrators are compelled to ask several penetrating questions:

- Does the new technology enhance academic achievement?
- Can technology be integrated into our existing classroom arrangement and educational programs without significant disruption?
- Will the new technological approach have the impact we expect?
- Is changing our technological program worth the financial expenditures required to upgrade or replace existing facilities, equipment, and programs?

- Are new technological advances on the horizon that will render our intended equipment purchases obsolete in the not-too-distant future?

- Where can we go as a school (or school district) to get the best advice about serving our technological needs for upgrading or staying current?

At present, research is showing a higher correlation between increases in student achievement and the use of technology in schools. Some citizens, however, still question technological changes in education when it is not clear to them that such resources are directly tied to student achievement. The reality is that new developments in technology, changing societal and career needs, and new learning strategies are challenging schools to accommodate a symbiotic relationship among technology, curriculum, and the learning environment.

Technology as a Tool in the Curriculum

The Internet was previously known as the information superhighway, but currently the phrase is rarely used—instead terms like *PDA* and *podcast* are as common as *accountability* and *standards* (Padgett, 2007).

Computer-based instruction (CBI) was a primary use of technology in years past. The broad term "computer-based instruction" referred to general use of the computer in an educational setting. Some of these uses included drill and practice, tutorials, simulations, instructional management, supplementary exercises, programming, database development, word processing, and networking.

Throughout the past decades, technology has been viewed as a lodestone for improving student academic performance and for increasing the flexibility of public schools. According to Cheryl Franklin (2008), assistant professor at the University of New Mexico, the Internet has to a large extent been a way to connect students with resources outside of the classroom as well as develop WebQuests and other Web inquiry projects for their students. Teachers also used the Internet to integrate the teaching of technology skills into student projects and to take advantage of existing software.

Franklin further noted ways technology influences elementary school teachers:

- *Availability and Access to Technology.* The availability of classroom technology correlates to teacher use of computers, and teachers who have more computers available in the classroom more often assign activities in which students use technology.

- *Teacher Preparation and Training.* Teachers who feel better prepared to use technology are more likely to assign students to use technology. If technology integration into curriculum is desired, the teacher must know how to integrate curriculum and technology.

- *Time.* Teachers need time released from their classroom duties to learn, practice, and plan ways to integrate technology into curriculum. There also needs to be time in the daily schedule for students to use technology.

- *Leadership.* A strong community of leadership within schools is vital to technology implementation. When principals believe technology to be important to teaching and learning they tent to impart this belief to their teachers.

Technology as an Integral Part of the Curriculum

Schools that are effectively using technology at both secondary and elementary levels are primarily using Web-based technology. As part of the effective transition of technology into classrooms, students continue to find many uses for technology, such as art programs to make scientific drawings of penguins and newspaper publishing to culminate a unit on the Great Depression. Fourth- and fifth-grade students are trained in some districts to assist with younger students and teachers' computer instruction. These students also work with some senior citizens who come to school to learn about technology. While computers and technology are tremendous assets to the learning community of any school, the integration of technology across the curriculum is where the real value is found.

Managing assessment through technology has helped to overcome one of the greatest hurdles to improving classroom instruction—that is, the collecting, management, and analysis of data. Over time, with professional development, teachers have become smarter about collecting, interpreting, and using data (Gallagher & Ratzlaff, 2007/2008). Wireless networks also make it easier for teachers to provide frequent formative assessment to all students.

One of the exciting technology tools to be integrated into the classroom has been the digital whiteboard (Solvie, 2003). The digital whiteboard is an electronic version of a dry-erase board. The board can be written on with dry-erase markers or can be used with electronic or "virtual" markers. It has proven to be a useful organizational tool for both lesson preparation and instruction. The electronic whiteboard is only one of the many new technology devices being used extensively in the classroom.

Technology as the Curriculum

With new developments technology has become a tool with which to deliver a total curriculum or course of study. For example, the Internet can yield rich resources for curriculum development. Educators now utilize a number of technology programs to deliver curriculum for a variety of uses in schools today. Some of these uses are offering dual college and high school credit for upper-level students in high schools; credit recovery; discussions; collaborations among students from various locations in the state, country, or world; virtual schools; alternative virtual schools; and homeschool uses.

Curriculum design can be greatly assisted by technology. Kristen Lee Howard (2004) shared how technology could be used in a Universal Design for Learning or UDL. Universal Design for Learning focuses on educators' using flexible curricula that provide students with multiple ways of accessing content, multiple means for expressing themselves, and multiple pathways for engaging their interest and motivation (see Exhibit 14.6 for an example of using the computer to manage curriculum). Howard advocates asking the following questions when planning curriculum, which are still applicable today:

- What is the basic idea that the students need to learn?
- What are different ways to learn this idea: Demonstration? Games? Shared experience?
- If reading is involved, do they have to read independently, or can they use other tools and strategies to get the information?

EXHIBIT 14.6 The Computer as Manager of the Curriculum

Developing the Curriculum

1. Storing and providing data on student achievement and interests

2. Locating and retrieving exemplary scope-and-sequence charts

3. Locating and retrieving objectives from objectives banks

4. Locating and retrieving exemplary learning activities

5. Locating and retrieving appropriate learning materials

Facilitating and Monitoring the Learned Curriculum

1. Using student achievement and interest data to identify appropriate objectives

2. Recording and storing student performance with individual learning objectives

3. Using performance data to suggest remediation, further exploration, or next new objective

Aligning the Curriculum

1. Storing written curriculum in retrievable form

2. Storing teacher reports of objectives taught; matching written and taught

3. Storing test items; matching test items with written and taught

4. Storing test scores; providing achievement data in usable form to teachers and administrators

5. Analyzing congruencies and discrepancies between two or more of the above

Evaluating the Curriculum

1. Storing, analyzing data on student and teacher perceptions

2. Storing, analyzing achievement data relevant to specific units, objectives

This type of curriculum planning greatly enhances the use of Web-based technology, which are designed to enhance communication between teacher and students. Technology makes it easier for teachers to engage in best practices, facilitate group discussions, and provide timely feedback.

Curriculum Tip 14.6

Technology and data analysis help indicate what students are doing as well as what they are thinking, thus enabling teachers to enhance the natural communication flow in the classroom.

Student Achievement and Technology

Developing wide-area wireless networks and other forms of advanced technology in schools has been taking place for a number of years. A growing body of evidence now substantiates the notion that, when implemented appropriately, technology does have a relevant impact on student achievement.

Several beneficial outcomes have been noticed when a symbiotic relationship is established among technology, curriculum, and the learning environment. Some academic benefits of technology include the following:

- Enhancing problem-solving skills
- Enhancing writing processes and content
- Increasing teamwork and collaborative inquiry
- Increasing performance in basic skills learning
- Widening the scope of instructional opportunities
- Increasing student career opportunities
- Enhancing higher-order thinking skills

According to the available research on the effectiveness of technology in the student-learning environment, a variety of conclusions and opinions are offered. The supporters of technology point out that, in addition to student achievement, creating a technology culture that is more indicative of student needs has made a significant impact in at least 10 areas:

1. **Increased student writing.** Simply measuring the degree to which students are using computers to write reveals one positive impact of technology. Students are writing more compositions and doing so more often. Many teachers now find that students are producing three times the amount of written documents than they did before word processors were made available to them. Teachers who carefully watch students find that it often appears to be easier for their pupils to use a keyboard rather than a pen or pencil to write. The direct result is that students are writing more often and with seemingly greater ease. This trend is likely to become even more pronounced with the advent of voice-recognition programs and other technological applications.

2. **Higher-quality student writing.** Analysis of student writing by numerous researchers has shown that word processing helps students become more effective writers. This is not surprising to anyone who uses word processing to any degree because today's user-friendly computers and powerful programs allow students to check grammar, spelling, and revise all or part of their work as often as they wish.

3. **Enhanced cooperative learning.** Schools whose teachers are using wide-area networked computers and a printer in classrooms are finding that this format enhances and supports cooperative learning strategies. By using classroom computer centers as learning stations, many teachers are finding it easier to have students engage in collaborative efforts. When collaborative learning is linked with technology, it is known to have a strong positive influence on student achievement.

4. **Enhanced integration of curriculum**. Teachers whose classrooms have access to the Internet and electronic scanning devices are finding that using technology can make it easier to integrate social studies, literature, math, and science into a more coordinated series of learning experiences for students. A practical example of this type of learning opportunity would occur when students use the Internet and scanner to create content-integrated presentations utilizing material from several disciplines. In addition, maps, graphs, tables, and illustrations from a variety of subject areas can be incorporated into student projects and visual presentations by means of multimedia applications.

5. **Greater application of learning style strategies**. A significant correlation exists between the use of technology and the ability to accommodate different student learning styles in the classroom. Research notes that technology is structured to enhance the visual, auditory, and kinesthetic components of student learning.

6. **Increased applications of cross-age tutoring**. Students having access to high-speed wide-area networked systems are now able to use computers at any site in the school district. As a result, teachers are finding that older students can work with younger students on cooperative or tutorial projects over the network.

7. **Increased teacher communication**. An analysis of message logs across school districts indicates an interesting trend. Teachers with access to e-mail and Internet services at their schools are communicating more with their administrators as well as with other teachers at the same grade level. Today's new wave of technological advances is allowing teachers to exchange information more easily with other educators on local, state, national, and international levels. A very positive consequence of this increased use of electronic communication is the improvement of communication among school staffs at all levels.

8. **Greater parent communication**. Voicemail, e-mail, and text-messaging capabilities have provided a promising new link between home and school. Many teachers can now have parents contact the school via Web-based applications and receive updated reports on homework assignments and upcoming school activities. Looking at schools' message logs also demonstrates the impact and effectiveness of how technology is helping to bridge the information and understanding gaps that can occur between school and home.

9. **Enhanced community relations**. Bringing the school and community together provides another compelling reason for implementing technology in schools. In many school districts, community residents and local business members are regularly invited to take part in on-campus training programs using classroom facilities and computer labs. As a result, adult-education classes using technical instructors and school multimedia facilities are on the rise. In addition, students and teachers across the country are helping civic groups and small businesses develop Web pages, formulate listservs, and use e-mail and text messaging.

10. **Enhanced global learners**. Never before have educators and students been able to develop a better understanding of other cultures and people than is possible today. Many schools are now using Web-based applications to access information from all parts of the globe. New advances in voice translation and voice recognition will improve this capability even more in the future. As one considers this phenomenon, it becomes increasingly evident that technology in schools is paving the way for students, teachers, and citizens to enter a new community of global learners.

Classroom Technology

New understandings of systemic leadership and management frameworks are melding with technological advancements to revitalize concepts and designs for the Web-based classroom of the future. These new designs direct educational technology away from using it merely as a tool to something that addresses the academic needs of a new generation of learners. The concentration of the melded leadership framework makes the implementation and regular use of technology student centered. The philosophy is to build awareness as well as a vision of how technology can advance education, enhance student opportunities for exploration, and provide a transition between present and future forms of learning.

This educational vision creates a suitable climate for the use of technological advances in classrooms. For those schools with access to computer labs, advances in technology are providing opportunities for teachers and students to use high-speed technology to access Web-based applications as well as to assist with curricula programs. For the first time in our educational history, teachers and students will have the speed, hardware, courseware, and service support to truly enhance curriculum and instruction in a lab setting.

Web-Based Applications

Wireless networks now link classrooms with multiple servers and provide powerful information-gathering Web-based tools for administrators and teacher leaders. Many teachers are now finding that they are learning to use technology effectively in their classrooms because they have open access to Web-based applications.

According to Barger, Edens, O'Neill, and Wilcoxen (2007), Web-based curriculum mapping tools are particularly useful because they align existing curriculum with state standards and allow teachers to operate collaboratively rather than independently.

Principals/Teacher–Leaders

Web-based curriculum mapping tools provide principals and teacher–leaders with access to what is happening in the classroom on a much broader scale than individual classroom visits. One can search teachers' maps by name, grade level, specific keywords, and content area. Communication is increased because Web-based mapping begins conversations with teachers about standards, assessment, curriculum, and instruction.

Teachers

Access to other colleagues' curriculum maps via the Web provides a treasure trove of ideas and quality resources, leaving time to focus on daily lesson plans. New teachers are especially benefited with collaboration in real time with teachers in other grade levels and/or in other schools. The Web site serves as a historical archive, allowing teachers to share from each other.

Impact on Teaching and Learning

Web-based curriculum mapping serves as a tool teachers can use to build a solid record of instruction by electronically documenting their instruction throughout the year. The ability to access, create, revise, view, and compare maps at any time provides teachers with a unique opportunity to collaborate both horizontally and vertically across classrooms, subjects, grade levels, schools, and districts, allowing them to more easily identify and address gaps and repetition in instruction.

District Access

The Web site becomes the center for a districtwide system that allows principals, teachers, and parents to access the district's core curriculum and common assessments as well as instructional strategies.

Innovative teachers and administrators have had access and use information from a wide array of multimedia formats for years. Technologically integrated classrooms now provide opportunities for using Read/Write Web, podcasts, video conferencing, automated libraries, voice-recognition software, electronic whiteboards, flex cams, hypertext presentations, Web-based curriculum mapping and materials, and down-linked feeds to improve learning opportunities for students. As a result, teachers in technologically advanced schools are discovering that the classroom of tomorrow is here today. Nevertheless, no technology program or curriculum can be truly successful without quality staff development.

A key to quality staff development and curriculum delivery via technology is the formation of a teacher-to-teacher mentoring program. According to principal Craig Mills (2007), mentoring and professional development are key to any successful technology-implementation program. At his school in Chesapeake, Virginia, 10 of the most computer-literate teachers were provided a full day of in-depth training and the other teachers received half-day training. For the rest of the year, the more intensively trained teachers provided additional training as needed. As his teachers began to implement the system in their classrooms, they appreciated knowing that there was a trainer two or three doors down the hall. Teachers were required to use technology weekly and post at least one digital lesson on the system.

The digital learning system and mentoring program helped allow teachers to customize existing lessons or build their own lessons to deliver targeted differentiated instruction to each student in accordance with that student's abilities. The professional training and mentoring system also encouraged collaboration. With the use of the school's technology system, teachers now had more time for direct instruction.

By training some teachers to train other teachers, and requiring all teachers to use the system's many technology tools, the school has become academically successful. Since adopting the mentoring program along with the digital learning system, the school has seen a steady rise in third-grade state test scores and was able to meet adequate yearly progress goals for the first time.

As seen above in the case of Chesapeake school and others, mentoring programs can make a powerful difference in school climate. One of the first steps in developing a mentoring program is to assess and increase the teachers' comfort levels. Once the teachers are committed to a plan, they should follow steps as noted below by authors Kathleen Gora, Janice Hinson, and Don Hall (2003–2004):

- Identify three or four topics or concepts to explore based on school goals.
- Submit a work plan with specific goals.
- Meet quarterly at designated times.
- Use expert teachers to learn new applications and techniques.
- Provide feedback on progress through group member surveys and mid- and end-of-year evaluations.

The development of a quality mentoring program to help integrate technology into the curriculum is an important aspect of the curriculum-planning process. To be effective, the mentoring process must be continually adjusted to enable every teacher to exhibit stronger technology-integration skills. With a quality mentoring program in place, teachers begin to see the real value of using technology in their classroom.

It has been said that we are living in a communication age, but some theorists are now suggesting we are entering a new phase called the "learning age." The reality is that many people are also living and working in an age of increasing interconnectedness. There seems to be little doubt that new advances in technology are capable of providing America's classrooms and citizens with a new and long-awaited window to the world. Because students thrive on creating and being a part of a community, this technology design is beginning to make a difference in teaching and learning, as it is in society.

Developing Local Community Awareness

Developing plans to fully integrate technology into instruction can make a good school better. The process can require innovative funding, training, and reassuring parents. What can result is a learning community in which teachers, students, and parents succeed in infusing technology seamlessly into classroom practices (Patterson, 2007).

In many districts, parents and community members are now communicating with teachers in their classrooms via electronic mail, text messaging, school hotlines, and interactive Web-based applications. In addition, some progressive schools are providing students and parents with their own portable laptops that can be used for homework or class projects.

Public involvement is growing in many schools as advances in educational technology occur, and, as a result, community members are beginning to revise their views about education. Increasingly, business leaders are recognizing the connection between students' technological skills and their ability to be successful in the world of work. This consciousness has led to the formation of school-to-work programs funded by state money and local taxpayers. As part of the concern about the United States no longer having the best educated workforce in the world, a new report, *Tough Choices or Tough Times* from the New Commission on the Skills of the American Workforce, helps focus educational leaders on global issues (Tucker, 2007).

At least, school/business partnerships are on the rise. Students and teachers routinely help businesspeople by doing such things as creating Web pages and Web-based links for them. In return, local businesses often donate equipment to schools in an effort to capitalize on a new market for educational products. An important byproduct of these various forms of contact between schools and citizens is that community members are often more willing to support tax levies for education when they understand where their tax dollars are going. The resulting interaction between schools and community members is being seen more and more as a positive outcome for both groups.

School Technology Goals

A key standard for school jurisdictions to consider is the provision of four clear and practical technological goals that will expand the boundaries of traditional schooling and help children reach new levels of learning development.

First, school administrators should coordinate school-based services and resources in order to heighten access to interactive technology for students in their schools. Statewide telecommunication infrastructures are usually most capable of providing the necessary level of linkage and delivery for schools.

Second, guidelines for equipment use and programs designed to enhance communication and technological awareness within communities need to be developed. Improved public awareness of the technology that is available often leads to a greater understanding of how technology can benefit students and citizens. Community appreciation also leads to the creation of shared vision and mission statements, joint technology committees, appropriate financing programs, infrastructure development, staff development, maintenance and service arrangements, favorable program evaluation, and, finally, successful public relations programs. Education leaders must expand traditional school boundaries to involve the community in planning, financing, implementing, and evaluating technology.

Third, school leaders would be wise to share school success stories with their communities. Data obtained from student assessments can add substantial credibility to the positive things happening in schools when effectively presented to the public. This information can be easily retrieved and presented with the aid of Web-based applications.

Fourth, data from student assessments can provide school administrators and teachers with a valuable mechanism for checking exam results to ensure that student performance meets or exceeds local, state, and national standards. If required, a statewide data-retrieval system for student performance could assist school leaders in determining aggregate achievement levels for all schools. As well, an accompanying item analysis of standardized test questions would provide administrators and teachers with a means of making a sound appraisal of strengths and weaknesses in the school or district curriculum and meeting government mandated guidelines such as Response to Intervention (RTI) requirements. For more information on RTI, see Chapter 15.

Curriculum Tip 14.7	Informative assessment is not an end itself, but the beginning of better instruction. (Tomlinson, 2007/2008)

It is through the development of clear public information programs that state legislators and citizens will best understand how technology is affecting student achievement. As community support increases, school leaders are better able to provide the administrative support necessary to accommodate the needs of teachers and students. Community support also breaks down classroom walls by making the positive activities in schools more visible and educators more accessible to parents. New technologies provide a practical avenue to connect teachers and students with learning opportunities that await them as they begin to make contact with the rest of the world. There is little doubt that leading-edge technology holds the promise of many positive elements for American education. A few of these positive outcomes would be the fostering of exploratory learning, the empowering of teachers, and the equipping of school leaders with advanced resources technology needed to manage schools. In reality, the task of illuminating the role of technology in our nation's classrooms is a complex and important one. It is only through an effective public information campaign that policymakers, practitioners, and citizens can be equipped with the facts needed to make wise decisions about the new electronic advancements available to their schools.

State and National Levels of Awareness

State and national organizations are now working to develop a shared vision that will establish a workable frame of reference for school technology programs. It is crucial that education leaders at state and national levels develop a coordinated plan directed at helping schools use technology. It is unfortunate that, at present, state and federal agencies often confound this process by duplicating each other's efforts. While numerous government agencies are capable of providing financial and technical support to schools, they are often unable to offer this aid efficiently. As a result, many schools are trying to work with a mishmash of networks, database providers, hardware and courseware applications, and all of the difficulties associated with such a technological conglomeration. In practice, this uncoordinated array of appliances and applications creates confusion for educators. Fortunately, a concerted effort is underway to eradicate this problem. In an effort to improve the situation, savvy school leaders are spearheading a movement to develop new frameworks for including influential noneducators into the brainstorming and implementation process before bringing new technologies into their districts.

The creation of national and state standards for the use of Web-based and other digital resources is a major factor in the development of an overall plan to deal with the complexity of today's high-tech educational landscape.

The International Society for Technology in Education (ISTE) and its National Educational Technology Standards (NETS) Project have gone a long way in helping guide all schools into effective technology integration. Joining ISTE in the NETS Project are organizations representing major professional education groups, government entities, foundations, and corporations (Exhibit 14.7).

EXHIBIT 14.7 NETS Project Partners

Associations and/or Organizations	Web Sites
American Association of School Librarians (AASL), a division of the American Library Association (ALA)	www.ala.org/aasl
American Federation of Teachers (AFT)	www.aft.org
Association for Supervision and Curriculum Development (ASCD)	www.ascd.org
The Council for Exceptional Children (CEC)	www.cec.sped.org
Council of Chief State School Officers (CCSSO)	www.ccsso.org
National Association of Elementary School Principals (NAESP)	www.naesp.org
National Association of Secondary School Principals (NASSP)	www.nassp.org
National Education Association (NEA)	www.nea.org
National Foundation for the Improvement of Education (NFIE)	www.nfie.org
National School Boards Association (NSBA)	www.nsba.org/itte
Software Information Industry Association (SIIA)	www.siia.net

SOURCE: ISTE and National Educational Technology Standards (2008, January 6). Retrieved February 18, 2008, from http://cnets.iste.org

In addition, The National Council for the Accreditation of Teacher Education (NCATE) requires schools of education to meet verifiable technology standards for program accreditation. This accreditation body recognizes the importance of advanced technology in schools and supports this stance by requiring technology to move from the periphery to the center of teacher education.

Many local and state educational leaders are considering a proposal to collaborate closely with the U.S. Department of Education on matters related to technology in schools. The results of these coordinated efforts will continue to be specifically directed at better understanding of Web-based applications, the integration of curriculum via technology, software and courseware development, and course content for technology classes. This organization will be composed of a consortium of capable people from the ranks of higher education, business, research institutes, and governmental agencies. The intention will be to share research information and data from many sources to develop a national technology initiative. The outcome of subsequent proposals made by the national and state technology task forces will be to place a greater emphasis on technology in classrooms by fostering close cooperation among teachers, administrators, parents, experts from higher education, and business. Individual states are also moving forward with initiatives designed to capitalize on the benefits of technology for schools and students. Some perceptive state lawmakers are advancing legislation to provide teachers with technology skills to allow for a wider use of multimedia in classrooms, while legislators in other states are establishing statewide standards to regulate the use of technology in schools and classrooms.

E-Learning

With 100% (see Exhibit 14.5) of the schools connected to the Internet, schools are increasingly adopting the use of the E-learning environment to increase their curricula and extend learning experiences for students (Remondino & Chen, 2004). As Daniel J. Hoesing (2004) pointed out,

> With all schools connected to the Internet, multimedia and Internet-based technologies have replaced satellite, microwave, cable, and broadcast television technologies that originally extended distance-learning opportunities for students. As a result, states, school districts, and individual schools are more open to promoting the use of the virtual classroom [bold added] to augment their curricula. (p. 4)

As shown in Exhibit 14.8, there are several sample online virtual high school programs that are offering courses.

Hoesing (2004) also drew the following conclusions:

1. Students indicated that they were able to establish interpersonal relationships with instructors in the E-leaning environment.

2. Based on the increasing numbers of distance-learning participants, there is a need for E-learning in high schools, especially in rural or economically disadvantaged areas.

3. Based on student perceptions, E-learning is expanding in popularity and becoming more widely accepted as an effective and economical educational delivery system at the high school level.

EXHIBIT 14.8 Online High School Programs	
Sample Online Programs	*Results*
University of Missouri–Columbia Virtual High School	Began in 1999 with approximately 20 courses that were entirely online. Three years later, the program increased to 203 students enrolled in over 991 classes with a dropout rate of less than one student per class or 4.8%.
Alabama Online High School	Initiated in an attempt to save small rural schools in the state from consolidation. In the fall of 1999, 40 students were enrolled in an online science course. The program has since expanded from an initial pilot science class to include online course in Spanish, mathematics, English, and language arts.
Illinois Virtual High School	Successfully opened in 2001 with the goal to provide advanced placement, dual credit, curriculum enhancement, remedial education, and curriculum enrichment courses to all secondary students, rather than just a selected segment of the school population.
Basehor-Linwood Virtual Charter School, Kansas	The school was created because of the State's interest to further integrate technology into the regular curriculum. In three years the enrollment increased from 63 students to 368 students.
South Dakota Center for E-Learning, Northern State University, Aberdeen, South Dakota	Since the opening in 2001, the numbers for Northern State University Center for Statewide E-Learning reached new highs for enrollment. The Center had an enrollment of 909 high school students from 81 school districts.
Coleridge, Laurel-Concord, New Castle, and Wynot Public Schools, Nebraska	Starting in 1998, the consortium is comprised of four schools with an additional eight schools receiving E-learning courses. Comprised mostly of core courses, 57 classes are offered with the majority of the course in a blended learning setting: asynchronous and synchronous.

SOURCE: From *Student Perceptions of E-Learning in South Dakota High Schools,* by D. J. Hoesing, 2004. Unpublished doctoral dissertation, the University of South Dakota, Vermillion. For information about the E-learning program at the Nebraska schools, access www.laurel.esu1.org or call Dr. Hoesing at 402-256-3133.

4. Based on survey responses, students' satisfaction, level of learning, and overall experience in the distance-learning environment is directly influenced by the quality of the instructors.

5. Based on class completion rates, attributes of the learner affect the probability of student success realized in an E-learning environment.

6. Student responded that course design and instructional methods contribute to the students' interest, satisfaction, and performance in the distance-learning environment.

7. Students indicated that Web-based interface supports a variety of effective tools that contribute to their level of understanding and facilitated communication with

instructors and students from other school districts in a blended E-learning environment. (pp. 74–75)

E-learning in many high schools, especially in rural communities, has established itself as a major alternative system for educating children in the 21st century. The E-learning concept confirms that barriers of time and place are diminishing as technology does offers alternative choices and opportunities for both students and educators.

STRATEGIES FOR SUCCESS

To be successful in our increasingly technological world, all learners and educators must be skilled in the use of technology. Also, to bring about change and establish equity, factors such as proper training programs, technical support, and time for learning must be provided simultaneously for educators. Goals to be successful with technology include the following:

- Community involvement in planning and implementing the use of technology in schools should be a high priority for school leaders.
- Developing quality technological leadership and planning for effective technology use within the jurisdiction must receive considerable attention.
- Finances for technology should come from the district's general budget.
- Emphasis should be placed on incorporating technology learning centers into classrooms.
- Curriculum should use technology but not be driven by it.
- Staff development involving technology should be made highly practical by having "teachers instruct teachers."
- Planning and implementation phases for the inclusion of new technology should include assessment and evaluation standards.
- A well-planned public relations program should be used to share the benchmarks of a successful program with the community.

In our rapidly changing world, the economic vitality of communities and individuals will depend more and more on the ability to access information, build knowledge, solve problems, and share success. Because technology will increasingly play a key role in this process, students must develop the necessary skills while they are in school (see Exhibit 14.9 for an example of proposed scope and sequence for information technology education). This means that today's students must be prepared now for the technological world that will be a very real part of their lives in the future.

FUTURE CHALLENGES

One might say that "technology is here to stay." The 88 million children of baby-boomer adults find using digital technologies no more intimidating than using a VCR or a toaster.

	Subjects		
Grade	English	Social Studies	How It Works
5	Talking with technology		Podcasts and video conferencing
6		Technology in our community	Lasers; sound and sight
7		Doing what's right with technology	Web-based applications
8	Using, not being used by, the new technology		Scientific discovery in the new technology
9	Technology as a communications medium	The new technology and politics	
10	The new technology as art		
11	Careers in the new technology	The new technology shapes our society	
12	The new technology and the future	Ethical choices and the new technology	

EXHIBIT 14.9 Proposed Scope and Sequence: Information Technology Education

These children are often referred to as the Net Generation because they are media literate and watch much less television than their parents did at the same age. Two thirds of the children today use a personal computer or a technological Web-based device either at home or at school, which implies that they want to be active participants, not just viewers or listeners. In fact, television to many in the current generation is somewhat old-fashioned. To meet the challenge for the future, the following questions need answers:

- How do we engage youth in our schools to be active participants in all of our classrooms with online activities?

- What must a school district do to make 100% of the teachers feel comfortable with technology?

The Western Rockies School District in Montana answers the question, "What must a school district do to make 100% feel comfortable with technology?" The school district developed a districtwide Educational Technology Master Plan. The document includes the following language:

Preparing Western Rockies School District community; [sic] students, faculty and parents to function successfully in the world today and tomorrow is one of the primary aims of education. As we have changed from an industrial society to an information society, the projected impact of technology on our lives makes the development of technology literate students an increasingly necessary goal of education. The students of the Western Rockies School District will be continuously educated in the effective use of technology at each grade level K–12.

Technology in the form of telecommunication networks, web-based applications, and multi-media equipment is becoming an increasingly important resource for instruction as well as an integral part of the worlds of work and home. We believe this document will ensure the delivery of a common core technology curriculum to all students and assist sites in their development of individual school technology plans. Furthermore, this document provides the guidelines for the integration of such technology into the instructional programs for the students in the Western Rockies School District. (Adapted from CUSD Instructional Center, 2005)

Today, with the heightened national interest in improved student performance, high-stakes testing, and school accountability, the school administrator's role must change. Traditionally, principals have been seen as managers responsible for implementing district policies. Until the arrival of the information age, the mentality of school administrators was, "If it ain't broke, don't fix it." At present, because investments in equipment have not always been accompanied by changes in teaching, school administrators must take on the role of leadership. Teachers need help to overcome obstacles and integrate technology into their instructional practice. The overriding question is, "What must school administrators do?" Also, if technology is to help create a more egalitarian society, disparities in the quality of home and school access across different socioeconomic groups must be addressed.

As educators give further thought to the impact of technology in our present world, and as they consider the nature of the world our children will inherit from us, it becomes readily apparent that we must carefully meld technologies into the current structure of individual classrooms. The potential for creating schools and school districts of high quality is possible only through the timely and adroit application of existing knowledge. To benefit from this knowledge, it is important that a comprehensive blueprint be adopted and followed. It is generally recommended that educators and community leaders carefully consider and adhere to suggestions in this book as they explore unique ways on how to integrate technology into the curriculum to enhance student learning.

MEDIA TECHNOLOGY

As our society continues to advance in the information and learning age, the importance of media within the school's overall curriculum increase. In today's technological world, the communication of information and ideas is channeled through a variety of Web-based technology applications; each is appropriate for a particular type of message. Information and ideas thus received can be assimilated, organized, and communicated to others using current technology.

Instructional programs must effectively integrate media throughout the curriculum. The basis of this integration is a media skills program that offers students the opportunity to (a) become fluent users and producers of media, (b) use media resources effectively in everyday learning process, and (c) demonstrate awareness of the manipulative power of the media.

Students need the tools to efficiently search through and make use of the ever-growing numbers of information source levels. Teaching should support continuous, natural, and increasingly sophisticated use of media and should include regular use of the library/media center. To the extent possible, assistive technology should be used to help learning-impaired children achieve their educational goals. Media literacy must take a vital place in our national school curricula.

SUMMARY

This chapter addresses curricular changes that transcend a single discipline. The major curricula changes include using writing to learn, improving thinking skills, speaking, listening, and the integration of technology throughout the curriculum. Transcending the discipline to address these skills requires both a different perspective on curriculum change and different processes for planning and implementation.

APPLICATIONS

1. Develop the outlines of a writing-to-learn project that could be used in a subject or discipline you know well. Use the framework suggested in Exhibit 14.1 to describe the major components of the program.

2. The "higher-order thinking skills" (HOTS) concentrate on the top three levels of Bloom's Taxonomy: analysis, synthesis, and evaluation. Review the curriculum guides and/or unit or daily lesson plans and identify several HOTS.

3. If you were charged with the responsibility of developing a district curriculum in critical thinking, would you recommend developing separate courses, integrating critical thinking into existing courses, or using both approaches? Provide a rationale for your recommendation.

4. Consider the four uses of technology in relation to the curriculum: technology applications as developer, technology applications as deliverer, technology applications as tools, and technology applications as the curriculum. As you assess the needs of a school system with which you are familiar, how would you prioritize these four approaches? What systematic processes would you use in making such a determination?

5. As reported in Chapter 2, the reform report *A Nation at Risk* identified "computer literacy" as one of the "Five New Basics" and recommended that a one-semester course in computer literacy be required for each high school student. What is your assessment of the wisdom of such a suggestion?

6. One of the issues dividing specialists in early childhood education is how much use should be made of technology as an instructional tool for the early elementary grades. Based on your knowledge and your values, explain the position you would take on this issue and the reasons you would advance in support of your position.

CASE STUDY   Developing and Sharing Strategies

This case study provides an example of how a teacher leader solves the problem with a colleague who is not using the writing to-learn project—a district-mandated curriculum program.

"I've noticed that some of our fifth-grade students are not using the school district's writing to-learn project," states teacher–leader Bill Drucker. "Is there a reason that we are not using this program?"

Fifth-grade teacher Pam Hollenbeck looks up from her desk. "That's correct. I just don't have the time to work this program into my schedule. There are so many other subjects during the day that I cannot get to it."

"I realize that time is a concern," sighs the teacher–leader. "Nevertheless, according to our curriculum and district policy in regards to that curriculum, we will have to find a way to incorporate the writing to-learn project. It's a mandatory project."

Mrs. Hollenbeck realizes her colleague is very concerned and quickly comprehends the seriousness of the situation. "Well, I suppose I can incorporate a writing-to-learn project in social studies."

"Yes," answers Drucker, giving a sigh of relief. "A writing-to-learn project in social studies would be great!"

Now smiling, Hollenbeck adds, "One of my students is participating in a writing-to-learn project involving a great story on Seaman, Captain Lewis's dog. This is the Newfoundland dog that accompanied the men throughout the Lewis and Clark expedition." She continues, "As part of the writing-to-learn project, my students can also make a PowerPoint presentation of the story." "Also, since the fourth grade is developing a unit on Montana history, this could be sent to all fourth-grade teachers in the district."

"Yes, I heard something about that from the fourth-grade teachers. They loved it!" he says, smiling. "It is really great that we can share materials with other grades!

The Challenge

Teacher Pam Hollenbeck uses technology successfully to improve student writing and thinking skills. What specific steps can teacher–leader Drucker take to get other teachers to use Hollenbeck's ideas and strategies? What kind of resistance might he encounter from other teachers and staff?

Key Issues/Questions

1. Is it possible to bring a school facing the problem of unsatisfactory student writing levels up to national standards with the use of technology? Why or why not?

2. What are your impressions of Pam Hollenbeck's program in this Montana school? Can this program be replicated in other states using their own history as a guideline?

3. What are some of the problems that educators face as they begin using technology in the classroom?

4. What other innovative technology strategies can be used to improve student writing and thinking skills? How can teacher–leaders and principals best initiate these strategies?

5. How does technology use in middle and high schools differ from how it is used in an elementary classroom setting?

WEBLIOGRAPHY

Center for Implementing Technology in Education
www.cited.org

National Staff Development Council—Data-in-a-Day technique provides a snapshot of teaching that motivates
www.nsdc.org/library/publications/jsd/ginsberg222.cfm

International Society for Technology in Education's National Educational Technology Standards
www.cnets.iste.org

Internet4Classrooms provides grade-level content skills
www.internet4classrooms.com/grade_level_help.htm

National Council of Teachers of English
www.ncte.org

National Writing Project
www.nwp.org

Teachers face handheld revolution
http://news.bbc.co.uk/1/hi/uk_politics/4230832.stm

Technology in Education Resource Center
www.rtec.org

Topmarks educational search engine
www.topmarks.co.uk

CHAPTER 15

Individualizing the Curriculum

Plato may have been one of the first writers to recommend individualization through tracking. In his *Republic*, Plato made clear his belief that children should be directed toward roles of philosopher, guardian, or artisan based on their talents. While contemporary educators reject such a deterministic differentiation, the search for curricula that respond to individual differences continues. The search is one that involves curricula promoting student choice, curriculum integration, differentiated learning, and self-assessment that engage students deeply in learning (Brown, 2002).

This chapter analyzes the types of individualized programs, reviews previous attempts to respond to individual differences, and assesses current models. The chapter concludes by examining the challenging problems inherent in providing for very special student populations.

Questions addressed in this chapter include the following:

- What early attempts were made to individualize curriculum?
- What are some examples of current individualized programs, and why are they considered to be successful?
- What individualized adaptive approaches are being used in gifted education, and are they considered successful?
- What are some examples of specialized curriculum, and how are they enhancing the concept of individualization?
- What role does bilingual education play in individualizing curriculum?

Key to Leadership

Successful curriculum leaders know that an important aspect of any curriculum change is that it relates to standards and that it can be translated into individual academic performance indicators.

TYPES OF INDIVIDUALIZED PROGRAMS

It would be useful to begin the analysis by clarifying the concept. Here it seems wise to substitute the clearer term *adaptive* for the more ambiguous *individualized*. Largely because of the vague and conflicting connotations associated with the latter term, specialists in the field often refer to *adaptive* curricula and *adaptive* instructional practices.

Curriculum Tip 15.1	**Adaptive curricula** are educational processes that arrange the conditions and materials of learning so that they fit individual learner differences.

Today's schools face unprecedented challenges in individualizing curriculum and preparing students for the unpredictable demands of the future workplace. Knowing what to do is the easy part. Actually doing it is what's hard (Wiliam, 2007–2008). According to Dave Brown (2002), professor of education at West Chester University Pennsylvania, adaptive and instructional practices involve students in developing their own curriculum; study methods and assessments are built around questions that are important to the students. Involving students in curriculum development encourages them to explore the topics they study deeply and allows them a voice of their own as well as opportunities to share their learning with the community. Students and teachers in this type of program are generally revitalized and refreshed as they experience the benefits of the processes' self-directed, integrated curriculum (Brown, 2002).

The National Association for the Education of Young Children (NAEYC & NAECS/SDE, 2004) drafted a series of indicators that best reflect the design of this type of curriculum. These indicators include the following:

- Children are active and engaged.
- Goals are clear and shared by all.
- Curriculum is evidence based.
- Valued content is learned through investigation, play, and focused, intentional teaching.
- Curriculum builds on prior learning and experiences.
- Curriculum is comprehensive.
- Professional standards validate the curriculum's subject-matter content.
- The curriculum benefits children.

As noted by the NAEYC, it is important to realize the overarching need to create an individualized and integrated curriculum that addresses the needs of all children. Such a curriculum has the capacity to support learning and development for children living in poverty, children with disabilities, children whose home language is not English, and children who need to be academically challenged. The focus needs to be on believing that students with the interest, motivation, and capacity for learning should be challenged in every classroom, each and every day (Page, 2000).

PREVIOUS ATTEMPTS TO INDIVIDUALIZE

A major challenge facing our schools today is the diversity of students. Examining how master teachers weave differentiation into their daily practice can help reluctant teachers take the plunge (Carolan & Guinn, 2007).

Consider the range of abilities present in most classrooms in U.S. education during its long history. As Grinder and Nelsen (1985) noted, attempts to individualize education in the United States go back to colonial times, a period they characterize as individualized instruction by default. One hundred youngsters would be seated in a large ungraded classroom, working on exercises, while one teacher monitored their work. The need to educate large numbers of children in a more systematic manner led 19th-century educational reformers to institute graded classrooms, each with a teacher in charge, presenting a standard program. While this self-contained graded classroom has persisted as the norm for at least 100 years, during this time numerous attempts have been made to break out of the constraints imposed by standardized education. Rather than presenting a comprehensive historical review of such attempts, the discussion that follows concentrates on those approaches that persist to the present (for a fuller discussion of the history of individualized instruction, consult the Grinder and Nelsen work).

Providing Elective Courses

During the first century of American education, educators seemed concerned solely with identifying the common curriculum for all students; electives as such were not even considered. Even though Charles Eliot was chairman of the Committee of Ten, he was not able to persuade the committee that electives were desirable; the only option provided in their recommendations was that bookkeeping and commercial arithmetic could be substituted for algebra (see Committee of Ten, 1893). The first official statement recommending elective courses was the *Cardinal Principles of Secondary Education*, published by the Commission on the Reorganization of Secondary Education in 1918. In their formulation of the ideal program, the commission recommended a balance between the constants (those courses to help all students achieve essential goals), curriculum variables (special courses determined by the student's specific educational and career goals), and free electives (courses chosen in response to special interests).

For the past 90 years the debate over what constitutes the best balance of these three components has continued unabated. The debate has not been informed by rational analysis and too often has produced prescriptions that reflect only the participants' biases about the need to control the education of the young.

Curriculum Tracking

Tracking of students should also be an area of discussion. A particularly difficult decision for educators is how best to balance comprehensive (one school for all) versus "selective" schooling. Thus, school systems that offer an elite academic track provide an incentive for affluent families to remain in the public school system—but often at a cost to children assigned to lower tracks (Rotberg, 2007). According to Janet Atkins and Judy Ellsesser (2003), conversations with an online teachers' network reveal different experiences with tracking and reflections on its implications for students. Curriculum tracking, sorting students into somewhat rigid tracks based on career and educational goals, was probably first formally recognized as a desirable practice by the Committee of Ten. Their report recommended four tracks, differentiated chiefly by the language studied: Classical, Latin Scientific, Modern Languages, and English. The committee was quite explicit about the relative qualities of those four: "The programs called respectively Modern Languages and English must in practice be distinctly inferior to the other two" (p. 48). Thus, the practice of tracking and the status accorded to certain tracks have continued for almost 100 years; all that changes are the number of tracks and their names. Most high schools now provide for three tracks, determined primarily by educational and career goals: college preparatory, general, and vocational/technical.

Curriculum Tip 15.2	Research suggests rather clearly that curriculum tracking is not a useful way of responding to individual differences.

Janet Atkins and Judy Ellsesser (2003) quoted a teacher from Alaska as stating,

Whenever we start leveling and tracking our students we send a loud, personal message to each student. It is important to never forget that these students will be next to voice opinions about what is right or wrong about their own children's education. (p. 46)

As a result, many schools have eliminated tracked classes and have adopted a universal accelerated program and instituted heterogeneous grouping, with dramatic results. Using this type of curriculum reform, high achievers seem to be doing better, and more students are becoming high achievers (Burris, Heubert, & Levin, 2004). Ultimately, "just one question might best serve diverse learners, their teachers, and their society. What can we do to support educators in developing the skill and the will to teach for each learner's equity of access to excellence?" (Tomlinson, 2003, p. 7). If teachers adhere to the principles shown in Exhibit 15.1, differentiation can liberate students from stereotypical expectations and experience equity of success to excellence.

Offering "Mini-Courses"

As noted in Chapter 2, many school districts in the past gave students content options within a field of study by developing mini-courses lasting from 6 to 18 weeks. Rather than

EXHIBIT 15.1 Principles for Fostering Equity and Excellence in Academically Diverse	
Principles	*Descriptors*
Good curriculum comes first.	The teacher's first job is always to ensure a coherent, important, inviting, and thoughtful curriculum.
All tasks should respect each learner.	Every student deserves work that is focused on the essential knowledge, understanding, and skills targeted for the lesson. Every student should be required to think at a high level and should find his or her work interesting and powerful.
When in doubt, teach up!	Good instruction stretches learners. The best tasks are those that students find a little too difficult to complete comfortably. Be sure there's a support system in place to facilitate the student's success at a level that he or she doubted was attainable.
Use flexible grouping.	Find ways and time for the class to work as a whole, for students to demonstrate competence alone, and for students to work with varied groups of peers. Using only one or two types of groups causes students to see themselves and one another in more limited ways, keeps the teacher from "auditioning" students in varied contexts, and limits potentially rich exchanges in the classroom.
Become an assessment junkie.	Everything that a student says and does is a potential source of assessment data. Assessment should be an ongoing process, conducted in flexible but distinct stages, and it should maximize opportunities for each student to open the widest possible window on his or her learning.
Grade to reflect growth.	The most we can ask of any person—and the least we ought to ask—is to be and become their best. The teacher's job is to guide and support the learner in this endeavor. Grading should, in part, reflect a learner's growth.

SOURCE: Adapted from Tomlinson and Edison (2003).

taking English II, students could choose from an array of offerings with titles such as *Women in Literature, The Mass Media,* and *The Search for Wisdom.* While such mini-courses were more often developed in the fields of English and social studies, they could also be found in science and mathematics; in fact, many schools prided themselves on offering more than 200 mini-courses.

The mini-course approach was highly popular with teachers, because it enabled them to develop and teach courses relating to their special interests and knowledge. Most schools using a mini-course curriculum reported high levels of student satisfaction. Most of these courses seemed poorly designed, however. They seemed not to have been produced with some overall conceptualization of that field and gave scant attention to important skills and concepts. Thus, the claim that this *smorgasbord curriculum* contributed to the decline in academic achievement seems warranted, even though no persuasive empirical evidence was evident on this point.

Open Classrooms

The open classroom popular during the late 1960s and early 1970s attempted to respond to individual differences in several ways. First, open classroom teachers felt less constrained by district curriculum guides and fashioned curricula that they believed responded to the special needs and interests of their pupils. While elementary teachers in open classrooms all taught language arts, social studies, mathematics, and science, they chose content that they believed would be most meaningful to their pupils, and that content typically involved the integration of several subject fields. Second, pupils had some options about their use of time: They could work in special learning centers any time during the day, unlimited by bells and artificial distinctions between subjects; and they could spend as much time as they needed. They also had some choice about activities and materials; the learning centers were usually provisioned with a rich assortment of materials for learning. Finally, there was an atmosphere of informality, which advocates believed was truly individualized: Pupils could talk together and move about the room as necessary.

The open-classroom movement was short-lived, succumbing to conservative pressures for more teacher control and higher achievement in the basics. Its rapid demise was probably unfortunate.

Self-Paced Instruction

During the 1960s and 1970s, there was also much interest in several varieties of self-paced instruction, usually called *individualized learning*. While these programs varied in their details, they shared several common elements:

- The curriculum is analyzed into several components, arranged in a tightly controlled sequence.

- The learner is assessed and placed appropriately along that sequence.

- The learner works on self-instructional packets or lessons, usually in isolation, in order to achieve clearly specified objectives.

- The learner gets feedback about progress and remediates where necessary.

In most such programs, only the pace of learning (and, concomitantly, the time spent on learning a particular set of objectives) is adapted to learner needs; every other important element is controlled and standardized.

An important aspect of self-paced programs is the emphasis on using a multitude of textbooks and packaged materials. According to Valerie Chapman, University of Texas, El Paso, and Diane Sopko, Tarleton State University, Fort Worth, Texas (2003), having students reading combined textbooks is much like peeling an onion. When students use textbooks, they read in layers. The layers include illustrations, informational text, and narrative text, as well as additional details such as directions and borders. Learning how to read a variety of texts helps develop a sense of organization for self-paced learners.

CURRENT ADAPTIVE APPROACHES

According to Carol Ann Tomlinson, there is no contradiction between effective standards-based instruction and differentiation. Curriculum tells us what to teach and differentiation tells us how. Thus, if we elect to teach a standards-based curriculum, differentiation simply suggests ways in which we can make that curriculum work best for varied learners (Protheroe, 2007). An important aspect of any adaptive approach is that it relates to curriculum standards and that it is able to be translated into academic performance indicators with well-organized unit plans and congruent unit objectives (March & Peters, 2002). Educational consultants Judith March and Karen Peters noted nine important factors for developing a new curriculum design or approach:

- Greater attention to problem solving
- Focus by the entire staff on the most important parts of curriculum
- Alignment of expected outcomes
- Connections between subject areas through curriculum mapping
- Inclusion of a variety of methods (inquiry, guided discussion, action research)
- Authentic performance assessments
- Multiple opportunities for teachers to collaborate
- High-quality materials
- Consistency in preparation of students for following grade

Curriculum Tip 15.3	Awareness and a willingness to actually restructure and realign the classroom curriculum is the key to developing successful adaptive change

To assist in the curriculum design process, five major adaptive approaches are prevalent: the adaptive learning environments model (ALEM), cooperative learning models, learning-styles models, mastery learning models, and computer-based models. In each case, the discussion below describes the models and reviews the research on its effectiveness.

Adaptive Learning Environments Model

The **adaptive learning environments model** (ALEM) was developed at the Learning Research and Development Center of the University of Pittsburgh. It is, in the views of its developers, an attempt to combine prescriptive or direct instruction with those aspects of open education that have been found to be effective. ALEM is a rather ambitious model that attempts to restructure the school environment, not simply alter the instructional system.

Cooperative Learning Models

Dedicated teachers are always looking for better ideas for meeting the many challenges they face in school, especially as diversity increases in the student population. **Cooperative learning models** provide teachers with effective ways to respond to diverse student bodies by promoting academic achievement and cross-cultural understanding (California Department of Education, 2004).

The Team-Assisted Individualized program (TAI) combines group and individual work for the teaching of mathematics. Students are assigned to four- and five-member heterogeneous teams and are given a placement test to determine placement. During the individualized portion of the program, they work on prepared curriculum materials that include an instruction sheet, several problem sheets, a practice test, and a final test. Students work on their units in teams, helping each other and assisting with the practice tests. The teams receive scores, with special recognition for high performance. The teacher works each day with groups of students who are at about the same point in the curriculum.

Learning-Styles Models

"Even the slowest and most reluctant readers can learn to read well when taught according to their individual learning styles," says Marie Carbo (2003), founder and executive director of the National Reading Styles Institute in Syosset, New York. **Learning-styles models** are built on the assumptions that learners differ significantly in their styles of learning, that those styles can be assessed, and that knowledge of styles can help both teachers and learners.

According to Carbo (2007), students who voluntarily read for their own pleasure improve their reading skills and their test scores at a much faster rate than those who do not. Dr. Carbo provides five effective reading strategies:

1. *Change Negative Perceptions.* Youngsters benefit from high-interest, challenging reading materials; structured choices; powerful modeling of texts; increasingly difficult stories; hands-on skill work; opportunities for mobility; and opportunities to work in groups.

2. *Reduce Stress.* When we reduce the stress associated with reading, students become excited about reading and learning experiences.

3. *Use Powerful Modeling Reading Methods.* Modeling methods help struggling readers bypass the decoding process, read fluently, and concentrate on meaning.

4. *Use Carbo Recordings.* These recordings have enabled students to read challenging reading materials with ease and to make high gains in reading fluency, vocabulary, and comprehension.

5. *Provide Student-Responsive Environments.* Young children—and at-risk readers in particular—tend to be global, tactile, and kinesthetic learners. These children prefer and do well in classrooms that allow for movement, have some comfortable seating and varied lighting, and enable students to work with relative ease in different groupings.

What else should educators do once a student's learning style has been identified? Many learning-style advocates recommend a matching strategy: Find the student's preferred learning style and then provide learning experiences that match that style.

What does the research say about the usefulness of the learning-styles models? First, a considerable body of evidence supports the aspects of cognitive style, especially, playing an important role in learning. Here the dimension of field independence/field dependence is perhaps the most studied. The field-dependent person in perceiving phenomena is less able than the field-independent person to keep an item separate from its context.

For additional information on learning styles, see the following Web resources:

- The National Reading Styles Institute Program, titled Research Update, at www.nrsi.com

- The Northwest Regional Educational Laboratory at www.nwrel.org

- Center for Comprehensive School Reform at www.centerforcsri.org (Carbo, 2003, p. 24)

Mastery Learning Models

As explained in Chapter 2, mastery learning principles were first enunciated by Benjamin Bloom; they have since been adapted in several different approaches. In a review of literature, Anderson (1985) analyzed all these **mastery learning model** approaches and found they have six features in common: clearly specified learning objectives; short, valid assessment procedures; current mastery standards; a sequence of learning units; provision of feedback on learning progress to students; and provision of additional time and help correct specified errors of students' failing to meet the mastery standard. In his review of all the research on mastery learning, Anderson concludes that learning-for-mastery students have outperformed students in conventional classrooms on measures of achievement, retention, learning rate, attitudes, and self-esteem.

He also calls attention to some important findings about the application of the mastery model. First, the research evidence suggests that standards between 85% and 95% correct are most appropriate; setting lower performance standards seems to result in no substantial improvement. Second, the effective use of corrective procedures is critical; in fact, he concludes that corrective instruction targeted to the needs of particular learners and their learning problems is more important than the clarity of the original instruction.

Computer-Based Models

As mentioned in Chapter 14, a number of schools are using a classroom model that involves a high-speed, wireless, Internet-accessible teacher computer, as well as an option of having individual student computers, LCD projector, electronic board, scanner, and access to a color printer. This model allows individual teachers to deliver Web-based technology in their own classrooms. The success of state-of-the-art classroom technology is creating a shift in curriculum design as to how technology best works in schools. For example, in today's classrooms, curriculum leaders are finding that new developments in technology are now helping to promote instructional change as well as enhance student academic achievement.

ADAPTIVE PROGRAMS FOR THE GIFTED

Curriculum leaders have long contended that what schools teach must reflect the needs of society, the needs of the learner, and the recommendations of scholars in various academic fields. Unfortunately, schools are narrowing the curriculum because they are under considerable pressure to show adequate yearly progress in reading and math. Any balanced curriculum should highlight the interconnectedness of various fields of knowledge. Restoring the curriculum balance will require vigorous and committed leadership (Cawelti, 2006).

Most researchers agree that special educational programming is advisable for academically gifted students, although the best type of programming is a matter of controversy (Swiatek & Lupkowski-Shoplik, 2003). The field of gifted education, like the fields of special education and child psychiatry, is experiencing rapid change. These changes are influenced by dramatic ideological, political, economic, and cultural shifts and by recent technological advances. For example, a shift in the intellectual and cultural zeitgeist has made gifted education more vulnerable to challenges from regular education and the inclusion movement and has raised troubling questions about the need for special programs (Pfeiffer, 2003). Focusing on gifted traits that are not solely cognitive provides educators with a way to understand how we can create conditions that will stimulate more people to use their gifts in socially constructive ways (Renzulli, 2002).

Curriculum Tip 15.4	Most adaptive models can be used in educating the gifted and talented.

Several programs have been especially designed to adapt to the special needs of this population. Before reviewing specific adaptive programs, however, it would be useful to identify some general guidelines for developing and evaluating programs for the gifted. In reviewing the literature those that seem to be most widely used by educators still today are the ones proposed by the Leadership Training Institute (as cited in VanTassel-Baska, 1985):

- The content of curricula for the gifted and talented (G/T) should focus on and be organized to include more elaborate, complex, and in-depth study of major ideas, problems, and themes that integrate knowledge within and across systems of thought.

- Curricula for the G/T should allow for the development and application of productive thinking skills to enable students to reconceptualize existing knowledge and/or generate new knowledge.

- Curricula for the G/T should enable students to explore constantly changing knowledge and information and develop the attitude that knowledge is worth pursuing in an open world.

- Curricula for the G/T should encourage exposure to, selection of, and use of specialized and appropriate resources.

- Curricula for the G/T should promote self-initiated and self-directed learning and growth.

- Curricula for the G/T should provide for the development of self-understanding and the understanding of one's relationship to persons, societal institutions, nature, and culture.

- Evaluations of curricula for the G/T should be conducted in accordance with prior stated principles, stressing higher-level thinking skills, creativity, and excellence in performance and products.

Parallel Curriculum for the Gifted

An inescapable truth is that gifted learners vary. Their abilities may be strong in one area and weak in another. Their capabilities may appear easy to some and difficult to others. A gifted student may find easy what a talented student finds difficult.

The concept of a parallel curriculum takes its basic definition from paralleling other forms of curriculum. For example, the overall or umbrella curriculum spans and parallels four different curriculum approaches for the gifted learner. They include: Core Curriculum, Curriculum Connections, Curriculum of Practice, and Curriculum of Identity (Tomlinson et al., 2002). The **Core Curriculum** parallels a discipline while the **Connective Curriculum** makes connections within and across times, cultures, places, and disciplines. The **Curriculum of Practice** guides gifted learners in understanding and applying the facts, concepts, principles, and methodologies of the discipline. The **Curriculum of Identity** guides gifted students to understand their own strengths, preferences, values, and commitment. Teachers who use a parallel curriculum approach do so by creating a challenging and overarching curriculum as well as a framework for thinking.

Compacting

Curriculum **compacting** was first developed by Joe Renzulli at the University of Connecticut. Once demonstrating a level of proficiency in the basic curriculum, compacting allows a student to exchange instructional time for other learning. Compacting is designed to help advanced or gifted learners maximize their use of time for learning. According to noted author Carol Tomlinson (2001), compacting has three stages.

Stage 1: The teacher identifies gifted and talented students who are candidates for compacting and assesses what they do and do not know. Students who are compacting are exempt from whole-class instruction and activities in content areas they have already mastered.

Stage 2: The teacher notes any skills or understandings covered in the study in which the student did not demonstrate mastery. The teacher then lays out a plan to make certain the student achieves those goals and meets those objectives. The plan may require the student to work with other individuals in the classroom.

Stage 3: The teacher and student design an investigation or study for the student to engage in while others are working with the general lessons. Project parameters, goals, timelines, procedures for completing tasks, and criteria for evaluation are determined at that time.

Compacting helps gifted or accelerated learners avoid having to go over mastered material while offering them a chance to challenge themselves in the classroom. This provides for invigorating and productive learning in school.

Discovery Method

The **discovery method**, occasionally referred to as the Socratic method, is often used by teachers when working with gifted and talented students, but it can certainly apply to all students. When children are exposed to the wonders of science, the doors to discovery are opened for them. The more we encourage our children to explore and appreciate the world through the lens of a discoverer, the more likely they will understand the value of global diversity (Connelly, 2007). The perception is that it is often better to "discover" how to perform a skill or tactic than to be directly taught the skill or tactic (Marzano, Pickering, & Pollock, 2001). Through a process of inductive and deductive reasoning, students can become better able to "discover" a deep understanding of a problem, hopefully leading to greater motivation or different levels of learning.

There is little research to substantiate the discovery method, according to Marzano and colleagues (2001). They state that some skills are not amenable to discovery learning. In mathematics, for example, students often are required or need to follow a series of specific steps to reach the solution to a problem. It is better to demonstrate those steps and then provide opportunities for the students than to alter the steps or change them in some way. The key to the success of the discovery-oriented approach probably lies with the teacher and with the student. Both the teacher's and student's awareness and interest in the problem will lead to a point of understanding or to a point of discovery.

Brain-Based Learning

Brain-based learning follows the belief that there are connections between brain function and educational practice (Jensen, 2008). Neurological research has discovered much about how the brain works, but educators need to be cautious when applying this research to teaching (Willis, 2007). Nevertheless, a teacher's ability to give sufficient examples relating to the students' experiences and to involve gifted and talented students in experiences makes the abstract concepts of brain-based learning at least a bit more understandable. According to Patricia Wolfe (2001), many of our strongest neural networks are formed by actual experience. It is often possible to take advantage of this natural proclivity by involving students in solving authentic problems in their school or community. In addition to the obvious benefits of engaging in authentic problem solving, teachers report that it also immeasurably enhances students' motivation, sense of efficacy, and self-esteem. The key is to make curriculum meaningful through brain-engaging problems, projects, and simulations that challenge the student.

Special Pace: Acceleration

Acceleration as an adaptive strategy helps gifted students advance through the grades and master advanced academic content at a rapidly accelerated rate. Thus, a highly gifted 10-year-old might be placed in a ninth-grade science class, or a very intelligent elementary school pupil might be studying the mathematics normally taught in high school. Also, high school students preparing for and taking the Advanced Placement (AP) examinations of the College Entrance Examination Board are experiencing a type of acceleration.

Classroom technology and the Internet can provide an alternative to advancing students into another grade level. Accessing the Internet to build Web sites or to obtain information globally allows gifted and talented students a way to enhance and accelerate learning and still remain in their classrooms. Adaptive hypermedia is a good example of how just one type of program can be used to keep gifted students in a classroom and yet move them into more advanced material.

According to Peter Brusilovsky (2004) of the Carnegie Technology Education Institute, adaptive hypermedia systems can build a model of the goals, preferences, and knowledge of each individual user. For example, a student in an adaptive educational hypermedia system might be given a presentation that is adapted specifically to his or her knowledge of the subject. Suggested sets of most relevant links are also given to the student to proceed further. An adaptive electronic encyclopedia helps personalize the content of an article to augment the user's existing knowledge and interests. A virtual museum can be adapted for the presentation, noting each visited object or path taken by the student. Hypermedia is just one example among hundreds of ways teachers can use technology to build an accelerated program for gifted and talented learners.

Special Curricula

It is crucial when formulating special curricula for the gifted and talented that teachers develop materials that clarify specific learning goals that are implicit in the standards (Hamilton & Stecher, 2004). It is sometimes necessary to supplement state standards with more detailed descriptions of goals and objectives so that teachers and administrators understand what students are expected to know and what they are expected to do. Curricular modifications for the gifted have in general taken two forms: offering special subjects and providing for enrichment activities. In many school districts, gifted students can study subjects ordinarily not included in the curriculum by following independent study programs or by receiving group instruction in a special program. The Philosophy for Children program has been used by many school districts for such purposes, with generally successful results.

Several enrichment models have been used in programs for the gifted. Two of those that seem in widest use are Renzulli's (1977; Renzulli, Reis, & Smith, 1981) triad/RDIM program and Meeker's (1985) SOI model.

Triad/RDIM Program

The **triad/RDIM (Revolving Door Identification Model) program** combines the enrichment triad model originally proposed by Renzulli (1977) with a relatively recent approach to selection, the revolving-door identification model (Renzulli et al., 1981). The enrichment triad model is based on three types of enrichment activities for the gifted. Type I activities are *general exploratory activities* in which learners explore areas of personal interest. Type II activities are *group-training activities*, consisting of materials and instructional techniques designed to develop critical and creative thinking skills. Type III activities are *individual or small-group investigations*, in which students have an opportunity to investigate real problems through research and inquiry.

The revolving-door identification model begins by identifying a pool of the top 15% to 20% of the student population. All these students are exposed to Type I and Type II activities on a regular basis. As these students work on these enriching activities, teachers remain alert for students who demonstrate signs of interest, creativity, task commitment, and advanced ability. As a student is so identified, the teacher encourages the student to move into a Type III activity, using either the resources of the regular classroom or the special "resource room" until the project is completed.

On the basis of implementation studies in 30 Connecticut schools, Reis and Renzulli (1984) were able to identify several key features that account for successful programs: thorough orientation of teachers, parents, and administrators; extensive planning by the local school team; in-service and administrative support; schoolwide enrichment teams composed of the principal, the resource teacher, classroom teachers, parents, and in some cases a student; developing in the entire staff a sense of ownership of the program; detailed orientation of the students; communication with prime interest groups; program flexibility; and evaluation and program monitoring.

The triad/RDIM program seems to be a very productive means for providing interesting learning experiences. The obvious question arises again, however: Why for only the top 20%?

Guilford's Structure of the Intellect Model

Over the course of several decades, J. P. Guilford (1977) has been conducting research on and refining his **structure of the intellect**, represented by a three-dimensional cube. The three dimensions are the five contents of the intellect, the six products of the intellect, and the five operations of the intellect. Of the 120 possible intellectual abilities that result from the intersection of these three dimensions, 96 have been substantiated through testing. Mary Meeker and her associates (Meeker, Meeker, & Roid, 1985) were able to validate 26 of those factored abilities as necessary for successful learning. Those 26 intellectual abilities have been used to develop several tests that have been very useful in identifying potentially gifted students, especially minority students. Meeker has found in her own work that Blacks, Hispanics, and Native Americans score higher on some SOI measures than do White students. The SOI model has also been useful in diagnosing and prescribing for the developmental needs of the gifted.

Special Resources

The third general approach is to provide special resources—that is, special schools (such as the Bronx High School of Science), special summer programs, or special mentors for the gifted. Of these, mentoring deserves perhaps a more detailed examination here. The mentoring approach involves associating a gifted student with an adult mentor who can serve as a role model, provide support and encouragement, and give the necessary direction on a one-to-one basis. VanTassel-Baska (1985) noted that some mentoring programs are more highly structured, requiring a contract between mentor and student that stipulates the tasks to be accomplished, the types of supports provided, and a schedule for completion.

Staffing for Gifted and Talented Students

Teachers around the country are entrusted with the task of fostering the academic and intellectual development of the students they teach. The conundrum is that each teacher is a unique individual just as each student is a unique individual. The challenge that arises is that some teachers who are particularly effective in teaching one group of students may not be equally effective in teaching other students.

The expertise, certain personality traits, and cognitive style preferences of teachers may be critical as to how they teach. Carol Mills, PhD, from Johns Hopkins University, recommends that we expose gifted students to many different styles of teaching and to teachers with many different cognitive preferences. In a study, Dr. Mills (2003) found that the personality types of teachers are similar to the personality types of the gifted students. This suggests that teachers who are judged to be highly effective in working with gifted students prefer abstract themes and concepts, are open and flexible, and value logical analysis and objectivity. Results suggest that a teacher's personality and cognitive style may play a role in his or her effectiveness in teaching gifted students. According to Dr. Mills, students need to understand styles other than their own.

PROVIDING FOR ACADEMICALLY CHALLENGED LEARNERS

Conceptions of how best to educate students with disabilities have shifted toward one of two extremes: denying that disabilities exist or accommodating them to the extent that there is no expectation of student progress toward realistic goals. The authors contend that both attitudes seem to defeat the primary educational aim of helping all students achieve their highest potential.

In this light the authors believe that education will change rather dramatically, because of the implementation of Response to Intervention (RTI). William Bender and Cara Shores (2007), in their book *Response to Intervention: A Practical Guide for Every Teacher*, noted that this change has been prompted by several legislative measures, including the No Child Left Behind (NCLB) legislation and more specifically the 2004 Reauthorization of Individuals with Disabilities Education Act (IDEA). This metamorphosis is much broader than merely a new way to document the existence of a learning disability. All educators will become involved in implementation of programs to demonstrate how students respond on an individual basis to various education interventions. Most of the early work required by the RTI procedures for a particular child will take place in the general education classroom. Thus, this initiative will not only affect special educators; all educators will be expected to implement this procedure in their classes.

Michael Giangreco's (2007), professor of education at the University of Vermont, views seem to follow with RTI guidelines in that he believes students rarely need both an individualized education program and individualized supports all the time. He believes the first placement option for each student with a disability is the regular classroom.

Dealing with disabilities is a lifelong process. James Kauffman (Kauffman, McGee, & Brigham, 2004), a professor of education at the University of Virginia, notes that many successful adults with disabilities express common themes when asked about their ability to succeed in the face of a disability. Tom Cray, a Rhodes Scholar who has a severe learning disability, claimed that having to deal with the hardest experiences gave him the greatest strength.

As explained in Chapter 4, Public Law 94-142 was landmark legislation that radically changed how the schools were to provide for these special students. Four basic rights and protections are specified in PL 94-142. According to Macmillan's (1982) analysis of the law, they are the right to due process in the classification and placement of learners, protection against discriminatory testing during assessment, placement in the least restrictive educational setting, and Individualized Educational Programs (IEPs).

Curriculum Tip 15.5	Response to Intervention (RTI) is likely to affect almost every classroom and every teacher in the nation.

Early Intervention

In reviewing the literature, a combination of school and teacher factors was found by researcher Barbara Taylor, EdD (2001), to be the most important factors in beating the odds in teaching all children how to read. Factors to use in **early intervention** include the following:

- Schools with strong links to parents

- Collaboration of teaching staff

- Shared system for assessing oral reading fluency, accuracy, and text level

- Extensive professional development on instructional practices

An emphasis on one-on-one instruction is also an important factor. Taylor (2001) notes some great strategies used in early intervention by teachers:

- Small-group instruction
- Time for independent reading
- Communication and reading with parents
- Applying word identification
- Asking higher-level questions

These are all excellent early-intervention strategies used by accomplished primary-grade teachers in effective schools. According to Barbara Taylor, they have been especially effective in large urban poverty environments.

Since the relationships between poverty environments and developmental learning problems have been clearly established, most early-intervention programs have focused on the children of the poor. Increasingly, such programs have attempted to reach infant children and their parents, on the theory that *the earlier, the better.*

Early-Intervention Programs

Reading Recovery, Reading for Success, and other interventions are now being used extensively in schools. Of all the early literacy interventions being used, Reading Recovery is the most well known and most widely implemented. To date, Reading Recovery teachers have taught 1.6 million children in the United States.

An independent review of experimental research by the What Works Clearinghouse (WWC, 2007), a branch of the United States Department of Education and the Institute of Education Sciences, clearly determined Reading Recovery to be an effective intervention based on scientific research. As shown in Exhibit 15.2, the WWC report findings indicated that Reading Recovery leads to positive effects on students' alphabetics skills and general reading achievement. A finding of positive effects is the WWC's strongest evidenced rating. For example, Reading Recovery was found to have positive effects on students' alphabetics skills and general reading achievement outcomes. Students average over 34 percentile points in alphabetic and over 32 percentile points in general reading achievement. They also found potentially positive effects, the next highest evidence rating, on fluency with an average of 46 percentile points and an average of 14 percentile points on comprehension.

Students in Reading Recovery are taught by a specially trained teacher individually one-half hour each school day for a total of 12 to 20 weeks. Each daily lesson includes the five essential components of reading instruction described in *A Principal's Guide to Reading Recovery* (Reading Recovery Council of North America, 2002). As soon as a student demonstrates that they have developed effective reading and writing strategies and that they are likely to show continued achievement in literacy, the intervention is discontinued. The student, in effect, has moved from a position of not being able to profit from the classroom literacy instruction and needing special assistance to a position of being able to profit from classroom literacy instruction without any additional special assistance.

EXHIBIT 15.2 Four Studies Found Two Positive Effects, Alphabetic and General Reading Achievement, and Two Potentially Positive Effects, Comprehension and Fluency of Students

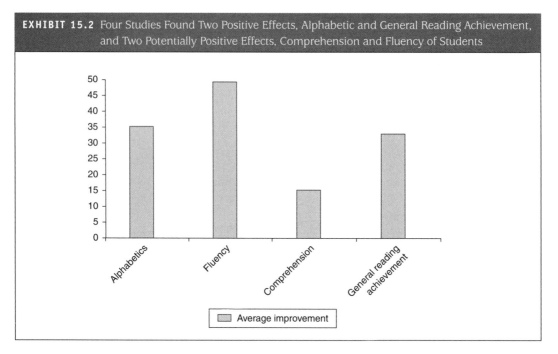

SOURCE: Adapted from What Works Clearinghouse (2007).

The hallmark of Reading Recovery is its accountability for student outcomes. According to *A Site Coordinator's Guide to the Effective Implementation of Reading Recovery,* (Reading Recovery Council of North America, 2006), the goal of Reading Recovery is to dramatically reduce both the number of students in first grade who are at risk of literacy failure and the cost of these learners to the school district. How effective is Reading Recovery? During the 2005–2006 school year, 108,000 Reading Recovery students were taught nationally. Seventy-six percent of the students who received a full series of lessons met the rigorous criteria for discontinuing the intervention. These students demonstrated that they were at or above their classroom average for reading and writing ability (Gomez-Bellenge & Rogers, 2007). As Dr. Garreth Zalud, trainer and director of the University of South Dakota Regional Reading Recovery Training Center, said, "These data are astounding when one considers the fact that the Reading Recovery program serves the lowest achieving students" (personal communication, September 28, 2007).

Reading Recovery may also be used as a pre-referral service or Response to Intervention as described by the Individuals with Disabilities Education Improvement Act (2004). Children who make progress in Reading Recovery but do not meet the rigorous criteria for discontinuing the intervention may be recommended for long-term support or additional assessment (Zalud, 2005–2006). In these instances, the assessment, strong documentation, and record keeping used by Reading Recovery are extremely beneficial to future planning for individuals.

Historically, schools developed concepts of **mainstreaming/inclusion** in schools. This approach advocated that special education children be allowed to remain in the regular classroom. Individuals supporting mainstreaming worked together to develop an awareness of the benefits of inclusion and how it may have a positive impact on mildly handicapped learners.

Today, the focus is less on mainstreaming and/or inclusion and more on a Response to Intervention (RTI) model. Below are guidelines that outline the RTI process.

1. Make certain that the reading curriculum utilized in the general education classrooms is a research-validated instructional curriculum and that teachers are trained in the use for that curriculum. If those conditions are met, then the "Tier One" intervention may become merely a "progress monitoring" of the child's progress on a weekly basis, and not a separate instructional intervention that must be implemented.

2. Train faculty in interventions that have a sound scientific base, in order to ensure treatment fidelity. In that sense, implementation of RTI can benefit all students, not only students who might be eligible for special services.

3. Use content experts as the independent observers for Tier One and Tier Two. In the case of reading disability, use a reading teacher, a master-level general education/special education teacher, or a school psychologist with expertise in instruction for those observations.

4. Using persons who would be spending time assessing the child under the traditional discrepancy-based paradigm (i.e., a school psychologist), as the observer offers the option of replacing one set of eligibility duties of that person with another. Thus, no additional resources are needed and fewer resources will be required because the eligibility determination no longer requires such extensive individualized assessment.

5. Use a different observer for the Tier One and Tier Two interventions when possible. In that fashion, more educators have actually seen how the student responds to intervention, and thus more will be qualified to suggest additional instructional ideas.

6. For Tier Two interventions, develop systems whereby students who need a Tier Two intervention may join in small-group instruction that is already ongoing in the school. For example, many Title One programs and/or various early intervention programs in reading or math involve small-group instruction (as is required in Tier Two). Thus, for Tier Two interventions, students may be assigned to those groups for one grading period, and their progress may be charted either daily or weekly.

7. Prior to Tier Three interventions, an eligibility committee must meet and formally determine that the child has not been responsive to instruction in Tier One and Tier Two. Thus, a committee meeting is called for whenever a student is unresponsive to Tier One and Tier Two interventions, and the Tier Three intervention takes place under the rubric of special educational services.

Tiers one, two and three refer to levels of instruction.

SOURCE: From *Response to Intervention: A Practical Guide for Every Teacher*, by W. N. Bender and C. Shores, 2007, Thousand Oaks, CA: Corwin Press & Council for Exceptional Children, p. 41.

More schools are now embracing the concept of RTI. As a result, fewer students are being pulled out of their regular education classrooms and placed in special education settings.

Special Curricula

The hope is that RTI and other curricular modifications will make an impact at both elementary and secondary school levels. In general, most curricula for the academically challenged students have emphasized the development of the basic skills, along with expressing a broader concern for improving social skills, helping learners manage their own behavior, and improving their cognitive skills. It is important, however, to avoid a "scattershot type of curriculum" when planning units and lessons for challenged learners. Scattershot approaches have insufficient planning, the objectives are not tied to goals, and goals are not tied to the school mission statement or vision. This form of curriculum planning is often unreliable and is hit or miss at best. It is a hodgepodge of instructional aims and subject matter whose content and expectations vary sharply from classroom to classroom (Jerald, 2003). It is important to have a focused and well-planned curriculum when developing and implementing cognitive skills for academically challenged learners.

The emphasis on the cognitive skills seems especially promising, because recent research has provided some productive insights into the special learning problems of the learning handicapped. A review of such research suggests that the following specific cognitive deficiencies are prevalent among this group: They are deficient in attention; have poor short-term memory; make inadequate use of memory strategies; have slower perceptual speed; are less efficient at categorizing incoming data into chunks; fail to organize input efficiently; use memory rehearsal strategies inefficiently; and cannot plan, select, sequence, and evaluate the use of such strategies.

BILINGUAL EDUCATION

In recent years, schools have made some progress in meeting the needs of culturally and linguistically diverse students, especially bilingual students with special education needs. Nonetheless, this area is fraught with controversy, and perhaps there is no area of the school's curriculum that has been the subject of such vehement controversy as bilingual education.

According to Klingner and Artiles (2003), the percentage of students from diverse cultures is growing in schools across the United States. For example, there are English language learners (ELLs) in all 50 states as well as Puerto Rico, the Virgin Islands, and Guam. These students speak a variety of languages and come from diverse social, cultural, and economic backgrounds. There are greater numbers of ELLs in the states that have historically been affected by them, but there are also many in states that until very recently had none (Hill & Flynn, 2006).

Adolescent ELLs come to the classroom with widely diverse education backgrounds and socioeconomic circumstances. The Carnegie Corporation of New York asked the Center for

Applied Linguistics to convene a panel of researchers, policymakers, and practitioners to identify ways to improve the academic literacy of adolescent ELLs. The advisory panel found that the U.S. education system faces major institutional obstacles in responding to the needs of this diverse and growing population (Perkins-Gough, 2007).

Curriculum Tip 15.6	Controversy regarding bilingual education has normally revolved around four issues: What is bilingual education? How extensive is the need for special education for those with limited English proficiency (LEP)? To what extent should local districts have flexibility in responding to those needs? Is bilingual education effective for such students?

As indicated in Chapter 4, bilingual educational programs were institutionalized in the law primarily as a result of political forces. The political controversies surrounding bilingual education continue, with partisans unable to agree on several issues.

What Is Bilingual Education?

Bilingual education refers to the practice of teaching non-English-speaking children in their native language. Developed in the 1960s, such programs were intended to allow children to progress in subjects such as math, science, and social studies while they learned English in a separate class. Bilingual education was meant as a transitional program, but students frequently linger in such programs for most of their school years.

Central to understanding all the controversy is having some clear understanding of several complex and somewhat ambiguous terms. As noted below, much of the controversy focuses on matters of definition, so to be as objective as possible, the following definitions have been drawn from a review of the literature (chiefly from Fillmore & Valadez, 1986).

- *Submersion programs.* These are sink-or-swim approaches—essentially non-programs that make no effort to accommodate the special needs of LEP students.

- *English as a Second Language (ESL) programs.* **ESL programs** are formal courses that teach English as a foreign language to nonnative speakers. In the strictest sense of the term, such courses should not be categorized as *bilingual education.*

Bilingual Education

The two significant characteristics of **bilingual education**, as Fillmore and Valadez (1986) defined the term, are these: Instruction is given in two languages—English (in the United States) and the home language of the LEP student; and instruction in English is given in a way that permits students to learn it as a second language. As will be noted below, the definition of the term has become a matter of much controversy.

Bilingual Transition Programs

There are several types of transitional programs that have the chief goal of enabling LEP students to move as quickly as possible into an all-English program of studies; dual language in instruction is offered only until LEP students have acquired enough English to deal with instruction in English.

Bilingual Maintenance Programs

In bilingual maintenance programs, the goal is to develop proficiency in both languages; students remain in these programs even after they have achieved proficiency in English.

How Extensive Is the Need?

Partisans in the debate about bilingual education cannot agree on even the extent of the need. Most states refer to federal guidelines involving English as a Second Language (ESL). For example, in Montana (Montana Office of Public Instruction, 2004), limited English proficiency (LEP) refers to the following:

- Individuals who were not born in the United States or whose native language is a language other than English

- Individuals who come from an environment where a language other than English is dominant

- Individuals who are American Indian and/or Alaskan Natives who come from environments where a language other than English has had significant impact on their level of language proficiency

Is Bilingual Education Effective?

The challenge is the increasing number of bilingual students who need special education help. Educators are becoming concerned about the overrepresentation of culturally and linguistically diverse students in certain special-education categories—learning disabilities, mental retardation, and emotional disturbance—and their underrepresentation in programs for the gifted and talented (Klingner & Artiles, 2003). One of the major problems has been the assessment of culturally and linguistically diverse students. This situation is being addressed through the No Child Left Behind Act and through the testing of subgroups. Nonetheless, it still continues to be fraught with theoretical misunderstandings and flawed practices (Klingner & Artiles, 2003).

Several possible solutions to this problem emerge. First, professional development needs to be provided to enhance professionals' understanding of culturally and linguistically challenged students. Second, administrators need to make sure that professionals with expertise in English-language acquisition should be present during meetings relating to the Student Assistant Team, Child Study Team, and the Individualized Educational Program. Incorporating these strategies will help develop a better understanding and awareness for our bilingual programs as well as provide needed help to some of our culturally diverse and linguistically challenged students.

SUMMARY

This chapter analyzes the types of individualized programs that promote student choice, curriculum integration, differentiated learning, and self-assessment that engage students deeply in learning. The chapter reviews previous attempts to respond to individual differences, and it assesses current models. The chapter concludes by examining the challenging problems inherent in providing for ESL students as well as other special student populations. Chapter topics include early attempts that were made to individualize curriculum and current successful examples of individualized programs. The chapter also includes individualized adaptive approaches that are being used in gifted education as well as examples of other specialized curriculum and how they are enhancing concepts of individualization. Finally, the role of bilingual education in individualizing curriculum is addressed.

APPLICATIONS

1. Some have argued that all learning is individualized: The learner makes individual meaning out of what is learned. They continue by disparaging the need for any type of individualized or adaptive instruction, contending that group-paced learning can be just as effective. How would you respond to such an argument?

2. Identify a subject or grade level you know well. Which of the adaptive approaches do you think would work best? Explain your choice and the reasons supporting it.

3. Some have suggested that knowledge about learning styles will produce an "educational revolution." Others are much less sanguine about the possibilities, pointing out that the research so far has not yielded significant gains for learning styles adaptations. As you review the models described in this chapter and analyze the research findings, what position do you take regarding this issue?

4. If teachers adhere to the principles shown in Exhibit 15.1, differentiation can liberate students from stereotypical expectations and experience and provide equity of success to excellence. What should be done in the school district where you are employed to make differentiation a reality?

5. Suppose you were not limited by laws, such as PL 94-142, that mandate mainstreaming and/or inclusion. As an educational leader, would you use mainstreaming and/or inclusion in your school? On what grounds would you justify your position?

6. How would you justify and present adding a Reading Recovery or similar program to the board of education?

7. Politicians often are afraid their votes against bilingual education will be perceived as hostile to minorities. This is ironic, since a READ Institute survey showed that 81% of Hispanics wanted their children to learn English first; only 12% wanted their children taught in Spanish. ProEnglish supports state initiatives to end bilingual education and believes the federal government should stop funding bilingual education programs exclusively and leave such decisions to states and local school districts. While ProEnglish endorses the teaching of second languages, it believes the first responsibility of our public school system is to teach children English. Should students spend one full school

year intensively learning English? Why? (See www.proenglish.org/issues/education/beindex.html to help with your response.)

CASE STUDY   Response to Intervention (RTI) Issues

Maintaining academically challenged students in the regular classroom can be rewarding, but it can also pose some difficulties. The following is an example of how one Colorado school principal handled a problem that involved keeping an at-risk student in the regular classroom.

Mr. Rusk, a sixth-grade teacher, meets with middle school principal Susan Thomas in her office.

He says, "I want to visit with you about a student remaining in my sixth-grade classroom." He appears to be angry. "I'm upset that this student is not being placed in special education."

"Well, I'm glad you were able to come down to the office so that we can talk about this," says the principal.

"And what are we going to do about this?" asks Mr. Rusk, still sounding agitated.

"Well, it is an interesting problem," says the principal, smiling. "As you already know, Response to Intervention is now a major focus of our program. RTI is mandated, and that means that we want our students to be in the regular classroom as much as possible. We expect that you will assist with providing the interventions needed to help this student." She further explains that she, as principal, has to follow the law and implement the RTI guidelines.

"Well, I will have to take the student," says Mr. Rusk.

The principal replies, "Yes, It will be great in having you help develop the intervention strategies for this student. Let me check around and ask some teachers what strategies they are using in their classrooms that meet the RTI guidelines. Maybe they'll have some suggestions. I'll get back to you as soon as possible."

The Challenge

Making sure the school addresses the needs of all students and follows federal guidelines is a critical component of any curriculum across the country. Analyze how the principal handled the situation. How can she best share her experiences as to RTI implementation with principals and teacher leaders from other schools?

Key Issues/Questions

1. What are your impressions of Principal Thomas and how she dealt with the issue of RTI? Did the principal adequately address the teacher's concerns? Why or why not?

2. What are your beliefs about RTI? How much in-service should administrators provide regarding RTI guidelines?

3. If the principal meets with a teacher about RTI, what should be discussed? When should the teacher be first involved in the discussion?

4. What are your feelings on mandated government programs? Do you feel that RTI is a viable option for academically challenged students?

5. What are some innovative approaches that principals and teacher–leaders might use to address RTI concerns? Identify specific strategies and explain why you think they might be effective.

WEBLIOGRAPHY

Assistive technology and inclusion
www.newhorizons.org/spneeds/inclusion/teaching/sax.htm

Association for Positive Behavior
www.apbs.org

Center for Evidence-Based Practice: Young Children with Challenging Behavior
http://challengingbehavior.fmhi.usf.edu

Council for Children With Behavioral Disorders
www.ccbd.net

Emotional intelligence resource
www.eq.org

George Lucas Educational Foundation's Edutopia site
www.edutopia.org

Institute for EQ Education/Emotional Intelligence
www.6seconds.org/school

Kentucky Department of Education and the University of Kentucky behavior home page
www.state.ky.us/agencies/behave/homepage.html

Learning Generation report on promoting the use of technology in special-education classrooms
http://learngen.org/cohorts/spedclass

PBS Misunderstood Minds—resources for instructional strategies
www.pbs.org/wgbh/misunderstoodminds

Reading Recovery
www.whatworks.ed.gov

SMARTer Kids Foundation online strategies to help teach special-education students
http://smarterkids.org

Using Technology to Raise the Achievement of ALL Students Initiative
www.accessibletech4all.org

Glossary

Academic Scientism. This describes the academic period from 1890 to 1916 that derives from the two influences: the academic and the scientific. The academic influence was the result of systematic and somewhat effective efforts of colleges to shape curriculum for basic education; scientific influence resulted from the attempts of educational theorists to use newly developed scientific knowledge in making decisions about the mission of the school and the content of the curriculum.

Acceleration. Acceleration is an adaptive strategy that helps gifted students advance through the grades and master advanced academic content at a rapidly accelerated rate.

Adaptive curricula. Adaptive curricula and instructional practices are educational processes that arrange the conditions and materials of learning so that they fit individual learner differences.

Adaptive learning environments model. This model is an attempt to combine prescriptive or direct instruction with those aspects of open education that have been found to be effective.

Affective education. The affective education movement emphasized the feelings and values of the child. While cognitive development was considered important, it was seen only as an adjunct to affective growth.

Anticipatory set. An anticipatory set helps students develop a mental set that allows them to focus on what will be learned.

Asynchronous. "When used to describe computer-mediated communication, it indicates that communication can take place without both parties being logged on at the same time, as messages can be left for subsequent reading" (Hoesing, 2004, p. 11 [see Chapter 14]).

Authentic task. An assignment given to students designed to assess their ability to apply standard-driven knowledge and skills to real-world challenges.

Back to the heart of education. The basic essence of teaching and learning.

Benchmarks. Benchmarks are points along a path toward learning a new skill or set of skills.

Bilingual programs. In bilingual programs the goal is to develop proficiency in both the formal language as well as a secondary language.

Blended learning. The term used to describe learning, training activities, or events where more traditional delivery methods are combined (Hoesing, 2004 [see Chapter 14]).

Brain-based learning. Brain-based learning follows the belief that there are connections between brain function and educational practice.

Charter schools. Charter schools are nonsectarian public schools of choice that operate with freedom from many of the regulations that apply to traditional public schools.

Child-centered curriculum. A child-centered curriculum is an approach whereby the child is the beginning point, the determiner, and the shaper of the curriculum. Although the developing child will at some point acquire knowledge of subject matter, the disciplines are seen as only one type of learning. Elements of child-centered curricula include affective education, open education, and developmental education.

Circle writing. Circle writing involves students creating a template for designing opening questions for discussion. The opening question becomes a starting point for circle writing. Each student adds his or her perspective as the paper is shared around the classroom.

Class diagnostic summary. A class diagnostic summary gives information about the test results of all the students in the class, objective by objective.

Committee of Fifteen. The Committee of Fifteen, commissioned by NEA in the early 1890s, was appointed to make recommendations for elementary-school curriculum.

Committee of Ten. The Committee of Ten, commissioned by NEA in 1893, was appointed to make recommendations for high school curriculum.

Community-based learning model. A community-based learning model is an approach based around an interdisciplinary theme that integrates educational experiences and closely parallels the way people learn. A community-based learning model makes it possible for teachers to draw on external communities that promote divergent thinking.

Compacting. Once demonstrating a level of proficiency in the basic curriculum, compacting allows a student to exchange instructional time for other learning.

Conceptual empiricists. Conceptual empiricists are those who derive their research methodologies from the physical sciences in attempting to produce generalizations that will enable educators to control and predict what happens in schools.

Conformists. Conformists are individuals who believe that the existing order is a good one—the best of all possible worlds.

Connective curriculum. Connective curriculum makes connections within and across times, cultures, places, and disciplines.

Content-oriented theories. Content-oriented theories are concerned primarily with specifying the major sources that should influence the selection and organization of the curriculum content.

Context evaluation. Context evaluation continually assesses needs and problems in the context to help decision makers determine goals and objectives.

Cooperative development. Cooperative development is an option usually provided only to experienced and competent teachers; it enables small groups of teachers to work together in a collegial relationship for mutual growth. It is intended to be a teacher-centered, teacher-directed process that respects the professionalism of competent teachers.

Cooperative learning models. These are models that provide teachers with effective ways to respond to diverse students by promoting academic achievement and cross-cultural understanding and to have students working in groups to reinforce concepts taught by the teacher.

Core curriculum. This curriculum is based on the concept there is a uniform body of knowledge that all students should know. Core curriculum parallels a discipline.

Core curriculum movement. The core curriculum movement is a movement that assumes there is a uniform body of knowledge that all students should know.

Correlating curricula. Correlating curricula is a process of aligning contents of two or more subjects. It is an interdisciplinary approach whereby teachers are organized into teams to plan for correlated lessons.

Course of study. A course of study is all the planned learning experiences for a period of 1 year or less in a given field of study.

Critical thinking skills. Critical thinking skills are skills that provide a set of information and belief based on intellectual commitment.

Curriculum alignment. Curriculum alignment is a process of ensuring that the written, taught, and tested curricula are closely congruent.

Curriculum-development team. A curriculum-development team is a team comprising administrators, teachers, and parents who review and plan curriculum for a district.

Curriculum evaluation. Curriculum evaluation is the assessment of the merit and worth of a program of studies, a field of study, or a course of study.

Curriculum guide. A curriculum guide has components that include specific learning objectives and the activities suggested for each objective. It is intentionally designed to meet district and state standards and is used to aid teachers in planning and developing teacher plans and strategies for specific subject areas.

Curriculum-objectives notebook. The curriculum-objectives notebook is a loose-leaf notebook that contains the following: a summary of the research on how to teach a given subject, a copy of the scope-and-sequence chart in reduced form, and a list of the objectives for those grade levels taught by the teacher to whom the guide is issued.

Curriculum of identity. Curriculum of identity guides students in coming to understand their own strengths, preferences, values, and commitment by reflecting on their own development through the lens of contributors and professionals.

Curriculum of practice. Curriculum of practice guides gifted learners in understanding and applying the facts, concepts, principles, and methodologies of the discipline.

Curriculum planning. Curriculum planning is the specification and sequencing of major decisions to be made in the future with regard to educational curriculum. Specific details of the curriculum-planning process are determined by the level and nature of curriculum work; designing a field of studies, improving a program of studies, and developing a course of study involve quite different processes.

Curriculum-scenario book. The curriculum-scenario book is a collection of learning scenarios, a practical account, to help determine what mix of learning activities, learning materials, and learning objectives can result in quality learning experiences.

· **Curriculum specialist.** The term *curriculum specialist* is used to designate any administrator or supervisor with responsibility for and training in curriculum development.

Curriculum theory. Curriculum theory is a way of noting philosophy of certain approaches and strategies to the development and enactment of curriculum. Theory is often considered a formalized, deductively connected bundle of laws that are applicable in specifiable ways to their observable manifestations.

Data-analysis report. Data-analysis report is a way of summarizing and aggregating results from individuals or groups about curriculum and school communities. If, however, an evaluation has been conducted that employs a control group, or measures changes in program participants over time, then it might be appropriate to employ *inferential* analysis in which a decision is made about whether the particular results of the study are "real." A data-analysis report provides data to analyze and utilize information

Descriptive curriculum. Descriptive curriculum is curriculum not merely based on what ought to happen but on what is actually happening in the classroom.

Developmental Conformism. Developmental Conformism (1941–1956) is a period marked by rather intensive interest in the educational implications of child and adolescent development. Dewey, among others, had long been concerned with delineating and responding to the stages of growth in children and youth. The two trends, developmental abilities and needs of youth and a concern with conformity, were the focus during this 15-year period.

Developmental education. A term referring to any curriculum theory that stresses the developmental stages of child growth as the primary determiners of placement and sequence.

Diagnostic–prescriptive model. A model that structures the field of study as a series of sequential nongraded levels of learning. It is an approach that represents observation, planning, teaching, obtaining feedback, monitoring, and revising instruction.

Differentiated professional development. Differentiated professional development is essentially a reconceptualization of the supervisory function, one that attempts to broaden the practitioner's view of supervision.

Discipline-based curriculum. This model uses the standard disciplines as the fields or organizing centers of learning.

Discovery method. The discovery method allows students to "discover" how to perform a skill or tactic rather than to be directly taught the skill or tactic.

Dynamic knowledge. Dynamic knowledge refers to metacognitive strategies, cognitive processes, thinking skills, and content-area procedural knowledge. In dynamic knowledge, curricula and teachers no longer serve solely as static knowledge options but assist in the development of a knowledge base that is student centered and enhances effective thinking on the part of the individual learner.

Early intervention. Early intervention is a system of coordinated services that promotes the child's growth and development and supports families during the critical years. Early-intervention services to eligible children and families are federally mandated through the Individuals with Disabilities Act.

Effective schools process. Effective schools process is a way of creating schools in which all children make progress and are ready for study at the next grade level.

E-learning. The delivery of a learning, training, or education program by electronic means. E-learning involves the use of an electronic device to facilitate and enhance learning by means of one-way and two-way interactive video, audio, personal computers, CD-ROMs, and the Internet (Hoesing, 2004 [see Chapter 14]).

Elective model. Individuals advocating elective models view the curriculum as a multipath network.

Elements of lesson design. Basic underpinnings of a lesson design.

Enrichment curriculum. Throughout the year each classroom teacher provides a number of special experiences and activities. These range from special programs and projects in the classroom to field trips and class excursions.

Equity principle. This involves teachers having high expectations and strong support for all students being able to learn.

ESL programs. English as Second Language (ESL) programs are formal courses that teach English as a foreign language to nonnative speakers.

Field of study. A field of study is all the planned learning experiences over a multiyear period in a given discipline or area of study.

Futurists. Individuals who, rather than being attuned to the present problems of the society, look to the coming age.

Goal-based design. Goal-based design is the setting of clear and practical goals that will expand the curriculum.

Goal-based model. A goal-based model is a curriculum model that aligns the district's educational goals with appropriate curricular fields. This model provides organizing strategies to determine the locus of control in decision making and what organizational structures are needed.

Guided practice. Posing questions that gradually lead students from easy or familiar examples to new understandings is a teaching strategy known as guided practice. The strategy is effective for teaching thinking skills as well as content.

Hidden curriculum. The hidden curriculum is the unintended curriculum—what students learn from the school's culture and climate. It includes such elements as the use of time, allocation of space, funding for programs and activities, and disciplinary policies and practices. For example, if an elementary school allocates 450 minutes each week to reading and 45 minutes to art, the hidden message to students is that "art doesn't matter."

Independent practice. The process of assigning independent practice of a process or skill, used to reinforce understanding.

Individual student report. An individual student report provides comprehensive information for each student; it also is distributed after each major testing. It gives the student's name and indicates the number correct and incorrect for all objectives.

Input. The process of giving students information about the knowledge, skill, or process they are to achieve.

Input evaluation. Input evaluation assesses alternative means for achieving those goals to help decision makers choose optimal means.

Integrated curriculum. A teaching method that attempts to break down barriers between subjects to make learning more meaningful.

Intensive development. It is an intensive and systematic process in which a supervisor, an administrator, or an expert teacher works closely with an individual teacher in an attempt to effect significant improvement in the essential skills of teaching.

Intentional curriculum. Intentional curriculum is the set of learnings that the school system consciously intends, in contradistinction to the hidden curriculum, which by and large is not a product of conscious intention. It has the following components: the written, the supported, the taught, and the tested.

Interdisciplinary courses. Interdisciplinary courses are those courses related to and/or characterized by participation of two or more fields of study. They are courses of study that either integrate content from two or more disciplines (such as English and social studies) or ignore the disciplines totally when organizing learning experiences.

International Reading Association (IRA). The International Reading Association is a professional organization created in 1956 to improve reading instruction.

Internet. The Internet is a global collection of networks connected together in different ways to form a single entity. It has broadcasting capability throughout the entire world and is a mechanism for information dissemination and a medium for collaboration or interaction between individuals and their computers without regard to geographic location (Remondino & Chen, 2004 [see Chapter 14]).

Knowledge-centered curricula. Curricula advocating a knowledge-centered approach whereby disciplines and/or bodies of knowledge are the primary determiners of what is taught.

Learned curriculum. The learned curriculum is the bottom-line curriculum—what students learn. Clearly it is the most important of all.

Learned (experiential) curriculum. This is the curriculum students are actually learning.

Learning scenario. A learning scenario is a sequence of concepts from domain knowledge represented by a series of activities. As the learning process proceeds the scenario is changed dynamically to better suit actual learner characteristics.

Learning-styles models. Learning-styles models are built on the assumptions that learners differ significantly in their styles of learning, that those styles can be assessed, and that knowledge of styles can help both teachers and learners.

Lesson. A lesson is a set of related learning experiences typically lasting from 20 to 60 minutes, focusing on a relatively small number of objectives.

Mainstreaming/inclusion. This approach advocates that special-education children be allowed to remain in the regular classroom whenever appropriate.

Mastery curriculum. Mastery curriculum proposes students work on a subject until they demonstrate mastery of it, which may be indicted by a grade of 90% or better on each and every assignment. Although most students complete their coursework on a timeframe similar to that in conventional schools, the mastery curriculum can accommodate students who may need more time on a particular subject or who want to speed up their progress.

Mastery learning models. Mastery learning models have six features in common: clearly specified learning objectives; short, valid assessment procedures; current mastery standards; a sequence of learning units; provision of feedback on learning progress to students; and provision of additional time and help to correct specified errors of students' failing to meet the mastery standard.

Mentorship. Mentoring is a form of teaching and sharing that invites an individual to learn from another's example.

Merit. The term *merit* refers to the intrinsic value of an entity—value that is implicit, inherent, and independent of any applications.

Metacognition. Metacognition is usually presented as a conscious and deliberate mental activity—we become aware that we don't understand a paragraph we read or a statement we hear.

Modeling. Demonstrating a process or skill.

Modern Conservatism. The academic period from 2000 to the present, evidenced by a move toward accountability. This period is marked by profound independence of the mind, intellectual equalitarianism, and distrust of traditional values. The No Child Left Behind Act (NCLB) and Response to Intervention (RTI) are typical federal programs of this time.

Monoethnic Courses (Phase 1). Originally, multicultural education was linked only to concerns about racism in schooling because African Americans demanded that schools respond to their needs and aspirations. Included in those demands were (a) textbooks that would accurately reflect African American history and culture, (b) community control of Black schools, and (c) Black teachers for African American youth (Banks, 1994 [see Chapter 2]).

Multicultural education. Multicultural education is a process that permeates all aspects of school practices, policies, and organization as a means to ensure the highest levels of academic achievement for all students. It should prepare students to live, learn, and work in a pluralistic world by fostering appreciation, respect, and tolerance for people of other ethnic and cultural backgrounds.

Multicultural Education (Phase 4). Phase 4 of multicultural education deals with the educational problems of all cultural groups—which includes women, the disabled, religious groups, and regional groups—and is cultural rather than merely focused on racial and ethnic minority groups (Banks, 1994 [see Chapter 2]).

Multiethnic Education (Phase 3). Multiethnic education summoned educators to develop a more unbiased educational reform that focused on the total school environment (Banks, 1994 [see Chapter 2]).

Multiethnic Studies Courses (Phase 2). The acceptance of ethnic courses for minority groups prompted White ethnic groups such as Jewish Americans and Polish Americans to demand separate courses that encompassed their histories and cultures in the curriculum (Banks, 1994 [see Chapter 2]).

Naturalistic process. The naturalistic process attempts to be sensitive to the political aspects of curriculum making, places greater emphasis on the quality of the learning activities, attempts to reflect more accurately the way curricula have actually been developed, and takes cognizance of the way teachers really plan for instruction.

Needs assessment. Needs assessment is a process used to obtain accurate, thorough data as to the strengths and weaknesses of a school and community to determine the academic needs of all students as well as to contribute to the improvement of student achievement.

Objective and purpose. That which is to be learned and how it will be useful.

Open education. A child-centered curriculum movement that emphasized the social and cognitive development of the child through informal exploration, activity, and discovery. Open education was an approach emphasizing a rich learning environment, one that modeled the use of concrete and interactive materials organized in "learning centers."

Operational curriculum. This is the observed curriculum—the curriculum one observes being taught in a classroom.

Planning report. A planning report summarizes student performance for each class on the previous year's summative examination.

Prescriptive curriculum. Prescriptive curriculum can be defined as what "ought" to happen in curriculum. It often takes the form of a plan, an intended program, or some kind of expert opinion about what needs to take place in the course of study.

Privatistic Conservatism. The academic period from 1975 to 1989, evidenced by substantially reducing federal spending, strengthening local and state control, maintaining a limited federal role in assisting states in carrying out their educational responsibilities, expanding parental choice, reducing federal judicial activity in education, and abolishing the Department of Education.

Process evaluation. Process evaluation monitors the processes both to ensure that the means are actually being implemented and to make the necessary modifications.

Process-oriented theories. Process-oriented theories are concerned primarily with describing how curricula are developed or recommending how they should be developed. Some process-oriented theories are descriptive in nature; others are more prescriptive.

Product evaluation. Product evaluation compares actual ends with intended ends and leads to a series of recycling decisions.

Proficiency movement. A proficiency movement is the commitment of educators to the concept of developing student and skill proficiency.

Program of studies. A program of studies represents all the planned learning experiences over a multiyear period for a given group of learners.

Progressive Functionalism. The era of Progressive Functionalism, which lasted approximately from 1917 to 1940, was characterized by the confluence of two seemingly disparate views: the progressive, child-centered orientation of the followers of John Dewey, and the functional orientation of curriculum scientists.

Radicals. Individuals who regard the society as critically flawed and who espouse curricula that would expose those flaws and empower the young to effect radical changes.

Rating. As per this text, the term *rating* is used in this sense: The process of making formative and summative assessments of teacher performance for purposes of administrative decision making.

Recommended curriculum. This is curriculum recommended by individual scholars, professional associations, and reform commissions; it also encompasses the curriculum requirements of policymaking groups, such as federal and state governments.

Recommended (ideal) curriculum. A curriculum determined by a set of recommendations proposed by the scholars and experts in the field. It is what teachers believe should be taught. The recommended curriculum should reflect the best current knowledge about that subject, tempered by the realities of the classroom.

Reconceptualists. Individuals who view education more as an existential experience. They are individuals who emphasize subjectivity, existential experience, and the art of interpretation in order to reveal the class conflict and the unequal power relationships existing in the larger society.

Reformers. Reformers are individuals who see society as essentially sound in its democratic structure but want to affect major reforms in the social order

Romantic Radicalism. The academic period from 1978 to 1974, evidenced by "rights," not responsibilities, being the dominant slogan: Black people, handicapped individuals, homosexuals, women, and nonnative groups all asserted their rights to liberation and to greater power. Educational reform was viewed as a political process.

Scholarly Structuralism. The academic period from 1957 to 1967, evidenced by educational leaders being convinced that rational, technological approaches could solve the schools' problems.

School vouchers. School vouchers are government grants aimed at improving education for the children of low-income families by providing school tuition that can be used at public or private schools. The thought behind school vouchers is to give parents a wider choice of educational institutions and approaches; it is also assumed that competition from private schools will pressure public schools into providing a better education for their students.

Self-directed development. A way for teachers to identify a small number of professional-growth goals for the year and work independently in attempting to accomplish those goals.

Six-trait analytical model. A model centered on the six traits of writing: ideas, organization, voice, word choice, sentence fluency, and conventions.

Society-centered curricula. Curricula that is based on the concept of social order being the starting point and the primary determiner of the curriculum.

Standards and outcome statements. Standards and outcome statements define knowledge and skills students need to possess at critical points during their education.

Structure of the intellect. This model of intelligence, designed by J. P. Guilford, is represented by three dimensions: the five *contents* of the intellect (visual, auditory, symbolic, semantic, behavioral), the six *products* of the intellect (units, classes, relations, systems, transformation, implications), and the five *operations* (evaluation, convergent production, divergent production, memory, cognition).

Structure-oriented theories. Structure-oriented theories are generally concerned with components of curriculum and their interrelationships. Primarily analytical in their approach, educators espousing structure-oriented theories often seek to describe and explain how curricular components interact within an educational environment.

Supported curriculum. The supported curriculum is reflected and shaped by the resources allocated to support or deliver the curriculum.

Synchronous. A term used to describe computer-mediated communication, indicating that communication takes place with both parties being logged on at the same time (Hoesing, 2004 [see Chapter 14]).

Taught curriculum. The taught curriculum is the one that teachers actually deliver. Researchers have pointed out that there is enormous variation in the nature of what is actually taught, despite the superficial appearance of uniformity.

Technological Constructionism. The academic period from 1990 to 1999, evidenced by the development of a standards-based and technological reform movement that gained support at national, state, and local levels.

Technological process. The technological process describes any curriculum-development model that emphasizes the importance of defining terminal learning objectives early in the process and then identifies the steps needed to accomplish those objectives.

Tested curriculum. The tested curriculum is the one embodied in tests developed by the state, school system, and teachers. The term *test* is used broadly here to include standardized tests, competency tests, and performance assessments.

Traditionalists. Traditionalists view curriculum as notions of class, teacher, course, units, and lessons. They are individuals concerned with the most efficient means of transmitting a fixed body of knowledge in order to impart the cultural heritage and keep the existing society functioning.

Triad/RDIM program. A triad/RDIM program is based on three types of enrichment activities for the gifted: general exploratory activities, group-training activities, and individual or small-group investigation activities.

Unit of study. A unit of study is a subset of a course of study that constitutes one education unit. The amount of contact hours and/or material covered for completion.

Universal design for learning. Universal design for learning focuses on educators' using flexible curricula that provide students with multiple ways of accessing content, multiple means for expressing themselves, and multiple pathways for engaging their interest and motivation.

Value-oriented theories. Value-oriented theories are based on the precept that central to the human condition is a search for transcendence, the struggle of the individual to actualize the whole self. Educators espousing a value-oriented philosophy tend to question their assumptions, to aspire to more worthy goals, and to reconceptualize the enterprise of curriculum making.

Virtual classroom. This is a classroom in which the physical room does not actually exist. Students are connected to the Internet and communicate through email and conferencing. The teacher is responsible for presenting learning material online and coordinating classroom activities.

Walkthroughs. "The practice of principals or other instructional leaders spend only minutes observing classrooms to form an impression about the quality of teaching and learning occurring" (Pitler & Goodwin, 2008, p. 9 [see Chapter 9]).

Ways of knowing. An educational approach espousing the view that there are multiple ways of knowing, not just one or two.

Worker Education and Training Program (WETP). This model program, under the auspices of the National Institute of Environmental Health Sciences, was given major responsibility for initiating a training grants program under the Superfund Amendments and Reauthorization Act of 1986. It encourages innovation for training difficult-to-reach populations by addressing issues such as literacy, appropriate adult education techniques, training quality improvement, and other areas unaddressed directly by the private sector. The program enhances rather than replaces private-sector training responsibility by demonstrating new and cost-effective training techniques and materials.

Worth. Worth refers to the context-determined, which varies from one context to another. For example, a curriculum may have a certain worth for teaching a particular child in a given year.

Writing across the curriculum. Writing across the curriculum can be defined as a comprehensive program that transforms the curriculum, encouraging writing to learn and learning to write in all disciplines. Also, writing and thinking are closely allied because learning to write well involves learning particular discourse conventions. Therefore, writing belongs in the entire curriculum, not just a course offered by the English department.

Writing process. Represents the complex act of creating written communication, specifically planning, drafting, revising, editing, and publishing.

Writing to learn. A writing-to-learn program is an approach that implies that students have something to say and that the process of writing implies at once a way for them to discourse and communicate.

Written curriculum. The written curriculum indicates a rationale that supports the curriculum, the general goals to be accomplished, the specific objectives to be mastered, the sequence in which those objectives should be studied, and the kinds of learning activities that should be used.

Written (formal) curriculum. The curriculum embodied in the school district's curriculum guides the written (formal) curriculum. It is the curriculum produced in written district guides that reflect synthesis of the recommended and the taught.

References

CHAPTER 1 REFERENCES

Achilles, C. M. (1997, October). Small classes, big possibilities. *School Administrator, 54*(9), 6–15.

Achilles, C. M., Finn, J. D., Prout, J., & Bobbett, G. C. (2001, February 18). *Serendipitous policy implications from class-size-initiated inquiry: IAQ?* Paper presented at Conference-Within-a-Conference, the American Association of School Administrators (AASA), Orlando, FL.

Allington, R. L. (2002). You can't learn much from books you can't read. *Educational Leadership, 60*(3), 16–19.

Anderson, C. S. (1982). The search for school climate: A review of the research. *Review of Educational Research, 52*(3), 368–420.

Apple, M. W. (1979, Winter). On analyzing hegemony. *Journal of Curriculum Theorizing, 1,* 10–43.

Azzam, A. M. (2007). The intervention called NCLB. *Educational Leadership, 65*(2), 92.

Banks, J. A., & Banks, C. A. M. (1996). *Multicultural education: Issues and perspectives* (3rd ed., pp. 385–407). Upper Saddle River, NJ: Prentice Hall.

Berliner, D. C. (1984). The half-full glass: A review of research on teaching. In P. L. Hosford (Ed.), *Using what we know about teaching* (pp. 511–577). Alexandria, VA: Association for Supervision and Curriculum Development.

Bobbitt, F. (1918). *The curriculum.* Boston: Houghton Mifflin.

Boles, K., & Troen, V. (2007). How to improve professional practice. *Principal, 87*(2), 50–53.

Booher-Jennings, J. (2006). Rationing education in an era of accountability. *Phi Delta Kappan, 87*(10), 756–761.

Brown, D. F. (2006). It's the curriculum, stupid: There's something wrong with it. *Phi Delta Kappan, 87*(10), 777–783.

Butzin, S. M., Carroll, R., & Lutz, B. (2006). Schools that like a challenge: Letting teachers specialize. *Educational Leadership, 63*(8), 72–75.

Carbo, M. (2007). Best practices for achieving high, rapid reading gains. *Principal, 87*(2), 42–45.

Caswell, H. L., & Campbell, D. S. (1935). *Curriculum development.* New York: American Book.

Century, J. (1994). *Making sense of the literature on equity in education. Draft one: ". . . A think piece . . ."* Newton, MA: Educational Development Center, Statewide Systemic Initiative Equity Leadership Institute.

Chambers, L. (1999, September). Sizing up the effects of class size. *Changing Schools, 8,* 1–2.

Cunningham, P., & Allington, R. (1994). *Classrooms that work.* New York: HarperCollins College.

Danielson, C. (2002). *Enhancing student achievement: A framework for school improvement.* Alexandria, VA: Association for Supervision and Curriculum Development.

Deutsch, N. (2004). *Hidden curriculum paper.* Retrieved December 15, 2007, from http://www.nelliemuller.com/HiddenCurriculum.doc

Dewey, J. (1902). *The child and the curriculum.* Chicago: University of Chicago Press.

Doyle, W. (1983). Academic work. *Review of Educational Research, 53*(2), 159–199.

Dreeben, R. (1968). *On what is learned in schools.* Reading, MA: Addison-Wesley.

Dugger, W. E., Jr., Meade, S., Delany, L., & Nichols, C. (2003, December). Advancing excellence in technological literacy. *Phi Delta Kappan, 85*(4), 316–317.

Ellis, A. K. (2004). *Exemplars of curriculum theory.* Larchmont, NY: Eye on Education.

Farber, S., & Finn, J. (2000, April). *The effect of small classes on student engagement.* Paper presented at the annual AREA meeting in New Orleans, LA.

Finn, J., & Achilles, C. (1990). Answers and questions about class size: A statewide experiment. *American Educational Research Journal, 27*(3), 557–577.

Fleck, F. (2007). The balanced principal: Joining theory and practical knowledge. *Principal,* 24–31.

Gagne, R. W. (1967). Curriculum research and the promotion of learning. In R. W. Tyler, R. M. Gagne, & M. Scriven (Eds.), *Perspectives of curricular evaluation.* Chicago: Rand McNally.

Giroux, H. A. (1979). Toward a new sociology of curriculum. *Educational Leadership, 37*(3), 248–253.

Giroux, H. A., & Penna, A. N. (1979). Social education in the classroom: The dynamics of the hidden curriculum. In H. A. Giroux, A. N. Penna, & W. F. Pinar (Eds.), *Curriculum and instruction* (pp. 209–230). Berkeley, CA: McCutchan.

Glatthorn, A. A. (1980). *A guide for developing an English curriculum for the eighties.* Urbana, IL: NCTE.

Goodlad, J. I. (1984). *A place called school: Prospects for the future.* New York: McGraw-Hill.

Goodlad, J. I., & Associates. (1979). *Curriculum inquiry: The study of curriculum practice.* New York: McGraw-Hill.

Guilfoyle, C. (2006). NCLB: Is there life beyond testing? *Educational Leadership, 64*(3), 13.

Hanley, M. S. (1999). The scope of multicultural education. *New Horizons for Learning.* Retrieved January 26, 2008, from http://www.newhorizons.org

Hargreaves, A., & Fink, D. (2006). The ripple effect. *Educational Leadership, 63*(8), 20.

Hass, G. (1987). *Curriculum planning: A new approach* (5th ed.). Boston: Allyn & Bacon.

Hopkins, L. T. (1941). *Interaction: The democratic process.* Boston: D. C. Heath.

Jackson, P. (1968). *Life in classrooms.* New York: Holt, Rinehart & Winston.

Kahlenberg, R. D. (2006). The new integration. *Educational Leadership, 63*(8), 22–26.

Karweit, N. C. (1983). *Time-on-task: A research review.* Baltimore: Johns Hopkins University, Center for Social Organization of Schools.

Kirschenbaum, V. R. (2006). The old way of reading and the new. *Educational Leadership, 63*(8), 49–50.

Kirst, M. W. (1983). Policy implications of individual differences and the common curriculum. In G. D. Fenstermacher & J. I. Goodlad (Eds.), *Individual differences and the common curriculum* (Eighty-Second Yearbook of the National Society

for the Study of Education: Part I, pp. 282–299). Chicago: University of Chicago Press.

Martinez, M. F. (2006). What is metacognition? *Phi Delta Kappan, 87*(9), 696–699.

Marzano, R., Pickering, D., & Pollock, J. (2001). *Classroom instruction that works: Research-based strategies for increasing student achievement.* Alexandria, VA: Association for Supervision and Curriculum Development.

McBrien, J. L., & Brandt, R. (Eds.). (1997). *The language of learning: A guide to educational terms.* Alexandria, VA: Association for Supervision and Curriculum Development.

McGill-Franzen, A., & Allington, R. (2006). Contamination of current accountability systems. *Phi Delta Kappan, 87*(10), 762–766.

Mosteller, F. (1995). The Tennessee study of class size in the early school grades. *Future of Children, 5*(2), 113–127.

National Education Association. (2007). *Class size.* Retrieved December 10, 2007, from http://www.nea.org/classsize/index.html

Oakes, J., Ormseth, T., Bell, R., & Camp, P. (1990, July). *Multiplying inequalities: The effects of race, social class, and tracking on opportunities to learn mathematics and science.* Santa Monica, CA: RAND.

Pellegino, J. (2007). Should NAEP performance standards be used for setting standards for state assessments? *Phi Delta Kappan, 88*(7), 541.

Pennsylvania Department of Education. (2007). *Curriculum alignment: Definition of curriculum.* Chapter 4, PA State Board of Education. Resource 1.D. Retrieved December 10, 2007, from http://smasd.k12.pa.us/pssa/html/CURRDEVL/res1-d.htm

Perkins-Gough, D. (2007). Giving intervention a head start. *Educational Leadership, 65*(2), 8–14.

Pinar, W. F. (1978). The reconceptualization of curriculum studies. *Journal of Curriculum Studies, 10*(3), 205–214.

Popham, W. J. (2007). Instructional insensitivity of tests: Accountability's dire drawback. *Phi Delta Kappan, 89*(2), 146–147.

Popham, W. J., & Baker, E. I. (1970). *Systematic instruction.* Englewood Cliffs, NJ: Prentice Hall.

Ragan, W. B. (1960). *Modern elementary curriculum* (Rev. ed.). New York: Henry Holt.

Rosenbaum, J. E. (1980). Social implications of educational grouping. In D. C. Berliner (Ed.), *Review of research in education* (Vol. 8, pp. 361–404), Washington, DC: AERA.

Rotberg, I. C. (2007). Schools making tough choices: An international perspective. *Principal, 86*(4), 32–37.

Rugg, H. O. (Ed.). (1927). *The foundation of curriculum making* (Twenty-Sixth Yearbook of the National Society for the Study of Education, Part II). Bloomington, IL: Public School Publishing.

Saylor, J. G., Alexander, W. M., & Lewis, A. J. (1981). *Curriculum planning for better teaching and learning* (4th ed.). New York: Holt, Rinehart & Winston.

Scherer, M. (2007). Playing to strengths. *Educational Leadership, 65*(1), 7.

Schmoker, M. (2007). Radically redefining literacy instruction: An immense opportunity. *Phi Delta Kappan, 88*(7), 488.

Secada, W. (1992). Race, ethnicity, social class, language, and achievement in mathematics. In D. Grouws (Ed.), *Handbook of research on mathematics teaching and learning* (pp. 623–660). Reston, VA: National Council of Teachers of Mathematics.

Shaywitz, S. E., & Shaywitz, B. A. (2007). What neuroscience really tells us about reading instruction. *Educational Leadership, 64*(5), 74–76.

Slavin, R. E., Chamberlain, A., & Daniels, C. (2007). Preventing reading failure. *Educational Leadership, 65*(2), 22–27.

Stallings, J. (1980, December). Allocated learning time revisited or beyond time on task. *Educational Researcher, 9*(4), 11–16.

Tagiuri, R. (1968). The concept of organizational climate. In R. Tagiuri & G. H. Litwin (Eds.), *Organizational climate: Exploration of a concept.* Boston: Harvard University, Graduate School of Business Administration.

Tanner, D., & Tanner, L. (1995). *Curriculum development: Theory and practice* (3rd ed.). New York: Merrill.

Tomlinson, C. A., Burns, D., Renzulli, J. S., Kaplan, S. N., Leppien, J., & Purcell, J. (2002). *The parallel curriculum: A design to develop high potential and challenge high-ability learners.* Thousand Oaks, CA: Corwin Press.

Tyler, R. W. (1957). The curriculum then and now. In *Proceedings of the 1956 Invitational Conference on Testing Problems.* Princeton, NJ: Educational Testing Service.

Villegas, M., & Lucas, T. (2007). The culturally responsive teacher. *Educational Leadership, 64*(6), 28–33.

Walcott, H. F. (1977). *Teacher vs. technocrats.* Eugene: University of Oregon, Center for Educational Policy and Management.

Walker, D. (1979). Approaches to curriculum development. In J. Schaffarzick & G. Sykes (Eds.), *Value conflicts and curriculum issues: Lessons from research and experience* (pp. 263–290). Berkeley, CA: McCutchan.

Waters, T., Marzano, R. J., & McNulty, B. (2003). *Balanced leadership: What 30 years of research tells us about the effect of leadership on student achievement* (Working paper). Aurora, CO: McREL.

Wilhelm, J. D. (1996). *Standards in practice, Grades 6–8.* Urbana, IL: National Council of Teachers of English.

Wilson, L. O. (2005). *What is curriculum? And what are the types of curriculum?* Retrieved December 15, 2007, from http://www.uwsp.edu/Education/lwilson/curric/curtyp.htm

Wolfe, P. (2001). *Brain matters: Translating research into classroom practice.* Alexandria, VA: Association for Supervision and Curriculum Development.

CHAPTER 2 REFERENCES

Allington, R L. (2005). *What really matters for struggling readers: Designing research-based programs.* Boston: Allyn & Bacon.

Archived information. (n.d.). *Goals 2000: Educate America Act* (H.R. 1804: 103rd Congress). Retrieved April 11, 2005, from http://www.ed.gov/legislation/GOALS2000/TheAct/intro.html

Banks, J. A. (1994). *Multiethnic education: Theory and practice* (3rd ed.). Boston: Allyn & Bacon.

Barton, P. E. (2006, November). Needed: Higher standards for accountability. *Educational Leadership, 64*(3), 28–36.

Bast, J., Harmer, D., & Dewey, D. (1997, March). *Vouchers and educational freedom: A debate.*

Retrieved February 7, 2004, from http://www.cato.org/pubs/pas/pa-269.html

Bender, W. N. (2007). *Response to intervention: A practical guide for every teacher.* Thousand Oaks, CA: Corwin Press & the Council for Exceptional Children.

Bernhardt, V. L. (1998). *Data analysis: For comprehensive schoolwide improvement.* Larchmont, NY: Eye on Education.

Bloom, B. S. (Ed.). (1956). *Taxonomy of educational objectives: The classification of educational goals: Handbook 1. Cognitive domains.* New York: McKay.

Bobbitt, F. (1913). *The supervision of city schools* (Twelfth Yearbook of the National Society for the Study of Education, Part I). Chicago: University of Chicago Press.

Boschee, F., Beyer, B. M., Engelking, J. L., & Boschee, M. A. (1997). *Special and compensatory programs: The administrators role.* Lanham, MD: Rowman & Littlefield Education.

Boschee, F., & Hunt, M. M. (1990). Educational choice and vouchers—Where do you stand? *NASSP Bulletin, 74*(524), 75–86.

Boyer, E. L. (1983). *High school: A report on secondary education in America.* New York: Harper & Row.

Bracy, G. W. (2003). The 13th Bracey report on the condition of public education. *Phi Delta Kappan, 85*(2), 148–149.

Bruner, J. S. (1960). *The process of education.* Cambridge, MA: Harvard University Press.

Center on Juvenile and Criminal Justice. (2000). *School house hype: Two years later.* Retrieved March 3, 2005, from http://www.cjcj.org/pubs/schoolhouse/shh2.html

Chamberlin, M., & Plucker, J. (2008). P–16 education: Where are we going? Where have we been? *Phi Delta Kappan, 89*(7), 472–479.

Commission on the Reorganization of Secondary Education. (1918). *Cardinal principles of secondary education.* Washington, DC: U.S. Government Printing Office.

Conant, J. B. (1959). *The American high school today.* New York: McGraw-Hill.

Cook, G. (2004, January). Vouchers, choice & controversy. *American School Board Journal, 191*(1).

Cuglietto, L., Burke, R., & Ocasio, S. (2007, March). A full-service school. *Educational Leadership, 64*(6), 72–73.

Cunningham, P. M., & Allington, R. L. (1994). *Classrooms that work: They can read and write.* New York: HarperCollins.

Curriculum Development Associates. (1972). *Man: A course of study.* Washington, DC: Author.

Czarra, F. (2002–2003). Global education checklist. *The American Forum for Global Education, 173.* Retrieved April 17, 2008, from http://www.globaled.org/fianlcopy.pdf

Danielson, C. (2002). *Enhancing student achievement: A framework for school improvement.* Alexandria, VA: Association for Supervision and Curriculum Development.

Dewey, J. (1900). *The school and society.* Chicago: University of Chicago Press.

Dewey, J. (1902). *The child and the curriculum.* Chicago: University of Chicago Press.

Dewey, J. (1916). *Democracy and education.* New York: Macmillan.

Dewey, J. (1938). *Experience and education.* New York: Macmillan.

Dewey, J. (1964). *John Dewey on education: Selected writings* (R. Archambaust, Ed.). New York: Random House.

Education Commission of the States. (1982). *The information society: Are high school graduates ready?* Denver, CO: Author.

Eisner, E. W., & Vallance, E. (1974). *Conflicting conceptions of curriculum.* Berkeley, CA: McCutchan.

Ferrandino, V. (2003, July 25). *A practical guide to talking with your community: Talking points on No Child Left Behind* [Newsletter to NAESP members]. Alexandria, VA: National Association of Elementary School Principals.

Ferrandino, V. (2007, January/February). Keeping up with the fourth graders. *Principal, 86*(3), 64.

Flexner, A. (1916). The modern school. *American Review of Reviews, 8,* 465–474.

Friedman, T. L. (2005). *The world is flat: A brief history of the twenty-first century.* New York: Farrar, Straus and Giroux.

Fullan, M. (2001). *Leading in a culture of change.* San Francisco: Jossey-Bass.

Gelman, R., & Baillargeon, R. (1983). A review of some Piagetian concepts. In P. H. Mussen (Ed.), *Handbook of child psychology* (Vol. 3, pp. 167–230). New York: John Wiley.

Giles, H. H., McCutchen, S. P., & Zechiel, A. N. (1942). *Exploring the curriculum.* New York: Harper.

Gilmore, J. (2005, August). Keep the home-school fires burning. *New American, 21*(17), 29–33.

Glass, G. V. (Ed.). (2003). *Education policy analysis archives.* Retrieved February 7, 2004, from http://epaa.asu.edu/epaa/board/darling-hammond.html

Glatthorn, A. A. (1975). *Alternatives in education: Schools and programs.* New York: Dodd, Mead.

Goens, G. A., & Clover, A. (1991). *Mastering school reform.* Boston: Allyn & Bacon.

Gorski, P. C. (1999, November). A brief history of multicultural education. *Research Room. EdChange Multicultural Pavilion.* Retrieved March 19, 2008, from http://www.edchange.org/multicultural/papers/edchange_history.html

Hall, G. S. (1904). The natural activities of children as determining the industries in early education. *National Education Association Journal of Proceedings and Addresses,* pp. 443–444.

Hall, G. S. (1969). *Adolescence.* New York: Arno Press and *The New York Times.* (Original work published 1904)

Hardy, L. (2004, March). A nation divided. *Education Vital Signs 2004* (An ASBJ Special Report), 2–6.

Havighurst, R. J. (1972). *Developmental tasks and education* (3rd ed.). New York: David McKay.

Haycock, K., & Huang, S. (2001, Winter). Are today's high school graduates ready? *Thinking K–16, 5*(1), 3–17.

Hewitt, T. W. (2008). Speculations on a nation at risk: Illusions and realities. *Phi Delta Kappan, 89*(8), 579.

Holt, J. (1964). *How children fail.* New York: Pitman.

InfoMedia, Inc. (1993). *Educational reform: A national perspective.* Ellenton, FL: Author.

Jones, R. (2000, September). Making standards work: Researchers report effective strategies for implementing standards. *American School Board Journal, 187*(9), 27–31.

Kliebard, H. M. (1985). What happened to American schooling in the first part of the twentieth century? In E. Eisner (Ed.), *Learning and teaching the ways of knowing* (pp. 1–22). Chicago: University of Chicago Press.

Knudsen, L. R., & Morrissette, P. J. (1998, May 12). Goals 2000: An analysis and critique. *International Electronic Journal for Leadership in Learning, 2*(4). Retrieved February 7, 2004, from http://www.ucalgary.ca/~iejll/volume2/knudsen2_html

Kozol, J. (2007, September/October). The single worst, most dangerous idea. *Principal, 87*(1), 56–59.

Marzano, R. J., Waters, T., & McNulty, B. A. (2005). *School leadership that works.* Alexandria, VA: Association for Supervision and Curriculum Development.

Murphy, J., & Shiffman, C. D. (2002). *Understanding and assessing the charter school movement.* New York: Teachers College Press.

National Center for Education Statistics. (2004). *Homeschooling in the United States: 1999.* Washington, DC: U.S. Department of Education, Office of Educational Research and Improvement.

National Commission on Excellence in Education. (1983). *A nation at risk: The imperative for educational reform.* Washington, DC: U.S. Government Printing Office.

National Education Association. (1893). *Report of the Committee on Secondary School Studies.* Washington, DC: U.S. Government Printing Office.

National Education Association. (1895). *Report of the Committee of Fifteen.* New York: Arno Press and *The New York Times.*

North Idaho State College. (2007). *Tech prep leads from high school to technical training, to college degrees and high demand careers.* Retrieved December 15, 2007, from http://www.nic.edu/techprep/Region1

Oliver, A. I. (1977). *Curriculum improvement: A guide to problems, principles, and process* (2nd ed.). New York: Harper & Row.

O'Shea, M. R. (2005). *From standards to success.* Alexandria, VA: Association for Supervision and Curriculum Development.

Palmer, L. B. (2007, December). The potential of "alternative" charter school authorizers. *Phi Delta Kappan, 89*(4), 304–309.

Parker, F. W. (1894). *Talks on pedagogics.* New York: E. L. Kellogg.

Physical Science Study Committee. (1961). *PSSC physics: Teacher's resource book and guide.* Boston: D. C. Heath.

Piaget, J. (1950). *The psychology of intelligence.* New York: Harcourt.

Potter, W. (2003, May 2). Report seeks to align state standards for high schools and colleges. *Chronicle of Higher Education, 49*(34), A31.

Provenzo, E. F. (2003). *Contemporary educational thought.* University of Miami School of Education. Retrieved December 21, 2004, from http://www.education.miami.edu/ep/contemporaryed/home.html and http://www.education.miami.edu/ep/contemoraryed/Eliott_Eisner/eliott_eisner.html

Purkey, S. C., & Smith, M. S. (1983). Effective schools: A review. *Elementary School Journal, 83*(4), 426–452.

Ravitch, D. (1983). *The troubled crusade: American education 1945–1980.* New York: Basic Books.

Ray, B. D. (2006). *Research facts on homeschooling.* Retrieved March 20, 2008, from http://www.exploringhomeschooling.com/ResearchFactsonHomeschooling.aspx

Rogers, C. (1969). *Freedom to learn: A view of what education might become.* Columbus, OH: Merrill.

Rugg, H. O. (Ed.). (1927). *The foundation of curriculum-making* (Twenty-Sixth Yearbook of the National Society for the Study of Education, Part II). Bloomington, IL: Public School Publishing.

Sarason, S. B. (1990). *The predictable failure of educational reform.* San Francisco: Jossey-Bass.

Schwab, J. J. (1969). The practical: A language for curriculum. *School Review, 78*(1), 1–23.

Schwab, J. J. (1971). The practical: Arts of eclectic. *School Review, 79*(4), 493–542.

Schwab, J. J. (1973). The practical 3: Translation into curriculum. *School Review, 81*(4), 501–522.

Schwab, J. J. (1978). Education and the structure of the disciplines. In I. Westbury & N. J. Wilk of (Eds.), *Science, curriculum, and liberal education: Selected essays of Joseph T. Schwab* (pp. 229–270). Chicago: University of Chicago Press.

Schwab, J. J. (1983). The practical 4: Something for curriculum professors to do. *Curriculum Inquiry, 13*(3), 239–265.

Silberman, C. (1970). *Crisis in the classroom.* New York: Random House.

Taylor, F. W. (1911). *The principles of scientific management.* New York: Harper and Bros.

Tomlinson, C. A., Kaplan, S. N., Renzulli, J. S., Purcell, J., Leppien, J., & Burns, D. (2001). *The parallel curriculum: A design to develop high potential and challenge high-ability learners.* Thousand Oaks, CA: Corwin Press.

Tomlinson, C. A., & McTighe, J. (2006). *Integrating plus differentiated instruction and understanding by design.* Alexandria, VA: Association for Supervision and Curriculum Development.

Tyler, R. W. (1950). *Basic principles of curriculum and instruction.* Chicago: University of Chicago Press.

Tyler, R. W. (1971). Curriculum development in the twenties and thirties. In R. M. McClure (Ed.), *The curriculum: Retrospect and prospects* (pp. 26–44). Chicago: University of Chicago Press.

US Charter Schools. (2008). *US Charter Schools history and overview.* Retrieved January 12, 2008, from http://www.uschaarterschools.org/lpt/uscs_docs/309

Van de Water, G., & Krueger, C. (2002). P–16 education. *Clearinghouse on Educational Policy and Management.* Eugene: College of Education, University of Oregon. Retrieved April 24, 2008, from http://eric.uoregon.edu/publications/digests/digest159.html

Van Til, W., Vars, G. F., & Lounsbury, J. H. (1961). *Junior high years.* Indianapolis, IN: Bobbs-Merrill.

Vu, P. (2007). *Govs call for more control over NCLB.* Retrieved March 18, 2008, from http://www.stateline.org/live/details/story?contentId=196302

Whitehead, B. M., Jensen, D. F. N., & Boschee, F. (2003). *Planning for technology: A guide for school administrators, technology coordinators, and curriculum leaders.* Thousand Oaks, CA: Corwin Press.

Willis, J. (2007, March). Toward neuro-logical reading instruction. *Educational Leadership, 64*(6), 80–82.

Wolfe, P. (2001). *Brain matters: Translating research into classroom practice.* Alexandria, VA: Association for Supervision and Curriculum Development.

Wormeli, R. (2006). *Fair isn't always equal: Assessing & grading in the differentiated classroom.* Portland, ME: Stenhouse; Westerville, OH: National Middle School Association.

Wraga, W. G. (2001, Winter). A progressive legacy squandered: The "cardinal principles" report reconsidered. *History of Education Quarterly, 41*(4), 494–519.

CHAPTER 3 REFERENCES

Abbot, J., & Ryan, T. (1999). Constructing knowledge, reconstructing schooling. *Educational Leadership, 57*(3), 66–69.

Apple, M. W. (1975). Scientific interests and the nature of educational institutions. In W. Pinar (Ed.), *Curriculum theorizing: For reconceptualists* (pp. 120–130). Berkeley, CA: McCutchan.

Atkins, E. S. (1982). *Curriculum theorizing as a scientific pursuit: A framework for analysis.* Unpublished doctoral dissertation, University of Pennsylvania.

Bambrick-Santoyo, P. (2007, December/2008, January). Data in the driver's seat. *Educational Leadership, 65*(4), 43–46.

Beauchamp, G. A. (1981). *Curriculum theory* (4th ed.). Itasca, IL: Peacock.

Bobbitt, F. (1918). *The curriculum.* Boston: Riverside Press.

Bowers, C. A. (1977, September). Emergent ideological characteristics of educational policy. *Teachers College Record, 79*(1), 33–54.

Bransford, J., Brown, A. L., & Cocking, R. R. (2001). *How people learn: Brain, mind, experience, and school.* Washington, DC: National Academy Press.

Brooks, M. (1986, April). *Curriculum development from a constructivist perspective.* Paper presented at the annual meeting of the American Educational Research Association, San Francisco.

Brooks, M., & Brooks, J. (1999). The courage to be a constructivist. *Educational Leadership, 57*(3), 18–24.

Brown, G. I. (1975). Examples of lessons, units, and course outlines in confluent education. In G. I. Brown (Ed.), *The live classroom* (pp. 231–295). New York: Viking.

Burks, R. (1998). *A review and comparison of Ralph W. Tyler's basic principles of curriculum. Curriculum and instruction.* Retrieved March 8, 2003, from http://www.randallburks.com/ critique.htm

Carolan, J., & Guinn, A. (2007, February). Differentiation: Lessons from master teachers. *Educational Leadership, 64*(5), 44–47.

Caulfield, J., Kidd, S., & Kocher, T. (2000). Brain-based instruction in action. *Educational Leadership, 58*(3), 62–65.

Christie, K. (2007, November). Stateline: Premature arrival of the future. *Phi Delta Kappan, 89*(3), 165–166.

Counts, G. S. (1932). *Dare the school build a new social order?* New York: Day.

Davis, S. H. (2007, April). Bridging the gap between research and practice: What's good, what's bad, and how can one be sure? *Phi Delta Kappan, 88*(8), 569–578.

Doll, R. C. (1986). *Curriculum improvement: Decision making and process* (6th ed.). Boston: Allyn & Bacon.

Eisner, E. (Ed.). (1985). *Learning and teaching the ways of knowing* (Eighty-Fourth Yearbook of the National Society for the Study of Education, Part II). Chicago: University of Chicago Press.

Eisner, E. W., & Vallance, E. (Eds.). (1974). *Conflicting conceptions of curriculum.* Berkeley, CA: McCutchan.

Faix, T. L. (1964). *Structural-functional analysis as a conceptual system for curriculum theory and research: A theoretical study.* Unpublished doctoral dissertation, University of Wisconsin, Madison.

Farmer, D. (1996, January). *Curriculum differentiation: An overview of the research into the curriculum differentiation educational strategy.* Retrieved April 5, 2005, from http://www.austega.com/gifted/provisions/curdifferent.htm

Foti, S. (2007, May). Technology: Did we leave the future behind? *Phi Delta Kappan, 88*(9), 647–648, 715.

Franklin, C. A. (2008, January/February). Factors determining elementary teachers' use of computers. *Principal, 87*(3), 54–55.

Freire, P. (1970). *Pedagogy of the oppressed.* New York: Herder and Herder.

Gagne, R. (1985). *The conditions of learning and theory of instruction* (4th ed.). New York: Holt, Rinehart & Winston.

Gagne, R., Briggs, L., & Wager, W. (1992). *Principles of instructional design* (4th ed.). Fort Worth, TX: HBJ College.

Gay, G. (1980). Conceptual models of the curriculum planning process. In A. W. Foshay (Ed.), *Considered action for curriculum improvement* (pp. 120–143). Alexandria, VA: Association for Supervision and Curriculum Development.

Given, B. (2000). Theaters of the mind. *Educational Leadership, 58*(3), 72–75.

Glatthorn, A. A. (1980). *A guide for designing an English curriculum for the eighties.* Urbana, IL: National Council of Teachers of English.

Glatthorn, A. A. (1987). Analysis of Glatthorn's (1986) curriculum-development process. In A. A. Glatthorn (Ed.), *Curriculum leadership* (p. 120). New York: HarperCollins.

Goodlad, J. I. (Ed.). (1979). *Curriculum inquiry: The study of curriculum practice.* New York: McGraw-Hill.

Hanson, N. R. (1958). *Patterns of discovery.* Cambridge, UK: Cambridge University Press.

Hess, F. M. (2008, January). The politics of knowledge. *Phi Delta Kappan, 89*(5), 354–356.

Hirsch, E. D., Jr. (1995). *What your fifth grader needs to know: Fundamentals of good fifth-grade education.* Los Alamitos, CA: Delta.

Hoer, T. R. (2007, December/2008, January). What is instructional leadership? *Educational Leadership, 65*(4), 84–85.

Huenecke, D. (1982). What is curricular theorizing? What are its implications for practice? *Educational Leadership, 39*, 290–294.

imagitrends. (2000). *Future primary educational structure.* Retrieved April 5, 2005, from http://pages.prodigy.net/imagiweb/reports/file00/oct1.htm

Kaplan, A. (1964). *The conduct of inquiry: Methodology for behavioral science.* San Francisco: Chandler.

Keat, R., & Urry, J. (1975). *Social theory as science.* London: Routledge & Kegan Paul.

Levine, M., & Barringer, M. (2008, January/February). Getting the lowdown on the slowdown. *Principal, 87*(3), 14–18.

Macdonald, J. B. (1974). A transcendental developmental ideology of education. In W. Pinar (Ed.), *Heightened conscience, cultural revolution, and curriculum theory* (pp. 85–116). Berkeley, CA: McCutchan.

Macdonald, J. B. (1977). Value bases and issues for curriculum. In A. Molnar & J. A. Zahorik (Eds.), *Curriculum theory* (pp. 10–21). Alexandria, VA: Association for Supervision and Curriculum Development.

Maheshwari, A. N. (2003). *Value orientation in teacher education.* Retrieved March 1, 2003, from http://www.geocities.com/Athens/Parthenon/2686/value.htm

Martinez, M. E. (2006, May). What is metacognition? *Phi Delta Kappan, 87*(9), 696–699.

McNeil, J. D. (1985). *Curriculum: A comprehensive introduction* (3rd ed.). Boston: Little, Brown.

Papert, S. (1993). *The children's machine: Rethinking school in the age of the computer.* New York: Basic Books. Retrieved March 9, 2004, from http://www.stemnet.nf.ca/~elmurphy/emurphy/papert.html

Parker, F. W. (1894). *Talks on pedagogics.* New York: E. L. Kellogg.

Patterson, P. (2007, January/February). Mission possible: Teaching through technology. *Principal, 86*(3), 22–25.

Perkins, D. (1999). The many faces of constructivism. *Educational Leadership, 57*(3), 6–11.

Pinar, W. F. (1978). The reconceptualization of curriculum studies. *Journal of Curriculum Studies, 10*(3), 205–214.

Popper, K. R. (1962). *Conjectures and refutations.* New York: Basic Books.

Posner, G. J., & Strike, K. A. (1976). A categorization scheme for principles of sequencing content. *Review of Educational Research, 46*, 665–690.

Purpel, D. E., & Belanger, M. (1972). Toward a humanistic curriculum theory. In D. E. Purpel & M. Belanger (Eds.), *Curriculum and the cultural revolution* (pp. 64–74). Berkeley, CA: McCutchan.

Racer, C. E. (2007, September). Best of the blog: In-response to "engaging the whole child," summer online. *Educational Leadership, 65*(1), 94–95.

Scherer, M. (1999). The understanding pathway: A conversation with Howard Gardner. *Educational Leadership, 57*(3), 12–16.

Schiro, M. (1978). *Curriculum for better schools: The great ideological debate.* Englewood Cliffs, NJ: Educational Technology.

Schon, D. A. (1983). *The reflective practitioner: How professionals think in action.* New York: Basic Books.

Schwab, J. (1970). *The practical: A language for curriculum.* Washington, DC: National Education Association.

Short, E. C. (1983). The forms and use of alternative curriculum development strategies: Policy implications. *Curriculum Inquiry, 13*, 45–64.

Shulman, J. (2003). *Institute for case development.* Retrieved March 2, 2004, from http://www.wested.org/cs/we/view/pj/173

Smith, M. K. (1996, 2000). Curriculum theory and practice. *The encyclopaedia of informal education.* Retrieved December 24, 2007, from http://www.infed.org/biblio/b-curric.htm

Suppe, F. (Ed.). (1974). *The structures of scientific theories.* Urbana: University of Illinois Press.

Swain, S. (2003). *Research and resources.* Westerville: OH: National Middle School Association.

Tomlinson, C. A., & McTighe, J. (2006). *Integrating + differentiated instruction and understanding by design.* Alexandria, VA: Association for Supervision and Curriculum Development.

Tyler, R. W. (1950). *Basic principles of curriculum and instruction.* Chicago: University of Chicago Press.

Vallance, E. (1985). Ways of knowing and curricular conceptions: Implications for program planning. In E. Eisner (Ed.), *Learning and teaching the ways of knowing* (pp. 199–217). Chicago: University of Chicago Press.

Weber, L. (1971). *The English infant school and informal education.* Englewood Cliffs, NJ: Prentice Hall.

Wiggins, G., & McTighe, J. (2005). *Understanding by design* (Expanded 2nd ed.). Alexandria, VA: Association for Supervision and Curriculum Development.

Willis, J. (2007, March). Toward neuro-logical reading instruction. *Educational Leadership, 64*(6), 80–82.

Willwerth, D. (2003). *Heuristics and curriculum theory.* (Originally cited in Schiro, M. [1978]. *Curriculum for better schools: The great ideological debate* [pp. 7–16]. Englewood Cliffs, NJ: Educational Technology Publications.) Retrieved March 1, 2004, from http://www2.bc.edu/-evansec/curriculum/index.html

CHAPTER 4 REFERENCES

Alexander, K., & Alexander, M. D. (2005). *American public school law* (6th ed.). Belmont, CA: Thomson West.

Atkin, J. M., & House, E. R. (1981). The federal role in curriculum development, 1950–80. *Educational Evaluation and Policy Analysis, 3*(5), 5–36.

Bell, T. H. (1986). Educational policy development in the Reagan administration. *Phi Delta Kappan, 67,* 487–493.

Bender, W. N., & Shores, C. (2007). *Response to intervention: A practical guide for every teacher.* Thousand Oaks, CA: Corwin Press & Council of Exceptional Children.

Berliner, D. C., & Biddle, B. J. (1997). *The manufactured crisis: Myths, fraud, and the attack on America's public schools.* White Plains, NY: Longman.

Christie, K. (2005, January). Stateline: Providing the facts. *Phi Delta Kappan, 86*(9), 341–342.

Christie, K. (2008). Stateline: An exponential payoff. *Phi Delta Kappan, 89*(5), 325–326.

Conners, J. (2007). Casualties of reform. *Phi Delta Kappan, 88*(7), 518–522.

Curriculum Development Associates. (1972). *Man: A course of study.* Washington, DC: Author.

Donaldson, G. A., Jr. (2007). What do teachers bring to leadership? *Educational Leadership, 65*(1), 26–29.

Doyle, D. P., & Hartle, T. W. (1985). Leadership in education: Governors, legislators and teachers. *Phi Delta Kappan, 66*(1), 21–28.

Elmore, R. F. (1997, Fall). The politics of education reform [Electronic version]. *Issues in Science and Technology Online, 1–3.*

Evans, M. (2008, January/February). Developing diverse communities. *Principal, 87*(3), 63.

Fugate, C. (2007). Vonnegut warned us. *Phi Delta Kappan, 89*(1), 71–72.

Gallagher, C. W., (2008). Democratic policy making and the arts of engagement. *Phi Delta Kappan, 89*(5), 340–346.

Garrison, W. H. (2008). Democracy and education: Empowering students to make sense of their world. *Phi Delta Kappan, 89*(5), 347–348.

Gregory, G. H., & Kuzmich, L. (2008, January/February). Jump-starting learning communities. *Principal, 87*(3), 57.

Harrison, C., & Killion, J. (2007). Ten roles for teacher leaders. *Educational Leadership, 65*(1), 74–77.

Harvest, D. (2008 January/February). Voices from the road: Succeeding with struggling learners. *Principal, 87*(3), 12.

Henig, J. R. (2008, January). The evolving relationship between researchers and public policy. *Phi Delta Kappan, 89*(5), 357–360.

Hertling, J. (1986, March 12). Block grants found to achieve gains. *Education Week,* p. 8.

Hess, F. (2008, January). The politics of knowledge. *Phi Delta Kappan, 89*(5), 354–356.

Hill, J. D., & Flynn, K. M. (2006). *Classroom instruction that works with English language learners.* Alexandria, VA: Association for Supervision and Curriculum Development.

Hoerr, T. R. (2007, December/2008, January). What is instructional leadership? *Educational Leadership, 65*(4), 84–85.

Holt, J. (1964). *How children fail.* New York: Dell.

Hubbard, R. (2007). Quoting Marc Tucker in backtalk: A real system-level change. *Phi Delta Kappan, 89*(1), 81.

Illich, I. (1972). *Deschooling society.* New York: Harper and Row.

Ingersoll, R. M. (2007). Short on power, long on responsibility. *Educational Leadership, 65*(1), 25.

Ingersoll, R. M. (2008). A researcher encounters the policy realm: A personal tale. *Phi Delta Kappan, 89*(5), 369–375.

Kliebard, H. M. (1979). Systematic curriculum development, 1890–1959. In J. Schaffarzick & G. Sykes (Eds.), *Value conflicts and curriculum issues* (pp. 197–236). Berkeley, CA: McCutchan.

Kozol, J. (1991). *Savage inequalities: Children in America's schools.* New York: Crown.

Lau v. Nichols, 414 U.S. 563 (1974).

Levine, E. L., & Wexler, E. M. (1981). *P.L. 94-142: An act of Congress.* New York: Macmillan.

Lewis, A. C. (2007a, March). Washington commentary, Looking beyond NCLB. *Phi Delta Kappan, 88*(7), 483–484.

Lewis, A. C. (2007b, September). Washington commentary, choices: Rational or otherwise. *Phi Delta Kappan, 89*(1), 3–4.

Llewellyn, G. (1991). *Teenage liberation handbook: How to quit school and get a real life and education.* Eugene, OR: Lowery House.

Lynch, K. L. (1986). *School finance policy formulation in Pennsylvania: A case study.* Unpublished doctoral dissertation, University of Pennsylvania.

Marshall, C. (1985, March). *Policymakers' assumptive worlds: Informal structures in state education policymaking.* Paper presented at the meeting of the American Educational Research Association, Chicago.

Mathews, J. (2003). *To educators, "No Child" goals out of reach.* Retrieved September 16, 2004, from http://www.washingtonpost.com/ac2/wp-dyn/A15836-2003Sep15?language = printer

Mills v. Board of Education, 348 F. Supp. 866 (D.D.C. 1972).

National Council for Accreditation of Teacher Education. (2007, updated May 3). *State relations FAQs.* Retrieved May 28, 2008, from http://www.ncate.org/states/StateRelationsFAQ.asp?ch = 104#stRfaqs4

Parents choose schools via vouchers. (2003). Retrieved May 3, 2004, from http://www.issues2000.org/VoteMatch/q10.asp

Partnerships 1990–2000: Ten years of supporting education. (2003). Retrieved November 20, 2003, from http://www.napehq.org/d.pdf

Payne, R. K. (2002). *Understanding learning: The how, the why, the what.* Alexandria, VA: Association for Supervision and Curriculum Development.

Phillips, M. (2007, May). Backwards into the future—Again. *Phi Delta Kappan, 88*(9), 712–714.

Popham, W. J. (2007, March). All about accountability: Another bite out of the apple. *Phi Delta Kappan, 64*(6), 83–84.

Ravitch, D. (1983). *The troubled crusade: American education, 1945–80.* New York: Basic Books.

Scherer, M. (2007, December/2008, January). An answer for the long term. *Educational Leadership, 65*(4), 7.

Schon, D. A. (1971). *Beyond the stable state.* New York: Random House.

Schugurensky, D. (2003). *History of education: Selected moments of the 20th century.* Retrieved November 20, 2004, from http://fcis.oise.utoronto.ca/~daniel_schugurensky/assignment1/1994goals2000.html

Shorr, P. W. (2006, October/November). Best of class. *Scholastic Administrator, 6*(3), 24.

Summary of the Individuals with Disabilities Education Act (IDEA). (2003). Retrieved November 20, 2004, from http://edworkforce.house.gov/issues/108th/education/idea/idea.htm

Tomlinson, C. A., & McTighe, J. (2006). *Integrating differentiated instruction & understanding by design.* Alexandria, VA: Association for Supervision and Curriculum Development.

Van Geel, T. (1979). The new law of the curriculum. In J. Schaffarzick & G. Sykes (Eds.), *Value conflicts and curriculum issues* (pp. 25–72). Berkeley, CA: McCutchan.

Waskiewicz, J. (2007). Best of the blog. *Educational Leadership, 64*(6), 96.

Wiles, J., & Lundt, J. (2004). *Leaving school: Finding education.* St. Augustine, FL: Matanzas Press.

Wiliam, D. (2007, December/2008, January). Changing classroom practice. *Educational Leadership, 65*(4), 36–42.

Young, E. (2008). Focus on global education: A report from the 2007 PDK summit. *Phi Delta Kappan, 89*(5), 349–353.

Zirkel, P. A. (2007). Courtside: True diversity? *Phi Delta Kappan, 89*(3), 238–239.

CHAPTER 5 REFERENCES

Bambrick-Santoyo, P. (2007, December/2008, January). Data in the driver's seat. *Educational Leadership, 65*(4), 43–46.

Berry, B., Norton, J., & Byrd, A. (2007, September). Lessons from networking. *Educational Leadership, 65*(1), 48–52.

Blanchard, J. (2007). New schools chief takes lessons during first day on job. *Seattle Post-Intelligencer.* Retrieved July 10, 2007, from http://seattlepi.nwsource.com/local/323031_schools10.html

Christensen, D. (2004). *2002–2003 state of the school report: A report on Nebraska public schools* [Electronic version]. Lincoln, NE: Department of Education.

English, F. W. (1980). *Improving curriculum management in the schools.* Washington, DC: Council for Basic Education.

Ferrandino, V. L. (2007, March/April). Postscript: Sizing up the competition. *Principal, 86*(4), 80.

Fleck, F. (2007, September/October). The balanced principal. *Principal, 87*(1), 24–26.

Goodlad, J. I. (2004). *A place called school.* New York: McGraw-Hill.

Kaufman, R. A. (1982). Needs assessment. In F. W. English (Ed.), *Fundamental curriculum decisions* (pp. 53–67). Alexandria, VA: Association for Supervision and Curriculum Development.

Keech, C., Stahlecker, J., Thomas, S., & Watson, P. (1979). *National Writing Project evaluation report.* Berkeley, CA: University Press Books.

Lattimer, H. (2007, September). To help and not to hinder. *Educational Leadership, 65*(1), 70–73.

Mills, C. (2007, January/February). Building curriculum with digital materials. *Principal, 86*(3), 26–28.

O'Shea, M. R. (2005). *From standards to success.* Alexandria, VA: Association for Supervision and Curriculum Development.

Owens, T. R., & Wang, C. (1996, January). *Community-based learning: A foundation for meaningful educational reform* (Topical Synthesis #8). Portland, OR: Northwest Regional Laboratory. Retrieved April 5, 2005, from http://www.nwrel.org/scpd/sirs/10/t008.html

Patterson, P. (2007, January/February). Mission possible: Teaching through technology. *Principal, 86*(3), 22–25.

Pollock, J. E. (2007). *Improving student learning one teacher at a time.* Alexandria, VA: Association for Supervision and Curriculum Development.

Protheroe, N. (2008, January/February). District support for school improvement. *Principal, 87*(3), 36–38.

Reeves, D. B. (2007, December/2008, January). Making strategic planning work. *Educational Leadership, 65*(4), 87.

Suarez-Orozco, M. M., & Sattin, C. (2007). Wanted: Global citizens. *Educational Leadership, 64*(7), 58.

Vermillion School District 13-1. (2004). *Lessons for standardized curriculum: Mathematics, Grades 7–12.* Vermillion, SD: Author.

Zmuda, A., Kuklis, R., & Kline, E. (2004). *Transforming schools: Creating a culture of continuous improvement.* Alexandria, VA: Association for Supervision and Curriculum Development.

CHAPTER 6 REFERENCES

Adler, M. J. (1982). *The Paideia proposal: An educational manifesto.* New York: Macmillan.

American Association of Colleges for Teacher Education. (2004, December 30). No Child Left Behind (NCLB) research [Electronic version]. *AACTE Education Policy Clearinghouse.* Retrieved December 30, 2004, from http://www.edpolicy.org/research/nclb/index.php

Ashton, A. (2004, May 5). Report: U.S. losing ground in science education. *USA Today.* Retrieved December 28, 2004, from http://www.usatoday.com/news/education/2004-05-05-sciteach_x.htm

Bernhardt, V. L. (1998). *Data analysis for comprehensive schoolwide improvement.* New York: Eye on Education.

Bracey, G. W. (2006). How to avoid statistical traps. *Educational Leadership, 63*(8), 78–83.

Bunting, D. (2007). Principals as classroom leaders. *Principal, 86*(3), 39–41.

Cawelti, G. (1982). Redefining general education for the American high school. *Educational Leadership, 39,* 570–572.

Educational Policies Commission. (1952). *Education for all American youth—A further look.* Washington, DC: National Education Association.

Friedman, T. L. (2005). *The world is flat: A brief history of the twenty-first century.* New York: Farrar, Straus and Giroux.

Goldys, P., Druft, C., & Subrizi, P. (2007). Action research: Do it yourself! *Principal, 86*(4), 60–63.

Goodlad, J. I. (2004). *A place called school.* New York: McGraw-Hill.

McConnell, S. (2007, March/April). Rescuing public education. *Principal, 86*(4), 16.

Northwest Mississippi Community College. (2004, October). *NWCC SCANS committee monthly minutes.* Retrieved December 30, 2004, from http://www.northwestms.edu/administration/scans.html

Olson, L. (2004). Researchers sort out data-analysis software. *Education Week, 23*(18), 6.

Reeves, D. B. (2006, December/2007, January). How do you change school culture? *Educational Leadership, 64*(4), 94–95.

Snyder, C. W. (2004). *Calendar of activities/itinerary narrative.* Unpublished paper completed for the University of Montana International Studies program.

Stallings, J. (1980). Allocated academic learning time revisited, or beyond time on task. *Educational Researcher, 9,* 11–16.

Wormeli, R. (2005). *Summarization in any subject.* Alexandria, VA: Association for Supervision and Curriculum Development.

Zellmer, M. B., Frontier, A., & Pheifer, D. (2006). What are NCLB's instructional costs? *Educational Leadership, 64*(3), 43–46.

CHAPTER 7 REFERENCES

Bender, W. N., & Shores, C. (2007). *Response to Intervention: A practical guide for every teacher.* Alexandria, VA: Association for Supervision and Curriculum Development & Council for Exceptional Children.

Cawelti, G. (2006, November). The side effects of NCLB. *Educational Leadership, 64*(3), 64–68.

Copperman, P. (1978). *The literacy hoax.* New York: William Morrow.

Corcoran, T., McVay, S., & Riordan, K. (2003). *Getting it right: The MISE approach to professional development.* Philadelphia: Consortium for Policy Research in Education.

Cusick, P. A. (1983). *The egalitarian ideal and the American high school: Studies of three schools.* New York: Longman.

Darling-Hammond, L., & Berry, B. (2006). Highly qualified teachers for all. *Educational Leadership, 64*(3), 14–20.

Education Commission of the States. (2005). Professional development database. Denver, CO: Author. Retrieved April 2, 2008, from http://mb2.es.org/reports/Report.aspx?ed = 425

English, F. W. (1980). Curriculum mapping. *Educational Leadership, 37*(7), 558–559.

Fugate, C. (2007). Vonnegut warned us. *Phi Delta Kappan, 89*(1), 71–72.

Goodlad, J. I. (1977). What goes on in our schools. *Educational Researcher, 6*(3), 3–6.

Guilfoyle, C. (2006). NCL: Is there life beyond testing? *Educational Leadership, 64*(3), 8–13.

Hillocks, G., Jr. (1972). *Alternatives in English: A critical appraisal of elective programs.* Urbana, IL: National Council of Teachers of English.

Jacobs, H. H. (2004). *Getting results with curriculum mapping.* Alexandria, VA: Association for Supervision and Curriculum Development.

Kozol, J. (2007, September). Letters to a young teacher. *Phi Delta Kappan, 89*(1), 8–20.

National Staff Development Council. (2001). *Tools for growing the NSDC standards.* Oxford, OH: Author.

Oliver, A. I. (1978). *Maximizing mini-courses: A practical guide to a curriculum alternative.* New York: Teachers College Press.

Reason, C., & Reason, L. (2007). Asking the right questions. *Educational Leadership, 65*(1), 36–40.

Schmidt, B. W. (2004, June 21). District's new leader plans better learning. *Argus Leader,* p. A2.

Snow-Renner, R., & Lauer, P. A. (2005). *Professional development analysis.* Denver, CO: McREL. Retrieved March 18, 2008, from http://www.mcrel.org/PDF/ProfessionalDevelopment/5051IR_Prof_dvlpmt_analysis.pdf

Snyder, C. W. (2004). *Calendar of activities/itinerary narrative.* Unpublished paper completed for the University of Montana International Studies Program.

Washburne, C. W., & Marland, S. P., Jr. (1963). *Winnetka: The history and significance of an educational experiment.* Englewood Cliffs, NJ: Prentice Hall.

Whitehead, B., Jenson, D. F. N., & Boschee, F. (2003). *Planning for technology: A guide for school administrators, technology coordinators and curriculum leaders.* Thousand Oaks, CA: Corwin Press.

Wormeli, R. (2006). *Fair isn't always equal: Assessing & grading in the differentiated classroom.* Alexandria, VA: Association for Supervision and Curriculum Development.

Ysseldyke, J. E., & Tardrew, S. P. (2003). *Differentiating math instruction: A large-scale study of accelerated math: Final report.* Wisconsin Rapids, WI: Renaissance Learning. Retrieved March 23, 2005, from http://research.renlearn.com/research/139.asp

Zellmer, M. B., Frontier, A., & Pheifer, D. (2006, November). What are NCLB's instructional costs? *Educational Leadership, 64*(3), 43–46.

CHAPTER 8 REFERENCES

Assessment Reform Group. (1999). *Assessment for learning: Beyond the black box* [Electronic version]. Cambridge, UK: Cambridge University School of Education.

Bambrick-Santoyo, P. (2007, December/2008, January). Data in the driver's seat. *Educational Leadership, 65*(4), 43–46.

Chrisman, V. (2005). How schools sustain success. *Educational Leadership, 62*(5), 16–20.

Christie, K. (2007). Stateline: States seek to leverage assistance. *Phi Delta Kappan, 88*(7), 485–487.

Glatthorn, A. A. (1987). *Curriculum leadership.* New York: HarperCollins.

Guskey, T. R. (2007, December/2008, January). The rest of the story. *Educational Leadership, 65*(4), 28–34.

Leithwood, K. A., & Montgomery, D. J. (1982). The role of the elementary principal in program improvement. *Review of Educational Research, 52,* 309–339.

McConnell, S. (2007). Rescuing public education. *Principal, 86*(4), 16–19.

Montana State University. (2007). *Montana university system position on Administrative Rule N. 10-55-907: Alternative Dual Credit Licensure for MUS Online Faculty.* Unpublished report presented to the Montana Distance Learning Task Force, January 15, 2008.

Packer, J. (2007). The NEA supports substantial overhaul, not repeal, of NCLB. *Phi Delta Kappan, 89*(4), 265–269.

Patterson, P. (2007). Mission possible: Teaching through technology. *Principal, 86*(3), 22–25.

Richardson, W., & Mancabelli, R. (2007). The Read/Write Web: New tools for a new generation of technology. *Principal, 86*(3), 12–17.

Schmoker, M. (2001). *The results fieldbook: Practical strategies from dramatically improved schools.* Alexandria, VA: Association for Supervision and Curriculum Development.

Sholten, C. (2003). *Developing acceptable use policies: How can I develop an acceptable use policy that will work for my school?* Learning to Teach With Technology Studio. Course TE 001.

Retrieved February 26, 2004, from http://ltts.indiana.edu

Snyder, C. W. (2004). *Calendar of activities/itinerary narrative.* Unpublished paper completed for the University of Montana International Studies Program.

Stiggins, R. J. (2002, June). Assessment crisis: The absence of assessment for learning. *Phi Delta Kappan, 83*(10), 758–765.

Tomlinson, C. A. (2007, December/2008, January).

Learning to love assessment. *Educational Leadership, 65*(4), 8–13.

Tucker, M. (2007). Charting a new course for schools. *Educational Leadership, 64*(7), 48–52.

Tyler, R. W. (1949). *Basic principles of curriculum and instruction.* Chicago: University of Chicago Press.

Wulf, K. M., & Schave, B. (1984). *Curriculum design: A handbook for educators.* Glenview, IL: Scott, Foresman.

CHAPTER 9 REFERENCES

Allen, T. (2004). No school left unscathed. *Phi Delta Kappan, 85*(5), 396–397.

Allington, R. L. (2002). *Big brother and the national reading curriculum: How ideology trumped evidence.* Portsmouth, NH: Heinemann.

Berliner, D. C. (1984). The half-full glass: A review of the research on teaching. In P. Hosford (Ed.), *Using what we know about teaching* (pp. 51–85). Alexandria, VA: Association for Supervision and Curriculum Development.

Boles, K. C., & Troen, V. (2007). How to improve professional practice. *Principal, 67*(2), 50–53.

Brophy, J. E., & Good, T. L. (1986). Teacher behavior and student achievement. In M. C. Wittrock (Ed.), *Handbook of research on teaching* (3rd ed., pp. 328–375). New York: Macmillan.

Costa, A. L., & Garmston, R. J. (2002). *Cognitive coaching: A foundation for renaissance schools.* Norwood, MA: Christopher-Gordon.

Danielson, C. (2002). *Enhancing student achievement: A framework for school improvement.* Alexandria, VA: Association for Supervision and Curriculum Development.

Elliot, D., & Woodward, A. (1990). Textbooks and schooling in the United States (Ninetieth Yearbook of the Society for the Study of Education). Chicago: University of Chicago Press.

Gersten, R., Green, W., & Davis, G. (1985, April). *The realities of instructional leadership: An intensive study of four inner city schools.* Paper presented at the annual meeting of the American Educational Research Association, Chicago.

Gilman, D. A., & Gilman, R. A. (2003). Standard-based teaching: Overcoming the side effects. *Principal, 83*(2), 44–47.

Glatthorn, A. A. (1984). *Differentiated supervision.* Alexandria, VA: Association for Supervision and Curriculum Development.

Glatthorn, A. A. (1987). *Curriculum leadership.* New York: HarperCollins.

Glickman, C. D. (2001). *Leadership for learning: How to help teachers succeed.* Alexandria: VA: Association for Supervision and Curriculum Development.

Glickman, C. D., Gordon, S. P., & Ross-Gordon, J. M. (2003). *Supervision and instructional leadership: A developmental approach.* Boston: Allyn & Bacon.

Glover, E. (2007). Real principals listen. *Educational Leadership, 65*(1), 60–63.

Harmon, M. B. (2004, March). Rewriting the book on literacy. *Scholastic Administrator, 3*(5), 18–22.

Hunter, M. (1984). Knowing, teaching, and supervising. In P. L. Hosford (Ed.), *Using what we know about teaching* (pp. 169–193). Alexandria, VA: Association for Supervision and Curriculum Development.

Komoski, P. (1985). Instructional materials will not improve until we change the system. *Educational Leadership, 42*(7), 31–37.

Lattimer, H. (2007). To help and not hinder. *Educational Leadership, 65*(1), 70–73.

McGreal, T. L. (1983). *Successful teacher evaluation.* Alexandria, VA: Association for Supervision and Curriculum Development.

Merrow, J. (2004). Meeting superman. *Phi Delta Kappan, 85*(10), 455–460.

Muther, C. (1985). *The pitfalls of textbook adoption and how to avoid them.* Alexandria, VA: Association for Supervision and Curriculum Development.

Penuel, W. R., & Riel, M. (2007). The "new" science of networks and the challenge of school change. *Phi Delta Kappan, 88*(8), 611–615.

Perspectives: What works in reading? (2004). *Educational Leadership, 61*(6), 5.

Piltch, B., & Quinn, T. (2007). Practitioner's corner: Don't throw in the towel just yet. *Principal, 87*(2), 54–55.

Pitler, H., & Goodwin, B. (2008). Classroom walk-throughs: Learning to see the trees and the forest. *Changing Schools, 58,* 9–11.

Reason, C., & Reason, L. (2007). Asking the right questions. *Educational Leadership, 65*(1), 36–40.

Reeves, D. B. (2007). Coaching myths and realities. *Principal, 65*(2), 89–90.

Richards, J. (2007). How effective principals encourage their teachers. *Principal, 86*(3), 48–50.

Riggins-Newby, C. G. (2003). Improving curriculum and instruction. *Principal, 83*(2), 8.

Rosenshine, B., & Stevens, R. (1986). Teaching functions. In M. C. Wittrock (Ed.), *Handbook of research on teaching* (3rd ed., pp. 376–391). New York: Macmillan.

Sergiovanni, T. J. (1985). Landscapes, mindscapes, and reflective practice in supervision. *Journal of Curriculum and Supervision, 1,* 5–17.

Sergiovanni, T. J. (2005). *Strengthening the heartbeat: Leading and learning together in schools.* San Francisco: Jossey-Bass.

Stallings, J. (1986, April). *Report on a three-year study of the Hunter model.* Paper presented at the annual conference of the American Educational Research Association, San Francisco.

Tomlinson, C. A., Kaplan, S. N., Renzulli, J. S., Purcell, J., Leppien, J., & Burns, D. (2002). *The parallel curriculum: A design to develop high potential and challenge high-ability learners.* Thousand Oaks, CA: Corwin Press.

Weeks, D. J. (2001, Winter). Standards and the impulse for human betterment. *Northwest Teacher, 2*(1), 2–5.

Weis, I. R., & Pasley, J. D. (2004). What is high quality education? *Association for Supervision and Curriculum Development, 61*(5), 24–28.

CHAPTER 10 REFERENCES

Baron, M. A., Boschee, F., & Jacobson, M. (2008). *Performance-based education: Developing programs through strategic planning.* Lanham, MD: Rowman & Littlefield Education.

Bradley, L. H. (1985). *Curriculum leadership and development handbook.* Englewood Cliffs, NJ: Prentice Hall.

Canadian Ministry of Education. (1992). *Language arts English primary–graduation curriculum guide.* (1992). Victoria, BC: Author.

Kizlik, B. (2008). Definitions of behavioral verbs for learning objectives. *ADPRIMA.* Retrieved May 12, 2008, from http://www.adprima.com/verbs.htm

Perkins-Gough, D. (2003/2004). Creating a timely curriculum. *Educational Leadership, 61*(4), 12.

Waters, J. T., & Marzano, R. J. (2006, September). *School district leadership that works: The effect of superintendent in student achievement* (Working Paper). Retrieved May 10, 2008, from http://www.mcrel.org/pdf/leadershiporganizationdevelopment/4005RR_Superintendent_Leadership.pdf

CHAPTER 11 REFERENCES

Arhar, J. M., (1997). The effects of interdisciplinary teaming on students and teachers. In J. L. Irvin (Ed.), *What current research says to the middle level practitioner* (pp. 49–56). Columbus, OH: National Middle School Association. (ERIC Document Service No. ED 427 847)

Bambrick-Santoyo, P. (2007, December/2008, January). Data in the driver's seat. *Educational Leadership, 65*(4), 43–46.

Baron, M. A., Boschee, F., & Jacobson, M. (2008). *Performance-based education: Developing programs through strategic planning.* Lanham, MD: Rowman & Littlefield.

Beane, J. A. (1997). *Curriculum integration: Designing the core of democratic education.* New York: Teachers College Press.

Bernhardt, V. L. (1998). *Data analysis for comprehensive schoolwide improvement.* New York: Eye on Education.

Bloom, B. S., Hastings, J. T., & Madaus, G. F. (1971). *Handbook on formative and summative evaluation of student learning.* New York: McGraw-Hill.

Danielson, C. (2002). *Enhancing student achievement: A framework for school improvement.* Alexandria, VA: Association for Supervision and Curriculum Development.

Duffy, G., & Kear, K. (2007, April). Compliance or adaptation: What is the real message about research-based practices? *Phi Delta Kappan, 88*(8), 579–581.

Fusarelli, L. D. (2008, January). Flying (partially) blind: School leaders' use of research in decision making. *Phi Delta Kappan, 89*(5), 365–368.

Gallagher, C. W., & Ratzlaff, R. (2007, December/2008, January). The road less traveled. *Educational Leadership, 65*(4), 48–53.

Herman, J. L., Baker, E. L., & Linn, R. L. (2004, Spring). Accountability systems in support of students learning: Moving to the next generation. *CRESST LINE.* Retrieved May 8, 2008, from http://www.cse.ucla.edu/products/newsletters/cresst_cl2004_2.pdf

Lyon, G. R., & Chhabra, V. (2004). The science of reading research. *Educational Leadership, 61*(6), 12–17.

Marzano, R. J., Waters, T., & McNulty, B. A. (2005). *School leadership that works: From research to results.* Alexandria, VA: Association for Supervision and Curriculum Development.

National Association for Core Curriculum. (2000). *A bibliography of research on the effectiveness of block-time, core, and interdisciplinary team teaching programs.* Kent, OH: Author.

Nichols, S. L., & Berliner, D. C. (2008). Why has high-stakes testing so easily slipped into contemporary American life? *Phi Delta Kappan, 89*(9), 672.

Stiggins, R. J. (2001). *Student-involved classroom assessment* (3rd ed.). Upper Saddle River: NJ: Prentice Hall.

Tomlinson, C. A., Kaplan, S. N., Renzulli, J., Purcell, J., Leppien, J., & Burns, D. (2002). *The parallel curriculum: A design to develop high potential and challenge high-ability learners.* Thousand Oaks, CA: Corwin Press.

Torff, B., & Fusco, E. (2007, December/2008, January). Teachers who know their stuff-but can't teach it. *Principal, 86*(3), 61–62.

Vars, G. F. (1996). Effects of interdisciplinary curriculum and instruction. In P. S. Hlebowitsh & W. G. Wraga (Eds.), *Annual review of research for school leaders* (pp. 147–164). Reston, VA: National Association of Secondary School Principals and Scholastic Publishing.

Vars, G. F. (1997). Effects of integrative curriculum and instruction. In J. L. Irvin (Ed.), *What current research says to the middle level practitioner* (pp. 179–186). Columbus, OH: National Middle School Association. (ERIC Document Service No. ED 427 847)

Vars, G., & Beane, J. A. (2000). *Integrative curriculum in a standards-based world.* Champaign, IL: ERIC Clearinghouse on Elementary and Early Childhood Education, University of Illinois, *ERIC Digest.* (ERIC Document Reproduction Service No. ED 441 618) Retrieved March 27, 2005, from http://www.eric.ed.gov

Weiss, I. R., & Pasley, J. D. (2004). What is high-quality instruction? *Educational Leadership, 61*(5), 24–28.

Whitehead, B. M., Jensen, D. F. N., & Boschee, F. (2003). *Planning for technology: A guide for school administrators, technology coordinators, and curriculum leaders.* Thousand Oaks, CA: Corwin Press.

CHAPTER 12 REFERENCES

Brandt, R. S. (Ed.). (1981). *Applied strategies for curriculum evaluation.* Alexandria, VA: Association for Supervision and Curriculum Development.

Eisner, E. W. (1979). *The educational imagination: On the design and evaluation of school programs.* New York: Macmillan.

Ferrero, D. J. (2006). Having it all. *Educational Leadership, 63*(8), 8–14.

Glatthorn, A. A. (1987). *Curriculum leadership.* New York: HarperCollins.

Guba, E., & Lincoln, Y. (1981). *Effective evaluation.* San Francisco: Jossey-Bass.

Guskey, T. R. (2007, December/2008, January). The rest of the story. *Educational Leadership, 65*(4), 28–35.

Holland, R. (2001, December). *Indispensable tests: How a value-added approach to school testing could identify and bolster exceptional teaching.* Retrieved March 17, 2004, from http://www.lexingtoninstitute.org/education/schooltesting.htm

Homan, P. (2003). *Sioux Falls School District 2002–2003 value-added analysis of student achievement and effective instruction.* Unpublished manuscript. Available from Sioux Falls School District, South Dakota.

Kohn, A. (1994). Grading: The issue is not how but why. *Educational Leadership, 52*(2), 40.

Mayer, R., Schustack, M. W., & Blanton, W. E. (n.d.). *What do children learn from using computers in an informal collaborative setting?* Retrieved March 28, 2005, from http://129.171.53.1/blantonw/5dClhse/publications/tech/mayer_schustak_blanton.html

National Educational Association. (1969). *Report of the Committee of Ten on secondary school studies.* New York: Arno Press and *The New York Times.* (Originally published in 1893 by the U.S. Government Printing Office)

Olson, A. (2004, March). Tailor tests for every student. *Scholastic Administrator.* Retrieved March 28, 2005, from http://www.scholastic.com/administrator/march04/articles.asp?article = opinion

Popham, J. W. (2001). *The truth about testing: An educator's call to action.* Alexandria, VA: Association for Supervision and Curriculum Development.

Scriven, M. (1972). Prose and cons about goal-free evaluation. *Evaluation Comment, 3*(4), 1–4.

Stake, R. E. (Ed.). (1975). *Evaluating the arts in education: A responsive approach.* Columbus, OH: Bobbs-Merrill.

Stufflebeam, D. L. (1971). *Educational evaluation and decision-making.* Itasca, IL: Peacock.

Tyler, R. W. (1950). *Basic principles of curriculum and instruction: Syllabus for Education 305.* Chicago: University of Chicago Press.

Worthen, B. R. (1981). Journal entries of an eclectic evaluator. In R. S. Brandt (Ed.), *Applied strategies for curriculum evaluation* (pp. 58–90). Alexandria, VA: Association for Supervision and Curriculum Development.

CHAPTER 13 REFERENCES

Allen, R. (2004, Summer). Shaking up science: Putting physics first changes more than sequence. *Curriculum Update, 1–2,* 6, 8.

Allington, R. L. (2001). *What really matters for struggling readers: Designing research-based programs.* New York: Addison-Wesley Educational.

American Council of Teachers of Foreign Languages. (1982). *ACTFL provisional proficiency guidelines.* Hastings-on-Hudson, NY: Author.

Americans for the Arts News. (2008). Standards for arts education. Retrieved March 10, 2008, from http://www.americansforthearts.org/public_awareness/artsed_facts/oo4.asp

Armstrong, T. (2003). *The multiple intelligences of reading and writing.* Alexandria, VA: Association for Supervision and Curriculum Development.

Beck, I. L., & McKeown, M. C. (2002). Questioning the author: Making sense of social studies. *Educational Leadership, 60*(3), 44–47.

Bohn, A. P., & Sleeter, C. E. (2000, October). Multicultural education and the standards movement: A report from the field. *Phi Delta Kappan, 82*(2), 156–159.

Boss, S. (2001, Winter). Teachers taking charge of change. *Northwest Teacher, 2*(1), 6–9.

Bracey, G. W. (2006). Research: Is literacy lagging? *Phi Delta Kappan, 87*(9), 713–714.

Camilli, G., & Wolfe, P. (2004). Research on reading: A cautionary tale. *Educational Leadership, 61*(6), 26–29.

Canadian Association for Health, Physical Education, Recreation and Dance. (2008). *Quality daily physical education.* Retrieved July 18, 2008, from http://www.cahperd.ca/eng/physicaleducation/about_qdpe.cfm

Carbo, M. (2003, November/December). Achieving with struggling readers. *Principal, 83*(2), 20–24.

Carbo, M. (2007). Best practices for achieving high, rapid reading gains. *Principal, 87*(2), 42–45.

Chalufour, I., Hoisington, C., Moriarty, R., Winokur, J., & Worth, K. (2004). The science and mathematics of building structures. *Science and Children, 41*(4), 30–34.

Chandler, H. (2003). Concept mapping & WebQuests in social studies. *Media and Methods, 39*(3), 38–39.

Coles, G. (2004). Danger in the classroom: "Brain glitch" research and learning to read. *Phi Delta Kappan, 85*(5), 344–351.

Colombo, M. W., & Colombo, P. D. (2007). Blogging to improve instruction in differentiated science classrooms. *Phi Delta Kappan, 89*(1), 60–63.

Connell, D. R., Turner, R. R., & Mason, E. F. (1985). Summary of findings of the School Health Education Evaluation: Health promotion effectiveness, implementation, and costs. *Journal of School Health, 55,* 316–321.

Cox-Petersen, A., & Olson, J. K. (2007). Alternate assessments for English language learners. *Principal, 87*(2), 32–34.

Crocco, M. S., & Thornton, S. J. (2002, Spring). Social studies in the New York City public schools: A descriptive study. *Journal of Curriculum and Supervision, 17*(3), 206.

Czarra, F. (2002–2003). Global education checklist. *American Forum for Global Education,* 173. Retrieved April 17, 2008, from http://www.globaled.org/fianlcopy.pdf

Daniels, Y. D., Queen, J. A., & Schumacher, D. (2007). Obesity and poverty: a growing challenge. *Principal, 86*(3), 42–47.

Darling-Hammond, L., & Berry, B. (2006). Highly qualified teachers for all. *Phi Delta Kappan, 64*(3), 14–20.

Department of Health and Human Services. (1995). *Strategic plan for promoting physical activity.* Dallas, TX: Centers for Disease Control and Prevention; American Heart Association.

Dunn, R., & Griggs, S.A. (Eds.). (2007). *What if? Promising practices for improving schools.* Lanham, MD: Rowman & Littlefield Education.

Education for Global Leadership. (2007). *Business and academic leaders endorse CED foreign language studies project.* Committee for Economic Development/Creative Commons Attribution. Retrieved March 10, 2008, from http://www.ced.org/projects/educ_forlang.shtml

Gay, G. (2003, December/2004, January). The importance of multicultural education. *Educational Leadership, 61*(4), 30–34.

Glendening, M. (2004, February/March). Learning through literature connections. *Reading Today, 21*(4), 10.

Gold, R. S. (1994). The science base for comprehensive school health education. In P. Cortese & K. Middleton (Eds.), *The comprehensive school health challenge: Promoting health through education* (pp. 545–573). Santa Cruz, CA: ETR Associates.

Gomez, L. M., & Gomez, K. (2007). Reading for learning: Literacy supports for 21st-century work. *Phi Delta Kappan, 89*(3), 224–228.

Hammerberg, D. D. (2004). Comprehension instruction for socioculturally diverse classrooms: A review of what we know. *Reading Teacher, 57*(7), 648–661.

Hammill, C. (2008). Finding value in the answers [Review of the book *What if? Promising practices for improving schools*]. *Principal, 87*(3), 57.

Harris, L., & Associates. (1989). *Health—You've got to be taught: An evaluation of comprehensive health education in American public schools.* New York: Metropolitan Life Foundation.

Hubbell, E. R., & Kuhn, M. (2007). Using technology to promote science inquiry. *Principal, 87*(2), 24–27.

Hunsader, P. D. (2004, April). Mathematics trade books: Establishing their value and assessing their quality. *Reading Teacher, 57*(7), 618–629.

International Reading Association. (2000, October). Excellent reading teachers. *Reading Teacher, 54*(2), 235.

International Reading Association. (2004, April/May). Setting an example. *Reading Today, 21*(5), 15.

Jarolimek, J. (1981). The social studies: An overview. In H. D. Mehlinger & O. L. Davis, Jr. (Eds.), *The social studies* (pp. 3–18). Chicago: University of Chicago Press.

Jensen, E. P. (2008). A fresh look at brain-based education. *Phi Delta Kappan, 89*(6), 412.

Keith, C. L. (2004, February/March). Libraries called key. *Reading Today, 21*(4), 1–4.

Kolbe, L. J. (1993a). Developing a plan of action to institutionalize comprehensive school health education programs in the United States. *Journal of School Health, 63*(1), 12–13.

Kolbe, L. J. (1993b). An essential strategy to improve the health and education of Americans. *Preventive Medicine, 22*(4), 1–17.

Lewis, C., Perry, R., & Hurd, J. (2004). A deeper look at lesson study. *Educational Leadership, 61*(5), 18–22.

Long, T. W., & Gove, M. K. (2004). How engagement strategies and literature circles promote critical response in a fourth-grade, urban classroom. *Reading Teacher, 57*(4), 350–361.

Loveless, T., & Coughlan, J. (2004). The arithmetic gap. *Educational Leadership, 61*(5), 55–59.

Lozanov, G. (1978). *Suggestology and outlines of Suggestopedia.* New York: Gordon and Breach.

Lyon, G. R., Fletcher, J. M., Torgeson, J. K., Shaywitz, S. E., & Chhabra, V. (2004). Preventing and remediating reading failure: A response to Allington. *Educational Leadership, 61*(6).

McDaniel, C. (2004). Critical literacy: A questioning stance and the possibility for change. *Reading Teacher, 57*(5), 472–473.

McGuire, M. E. (2007). What happened to social studies? The disappearing curriculum. *Phi Delta Kappan, 88*(8), 620–624.

Melber, L. M. (2003, Fall). Partnerships in science learning: Museum outreach and elementary gifted education. *Gifted Child Quarterly, 47*(4), 251–258.

National Association for Sport and Physical Education. (2008, Winter). On pace: Physical activity in contemporary education. *NASPE News, 77,* 7.

National Council for the Social Studies. (1984). In search of a scope and sequence for social studies. *Social Education, 48,* 249–262.

National Council of Teachers of English. (2005). *IRA/NCTE standards for the English language arts: The 12 standards.* Retrieved on March 28, 2005, from http://www.ncte.org/about/over/standards/110846.htm

National Council of Teachers of Mathematics. (1989). *Curriculum and evaluation standards for school mathematics.* Reston, VA: Author.

National Council of Teachers of Mathematics. (2004). *Principles and standards for school mathematics.* Reston, VA: Retrieved April 22, 2004, from http://standards.nctm.org/document

National Education Association. (1969). *Report of the Committee of Fifteen.* New York: Arno Press. (Original work published in 1895 by New England Publishing)

National Institute of Child Health and Human Development. (2000). *Report of the National Reading Panel: Teaching children to read: An evidence-based assessment of the scientific research literature on reading and its implications for reading instruction.* Washington, DC: U.S. Department of Health and Human Services.

National Standards in Foreign Language Education Project. (1996). *Standards for foreign language learning: Preparing for the 21st century.* Yonkers, NY: Author. (ERIC Document Reproduction Service No. ED 394 279)

North Central Educational Regional Laboratory. (n.d.). *Integrating technology into the curriculum: Technology in social studies.* Retrieved March 28, 2005, from http://www.ncrel.org/tplan/guide/int7.htm

O'Brien, T. C. (2007). The old and the new. *Phi Delta Kappan, 88*(9), 664–668.

Padgett, R. (2007). New developments in K–8 science instruction. *Principal. 87*(2), 6.

Perkins-Gough, D. (2004). Web wonders. *Educational Leadership, 61*(6), 91–92.

Ponder, G. (1979). The more things change: The status of social studies. *Educational Leadership, 36*(7), 515–518.

Protheroe, N. (2007). Differentiating instruction in a standards-based environment. *Principal, 87*(2), 36–40.

Reys, B. J., Reys, R. E., & Chavez, O. (2004). Why mathematics textbooks matter. *Educational Leadership, 61*(5), 61–66.

Richardson, W., & Mancabelli, R. (2007). The Read/Write Web: New tools for a new generation of technology. *Principal, 86*(3), 12–17.

Roberts, H. D., Kaulfers, W. V., & Kefaurer, G. N. (Eds.). (1943). *English for social living.* New York: McGraw-Hill.

Robertson, W. C., Gallagher, J., & Miller, W. (2004, March). Newton's first law: Not so simple after all. *Science & Children, 41*(6), 25–29.

Roschelle, J., Penuel, W. R., & Abrahamson, L. (2004). The networked classroom. *Educational Leadership, 61*(5), 50–53.

Santos, R. M. (2004, January). Ensuring culturally and linguistically appropriate assessment of young children. *Young Children, 59*(1), 48–50.

Scherer, M. (2004). Perspectives: What works in reading? *Educational Leadership, 61*(6), 5.

Schleicher, A. (2008). PISA, PIRLS spotlight global trends and literacy skills: Foundation for success. *Reading Today, 25*(4), 4.

Schmidt, W. H. (2004). A vision for mathematics. *Educational Leadership, 61*(4), 6–11.

Schneider, E. (2000). Shifting into high gear. *Educational Leadership, 58*(1), 57–60.

Schulte, P. L. (1996, November/December). A definition of constructivism. *Science Scope, 20*(6), 25–27.

Schutz, R. (2007). *Stephen Krahsen's Theory of Second Language Acquisition.* Retrieved March 10, 2008, from http://www.sk.com.br/sk-krash.html

Seffrin, J. R. (1990). The comprehensive school health curriculum: Closing the gap between state-of-the-art and state-of-the-practice. *Journal of School Health, 60*(4), 151–156.

Shaver, J. P., Davis, O. L., Jr., & Helburn, S. W. (1979). The status of social studies education: Impressions from three NSF studies. *Social Education, 43*(2), 150–163.

Shaywitz, S. E., & Shaywitz, B. A. (2004). Reading disability and the brain. *Educational Leadership, 61*(6), 7–11.

Slavin, R. E., Chamberlain, A., & Daniels, C. (2007). Preventing reading failure. *Educational Leadership, 65*(2), 22–27.

Snow, C. E., Burns, M. S., & Griffin, P. (Eds.). (1998). *Preventing reading difficulties in young children.* Washington, DC: National Academy Press.

Stepanek, J. (2001, Winter). Using standards to illuminate big ideas in science. *Northwest Teacher, 2*(1), 10–13.

Stigler, J. W., & Hiebert, J. (2004). Improving mathematics teaching. *Educational Leadership, 61*(5), 12–17.

Stoskopf, A. (2001). Reviving Clio: Inspired history teaching and learning (without high-stakes testing). *Phi Delta Kappan, 82,* 468–473.

Strong, R., Thomas, E., Perini, M., & Silver, H. (2004, February). Creating a differentiated mathematics classroom. *Educational Leadership, 61*(5), 73–78.

Superka, D. P., Hawke, S., & Morrissett, I. (1980). The current and future status of the social studies. *Social Education, 44*(5), 362–369.

Thornton, S. J. (2007). Geography in American history courses. *Phi Delta Kappan, 88*(7), 535–536.

Tomlinson, C. A., & McTighe, J. (2006). *Integrating differentiated instruction & understanding by design.* Alexandria, VA: Association for Supervision and Curriculum Development.

Vitaska, D. (2002, September/October). The new language classroom. *Media & Methods, 39*(1), 10–13.

Walling, D. R. (2001). Rethinking visual arts education: A convergence of influences. *Phi Delta Kappan, 82*(8), 626–631.

Weiss, I. R., & Pasley, J. D. (2007). Teaching math and science: Improving instruction through local systemic change initiatives. *Phi Delta Kappan, 88*(9), 669–675.

Whyte, D. (2008). Focus attention on high-impact activities. *Phi Delta Kappan, 1*(15), n.p. Retrieved May 13, 2008, from http://www.pdkintl.org/publications/Sparks_080512.pdf

Willis, J. (2007). Toward neuro-logical reading instruction. *Educational Leadership, 64*(6), 80–82.

Wolfe, P. (2001). *Brain matters: Translating research into classroom practice.* Alexandria, VA: Association of Supervision and Curriculum Development.

Yager, R. E., Aldridge, B. G., & Penick, J. E. (1983). Current practice: School science today. In F. K. Brown & D. P. Butts (Eds.), *Science teaching: A profession speaks* (pp. 1–22). Washington, DC: National Science Teachers Association.

Young, B. (2007). Rewriting the book on science instruction. *Principal, 87*(2), 28–31.

CHAPTER 14 REFERENCES

Bambrick-Santoyo, P. (2007, December/2008, January). Data in the driver's seat. *Educational Leadership, 65*(4), 43–46.

Barger, S., Edens, D., O'Neill, B., & Wilcoxen, S. (2007). Strengthening instruction through Web-based curriculum mapping. *Principal, 87*(2), 56–57.

Brown, D. (2002). Self-directed learning in an 8th grade classroom. *Educational Leadership, 60*(1), 54–59.

CUSD Instructional Center. (2005). *Educational technology master plan.* Retrieved March 29, 2005, from http://www.cusd.claremont.edu/tech/plan/intro.html

Dahl, K., Bart, A., Bonfils, A., Carasello, M., Christopher, J., Davis, R., et al. (2003–2004). Connecting developmental word study with classroom writing: Children's descriptions of spelling strategies. *Reading Teacher, 57*(4), 310–321.

Ferrandino, V. L. (2007). Keeping up with fourth graders. *Principal, 86*(3), 64.

Franklin, C. A. (2008). Factors determining elementary teachers' use of computers. *Principal, 87*(3), 54–55.

Gallagher, C. W., & Ratzlaff, S. (2007, December/2008, January). The road less traveled. *Educational Leadership, 65*(4), 48–52.

Gibbons, M. (2004). Pardon me, didn't I just hear a paradigm shift? *Phi Delta Kappan, 85*(6), 461–467.

Glatthorn, A. A. (1984). *Writing to learn.* Unpublished manuscript, University of Pennsylvania.

Glatthorn, A. A. (1985). *Teaching critical thinking: A teacher-centered process.* Unpublished manuscript, University of Pennsylvania.

Gora, K., Hinson, J., & Hall, D. (2003–2004, December/ January). Teacher-to-teacher mentoring. *Learning & Leading With Technology*, pp. 36–39.

Henk, W. A., Marinak, B. A., Moore, J. C., & Mallette, M. H. (2003–2004). The writing observation framework: A guide for refining and validating writing instruction. *Reading Teacher, 57*(4),322–333.

Hoesing, D. J. (2004). Student perceptions of e-learning in South Dakota high schools (Doctoral dissertation, the University of South Dakota). *Dissertation International Abstracts, 65*, 4532A.

Howard, K. L. (2004). Multidisciplinary Universal Design: Meeting the needs of all students. *Learning & Leading With Technology*, p. 26.

Johnson, D. (2004). Plagiarism-proofing assignments. *Phi Delta Kappan, 85*(7), 549–552.

Layton, T. (2000). Digital learning. Why tomorrow's schools must learn to let go of the past. *Electronic School.Com*, p. 6.

Lewis, A. C. (2004). Schools that engage children. *Phi Delta Kappan, 85*(7), 483–484.

Liben, D. M., & Liben, M. (2004). Our journey to reading success. *Educational Leadership, 61*(6), 58–61.

Lieberman, A., & Friedrich, L. (2007). Teachers, writers, and leaders. *Educational Leadership, 65*(1), 42–47.

March, J., & Peters, K. (2002). Curriculum development and instructional design in the effective school process. *Phi Delta Kappan, 83*(5), 379–381.

Martinez, M. E. (2006). What is metacognition? *Phi Delta Kappan, 87*(9), 696–699.

McCaulley, R. J. (1992). The effects of a semester-long listening skills program on listening comprehension and reading comprehension (Doctoral dissertation, University of South Dakota, 1992). *Dissertation International Abstracts, 53*, 1432A.

MIT Online Writing and Communication Center. (1999). Massachusetts Institute of Technology. Retrieved May 24, 2008, from http://web.mit .edu/writing/Writing_Process/writingprocess.html

National Council of Teachers of English. (2008). NCTE beliefs about the teaching of writing. Retrieved May 24, 2008, from http://www.ncte.org/prog/ writing/research/118876.htm

Noddings, N. (2004). War, critical thinking, and self-understanding. *Phi Delta Kappan, 85*(7), 489–495.

Northwest Regional Educational Laboratory. (2001, March/April). *6 + 1 Trait Writing Program: Study findings on the integration of writing assessment & instruction*. Retrieved April 10, 2005, from http:// www.nwrel.org/assessment/department.php?d = 1

Padgett, R. (2007). Helping you embark on a new frontier. *Principal, 86*(3), 63.

Panel on Educational Technology. (1997, March). *Report to the president on the use of technology to strengthen K–12 education in the United States*. Washington, DC: President's Committee of Advisors on Science and Technology.

Patterson, P. (2007). Mission: Teaching through technology. *Principal, 86*(3), 22–25.

Remondino, F., & Chen, T. C. (2004). 35 years of Internet—10 years of ISPRS online [Electronic version]. *British Library Direct, 35*(6), 111–122.

Schmoker, M. (2007). Reading, writing, and thinking for all. *Educational Leadership, 64*(7), 63–66.

Simkins, M., Cole, K., Tavalin, F., & Means, B. (2002). *Increasing student learning through multimedia projects*. Alexandria, VA: Association for Supervision and Curriculum Development.

Smith, B. M. (2004). No time for thinking [Editorial]. *Phi Delta Kappan, 85*, 482.

Solvie, P. A. (2003). The digital whiteboard: A tool in early literacy instruction. *Reading Teacher, 57*(5), 484–487.

Sternberg, R. J. (2008). Assessing what matters. *Educational Leadership, 65*(4), 25.

Taylor, B. O. (2002). The effective schools process: Alive and well. *Phi Delta Kappan, 83*(5), 375–378.

Tomlinson, C. (2007, December/2008, January). Learning to love assessment. *Educational Leadership, 65*(4), 8–13.

Tucker, M. (2007, April). Charting a new course for schools. *Educational Leadership, 64*(7), 48–52.

Weiss, I. R., & Pasley, J. D. (2004). What is high-quality instruction? *Educational Leadership, 61*(5), 24–28.

Whitehead, B. M., Jensen, D. F. N., & Boschee, F. (2003). *Planning for technology: A guide for school administrators, technology coordinators, and curriculum leaders*. Thousand Oaks, CA: Corwin Press.

CHAPTER 15 REFERENCES

Anderson, L. W. (1985). A retrospective and prospective view of Bloom's "Learning for Mastery." In M. C. Wang & H. J. Walberg (Eds.), *Adapting instruction to individual differences* (pp. 254–268). Berkeley, CA: McCutchan.

Atkins, J. T., & Ellsesser, J. (2003). Tracking: The good, the bad, and the questions. *Educational Leadership, 61*(2), 44–49.

Bender, W. N., & Shores, C. (2007). *Response to intervention: A practical guide for every teacher.* Thousand Oaks, CA: Corwin Press & Council for Exceptional Children.

Brown, D. F. (2002). Self-directed learning. *Educational Leadership, 60*(1), 54–59.

Brusilovsky, P. (2004). Adaptive hypermedia: From intelligent tutoring systems to Web-based education. *Carnegie Technology Education and HCI Institute.* Retrieved April 24, 2004, from http://www.sis.pitt.edu/~peterb/papers/ITS00inv.html

Burris, C. C., Heubert, J. P., & Levin, H. M. (2004). Math acceleration for all. *Educational Leadership, 61*(5), 68–72.

California Department of Education. (2004). *Cooperative learning: Response to diversity.* Curriculum Instruction Web Team. Retrieved April 25, 2004, from http://www.cde.ca.gov/iasa/cooplrng2.html

Carbo, M. (2003). Achieving with struggling readers. *Principal, 83*(2), 20–24.

Carbo, M. (2007). Best practices for achieving high, rapid reading gains. *Principal, 87*(2), 42–45.

Carolan, J., & Guinn, A. (2007). Differentiation: Lessons from master teachers. *Educational Leadership, 64*(5), 44–47.

Cawelti, G. (2006). The side effects of NCLB. *Educational Leadership, 64*(3), 64–68.

Chapman, V. G., & Sopko, D. (2003). Developing strategic use of combined-text trade books. *Reading Teacher, 57*(3), 236–241.

Commission on the Reorganization of Secondary Education. (1918). *Cardinal principles of secondary education.* Washington, DC: U.S. Government Printing Office.

Committee of Ten. (1893). *Report of the Committee of Ten on secondary school students.* Washington, DC: National Education Association.

Connelly, G. (2007). Opening the doors to discovery. *Principal, 87*(2), 68.

Fillmore, L. W., & Valadez, C. (1986). Teaching bilingual learners. In M. C. Wittrock (Ed.), *Handbook of research on teaching* (3rd ed., pp. 648–685). New York: Macmillan.

Giangreco, M. F. (2007). Extending inclusive opportunities. *Educational Leadership, 64*(5), 34–37.

Gomez-Bellenge, F. X., & Rogers, E. M. (2007). *Reading recovery and Descubriendo la Lecura (National Report 2005–2006).* Columbus: Ohio State University College of Education, National Data Evaluation Center.

Grinder, R. E., & Nelsen, E. A. (1985). Individualized instruction in American pedagogy. In M. C. Wang & H. J. Walberg (Eds.), *Adapting instruction to individual differences* (pp. 24–43). Berkeley, CA: McCutchan.

Guilford, J. P. (1977). *Way beyond the IQ.* Great Neck, NY: Creative Synergetic Associates.

Hamilton, L., & Stecher, B. (2004). Responding effectively to test-based accountability. *Phi Delta Kappan, 85*(8), 578–583.

Hill, J. D., & Flynn, K. M. (2006). *Classroom instruction that works with English language learners.* Alexandria, VA: Association for Supervision and Curriculum Development.

Individuals with Disabilities Education Improvement Act of 2004, P.L. 108-446 (2004).

Jensen, E. P. (2008). A fresh look at brain-based education. *Phi Delta Kappan, 89*(6), 408–417.

Jerald, C. (2003). Beyond the rock and the hard place. *Educational Leadership, 61*(3), 12–16.

Kauffman, J. M., McGee, K., & Brigham, M. (2004). Enabling or disabling? Observations on changes in special education. *Phi Delta Kappan, 85,* 613–620.

Klingner, J. K., & Artiles, A. J. (2003). When should bilingual students be in special education? *Educational Leadership, 61*(2), 66–71.

March, J. K., & Peters, K. H. (2002). Curriculum development and instructional design in the effective schools process. *Phi Delta Kappan, 83,* 379–381.

Marzano, R. J., Pickering, D. J., & Pollock, J. E. (2001). *Classroom instruction that works: Research-based strategies for increasing student achievement.* Alexandria, VA: Association for Supervision and Curriculum Development.

Meeker, M. N. (1985). SOI. In A. L. Costa (Ed.), *Developing minds: A resource book for teaching thinking* (pp. 187–192). Alexandria, VA: Association for Supervision and Curriculum Development.

Meeker, M. N., Meeker, R., & Roid, G. (1985). *The basic SOI manual.* Los Angeles: WPS.

Montana Office of Public Instruction. (2004). *Montana comprehensive assessment: Limited English proficiency.* Helena, MT: Author.

NAEYC & NAECS/SDE. (2004, January). Where we stand on curriculum assessment and program evaluation. *National Association for the Education of Young Children, 59*(1), 51–63.

Page, S. W. (2000). When changes for the gifted spur differentiation for all. *Educational Leadership, 58*(1), 62–65.

Perkins-Gough, D. (2007). Focus on adolescent English language learners. *Educational Leadership, 64*(6), 90–91.

Pfeiffer, S. I. (2003, Spring). Challenges and opportunities for students who are gifted: What the experts say. *Gifted Child Quarterly, 47*(2), 161–169.

Protheroe, N. (2007). Differentiating instruction in a standards-based environment. *Principal, 87*(2), 36–39.

Reading Recovery Council of North America. (2002). *A principal's guide to Reading Recovery.* Worthington, OH: Author.

Reading Recovery Council of North America. (2002). *More than one million children served: Results 2000–2001.* Columbus: Ohio State University College of Education, National Data Evaluation Center. Retrieved April 20, 2005, from http://www.readingrecovery.org/pdfs/FinalARlayout.pdf

Reading Recovery Council of North America. (2006). *A site coordinator's guide to the effective implementation of Reading Recovery.* Worthington, OH: Author.

Reis, S. M., & Renzulli, J. S. (1984). Key features of successful programs for the gifted and talented. *Educational Leadership, 41*(7), 28–34.

Renzulli, J. S. (1977). *The enrichment triad model: A guide for developing defensible programs for the gifted.* Mansfield Center, CT: Creative Learning.

Renzulli, J. S. (2002). Expanding the conception of giftedness to include co-cognitive traits and to promote social capital. *Phi Delta Kappan, 84*(1), 33–58.

Renzulli, J. S., Reis, S. M., & Smith, L. H. (1981). *The revolving door identification model.* Mansfield Center, CT: Creative Learning.

Rotberg, I. C. (2007). Schools making tough choices: An international perspective. *Principal, 86*(4), 32–37.

Swiatek, M. A., & Lupkowski-Shoplik, A. (2003, Spring). Elementary and middle school student participation in gifted programs: Are gifted students underserved? *Gifted Child Quarterly, 47*(2), 118–120.

Taylor, B. M. (2001, Spring). Beating the odds in teaching all children to read. *Of Primary Interest. National Association of Early Childhood Specialists, 8*(2), 1–2.

Tomlinson, C. A. (2001). *How to differentiate instruction in mixed-ability classrooms* (2nd ed.). Alexandria, VA: Association for Supervision and Curriculum Development.

Tomlinson, C. A. (2003). Deciding to teach them all. *Educational Leadership, 61*(2), 6–11.

Tomlinson, C. A., & Edison, C. C. (2003). *Differentiation in practice: A resource guide for differentiating curriculum, Grades 5–9.* Alexandria, VA: Association for Supervision and Curriculum Development.

Tomlinson, C. A., Kaplan, S. N., Renzulli, J. S., Purcell, J., Leppien, J., & Burns, D. (2002). *The parallel curriculum: A design to develop high potential and challenge high-ability learners.* Thousand Oaks, CA: Corwin Press.

VanTassel-Baska, J. (1985). Appropriate curriculum for the gifted. In J. Feldhusen (Ed.), *Toward excellence in gifted education* (pp. 45–67). Denver, CO: Lows.

What Works Clearinghouse. (2007, March 19). *WWC intervention report: Reading Recovery.* Washington, DC: U.S. Department of Education, Institute of Education Sciences.

Wiliam, D. (2007, December/2008, January). Changing classroom practice. *Educational Leadership, 65*(4), 36–42.

Willis, J. (2007, May). Which brain research can educators trust? *Phi Delta Kappan, 88*(9), 697–699.

Wolfe, P. (2001). *Brain matters: Translating research into classroom practice.* Alexandria, VA: Association for Supervision and Curriculum Development.

Zalud, G. (2005–2006). *Reading Recovery executive summary 2005–2006.* Vermillion: University of South Dakota, Regional Reading Recovery Training Center.

Index

About the Authors

Allan A. Glatthorn (1924–2007) was a Distinguished Research Professor of Education (Emeritus) at East Carolina University, Greenville, North Carolina. He formerly was a member of the faculty at the University of Pennsylvania Graduate School of Education. During his 55 years of working in education, he served as a teacher, principal, supervisor, and professor. He was also the author of more than 20 books in the fields of curriculum and supervision and consulted with more than 200 school districts, assisting them in developing and implementing their curricula.

Floyd Boschee has an extensive background in teaching and educational leadership. He has served as a teacher, coach, and school administrator in the public schools and as a professor and chairman of departments of education at the collegiate level. He is Professor Emeritus in the Division of Educational Administration, School of Education, at the University of South Dakota and a former school board member of the Vermillion School District, Vermillion, South Dakota. During his tenure as a university professor, he consulted with school districts on reorganization, published numerous articles in major educational journals, and conducted workshops on curriculum development and implementation, the teaching and learning process, and school administrator evaluations. He is the author or coauthor of 10 books in the fields of school administration and curriculum leadership.

Bruce M. Whitehead serves as an elementary school principal in School District #4, Missoula, Montana, and as an adjunct professor at the University of Montana. His career includes appointments to numerous national and international committees as well as being elected as president of the Montana Association of Elementary School Principals and president of the Montana State Reading Association. He also served as chairman of the Montana Governor's Task Force on Technology. As a Distinguished Alumni recipient at the University of Montana, he has authored or coauthored six books in the fields of administration, reading, and technology and has written numerous articles published in major educational journals. Additional honors and awards include the International Reading Association's Presidential Service Award, NAESP's National Distinguished Principal Award, Milken Family Foundation's National Outstanding Educator Award, the John F. Kennedy Center's Award for Arts in Education, and Japan's International Mathematics Soroban Institute Award.